MUSSOLINI'S WAR

MUSSOLINI'S WAR

FASCIST ITALY FROM TRIUMPH TO COLLAPSE 1935-1943

JOHN GOOCH

PEGASUS BOOKS
NEW YORK LONDON

Mussolini's War

Pegasus Books, Ltd.
148 West 37th Street, 13th Floor
New York, NY 10018

ISBN: 978-1-64313-548-9

10 9 8 7 6 5 4 3 2 1

Printed in the United States of America
Distributed by Simon & Schuster
www.pegasusbooks.com

*The character of a leader is a large
factor in the game of war . . .*
                General William Tecumseh Sherman

Contents

Acknowledgements

Once again I am deeply grateful to the personnel who man the Ufficio Storico dello Stato Maggiore dell'Esercito in Rome for their help and support while I was researching this book. Colonel Filippo Cappellano, first as *cap'archivio* and latterly as Head of the Office, a distinguished historian in his own right, has welcomed me on numerous occasions and shared with me his unbounded knowledge of the archives. His predecessor, Colonel Cristiano Dechigi, was no less supportive in his turn. Lieutenant-Colonel Emilio Tirone, currently head of the archive, has been – and is – no less welcoming and has given me much unobtrusive but invaluable assistance. Trawling through the archives themselves was made infinitely easier with the advice and guidance of the principal archivist, Dottore Alessandro Gionfrida. My thanks go to him, to his deputy Dottore Filippo Bignato, and to the unfailingly cheerful and friendly staff who ferry the files to and fro. With the help of *caporale maggiore* Claudio Piddini, and some much-appreciated cups of *espresso* coffee, I was able to make a brief raid on the photographic archives – a source of extraordinary depth and richness which remains under-exploited by historians.

My entry into the Italian Air Ministry was made simple and straightforward thanks to the friendship, help and hospitality of Lieutenant-General Basilio Di Martino. The head of the Ufficio Storico dell'Aeronautica Militare, Colonel Luigi Borzise, opened its resources to me without hesitation. He and his staff, Dotoressa Monica Bovino and Signore Marcello Neve, were friendliness personified and made my brief time with them both productive and delightful.

Getting into Service archives in Italy requires jumping through bureaucratic hoops. Signora Palmina Cerullo of the British Embassy in Rome has come up trumps every time yet another of my requests for help has landed on her desk. Thanks, Palmina.

In Genoa, Dr Gianni Franzone, director of the Centro Wolfsoniana, kindly found me room and time in which to consult his archive. And at

Castiglione delle Stiviere, Professoressa Dr Silvana Greco and Professor Giulio Busi, directors of the Fondazione Palazzo Bondoni Pastorio, were the most hospitable and kindly of hosts.

My visits to the outstation of the Imperial War Museum at Duxford were among my most enjoyable outings thanks to the presence there of Stephen Walton as Senior Curator. Stephen provided everything a researcher could want: swift and comprehensive guidance through the holdings, ready help when needed, relaxing surroundings – even coffee and a biscuit!

In Rome, long-time friends Dr Ciro Paoletti and Professor Andrea Ungari made my visits even more of a pleasure than they would otherwise have been. And in London Drs. Jenny and Michael Sevitt provided home comforts while I visited the ever-efficient National Archives at Kew.

Assembling the materials for a book such as this is not straightforward and I am deeply grateful to friends old and new for helping me do so. My warmest thanks go to Professor Holger Afflerbach; Dr Fabio De Ninno; Dr Jurgen Foerster; Dr Emilio Gin; Dr Richard Hammond; Professor MacGregor Knox; Dr Jacopo Lorenzini; Professor Evan Mawdsley; Dr Steven Morewood; Professor Rick Schneid; Dr Matteo Scianna; Dr Brian Sullivan; and Dr Nicolas Virtue.

Many years ago a professor in my college remarked that historians should not marry. For me at least, he was wholly wrong. Ann has lived patiently with Italian matters military for a very long time, managing our lives together here in England and in Rome. Without her as a partner this book would not have been written, so it is at least as much hers as it is mine.

Dramatis Personae

AMBROSIO, General Vittorio (28 July 1879–20 November 1958)

Commissioned as a cavalry officer, Ambrosio served as a divisional staff officer during the First World War and a divisional and then corps commander in the years that followed. In 1939 he was given command of 2nd Army on the Yugoslav border, leading the Italian offensive against the Yugoslavs in April 1941. Exchanging posts with Mario Roatta, he became chief of the army general staff in January 1942. On 1 February 1943 Mussolini appointed him chief of the armed forces general staff. A dyed-in-the-wool monarchist, he played a major part in the plotting that led to Mussolini's downfall after repeated but fruitless attempts to persuade Mussolini to change course. On 8–9 September, after the announcement of the armistice, he left Rome along with the king, Badoglio and others, serving under the rump Italian government as inspector-general of the army until November 1944.

AMÉ, General Cesare (18 November 1892–30 June 1983)

Amé joined the Italian Military Intelligence Service (*Servizio Informazioni Militari* – SIM) in 1921, serving first in the counter-espionage centre at Turin and then in Vienna and Budapest. Leaving SIM in 1929, he held a command post in Perugia and then taught at the Air Force Academy at Caserta from 1933 to 1935. Promoted colonel in 1937, he commanded an infantry regiment and served first as a divisional and then as corps chief of staff. Recalled to SIM as vice-chief with Mussolini's approval at the beginning of January 1940, he was appointed head of SIM on 20 September 1940. By the end of 1941 he commanded an organization of 1,500 officers, non-commissioned officers and specialized troops, double the size of the one he took over. He was removed by Badoglio on 18 August 1943.

ARMELLINI, General Quirino (31 January 1889–13 January 1975)

A faithful follower of Badoglio, Armellini commanded an Eritrean battalion during the reconquest of Libya. In November 1935 Badoglio made him operations chief in Ethiopia. From 1936 until 1938 he served as military commander of the Amhara district. Following divisional commands in Italy, he served as Badoglio's chief staff officer at the *Comando Supremo* from June 1940 until he was replaced in January 1941 following his master's fall. He commanded the *La Spezia* infantry division and then XVIII Corps in Dalmatia and Croatia until he was replaced in July 1942 following a clash with the civil governor of Dalmatia, Giuseppe Bastianini. When Mussolini fell on 25 July 1943, Armellini was tasked by Badoglio with dissolving the Fascist militia (*Milizia Volontaria per la Sicurezza Nazionale*) and incorporating it into the army. After the armistice he joined the resistance in Rome, heading the clandestine military front there from March 1944.

BADOGLIO, Marshal Pietro (28 September 1871–1 November 1956)

Badoglio enjoyed a meteoric rise during the First World War, climbing from lieutenant-colonel to lieutenant-general in only two years. His XXVII Corps front collapsed during the battle of Caporetto (24 October 1917), giving rise to accusations of failure and then of a cover-up which dogged him throughout his life – as they continue to do. After serving as ambassador to Brazil between 1923 and 1925 he became army chief of staff and then *Capo di stato maggiore generale* (chief of the armed forces general staff) from 1925 to 1940. Between 1929 and 1933 he was governor of Libya and then from November 1935 to May 1936 he directed the war in Ethiopia, all the while still holding his position in Rome. He both solicited and received rich rewards: the king made him duke of Addis Ababa in July 1936. His direction of military affairs was generally unimpressive. Uncharacteristically, he openly criticized Mussolini after the Greek debacle in November 1940 and lost office as a result. His deep-seated dislike of the Germans was probably only exceeded by his visceral hatred of Cavallero, in whose death he may have had an indirect hand. Appointed head of the government on

25 July 1943, he fled Rome for Brindisi with the king and others on 8–9 September 1943, continuing to head the rump Italian government until June 1944.

BALBO, Italo (6 June 1896–28 June 1940)

Fascist *ras* (Party chief) of Ferrara and one of the four men appointed by Mussolini to lead the March on Rome in October 1922, Balbo became first under-secretary (1926–9) and then Minister of Aviation (1929–33). Courageous, energetic and charming, he made an international reputation by leading four long-distance training flights, including a double crossing of the Atlantic. A good organizer, he was unable to overcome deep-seated inter-service rivalries or to impose a uniform doctrine on the air force. In January 1934, seeing him as a dangerous rival and potential successor, Mussolini 'exiled' him to Libya as governor. In June 1940, his plane was misidentified as a British fighter shortly after an enemy attack and shot down over Tobruk by Italian anti-aircraft batteries. Balbo Drive, a street in Chicago where he was fêted on reaching America, is still named after him.

BASTICO, General Ettore (9 April 1876–1 December 1972)

Bastico's fifty-three-year military career began, like many others, with the Italo-Turkish war in Libya (1911–12). After distinguished service during the First World War he rose through the ranks during the inter-war years, establishing a reputation as something of a thinking general with his book *The Evolution of the Art of War* in which he took on Giulio Douhet, who he thought had over-emphasized the mechanized aspect of war at the cost of the human element. He also developed a close friendship with Mussolini. During the Abyssinian war he commanded the 1st Blackshirt/23 *Marzo* division, and in 1937 he briefly led the *Corpo di Truppe Volontarie* (CTV) in the Spanish Civil War. In December 1940 he was appointed military governor of the Dodecanese and on 19 July 1941 Mussolini made him governor of Libya and nominal commander of the Axis forces in North Africa. Rommel, who clashed frequently with him over his logistical and strategic caution, nicknamed him 'Bombastico'. Promoted *Maresciallo d'Italia* (Marshal of Italy) on 12 August 1942 so as not to be junior to Rommel, he was relieved in February 1943 after Tripoli fell.

CAMPIONI, Admiral Inigo (14 November 1878–24 May 1944)

Widely regarded during the latter years of his peacetime career as the most promising officer in the *Regia Marina*, Campioni served on battleships and then commanded convoys during the First World War. His interwar career, during which he rose to flag rank in 1932, included time as naval attaché in Paris, command of the battleship *Duilio* and a heavy cruiser, and service as Admiral Cavagnari's office chief. In 1938 he was made deputy chief of the naval staff and in 1939 he was appointed to command the 1st Naval Squadron – the main Italian battle fleet. Criticized after the battles of Punta Stilo and Capo Teulada in July and November 1940 for being over-cautious and failing to press home his advantage, he was replaced on 8 December 1940. He returned to the post of deputy chief of the naval staff and then in October 1941 became governor of the Dodecanese, surrendering them to the Germans on 11 September 1943, three days after the armistice. Imprisoned by the Germans, he was handed over in January 1944 to Mussolini's Italian Social Republic (*Repubblica Sociale Italiana* – RSI), which convicted him of high treason after he repeatedly refused to collaborate with it. Offered a pardon if he recognized the RSI as Italy's legitimate government he rejected it outright and was shot in the city square of Parma. In November 1947 he was posthumously awarded Italy's highest decoration for valour, the *Medaglia d'Oro*.

CAVAGNARI, Admiral Domenico (20 July 1876–2 November 1966)

During the First World War Cavagnari commanded a squadron of destroyer leaders (*esploratori*). From 1929 to 1932 he was head of the Italian Naval Academy at Livorno. His time there coincided with a change of tone in the navy's relationship with the regime and an increased emphasis on the positive virtues of Fascism. As undersecretary of the navy from November 1933 and chief of the naval staff from June 1934, Cavagnari shaped the navy that went to war in 1940, keeping a tight hold on everything and insisting on uniformity and obedience. A 'battleship' admiral, he showed little interest in aircraft carriers (like his master) or in radar, effectively closing down research and innovation in January 1934 with the declaration that 'at sea a simple device, resistant and which functions reliably is preferable to another which, though more sophisticated and faster, is more complex, fragile and less reliable'. He did, though, oversee the construction of sixty submarines, intended to attrite enemy battleships and carriers, between 1935 and 1940. The indecisive battle of Punta Stilo and the successful enemy strike at Taranto in November 1940 ended his career.

CAVALLERO, Marshal Ugo (20 September 1880–13 September 1943)

During the First World War Cavallero, who was popular with the rank and file there for his easy-going attitude, served first on Cadorna's head-quarters and then as operations chief under Badoglio, deputy chief of staff to Cadorna's successor Marshal Diaz. In 1920, sensing that peace-time promotion would be slow, he left the army for private industry. In 1925 Mussolini made him under-secretary of state for war, a position he held for three years, during which time he and Badoglio became bitter rivals and from which he was removed after direct intervention from the king. He then worked for five years for Ansaldo, as a result of which he was suspected for the rest of his life of profiteering from the firm's supply of poor-quality steel for the armed forces. After a period commanding the troops in Italian East Africa he was sacked by the viceroy, Amedeo Duke of Aosta. In June 1939 Mussolini sent him to Berlin to handle the negotiations that followed the signing of the Pact of Steel on 22 May. On 6 December 1940 he succeeded Badoglio as chief of the armed forces general staff and was immediately sent to Albania to take over the conduct of the Greek war from Ubaldo Soddu, returning to Rome in May 1941. Somewhat too accommodating to the Germans for some of his fellow generals, Cavallero held office until 31 January 1943, chiefly perhaps because, unlike his successor Ambrosio, he never questioned the *Duce*'s direction of the war. In July 1943 Badoglio had him arrested and then, when he was released after the king's intervention, had him arrested again. During his imprisonment he wrote a memorandum in which he claimed to have conspired against

Mussolini from November 1942. When Badoglio fled Rome he left the '*memoriale Cavallero*' on his desk. The Germans found it. With this in his hands, Kesselring offered Cavallero command of the armed forces of what would become the RSI. On 13 September 1943 Cavallero had supper with Kesselring. Next morning he was found dead in the garden of the hotel in Frascati in which he was staying, having apparently committed suicide. Some suspect that he was murdered.

CIANO, Count Galeazzo (18 March 1903–11 January 1944)

The son of an admiral and a minister in Mussolini's cabinet who was close to the *Duce*, Ciano married Mussolini's daughter Edda in April 1930. His rise thereafter was rapid: under-secretary and then minister for propaganda (1934–5), he was promoted Foreign Minister by his father-in-law on 9 June 1936, a post he held until February 1943 when he was demoted to ambassador to the Holy See. Vulgar, ambitious and opportunistic, Ciano was at first little more than a placeman. Mounting anxiety about Italy's vulnerability to a dominating Nazi Germany changed that and led ultimately to Ciano's voting for his father-in-law's dismissal at the meeting of the Fascist Council on 24–25 July 1943. That cost him his life. After foolishly fleeing to Germany he was handed over to the RSI, tried and convicted as a traitor, and shot in the back. For anyone so minded a video of his execution can be found on YouTube.

FAVAGROSSA, General Carlo (22 November 1888–22 March 1970)

An engineer, Favagrossa served as a junior officer in the Libyan war and the First World War. After presiding over the control commission for the observation of the armistice in Vienna in 1919 he served in Cyrenaica and then on military and diplomatic duties in France and Czechoslovakia. Following regimental command and then service as deputy commandant of the Artillery and Engineers' Academy, he was given command of Italy's lone motor-mechanized brigade in June 1936. Sent to Spain in the aftermath of Guadalajara, he completely reorganized the Intendance (supply) service. After divisional commands he took over the presidency of the General Commissariat for War Production (*Commissariato Generale per le Fabbricazioni di Guerra* – COGEFAG) on 1 September 1939. On 23 May 1940 he was renamed an under-secretary of state for war production, and on 6 February 1943 raised to the rank of minister. In office he controlled the allocation of raw materials (though always having to contest this with various branches of the Fascist Party), but not weapons procurement.

FOUGIER, General Rino Corso (14 November 1894–24 April 1963)

Fougier began war service in 1915 with the *Bersaglieri* (light infantry) but transferred to the air wing in 1916, winning three silver medals for valour. After the war, as successively a squadron, wing and group commander he impressed the air minister Italo Balbo, who when governor of Libya called him to Tripolitania between 1935 and 1937. Put in command of the *1a Squadra Aerea* in May 1940, he commanded the air expeditionary force (*Corpo Aereo Italiano*) in Belgium which joined in the bombardment of Great Britain between 10 September 1940 and 28 January 1941. On 15 November 1941 he succeeded Pricolo as under-secretary of state for air and chief of the air staff. He was removed from office on 27 July 1943.

GAMBARA, General Gastone (10 November 1890–27 February 1962)

Gambara began his military career as a non-commissioned officer before graduating from the Modena Military Academy via a special course for promising NCOs. During the First World War he served in the *Alpini* (specialized mountain troops), winning two *Medaglie d'Argento* (silver medals, Italy's second highest award for gallantry) in nine months in 1918. After commanding an *Alpini* battalion in the early 1920s he held a variety of staff posts. He fought in Ethiopia and then in Spain, where he was chief of staff to the CTV. After commanding XV Corps in the brief battle in the French Alps in June 1940, he next commanded VIII Corps in the war against Greece from 5 February 1941. On 11 May 1941 he was transferred to Tripoli, first as Gariboldi's, and them Bastico's chief of staff, and then as commander first of the *Corpo d'Armata Corazzato* (Armoured Corps) and subsequently the *Corpo d'Armata di Manovra* (Manoeuvre Corps). After falling out with Rommel and Cavallero he was recalled on 6 March 1942 and sent to Slovenia in September to command XI Corps, staying there until 5 September 1943. After the armistice Gambara sided with the Fascist *Repubblica Sociale Italiana* and on 20 October 1943 he was appointed chief of staff of the Republican National Army. Mussolini removed him on 12 March 1944 for 'excessive pessimism'. His name was on the 1947 Anglo-American list of war criminals, but like others he escaped arraignment either in Italy or abroad.

GARIBOLDI, General Italo (20 April 1879–9 February 1970)

Gariboldi served in staff posts during the First World War. Between 1920 and 1925 he led the Italian delegation determining the Yugoslav frontier. Regimental and brigade command was followed by command of the Military Academy at Modena and the School of Application at Parma. In 1936 he commanded the *Sabauda* division in the march on Addis Ababa. As chief of staff to the governor of Italian East Africa he participated in the brutal repression of Abyssinian resistance. Recalled in February 1938, he commanded an army corps and then from 11 June 1940 to 11 February 1941 5th Army in Tripolitania, at which time he took over from Graziani as commander-in-chief and governor general. Tense relations with Rommel, of whose lightning re-conquest of Cyrenaica he disapproved, led to his recall on 19 July 1941. In spring 1942 he was appointed to command 8th Army (ARMIR) in Russia. Gariboldi was at Parma rebuilding the shattered 8th Army when, on 15 September 1943, he was arrested by the Germans. Refusing to collaborate with them, he was first interned in Germany and then handed over to the RSI, which condemned him to ten years' imprisonment.

GELOSO, General Carlo (20 August 1879–23 July 1957)

An artilleryman, Geloso won three silver medals for valour during the First World War. Emerging from it as a colonel, he went into the special reserve until recalled with the advent of Fascism. After regimental command and staff service he fought in Somalia in 1936 and then participated in the 'pacification' of Ethiopia, using methods which even Roberto Farinacci, a hard-line Fascist, judged 'often disproportionate and unjustified'. In December 1939 he commanded XXVI Corps in Albania, succeeding Guzzoni, but was replaced in the summer of 1940 by Visconti Prasca at Ciano's behest. Recalled to Albania in November 1940, he commanded 11th Army until April 1941. He then served as military governor of Greece until unseated by a scandal in May 1943 after which his pleading letters to Mussolini were studiously ignored. Following the armistice in September 1943 he was captured and interned by the Germans at Poznan until freed by the Red Army. The Ethiopian government tried unsuccessfully to extradite him for war crimes in 1947, a year after the Greek government, then in the midst of a civil war, announced that it did not intend to pursue the extradition of any Italians held to have carried out illegal actions in their country.

GRAZIANI, Marshal Rodolfo (11 August 1882–11 January 1955)

After gaining his university matriculation Graziani enrolled for a two-year course in law but never completed his studies. Too poor to attend one of the military academies he was conscripted into the army, serving as a non-commissioned officer and then as a second lieutenant before winning a permanent commission in 1906. In Libya throughout the First World War, he emerged from it the youngest colonel in the army and one of the most decorated. After briefly abandoning the army but failing to make his way in the civilian world he returned to Libya in 1921 and stayed for thirteen years, taking a leading part in the repression and re-conquest of the colony and carving a reputation for himself as one of Italy's most aggressive – and successful – soldiers. Promoted to *generale di corpo d'armata* (lieutenant-general), he was recalled to Rome in 1934 but left again in February 1935 to take command of Italian forces in Somalia. His success there earned him the baton of *Maresciallo d'Italia*. As viceroy of Ethiopia he hanged and shot 'rebel' leaders, becoming markedly more ruthless after an attempt on his life on 19 February 1937. Returning to Rome in January 1938, Graziani was appointed chief of the army general staff on 1 November 1939 (apparently learning of his appointment on the 1 o'clock news) and then, in June 1940, governor of Libya. He was relieved of command on 8 February 1941 and was not employed again until Mussolini made him War Minister of the RSI in late 1943. On the partisans' list for execution, Graziani escaped retribution when he fell into American hands. First an Allied prisoner of war and then imprisoned in Italy, he was tried in May 1950 'for military collaboration with Germany' and condemned to nineteen years incarceration, but released four months later. The Abyssinian government's attempt to extradite and try him for war crimes came to nought.

GUZZONI, General Alfredo (12 April 1877–15 April 1965)

Guzzoni served as a front-line staff officer for most of the First World War, during which he won two *Medaglie d'Argento*, and afterwards on the inter-Allied control commissions for Austria and Hungary. Regimental, brigade and divisional commands followed. In November 1935 he was sent to Eritrea, where he stayed as governor from June 1936 to April 1937. After leading the forces that invaded Albania on 7–8 April 1939, he commanded 4th Army during the brief campaign against France in June 1940. On 30 November 1940 he was nominated under-secretary of state for war and deputy chief of the armed forces general staff, a job he seems to have done fairly well. Cavallero abolished his deputy's post on his return to Rome after the Greek war ended and forced Guzzoni to resign as under-secretary in May 1941. On 1 June 1943 Guzzoni was given command of 6th Army and made responsible for the defence of Sicily, a difficult role in which he failed to shine. He was imprisoned by the RSI on 26 October 1943 following an attack on his record in Sicily by Roberto Farinacci but released two weeks later after pressure from the German high command.

IACHINO, Admiral Angelo (24 April 1889–3 December 1976)

Iachino spent the early part of the First World War on board the battleship *Giulio Cesare* before commanding a torpedo boat in the Adriatic and winning a *Medaglia d'Argento* (Silver Medal). After serving as naval attaché in China between 1923 and 1928, he commanded a destroyer, a light cruiser and then two groups of light ships during the Spanish Civil War. In August 1940 he was given command of the 2nd Naval Squadron. He took part in the battle of Cape Spartivento in November 1940 and replaced Campioni as commander of the battle fleet the following month. Much criticized for his handling of the battle of Cape Matapan, during which he lost an entire cruiser division, he survived until 5 April 1943 and was then replaced by Admiral Carlo Bergamini. He was restored to active service in 1948 and finally discharged in 1962.

MARRAS, General Efisio (2 August 1888–29 January 1981)

An artilleryman, Marras was selected as Italy's military attaché in Berlin in October 1936. He stayed in post for seven years, apart from a short interlude in the summer of 1939 when he was replaced by General Mario Roatta. Acting as the *Comando Supremo*'s eyes and ears there, he reported and interpreted Nazi military policy. After the armistice he was interned by the Germans and then handed over to the RSI and imprisoned. In August 1944 he escaped and reached Switzerland. After the war he served first as army chief of staff and then from 1950 to 1954 as chief of the defence staff, playing a major role in the reconstruction of the Italian army.

MESSE, Marshal Giovanni (10 December 1883–18 December 1968)

Italy's finest general, Messe took a major part in training and then leading elite *Arditi* infantry units during the latter years of the First World War, winning a *Medaglia d'Argento*. After service as a royal aide-de-camp between 1923 and 1927, he commanded a *Bersaglieri* unit and then a motorized brigade, which he led during the war in Ethiopia and from which he emerged as a major-general. Deputy commander during the invasion of Albania in April 1939, he then commanded the *Celere* ('rapid') corps between June and December

1940. His success during the Greek war, in which he commanded the *Corpo d'Armata Speciale* (Special Army Corps), led to his being appointed to command the *Corpo di spedizione italiano in Russia* (CSIR) in July 1941 when the first choice fell ill. After failing to persuade Cavallero and Mussolini not to expand the CSIR to full Army size, rubbing up against the Germans, and disagreeing with the new 8th Army commander, Gariboldi, over strategy, Messe asked to be relieved and left Russia in November 1942. In February 1943 Mussolini handed him a poisoned chalice, appointing him to command Italian forces in Tunisia. After the surrender of Axis forces in North Africa in May 1943 he was confined along with other senior captives in England, his conversations bugged by his captors. In September 1943 he was made chief of staff of the Italian Co-Belligerent Army, a post he held until the end of the war.

PIRZIO BIROLI, General Alessandro (23 July 1877– 20 May 1962)

The son of one of Garibaldi's volunteers, Pirzio Biroli was commissioned into the *Bersaglieri*. During the First World War he first served on the staff in Rome and then as a staff officer in Macedonia before transferring to the Italian front after Caporetto. Between 1922 and 1927 he headed a military mission to Ecuador, following this with divisional and corps command. He commanded the Eritrean corps during the Abyssinian war and then, as a full general, held office as governor of Amhara. After attempting and failing to crush the revolt which broke out there in August 1937, for which Graziani held him responsible, he was dismissed in December 1937. Unemployed until February 1941, he was then made commander of 9th Army in Albania. As governor and military commander in Montenegro from October 1941 he used the ruthless methods practised in Abyssinia to hold down his fiefdom. In June 1943 the *Comando Supremo* created Army Group East, leaving Pirzio Biroli with only civil powers. He returned to Rome the following month. Following the armistice he was offered the post of Minister of National Defence by Mussolini but declined it. Passing through the German lines, he escaped to Brindisi and in October 1944 he was recalled to temporary service to head a commission examining awards for valour. On the Allied list of war criminals, he too escaped retribution. Reportedly a crack shot with a pistol, Pirzio Biroli won a silver medal in the team sabre event at the 1908 London Olympics.

PRICOLO, General Francesco (30 January 1891–14 October 1980)

Commissioned as an engineer, Pricolo flew dirigibles in the Italo-Turkish war and then in the First World War, winning two Silver Medals for valour. After filling a variety of command and staff posts, including deputy chief of the air staff for ten months in 1932–3, he was appointed under-secretary of state for air and chief of the air staff on 10 November 1939. Used by Mussolini as a personal channel of information on the mishandling of the early stages of the Greek war, he had disagreements with Cavallero and was distrusted by Rommel, who accused him of 'fickleness'. He was fired on 14 November 1941 after failing to send the new Macchi 202 fighters to North Africa as ordered, on the grounds that the personnel to fly them were not yet trained and the planes lacked sand filters. He was put on permanent leave in August 1945 and finally retired in 1954.

RICCARDI, Admiral Arturo (30 October 1878–20 December 1966)

Riccardi began his career serving with the Italian marines in the Boxer rebellion (1900–1) and then in the Far East campaign of 1905. Following war service he held several important staff posts in the main office of the Navy Ministry, becoming director-general of personnel and military services in August 1935, three years after he made admiral and one year after he joined the La Spezia branch of the Fascist Party. On 8 December 1940 he succeeded Cavagnari as under-secretary of the navy and chief of the naval staff. He was removed from both offices by Badoglio on 27 July 1943, following Mussolini's downfall.

ROATTA, General Mario (2 January 1887–7 January 1968)

A highly intelligent, equally controversial and somewhat elusive figure, Roatta served in Italy and France during the First World War and then as military attaché in Warsaw between 1924 and 1930. In 1934 he was chosen to head the *Servizio Informazioni Militari* (Italian military intelligence – SIM). Likely involved in the assassination of King Alexander of Yugoslavia in October 1934 (and shadowed thereafter by French intelligence during his visits to France), he planned in January 1936 to kidnap or assassinate Haile Selassie but was prevented from doing so by Mussolini. As the first commander of the CTV in the Spanish Civil War he failed to distinguish himself, losing the battle of Guadalajara. After acting as military attaché in Berlin between August and October 1939 he served first as Graziani's deputy chief of army staff from 31 October 1939 and then as chief of army staff until 20 January 1942, when he took over command of the occupation forces in Slovenia and Dalmatia. He left the Balkans in February 1943 and after briefly being responsible for the defence of Sicily became chief of army staff for the second time in June 1943, fleeing Rome with Badoglio in September. He was sacked by Badoglio on 12 November 1943 on Allied insistence after being charged by the Yugoslavs with war crimes. In circumstances that are still unexplained he escaped from a prison hospital in Rome on 5 March 1945 and took refuge in Spain, where he stayed until 1966. In Italy he was sentenced *in absentia* to life imprisonment and a year's solitary confinement, a sentence that was overturned by the High Court of Appeal in 1948. Allied opinions of him varied from the uncomplimentary to the unprintable.

SODDU, General Ubaldo (23 July 1883–20 July 1949)

Soddu spent most of the First World War in Cyrenaica, returning in May 1918 and serving in France where he won a *Medaglia d'Argento*, a *Croix de Guerre* and the *Légion d'Honneur*. Much of his interwar career, during which he took a law degree, was spent teaching at various military institutions and publishing military studies. He caught the *Duce*'s eye first as head of the War Minister's office between 1934 and 1936 for his skill in shaping military legislation and then as author of a book proclaiming the virtues of 'rapid decisive war'. In December 1937 he was made deputy chief of army staff for operations and in October 1939 under-secretary of state for war, a post he held until 30 November 1940. On 8 November 1940, promoted full general, he was given command of the war against Greece, a position he held for only fifty-two days before being replaced first unofficially and then officially by Cavallero.

Placed in reserve thereafter, he was arrested twice and imprisoned once following the fall of Mussolini on 25 July 1943 and freed by the Germans on 12 September 1943. He spent the rest of his life in retirement.

VISCONTI PRASCA, General Sebastiano
(23 January 1883–25 February 1961)

After service during the First World War, Visconti Prasca served as military and air attaché in Belgrade between 1925 and 1930 before commanding the Italian corps in the Saar in 1934. He served as military attaché in Paris from 1937 to 1939. A proponent of the new-style Fascist 'lightning war', as commander of the Italian forces invading Greece he failed dismally and was replaced by Ubaldo Soddu after only two weeks. He was immediately retired. In September 1943 he joined the resistance movement. Captured by the Germans and sentenced to death, subsequently commuted to life imprisonment, he escaped and reportedly fought with the Red Army, taking part in the battle of Berlin.

Maps

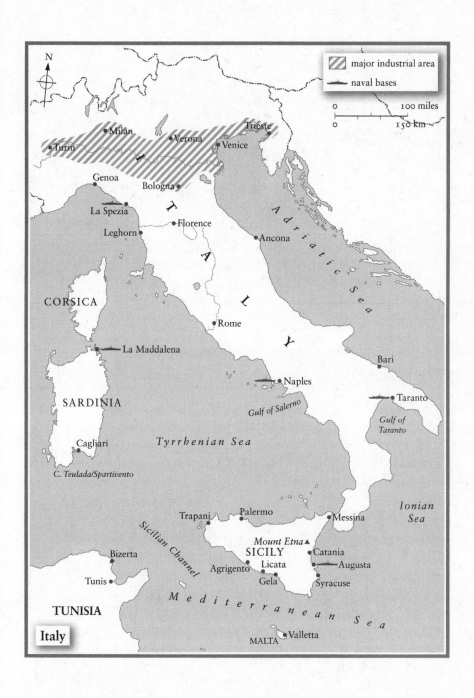

N

major industrial area
naval bases

100 miles
150 km

Milan
Turin
Verona
Trieste
Venice
ITALY
Genoa
Bologna
La Spezia
Leghorn
Florence
Ancona
Adriatic Sea

CORSICA

Rome
La Maddalena
Bari
Naples
Taranto
SARDINIA
Gulf of Salerno
Gulf of Taranto
Cagliari
Tyrrhenian Sea
C. Teulada/Spartivento

Ionian Sea

Trapani
Palermo
Messina
Mount Etna
SICILY
Catania
Bizerta
Agrigento
Licata
Augusta
Tunis
Gela
Syracuse

TUNISIA

Mediterranean Sea

Italy

MALTA
Valletta

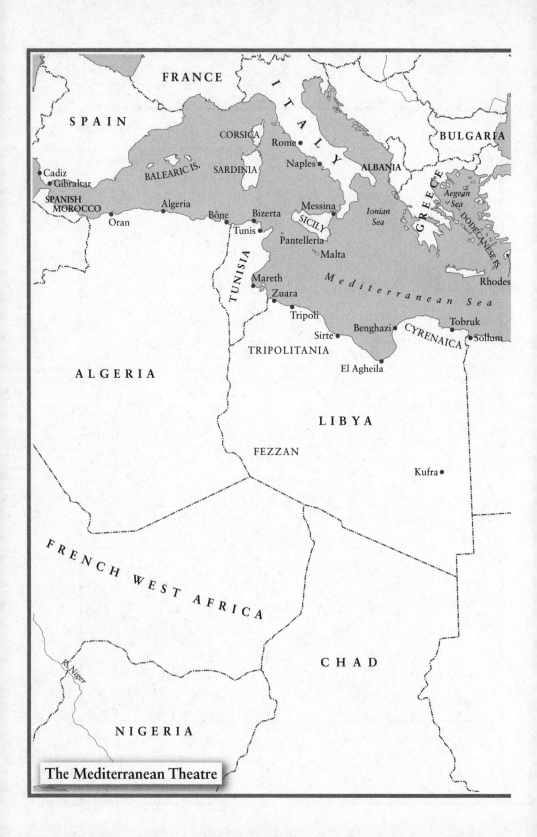

The Mediterranean Theatre

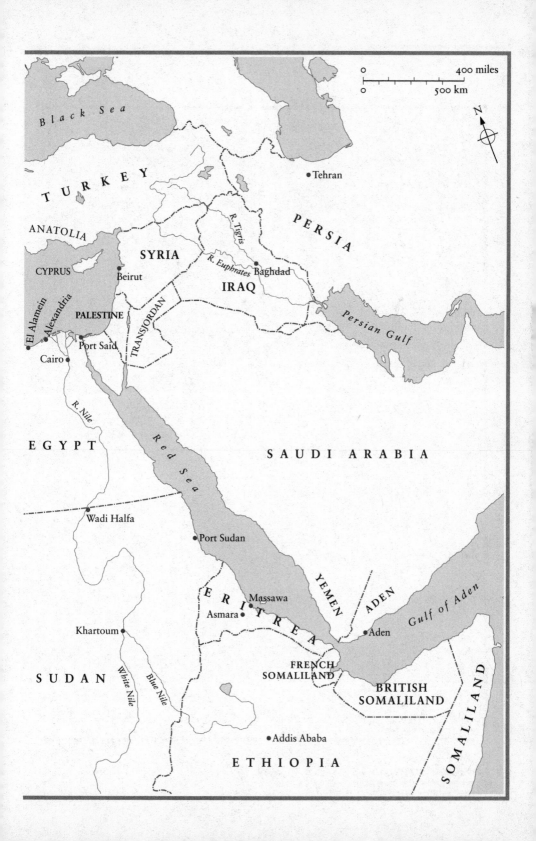

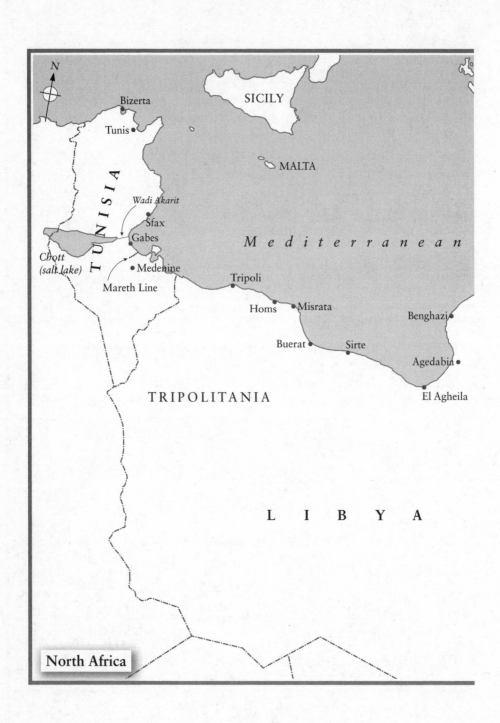

N

Bizerta

Tunis

SICILY

MALTA

T U N I S I A

Wadi Akarit

Sfax

Gabes

Chott
(salt lake)

Medenine

Mareth Line

M e d i t e r r a n e a n

Tripoli

Homs   Misrata

Buerat   Sirte

Benghazi

Agedabia

El Agheila

TRIPOLITANIA

L I B Y A

North Africa

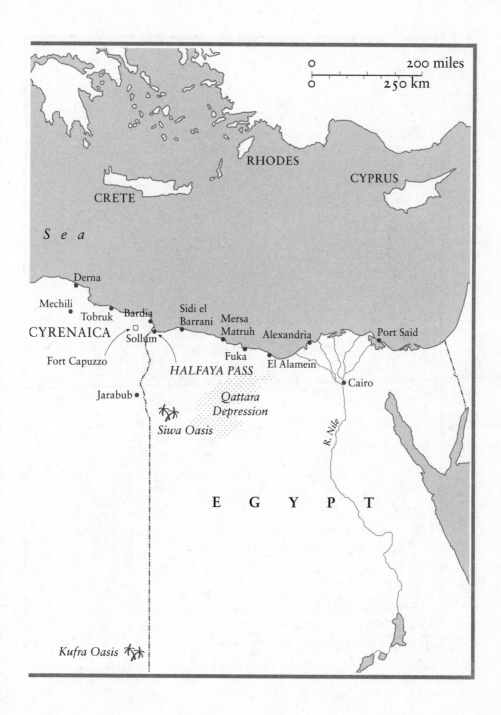

200 miles

250 km

RHODES

CYPRUS

CRETE

S e a

Derna

Mechili

Tobruk　Bardia

Sidi el
Barrani

Mersa
Matruh

Alexandria

Port Said

CYRENAICA

Sollum

HALFAYA PASS

Fuka

El Alamein

Fort Capuzzo

Cairo

Jarabub

*Qattara
Depression*

R. Nile

Siwa Oasis

E　G　Y　P　T

Kufra Oasis

N

AUSTRIA

HUNGARY

0   50 miles
0   100 km

under
German occupation

Ljubljana

Mount Krim

ITALY

Fiume

Senj

Italian Zone

Bihać

Zagreb

Karlovac

R. Sava

German Zone

KINGDOM OF CROATIA

Banja Luka

Tuzla

R. Drina

under
German
occupation

SERBIA

Zara

Sebenico

DALMATIA

Knin

Livno

Zone II

Spalato

HERZEGOVINA

Mostar

BOSNIA

Sarajevo

Zone III

Foča

SANJAK

Pljevlja

Italian-German demarcation line

A d r i a t i c   S e a

Ragusa

Cattaro

Cetinje

Podgorice

ALBANIA

annexed by Italy (Zone I)

independent State of Croatia

under Italian occupation and administration

annexed to Albania

annexed or occupied by Hungary

Kingdom of Yugoslavia 6 April, 1941

Yugoslavia

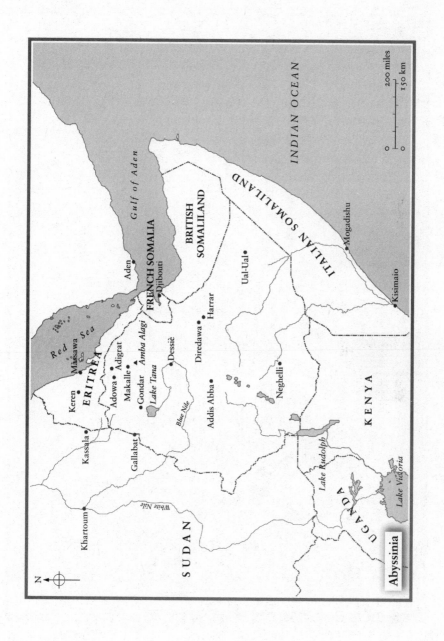

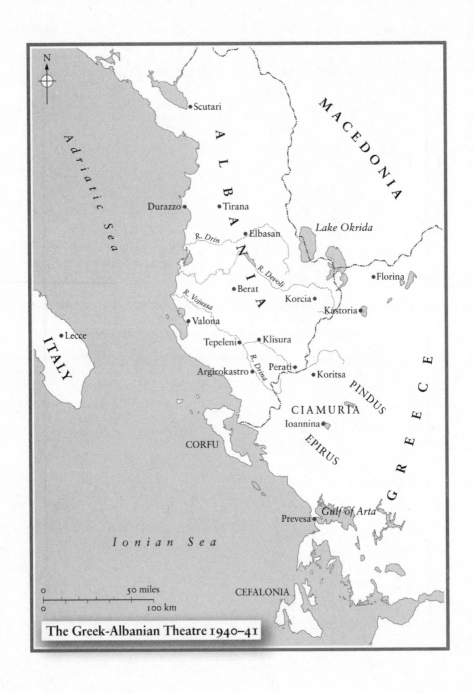

N

Adriatic Sea

•Scutari

A L B A N I A

Durazzo• •Tirana

R. Drin •Elbasan

M A C E D O N I A

Lake Okrida

R. Devoli

•Berat Korcia• •Florina

R. Vojussa Kastoria•

•Valona

Tepeleni• •Klisura

R. Drina Perati•

Argirokastro• •Koritsa

I T A L Y •Lecce

CIAMURIA

Ioannina•

CORFU **EPIRUS**

PINDUS

G R E E C E

Ionian Sea

Prevesa• *Gulf of Arta*

0 ——— 50 miles
0 ——— 100 km

CEFALONIA

The Greek-Albanian Theatre 1940–41

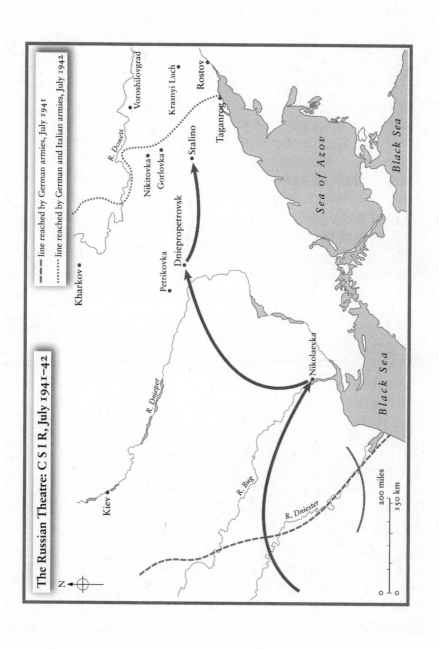

The Russian Theatre: C S I R, July 1941–42

- - - line reached by German armies, July 1941
········ line reached by German and Italian armies, July 1942

Kharkov

Voroshilovgrad

R. Donets

Krasnyi Luch

Nikitovka

Gorlovka

Stalino

Rostov

Taganrog

Petrikovka

Dniepropetrovsk

R. Dnieper

Kiev

Nikolaevka

Sea of Azov

Black Sea

Black Sea

R. Bug

R. Dniester

200 miles
150 km

N

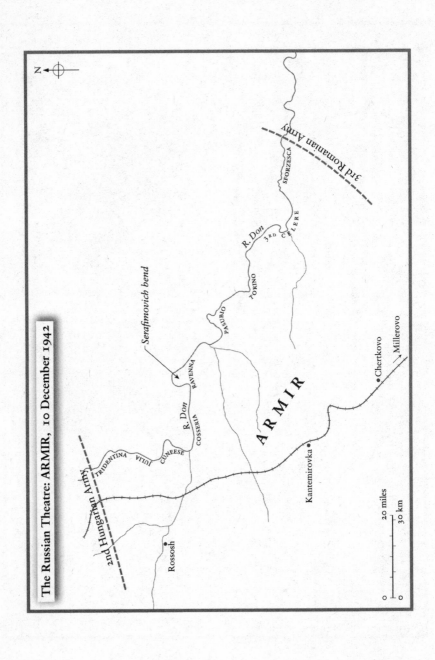

The Russian Theatre: ARMIR, 10 December 1942

N

2nd Hungarian Army

TRIDENTINA
JULIA
CUNEESE
R. Don
COSSERIA
RAVENNA

Serafimovich bend

PASUBIO
R. Don
TORINO
3RD CELERE
STORZESCA

3rd Romanian Army

A R M I R

Rossosh

Kantemirovka

Chertkovo
Millerovo

20 miles
30 km
0
0

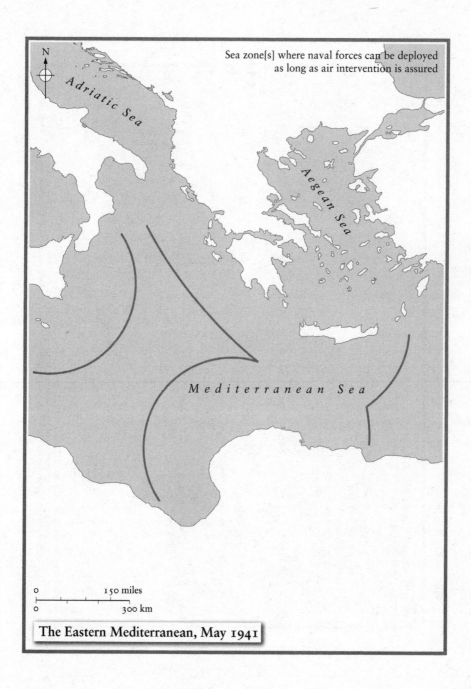

Sea zone[s] where naval forces can be deployed
as long as air intervention is assured

Adriatic Sea

Aegean Sea

Mediterranean Sea

150 miles

300 km

The Eastern Mediterranean, May 1941

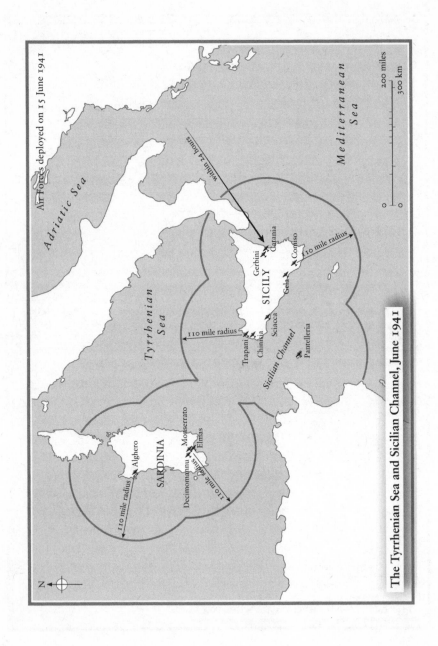

The Tyrrhenian Sea and Sicilian Channel, June 1941

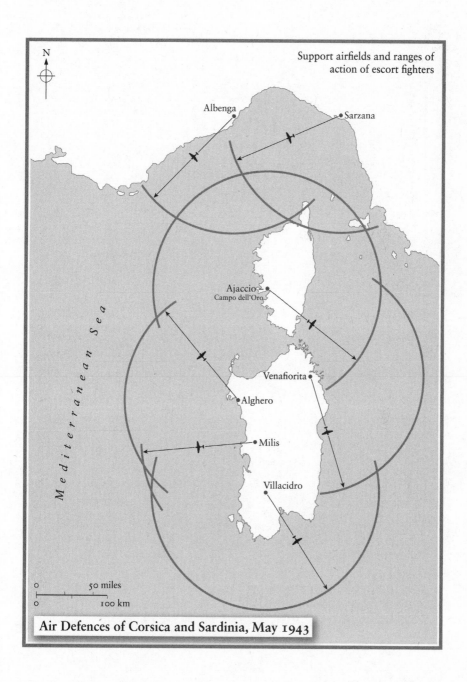

N

Albenga

Sarzana

Ajaccio
Campo dell'Oro

M e d i t e r r a n e a n   S e a

Venafiorita

Alghero

Milis

Villacidro

50 miles

100 km

Air Defences of Corsica and Sardinia, May 1943

Introduction

When, on 30 October 1922, Mussolini took charge of Italy and inducted the country into Fascism – a revolution that he would begin to try to enforce three years later after defeating the radical wing of his own party – his intention was to forge a new, resurgent state and force the international community to recognize that his fiefdom was no longer 'the least of the Great Powers'. Carving out a new Roman empire that would cover the Mediterranean and North Africa, include a substantial slice of the Balkans, and open gateways onto the Atlantic and the Indian Ocean would give Fascist Italy its rightful place in world affairs. Parts of this agenda were not new – Liberal Italy had unveiled its colonial ambitions when it set foot in Massawa on the Red Sea in 1885 and again when it fought the Turks in Libya in 1911–12 and won possession of a new colony. Nor were Italian ambitions in the Balkans and even, briefly, in Anatolian Turkey signs of a new appetite for expansion. The continuities between the foreign policies of Liberal and Fascist Italy have given historians plenty of ammunition for debate and disagreement. What was new was the interlocking of these goals into a composite programme – and the ambitious drive that Mussolini gave to achieving them. To conquer what he and many in his entourage regarded as Italy's *spazio vitale* ('living space') meant dealing both with legacies from the past and the contextual circumstances of the present. For a while, Mussolini seemed to succeed on both fronts.

Before the First World War, Italian diplomats had worked pragmatically, avoiding antagonizing the Great Powers, seeking openings to advance where there was no powerful resistance, and using force when it looked as though they could do so without causing a hostile international reaction. One consequence of this was that on the eve of the world war Italy's military record was mixed at best. Allowed by the Great Powers to establish a foothold in Eritrea and encouraged by their politicians, Italian soldiers had pushed inland, challenging the independent warrior empire of Ethiopia. Reach was not matched by grasp, and Italian arms suffered a total and humiliating defeat at the battle of Adowa on 1 March 1896.[1] This put a stop to Italian initiatives in the region. Mussolini would breathe new life into them in 1935. This confirmed the low opinion that many Italian politicians – notably the pre-war premier Giovanni Giolitti – had of Italian military capacity. His army won Libya for him in the Italo-Turkish war, but it was only partially a victory: the troops on the ground suffered some serious setbacks, the Turks only backed out of this war when they faced another in the Balkans, and thereafter Istanbul backed an ongoing guerrilla war in Libya which lasted throughout the world war that followed, during which Italians were able to keep only four coastal footholds. In both colonial wars Italian armies used brutal methods against the local populations.

If the record of the peacetime Liberal administrations appeared to leave a lot to be desired – and much to improve upon – so did Italy's performance during the First World War. Coming late into the war – she joined in on the Entente's side in May 1915 after extensive parlaying with both parties – earned her international disapprobation which only increased with time. Her entry into the war also deepened pre-existing fault lines in society, with right-wing and conservative interventionists ranged against left-wing and democratic neutralists (though, confusingly, democrats could also back the war in support of Belgium), while the official socialist party stood somewhere in the middle, neither for the war nor against it.

For three years the Italian and Austro-Hungarian armies grappled with one another in the mountains and limestone uplands along their common border. It was, as an on-the-spot British observer remarked, 'a desperate country to fight in'. Then, on 24 October 1917, Italy suffered an almost catastrophic defeat when German and Austro-Hungarian forces broke Marshal Cadorna's army at Caporetto and pursued it as far as the Piave river. There the army held – before the Anglo-French forces that were coming to its support had got into position to lend a hand – and began first a recovery and then a fightback that ended in

October 1918 when it in turn broke the Austro-Hungarians at the battle of Vittorio Veneto.*

The First World War cost Italy some 650,000 dead. If this casualty list more or less matched that of Great Britain, who lost 750,000 men and fought for nine months more (a macabre form of calculation and not in itself of great value), it did not earn Italy much in the way of international acknowledgement or recognition. In the aftermath both Georges Clemenceau and David Lloyd George denigrated Italy's military record, the Welshman declaring that when compared with his own countrymen the Italians had 'no idea what fighting meant'.[2] At the Paris Peace Conference in 1919, Italy's territorial claims were made to look grasping and cynical – which by no means all of them were.

In Italy, Mussolini poured criticism on the government in the pages of his newspaper *Il Popolo d'Italia*. By making only 'vague and high-sounding' public declarations but failing to equalize the burdens paid by town and country in terms of both blood and money, it had failed 'morally and economically'. How Italy had come to lose the twelfth battle of the Isonzo (i.e. Caporetto) was something of a mystery, but as a front-line soldier himself Mussolini was certainly not inclined to blame the ordinary *fante* (infantryman), despite Cadorna's talk of 'deficient resistance by some detachments'. The future, Mussolini declared, would now be in the hands not of the old elites, civilian or military, but of the 'trenchocracy' which come peacetime would unite class and nation.[3]

The First World War would have dramatic consequences for Italian politics. No less important, though much less obvious at the time, were the strategic lessons it offered – and those it did not. Before the war, soldiers and politicians had agreed that Italy was strategically vulnerable: her lengthy coastline and her islands were wide open to attack, and the mountains along which her northern borders ran to penetration. With the two major naval powers in the Mediterranean – Great Britain and France – on her side her vulnerability to enemy sea power was never really exposed. Wartime Italy faced only minor naval threats from Austro-Hungarian and German units in Pola and Trieste, and by

* The battle of Caporetto has become part of the everyday Italian lexicon: when Ferrari were beaten in the Japanese Grand Prix, Italian sports papers talked of a 'Singaporetto'.

the war's end had support in the shape of British, American, Australian and Japanese naval vessels and a mass of nets and mines closing the neck of the Adriatic. So, with no great sea battles in prospect, the major task the Italian navy faced was shepherding convoys across the Mediterranean alongside her Entente allies. Coal, food and weapons from her Western partners, not least the United States, flowed along the arteries formed by well-defended sea lanes. None of this would Italy enjoy when Mussolini took her into another war.

When compared with the war fought by the powers that would, in 1940 and 1941, become her enemies, the land war that the Italian armies fought between 1915 and 1918 was characterized by particular local conditions and circumstances which would not be repeated. The stage was smaller and the cast of combatants limited – though the action was just as bloody. With France on her side and Switzerland neutral the fighting front was, relatively speaking, small, clearly defined and unambiguous. There were 'side-shows' to be sure – Italian units fought in Greece and were present, albeit in very small numbers, with General Edmund Allenby in Palestine – but in strategic terms this was essentially a single-theatre war. It was also a static war. For most of the time the Italian armies were nailed to the mountains. There they fought their enemy at close range, relying on infantry assaults backed by artillery (of which they never had enough). No mechanized warfare here and no mobile warfare to speak of either. Nor did the Italian armies have much experience of fighting alongside allies: eight British and French divisions were entrained for Italy after Caporetto, but then five of them were hastily withdrawn again when the Germans launched their March offensive in 1918. Thus much of the first-hand lesson-learning which took place at the time and subsequently in the British, French and German armies had to be done by Italy at second-hand.[4]

Under Fascism, all three services had to prepare themselves for modern war. Exactly what war in what circumstances would depend entirely on how the *Duce* read the international situation – an element of continuity with the past here. All would be expected to be ready to shoulder whatever burdens came their way. All would be under pressure – but the army was under a particularly strong spotlight. Mussolini required his soldiers to shake off a legacy of defeats and partial victories which went back past Caporetto and Adowa to the wars of the

Risorgimento and beyond, and give the lie to the old calumny that *italiani sunt imbelles* ('the Italians can't fight').

Joining in a second major war, at first European and then global, would entail grasping, assessing and then mastering complex strategic challenges. Neutrality was one such challenge. In the First World War it had simplified Italy's fight; now a neutral Spain at one end of the Mediterranean and a neutral Turkey at the other would act as geopolitical 'book-ends' which Mussolini could do nothing about and which would ultimately play to Allied advantage. Theatre warfare was another. The army, navy and air force had to win their campaigns if Italy was to be victorious, but they had to be the right campaigns fought (if possible) at the right time and in the right place. In 1940 the strategic chequer board was not yet as complex as it would become the following year. There are 'lost opportunities' for every combatant in every war, and readers will be able to judge for themselves how much Mussolini's obdurate refusal to accept German assistance in North Africa in the autumn and winter of 1940–1, when the Wehrmacht was between campaigns of its own, cost him. Then there is resource allocation. Parcelling out men, guns, planes and ships to meet competing demands in ever more widely divergent theatres would be an increasingly demanding task for a combatant that was still the least of the Great Powers. Mussolini's military chiefs would spend increasing amounts of time and energy on a problem they were unable to resolve.

The Second World War was the supreme test for every combatant. Fascist Italy, eighteen years in the making when that test came in May 1940, was no exception. How did warlord Mussolini and the armed forces that served him fare in meeting the challenges that he and they faced between 1940 and 1943? The balance sheet is set out in the story that follows.

Chapter 1
On the March

For Italy the first post-war years were difficult ones. Demobilization was slow: at the end of 1919 there were still half a million men in the army and the process only came to an end in 1921. There was mounting internal disorder as Italian labour joined an international general strike in June 1919 and two violent years of internal strife began. And to many who had worn or were still wearing a uniform the peace settlement and the 'mutilated victory' that the politicians brought back from Versailles confirmed the feeling that the fighting had all been for nothing. 'No march on Vienna,' a disenchanted *Arditi* captain moaned in July 1919, 'no affirmation of victory, no colonies, no Fiume, no indemnity, nothing of any merit.'[1] Economies hit the army hard. All promotions were suspended for five years, several thousand mostly junior officers were retired, and officers' pay was cut. Benito Mussolini's assurance that officers would get a decent salary, made some six months before the March on Rome that brought him to power in October 1922, was welcome. Some of Fascism's goals dovetailed with those nursed by the soldiers, so the army happily collaborated with the Fascist Blackshirts in restoring order after the occupation of the factories and the wave of civil strikes in 1920. It also found Fascism's expansionist agenda very much to its taste. Against that, the early Fascist party looked rather too republican. In August 1922 a group of officers warned it not to set itself against the Crown. They got only an ambiguous reply.

For six years between 1919 and 1925, while Mussolini first took power and then consolidated his hold on it by shedding the radical aspects of Fascism, the generals argued with one another and the politicians over how many men were to be conscripted into the army each year, how long they were to serve in it, and how large it ought to be. Finally, in April 1925, Mussolini took over the reins of the War

Ministry himself (holding them until September 1929) and settled the
question. A force of 250,000, mostly conscripts serving eighteen
months, would form thirty 'triangular' divisions each made up of nine
battalions. Numbers would vary, re-balancing the force over the year
in order to keep within the budget. The measure was one of a raft of
seven laws intended to create the institutions that would shape the
nation's defences in peace and in war. They included the creation of
a Supreme Defence Commission to determine in peacetime what the
army would need in war, and the position of chief of the armed forces
general staff, whose occupant would be the 'technical consultant to
the head of government for matters to do with the co-ordination of
the defensive arrangements of the State and planning for future operations of war'. The new post was given to General Pietro Badoglio, a
conservative Piedmontese professional with a good though not unblem-
ished wartime record – some thought him at fault for the collapse at
Caporetto on 24 October 1917. His appointment reassured the king,
pleased the army and went down well with the public. For two years
he held the new post together with the position of chief of the army
general staff. Then Mussolini split the two offices apart and watered
down Badoglio's powers.[2]

During the latter half of the 1920s the soldiers rebuilt an army that
looked very much like the one that had gone to war in 1915. The Stokes
mortars, rifle grenades, flamethrowers and semi-automatic weapons
that had given small units the heavy firepower they needed in 1918
were discarded and the army went back to old-fashioned rifle companies. Artillery lagged badly: well into the 1930s pre-war guns were
being 'improved' by lengthening their barrels and supplying them with
better ammunition. Some of the best guns at the army's disposal were
Skoda 75mm and 100mm howitzers captured from the Austrians. As
the decade went on the authorities put increased emphasis on physical training and the concepts guiding the army in war began to take
on a distinctly nineteenth-century look. Combat regulations envisaged
offensives in which artillery barrages would prepare the way for the
infantry battalions to strike their blows, and stated flatly that the basis
of any manoeuvre on the battlefield was 'the principle of mass'. They
acknowledged the importance of air-ground co-operation in reconnaissance and tactical strikes but said little about tanks, mainly because
everything was tailored to mountain warfare on the assumption that a

new war would share the characteristics of the old, with Germany and Austria the likely enemies. In 1930 regulations made technology a second-order issue, declaring that war was in its essence 'the struggle of spirit and will'. This was something on which the new generation of Fascistized generals would build in the 1930s.[3]

In 1921 the Liberal government decided that Italy must win back possession of Libya, taken from the Turks in the war of 1911–12 and mostly lost during the world war. The reconquest began the following year. First the army began to spread its reach along the coast of Tripolitania and penetrate inland, using co-ordinated columns of Eritrean battalions and local levies and inflicting harsh punishment on the 'rebels'. It was now that Colonel – later Marshal – Rodolfo Graziani began to make his name as an expert leader of these light mobile forces. By the end of 1925 Graziani and his fellows had reconquered northern Tripolitania, killing some 6,500 Arabs at a cost of 2,582 Italians dead, wounded and missing. In Cyrenaica General Ernesto Mombelli carried out sweeps using columns co-ordinated by wireless and supported by air to hunt down the Senussi tribesmen being led by Omar el-Mukhtar, destroying encampments and tents, seizing sheep and camels, and killing 400 'rebels' at a cost of six dead and twenty-five wounded.

In July 1925 Mussolini decided that it was time for a new man to take over and appointed fifty-nine-year-old General Emilio De Bono as governor of Libya. While Graziani pushed into the interior of Tripolitania, using nomadic tribesmen and forging links with tribal leaders, De Bono sentenced rebels to death without a qualm and approved the use of phosgene gas on at least four occasions. Thanks partly to the effective use of aircraft in carrying out long-range and tactical reconnaissance, transporting troops and materiel, and co-ordinating the movement of columns, hunting down and killing rebel bands produced results. Graziani was particularly good at it. But clearing and controlling the vast desert hinterland was another matter. Also subduing the Senussi needed a higher level of direction and order than De Bono was able to provide, so in December 1928 Mussolini replaced him with Badoglio.

Over the next three years Badoglio and Graziani set about breaking down Libya's entire socio-political order, confiscating Senussi property, disarming the tribes that submitted, and carrying out a series of public trials and executions. To separate the armed Senussi in

Cyrenaica from the tribes who directly or indirectly supported them, they set up barbed-wire enclosures on the coastal strip and by the end of 1930, 80,000 tribespeople were confined in them. The internment camps made their contribution to the final death toll in Cyrenaica, which probably amounted to between 50,000 and 60,000 people.[4] At Graziani's suggestion a 270-kilometre long barbed-wire barrier was put up along the Egyptian border. Penned inside it and hunted down, Omar el-Mukhtar was captured on 11 September 1931 and hanged five days later in front of a crowd of 20,000 Arabs. On 24 January 1932 Badoglio announced that the rebellion in Cyrenaica had been defeated. Rome was triumphant. Libya was now entirely in Italian hands for the first time in almost two decades, the Fascist armed forces had won their first campaign, Badoglio had polished his credentials as Fascist Italy's leading soldier, and the new Italy had shown itself to be efficient, effective and merciless towards its enemies – exactly what Mussolini wanted the world to see.

WAR IN ABYSSINIA

The road to Mussolini's first major war opened in July 1925 when his Colonial Minister, Pietro Lanza di Scalea, proposed reinforcing the Italian colonies of Eritrea and Somalia and blocking any movement of arms to Addis Ababa and to the Abyssinian *ras* (tribal chiefs). The *Duce* was ready to begin positioning Fascist Italy for expansion and conquest. At some time in the future the Ethiopian Empire might collapse and Italy must prepare herself militarily and diplomatically, working as far as possible in collaboration with the English and 'chloroforming the official Abyssinia world' in the meantime.[5] At first things moved slowly. In June 1926 Mussolini agreed that Badoglio send a personal representative to assess the military conditions of Eritrea in view of a possible future conflict. General Giuseppe Malladra duly told Rome what it wanted to hear – that peace was precarious and war with a belligerent Abyssinia could break out at any moment.[*] To be able to defend itself, the colony needed 160,000 white troops on top of the

---

[*] At the time and since Italians have used the terms Ethiopia and Abyssinia interchangeably, with a preference for the former.

30,000–40,000 Eritreans available. Badoglio thought 40,000–50,000 Italian troops and a strong air force would be enough. For the moment, though, Italian policy still concentrated on 'chloroforming' the Abyssinians. Local representatives negotiated a treaty of friendship and good neighbourliness, and a convention on road building was signed 2 August 1928. When *ras* Tafari became emperor two months later relations worsened over the road contract and over Rome's refusal of the new emperor's request for aircraft. On the ground a new governor of Eritrea, Corrado Zoli, attacked his predecessor's weak policies. Half-hearted attempts at an agreement with France were abandoned when the Italians could see no advantage to themselves.

Many of the leading figures in the foreign policy establishment were four-square behind an Italian bid for another African colony. In April 1930 Dino Grandi, Minister of Foreign Affairs, told the Fascist Grand Council that a strong Italy could not for ever remain clinging to the extreme edge of the Eritrean *altopiano* (highland plateau) and stuck in the restricted space of Italian Somalia. The nation had a civilizing mission in the black continent to carry out and the current generation had a problem to resolve – 'the colonial problem'.[6] At the Foreign Ministry Raffaele Guariglia believed it was Italy's destiny to become a major African colonial power, as did Alessandro Lessona at the Colonial Ministry. As the history of colonization proved, 'nothing great is done in the world without getting blood on one's hands'. A war would be easier for Italy now than it had been in the past. Abyssinia had lots of guns, though not of modern types, her territories were well suited to defensive war and her soldiers particularly adapted to fight it, but modern European military technology and particularly aircraft would give Italy the whip-hand. The moment had come to consider 'this whole question, pregnant with dangers, but also with real possibilities for our country'. However, Italy could not act alone. Given the current political and military situation, Guariglia believed that prior accords with France and Great Britain were 'indispensable'.[7]

In 1932 Mussolini singled out Ethiopia – as the Italians liked to call it – as his next objective. As a first step he sent his favourite general to scout the ground. Emilio De Bono returned with the news that the Negus (Emperor Haile Selassie) was consolidating his power and intended at some future time to take up arms against Italy. Italy must prepare for a preventive war in the future. For the moment, though, armed intervention was out of the question.[8] In August the army approached De Bono about naming a commander designate in order to begin planning. De Bono went straight to Mussolini, who immediately gave him the role. De Bono planned to conquer northern Abyssinia with 35,000 white troops, 50,000 Eritrean *ascari*, 100 aircraft – and only a month's preparation. Now ensconced at Tripoli, where he was masterminding the brutal suppression of the local tribes, Badoglio was happy to see that 'this very important problem' was finally being addressed.[9] The army general staff was not. Its chief, General Alberto Bonzani, excoriated a rash plan that proposed to push two separate forces 80 kilometres forward onto the *altopiano*, fight the enemy when he was mobilized and had been allowed to close up to relatively close range, and then after a successful battle pursue him in depth. Having just expressed 'lively satisfaction' with De Bono, Badoglio now put up a plan of his own: stand on the defensive, wait until the enemy had assembled, strike with air power, and follow that up with a counter-offensive to liquidate him 'definitively'. His suggestions for a designated commander were clearly designed to exclude De Bono.

On 1 January 1934 Badoglio came back to Rome. Over the next three months the top brass struggled for control over the shaping of Mussolini's first war. Badoglio thought that accords with London and Paris were the essential diplomatic foundation for action, otherwise at the least they might arm the Abyssinians. The army general staff too wanted the whole venture set in a broad scenario which took account of whether Italy was in alliance with France or at war with her. Mussolini wanted action in 1935. Either there would be peace in Europe during the next few years, in which case a defensive position could act as the base either for an offensive or a counter-offensive, or a worsening European situation would not allow Italy to deploy force in Africa, in which case a defensive organization 'will allow us to break [down] any attempt by the Abyssinians'.[10] In late March, with the French now apparently favouring an accord, Mussolini announced that he had decided to finish off Abyssinia. Rather than put De Bono in complete charge he accepted Badoglio's argument that it was the army general staff's responsibility to do the planning. A letter duly winged its way to De Bono. Its recipient exploded. 'That pig of a Badoglio' had tried to do him down – and had succeeded.[11] With no choice De Bono gave way, though the actual conduct of the campaign still lay in his hands.

The chiefs of staff met briefly at the Palazzo Venezia on 7 May 1934 to discuss force levels for the proposed operation. Immediately Badoglio tried to apply the brakes – as he would do again in 1940. A war would cost six milliards and would put the army in crisis during the campaign and then afterwards as it struggled to refill its magazines and stores. And there would be a permanent burden of occupation. Was it worth it?[12] When he was told that preparing for a campaign in Ethiopia would take three years, the *Duce* called Badoglio and De Bono to the Palazzo Venezia on 31 May and laid out the modus operandi for the next few months. Defensive arrangements must be made as quickly as possible, after which the problem of provoking the Abyssinians into action would be addressed. In the meantime everything was to be done in the colony and internationally to avoid giving the game away.[13] Juggling his multiple offices – and his mistresses – the *Duce* forged ahead, leaving unresolved issues in his wake. How was De Bono's determination to take offensive action as soon as possible to be reconciled with Badoglio's to proceed slowly and cautiously? Whose budget was going to pay for it all? And could the country afford it? The general staff estimated that a six-month war in which four divisions took part would cost about 3,500,000,000 lire and a year-long campaign would increase the bill to just short of 5,000,000,000 lire.

The murder of the Austrian chancellor Engelbert Dollfuss on 25 July 1934 left Mussolini unwilling for the moment to do anything that might weaken his military strength in Europe, but still ready to act. Defensive preparations in Eritrea must be accelerated. If the Abyssinians attacked they were to be checked 'decisively', followed by a counter-offensive 'in directions and with objectives that the situation at the time suggests'.[14] That autumn two incidents ratcheted up the temperature. On 4 November the Italian consulate in Gondar was attacked, and on 22 November there was an armed stand-off between Abyssinians and Italians at the wells of Ual-Ual, in an area where the frontier was not defined and where the Abyssinians contested the Italian occupation. Haile Selassie appealed to the League of Nations.

The open challenge to Mussolini's prestige made him all the more determined to solve the Abyssinian problem with force before the tribes could benefit from an ongoing programme of rearmament and training by European instructors. Time was working against Italy. The problem had to be resolved as soon as possible, 'that is, as soon as our military preparations give us the certainty of victory.' There could only be one objective: 'the destruction of the Abyssinian forces and the total conquest of Ethiopia'. Glancing over the international scene, Mussolini could see no likelihood of war in Europe during the coming two years. Accords with France, the consequent easing of relations with Yugoslavia, and the fact that Germany was as yet still too weak to contemplate attacking Austria, all gave him grounds for certainty. Everything and everyone must be on the spot and ready for October 1935. Until then, foreign policy must ensure that premature conflict was avoided. The 'Gordian knot' of Italian-Abyssinian relations had to be cut before it was too late.[15]

The armed forces prepared to fight a war without quarter against a 'barbarous' enemy. No 'false scruples' were to be entertained, and no potential weapon was to be overlooked.[16] Air power would be one of those weapons. Indeed, Mussolini intended Italian air power to play a leading role in the coming campaign. As well as destroying the only Abyssinian railway, he wanted troops, population, material resources and all the 'bases of life' bombed. The airmen welcomed his directives, which gave them operational and therefore strategic independence from the army, played to the publicity campaign waged by the air minister, Italo Balbo, and would allow them to try out General Douhet's theories of terror-bombing to which their leaders were oriented.[17] The chief of the air staff, General Giuseppe Valle, obediently fell in line. In the closing months of 1935 the air force would wage a defensive war, 'halting and perhaps breaking any enemy offensive inclination' and engendering in the enemy 'a salutary terror, from which we can profit in 1936'. Italian aircraft operating from bases along the Eritrean coast would sweep the entire zone of operations, carrying out whatever actions were required, 'including the destruction of Addis Ababa, of Gondar, of Harrar and the systematic burning of the entire Somalian highlands'.[18] Gas would play an integral part in the coming war: 10 per cent of the munitions were to be gas bombs.

The New Year brought unwelcome news. Badoglio told Mussolini that the air force would not be ready to fight before October and an expeditionary corps could not be in place on the Abyssinian *altopiano* until the following February. A rapid campaign needed foresight and meticulous preparation. Italy would need 'all of 1935 and the first eight months of 1936 to be in a position to take on such an arduous task with the certainty of success'.[19] Valle concurred: fighting an offensive war would not be possible until the end of 1936, because of the lack of roads and infrastructure. Admiral Cavagnari, chief of the naval staff, warned that British and French agreement to action was essential and League of Nations sanctions were very likely. Mussolini's response was to order his subordinates to press ahead quickly with war preparations. With Fascist Italy's prestige, and his own, increasingly in play he was ready to fight if he had to, but also ready to garner his reward from the mere threat of aggression if that sufficed. 'Only if they [the League of Nations and especially Great Britain] see that we are ready to go to extreme lengths', he told Alessandro Lessona, 'will they perhaps be induced to allow the situation to resolve itself with honour and without war.'[20]

On the diplomatic front things looked promising. Pierre Laval, France's Foreign Minister, arrived in Rome at the beginning of January and concluded an accord with Italy containing a secret clause giving Mussolini a free hand in Abyssinia. Whether this included a rider excluding war, as Laval afterwards claimed, is still contested but there were grounds enough for Mussolini to assume that the French were not likely to try to stop him. The Italian Foreign Ministry advised that Great Britain too was unlikely to put up serious opposition to a war against Ethiopia, and its under-secretary Fulvio Suvich suggested that it would be possible to reach an understanding with her even after Italy had conquered Abyssinia. Italian soldiers and war materiel began transiting the Suez Canal, unmistakable signs that action was in the offing.

Making a determined bid to take charge of the coming war, Badoglio put his war plan to Mussolini. Either the Abyssinians would attack en masse, in which case they would be beaten as long as best use was made by 'an able and energetic command[er]' of Italy's superiority in both means and technical capacity, and could then be harried by Italian air power, or they would hold back, in which case the Italians could advance slowly in stages to Adigrat and Adowa, preceded by a violent air bombardment. Everything in the 700 kilometres between the frontier and Addis Ababa should be destroyed and terror disseminated throughout the empire.[21] The barely disguised move to push De Bono off his perch failed. On 8 March 1935, a day before Hermann Goering announced the creation of the *Luftwaffe* and a week before Hitler announced that conscription would be revived in Germany, the *Duce* told De Bono he was sending not two but ten divisions along with 300 to 500 planes and 300 fast tanks. He was not going to make the same mistake as his predecessor, Francesco Crispi, had made in 1896 when, in a national humiliation, he had lost a campaign in Ethiopia for want of 'a few thousand men'. Operations must start at the end of the coming September or in October.[22]

To men like Alessandro Lessona the war that was about to start would be the completion of a colonial programme begun fifty years before when Italian soldiers first set foot on Assab on the Red Sea coast, and would put Ethiopia's natural resources at Italy's disposal. To others it was the first step in the planned progress to imperial grandeur, as indeed schoolchildren would be taught shortly after the war ended. 'Young Turks' wanted war to liberate the regime from the stagnation into which it was sinking and remake a party that was no longer the guarantor of the original ideals of the Fascist revolution. War was also welcomed as a mobilizing force that could reawaken the feelings of nationalism and patriotism which had flourished between 1915 and 1918 before being supposedly submerged beneath a Red tide.[23]

On 25 May 1935, addressing the Italian chamber of deputies, Mussolini told them to look beyond the immediate issue of Austria and the defence of the Brenner Pass to the growing threat to Italian East Africa. No one should think of turning Abyssinia into a pistol 'perennially pointed at us'. 'We have some old and some new scores to settle,' he told the *Sabauda* division in June on the eve of its departure for East Africa, '[and] settle them we shall.' At the end of July, in an article in *Il Popolo d'Italia*, his personal newspaper and the mouthpiece of the Fascist Party, he brushed aside slavery, race and civilization as the basic causes of Italy's conflict with Ethiopia. There were only two 'essential, irrefutable' matters at issue: 'the vital needs of the Italian people and the military security of East Africa'. The latter was the decisive one. If Italy were to find itself committed in Europe the threat that Ethiopia would pose would be strategically unsustainable, and until the 'looming military menace' was eliminated, Eritrea and Somalia would never be safe. The solution could only be 'totalitarian'. The Abyssinian threat was about to be eliminated not by diplomacy but by brute force.[24]

In June Mussolini had written off Great Britain as likely to be bother-some only in the League of Nations. Then, at the start of August, came the news that the British Home Fleet was in fact being sent to the Medi-terranean. Ordered to prepare plans for war with England, Badoglio summoned the chiefs of staff. Admiral Cavagnari and General Valle were unequivocal: neither the navy nor the air force was in any condition to fight England.* Only the army was ready to take her on, and its contri-bution could not save the Mediterranean from falling under British dominance.[25] Badoglio warned Mussolini: a war with England would face Italy with a situation that would be 'by a long way the gravest that our country has traversed throughout the eventful story of her formation and her national consolidation'.[26] Next day brought better news from London. Grandi, now the ambassador to England, told the *Duce* that the Admiralty had advised that war with Italy should be avoided as the military efficiency of the Mediterranean Fleet was not such as to guaran-tee success against the Italian navy and air force. On 21 August Mussolini ordered De Bono to be ready to start the war at any time after 10 September. De Bono asked for a further eight to ten days' grace and got it.[27] With this Badoglio came into line, assuring Mussolini that with six metropolitan divisions as well as two native divisions and another eight battalions to hand, De Bono could begin operations.[28]

An immense logistical effort put the resources in place for the war Mussolini demanded. The navy built a railway, reservoirs and wharves at the port of Massawa on the Red Sea, increasing its unloading capacity from 400–500 tons a day to 2,000 and then finally 4,000 tons a day. Spending 950,000,000 lire on hiring ships and paying Suez Canal dues, the navy carried 595,204 men, 634,900 tons of supplies, 10,084 vehicles and 40,859 animals to Eritrea and Somalia between February 1935 and July 1936. In the months before the war began, it shipped in enough materials for the air force to build six main bases, eighteen airports and eighty-four field landing strips, as well as bring-ing in 49,500 tons of fuel and lubricants and 14,500 tons of munitions. A surge of effort by all the military agencies produced a vast panoply of essential war goods from refrigerator ships and hospital ships at one end of the spectrum to maps and khaki uniforms at the other.[29]

* At the time, contemporaries generally used the term England rather than Britain or Great Britain.

The prospect of a war in Abyssinia galvanized the officer corps. Four thousand active officers and 17,000 reserve officers put in requests to serve, some using the normal route of the war office, others going via the royal household or members of the government. The Fascist propaganda machine went full blast, churning out simple messages about national pride and the need to escape from the position imposed on Italy by the egoism and fear of the rich nations. The Catholic Church joined the cause. Although the Pope remained studiously neutral, the hierarchy and the rank and file fell in behind Mussolini. Three weeks after the war began Cardinal Schuster told the congregation assembled in the *duomo* in Milan that their army was spilling its blood 'to open the doors of Ethiopia to the Catholic Faith and to Roman civilization'. The bishop of Terracina assured Mussolini that the hearts of all Italians were beating in unison with his, and the bishop of Ozieri told his flock that the war was neither a colonial nor a political issue but a moral and religious one in which Protestantism, Freemasonry, Communism and anti-Fascism were trying to destroy the civilization of Rome because it was Catholic.[30]

At 5 a.m. on the morning of 3 October 1935 four Italian and two Eritrean divisions, 110,000 men in all, crossed the frontier and marched into Abyssinia. At De Bono's direction, a three-pronged advance drove the fifty or so kilometres to Adigrat and Adowa. At first there was little resistance. What the Italians did not know was that the local chieftain had been ordered by Haile Selassie to avoid battle and stick to guerrilla action. The Italians were in Adigrat in two days and Adowa in three. With Dino Grandi in London warning of the danger that an incident with British forces in the Mediterranean or the Red Sea might expand the conflict, and his under-secretary Suvich pressing for a further advance, Mussolini decided to send Badoglio and Lessona to Eritrea to see what could be done there if the conflict did balloon. For the moment, though, France was evidently in the mood for conciliation and London denied any intention of preparing for war. A telegram was despatched from Palazzo Venezia ordering De Bono to push on quickly to Makalle. Like many of the objectives in the first phase of the war, it had great historical significance for the Italians. In January 1896, only weeks before the disaster at Adowa in which he was killed, Major Galliano and a force of 1,350 soldiers had held out under siege there for nine days before being granted a safe conduct by Menelik II.

De Bono dug in his heels and refused to move before 10 November. With a British election due very shortly and the possibility that sanctions, voted by the League of Nations on 19 October and currently not including oil, would be tightened, Mussolini needed action. De Bono was instructed to begin the next stage of the advance on 3 November. When all the territories lost in 1896 were back in Italian hands, Mussolini declared, he intended to suspend hostilities. The pressure on him at that moment was as much financial as international: imports were set to rise considerably, exports were likely to be down by half in the coming year, and gold was flowing out of the Banca d'Italia. Instructions came down from on high that military orders were to be kept 'rigorously' within the bounds of previously agreed imports of raw materials, and war materials only to be acquired from countries that were not imposing sanctions.[31]

Badoglio's report landed on Mussolini's desk early in November. De Bono was tired to the point of complete exhaustion (he was sixty-nine, five years older than Badoglio), the high command in Eritrea was static in spirit and in function, and the chief staff officers were being run on a loose rein. What the whole force lacked was the guidance of a commander with prestige and authority.[32] Reluctantly De Bono recommenced his attack. Once again there was little enemy resistance, but advance was difficult: the rains had degraded the mule tracks so that it took several days for the guns and light tanks to catch up with the foot soldiers ahead of them. De Bono's men reached Makalle on 8 November. Again Mussolini urged his hesitant commander forward, telling him to push his Eritrean troops out to Amba Alagi. It too carried huge symbolic significance: on 7 December 1895 it had been the scene of a hopeless battle in which 2,350 Italian troops, mostly *ascari*, had been overwhelmed by 30,000 Ethiopians. This was a war in which deep wounds could at last be avenged. De Bono protested: he was at the end of a 500-kilometre supply line, his artillery had not yet come up, his reserves were strung out along the road network, and his defences were far from complete. Mussolini had had enough. On 14 November De Bono was relieved, his reward for a job rather less than half done the baton of a *Maresciallo d'Italia*, and Badoglio took over the war.

Badoglio left Naples on 18 November 1935 and by the end of the month he was at Asmara on the *altopiano*. Waiting for him was intelligence suggesting that 150,000 Ethiopians were on the march. As far as he was concerned, the aim of the war was the total destruction of the Abyssinian armed forces and the complete conquest of Ethiopia. But first things must be properly organized so that 'we are not up in the air as we are now'. Then, and only then, active military operations could and would follow.[33] While Mussolini waited to see whether Geneva would apply petrol sanctions, Badoglio set about methodically establishing a secure defence.

In the febrile world of Fascist military politics, Badoglio's appointment challenged the status of a new generation. The chief of the army general staff, General Federico Baistrocchi, busy disseminating his own ideas for a new kind of *guerra lampo* ('fast war'), thought Badoglio lacked the necessary Fascist dash and genius and feared that he would conduct operations at a slow and steady pace 'with heavy forces anchored to the terrain'. What were needed were light, agile columns that could move quickly to take advantage of surprise. He urged Mussolini to recall the chief of the armed forces general staff to Rome where he belonged and to take personal command, aided by 'a technical expert with a broad viewpoint, without preconceptions, a Fascist devoted to You' – in other words himself.[34] The men on the spot – Badoglio, General Rodolfo Graziani on the Somalian front, and Italo Balbo, now governor of Libya – were, he claimed, each seeing the war from their own perspective. What was needed was centralized control and only Mussolini could see the whole war in the round and issue 'orders, which everyone will obey'.[35] Orbiting above the squabbling, Mussolini was prepared to give his new field commander time – as long as he did not waste it.

Reading the cultural mindset of his opponent with some accuracy, Badoglio thought that a battle could develop spontaneously on one or more sectors of his front regardless of the emperor's intentions as a result of the independence and rivalry of the Ethiopian *ras*. The immediate threat was an attack on the nodal point of his line at Makalle by up to 200,000 Ethiopians. After a quick tour of the line he explained to his corps commanders why nothing was happening just now. The first priority was organizing a defensive line that would allow 'secure and continuous replenishment for the troops gathered in the Makalle area'. So for some time they would be standing still – but offensive operations would then follow.[36]

Badoglio had good reason to be cautious, for De Bono had left him in a precarious strategic situation. His forces were split into two separate parts, one around Adowa and the other at Makalle. Although they were only 100 kilometres apart, there were no direct communications between them. The troops at Adowa had to be supplied along two mule tracks that could be cut by the Ethiopians, and both flanks of the Makalle position were wide open as far back as the frontier with Eritrea 170 kilometres away. With threats developing to Adowa and Axum on his right and to Makalle on his left, Badoglio made his only mistake of the campaign, leaving the central stretch of his line at Tembien guarded by four Blackshirt divisions. The result was a minor but annoying setback when the Blackshirts retreated in the face of an Ethiopian attack, potentially opening up a route through the Italian positions. Badoglio swiftly moved his Eritreans into the line, countering the threat.

On the right *ras* Immirù and 30,000–40,000 Ethiopians pushed back General Maravigna's forward defences at Dembeguina, forcing the Eritrean troops who were holding the pass to withdraw at a cost of 401 casualties. On 15 December a small detachment of eight light tanks with no infantry support allowed itself to be drawn into combat with Ethiopians advancing on the Dembeguina Pass. Two tanks were destroyed, two crewmen decapitated, and the other two carried off to meet an unknown fate. The remaining six tanks withdrew across rough ground and were eventually brought to a standstill when the Ethiopians disabled their tracks and guns (Italian machine guns, it emerged, could simply be bent) and knocked out their radiators with hand grenades. All eight tanks were destroyed or abandoned, and only four Italians, two of whom were wounded, got out of the imbroglio.[37]

Mussolini was put out at the setback, which created a very poor impression. Badoglio reassured him: such minor annoyances were no real threat to the situation and might even be beneficial. 'Sad events' like this were needed 'to convince officers and men that we are [actually] in enemy territory'.[38] The air force had been unable to prevent the assembling of the Ethiopian forces – after the first bombing they dispersed and moved up out of sight of the watching aircraft. So, to protect the slow advance of his own troops, Badoglio ordered the air force to use all means available to slow down the advance of the enemy columns. On 23 December 1935 the *Regia Aeronautica* dropped six gas bombs – the first of the campaign – on Ethiopian troops. Five days later Mussolini formally authorized Badoglio to use both gas and flamethrowers. In February 1936 he would propose using bacteriological warfare, which Badoglio refused to do.

The Italians quickly learned that aerial war had to be used with at least some circumspection. The news that Italian aircraft had bombed a Swedish Red Cross hospital threatened to turn international opinion further against Italy. Immediately, fresh instructions went out from Rome. The bombing of Abyssinian cities, including Addis Ababa, was suspended and so was attacking, or even over-flying, communications between Abyssinia and the outside world. 'No one is more in favour of harsh war than I am,' Mussolini told Badoglio, but 'the necessary reprisals must be intelligent.'[39] Unsure whether the Ethiopians were going to operate in accordance with some overarching strategic plan formulated by the emperor or fight a series of local actions, and with a 250-kilometre front to defend, Badoglio needed more men. He asked for two more divisions and Mussolini sent him three, urging him to get on and win the war as soon as he could.

After making sure that his supply lines were secure and fully functional, Badoglio was ready to move. In front of him were three separate Ethiopian armies. On his right, facing Adowa, stood *ras* Immirù with 40,000 men; in the centre *ras* Cassa and *ras* Sejum with 30,000 men; and on his left facing Makalle *ras* Mulughueta with 80,000 men. Mussolini urged Badoglio forward. The *parola d'ordine* was not to wait passively for the enemy to take the initiative but to defeat him 'in battles which will be large or small according to circumstance, but victorious'.[40] Badoglio hoped to launch his main offensive south from Makalle to Amba Aradam soon. He was also aware of the possibility that his right wing at Adowa – Axum might be attacked. In the event, his first battle was fought not on the right or left of his line but in the middle. To secure his centre, and to pre-empt an offensive by his opponent, Badoglio decided to adopt a plan proposed by General Pirzio Biroli and attack *ras* Cassa. The first battle of Tembien (19–22 January 1936), fought by Pirzio Biroli's Eritrean corps, ended with *ras* Cassa's withdrawal, but all was not plain sailing. At one point, when a Blackshirt division had lost 450 dead and wounded, Badoglio ordered his staff to begin work in strictest secrecy on a plan for a complete withdrawal from Makalle but was persuaded by subordinates to suspend it.

However, the crisis soon passed and on 24 January Badoglio informed Rome that the enemy had fallen back.

Tembien was an important battle. Tactically neither side had won an outright victory, but strategically the Italian position was now secure. The air force had demonstrated the importance of air intervention and the role it could fulfil, not only (according to its commander, Ajmone Cat) 'contributing to the resolution of the tactical situation, as in all other phases of the campaign, but reversing it'.[41] Throughout the rest of the campaign air power would play a crucial role, hammering retreating enemy columns, sealing off rear areas with gas, and protecting and resupplying the columns that would soon advance on Gondar, Lake Tana and Addis Ababa. During the battle Badoglio had been able to take advantage of intercepted Ethiopian radio messages – these would become an increasingly valuable ace in his hand as the war went on. Rome provided more intelligence from intercepted messages from the Abyssinian delegation at Geneva. Perhaps most importantly, Tembien enabled Badoglio to test the effectiveness of European training and modern weapons on Ethiopian fighting power and also gauge how far the Negus was able to co-ordinate and control his factious tribal chiefs. The encouraging conclusion was that the military progress Abyssinia had appeared to be making with European help before the war was purely superficial. The Ethiopians did indeed have better weapons than before and their warlike spirit was high, but the Negus had clearly not been able to impose a modern organization on his tribal levies or exert a co-ordinating authority over them. The intercepts told Badoglio that Haile Selassie did not know what to do next and was far from sure of the loyalty of the *ras*.[42]

While Badoglio was preparing and fighting his battle in the north, General Rodolfo Graziani pulled off a dramatic success in the south. After fending off an Ethiopian attack on 12 January, he launched a column of 7,000 men into the southern Abyssinian province of Sidamo, taking Neghelli and forcing Haile Selassie to switch troops to the south. Addis Ababa was now only 365 miles away along a motor road, but instead of pushing on into the heart of enemy territory Graziani obeyed instructions from Mussolini and sent columns out west to the border with Kenya, penetrating 130 kilometres into enemy territory. In March the annual rains arrived and movement in the south came to a halt.

Tembien had cost the Abyssinians some 5,000 casualties but they still had 150,000 men in the field and another 25,000 to 30,000 on their way. With his supply services ready at last to back up a large-scale advance, Badoglio laid his plans for a great offensive which would break Ethiopian resistance. Collecting together a force of forty battalions (40,000–50,000 men) and 230 guns, he would press forward from Makalle on the left end of his line against *ras* Mulughueta and his 80,000 Abyssinians. This was the largest of the three Ethiopian armies and its focal point, the well-defended mountain of Amba Aradam, commanded all the main communications in its vicinity. Mulughueta would either have to fight, in which case Badoglio was confident of winning, or withdraw and expose the lines of communication running to the two other Abyssinians forces facing the Italians' centre and right. Either outcome would then offer him the opportunity to defeat the other two armies in detail. Tactically, Badoglio was playing to Italian strengths and Abyssinian weaknesses. His advancing troops would rely heavily on artillery and air power, defending their flanks with strong defensive positions and drawing out the fight in order to wear down Abyssinian nerves and use up the enemy's limited supplies of ammunition before turning his flanks and then smashing his centre.[43] The plan was submitted to Mussolini, who approved it.

At dawn on 11 February 1936 the Italian artillery opened up on the Ethiopians, firing shells charged with arsine. Gas shells were used again next day and on the day the battle took place. In all, 22,908 rounds were fired during the battle, of which 1,367 were gas shells. Though gas-charged rounds continued to arrive in Eritrea they would not be used again, probably because they seemingly had little effect in mountainous terrain. After advancing in alternate bounds for three days, the two army corps that would fight the battle paused for two days to reposition their artillery and improve communications. A lone Ethiopian chief, Maconnen Demissié, understanding that the Italians were going to encircle Mulughueta's forces, tried to surround one of the advancing infantry regiments but was fought off. Badoglio was sublimely confident. 'We shall win the war with a lightning campaign the like of which has not been seen since Napoleon's day,' he told a group of embedded journalists on the eve of the battle. The war would be won and the Ethiopian Empire would collapse under Italian blows in little more than two months, he assured them.[44]

The battle of Endertà, which took place on 15 February, was the largest engagement of the war. At dawn the battlefield was swathed in a dense fog, hindering Italian observation from the air and limiting the effectiveness of the guns, but as the sun rose it dissolved and at about nine in the morning the fighting began. Two pincers drove into the Abyssinian mass from the flanks, while a smaller column fixed them in the centre. The Ethiopians launched three fierce counter-attacks during the morning and early afternoon, but the Italian guns broke them all. Artillery played a big part in the Italian victory – in the course of the day 280 guns fired 23,000 rounds. So too did air power, the *Regia Aeronautica* carrying out forty-four missions on the day and dropping 13,388 kilos of explosives. Afterwards Ajmone Cat claimed that air action during the battle had reduced Italian casualties from an estimated 3,000 to only 300. At noon Mulughueta left the field of battle and three hours later air reconnaissance reported that the Ethiopians were retiring. A battalion of the 23 *Marzo* Blackshirt division was allowed the credit of taking the summit of Amba Aradam, though the *Alpini* had done the lion's share of the fighting and probably got there first.

Although at the end of the day he had won a victory, again Badoglio's battle did not go entirely as he intended. The two Italian wings failed to join up, leaving a gap three kilometres wide through which Mulughueta was able to slip away. Only a handful of tribesmen managed to flee with him. The Ethiopians lost some 20,000 men on the field of battle and more in the retreat that followed. Galla tribesmen joined in against their traditional enemies, and the air force played its part: 16 February saw the heaviest day's bombing in the entire war. Gas, dropped from the air on the retreating Ethiopians, added to the slaughter. Italian losses numbered 134 dead and 523 wounded in the white units and sixty-three dead and eighty-three wounded in the native units. Mulughueta himself was killed during the retreat.[45]

The enemy was now in disarray, as Badoglio knew from intercepts. Haile Selassie wanted the remaining two tribal armies to pull back towards Amba Alagi to form a single compact force but lacked the authority to enforce his wishes. *Ras* Immirù on the Ethiopian left was standing on the defensive, and *ras* Cassa in the centre, now worried about what might have happened to Mulughueta's men on his own right flank, intended to move to his left to join Immirù. Daily intercepts told the Italians much about the confusion and lack of co-ordination in the enemy's camp. The Abyssinians were now wide open to defeat in detail. Along the Italian front five army corps began to move. In the fighting to come, Badoglio shaped Italian combat methods to negate the enemy's strengths – rapidity and fluidity of movement, lightning attacks and a complete disregard of casualties. Italian forces accompanied by lots of guns and machine guns and copious supplies of ammunition would advance leap-frog style in bounds so that the elements on the move were always supported by those that had momentarily halted.[46]

Following Mulughueta's retreating tribesmen, the three divisions of General Santini's I Corps pushed south to Amba Alagi, meeting no real resistance, and on 28 February the Italian *tricolore* flew again over the fort where, in December 1895, Major Pietro Toselli and three-fifths of his garrison of 2,350 men had perished after trying to fight off 30,000 Ethiopians. Meanwhile, General Pirzio Biroli's Eritrean corps went after *ras* Cassa. To reach their target his men had to cross a range of rocky peaks dotted with patches of vegetation and broken by innumerable caverns which offered shelter for occasionally stiff resistance. Once again Italian logistics worked a minor miracle, bringing forward 48,000 rounds of artillery ammunition and 7,000,000 rounds of smallarms' ammunition along rough tracks where trucks sank up to their axle hubs in sand. The Eritreans smashed Cassa's men in the second battle of Tembien (27–29 February 1936) before joining up with General Ettore Bastico's III Corps and cutting off their retreat. Italian aircraft again played an important role in the battle, dropping 100 tons of explosives and harassing the retreating Ethiopians with thousands of incendiaries. Gas bombs were used to make fords impassable to retreating Ethiopians. The battle cost the Abyssinians 8,000 men, the Italians 393 dead and wounded, and the Eritreans 188.[47]

It was now *ras* Immirù's turn to experience the Fascist war machine. Again, the battle of Scirè (29 February–3 March 1936) did not go quite according to plan. According to the original battle plan, Maravigna's II Corps advancing from the east and Babbini's IV Corps coming from the north would converge from opposite directions and crush the enemy in a concentric manoeuvre.[48] Maravigna's troops had only thirty kilometres to cover through easy country, part hills and part plain and crossed by a motor road, but they faced determined resistance which slowed them down by a day. Babbini's men, on the other hand, faced a ninety-kilometre march across very broken ground covered with thick, spiny vegetation and entirely without water in territory that was completely unknown. Since the plan offered Immirù the opportunity to strike each of the two Italian corps in turn, Badoglio changed it: now II Corps would attack the enemy head on while IV Corps threatened his flank and rear. Maravigna's troops began moving in the early hours of 29 February but were slowed down when the advance guard of one of his divisions ran into some stiff resistance. Next day he had to ask for twenty-four hours' pause to reorganize his forces and restock with more munitions. Whether or not Badoglio was responsible for the delay, as Maravigna claimed years later, it was certainly true that timing the movement of the two corps had not been managed as well as it could have been.[49]

Maravigna's men resumed their march on 2 March and were again slowed down by the enemy. Neither newly arrived flamethrowers nor tanks which continually shed their tracks proved of much assistance. Aware of the threat that was developing, Immirù took advantage of the two-day pause in II Corps' advance to break off the engagement and retreat. IV Corps marched undisturbed to its designated target ground, making no contribution to the battle. Immirù left 4,000 dead on the field and lost another 3,000 men to Italian air attacks during the withdrawal, gas again playing its part. Totally demoralized, his remaining force dissolved and Immirù himself fled towards Gondar with a few hundred men. The last Ethiopian army left on the northern front had been neutralized at a cost of 868 Italian and Eritrean dead and wounded.

The success of the Tigray operations owed a great deal to skill and effectiveness with which the Italian *Intendenza* had managed the logistics. Five army corps had been kept supplied in mountainous regions lacking any resources more than 400 kilometres from the coast and 4,000 kilometres from the Italian *patria*. Over 900 trucks had transported weapons and munitions, and two army corps (III and IV) had been partially resupplied by air. An entire division had been moved from the coast to the front at Makalle in only thirty-eight hours, using 650 vehicles. In the first two weeks of February alone the supply services carried 200,000 rounds of artillery ammunition, 22,000,000 rounds of small-arms ammunition and tens of thousands of grenades to front-line units, as well as dozens of cannon and hundreds of rifles and sidearms. Every day the trucks, 6,000 camels and 4,000 mules sent forward 5,000 kilos of flour, 400 kilos of frozen meat, 150,000 cartons of milk, 4,000 hectolitres of wine, 900 kilos of jam, 450 kilos of dried fruit, 1,200 kilos of biscuit, 15,000 kilos of tobacco, 150,000 bottles of mineral water, and 500,000 cans of meat and soup. Every division had two field hospitals, every corps had a surgical centre, and three central field hospitals were set up with 1,800 beds.[50]

Thanks to intercepts, Badoglio knew that Immirù had only a handful of men left, that only Haile Selassie's imperial guard together with a handful of irregulars and the few survivors of the earlier battles, amounting to between 30,000 and 50,000 men, now stood between him and outright victory in the field, and that at an imperial council of war on 26 March a reluctant emperor had sided with the aggressive majority and now intended to advance against him.[51] In what would turn out to be the last act of the war the Ethiopians were playing straight into the Italians' hands. Having forsworn guerrilla war at the outset as being beneath their warrior mentality, they should now have drawn Badoglio deeper into the country and away from his supply bases – as he feared they might do. Instead they allowed themselves to become victims as much of their own traditions as of Italian material and organizational superiority.

Knowing that he was facing 31,000 Ethiopians, and that the Negus intended to try to break into the fortified lines he had set up to secure the occupied territories, Badoglio laid out the timetable with which he intended to finish the war. The Negus would be beaten at the beginning of April, he would enter Addis Ababa as its conqueror on 30 April, and ten days later he would leave the country and return to Italy. 'I am only here to make war', he told Colonel Quirino Armellini.[52] Staying in Abyssinia would mean taking on the complex and unrewarding task of building a new colonial administration there. It would also keep him away from Rome and thereby expose him to the consequences of the political infighting that was part and parcel of life at the top of the Fascist regime. Returning in triumph to the capital of Mussolini's new Roman Empire, on the other hand, would give him an undeniable claim to the rewards that the *Duce* was ready to dish out to those in favour – or those he did not wish to antagonize.

Badoglio tightened the vice on the remaining Ethiopian resistance. A motorized column led by the Fascist boss Achille Starace set out on 15 March from Asmara and after crossing more than 300 kilometres of unknown terrain, initially desert and then high mountain passes, without meeting any resistance it reached Gondar, formerly the capital of Ethiopia, on 1 April at the same time as an Eritrean column. The native troops were held back to give the Fascist the laurels. By the end of the month Lake Tana and the entire region were in Italian hands. I Corps pushed steadily south towards Lake Ashenge, building a road as it went, while Italian aircraft dropped gas bombs on concentrations of Ethiopian troops ahead of it. Then came what was to Badoglio welcome news: rather than retreat back to Dessié, the Negus proposed to fight. Taking his time, Badoglio paused for two weeks to finish building the roads and bring up the troops and munitions he needed for what he told Mussolini would be 'a grandiose action that could be truly decisive'.[53] He planned to complete the concentration of his forces on 31 March and start his advance on Dessié next day. Then, unexpectedly, the Ethiopians began to advance. Armed only with picks and shovels, the Italians hastily threw up a makeshift defensive line consisting mostly of dry stone walls and branches of trees and defended only by light-calibre guns, and awaited the enemy. Three Italian front-line divisions, some 40,000 men, faced about the same number of Ethiopians.

The battle of Mai Ceu began at 5.45 a.m. on 31 March 1936 with a head-on attack by Ethiopians on General Luigi Negri's *Pusteria* division. The troops held their ground in the face of what seemed like a human flood as wave after wave threw themselves against the defences and were cut down by bursts of rifle and machine-gun fire. Then the Ethiopians shifted their attack to the east of Negri's position, aiming for the Mecan Pass defended by the 2nd Eritrean division, hoping that resistance there would be less determined and that they could open up a gap in the centre of the Italian line. Shortly after 8.00 in the morning the *Regia Aeronautica* joined in the fray. Seventy Italian bombers, one of them piloted by Mussolini's son Bruno, began bombing the battle-field, the Ethiopians' rear and their supply lines. The Negus threw in his imperial guard, and for three hours a fierce fight raged for control of the pass. A counter-attack with the bayonet led by the divisional commander, General Renzo Dalmazzo, gradually ran out of steam as the *ascari* paused to loot the battlefield and was forced back to its starting line. Throughout the afternoon, attack was met by counter-attack. At about 4 p.m. three columns of fresh Ethiopian troops attacked both wings of Negri's line. Bitter fighting went on for two hours and then, as twilight began to fall, Haile Selassie ordered his forces to withdraw. The battle had lasted more than fourteen hours. The Italians lost 89 dead and 291 wounded, their Eritrean *ascari* 204 dead and 669 wounded. Ethiopian losses are unknown but probably amounted to between 5,000 and 8,000. The emperor – in a telegram to his empress that night which, like so many others, was intercepted and deciphered – praised his troops' determination but admitted that they were 'unable to carry out European-style combat'.[54]

The attack was renewed next day, but although Italian aircraft were hampered by bad weather three more Italian divisions came into line. Demoralized by their failure, the losses suffered in battle and the desertions that were now occurring, the Ethiopians began to retreat. With that the weather cleared, enabling the Italian air force to strike them at will. With only 5,000 tribesmen blocking Badoglio's route to the capital, where the emperor's imperial guard faced the likelihood of being surrounded, the Ethiopian Foreign Minister (in yet another intercepted telegram) warned that the military situation was becoming 'unsustainable'. The Italians were halfway to Dessié and there was no army to stop them.[55] Pirzio Biroli's Eritreans pursued the fleeing Ethiopians, who moved at night to escape the watching eyes of Italian aircraft. Advancing more than 250 kilometres in a week thanks to a well-organized aerial resupply service, they reached Dessié, an important crossroads for caravan routes which was also the Ethiopians' strongest strategic bulwark, on 15 April. At the same time Graziani was ordered to attack from the south.

While Mussolini sprayed out ambiguous telegrams from Rome suggesting that he was willing to treat with Haile Selassie, the war in Ethiopia moved inexorably towards its end. As Badoglio prepared to strike the last blow Graziani, who had spent most of February and March intriguing with Baistrocchi in Rome to get control of the army and the colonial forces after the war, launched his attack on Harrar. Graziani's 38,000 troops faced some 30,000 Ethiopians spread out in depth in front of him. He planned a lightning advance into enemy territory by three columns. His intention was to fight a different kind of campaign from the one Badoglio was masterminding. A more elastic tactical organization freed from supply bases was designed to contrast sharply with the ponderous war machine that was grinding its way down to Addis Ababa in the north.[56] Graziani's attack on the Ogaden, spearheaded by colonial troops, began on 15 April. After overcoming some determined resistance, he fought a major battle on 24–25 April, losing 2,000 dead and wounded, and then paused to reorganize and resupply his men. Anxious to get his venture over as quickly as possible, Mussolini promised Graziani the baton of a Marshal of Italy if and when he conquered Harrar.

It took the Italian engineers and supply services ten days to create a viable line of communications from Mai Ceu to Dessié and bring up the stores and munitions needed for the final push. On 24 April 1936 the assault on the capital began. Twenty thousand Italian and Eritrean troops, supported by 1,725 lorries and trucks, advanced on Addis Ababa along the two main routes to the capital. So did twelve generals, the under-secretary of the Colonial Ministry Alessandro Lessona, the Fascist hierarch Giuseppe Bottai, two senators, a prince, twenty-one journalists, Badoglio's two sons, and his nephew. A motorized column under General Gariboldi and a separate group of four battalions of Eritreans on foot went down one route, while another column at brigade strength marched down the other. The two marching columns started first, ready to deal with any substantial Ethiopian resistance – but there was none worth the name. Once this was apparent, the main motorized column leap-frogged ahead of its supports. By the evening of 4 May the capital was in sight. The Eritrean column had already been encamped within sight of Addis Ababa for two days – but the honour of taking the capital had to go to white troops. At 4 p.m. on Tuesday, 5 May, a victorious Badoglio led his soldiers into the capital – not on horseback as he would have liked but in a motorcar, because of the rain. Haile Selassie had already gone. Advised by the French minister resident not to put the 6,000 foreign residents of Addis Ababa at risk by trying to defend it, he left three days before the Italians arrived, boarding the British cruiser *Enterprise* at Djibouti on 3 May and sailing to Haifa. Three days later, in appalling weather, Graziani's troops entered Harrar. The war was over.

In all, some 18,000 officers and 477,000 troops took part in the conquest of Abyssinia, backed by 1,500 guns, 500 tanks and 450

aircraft, supported by 103,000 pack animals and 19,000 motor vehicles. Military casualties were relatively light: 2,988 white soldiers and
1,457 *ascari* died, and 7,815 white and 3,307 native soldiers were
wounded. The official Ethiopian death toll numbered some 275,000.[57]
The air force, which flew 50,000 hours and dropped 1,800 tons of
bombs, had eight aircraft shot down by the Abyssinians (who had
only a few modern Oerlikon anti-aircraft guns) and lost 131 officers
and men in air and ground combat and flying accidents.[58] The cost
was officially put at 12,111,000,000 lire, but to persuade both the
populace and the outside world that Fascist Italy could conquer an
empire without upsetting the balance between income and expenditure much of it was kept 'off balance sheet' and deferred to
subsequent years. Funding it took a third of Italy's gold and foreign
currency reserves, and by 1940 the new East African Empire had cost
46,000,000,000 lire or 21 per cent of total state spending, paid for by
debt mostly in the shape of Treasury bonds.[59]

In six months the Italian armed forces had conquered a country
bigger than France and Germany put together, much to the surprise of
'expert' international opinion which had believed that the war was
beyond Italy and would probably last at least two years. With means
enough, Italian army commanders showed themselves capable of
organizing and fighting a mobile war in which they manoeuvred tens
of thousands of men. In the overall balance of things the Abyssinians
stood little or no chance against the avalanche of troops, munitions
and supplies that Mussolini poured into the campaign. To provide it,
Baistrocchi and the army general staff had to strip the country's military resources almost to the bone. The fifteen divisions that fought in
Abyssinia, together with another five sent to Libya, took with them
enough weapons, munitions and supplies to equip seventy-five metropolitan divisions. Logistically, the war was a triumph for the supply
services. For the first time a large army had been kept in the field largely
by motor vehicles and aircraft across very broken and difficult ground.
Gas had played its part, but the Italians were not persuaded that its use
had been decisive and neither, it has been claimed, were the Ethiopians,
who feared incendiary bombs more than gas and learned to disperse
their troops in order to avoid its effects.[60]

Success gave rise to dangerous illusions. Badoglio claimed that the
war had shown that the three-regiment *divisione ternaria* was too

heavy and unmanoeuvrable, thereby backing the idea of a 'light' two-regiment *divisione binaria* which would be implemented by the next chief of the army general staff, Alberto Pariani. Some of his subordinates were more sceptical about drawing false lessons from 'exceptionally favourable situations which will be difficult to repeat in other wars'.[61] Mussolini could with some reason believe that his Fascist army was capable of feats that were beyond its pre-war Liberal predecessor, and Badoglio encouraged him in this dangerous belief. 'With soldiers like these,' he told the *Duce* and the public, 'Italy can dare all.' Baistrocchi warned Mussolini against misreading the immediate past. The war which the *Duce* predicted was coming would be not be a lightning war as the 'strategic utopians' were maintaining. That was 'a pleasing aspiration' only achievable when there was an enormous discrepancy of force between belligerents – as there had been in Abyssinia. In a world war which would see 'two opposing camps [fighting] a war without quarter', the winner 'will be the side that has been best able to prepare itself'. Italy was not yet ready to follow the Great Power policy upon which Mussolini had decided. That required 'time, money, raw materials, [and] an understanding of the necessities of war'.[62] This was not the kind of advice that Mussolini wanted to hear. By now involved in another military gamble, he sacked Baistrocchi, replacing him with the most committed proponent of a fast, Fascist-style war – General Alberto Pariani.

There is a general belief that Mussolini's regime was at the height of its popularity during the Ethiopian war. Fascist propaganda certainly made it look that way, but in the major cities the consensus was weak. As the war approached there were signs of 'apathy' in Pistoia and of 'great nervousness' in Rome where many feared the worst. In Turin, Florence and Trieste there was considerable anxiety at the prospect of a war against England or even Europe as a whole, which would demand huge sacrifices and might lead to the complete overturning of the nation. The pause at the end of the year while Badoglio made his preparations produced a bout of nervous agitation in Turin. In the months after the war officially ended the popular mood worsened as returning soldiers told of continuing combat with rebel bands. In Rome, Milan and Modena the authorities reported widespread feeling that the new empire was 'a delusion, [and] a huge burden for the Italian people'.[63] The war did nothing to improve the lot of the average Italian family.

Between 1935 and 1936 the cost of living rose by 7.15 per cent, and in the next twelve months it climbed again, this time by 9.5 per cent. In all, domestic prices rose by one-third between August 1934 and the second half of 1936.[64]

THE SPANISH QUICKSAND

No sooner had one war ended than another began. Early in June 1936 the Italian military attaché in Tangiers, Major Giuseppe Luccardi, reported that a military coup was in the offing. In the early 1930s conservative Spaniards had come to Rome every year to ask for Mussolini's help in unseating the Republican government, and every year they had gone away empty-handed. This time things were different. The Nationalist insurrection began on 18 July and General Francisco Franco immediately asked Rome for eight Caproni bombers. Italian military intelligence strongly advised against involvement. Franco's Moroccan *pronunciamiento* had failed in all but three of the peninsula's major cities. Spain was a morass into which the army could all too easily be sucked to no benefit. Then on 24 July came the news that the French were sending twenty-five aircraft to aid the Republicans. A Republican victory would put Spain firmly in France's orbit and that would be an intolerable threat both politically and strategically. Count Ciano, Mussolini's son-in-law and newly promoted Foreign Minister, was authorized to give the *Franchistas* a dozen planes in return for over £1,000,000 in cash.[65] At dawn on 30 July 1936 twelve unmarked SM 81 three-engined bombers took off from Elmas airport in Sardinia bound for Melilla in Spanish Morocco. Three were lost, but the remainder were soon in action, along with twenty-seven fighters, escorting Franco's forces across the Straits to the mainland and attacking Republican shipping, their true nationality concealed in the Italian press.

Why did Mussolini decide to get involved so soon after winning the Abyssinian war? Prestige was an issue to be sure, especially once the *Duce* had committed his armed forces to the struggle. The need for a distraction from economic hardship and the pressures of an increasingly intrusive and repressive regime may also have played its part. Political calculation certainly did. The war offered an opportunity to split apart Great Britain and France, both of whom were in any case likely for different reasons to be weak supporters of the Republicans. As well as reinforcing the ongoing 'parallel action' with Germany on which Mussolini was already focusing, the civil war in Spain could also threaten it: without a counterweight the country might fall entirely within the German sphere of influence. Then there was the opportunity to install a regime more in line with Fascism than Western democracy. And it would be a mistake to leave ideology out of the picture. Mussolini's view, expressed in the Axis protocol signed on 23 October 1936, was that Italy and Germany were partners in a common international action which identified communism as 'the greatest danger to the peace and security of Europe'.[66] Talking on the record to an American journalist in May 1937, he denied that Italy had 'ambitions' in Spain, but added that she was determined that bolshevism – 'the greatest threat to Europe' – would never set foot there.[67]

The public was presented with a war in which the issues were clearcut and simple: civilization in the shape of Christianity was fighting barbarism in the form of bolshevism. Ten per cent wage increases in April 1937, March 1939 and again in March 1940 helped keep the population quiescent while newspapers, radio and the *Luce* newsreel films, all firmly in the Fascist Party's hands, drove the message home. So too did the Catholic press, which gave its readers the impression that the Church in Rome was wholly on Franco's side.[68] As the numbers of murdered priests and nuns rose – 6,238 members of religious orders were killed, most in the first months of the war – the Church grew more wholehearted in its opposition to what it saw as godless barbarity. On 19 March 1937 Pope Pius XI published the encyclical *Divini Redemptoris* attacking Communism for peddling a 'pseudo ideal of justice, equality, and fraternity in labour' wrapped up in a 'false mysticism'.[69] Later he refused explicitly to condemn the bombing of Guernica (26 April) despite pleas from Basque priests to do so.

During August, 1936 Franco's African army marched up the western side of Spain towards Madrid, taking Badajoz with the help of Italian bombers on 14 August and Talavera on 3 September. The first aerial combat over mainland Spain took place on 21 August, and by 10 September Italy had its first 'ace' – Adriano Mantelli had shot down a dozen Republican planes. At first Italian pilots of the *aviación del Tercio*, along with Germans, had the best of the air war, largely thanks to the manoeuvrability of their Fiat CR 32 biplanes. In the hands of pilots whose training emphasized aerobatics they were able to rule the skies. In November 1936 things changed when Soviet fighters arrived: first I-15 Polikarpov biplanes and then soon after I-16 monoplanes and fast Tupolev SB 2 twin-engined bombers. As the attrition rate mounted, the Italian air force changed its tactics. Individual duels were abandoned in favour of large formations of fifteen or more aircraft in three flights of five echeloned at different heights. The two lower-level flights attacked first and the third flight dived down from above the fray to help when needed.[70] These tactics proved so successful that they were used for the rest of the war. The arrival of increasing numbers of Messerschmitt Bf 109 fighters after March 1937 helped cement Axis superiority in the air.

In September General Mario Roatta, head of SIM (*Servizio Informazioni Militari*, Italian military intelligence), arrived in Spain to assess the possibilities for further Italian intervention. A tour of the Nationalists' positions revealed gaps in the defensive lines and poor co-ordination between fronts. The Nationalist high command needed to get active operations under way as soon as possible, but advice alone was likely to have no impact unless accompanied by 'an adequate material support'. Without it the Nationalists were incapable of acting 'with the speed and decisiveness that are desirable and desired'.[71] There was another aspect to intervention too. Even though the Spaniards took a friendly view of the Italians there was every likelihood that after comparing the ways and means of the Germans and the Italians they would in the future opt for the former.[72] Meanwhile, on 29 October Soviet tanks appeared on the battlefield for the first time near Madrid and Republican aircraft began dropping Soviet bombs. Roatta had no doubt about what would happen next. In order not to lose the game the Soviets would ramp up their aid to the 'Reds'. At the back of it all was Stalin's expectation that a great war would lead to a general revolution – to his advantage.[73]

On 6 December 1936 Mussolini gathered his senior military advisers at Palazzo Venezia. On the table was a lengthy report from Roatta criticizing Franco for underrating the likely opposition and castigating the Spanish military. Its generals were using the outdated methods that had won the Rif War in Morocco a decade earlier and the Spanish command belonged in the Napoleonic era. However, if the aid being poured into Republican Spain was matched by equivalent aid to the Nationalists,

Roatta was confident that Franco would win.[74] A paper from Pariani favoured sending a division-sized unit of volunteers.[75] From Berlin came a report that the Germans were united in not wanting Italian influence in Spain to surpass their own.[76]

Mussolini emphasized the importance of aiding Franco against communism. Both Italy and Germany, while trickling men into Spain, should prepare division-sized units but commit them only after it was clear that the Soviets had committed military contingents of their own. Somewhat contradictorily, he next announced that 'the solution to the Spanish situation' could be secured at sea by blockading the Republican ports during the time it would take to train divisional-sized units, a task he was ready to take on alone using Italian submarines operating in Spanish waters. Admiral Cavagnari as chief of the naval staff demurred, but his reservations were shunted aside. General Valle as chief of the air staff proposed sending more fighter aircraft, an idea Mussolini quickly developed into a division of labour in which Germany would be chiefly responsible for providing bombers. The group then went over a few of the finer details, and that was that. A policy of sorts had been devised that met the regime's ideological requirements, supported the goals of national strategy, and furthered Axis solidarity.[77]

Four days after the Palazzo Venezia meeting Mussolini ordered the Ufficio Spagna, newly created within Ciano's Foreign Office to take charge of the adventure, to send out 3,000 volunteers 'to put some backbone into the Spanish National formations'.[78] The first Blackshirt Militia volunteers arrived in Cadiz at 3 a.m. on 22 December 1936. Over the next two months the numbers mounted and by mid-February 1937 there were 48,230 Italian troops in Spain, together with 46 light tanks, 488 guns, 706 assault mortars and 1,211 machine guns. The spur to this dramatic escalation was the news that Great Britain seemed set on persuading the international community to block sending volunteers to Spain. In Rome, Goering and Mussolini agreed that Franco was dragging his feet and that the general conduct of the war had to be 'radically changed'. Out of this came the plan to feed in more troops and materiel before the international community closed the door.[79]

Rome was determined that the Italian contingent must fight as a single entity under the command of an Italian general, Roatta, and must be deployed against decisive objectives. After two Nationalist attacks on Madrid in early January 1937 both failed, Franco was ready to agree to an Italian offensive which he hoped would divert Republican forces away from the capital. Pariani chose the objective. Malaga was closest to where the Italians were based and although less decisive it was a less complex operation than the alternatives.[80] The plan, for a fast surprise attack after a feint elsewhere and with no prior reconnaissance or preparatory bombardment by guns or planes, was shaped to fit the Fascist doctrine of the day for *guerra lampo*.

At 6.30 a.m. on 5 February 1937, Roatta launched his attack. Early morning fog lifted within an hour, the skies cleared and the sun shone. Three Italian columns, headed by tanks and machine-gun carriers and supported by Italian and German aircraft, drove south-west towards the hills protecting Malaga, supported by four Spanish columns on their right and one in between them of slower-moving troops. In all, 10,000 Italians faced 20,000 to 40,000 poorly armed defenders without tanks, armoured cars or anti-tank guns and with only a few machine guns. The Italian forces enjoyed complete command of the air – Malaga's defenders had only a single anti-aircraft gun and three machine guns – and the dry weather was on their side. By the end of the next day, despite some determined resistance by Republican militia bands, the Italians were masters of the heights surrounding the town. The rest was literally all downhill. At 6 a.m. on 8 February troops of the centre column entered Malaga and a unit of the *Carabinieri* took possession of the Banca di Spagna. After a slow start, a motorized column chased Republicans retreating along the coast, taking the town of Motril on 10 February just as evening began to fall. There the battle ended, at a cost to the Italians of 90 dead and 250 wounded.[81] During the fighting Italian troops shot those communists who waged what they termed a 'guerrilla war' against their columns and any Republicans who had stayed in their villages to defend them. They then handed over some 2,000 prisoners to the Nationalists, who promptly shot them.

Mussolini wanted Roatta to press on to Almeria and Madrid, but the next strategic decision was made by Franco. 'I will probably ask you to attack Guadalajara,' he told Roatta's chief of staff, Colonel Emilio Faldella.[82] This suited Roatta, who did not want his troops, shaped for a fast war of movement against distant objectives, to be locked up in the siege of Madrid.[83] Two days before the battle, the plan

– a simultaneous double offensive by the Spanish at Jarama and the Italians at Guadalajara to cut Madrid's lines of reinforcement – went by the board when Roatta learned that the Spaniards had no intention of attacking until the Italians reached Guadalajara.[84]

The ground over which the new battle would be fought was high and desolate table-land, dissected by rivers and deep erosions and beaten during winter by strong winds, rain and snow. Apart from the main highway, the '*strada di Francia*', roads were few and manoeuvring meant going off-road. Heavy rain during the night before the battle turned the soil into mud, and bad weather made the airfields unusable and kept the planes grounded. Disregarding a forecast of more bad weather to come, Roatta refused to postpone the operation. His subordinates were apparently unruffled, General Rossi remarking that if the *aviazione legionaria* could not fly then at least his troops would not be bombed by their own side, as had happened at Malaga.[85] The Italian guns opened up at 6.50 a.m. on 8 March and forty minutes later the attack began. Thirty thousand Italians, supported by 160 guns, 81 light tanks and 2,400 trucks, faced some 10,000 Republicans at the start of the battle – the latter's numbers would triple by the end – manning three lines of defences protecting the roads.

The Italians pushed down the *strada di Francia*, covering seventeen kilometres in the first day, but sleet blinded the troops and their commanders and turned the ground surrounding the road into a gigantic sea of mud. After two days the attack began to stall against determined resistance from units of the International Brigades. Failure to launch the Jarama offensive allowed the Republicans to pour in troops supported by Russian aircraft and tanks. After five days Roatta wanted to call off the offensive. Mussolini agreed but Franco did not, insisting that the Italians continue to fight where they were. Retreat would be an admission of defeat. A brief pause was followed by a massive Republican counter-attack on 18 March backed by several waves of bombers with fighter escorts. Panic began to take hold and troops started abandoning the lines. The Fascist 1st Blackshirt division partially collapsed and withdrew, forcing the two regular divisions to retreat to a second line, where they held off weakening assaults. Finally, late in the evening of 22 March, the exhausted Republicans withdrew. The battle of Guadalajara was over. The resounding setback cost the *Corpo di Truppe Volontarie* (CTV: the name adopted by the Italians on 16 February

1937) some 600 dead and approximately 2,000 wounded, along with twenty-five guns, ten mortars, eighty-five machine guns and sixty-seven trucks. The Republican IV Army Corps may have lost as many as 2,200 dead and 4,000 wounded.[86]

Roatta found plenty of reasons for losing what Ernest Hemingway a week later called one of the decisive battles of the world. The Spanish had not pressed their attack on Jarama; 'inept officers', both regulars and militia, had put the divisional commanders in the position of someone 'driving a good vehicle, who realizes that the steering wheel is made of rubber'; and his troops, though *ottimo* ('the best'), had contained 'a strong contingent of old men' who were 'not very combative'. The Republican international troops, generally well-led, had fought with skill, fanaticism 'and hatred'.[87] Roatta's troops, many attracted by the extra pay and allowances on offer, were indeed a motley crew: a quarter of them had criminal records and fifteen per cent were over forty, many suffering from hernias, varicose veins, appendicitis and the symptoms of syphilis.[88] 'Poor Italians', the great Sicilian novelist Leonardo Sciascia wrote later, 'were sent to fight poor Spaniards.'[89] The officers blamed their generals and the logistic services but not their under-trained troops.[90]

The battle encouraged the Spanish Republicans – in the streets Spanish children sang that the CTV needed *menos camiones y más cojones* ('fewer lorries and more balls'). It also made Mussolini determined to avenge the defeat and do all he could to ensure that the Nationalists won. Roatta was demoted and replaced by General Bastico. Arriving at Salamanca to take up his new command on 14 April, Bastico found a force that was 'materially disorganized, [and] low in morale'. Discipline everywhere was 'very relaxed', training was 'deficient in every respect' and administration was 'chaotic'. None of the officers from divisional commanders down were up to the job.[91] The new commander swiftly took matters in hand. The regular *Littorio* division was retained but two of the three Blackshirt divisions, whom Roatta had praised to the skies after Malaga, were dissolved and 3,700 men were sent home. A hundred-odd officers, among them two Blackshirt divisional commanders and one regular army general, were fired. The better elements were used to reinforce the single remaining *Fiamme Nere* militia division under General Luigi Frusci and the 23 *Marzo* group. A directive went out to divisional commanders on how to wage all-arms co-operative warfare, and battalion commanders were instructed on how to get round the 'curious legend of power and almost of invincibility' that had come to surround the enemy's tanks thanks to 'the scarce number of anti-tank weapons available and the lack of practice in using them'.[92]

Reorganizing the Italian forces was one thing. Fighting alongside the Nationalists was quite another. Neither the Germans nor the Italians were finding the Spanish army easy to work with. According to Admiral Canaris's liaison officer the Nationalists lacked alacrity, energy, and above all unified and authoritative direction. Franco gave the impression of 'mediocre capacity [and] restricted views, in thrall to the old agrarian aristocratic caste'. The Reds were more effectively organized than the Nationalists.[93] The Italian intelligence section in Spain found working with the Spanish next to impossible. 'Deeply and irremediably saturated with pride and vanity', after Guadalajara they had adopted an intolerable air of friendly superiority. The only way to treat a race that had inherited 'the ferocity of the Inquisition, the duplicity and untrustworthiness of the Arabs, [and] the air of Spanish grandees' was to be like the Germans: tough, unbending and overbearing.[94]

Franco's targets were now the Basques and the Asturias, particularly the port city of Bilbao. Cutting his ally down to size after Guadalajara, he ordered that in future the CTV fight only as part of larger Spanish units commanded by Spanish generals. The job of taking Bilbao was given to the Spanish general Emilio Mola. Mussolini ordered Bastico to keep the Italian forces united and to use them on decisive objectives. That meant doing everything possible to secure the fall of Bilbao.[95] Well aware of the need for an Italian success 'or one predominantly Italian', Bastico was infuriated when Franco turned down his offer to take a larger part in a major co-ordinated attack on Bilbao on the grounds that Italian troops were not sufficiently 'tempered' to attack a well-fortified bastion such as the city now was.[96] The way the Spanish went about things was wrong from top to bottom. Italian operational doctrine was for a war of movement and breakthrough, which gave the enemy no respite and which therefore needed 'very deep planning'. The Spanish, who had no organic plan and no concept of mass and manoeuvre, lived for the day and thought only in terms of short-range actions. As for Spanish generals, from the high command downwards they limited themselves to generic suggestions and participated in operations 'like mere spectators from positions well in the rear with no connections [to the front]'.[97] Finally, after repeatedly changing his mind, Franco accepted Bastico's plan to use the CTV to cut off the Republicans' retreat from Bilbao to Santander.[98]

Italian plans were disrupted first by the Spaniards, who were not ready to start the attack when planned, and then by the Republicans, who launched their own Brunete offensive on 6 July. Italian input to the massive battle outside Madrid, which sucked in a quarter of a million men and lasted three weeks, was limited to air power and artillery. When it was over the Republican air force had lost at least half of its 158 aircraft and was never again able to put overwhelming numbers of planes into the air. No less importantly Russian resupply dwindled, due partly to a change in Soviet policy as Moscow turned its attention to the Japanese attack on Nationalist China but also partly to the effects of Italian naval activity. Although she had signed the non-intervention treaty in August 1936 outlawing the handing over of warships of any kind to either side in the civil war, Italy had no intention of being bound by it. In April 1937 she gave the Nationalists two submarines and in October added four old destroyers to Franco's fleet of one. Between January and August 1937, Italian submarines and surface warships sank nine ships supplying the Republicans, six of them Spanish, one British and one Russian. On 3 September 1937 Mussolini ordered the recall of all Italian naval units. The Italian submarine campaign ended when the *Procida* returned to base ten days later.[99] Although its practical effects had been limited, its impact on morale and on international politics had been all that Mussolini could have hoped for.

Mussolini now wanted the war over quickly, before international pressure could intrude into operations. Franco was to be told in no uncertain terms that the Italian legionary forces 'must absolutely be employed and within the briefest space of time possible' against Santander, after which Valencia should be the next target. Franco's 'somewhat vague and prolix' reply was that he wished to do things which would be pleasing to the Duce.[100] Convinced that the Basques must be beaten and that Franco was dragging his heels, Mussolini resorted to threats: if the Italian volunteers did not fight now they would return home.[101] Now willing to be co-operative, Franco gave Bastico the task of taking Santander. The port was shielded by a chain of mountains some fifty kilometres from the coast rising to over 1,000 metres, dissected by five passes with good roads, which became the focus of the military operations. Defence was easier than attack in a harsh landscape and the Republicans had had months to improve their defences, during which time they had amassed 80,000 men, 180 guns and some 70 aircraft. However, the gains from the six-week delay in starting the operation were not all one-sided. Bastico had time thoroughly to reconnoitre the ground and gather intelligence about the enemy.

The battle began at 6.48 a.m. on Saturday 14 August when fifteen Italian aircraft bombed Republican lines facing Bastico's central column. One-third of the 90,000 attacking force were Italians. The bulk of the CTV was concentrated in the central one of three converging vectors, with Roatta's *Frecce Nere* brigade on the right flank. The artillery opened up twelve minutes later and after another twenty minutes the first Italian division attacked. On their right, the *Fiamme Nere* went into action two hours later. After two days the Italians had opened up the road through the mountains to Santander. Another two days were taken up in clearing the area and preparing for the next bound forward. The second stage of the advance began on 19 August in thick fog. To ensure that the Nationalists did not get into Santander first, Bastico relied mainly on his mobile divisional artillery: the advance echelons were given one or two guns each so that they could overcome resistance quickly without having to wait for entire batteries to come up. By 23 August the CTV had reached the last line of Republican defences above the coastal plain, and the next day some well-planned moves turned the enemy's defences. Under clear skies, the Italian forces closed in on the city.

At 7.35 a.m. on 26 August a Republican delegation arrived at the CTV headquarters to negotiate the surrender, knowing that their officers' lives were forfeit but hoping that the Italians would at least save the lives of their men. Bastico could offer no guarantees but was prepared to intercede on their behalf. The defenders surrendered at noon and Bastico entered the city in triumph an hour later – greeted with such enthusiasm that he reportedly had to abandon his car and walk to the town hall, where he met his opposite number, the Nationalist general Fidel Dávila, and drank toasts to the Spanish and Italian people and then to Franco and Mussolini.[102]

For the CTV, which had taken 20,000 prisoners at a cost of 424 dead, 1,556 wounded and three missing, and for Bastico, the battle of

Santander had been a striking success – and it was duly trumpeted as such in the Italian press. In his after-action report Bastico praised his troops, who had fought like veterans in the open field, but noted how easily their enthusiasm could change to discouragement without experienced professional officers to get the best out of them. The light tanks had worked well in mountain terrain and so had the machine-gun carriers and the artillery, though a lot of it was old and needed replacing. His chief reservation was over the two *binaria* divisions (*Littorio* and 23 *Marzo*). With only two regiments and not three like the only *ternaria* division (*Fiamme Nere*), they lacked 'the degree of strength needed to resolve a complex situation'.[103] The consequences of his victory were dramatic. Republican morale in the region collapsed and when on 21 October Franco's men took Gijón with the aid of a Blackshirt division the war in northern Spain was over.

Relations between the Italians and the Spanish got no better after Santander – indeed, if anything they got worse. There was tension over the fate of Basque prisoners, over what to do with captured Republican materiel, over supposed misuse of Italian artillery during the battle, and over who actually commanded the mixed Italian-Spanish *Frecce* division.[104] Bastico claimed the credit for the victory on the grounds that the entire battle had been directly influenced by 'our way of think-ing and acting', but his days were numbered. A report landing on Pariani's desk at the start of September spoke of troops who were not deeply committed to the war, of split direction and of a top-heavy command structure.[105] At this point Franco intervened. Incensed by Bastico's interference over captured Republicans, whom Franco intended to shoot, he demanded his replacement. On 27 September Bastico was recalled to Rome and two weeks later General Mario Berti replaced him.[106] Ciano was not enthused. 'Berti gave me the impression of a man who will not give us trouble,' he recorded in his diary, 'but neither does he have any brilliant surprises in store for us.'[107] Berti was certainly prepared to give Franco trouble. Asked what help the Italians could give in the forthcoming Aragon offensive, he told *el Caudillo* that he wanted the CTV held in reserve for the time being. With absolutely no faith in Spanish operational planning, he had no intention of play-ing second fiddle to a Spanish high command for which he felt both annoyance and contempt. 'I've never yet seen in Spain a battle start on the planned day,' he told Pariani.[108]

On 30 November Franco decided to suspend operations in Aragon and launch another attack on Madrid instead. Over the next few days Spanish plans changed several times. With no faith in the Spanish general staff's ability to organize and carry out large-scale manoeuvres, or in the ability of most of the Spanish corps and divisional commanders to prepare and direct a large battle, Berti was only prepared to take part on his own terms. The most important of these was that his offensive should start a day later than the Spanish attack to ensure that he was not left high and dry by his ally.[109] Pariani was inclined to go along with the new plan and so was Mussolini, who regarded it over-optimistically as 'the last battle'.[110] Then, on 4 December 1937, the Republicans launched a surprise attack on Teruel to pre-empt a Nationalist attack on Madrid. Franco's slow response confirmed all Berti's convictions about Spanish military mismanagement. Hot-footing it to Rome at Mussolini's request, he told the *Duce* that Franco, whose generals each had his own following and did not obey him, was honest and intelligent but weak and 'always a Spaniard'.[111] He thought the entire CTV should be withdrawn. Ciano, Pariani and Mussolini all agreed: Italian prestige might be at risk if the twenty infantry battalions in Spain met with another setback, but much more was to be lost if Italy pulled out. Berti was handed written instructions for Franco. The CTV would remain in Spain but was to be used in decisive actions and not in battles of attrition, the war should be speeded up, and the object must be the complete military defeat of the Republicans.

Teruel dragged on until 23 February 1938. Italian aviation and artillery took part in the battle to retake it, but Franco kept Italian ground forces in reserve. Mussolini demanded that the CTV be used to fight, otherwise it would be brought home. The reply – that Teruel showed the need for caution, that Franco accepted Mussolini's argument that victory had to be won on the battlefield, and that Italian forces would be an important element in that victory both physically and morally – is said to have won Mussolini over.[112] Maybe so, but Mussolini had committed Italy too far to back out now. All that the *Duce* could do was to urge that his forces be given the chance to fight 'one good decisive battle'.[113] He got his wish with the Aragon offensive. The Nationalists intended to cut Catalonia off from Valencia and the heart of Republican Spain. The CTV, which had not fought a battle for more than six months, was tasked with taking Alcañiz. To do so, it would have to advance across mountainous, mostly open ground where the only way to get heavy weapons and supplies forward was by pack animal. Defenders manning scattered field fortifications would have to be dislodged from high ground by attacks up steep slopes if they could not be turned. Berti's troops now had one truck for every fourteen to sixteen men and a massive superiority in artillery: the CTV alone had 236 guns, as well as ninety-four anti-aircraft and anti-tank guns, against a Republican park of as few as seventy-four guns.[114]

On 9 March 1938 the Italian artillery opened an hour-long bombardment at 8 o'clock in the morning, after which the air force hammered the Republican positions for fifteen minutes. At 9.30 the infantry went in. Roatta's *Frecce Nere* division opened the attack with a frontal assault, and by the end of the day they had forced a breach in the enemy lines eight kilometres wide and fourteen kilometres deep. After pushing forward for three days, the Spaniards tried briefly to alter the plan and use Berti's forces to support the two Spanish thrusts on either side of him, before reverting to the original scheme. As dawn broke on 14 March, Francisci's 23 *Marzo* division took Alcañiz. The first phase of the campaign had succeeded thanks to the speed and tactical manoeuvring of the Italians, the action of their artillery and aircraft – and the relative lack of resistance of the enemy.[115] Two days later, after learning that France was about to start a large-scale resupply of the Republicans and a few minutes before he went in front of parliament to announce Hitler's success in the *Anschluss*, Mussolini ordered General Valle to bomb Barcelona. In three days Italian bombers dropped 44 tons of explosives on the city. Republican sources put the casualties at 550 dead and 989 wounded.

After a pause to allow the Spanish columns to reach their allotted positions, the Italian divisions continued their advance on Gandesa and Tortosa. The ground was now more difficult and enemy resistance more determined. After another enforced three-day pause the Italians advanced again and by 3 April they reached the passes of the high Sierra del Montenegrelo. It took them five days to force their way through. After another six-day pause, during which Italian engineers converted a mule track into a roadway that could take artillery, the final assault began on 15 April. At 7.30 on the evening of 18 April retreating Republican forces blew the bridges over the Ebro and

Tortosa fell. Italian artillery had been heavily employed but rocky ground and well-protected defensive positions had combined to lessen its effectiveness. The air force had more than compensated for the gunners' difficulties, flying 4,000 sorties and dropping 1,000 tons of bombs, while bombers based in the Balearics struck the rear positions between the Sierra and the sea. The troops had fought well under the effective direction of Berti, who was promoted *generale di corpo d'armata* (lieutenant-general). The campaign cost the Italians 530 dead and 2,482 wounded – half as many again as the Nationalists. Undervalued afterwards by some and overvalued by others, the CTV had been the wedge that had forced open the Republican defences.[116]

Franco's next objective was Valencia. The Italians' share in the first phase of the Levante campaign, which lasted from 23 April to the middle of June, was limited largely to artillery and air support. Having just concluded the so-called 'Easter Accords' (16 April 1938) with Great Britain, Mussolini wanted to calm turbulent waters. Berti was instructed that while the CTV would remain in Spain as a mark of solidarity it was not to be used in mass actions, and only in 'exceptional cases' could the employment of small detachments be allowed. The 'volunteers' would leave Spain when the war had ended 'or if and when the non-intervention [committee] will have taken some decision'.[117] Berti went to Rome to beg for more troops. CTV companies were down to 100 men and almost half the legionaries were tired and needed replacing.[118] Abundant supplies of war materiel were continuing to flow across the Pyrenees to the Republicans, and the slowness with which the Spanish were conducting the first phase of the Levante campaign was allowing the enemy time to reorganize replacements and reserves.[119] Mussolini agreed to trickle 2,000 men wearing civilian clothes into Spain in small groups and by mid-July the numbers had risen to 5,500, still not enough to bring the CTV back up to its organic strength.

The second phase of the campaign for Valencia began on 13 July 1938. Berti expected to face an enemy over 100,000-strong supported by 1,300 machine guns, 130 to 150 guns, 70 to 80 tanks and 200 aircraft. Once again the Italians had to fight across a high mountainous zone intersected by numerous rivers before descending through foothills to the coastal plain. They attacked from the north-west, the *Littorio* and *23 Marzo* divisions flanked on either side by Spanish divisions, while a second prong of the assault drove down on Valencia from the north. A seventy-five-minute artillery barrage from 205 guns was followed by thirty minutes of aerial bombardment. In three days, aided by clear skies and moderate temperatures, the Italians broke through the Republican defences. There were more pauses before the armies got moving again on 19 July. As daytime temperatures climbed, the woods through which the troops had to advance caught fire. Six days later news that the Republicans had attacked in force on the Ebro brought the battle to a premature close. The Italians had pushed forward fifty kilometres in thirteen days, taking a thousand prisoners at a cost of 246 dead and 1,513 wounded. This time, things had not gone so well. Berti had been much more cautious than in the Aragon offensive, Italian artillery had fired on their own troops, and Italian aircraft had bombed them.[120]

Between July and November 1938 the Nationalist and Republican armies fought a bloody and brutal battle along the River Ebro. Where the Aragon offensive had been a war of movement, this was now a war of attrition. Italian Breda 65 planes bombed the bridges linking the Republican forward lines to their supply bases, then switched their attack to the enemy troops and their bases while aircraft from the Balearics bombed the Republican rear areas, targeting railways and ports. Reports reaching Rome suggested that the Republicans still had plenty of fight left in them – and plenty to fight with. Weapons and munitions had been pouring across the French border: the Italian consul in Toulouse estimated that over the past eighteen months an average of five trainloads a day had been reaching the Republicans, and his opposite number in Marseilles reported that Russian aircraft had been coming in via Honfleur and Le Havre in crates labelled 'agricultural machinery'.[121] The Italians could not get into Republican territory to see things for themselves, but neutrals could. The American naval attaché reported that morale was high in Catalonia, where the troops trained like regulars and the civil population had adapted to the rigours of war. In the south morale was much lower, and there were evident signs of tiredness.[122]

His attention now zeroing in on the mounting crisis over Czecho-slovakia and the forthcoming Munich conference, Mussolini offered Franco the choice between a withdrawal of the Italian infantry, sending out 10,000 more men, and despatching a force of one or more fresh divisions. Franco opted for 10,000 fresh troops. Angry at the 'anaemic' conduct of the war and foreseeing Franco's defeat, Mussolini ordered the *Littorio* and 23 *Marzo* divisions to be combined into one and 10,000 men repatriated back to Italy. After changing his mind again, and informing Franco that he would withdraw all the Italian infantry, he finally settled on the one-division option.[123] Withdrawing 10,000 'volunteers' would, he reckoned, trigger British recognition of the East African Empire. In the aftermath of the Munich conference the move worked, and on 16 November Great Britain indicated that it was ready to bring the Easter Accords into force.* Ten days later, 360 officers and 10,000 men embarked from Cadiz and sailed home.

The Italian stake in Spain now shrank from 39,000 soldiers to 19,300 along with 9,000 Fascist militiamen. Berti, briefly promoted to *generale designato d'armata* (roughly full general) until Mussolini realized that he was still a bachelor and demoted him for not fitting in with Fascist doctrine on the importance of generating future manpower, was replaced by his chief of staff, Gastone Gambara. Still a lowly brigadier-general, Gambara replaced his divisional commanders with more junior officers, all but one of whom were new to the war. He saw himself as running the test-bed for the new army doctrine, his main task to test the effectiveness of the *binaria* division 'in relation to its new concepts of employment' in Pariani's doctrine of *guerra di rapido corso* ('fast-paced war').[124]

Mussolini wanted Franco to strike against Catalonia, and Franco concurred. The offensive began on 23 December 1938. Once again, the Italians' superiority in artillery was crushing. 'In a stretch of barely four kilometres,' Gambara wrote afterwards of the opening bombardment, 'almost 500 guns were deployed, that is one gun every eight metres or so, almost like [it was] in the Great War!'[125] In the first phase of the battle, which lasted until 5 January 1939, the CTV struck towards Tarragona; then in the second phase it pushed west, outpacing the Spanish units on its flank. By 16 January organized Republican resistance had ended, and ten days later Italian *Celere* units and Spanish troops entered Barcelona. The CTV pressed on towards the French

---

* Under the terms of the Easter Accords (16 April 1938), Great Britain agreed to recognize the Italian Empire in Abyssinia once there was a settlement of the Spanish question and Italy reasserted the pledges it had made in the Gentlemen's Agreement in January 1937 not to seek to modify the status quo in the Mediterranean.

frontier, occupying Gerona on 31 January before being halted thirty kilometres from the border. With the Republican government in tatters and its military commander urging that the war be ended, Franco launched his last offensive against Madrid on 26 March. Resistance collapsed immediately. On the morning of 28 March 1939 Spanish troops entered Madrid and at 7.45 that evening a motorized column of CTV troops entered Guadalajara. In a jubilant Rome, Ciano delighted in 'a new formidable victory for Fascism: perhaps, up to now, the greatest'.[126]

Italy committed a total of 42,715 soldiers and 32,216 Blackshirt militiamen to the civil war in Spain and lost 3,318 dead and 11,763 wounded. Rafts of statistics charted the contribution that Fascism made to Franco's victory. In the course of the war, the army's 1,604 guns had fired some 10,000,000 rounds. The CTV took 108,385 prisoners, captured 137 guns, 1,022 machine guns and 65 tanks, and shot down 544 aircraft. The *Regia Aeronautica* calculated that it had sent 213 bombers and 414 fighters along with 132 other warplanes, together with 372,261 bombs and 9,500,000 rounds of machine-gun ammunition. As well as handing over ten ships, the navy had organized ports at both ends of the supply lines, had used 87 transports to make 193 trips for a total of 250,000 miles, and among other things had provided the Nationalists with an interception and decryption service.[127] The direct cost worked out at 6,086,003,680 lire. The overall costs caused state expenditure to more than triple in 1936 to 66.9 billion lire, creating a deficit of 40.4 billion lire.[128]

For Fascist Italy the Spanish venture had been a war of limited liability. However, for a country with a relatively weak industrial base and one which had just fought a colonial war in East Africa, even limited liabilities were a serious burden. As well as sustaining her own legionaries Italy handed the Nationalists 1,930 guns, 7,514,537 rounds of artillery ammunition and 7,668 motor vehicles as well as sundry other items. Reinstating all the material sent to Spain cost the War Ministry 5,780,210,000 lire.[129] The Italian air force gave Spain 517 aircraft, 350 of which were left behind when the *aviazione legionaria* was disbanded, and amassed a total bill of 1,000,506,000 lire. Fighting a war in Spain undoubtedly weakened the army, and if the 442 medium-calibre guns and 7,500 motor vehicles which went to the Nationalists had been available in June 1940 they would have given Graziani more to fight with, though they would probably not have altered the outcome.[130] But counterfactuals are tricky things: had those armaments not been sent then Franco's forces would have been the weaker and the civil war might have dragged on longer, with who knows what consequences.

The Italians looked to learn from Spain, though they kept reminding themselves that this was not the kind of full-scale war that would be fought by two industrialized powers: the Republicans were poorly armed, poorly trained and lacked capability in defensive operations. It was, one observer remarked, a war *sui generis*, halfway between a colonial war and a war between regular armies. Neither side had many of the modern means of offence and defence: heavy guns, heavy tanks, chemical weapons and solid, continuous lines of fortifications.[131] The air force delighted in the manoeuvrability of the CR 32 biplane fighter (replaced in 1939 by the CR.42 – another biplane) and the opportunity it gave individual pilots to show off their aerobatic prowess. The bombing campaign waged against Spanish cities and ports appeared to demonstrate the validity of Douhet's theory of 'terror bombing', and General Pricolo for one thought that using the air weapon for any other purposes than to instil terror was 'the fundamental error'.[132] Ciano chortled over the bombing of Barcelona, which he took as 'a good lesson for the future'. It showed, he thought, that planning air-raid protection and building shelters was useless: 'the only means of escape from air attacks is the evacuation of the cities'. From 1942 onwards, night-time mass flight from Italian cities that had no public shelters and few anti-aircraft guns would cause huge problems that the authorities were never able to solve.[133]

The Italian army's equipment, doctrine and practice were all shown to be wanting in various degrees. Spanish conditions meant that the lightly armed *carri d'assalto* ('assault tanks') did not always perform as was hoped or expected, and experience suggested that the infantry needed 'breakthrough' tanks armed with guns as well as 'assault tanks', which had only machine guns. This finding got rather lost when the tank men claimed that the *carro d'assalto* had 'won its battles' – against adversaries who lacked the solidity of regular forces and had few anti-tank weapons.[134] The artillery was generally believed to have performed well, but infantry–tank co-operation had been poor and the infantry were criticized for attacking in close order instead of spreading out.[135] Perhaps the most serious weakness of all was a structural one. General

Bastico tried to convince the authorities of the superiority of the three-regiment *divisione ternaria*, arguing that far from being 'heavy' it was just as flexible and manoeuvrable as the two-regiment *divisione binaria* when used properly, and would not need rotating out of line so frequently.[136] Gambara favoured the *binaria*, which the chief of the army general staff, General Pariani, was busy cementing into doctrine. Bastico lost the argument. The *binaria* had been tested in the final Catalonian campaign and as far as the army was concerned, 'the outcome could not have been more flattering'. Its 'extreme manageability' had allowed commanders rapidly to change direction, it had penetrative capacity because it could be redirected away from 'centres of strong resistance', and it had shown itself able to get in between major Republican units.[137] For a time Gambara became Mussolini's favoured general.[138]

Chapter 2
The Reluctant Neutral

During the 1930s a younger generation of generals devised a new Fascist theory of war which they labelled *la guerra lampo* ('fast war'). The revolution in Italian military affairs they intended to carry out was partly based on their reading of their fellow citizens' weaknesses and strengths. In November 1914 General Luigi Cadorna had advised the government that Italy needed to fight a fast, short war not so much for economic reasons as because of 'the moral and disciplinary conditions of our country, on which success largely depends'.[1] Certainly some of the younger Fascist generals believed that another war of attrition would grind down their own nation at least as much as the enemy, if not more. Then there was the lesson of the collapse at Caporetto in October 1917, which seemed to suggest that large armies of semi-trained Italian conscripts could be swept aside by relatively small, well-trained and well-armed forces.[2] Finally, there was international evidence that the winds of change were blowing elsewhere: experiments in motorization and mechanization were going on in Great Britain, Russia and latterly Germany.

In July 1933, dissatisfied with the slow progress that was being made in modernizing the army and the defensive mindset that dominated its upper reaches, Mussolini fired his War Minister and again took over the reins himself. The job of shaking up the conservative soldiery was given to General Federico Baistrocchi, under-secretary of state for war from 1933 to 1936 and chief of the army general staff from 1934 to 1936. 'Fascism,' he announced as he went through the doors of the war ministry, 'enters here with me.' It was soon fully ensconced. In very short order the Fascist hymn 'Giovinezza' was being played at military ceremonies and officers were being allowed to join the Fascist Party, something even Mussolini had previously resisted. Turning his mind to the problems of modern war, Baistrocchi devised a formula in which motorization, which would make manoeuvre easier and surprise possible, was coupled with mechanization in the shape of light, fast tanks.[3] In 1936 he planned to have fifteen motorized divisions by 1947, an ambitious target that would prove way beyond Italy's capabilities.

Baistrocchi expected that war, when it came, would break out suddenly and unexpectedly after a brief period of political tension. The regulations he bequeathed to the army in 1935 mixed together classical forms and modern dynamics. The enemy would be defeated by a combination of speed, surprise and manoeuvre. Air action and fast attacks by the *Celeri* divisions (a combination of cavalry, light tanks and bicycles) would open the fighting, followed by break-in and manoeuvre. Artillery would flatten the enemy and so smooth the path for the infantry – still the decisive instrument of combat. All arms co-operation was the order of the day, and the air force would play a big part, bombing the enemy's centres of population and hitting him on the battlefield and in the rear areas. Everything was saturated with Fascist values: war was above all a spiritual reality in which the moral qualities of devotion and sacrifice that the regime relentlessly propounded were given pride of place.

As a reformer Baistrocchi was imaginative, but as a strategic assistant he was a deal too cautious for the *Duce*. In 1934 he had counselled against the Ethiopian war, which would compromise the reconstruction of the army, and in 1936 he warned Mussolini not to get involved in Spain for much the same reason. He was promptly jettisoned and replaced as chief of the army general staff by General Alberto Pariani. A fluent German speaker (he was the illegitimate son of a German banker), Pariani was financially well off and widely read, his tastes ranging from philosophy to mild erotica. He was also in the grip of a strategic concept of his own – the *guerra di rapido corso*. This was fast war somewhat along the lines of his predecessor, but to fight it Pariani decided that the army needed to be *lighter* and faster. His scheme, road-tested in Spain, which reduced divisions from three regiments to two and took away some of their artillery and heavy machine guns, was officially tested in summer manoeuvres in Sicily in 1937 and introduced the following year. The so-called *divisione binaria* would prove to be a disastrous mistake. Only two-thirds the size of the divisions it would have to face in the field, and dependent on 54mm and 81mm mortars and 47mm anti-tank guns for its firepower, and on non-existent lorries to move fifteen 'auto-transportable' divisions, the new formations were little more than attack columns. Nor was the force especially mobile. The bulk of the infantry – thirty-six divisions – would march to war alongside two armoured divisions, two motorized divisions, three *Celeri* divisions and five divisions of *Alpini* mountain troops.[4]

Most of the generals fell in line behind Pariani. There was some opposition from old soldiers in the Senate, and Badoglio, chief of the armed forces general staff, was reportedly not in favour, even though he had said in print after the Ethiopian war that three-regiment divisions had proved too heavy. Pariani used theatrical methods to win over doubters. Summer manoeuvres in the Abruzzo in 1938 ended with the *binaria* Torino division laying every weapon it had except rifles and pistols out on the ground in the sun – an experiment intended to convince doubters that in the age of wars of movement the new units had all the strength they needed.[5]

THE AXIS AND THE PACT OF STEEL

As the Fascist and Nazi regimes travelled along their converging courses, the idea that there should be links between their respective armed forces also began to take hold. In May 1936 an Italian delegation went to Berlin, and in July the chief of the German armed forces training department led a reciprocal visit. Both sides issued polite invitations to send officers to each other's war academies and to observe each other's manoeuvres but nothing of substance transpired. Institutionally neither side set much store by the other – though for different reasons. General Werner von Blomberg, commander-in-chief of the German armed forces, visited Italy in June 1937. He was impressed by Mussolini and liked Pariani but was profoundly unimpressed by what he saw of the Italian army, whose solidity, weaponry and training all fell short of his standards. As yet there would be no military alliance, though Blomberg was willing to go along with an exchange of information between the two armies.[6] Pariani attended manoeuvres in Mecklenburg in September 1937, along with Mussolini and Badoglio, and returned to Germany for another visit in July 1938. He was impressed by much of what he saw: recruit training was excellent, officer education stressed character and decision-making, and training was almost all practical – 'very little place is given to theory'. Equipment was a different matter. German machine guns, mortars and light artillery were, Pariani asserted, mostly no better than the Italian equivalents, and in some cases worse.[7] On his return he told Mussolini that the German army would be ready to fight by 1941–2. If Italy wanted to travel along a parallel path, she could not afford to lose time.[8] Mussolini at once authorized an extraordinary additional budget of 5,000,000,000 lire. At more or less the same time he also told General Carlo Geloso that 'Italy needs ten years of peace and she will have them.'[9]

After announcing the creation of the Italo-German Axis on 1 November 1936, and standing by while Hitler occupied Austria in March 1938, Mussolini played his part in the dismemberment of Czechoslovakia at Munich in September 1938 by loyally reading from a script written by Hitler. German diplomats were now ready to tighten military links even if their own soldiers were not so keen, and so was Pariani. In November an invitation to open staff talks arrived from the German Embassy in Rome and Mussolini at once consented. Pariani assumed, wrongly, that it came as a result of the Germans' recognition of the excellent results Italy had registered in studying the technical means of war in which Italians were, he supposed, at the vanguard. At this point, with far greater combat experience than the Germans, the Italian military could plausibly assume some superiority. Hitler set the parameters for the forthcoming conversations. Discussions would be around a war between Germany and Italy on one side and France and Great Britain on the other, and the primary objective was to knock France out of the ring. The partners would act jointly but independently. Italy's role would be to immobilize as many French troops as possible on the Alpine frontier, attack French North Africa, and take Corsica. The Italian navy would act against French communications with North Africa and eliminate Gibraltar, while the Italian air force attacked France and her North African colonies.[10]

The Germans were in no hurry to formalize their partnership with Italy, but with the end of the Spanish Civil War close at hand and Albania now among his targets – he would invade it on 7 April 1939 – Mussolini pressed his suit. The *Duce* thought it advisable in view of 'the current state of affairs' for the general staffs to set up some formal agreements. What he had immediately in mind was a single-handed war with France for which he wanted not German manpower but German weapons, equipment and raw materials.[11] After occupying the rump of Czechoslovakia on 15 March 1939, Hitler gave permission to start conversations with the Italians over a possible war – but not to talk about operational goals.[12] The international atmosphere was already starting to grow febrile. General Efisio Marras, Italy's long-term military attaché in Berlin, warned Rome that the Germans were likely very shortly to strike new blows. This time they would use military force and face the risk of a European conflict. Their ultimate objective was the resources of the Ukraine and to get to them would mean crossing Polish territory. This move would certainly meet with armed resistance. When this would happen was unclear. As the tension over Danzig and the Polish corridor mounted, that moment began to look nearer.[13]

Pariani and General Wilhelm Keitel, appointed by Hitler as head of the then newly created OKW (Oberkommando der Wehrmacht) a year earlier, duly met at Innsbruck on 5 April 1939. Keitel began by passing on Hitler's assurance that in any war Germany would be at Italy's side. Pariani thought that war with the Western democracies at some future time was unavoidable. Previously his planning had focused on invading Egypt and reaching the Suez Canal, thereby knocking out England as a rival Mediterranean power. Now, though, England was no longer Italy's immediate target. Pariani produced a scheme for a localized 'colonial' war with France, for which Italy would need material aid from Germany. Keitel unceremoniously rejected the idea. A European war would then be inevitable and England would likely join in if things were going badly for France – 'this we would not have'. Pariani at once abandoned his scheme. The two men agreed that a war with the Western powers was inevitable and that it would be best for Italy and Germany to attack together. Pariani suggested that 1941–2 would be a good time for Italy, but Keitel only said that it could come 'in a few years' time' when their rearmament was complete. Then, and over a key issue, the two men parted company. Keitel came away from the meeting believing that they had agreed that a war, when it came, must be decided quickly, as Italy was even more poorly placed to endure a long war than Germany. Pariani thought they had agreed that war might be either long or short, and that both countries would give one another economic as well as military support.[14] Marras added to the confusion by observing that at the present time Germany was not in a state to face either a short or a long war 'in full efficiency', as she lacked the heavy artillery for the former and the raw materials for the latter.[15]

Military Italy was certainly going to need Germany. Anticipating the joint conversations that were expected to follow shortly, Pariani had schedules of Italy's needs prepared. In the case of immediate mobilization she would be asking for 570,220 rifles and machine pistols, 3,420 mortars, 2,490 small-calibre guns (47mm–100mm), 51,830,000 rounds of ammunition of all types, 6,700 trucks, and 460 'L' and 'M' model Italian tanks. To fight a year-long war would add another 1,103,000 rifles and machine guns, 9,100 mortars, 2,200 small-calibre guns and 2,612,534 rounds of ammunition to the bill. All this was needed not just to replace combat wastage, but also to equip the forty-one new divisions Pariani planned to raise. Nor was it just military hardware that Italy needed to fight for a year. A separate schedule listed her raw materials requirements. They included 700,000 tons of iron, 40,000 tons of copper, 6,000 tons of steel, 4,000 tons of nickel, 20,000 tons of rubber, 1,300,000 tons of liquid fuels and 150,000 tons of meat.[16]

The British guarantee to Greece and Romania on 13 April momentarily put Greece at the epicentre of Mussolini's targets. He saw the country, which he had wanted to attack in the early 1930s, as Great Britain's outstation in the eastern Mediterranean, not least because of the strong historical, psychological and economic links between Greece and Great Britain, which held 80–90 per cent of Greek public debt. After the Munich agreement the Greek Prime Minister, General Ioannis Metaxas, had taken pains to reassure Mussolini that, despite appearances to the contrary, he was sincere in his attachment to Italy (he had spent four years of political exile in Siena) and in his admiration for the *Duce*. There was, he said truthfully, no political accord with Great Britain.[17] In spring 1939 things began to change. Articles in the Italian press advancing Fascist territorial aspirations in the region aroused strong public hostility, which only intensified after the Italian move into Albania on 7 April 1939, though the attitude in official circles was reported to be 'not only correct but favourable'.[18] By mid-August tensions were running high: the Italians had moved four of the five divisions in Albania to the common frontier, and the Greeks responded by ordering a partial mobilization. The Greek permanent under-secretary told the German minister in Athens that the Greek government would react to any violation of its territory with force if necessary.

On 7 April 1939 Italy invaded and annexed Albania. The move had been in Mussolini's mind since May 1938, but the spur to action was Hitler's occupation of the rump of Czechoslovakia on 15 March. Ciano, pursuing a personal agenda of aggrandizement, claimed that it 'conform[ed] to the spirit of the Axis', Mussolini needed to assert himself with a 'parallel' move, and the strike would enable Italy to threaten Greece and Yugoslavia.[19] Things did not go smoothly. The commander, General Guzzoni, was only told about the attack a week before it took place; some units scheduled to take part in it could not be mobilized, because they lacked equipment and had to be substituted at the last minute; the force allocated to do the job (22,000 men) looked thin when weighed against up to 60,000 defenders; and many of the *Bersaglieri* called up to take part, aged between thirty-five and thirty-eight, did not know how to fire the new weapons the army now used.[20] Fortunately for the invaders resistance turned out to be minimal. Perhaps for this reason the notion that such ventures needed training and preparation failed to take root in the *Duce*'s mind.

On 28 April Hitler denounced both the Polish-German accord of 1934 and the Anglo-German Naval Treaty of 1935. At the beginning of May an indirect warning arrived from Admiral Wilhelm Canaris, head of the *Abwehr* (German military intelligence), that Germany would soon move to occupy Poland. SIM passed the warning on to Mussolini.[21] Two weeks later, on 22 May 1939, the Foreign Minister Galeazzo Ciano signed the Pact of Steel in Berlin committing Italy and Germany to come immediately to one another's aid if either power got itself into a war with a third party or parties, regardless of the circumstances. Five days after that Mussolini took up his pen to spell out for Admiral Cavagnari how he saw the future. War between the 'plutocratic and therefore selfishly conservative nations' and the 'populous but poor' ones was inevitable. He had already told the German Foreign Minister Joachim von Ribbentrop at the Milan meeting that Italy would not be ready to fight until 1943, by which time Ethiopia would be pacified and would provide an army of six million men, the six battleships undergoing construction or modernization would be ready, the new medium and heavy artillery would be with the troops, and Italy would be prepared for what was inevitably going to be a war of economic attrition. Since the Axis 'will receive nothing from the rest of the world', the whole of the Danube basin and the Balkans would have to be seized immediately the war began, regardless of declarations of neutrality. As for the war plan, Italy would contribute more manpower than materiel and Germany more materiel than manpower. Would all this meet with Hitler's approval? If it did, then the military staffs would prepare detailed directives.[22] Immediately afterwards Mussolini sent General Ugo Cavallero to Berlin with a memorandum explaining that Italy needed at least another three years of peace to put her defences in order and get her armed forces equipped for war.

At the end of May, General Erhard Milch came to Rome and agreed to exchanges of information on the British and French air forces. Again, Hitler set limits on the talks: all information about new German weapons under development was to be kept strictly under wraps and for the present there was to be no joint liaison staff. On 20 June Cavagnari met his German opposite number, Admiral Erich Raeder, at Friedrichshafen in southern Germany. When the discussion turned to strategy a chasm opened up. The Germans intended to focus their surface and submarine forces on the North Atlantic to begin with and wanted Italian submarines in the Atlantic south of Lisbon. Cavagnari wanted the Germans to keep the five British fast battleships out of the Mediterranean, which would give the two fast *Littorio* class Italian warships their best chance of using their central position against at least four slower Anglo-French battleships in the western Mediterranean and six in the eastern Mediterranean. When Raeder suggested action against the French navy in the western Mediterranean, Cavagnari was evasive, leaving the Germans with the impression that as far as their ally was concerned a defensive position was 'the only possibility' at either end of the Mediterranean.[23] Cavagnari made out that the Germans were in full agreement with his strategy of concentrating on the central Mediterranean and looking to act in the Indian Ocean, a goal that expressed the expansive naval ambitions nursed by him and by his staff in peacetime and in the war that was to come. In fact the Germans, having learned that the Italian navy prioritized keeping open the sea route to Libya, were determined to try to ensure that their ally 'does not go running after all sorts of prestige targets (protection of Libya or taking possession of Tunisia or Egypt) but . . . in the interests of our common goal . . . displays the most vigorous activity in the Western Mediterranean . . .'[24]

Four days after the admirals' encounter, General Valle paid a return visit to Berlin. He got some insight into Goering's air strategy for a war with England, which was to starve her out by dive-bombing her merchant and naval shipping, but apart from an agreement to divide their respective spheres of air command at the Alps nothing of any substance came out of the meeting. The Germans fed the Italians with exaggerated claims about their air strength, boasting 4,000 front-line aircraft (a figure they did reach in 1940), and Valle returned to Rome and fed Ciano with the wholly misleading information that Italian bombs and torpedoes were better than German ones.[25]

International tensions now rose rapidly as Germany and Poland squared up to one another. On 4 July the British ambassador to Rome, Sir Percy Loraine, warned that if Germany put unacceptable pressures on Danzig and if Italy promised her military support then there would be war. Mussolini replied that if England was ready to back Poland's position with force, 'Italy will do the same for Germany's demands.'[26] On 24 July, with reports coming in that the Germans were feverishly arming their supporters in Danzig and moving men and weapons to the Polish frontier, Ciano sent confused instructions to the Italian ambassador in Berlin, Bernardo Attolico. A war just now was a questionable idea since it would certainly bring in the Western powers, but if Hitler thought it was an opportune moment then 'Italy is disposed to consent to it 100 per cent.'[27] With his gold reserves almost gone and his military preparations far from complete, Mussolini now looked for a way out. If the crisis came then Italy would fight 'to save its honour', but war had to be avoided.[28] Ciano would go to Salzburg to meet the German Foreign Minister, Ribbentrop, and persuade him that there must be no conflict with Poland, because that would lead to a general war which would be disastrous for everybody.

From Rome's point of view the meetings with Ribbentrop and Hitler at Salzburg and Berchtesgaden between 11 and 13 August were a shipwreck. Ribbentrop, showing 'an obstinate and unreasonable desire for battle', shrugged off all the Italian arguments, while Hitler, clearly determined to fight Poland in what he was convinced would be a localized war, advised Italy to dismember Yugoslavia at the first favourable opportunity. The only crumb of comfort to be had was Hitler's assertion that he would not require Italian aid under the terms of the Pact of Steel.[29]

Ciano's office was furious at what they saw as a flagrant violation of the Pact of Steel. Every conversation between Italian and German diplomats over the previous six months had taken it as read that there would be no war for at least three years and maybe five. The country could not undertake hostilities – she was 'the weakest point' against whom the British and French would have the greatest chance of success.[30] Mussolini thought a little differently. If Great Britain and France intervened to support Poland, he told Badoglio on 16 August, then Italy would maintain a strict defensive position and do nothing to suggest that she supported the Germans. If, on the other hand, Italy was attacked, then as soon as she had secured her frontiers at home and overseas she would attack Greece, aiming for Salonika. On 16 August Mussolini ordered General Alfredo Guzzoni, currently commanding in Albania, to prepare a draft invasion plan for Greece.

Plans were also to be readied at once for an offensive against Yugoslavia. As far as she was concerned, Mussolini wanted to bite off Croatia to get possession of its natural resources after having 'unleashed' internal riots in Yugoslavia. Warned by Badoglio that a conflict would catch Italy off-guard in the middle of its programme of military re-equipment, and that preparations for war in North Africa were notably behind schedule, Mussolini replied nonchalantly that the situation in Libya was 'truly precarious' and ordered his armed forces to study offensives against Greece and Yugoslavia 'with maximum urgency'.[31] Badoglio passed on the *Duce*'s instructions, but warned Mussolini that the military were facing a triple crisis of personnel, armaments and munitions, 'not to mention the disorder due to the recent reforms in the divisional structure' – an innovation he had originally supported.[32] The planners were warned to be ready to sustain a twelve-month war.[33]

The soldiers got to work at once. Numbers were tight: fifty-two of the seventy-two divisions available were needed for defence at home and in the colonies, leaving only twenty divisions for both the Balkan and North African operations. Pariani's grandiose plans for the two campaigns, which he thought would complement one another, soon came unstuck. Greece would be struck by a three-pronged assault in which eight divisions, one of them armoured, would drive on to Salonika supported by a subsidiary drive into the Epirus and landings on the Greek islands of Cefalonia, Zante and St Maura by four divisions. A simultaneous attack on Yugoslavia by between fourteen and sixteen Italian divisions would only work if there were anti-Serbian riots and the Yugoslavs had to deploy some of their divisions to guard other frontiers – and Italy had only eight divisions left. So unless Yugoslavia dissolved in turmoil and Italian numbers were boosted by at least six German and three Hungarian divisions, the Salonika offensive would have to be called off.[34] It was already becoming apparent that Mussolini's appetite was dangerously outrunning the means required to assuage it.

Confirmation that war was definitely in the air now came from one of the best-placed sources in Berlin. Arriving there in August to take over briefly from Marras as military attaché, General Mario Roatta was immediately taken up by Admiral Canaris as a back-channel to Rome. Canaris told Roatta that, although some in the German military had faith in a short war, others feared that the war would be long and that Germany would lose it in the west just as she had done in 1917–18. Perhaps, Canaris suggested, even after the Salzburg meeting Hitler might yet be dissuaded from acting if the Italian government said explicitly that it would not make common cause with the Third Reich.[35] As Roatta quickly discovered, Germany's preparations for war were continuing apace. Driving around outside Berlin, he and his staff identified a dozen parallel routes to the east already marked out for use. On 18 August he reported that Germany was now clearly readying herself to undertake large-scale military operations in order to recover the eastern territories she had lost at Versailles, 'if not more'. German commanders reckoned they could knock out Poland in two to three weeks. Roatta was inclined to overrate Poland's powers of resistance (he had been military attaché there in the 1920s), and also believed that Germany would have to make greater strides in defending her western frontier before she would move, which may have misled some in Rome into believing that there was yet more time in which to manoeuvre.[36] On the evening of 25 August he was dining with a gloomy Canaris – 'we're at the end', his host told him – when a telephone call came in telling him that Hitler had halted mobilization. A 'solution' had been found and it looked as though war had been avoided. Roatta's report went to Mussolini next day.[37]

As the last days of peace drained away, the practicality of an Italian grab at the Balkans vanished. Mussolini ruled out any immediate possibility of Hungarian or Bulgarian assistance and Badoglio's staff pointed out that even if Italy put up fourteen divisions against the same number of Yugoslav divisions the enemy formations were half as big again as the *binaria* divisions, which left no margin for error. Badoglio threw in what was clearly intended to be the clincher: intelligence suggested that if Italy did undertake the proposed operations the French would immediately launch a double offensive against her (presumably across the Alps and into Libya from Tunisia). The first charge on the armed forces was to put the country in a position to be able to resist an attack on the *madrepatria* (motherland). Only then should they take up the question of offensives against Greece and Yugoslavia. The chances of success in the former would depend on Bulgarian and Hungarian 'benevolence'. The latter could be considered only if Yugoslavia were demonstrably coming apart internally.[38]

By the end of August, Mussolini had to accept that he could not go to war yet, no matter how much he might want to. The king, Vittorio Emanuele III, opposed war, Badoglio warned that Italy was vulnerable to French attack, military plans showed all too clearly that the country could not wage a war in the Balkans in anything less than optimal circumstances, and everyone knew that realistically Libya was barely capable of defending herself let alone acting as the launching pad for an attack on Egypt. As Germany went to war on 1 September 1939, Italy declared her 'non-belligerence'.

Knowing the state of public opinion was always one of Mussolini's foremost priorities: his working day normally began with audiences with the commandant of the *Carabinieri*, the chief of police and the head of OVRA (a branch of the political police that operated separately from it and reported directly to the chief of police), and the secretary of the *Partito Nazionale Fascista*. In the months leading up to the outbreak of the world war the reports coming in to the head of OVRA, Guido Leto, spoke of a virtually unanimous feeling of anxiety among the population at the prospect of war, and of a widespread sense that Italy's military preparations left much to be desired. At the end of August 1939 the chief of police, Arturo Bocchini, gave Mussolini an OVRA report showing that the overwhelming majority of Italians feared war and were not prepared for it. At the same meeting the Party secretary, Achille Starace, offered the *Duce* a diametrically opposed opinion. Forty million Italians were ready to throw themselves into the fray as soon as he ordered them to do so, he told Mussolini. Starace was privileging loyalty whereas Bocchini was prioritizing reality. Faced with this unwelcome dissonance Mussolini dismissed them both from the room. In the ante-room they almost came to blows. Bocchini's reports were much the most reliable. In September 1939 his agents reported widespread uncertainty. Non-belligerence was popular, but would it last? Informers among the mobilized troops relayed their feeling that the *Duce* would keep their country – and them – out of the conflict.[39]

Italy's non-belligerence met with massive popular approval – but though he saw it as unavoidable it was not what Mussolini wanted. 'The Duce is convinced of the need to remain neutral,' Ciano recorded in his diary, 'but he is not at all happy. Whenever he can he reverts to the possibility of our action.'[40] Joining the war would require more than just military preparation. 'Miserable dead-weights' were lurking in the alleys, in the out-of-the-way places and in the dark corners, Mussolini told the Fascists of Bologna. The corners where 'this Masonic, Jewish, foreign-loving rubbish' was lurking had to be cleaned up.[41] The leaders of the Genoa Fascists were told that the country was preparing militarily. There were notable difficulties, but they were being over-come. And then, if it came to war, 'the Italian people will fight'.[42] The Minister of Popular Culture, Alessandro Pavolini, set the Fascist press to work to persuade the populace that conflict was inevitable, not because the Fascists wanted it but because it was being forced on them by Great Britain and France.

Pariani was again looking to North Africa as his favoured option. He had believed that he could fight campaigns against both Greece and Yugoslavia while the bulk of the army was at only 50 per cent of its war footing. In the last week of August, with two regular army divisions about to leave for Libya, another twenty-four being readied to go there if needed and fourteen Fascist 'Blackshirt' militia divisions mobilized to cover the western frontier, he decided on further mobiliza-tions.[43] The day after Hitler launched his attack on Poland, Pariani proposed building up Italian forces in North Africa and then launching offensives against both Tunisia and Egypt. At the end of the first week in September, with the Greek option fading but the Yugoslav one apparently still a possibility, he decided to mobilize most of the rest of the army. During September and October four regular army divisions and four divisions of Blackshirts were sent to Libya, where they joined four metropolitan and two Libyan divisions, and by early November there were 90,000 Italian troops in Cyrenaica and 40,000 in Tripolitania. Over the following months tents, uniforms, trucks, tanks, artillery and ammunition were shipped across, but during the winter and spring of 1939–40 the troops had to put up with wretched conditions.[44] Several months later the governor of Libya, Italo Balbo, remarked that if war had broken out in September in anything other than 'the most fortunate circumstances, the outcome could not have been favourable for us'.[45]

On 20 September Mussolini told Guzzoni that the war with Greece was off. The country was 'a bare bone, and is not worth the loss of a single Sardinian grenadier'.[46] In the intervening weeks Metaxas had sent placatory signals. The notion that there were over 200,000 men under arms was a gross exaggeration, he told the Italian minister Emanuele Grazzi; there were only 110,000 soldiers in the ranks in the entire country. Greece would have to be mad to think of attacking Italy. Metaxas was ready to revoke the precautionary measures he had taken in the face of the Italian moves if they would partially withdraw.[47] He asked for an extension of the Italo-Greek pact of friendship signed in 1929, and on 30 September diplomatic notes were exchanged in which the Greek government expressed its pleasure that Italian troops were being withdrawn from the Albanian frontier and confirmed that it was still inspired by the principles of friendship and collaboration that were embodied in the pact. The Italian note protested its intention to continue the peace policy and hoped for a new period of friendship and understanding.[48] For the moment, it was Yugoslavia and not Greece that was back in Mussolini's cross hairs.

By 1 October 1939, 1,310,000 Italian men had been nominally re-enrolled. The process was a complete fiasco. Reports landing on Mussolini's desk spoke of rations for ten men being distributed to one hundred, of soldiers dressed in civilian clothes because there were no uniforms for them, of some men sleeping in public buildings or doorways and others going home because there was no room for them in the barracks. An alarmed public began asking itself why so many men were being called up if the government was not intending to go to war?[49] Mussolini was furious. The 'inconveniences' suffered by the conscripts had been too many and too widespread, but what was no less worrying was that discontent which was widespread in the army was spreading to the country at large as the story got out.[50]

In May Pariani had boasted in the chamber of deputies that the transformation of the army into *binaria* divisions would be completed during the year 1939–40. At the beginning of November he claimed that thirty-eight divisions were complete and that by 1 May 1940 another twenty-six would be too. Badoglio's report on the state of the armed forces told a very different story. Only ten of the seventy-two divisions in the army were fully manned and equipped and a further twenty-two planned divisions did not exist at all. There were shortages of junior officers, of modern artillery (all the guns dated back to the First World War and no new ones were due until May 1940), of motor vehicles, of tanks (there were no medium-sized tanks at all), and only enough fuel for four and a half months. The navy was not in much better shape. It had only two battleships afloat and the four due in 1940 would take time to be worked up for action, it had enough fuel for five months at most and not enough storage capacity for any more, and its anti-aircraft guns all dated back to the First World War. Nor was the air force anything to write home about. There was enough fuel to fly its 1,769 planes for two months, and enough munitions for three or four months, it was short of 4,000 motor vehicles and thousands of fuel drums; there were minuscule numbers of anti-aircraft guns, and the anti-aircraft defences of the fifteen most important targets would take ten months to set up. Nothing at all had been done about another forty-seven potential enemy objectives.[51]

NAVAL PREPARATIONS FOR WAR

For most of the interwar period the problem that preoccupied the Italian navy was the protection of the country's sea communications. The First World War had shown how dependent Italy was on outside sources of supply for the raw materials she needed to sustain her industries and her people. Those who saw a glass half full believed that Italy's central position in the Mediterranean gave her tactical and strategic advantages. Those who saw a glass half empty believed that it gave her neither. The theme that dominated much of the thinking about naval war during the interwar years was vulnerability. From this it followed that the first charges on the navy were ensuring that the country's essential supplies made it to home ports, protecting troop transports for North Africa and defending Italy's lengthy coastline. Attacking the enemy's supply lines and coasts – the enemy in this case being France – came second.[52]

The navy's strategic analysis of the challenges it faced and the options it had as the European war began made for gloomy reading. Even without aid from other Mediterranean naval powers the British and French battle-fleets, with three battleships each, could control both ends of the Mediterranean. They would also in all probability challenge Italy's control of the Sicilian Channel and the central Mediterranean. With fewer battleships, 'actions in grand style' at either end of the Mediterranean were out of the question. The main charge on the navy – apart from protecting the coasts and ports of metropolitan Italy – was escorting convoys to Libya. Troops could go to Libya on fast steamships, but almost the whole surface fleet would have to be deployed each time equipment and supplies had to be shipped there. The navy thought this 'extremely risky' as its surface fleet would then be exposed not only to superior surface forces but also to enemy aircraft flying out of bases in Tunisia, Egypt and Greece. What all this meant was that the navy was going to hang back, hoping to erode enemy forces through submarine and surface force attacks and wait to seize the only opportunity it could see for a major fleet action – if the enemy got into difficulties while trying, for example, to take the Balearic islands.[53] Challenged by Mussolini in a ministerial meeting, Admiral Cavagnari as good as admitted that the navy had no workable strategy for a war against Great Britain and France, telling the *Duce* that the navy would 'do its duty and fight, but no more'.[54] His stance when faced with a war to fight, as he afterwards acknowledged, was dominated by 'the grave risk of irremediably worsening the existing power relationship through an incautious action'.[55]

If the navy was not enthusiastic about going to war, it had good reason. Cavagnari had built a battle-fleet that looked impressive, but beneath its armour cladding it was fragile. An internal analysis carried out at the end of February 1940 exposed deficits and deficiencies almost everywhere. The peacetime navy needed 100,000 lower-deck reservists to reach its fighting strength of 170,000 men. They could be found, but the specialist functions such as radio-telegraphists, mechanics and fire directors would be about 25 per cent undermanned. Short of officers even in peacetime, the navy would be over a thousand short of its wartime strength of 9,000. For anti-aircraft defence it relied mainly on thirty-year-old 76mm guns which could not fire as high as modern planes could fly. There were no bomb-proof shelters anywhere on naval property. There were not enough vessels in the whole national fishing fleet to provide the 870-odd auxiliary minesweepers the navy believed it needed, and no specialized submarine-hunters at all. Supplies of ordnance were less than they were designed to be – there were enough anti-aircraft shells for five months of war – but industry could make good the deficiencies by the end of 1941 unless short of raw materials. There was enough diesel fuel in the reserves in Italy and Libya to fight for five months or so, but only enough aviation fuel to keep navy planes flying for one month.[56]

THE POLISH CAMPAIGN AND ITALIAN-GERMAN MILITARY COLLABORATION

The rapid success of Hitler's Polish *Blitzkrieg* unveiled a new face of war. The essentials of the Wehrmacht's land campaign were quickly apparent. The German army had shown that it had lost none of its skills in organization and manoeuvre on the battlefield, and although the rank and file of the Polish army had fought bravely their leaders had proved totally incapable. This suggested to more than one Italian observer that the German armed forces had not been seriously tested.[57] Working from open German sources, SIM summarized the main strategic lessons of the campaign. Contrary to the opinion of many pre-war critics, long-range turning movements that could lead to the complete annihilation of enemy forces were now possible. Speed was a key factor, paralysing the Polish high command and protecting the German forces from surprise, and so was the Germans' readiness to advance without bothering about open flanks or rear areas, leaving pockets of resistance to be mopped up later. Another major difference between the battles fought during the Great War and the ones the Germans had just won in Poland was the direct intervention of divisional commanders on the field of battle, made possible by motor vehicles. Rapid German domination of the skies and the use of air power in close support of land action was clearly a factor of huge weight: SIM warned that it exposed 'the sinister consequences' for an army whose own air force lost dominance of the skies from the outset of its operations.[58]

Air intelligence noted the change in bombing tactics. After initially bombing Warsaw at low level and suffering some losses, the Luftwaffe switched to higher-level attacks by larger formations. On a visit to the front at the end of September the Italian air attaché, Colonel Giuseppe Teucci, was not impressed by the high-level bombing, which was what the Germans had done in Spain. To judge by the percentage of craters that were distant from their targets, Italian formations 'would have done much better'. He was, however, impressed by the effects of twelve hours' bombing of the Warsaw Citadel which had left nothing standing except for a few partially demolished walls.[59] The role played by the light bombers – Dornier 17s (a newer type than had been seen in Spain, the air attaché noted), Junkers 88s and Heinkel 123s – in attacking forts, batteries and concentrations of enemy troops was repeatedly remarked on in Italian reports and emphasized in the official German report on the campaign. The bombers' actions had undoubtedly saved the army from 'an infinity of blood[-letting]' and had played a very large part in the overall success.[60] Teucci also noted, somewhat ominously for Italy, that Polish aircraft which four years ago had been reckoned the best in the world were now too slow to compete with the current generation of German aircraft.[61]

When it came to making overall judgements about why the Germans had won, Teucci acknowledged that this had been made possible thanks to their numerical and qualitative superiority. This had given them complete dominance in the air, which was 'beyond anything foreseeable'. Above all, though, the Germans had been helped by 'grave deficiencies' in Polish command and the 'incredible lack of preparation' of Polish support services. Polish aircraft had been unable to refuel at their temporary airfields, their resupply services were inadequate, and when deployed by a 'criminally deficient' air force command their attacks on German bombers and armoured columns had been no more than 'small change'.[62] Goering's description to Teucci of the air war, in which he emphasized his personal direction of a mass air strike by 400 to 500 planes against the Polish army and rather downplayed the importance of the close air support provided by Wolfram von Richthofen's X

Fliegerkorps, did little to encourage the heads of the *Regia Aeronautica* to adopt a more positive attitude towards collaboration with the other two armed services.[63]

Clearly there were lessons to be had and the Italian chiefs of staff were enjoined to learn them, not only from the Polish campaign but also from the actions which would develop in the German-French-British theatre. There must be no repeat of May 1915, when Italy had gone to war having failed to absorb the lessons of a conflict that was by then already ten months old.[64] When the chiefs did meet, Badoglio passed quickly over the issue. If there was a conflict it would be followed carefully to draw the appropriate lessons but, Badoglio reminded his audience, no two wars were the same.[65] Italian sensitivities also played a role in limiting the impact of the Polish campaign on their own practices. In the spring of 1940 the Germans offered to send Colonel Ritter von Thoma to Rome to share his experiences of using tanks in Spain and Poland. Unwilling at that time to see closer links forged with his partner, Mussolini vetoed the visit.[66] The general attitude seemed to be that there was not much to be learned from the Polish campaign: Roatta thought that what the Germans had done was very similar to Italian ideas of the *guerra di rapido corso*.[67]

As the 'Phoney War' began, the questions of when, where and how the Italians would join their Axis partner were still very much undecided. Four days into the Polish campaign, Germany's military attaché in Rome, General Enno von Rintelen, reported 'absolute readiness' among Mussolini's leading people to participate – if necessary.[68] The Germans assumed that their ally would not be in at the start of their coming offensive against the West but would come in at some point, Hitler expecting that the Italians would take advantage at 'a certain moment' of 'the favourable possibilities that will present themselves in order to join resolutely in the fray'. Mussolini was indeed ready to join a war at some as yet undecided point in the future 'when we are well prepared', but only in accordance with Italy's own objectives and her own strategy. On one thing he was quite determined – that Italy would fight a 'parallel war' independently of Germany.[69]

Reports reaching Berlin from Rome suggested that the Italians were seriously preparing to be ready to fight in the spring. They were, it seemed, very sensitive to any criticism on Germany's part that they had not so far participated.[70] In reality things were moving rather more slowly in Italian military circles. With Europe at war and Italy standing uneasily to one side, Badoglio called the heads of the armed forces together in mid-November. After welcoming Marshal Graziani, Pariani's successor as chief of the army general staff (whom he loathed), he warned all three men that the *Duce* had had enough of things being reported as done when they had not been done. Whether Italy went to war or not, whether she fought in the east or the west, was not their business. Their job was to see that every unit had reached a state of efficiency in which it could be 'securely' employed. The first task was 'to close the doors to the house both west and east'. Only after that should the chiefs study operations that could be carried out in favourable circumstances.

Jettisoning both Pariani's plans for an attack on the Suez Canal and his guiding conception of modern war, Badoglio announced that in the present circumstances 'a fast war must be excluded'. A run through the overseas territories confirmed what everyone very well knew – that they had only about half the fuel and munitions they would need to last for twelve months in war. A general count of stocks was now to be undertaken – a difficult task because each of the three services had its own way of doing things. Moving on to anti-aircraft defences, the heads of the armed forces registered yet more shortcomings. The navy alone, which was singled out for praise as the best prepared of the three services, had 1,264 guns to defend fifteen bases; to defend five times that number, as was now being advised, it would need 5,000 to 6,000 guns. The deputy chief of army staff responsible for anti-aircraft defence, General Claudio Bergia, reckoned that Italy could have most of the modern guns it needed by the end of 1942. As potential squabbles emerged, Badoglio told the three services not to be separate churches but to collaborate with one another 'altruistically' in dividing up what monies there were – something they had never done before and would not do now. Closing the meeting, he ordered the generals and admirals to be realistic in what they said they could do. It was everyone's duty to give the *Duce* accurate information 'so that he can know what he can and cannot decide to do'.[71]

In mid-December Mussolini told Graziani he wanted a million men trained and formed into sixty divisions and able to fight for a year by August 1940.[72] Recalculating the numbers and rewriting their tables, the soldiers reckoned they could raise an army of sixty-seven divisions, along with four divisions of Blackshirt militia. Their equipment might be reduced, which would inevitably reduce their firepower but would not prejudice their overall efficiency.[73] Graziani said that if he were to undertake a major offensive he would need a hundred divisions – and was told by Mussolini's deputy at the War Ministry, General Soddu, to stay in the realms of reality. In February and March 1940 a million men were called up, and in April and May another 700,000.

As 1940 opened Mussolini knew, thanks to a visit from the German labour minister Robert Ley in December, that the Germans were anticipating attacking Holland and that a war with Russia was on the cards at some time in the future. This last was something Mussolini was prepared to swallow and even to encourage. Russia was where Germany could solve its problem of *Lebensraum*. Once bolshevism was demolished, it would be the turn of the Western democracies. The *Duce* was in no hurry to fight them, partly because he was not sure that Great Britain and France could ever be brought to their knees – 'the United States would never permit the democracies to suffer such a total defeat' – and partly because he was sure that they would ultimately collapse from within thanks to the 'cancers' they nurtured within themselves. Italy's military preparations were gathering pace, he told Hitler, but she could not and would not involve herself in a long war. Her intervention, which must be an aid and not a burden to Germany when it came, must occur 'at the most rewarding and decisive moment'. Exactly when was a question to be examined by the soldiers.[74] In the event, that decision was one which Mussolini would take over their heads.

Mussolini may not have thought that the Western democracies could be crushed but he was sure, he told his council of ministers a couple of weeks later, that England and France 'can now no longer win the war'. Perhaps Germany might not win it either, but Italy must enter it at some point – to remain neutral throughout would be to reduce her status to that of a second-rate European power. By July, Italy would have the men and the aircraft she needed 'to confront the situation'. He wanted to make his move in the second half of 1940, or better still during the early part of 1941. This would be a *guerra parallela* – a specifically Italian war, with Italian objectives, separate from those of the actual contestants. As to what that move might entail, 'he speaks of terror bombings over France, of control of the Mediterranean'. The immediate task, though, was 'to throw mountains of cement on mountains of stone' and block the Alpine valleys.[75] At the start of the New Year, the army set out plans based specifically on experience in the Great War for an extensive programme of defensive fortifications along all Italy's frontiers which would be completed by the end of the year and which would be able to absorb and repel enemy attacks.[76]

ECONOMICS AND ARMAMENTS

As the summer of 1939 turned to autumn and peacetime gave way to 'non-belligerence' a cascade of economic statistics coming from General Carlo Favagrossa, head of the General Commissariat for War Production (COGEFAG) from 26 August, began to land on Mussolini's desk at the Palazzo Venezia. Coal imports were 60,000 tons a month less than what was necessary and scrap iron fell short by 42,000 tons a month. Partly as a result, monthly steel output fell in October by 50,000 tons to a total of 110,000 tons, which was 30,000 tons less than the minimum amount required. The shortfalls could not be made up by buying raw materials in from abroad: Italy needed 9,000,000,000 lire a year in gold, silver and foreign currencies to pay for what she needed but she had total reserves of only 4,000,000,000. In early December 1939, using the statistical data he had gathered, Favagrossa handed Mussolini his calculations of the time needed to get the armed forces ready to fight. There were already holes in the fabric of the economic war machine: the projections depended on there being enough raw materials to work two ten-hour shifts a day, and since it was already evident that there were not enough of them to fulfil the military needs, the gap would have to be plugged by exporting war equipment in order to get the means to import more raw materials. The data were not encouraging. The air force could be ready to begin fighting by the end of 1940, but it would not get everything it needed to sustain it for a year until the middle of 1941. The navy would be in a position to begin fighting during the second half of 1941, though it would not complete its construction programme or get the medium- and heavy-calibre guns it needed for a year's fighting until September 1942. The army was in the worst position of all. Individual side-arms, infantry mortars, tanks and tractors that were required before the fighting could start would be available during 1941, a full stock of mortar rounds and explosives during 1942, and infantry guns, munitions and machine guns not until the end of 1943. The full inventory of artillery would not be ready until the end of 1944. The message Favagrossa wanted to put across was crystal clear: Italy was not yet ready to fight and would not be fully ready even to begin to do so until 1945. Only in 1949 would she be fully ready to fight for a year and if labour only worked one ten-hour shift a day that date would be set back by a decade.[77]

As the selective British blockade, which indirectly affected particularly Italian imports of German coal which came via Rotterdam, began to bite, the seriousness of Italy's economic position became increasingly apparent. With industry only getting by from day to day and the country short of its most essential supplies, Luca Pietromarchi, head of the office of war economics at the Foreign Ministry, believed it would be 'suicidal' to line up with Germany. With no chance of buying more stocks despite her earnings from arms sales because Great Britain had cornered all the raw materials, the only way that Italy could reconstitute her supplies was to link herself to the Allies.[78]

In the months that followed, an avalanche of statistical evidence piled up, all of which went to confirm Mussolini's belief that Italy could only fight a short war. In mid-February Favagrossa reported that thanks to changes in the December programmes the time the navy would need to be ready to fight had been reduced by a year, and the army by two years – but only if both programmes started at once and if production was increased. If there were no shortages of raw materials, the armed forces would be ready to fight for a year by the end of 1943. The sums of money he needed simply did not exist. Three days after putting his memorandum on Mussolini's desk, Favagrossa asked for 4,400,000,000 lire for raw materials. He was given 2,096,000,000 lire, reduced on 21 May to 700,000,000 lire. A detailed summary of the raw materials situation in mid-May told Mussolini that in some sectors such as scrap steel and tin Italy was living from day to day, in others such as nickel and lead the supplies were running down rapidly thanks to the Allied blockade. On 1 June 1940, nine days before Italy went to war, Favagrossa pointed out the weaknesses in the army's situation as far as munitions were concerned. Its own estimates suggested it had enough for between fifty and sixty days of fighting, but the amounts of ammunition fired during the battle of the

Ebro showed that it grossly underestimated its needs. Favagrossa reckoned it would run out of ammunition after a month.[79] Whether all this information swayed Mussolini one way or another is doubtful. Aside from the fact that he had been deluged with statistics for years, he probably suspected that Favagrossa's figures were being exaggerated – as their author later admitted they were 'so that the nail went in'. And some of the numbers mysteriously improved: at the end of May, Favagrossa told Mussolini that he only had 25 tons of nickel left, but a month later he had 110 tons.

The seventeenth – and last – annual meeting of the Supreme Defence Commission (*Commissione Suprema di Difesa* – CSD) opened on 8 February 1940. According to one civilian minister who was present, no one was nursing any alarmist tendencies. Instead 'a reassuring quietism prevailed', partly because the Maginot Line was talked of as unbreakable and partly because 'we who knew him [Mussolini] did not fear the possibility that we would be overtaken by war of our own volition knowing the military and economic conditions of the country and well knowing the difference between talking of war and making it'.[80] The *Duce*, who had just told an audience of Fascist militia that he had decided on war in a speech which he ordered should not be published in the press, would shortly prove him wrong.

The twenty or so civilian and military leaders who gathered that day had in front of them a forbidding pile of position papers and memoranda. None of them made for comfortable reading. The navy had run down its stocks of raw materials to the point where they were practically non-existent. Its wish list of what it needed to survive five months of war was costed at 130,000,000 lire, but so far the Ministry of Defence had not released any funds to pay for it. Its building programme was therefore currently on hold.[81] The War Ministry's stocks were in slightly better shape, but it too was concerned about the supplies of raw materials. If war came, then even though the arms export trade that Italy was currently engaged in would be curtailed there would be a raw materials crisis that would bring production almost to a standstill. To get round this the War Ministry wanted 'an untouchable stockpile' built up with reserves that would last for six months' wartime consumption. It also highlighted an awkward fact: if new and secure sources of raw materials were not found then replacing consumption in wartime presently appeared 'highly chancy'.[82] As Mussolini well knew, the army was already in difficulties. To complete its planned replacement artillery programme it needed 236 tons of nickel, but even with an exceptional allocation it had only 34.5 tons. As a result, the programme could not now be completed before 1943.[83]

The commission began its work by examining anti-aircraft defence – or, more accurately, the lack of it. It soon appeared that not much had been or could be done. The mass of the population could not afford the gas masks that were on sale at 35 lire each; evacuating cities would be no defence since it would merely produce overcrowding elsewhere; and publicly funded shelters were regarded as unnecessary, because people could take shelter in their cellars. Plucking a number out of thin air, Mussolini declared that the country needed 4,000 of the new 90mm anti-aircraft guns – not one of which would be available before the end of the year. Meantime, and in the face of all this, the best protection was the threat of reprisals. If the air-raid sirens did not work very well, that did not matter – in such circumstances, Mussolini told his audience, it was well known that some people developed a very acute sense of hearing.[84] With that, the committee moved on.

Over the six days of meetings military men and civilian ministers put down markers for the enormous amounts of raw materials they would need if and when Italy went to war. Mussolini himself was first into the lists. The navy would need two million tons of fuel oil, enough for up to twelve months of war, by 1942 – partly because the two new 35,000-ton battleships 'will drink rivers of fuel'. Even though the Soviet Union had stopped supplying Italy with diesel fuel, adequate supplies were arriving from Mexico and the United States. The air force would need at least 400,000 tons of fuel – 'because without petrol you can't make war', the *Duce* explained – and the army would need 500,000 tons. By June 1941 he expected that domestic refineries would be able to produce about a quarter of those amounts each year.[85]

The list of raw materials demanded by the armed services seemed endless. The navy wanted 20,000 tons of steel, 3,000 tons of copper, 1,500 tons of lead and smaller amounts of other metals to keep going for the first five months of war. If the private shipbuilding industry were to remain viable during the first year of a war, it would need 95,000 tons of steel, 8,700 tons of copper, 2,300 tons of lead, 2,250 tons of zinc and more besides. Its demands paled into relative insignificance when compared with the army's calculations. The soldiers said they needed 1,300,000 tons of iron, 160,000 tons of copper, 40,000 tons of lead, 14,000 tons of rubber, 3,000 tons of tin and 1,000 tons of nickel – all of it from abroad – as well as substantial amounts of domestically sourced raw materials. General Favagrossa pointed out that just building factories to process the requisite metals would not be enough. They needed electricity, which meant in turn expanding the capacity of power plants. Mussolini skated dextrously over the surface of the problem. Italy needed to produce four million tons of steel a year to meet the needs of peace and war. She must reach an output of 2,500,000 tons during 1940, and the rest would become available once the steel-making process had become 'fully integrated'. As for where the metals were going to come from, the *Duce* had some answers. There was enough iron ore up and down Italy to enable the country to develop a great steel-making capacity, the Dolomites contained 'incalculable amounts' of magnesium, and the common clay in Istria and on the Gargano could be worked to produce aluminium. He had already convinced himself that there was plenty of scrap metal to be collected in Italy from metal railings, pots and pans and the like.[86]

One of Mussolini's techniques when chairing these meetings was to address specific issues for which he had an answer and ignore those for which he did not. Another was to show that he had a greater mastery of all the relevant data than anyone else. When the discussion moved on to autonomy in foodstuffs and textiles he deluged his audience with production statistics for olive oil, meat, fish, cellulose, wool and more besides, even telling them how many sheep and goats there were in the country (ten million). Some shortages would not matter: the meat situation was of no real concern since 'twenty million Italians have the wise habit of not eating it and they do very well'. Others could be solved very easily: coal consumption could be reduced by cutting the number of trains using it and by making sure that when they were in stations they stood still for as short a time as possible.[87]

If Mussolini thought that no one would question the economics of the Potemkin village he was building, he was wrong. When the Minister for Communications, Giovanni Host-Venturi, told the group that Italy would need to import twenty-two million tons of goods in 1940, Raffaele Riccardi, Minister for Currency and Foreign Exchange, told the commission that it might as well stop calculating there and then, because its feet were not on the ground. The studies it was examining had been drawn up by people who were still living in the pre-1914 world 'with freedom of the seas, abundant means to pay and secure [sources of] provisioning'. How was Italy going to pay for the imports she needed? In the best possible scenario she would still need to find 2,245,000,000 lire, far more than could be met by using up all Italy's gold reserves. And how, he asked the servicemen, did they propose to import seven million tons of liquid fuels in wartime when all three entrances to the Mediterranean were going to be closed to traffic? Italy's export trade was being sacrificed to the need to meet military orders, income from tourism had more or less disappeared, and the money coming in from Italians living abroad was merely a drop in the bucket. The only way to try to square the circle was to cut back on everything that was not militarily strictly essential and reduce domestic demand. Hannibal was not yet at the gates, Riccardi told his listeners, 'but he has crossed the threshold'.[88] Badoglio batted Riccardi's specific criticisms of the military aside – 'We must say to the DUCE: if this is what is wanted, this is what we need.' Mussolini could only waffle.

When the committee got round to considering North Africa, it was faced with another huge list of wants. Marshal Balbo's written submission made no bones about the things that needed to be done. He had 105,000 active troops – he should have had 170,000 but releases and leaves had whittled them down – and was short of officers, modern weapons, especially anti-tank guns and mortars, suitable motor vehicles and pack animals, without which his troops were roadbound, and anti-aircraft defences. Tobruk, for example, had only twenty 76mm guns to protect it. Fortifications had been built but they lacked internal fittings, guns and munitions. Of Balbo's 400-odd aircraft only 240 were fit for action and they included two groups of S-81 bombers that were on their last legs. Should it come to war, the colony had enough fuel and artillery ammunition to last for eighty days and enough smallarms ammunition to last one hundred days. If all his wants were met, then Libya would be able to put up an effective defence, break up probable enemy offensives and 'think of the possibility of offensive action'.[89] Badoglio gave his paper short shrift: if Balbo were to be given everything he was asking for, Italy would have to be 'completely emptied out'. Mussolini had nothing of substance to offer by way of solutions. Some of the divisional magazines needed filling; the fortifications were short of seventy-four steel turrets; and since Italy possessed 'the best anti-tank guns in Europe', they should be sent across to Libya as soon as possible. All in all, he concluded, things were not too bad and they could look to the future, 'I would not say with tranquillity but with firmness.'[90]

The committee soldiered on through the jungle of Fascist bureaucracy, picking up more bills as it went along: the navy asked for 131,000,000 lire to make basic improvements to its bases at Taranto, Trapani, Pantelleria and Tobruk, and 160,000,000 lire to complete a base at Kisimaio in Somalia and open a window onto the Indian Ocean. What it learned on its travels should have sounded alarm bells. Three-quarters of the machine tools used by the aircraft industry had to be imported. Italy's pre-war production of general purpose machine tools, and her dependence on specialized machine tools imported from the United States and Germany, would be important 'multipliers' in reducing her manufacturing capabilities during the war.[91] No significant progress had been made in relocating Italian industry to the south, out of reach of enemy air power. There was no proper plan for agricultural mobilization in wartime (the commission's secretary had to point that out). The agriculture minister was told to draw one up as quickly as possible. During the discussion on supply it was suggested that the problems could be solved by reaching agreements with neutral countries and especially Germany, which would necessitate building more merchant shipping and more railway stock. Later on, Host-Venturi told the commission that Italy needed at least 7,500 more railway wagons – another addition to the bill. Sometimes alarm bells were carefully muffled. While the Duke of Aosta was struggling with a simmering rebellion in Ethiopia, the commission was reassured that the situation in Italian East Africa was generally fine and that political activity, 'backed where necessary by military force', was winning over the rebels.[92]

Closing the sixth and last meeting of the commission, which lasted only ninety minutes, Mussolini brushed aside Riccardi's money worries. He had been told innumerable times during the Abyssinian war that the ship was going down, but it would undoubtedly still be afloat at the year's end. During its third session he had expressed 'ample reservations' about whether there would be a Franco-German land battle in the coming spring. France, he thought, would not risk another generation of men, and the Germans could say 'Advance, we're waiting for you.' Now he asserted that the army's programmes were not 'idiotic' but matched the means available and the domestic possibilities. The armed forces' requests must be met because they were the necessary minimum requirements below which Italy could not go. Finally, he endorsed a demand made by Marshal Graziani during that last afternoon to prioritize the defence of Italy's borders by fortifying all Italy's northern land frontiers. Giuseppe Bottai, who as Minister for Education attended the meetings, noted afterwards that he had never seen so much paper and so many plans and forecasts with no firm check on whether any of them had actually been put into effect. Now everyone was signing up to 'a mythical date' between the end of 1941 and the beginning of 1942. 'Everyone says they will be ready by then, if they are given the money.'[93]

A week after the final CSD meeting, the soldiers met to discuss their tasks. Concrete – for the fortifications that Mussolini had ordered – was the top item on their agenda. That needed coal, and, as Favagrossa pointed out, Italy could soon be wholly dependent on overland supplies from Germany. The Allied blockade would cut off seaborne supplies from Rotterdam from 1 March, and the Germans might well decide that coal coming from Great Britain was contraband and sink the ships. The soldiers quickly tacked away from these economic reefs to set themselves some priorities. The northern frontier would have top billing, followed by the western and then the eastern borders – which suggests that at this moment they saw a greater Germany as a more potent long-term threat than France. More generally, priority would be given to weapons and ammunition for the infantry, tanks, motor vehicles, and 90mm guns and the munitions for them. What remained would be used to build the frontier fortifications. Nothing more was going to Libya or to the Aegean. 'What they [can] have is what they've got,' General Soddu declared.[94]

Graziani wanted to know when, on the basis of what was currently available, sixty divisions could be ready. At the start of 1941, though with no reserve supplies, Roatta told him. Favagrossa tried once more to get the military to face up to economic reality. That could only be done if the factories worked two ten-hour shifts a day and Italy had three times the supplies of raw materials currently on hand. If the factories continued working at their current rate, it would take three times as long. Five days earlier Favagrossa had told Mussolini that with all the necessary raw materials to hand and working two shifts a day it would take at least four years before the armed forces were ready to fight for one year.[95] The soldiers decided to work on readying blocs of ten divisions at a time. They were, Roatta pointed out, in a circle they could not square. For the moment the army was not strong enough to fight an offensive war outside Italy and not well enough equipped to fight a defensive war in the open field inside the country. Therefore it needed to give battle based on a system of fortifications. These had to run along the frontier, which was often not the best site for defensive works. And they needed to save funds, or at least raw materials. The basic principle now was to leave Italy overseas entirely to its own devices. 'To give [them] any more is, in the present circumstances, impossible,' Roatta declared. 'We must concentrate everything on the mainland.'[96]

The army's needs were gargantuan. In the second half of March, Soddu gave Mussolini the figures for readying all seventy-one army divisions. That would require 6,230 guns, 2,000 anti-tank guns, 7,100 anti-aircraft guns plus munitions and transport. The bill came to some 19,000,000,000 lire. Mussolini approved the plan, dependent on having the necessary raw materials. This was not the only obstacle to achieving the planned outputs. In January 1940 the small-arms industry had only 13 per cent of the capacity needed to meet estimated needs, and by the end of 1942 it could only reach 30 per cent of what was required. In April, Favagrossa's office began talks with the main manufacturer, Breda, to double its output of medium machine guns and triple its output of light machine guns by mid-1942. Robbing Peter to pay Paul, Breda was given machine tools intended for other firms. For its part, Breda asked for orders for four times the amount of weaponry the army wanted. In the event it would achieve the planned outputs.[97]

When Mussolini made a move – and also what that move was – depended less on the state of Italian armaments and military readiness and more on what the Germans did. That was a matter of guesswork. As the German generals told the Italians, Hitler made the decisions and even they were not sure what was coming next. As the New Year began it seemed that only bad weather was delaying a German offensive against Belgium and Holland, that a peaceable solution with Great Britain now appeared impossible and that, in General Franz Halder's words, 'a great battle seems inevitable'. The German high command seemed hesitant and uncertain. The only certainty was that a long war had to be avoided and that therefore the Germans must take the initiative.[98] A month later, Hitler appeared to be thinking about delaying the long-expected air-land offensive against France and launching an aero-naval offensive against Great Britain first. There was also talk of a German intervention in the Balkans in tandem with a possible Soviet action against Bessarabia.[99] In early March, on the eve of Mussolini and Hitler's meeting at the Brenner Pass, General Marras had a meeting with Kurt von Tippelskirch, a member of the operations department of the OKW. Von Tippelskirch detected signs that the Allies were losing faith in a long blockade as a war-winning strategy and might review their hitherto intransigent attitude. Hitler might again put off unleashing the expected offensive, in part because the ground was unsuitable. As far as Italy was concerned, his advice was that the Alpine theatre bristled with difficulties and that principal operations might best be developed in North Africa, though action on both frontiers there would need a force of perhaps thirty divisions. Another possibility was that Italy might invade Greece.[100]

What the Italians were going to do if it came to war, and when, were questions that were as yet quite unresolved. Mussolini's determination to keep policy matters – and therefore strategy making – entirely in his own hands was a brake on progress. So was Badoglio's determination to keep Italy's ally at arm's length. Not everyone was happy about the situation. Despite having been personally snubbed by Hitler the previous autumn, when the Führer had denied him sight of German plans for the *Westwall* defences on the grounds that such confidential military information could only be given to effective allies in wartime, Roatta made sure that the Germans knew on the eve of the Brenner conference that there was another view about Italy's military partnership with Germany. What was needed now was an agreement on the preparation of a common conduct of the war. Mussolini was willing to intervene on the German side as soon as Italian intervention would be useful to Berlin. It was time, Roatta believed, to put an end to the unjustified lack of faith the Germans were showing in their ally.[101] This was not going to happen. Already the view was taking root in German military circles that the Italians could not keep secrets and were not going to be treated as absolute equals by the Wehrmacht.[102]

On 18 March 1940, Mussolini and Hitler met at the Brenner Pass. The destinies of Italy and Germany were, the Führer declared, 'indissolubly linked'. A lengthy explanation of why he had attacked Poland

and a somewhat less wordy explanation of why he had signed a pact with Stalin followed. Although he gave Mussolini no clear indication of what he planned to do next, there was a hint that more military operations were on their way. The 'apparent inactivity of the front' which had been imposed on Germany as a consequence of adverse weather conditions was being used to prepare troops and maximize the production of arms and munitions. The only concrete piece of advice was not to try any revisionism in the Balkans, which could have incendiary results.[103] Mussolini confirmed that he would intervene in the war as soon as Germany had created 'a favourable situation', ideally in three to four months when Italy's new battleships would be ready, or, if the war turned out to be a long one, at the moment when her intervention could be 'of real help' to Germany. Hitler suggested that instead of attacking the French in the Alps when the moment came, the Italians should attack on the Upper Rhine with twenty divisions.[104]

Mussolini saw the 'Phoney War' as a time of promise. Both sides were being weakened by the other's blows, and when they were both exhausted he could seize his opportunity and stab them both in the back – or so he boasted to his mistress, Claretta Petacci. The only fly in the ointment was that with Russia standing outside the fray bolshevism might be the ultimate winner. When Germany moved again he believed that she would win the war quickly, but that moment was not yet close at hand. Two weeks after meeting Hitler he summed up the strategic situation. There would be no compromise peace, because the democracies could never accept one. Great Britain and France would not attack the German West Wall; instead they would go on the counter-offensive at sea and in the air and look to tighten their blockade of Germany. Unless she had 'the mathematical certainty of a crushing victory' or could see no other way forward, Germany would not attempt a land offensive against France, Belgium or Holland. She had already secured her war objectives and had no need to attack. If she did so it would be running the risk of setbacks and an internal crisis. Instead she would concentrate on resisting the blockade. Italy would join in but because she could not fight a long war her entry must be delayed for as long as possible, 'compatible with honour and dignity', so that her intervention could determine the outcome. Military action was only vaguely defined and not moored to any clear political objectives. Defensive positions everywhere, excepting only in the 'improbable' case of a complete French collapse, was the watchword for the army. It could, though, think about an offensive against Yugoslavia in the event of an internal collapse there. When Italy did finally join in, there would be offensives in East Africa against Kassala in the north and Djibouti in the south. The air force would take the offensive or the defensive 'according to the fronts and the enemy's initiatives'. The navy was to take the offensive 'all along the line in the Mediterranean and beyond'.[105]

COUNTDOWN

On 7 April 1940, General Alfred Jodl, head of the operations section of the OKW, told General Marras that the Germans wanted to follow up the Brenner meeting with accords on operations. The war would be decided in France. Given that Italy did not want to face a long war, and that therefore her intervention could occur after the Germans had dealt the Franco-British forces a severe blow, would the Italians consider sending, say, twenty divisions to the Upper Rhine to fight on the German left flank? They could be in action, Jodl suggested, 'towards the start of the summer'.[106] Calling the chiefs of staff together two days later, just as the Germans were invading Denmark and Norway, Badoglio told them that Italy could try offensive action only if and when her enemies were in a state of complete collapse. Until then the defensive position was the order of the day on all fronts. The Germans were to be held at arm's length in case they dragged Italy into doing things that were not what Mussolini wanted or put him under pressure to intervene when he was not ready to do so.

The military were being told effectively to be prepared for anything – except co-operating with the Germans. It was left to the air force chief of staff, General Francesco Pricolo, to point out that it was difficult to draw up operational plans without a clear idea of whom the enemy or enemies might be. 'That', Badoglio told the chiefs of staff, 'is a consequence of the unusual situation in which we find ourselves.'[107] Summarizing the meeting for Mussolini, Badoglio warned him that the army general staff was heading down the path of working accords with the Germans, 'something that I think [is] highly dangerous, given the extreme delicacy of the present moment which requires that You be given complete freedom of action'. As far as future operations were concerned, the armed forces would not be up to a decisive effort in any theatre even if their preparations were complete. Only if the Germans undertook 'a weighty action' which prostrated the enemy's forces would Italian intervention be rewarding – and that was something which did not look likely either on land or at sea.[108]

The German invasion of Denmark and Norway on 9 April 1940 dramatically compressed the timescales. Mussolini had spent more than three years preparing to fight the Ethiopian war. Now he was being propelled into action by events that were beyond his control. 'At a certain moment,' he told Claretta Petacci two days later, 'we're going to face a dilemma – either be strangled or join in the war.'[109] In Rome, General von Rintelen presented Italy with three options: supporting the German left flank in the attack on France, which the OKW much preferred, attacking France on the Alpine front, or attacking in Libya. Marshal Graziani was not disposed to agree to any of them. A Libyan offensive was impossible without German tanks, armoured cars and artillery which, if shipped in advance, would certainly start a conflict prematurely. An Alpine offensive would be easier to prepare because it was all-Italian, but breaking through and then penetrating beyond the mountains would be 'notably more difficult' than fighting on the German left. However, that would require the assurance of Yugoslav neutrality and German tanks and guns. The defences of Libya and the Alps all needed strengthening and that required raw materials which only Germany could provide, and in the case of North Africa armoured cars and medium tanks too. If war came, then Germany would also have to supply raw materials to help replace Italian consumption.[110]

With Franco-British naval forces now apparently turning to the Mediterranean, Cavagnari wasted no time in alerting the *Duce* to the navy's parlous position. Italy's control of the Sicilian Channel was now valueless as the British and French had already deployed their troops in North Africa and so did not need to transit the Mediterranean. The navy could not do much in the Atlantic, which it could not access and where it lacked bases. The absence of merchant traffic in the Mediterranean meant submarine warfare would have little effect. The Allied navies, on the other hand, had a large margin of superiority. If they chose to take the offensive to neutralize Italy quickly then the decisive encounter could take place very soon 'with huge losses on our part'. Mussolini had ordered the navy to take the offensive 'all along the line', but no strategic objectives had been defined. Without them, and without any possibility of defeating the enemy's forces, entering the war voluntarily 'does not seem justified'. Whatever happened, Cavagnari told Mussolini, things were going to end badly. Naval losses were bound to be heavy and Italy could arrive at the peace-table without either a navy or an air force.[111] Mussolini was in no mood to listen. Days before receiving Cavagnari's gloomy forecast he had assured Hitler that his navy was ready. What was the use of building 600,000 tons of warships, he exploded, if Italy did not take this opportunity to pit its forces against the British and French?[112]

Badoglio advised Mussolini against both the Rhine option – 'we would be playing a second-order part' – and the Libyan option. He did not 'exclude absolutely' a possible future action on the Alps: it would be a difficult theatre to operate in, but strong pressure there would oblige the French to keep sizeable forces away from the northern battlefields. One thing he was sure of – that no strategic undertakings should be given to Germany. She had jumped the gun by three years. 'It is indispensable,' he told Mussolini, 'that You, Duce, must have complete freedom to select the time and the place of our intervention.'[113] The Germans now made a final bid to shape Italian strategy to their own ends. On 4 May, six days before they began their attack in the West, Halder's deputy, General Carl-Heinrich von Stülpnagel, again suggested that since a Libyan operation was no longer a viable possibility and the Alps were difficult the Italians might contemplate sending twenty divisions to Germany's western frontier.[114] At that moment Mussolini was worried about Libya, where 130,000 Italians faced an estimated 314,000 French troops in Morocco, Algeria and Tunisia, and another 100,000 British troops in Egypt. All the doors must be closed in all the sectors, Badoglio told the chiefs. They found another 80,000 men for Libya but no more trucks, tanks or guns. 'It is useless to send me thousands more men,' Balbo complained to Mussolini, 'if I cannot give them the means to move and to fight.'[115]

By 8 May there were strong indications that German action was imminent and 'reliable sources' were reporting that an offensive in the west within the next few days was certain.[116] When the Germans attacked France and Belgium two days later, giving Mussolini only a few hours' notice, the *Duce*'s strategic gaze turned east. With his leading military advisers, Soddu and Badoglio, both convinced that the Maginot Line was unbreakable – at least in the short term – his first thought was to attack Yugoslavia. 'We must act quickly,' he told Ciano.[117] There were indeed reasons for him to worry about the Balkans, where his goal had long been Italian predominance. The Croats, eager for independence, were showing signs of moving into the German camp, German ambitions to make the Balkans into the advanced base for its 'living space' were causing concern, and there were rumours that Germany was promising Hungary an outlet on the Adriatic if she joined the war. Reports suggested that the Yugoslavs had half a million men under arms and that their animosity towards Italy was increasing.[118] Three days later Mussolini changed his mind. No longer thinking of taking up arms against Yugoslavia, a 'humiliating alternative', he went back to his earlier strategic design to attack England and France in the air and on the sea. 'I shall declare war within the month,' he told Ciano.[119]

General Favagrossa now tried yet again to bring Italy's parlous economic situation home to the *Duce*. If scrap iron from abroad ceased to arrive then current steel production of 130,000 tons a month, which was barely enough to meet present national needs, could only be assured for three months. There was six months' supply of copper, Italy was living from month to month as far as tin was concerned, and the situation regarding nickel was 'very serious' and threatened to become 'tragic'. Aluminium supplies were half of what was needed. Lead from America and Spain was being blockaded by the Allies and supplies from Yugoslavia, the other major source, were arriving more slowly than scheduled. The list went on and on. The inevitable consequence of the situation was that munitions production would not reach its targets until the first half of 1942.[120]

Mussolini was not listening. The epochal events now unfolding in the West changed everything. With the French front on the Meuse collapsing, the British Expeditionary Force retreating in Belgium, and panic breaking out in Paris, he rehearsed his reasons for joining the war to a group of the Party faithful from Trieste. If Italy stayed out of the war then peace would be made without her and she would decline to the status of 'a second-order nation'. That was something he would never permit. If she did not now honour her signature of the Pact of Steel, the world's judgement of her would be 'inexorable'. The war was now on Italy's doorstep. She could not stay out of it.[121] Two days later he told the American ambassador William Phillips that Italy could not remain absent at a moment when the future of Europe was being decided, and in letters to Roosevelt and Churchill that day he said more or less exactly what he had told the Fascist hierarchs from Trieste.[122]

On 20 May German panzer units reached the English Channel. A day earlier Mussolini had told Hitler that important news would be coming from Rome in the next few days. Now, events were forcing him to come to decisions about when and where to start fighting. Ciano had an answer. Calling in General Geloso in the evening of 23 May, he told him that Italy would probably enter the field within two or three weeks and that the target would be Greece, which was becoming an aero-naval base for the British and the French and must be eliminated. Where, Ciano asked, should she be attacked? Salonika, which would cut Greece off from Turkey, along with minor operations in the Epirus, was the answer. It could be done, Geloso thought, with seven or eight divisions, two motorized and one armoured, plus another three to guard the Yugoslav frontier and maintain internal order. To succeed, it must start only when everything was ready to go and then be carried through 'with great speed'. It would need strong support from the air force.[123]

Prompted, he told the *Duce*, by the fact that, while until recently war had seemed likely in the spring of 1941, the moment of intervention now seemed 'considerably advanced', Graziani sent Mussolini another long memorandum. The army could mobilize seventy-five divisions. The two armoured divisions had only seventy medium M11 tanks between them, the rest being light tanks, and no heavy vehicles or armoured cars. The infantry divisions had only three-fifths as many guns as French divisions, and the new 75mm, 149mm and 210mm guns were not due to come into service until the end of the year. There were only 152 anti-aircraft guns in the whole of Italy, most dating back to the First World War. The army was almost 8,000 trucks short of the number it needed to mobilize, and had only seven to eight months' fuel when it needed at least a year's worth. Because of its lack of armour and modern equipment, the Italian army was in no position to be able to conduct a campaign of the kind the Germans had recently carried out in Poland. It could fight a static war, but 'it is in no condition to operate on the move'.[124] 'If I had to wait for the army to be ready,' an exasperated Mussolini, who was holding Graziani's memorandum in his hand, told General Rossi, 'I would have to wait years to enter the war, but I have to enter it now. We shall do what we can.'[125]

The Dunkirk evacuation began on 26 May. Three days later Mussolini called the heads of the armed forces together and told them he was going to join in the war at any time from 5 June. Waiting for a fortnight or a month would not improve things and would risk giving Germany the impression that the Italians were arriving 'when the job was done'. Joining in when the risk was minimal would do Italy no good when it came to peacemaking. Operations would begin in the air and at sea, but not on land, where 'we could do nothing spectacular' – though something might be done on the eastern frontier against Yugoslavia. Graziani's account of the army's deficiencies was brushed aside: the situation was 'not ideal but satisfactory'. With France reeling but still just about standing, Mussolini assured his centurions that it was 'not our moral custom to strike a man when he is about to fall'.[126]

In the country at large the population girded itself for what now looked like inevitable war. The German invasion of Norway had produced a wave of general apprehension, which turned into admiration for the German war machine when the attack on France began. It was only superficial. Sympathy for Belgium and Holland sharpened persistent anti-German feeling. The recall of reservists produced alarm and anxiety as the public waited for what now looked unavoidable. Economic hardship was just beginning to bite, the shortage of raw materials was growing ever more obvious, and there was concern about the effectiveness of the Italian armed forces. The government organized 'popular' demonstrations in an attempt to recreate the so-called 'radiant days' of 1915 which had led to Italian intervention in the First World War, but only Sardinia and parts of the South were in favour of joining the war on Germany's side. As the *Blitzkrieg* campaign in the West rolled over France, police agents reported expectations that the war would be short and the sacrifices limited, and a widespread feeling that Italy needed to join in so that she could get something out of it. Dunkirk reinforced feelings that Germany was invincible. A sense of fatalism combined in the public's mind with hopes fanned by the Fascist press for quick, cheap gains that would produce big industrial and commercial advantages.[127]

On the day that Mussolini gave the military chiefs the news that Italy was going to war, Cavagnari, who had apparently been told four days earlier, issued his general orders for a Mediterranean war. He expected 'intense and immediate action' by the British and French fleets to 'blunt our capacity to resist'. There were many possible scenarios, any or all of which might occur: action against mobile units in the Sicilian Channel, interdiction of traffic routes and interception of supplies to the overseas possessions, air and sea bombardment of Tobruk, Tripoli, the coastal cities of Sicily and Liguria, and using any of these options to draw the Italian high seas fleet into action in adverse circumstances. The fleet was tasked with taking offensive or counter-offensive action in the central Mediterranean to prevent the junction of enemy units from the east and west Mediterranean, acting with light forces and 'insidious means' (torpedo boats or human torpedoes) against enemy bases and lines of communication, protecting the lines of communication with Libya, Albania and the Aegean islands, and taking advantage of any opportunities for encounters in conditions of superiority or parity of strength. Battleships would only be committed when such encounters could take place nearer to Italian bases than enemy ones and only if the enemy's forces in the Mediterranean were not significantly strengthened.[128]

Writing to Hitler on 30 May, Mussolini informed his ally of his chosen date – 5 June – but offered to delay Italy's entry into the war if that fitted better with Hitler's plans. He had some seventy divisions 'in a state of good efficiency' to throw into the fray, and had the manpower to field seventy more but not the means to equip them. The navy and the air force were now on a war footing. When Hitler pointedly asked Dino Alfieri, the bearer of the *Duce*'s news, what Italy's actual plans were, the new Italian ambassador (who had replaced Attolico on 16 May) appeared to have swallowed his tongue. 'It was clear that they had no serious plan[s] at all,' the Führer railed afterwards. Delaying Italy's entry into the war by three days would indeed be welcome, Hitler told Mussolini next day. This would give the Luftwaffe time to knock out French air bases before the second and final stage of the crushing of France.[129]

Calling the heads of the armed forces together, Badoglio ordered the army to be ready to repel any attack by the French across the western Alps. The fleet was already formed up, Cavagnari reported. He was awaiting instructions from Mussolini about when and how to deploy his eighty-three submarines. A lot seemed to depend on the *Regia Aeronautica*: Badoglio wanted Pricolo's airmen to be ready to counter possible incursions by French aircraft coming across the western frontier and by enemy tanks crossing the western and eastern frontiers of Libya. The chief of the air staff pointed out that up to now it had looked as though the most likely operation would be against Yugoslavia. The moment to go into operational matters had not yet arrived, Badoglio told him. 'I would have liked at least to know by now what operations I am most likely to be ordered to carry out,' Pricolo remarked drily. Badoglio's reply spoke volumes about the direction – or lack of it – being given to Italy's coming war. If an action had not been studied, it would not be ordered. 'I shall get the chiefs of staff together again and we shall see what can be done.'[130] The meeting had lasted only forty-five minutes. Next day a worried Marshal Balbo told Mussolini that, if Italy entered the war against France, French troops would be in Tripoli in ten days. If colonies were lost then victory in Europe would recover them, Mussolini replied off-handedly.[131]

Last-ditch attempts were made to stay the warlord's hand. Badoglio expected that the final act in the war against France would take longer than the six or seven weeks the Germans were timetabling. That, he told Mussolini, gave the Italians plenty of time to intervene 'without looking like crows'. His concern at this moment was not specifically the weakness of Italy's military, though that was in itself considerable: only twenty-two out of seventy-one divisions were deemed 'complete', and they lacked a third of their full complement of trucks; thirty divisions were 'efficient' but lacked many of the 81mm mortars and 47mm guns they were supposed to have, and the remaining nineteen were 'incomplete'; only 169 of the 9,130 small-calibre and 4,385 medium- and large-calibre guns were modern weapons.[132] What was bothering Badoglio was the situation in Libya, where Balbo needed the whole of June to get the means in place to be able to put up 'an honourable defensive'.[133] Favagrossa weighed in. The army had only enough machine-gun and artillery ammunition for forty to sixty days' fighting – on the basis of estimates of consumption that had been shown during the Spanish Civil War to be too low. If Italy went to war now, the munitions factories could produce ten days' ammunition for machine guns, seven days' ammunition for light field guns and one and a half days' ammunition for medium artillery each month. With extreme effort, this might be tripled.[134]

Badoglio's staff thought their boss had won over Mussolini and that Italy would not be going to war until July. That delusion lasted a mere twenty-four hours. On 2 June, Mussolini told Hitler that he would declare war eight days later and start fighting the following day. He was minded to intervene directly, but only with a token force. Before the war began he had the staff write him a summary of Italy's pre-1914 plans to send an army to fight on the Rhine alongside the Germans, and he now offered Hitler a couple of *Bersaglieri* regiments for stage two of his French campaign.[135] Rather than send half a dozen infantry battalions, Graziani and Roatta, both in favour of closer strategic co-operation with the Germans, believed it would be better to send the *Trento* and *Trieste* motorized divisions. Well equipped and well trained, unlike most of the rest of the Italian army, they could make good use of the dense road network in northern France. Badoglio passed the suggestion on to Mussolini.[136] Roatta instructed the army planners to study offensives across the upper and lower French Alps.

At the Quirinale Palace, Vittorio Emanuele III assessed the alternatives facing the head of state. If he refused to sign the war decree then there would be a civil war, the Germans would come in, and a European war would inevitably follow. If he abdicated, there would be a war anyway. If the Axis lost it then the monarchy would be back but without a shred of respect left. If he signed and said nothing then, win or lose, Italy would become a republic and the days of the monarchy would be over.[137] The Crown, it seemed, could not win. Meanwhile the Fascist propaganda machine went into overdrive. *Relazioni internazionali*, the official bulletin on Fascist foreign policy, rang the patriotic bells. This would be 'the supreme war of independence', its spirit at one with that of the soldiers who had defended Italy on the Piave in November 1917 after the collapse at Caporetto. Alessandro Pavolini, the Minister of Popular Culture, mobilized the newspapers to put across the message that this would be a 'dynamic, rapid war of quality' – and therefore different from past wars.[138]

With war now only days away, Badoglio set out how things were going to be managed. As supreme commander of the armed forces, with authority delegated to him by the king, Mussolini exercised his powers through the chief of the armed forces general staff. Badoglio would keep him up to date with the day-to-day situation and the operational possibilities, receiving the *Duce*'s orders and general directions for the conduct of the war and converting them into strategic and operational directives for the three chiefs of staff. He would then follow the development of operations in the field, intervening when necessary 'to ensure the co-ordinated and timely employment of the armed forces'. The chiefs were forcibly reminded that they exercised command over their respective arms only as chiefs of staff and not as senior commanders. To ensure constant close contact with them, Badoglio undertook to hold frequent meetings and exchanges of ideas. What it all boiled down to, he told the chiefs, was a 'unitary and totalitarian concept of command' exercised personally by the *Duce*.[139] The naval general staff, now rechristened the *Supermarina*, issued its own operating rules. It would send out general directives for the conduct of the naval war, general operational orders and orders for special operations, circulate information about the movements of Italian and enemy ships, and secure intervention by the air force where and when necessary.[140] Cavagnari intended to keep his sea-going admirals on a tight rein.

On 5 June the chiefs of staff gathered once more – this time for fifty minutes – to have their previous instructions confirmed. No action was to be undertaken against France, which had given an assurance two days earlier that she had no intention of launching a lightning attack on Italy, but action against the British in the Mediterranean was on the cards. Not much was said about what that action might or should be. Pricolo was advised that air actions against Malta and Alexandria might be undertaken, but Gibraltar was to be left alone until the *Duce* had been consulted. The chiefs were told to begin studying the possibility of landing on Malta. Discussion rambled, as it often did under Badoglio's chairmanship, until he brought things to a close with the comforting remark that everything which could possibly be done had been done.[141]

Pricolo's instructions to his airmen, issued three days later, were not exactly in line with what he had been told to do. Unless ordered otherwise, he intended the first offensive actions to be directed against enemy bases in Tunisia, on Corsica, on Malta and in the Rhône–Saône basin. The latter were the most rewarding and therefore the most important targets. Strikes were to take place at first light using all available aircraft. Once that had been done every bomber group was to keep at least one squadron bombed up and ready for immediate action against enemy naval units. The German air force's daring and perfectly co-ordinated actions were the model to be followed. It could even be bettered, Pricolo told his airmen, because 'the quality, dash, courage, skill and unconditional dedication to duty of Fascist Italy's aviators have never been less than those of any other air force'.[142]

Chapter 3

First Moves

When war came in 1940 the army had seventy years' experience of planning, both to defend the frontier with France and to attack across it. Staff rides had examined the pros and cons of moving troops through the narrow valleys and mountains that ran the length of the frontier since before the First World War, and local district commanders had drawn up plans for action in their sectors of the front. In the last year before the war some of the most promising brains in the armed forces examined the problem of getting through the French Alps to the Rhône. After assessing the possibilities of half a dozen routes across the mountains, they opted for the two southern routes via the Corniche and the Colle di Tenda that seemed to offer the best opportunities for a *guerra di rapido corso*, something which, the War College team declared, 'we must always have in mind'. The fact that this was the zone where the French had the strongest defences was confirmation that it was 'greatly vulnerable'. Once Italian units had got through a twenty-kilometre strip of mountains – a task to which they paid remarkably little attention – 'we shall have the chance to operate in a less prohibitive region which will allow us to employ sizeable forces'.[1]

On the penultimate day of 1939 General Roatta asked SIM for its best guess on what operations the French intended to carry out against Italy in the Alpine region. The intelligence division thought that the French would probably take offensive action but, without enough reserve strength to carry out a major offensive, they would in all likelihood develop offensives at the northern and southern ends of the Italian mountain frontier.[2] His operations office interpreted the evidence differently, seeing French deployments as defensive moves designed to resist presumed Italian offensives across the Alpes Maritimes and towards Modane.[3] In the months that followed, SIM produced extensive reports analysing the defences, armaments, garrisons and munitions of the *Ligne Maginot Alpine*, which had been begun in 1928 and which by the start of the war consisted of a collection of concrete and steel positions covering the access routes and mule tracks that crossed the common frontier.[4] As to what they would actually do, the Italian military attaché in Paris reported at the end of May 1940, correctly if perhaps rather confusingly, that the French army was orienting itself towards the new style of war which demanded agility from commanders, officers and troops alike, but that would be difficult for an army that had made defence and counter-offensive its dogma.[5]

Without any clear strategic directives, planning for Alpine operations was dilatory. In late September 1939 1st and 4th Armies, responsible for the southern and northern portions of the frontier with France, were requested to study the offensive possibilities in their regions, but this was not followed up. On 1 March 1940 the main war plan, PR 12, was updated. Although it did note the possibility of offensive action across the Alpes Maritimes in Upper Savoy towards Albertville and Annecy if circumstances were favourable, the general directive was to maintain a defensive stance everywhere except in Italian East Africa and ensure that Italy's frontiers were inviolable. Fourth Army command did not get round to asking the *Alpini* army corps to study operations across the Piccolo San Bernardino Pass towards the two French towns until 8 April 1940. As the Germans penned in the British and French forces around Dunkirk, immobility seemed to be the order of the day as far as Italy was concerned. On 30 May Marshal Graziani ordered that the PR 12 deployments be put into effect within the next five days, and at the end of the first week in June a direct order went from Mussolini to Army Group West that in case of hostilities they were to maintain 'an absolutely defensive stance, on land and in the air'.[6]

As well as being told to stand still and defend themselves, the army commanders in the west were also ordered to make arrangements for detailed studies of offensive operations in their theatre in case the 'particularly favourable circumstances' that were vaguely alluded to in PR 12 should actually come to pass. The responses arrived in Rome at the end of the first week in June. General Pietro Pintor's 1st Army produced a plan for a First World War-style attack from the Colle della

Maddalena (Col de Larches). Preparations would take two months, and he would need *Alpini* and lots of guns. General Guzzoni's 4th Army produced a plan for an attack across the Piccolo San Bernardino, which was much more in line with current Fascist doctrine. Wildly optimistic assertions were made about moving motorized and armoured troops along what was little more than a cart track, and much depended on air strikes knocking out the French forts at Bourg-en-Bresse that guarded the French side of the frontier. The attack would take a month to be ready, Rome was told.[7]

THE FOUR-DAY WAR

On 10 June 1940 Italy declared war on France. Four days later the German army entered Paris. As Paul Reynaud's government collapsed, the Italian army commanders on the French frontier were ordered to start small offensive actions and engage enemy troops in order to keep 'the aggressive spirit of [our] troops high' and ready them 'technically and morally for larger future operations'. If the French collapsed, as talk was suggesting could happen, they should be ready to advance.[8] Next day Mussolini ordered the army to attack across the French Alps in three days' time – and then agreed to a two-day delay. With PR 12 now past history, Badoglio ordered Roatta to assume the deployment necessary for the offensive actions against both the Piccolo San Bernardino and the Colle della Maddalena.[9] Over the next two days small French patrols probed Italian positions and the Italians retaliated, taking a handful of prisoners and pushing across the frontier at several points. Then, on 16 June, came the news that the French government had fallen and that Marshal Pétain had taken over the reins. Graziani's orders went out that day. The generals had ten days in which to start operations against Moncenisio in the centre and the Piccolo San Bernardino in the north. Graziani clearly expected a rapid breakthrough on the mountains and so little or no account was taken of the difficulties the soldiers might face. After breezily dismissing any likelihood that the enemy would mount counter-offensives, the chief of the army general staff exhorted his subordinate commanders to 'Dare, that is the order of the day for everyone.'[10] The orders only reached Pintor and Guzzoni in the small hours of 19 June.

The French request for an armistice reached Berlin at 3 a.m. on 17 June, and Pétain's broadcast '*il faut cesser le combat*' ('the fighting must cease') was heard in Italy at 1.30 that afternoon. Fascist Italy now had to take Fortune on the fly. Furious that France was asking for peace, and faced with the possibility that any gains might suddenly be taken off the table, Mussolini was in a hurry to unleash the offensive along the western front. Badoglio's warnings about the difficulties of the terrain and the state of Italian deployment were dismissed. The order was given to accelerate the deployment at the Colle della Maddalena and limit the attack to this direction alone. *Superesercito* (the new title of the army general staff) thought differently and ordered the generals in the west to start actions along all three possible axes of advance – the Piccolo San Bernardino Pass, the Colle della Maddalena and the Corniche – as soon as possible and no later than 23 June. The troops were to turn the flanks of the enemy's permanent fortifications and get behind them and then 'decisively exploit success in depth'. The target was Marseilles.[11]

What looked straightforward to Rome was a much more difficult proposition on the ground. A series of confusing orders did not make things any easier. Planning axes shifted to and fro and divisions appeared and disappeared as the establishment tables of Pintor's and Guzzoni's armies changed. In mid-afternoon Roatta instructed them both to keep up the pressure on all fronts and be ready to pursue the French rear-guard. Half an hour later his chief of operations sent out a staccato injunction: 'Keep on the enemy's heels – Be Audacious – Dare – Throw yourselves [on them] – Don't let yourselves get caught by the armistice too far behind.' Not untypically, 1st Army got the injunction but 4th Army did not.[12] After a brief flurry of activity in which both sides' artillery exchanged fire and the Italians suffered three dead and three wounded the skirmishing died down shortly after six in the evening. That same afternoon an invitation arrived in Rome for Mussolini to meet Hitler and discuss French surrender terms. Military operations were momentarily suspended and the *Duce* sped off to Munich, taking Foreign Minister Ciano and a couple of generals with him. On the frontier, Italian soldiers tried to fraternize with their erstwhile enemy.

On the face of things, the Munich meeting went moderately well for the Italians. Hitler was affable, sitting on the edge of his desk or the arm of a chair while talking, laughing and shaking Mussolini by the arm. General Roatta, one of Mussolini's team of advisers, was left with the impression of 'a man of very great intelligence, good sense and prompt decision'.[13] Mussolini went into the meeting armed with a wish-list of armistice goals constructed by his military advisers. It comprised Italian occupation of France up to the Rhône with bridgeheads on the west bank of the river, Corsica, Tunisia, the coast of French Somalia, occupation of the French naval bases at Algiers, Oran (Mers-el-Kébir) and Casablanca, the neutralization of Beirut and the immediate hando-ver of the French fleet and air force. Hitler, who had his own objectives, was unwilling either to put too much pressure on France or to occupy the whole of the country. He was even reluctant to occupy any cities other than Paris and Bordeaux, though General Keitel persuaded him that a 'peripheral' occupation of Lyons and Marseilles 'at a certain distance' would be desirable. The one thing he was not prepared to do was to make demands on the French navy which might lead Pétain and his government to hightail it for North Africa. The best outcome would be for the French fleet to be held in bases under German control or in neutral ports. No one mentioned the French air force. Reluctantly Mus-solini fell in line. The diplomatic talks went less well for Italy. Foreign Minister Ribbentrop brushed aside Ciano's bid for Algeria, Egypt and the Sudan, leaving him with the strong impression that Germany was exploring the possibility of coming to terms with England. There was perhaps some consolation to be had in Hitler's undertaking that there would be no Franco-German agreement until France had first come to terms with Italy – though Ciano's hopes for joint negotiations along-side the Germans were summarily squashed.[14]

Once back in Rome, Mussolini began to fear that he was being relegated to a secondary role, and that the Germans were going to snatch the glory of a peace forged on the field of battle before he could do likewise.[15] Italian armies had to score a victory, not least because Italian appetites had grown. On the trip back to Rome it was decided that when she sat at the peace table Italy would seek consider-ably more than just the agreed armistice conditions. As well, she wanted Algeria, a link between Libya and the empire in East Africa, the neutralization of both sides of the Straits of Gibraltar, Egypt's abandonment of its alliance with England, and its replacement with an Italian alliance which would give Rome access to the oceans via the Red Sea and the Indian Ocean. For both Mussolini and the Italian navy this last was a goal long sought.[16]

At Munich, Roatta told Keitel that the Italian army would be ready to attack across the Alps along three main routes – the Piccolo San Bernardino Pass, the Colle della Maddalena and the Corniche – in three to four days. Keitel in turn promised to give orders for German columns to advance on Chambéry and Grenoble in support of the Italian action. With everyone back in Rome, Marshal Graziani suggested launching a full-scale attack along the French frontier on 23 June, timed to coincide with the German advance. Badoglio was reluctant to move. The two soldiers were called to Palazzo Venezia in the afternoon of 20 June along with the air force commander General Pricolo. Graziani suggested attacking the northern sector of the common frontier first to take advantage of the German thrust towards Lyons, and then following up with attacks in the centre and the south. Overriding any objections, including more heel-dragging by Badoglio, the *Duce* ordered a simultaneous attack all along the line to begin at 3.30 the next morning.

During the next few hours Italian strategy descended into something approaching chaos. With the Germans apparently near Lyons (they were actually already there), Roatta was confident: the troops manning the enemy's fortifications might still be in place, but French resistance was being overvalued and would amount to no more than 'a defensive crust'.[17] Then, a tap on the military's phone calls revealed that Pintor was wholly unprepared to attack next day.[18] In fact neither army commander was ready: Guzzoni told Army Group West that he could not begin the attack on the Piccolo San Bernardino before 23 June and that to do it he needed a motorized division, an armoured division and an engineer battalion. Incoming diplomatic intelligence suggested that an Italian attack might conceivably hamper both German and Italian peace negotiations. To avoid making the wrong move Mussolini decided not to move at all and countermanded his earlier order. Then news came that the Germans were indeed going to attack south from Lyons. Dreams of military glory trumped diplomatic hesitations and Mussolini changed his mind again. At 9.00 that evening Badoglio was told that the attack was going ahead the following morning, but only in the northern sector of the Piccolo San Bernardino Pass – as he and Graziani had recommended that afternoon. Roatta sent out orders to 4th Army to attack the Piccolo San Bernardino next day while all the remaining units of both armies kept contact with the enemy 'by means of small columns'.[19]

The soldiers assumed that the fates were on their side – even if material calculations suggested otherwise. Pétain had ordered French soldiers to stop fighting. Locally Italian commanders expected that French morale would be plummeting, and in Rome the generals expected that the German push towards Lyons would force the French high command to dismantle its garrisons in the mountains. Neither expectation was met. The local French commander and his men decided to fight, and the Germans were slow in getting started. At midday on 22 June – the second day of what would be a four-day war against France – Rome learned that the Germans would not be able to get going until the following afternoon as they were waiting for the arrival of mountain troops. The 'Lyons Group' only began its advance on 23 June 'without taking any risks and at a more leisurely pace than Rome would have liked'.[20]

Badoglio's orders for the first day of the battle were that the attacks across the Piccolo San Bernardino be pressed forward 'decisively' in concurrence with two German columns advancing on Grenoble and Chambéry from Lyons. The attacks on the Colle della Maddalena and along the Corniche were to be developed without getting wholly committed unless favourable conditions occurred, in which case all advantage must be taken of them. Once the northern thrust was successful, the attack should be pressed home all along the front with the aim of reaching the Rhône valley.[21] The first assault began at 6 a.m. on 21 June, and the main attack went in at 10.00 after a preliminary bombardment by thirty-nine Italian aircraft. With only minimal knowledge of where the French gun emplacements were, Italian units were quickly overwhelmed by enemy fire, bogged down in snow, and ambushed on the winding mule tracks by French ski units. Land-air co-ordination was minimal, Italian pilots lacking both training and detailed maps. Heavy fog and blizzards hampered air activity: half the bombing missions between 21 and 24 June did not even locate their objectives and some bombed their own troops. By mid-afternoon on the first day 4th Army was reporting some progress, but 1st Army was encountering strong resistance. As dusk began to envelop the battlefields a teletype from Berlin relayed Germany's formal submission of armistice terms to the French. Mussolini called in Badoglio and Roatta and told them that he intended to renounce any territorial occupation. His chief concern, then and subsequently, was that if he made unjustified demands 'Hitler might accuse me of having upset my [i.e. Hitler's] armistice.'[22]

The attacks began again next morning but by the afternoon it was clear that not much progress was being made. Both 1st and 4th Army were meeting strong resistance from enemy artillery and from French defensive works that were not being suppressed by Italian guns. Bad weather again hampered air activity. The German military attaché, Enno von Rintelen, assured Rome that when the German attack started the following afternoon fast German armoured columns would push forward as quickly as they could to give French troops fighting on the Alpine frontier the feeling that they were being cut off.[23] On 23 June a fresh assault met with more setbacks. Everywhere Italian attacks slowed or stalled in the face of the enemy's guns. Bad weather did not help the Italian airmen or the gunners. Nor did Italian planning: thanks to a mistake in identifying two capes that were ten kilometres apart, Italians targeted their own artillery. Next day the Italians again made little progress in the face of snowstorms and continued enemy resistance.

At 7.15 p.m. on 24 June Badoglio and the French general Charles Huntziger signed an armistice convention at the Villa d'Incisa in the suburbs of Rome and the brief Franco-Italian war came to an end. When General Huntziger learned the armistice terms he was delighted. They were, he told the government in Bordeaux, 'better than we could ever have expected'.[24] To Roatta's relief they signalled the demise of a project to fly Italian battalions into Lyons and Grenoble, an idea he did not favour. Hostilities ended at 1.15 a.m. Italian time next day. Soon afterwards, Mussolini ordered his negotiators not to pursue a request for Oran in order not to have France a potential belligerent at Italy's back in North Africa.[25]

At the final count the four-day campaign in the French Alps cost the army 642 dead, 2,631 wounded and 616 missing. Another 2,151 soldiers got frostbite – more than twice the number reported in the official after-battle summary. The brief fight showed up numerous deficiencies in Fascist Italy's military machinery. None was more freighted with implications than the shortcomings of the *binaria* divisions. They were intended to attack in a single direction with their component regiments leap-frogging over one another, but in June 1940 the two brigades invariably advanced in parallel columns along different axes. Both were quickly worn down, the attackers were soon exhausted, and commanders then had to replace them. *Alpini* divisions were differently equipped from ordinary infantry divisions and the artillery of the two was not interchangeable, which added to the problems.[26] With the armistice agreed, Mussolini went off to inspect the scene of the action at the Piccolo San Bernardino Pass. Deluding himself that the episode had been a triumph, the *Duce* expressed his pleasure at his troops' thirty-two-kilometre advance. 'Our soldiers overcame very strong resistance,' he boasted to his mistress.[27] Nothing was learned from the episode. There was next to no time to learn lessons, to be sure, but those that were there to be learned suggested that politico-military co-ordination was very far from perfect and the military machine sluggish and poorly articulated.

SUMMER STORMS

Even as Italian troops were trying to shoulder their way through the French Alps ideas were starting to come into focus about the next campaign – or campaigns – that Mussolini wanted to fight. There were three potential targets. One was Yugoslavia, long a thorn in Mussolini's side. War plans had been 'archived' in mid-June, but one day he intended to have a reckoning with her. Shortly they would reappear on the strategic menu. A second was Greece. The longer the British position in the Middle East survived the greater the likelihood that Greece might host British ships, aircraft and even men. And if Bulgaria, keen to get hold of the long-coveted region of Macedonia, moved against Greece then Italy too would have to intervene before the British arrived there to help the Greeks. Called to Rome, General Carlo Geloso produced an operational plan predicated on Greece being paralysed by threatened or actual Bulgarian aggression. Ten divisions in Albania, one of them armoured and another motorized, would be enough to do the job, half of them actually attacking while the rest watched the Yugoslav frontier and maintained internal order. If, on the other hand, the Italians faced all twenty-four divisions of the Greek army, then eighteen to twenty divisions, including double the number of armoured and motorized units, would be needed. All of them would have to be in place before the Greek army finished deploying, a process which would take the bulk of the enemy divisions only a month.[28]

The third target was Egypt, the missing piece in Mussolini's African empire. Taking it had obvious prestige value. Geo-strategically it would be the link with Italy's East African Empire and a base from which to expand Italian influence in the Middle East.[29] Possession of the Suez Canal would also give the Italian navy a chance to realize its strategic dream of establishing a base at the mouth of the Red Sea and pushing Fascism out onto the broad reaches of the Indian Ocean. Anticipating success, the army began planning the carve-up of Africa. Italy, Germany, Spain and Portugal would share out African territory, leaving France with a minimal stake and allowing Egypt and the Union of South Africa to remain in existence, free of British influence, as the only two independent states.[30]

Over the coming months each of these three scenarios appeared, disappeared and then reappeared on Mussolini's agenda, sometimes changing status over a matter of days or even hours. To them Mussolini added extra tasks, instructing the armed forces to plan for the occupation of the Rhône valley and Corsica as he sought to remedy his failure to squeeze territorial concessions out of the now defeated but still far from submissive French. Even Switzerland became a potential theatre of operations: by mid-July the army had a plan for the joint dismemberment of the country with Germany. 'We're still "up in the air" as regards operational intentions,' Roatta complained at that time. Switzerland was not definitively abandoned until late September, when even so there were five different war scenarios in play 'and no decision [on them] taken yet'.[31]

On 20 June Mussolini ordered the armed forces to be ready if necessary to invade Egypt 'without bothering yourselves about the possible future political consequences'. Five days later Badoglio gave the chiefs of staff fresh orders. Libya was now the principal theatre of operations. The French in Tunisia would not cause any problems, so the army general staff could examine the possibilities for an offensive into Egypt. Distances would be a problem – to get to Mersa Matruh the army would have to cross 220 kilometres of desert, and more beyond it – but 'the English soldiers are certainly less well adapted than ours to master such difficulties'. East Africa was a different matter, and needed planes and fuel. Air action would bomb Gibraltar and 'sterilize' Malta

(Mussolini's favourite term). This last idea foundered when Spain refused to allow Italian aircraft to land on her soil.[32]

'Things are moving very quickly,' Badoglio warned the governor of Libya. If she did not want to be left with empty hands at the peace conference Italy could be obliged very soon to attack Egypt.[33] Balbo was far from confident. A month earlier he had told the German assistant military attaché, Major Heggenreiner, that thanks to low supply levels, weak fortifications and the lack of modern tanks, guns and aircraft the situation in Libya was 'practically hopeless'.[34] Now he asked for fifty German tanks (Mussolini offered him seventy Italian M tanks), a thousand trucks, anti-tank guns and more besides. Expecting the invasion of England to begin in the first week of July, Mussolini wanted Balbo to go into action as quickly as possible.[35] Two days later Balbo was dead, shot down by his own anti-aircraft guns over Tobruk during a British bombing raid on the airfield. Badoglio suggested Graziani as his replacement. Graziani had extensive experience in North and East Africa, which certainly qualified him for the job – but he was also Badoglio's least favourite general, so sending him off to North Africa would get a potentially troublesome rival out of the way. For the time being, planning and organizing the army's war would be done in Rome by the deputy chief of staff, Mario Roatta.

While the army was focusing on North Africa, news arrived in Rome that revived Mussolini's deep-rooted ire against Yugoslavia. On 1 July Hitler told ambassador Alfieri that documents discovered in a French railway wagon at Charité-sur-Saône showed the extent of pre-war collaboration between Belgrade and Paris. 'At the opportune moment,' the Führer declared, Italy should settle accounts with this hostile power.[36] Mussolini needed little encouragement. Hearing about the cache of incriminating documents, he immediately ordered that the mass of the military forces now on Italy's western frontier be moved east and the air force start preparing temporary airfields along the Yugoslav frontier. But Germany now tried to direct Italy's military power where it might best help her. During the first week of July, Hitler twice offered heavy bombers to support an Italian attack on Egypt, telling Ciano that he intended to make a gesture towards a negotiated peace with England but was personally convinced that the war would continue. He also warned the Italians to steer clear of Yugoslavia at least for the time being, but was rather less discouraging about Greece.

Italian air component flew three raids against Portsmouth and Harwich between 29 October and 11 November.[47]

At this moment Mussolini's right-hand man at the War Ministry, General Ubaldo Soddu, came up with the idea of demobilizing part of the army. At the beginning of July he proposed cutting it to one million men and holding the units now spread out along the northern Alpine chain, in the Po valley and in Albania to 75 per cent of their war strength. Although an Egyptian operation was evidently in the offing, he passed over the need to bring Italy's two armoured and two motorized divisions up to full strength. There was a logic to the proposal: demobilizing some units would make men and materiel available for those units it was intended to deploy 'and thus create a body of troops smaller in proportion than at present, but perfectly efficient'.[48] Hitler was at that moment demobilizing units of the Wehrmacht, which may have led Soddu to think that Italy could and should do the same. But what would be readily reversible in Germany's well-oiled war machine would likely be disruptive in Italy's more delicately balanced system. In Badoglio's office, General Quirino Armellini was in despair: 'Units are being readied with 50–75 per cent equipment, raw materials are being exhausted, resupplies don't arrive ... If the war doesn't end soon there will be a collapse.'[49] Soddu would get his way in October, on the eve of the Italian attack on Greece.

Mussolini was willing to give Graziani the time to organize a wide-ranging in-depth manoeuvre, which he might be called on to launch early in August. In the meantime he was to launch preliminary attacks on Sollum–Halfaya as soon as he was ready. 'I hope to unleash the offensive at the same time as your attack [on England],' Mussolini assured Hitler.[50] Graziani's staff looked into attacking Alexandria – and blenched. It was 'a very arduous task', and would require 'adequate preparation and the availability of very large means' to succeed. At the end of July Graziani told Rome that it would be impossible to launch an operation until the hot season ended in October. Besides the heat, and the scarcity of water resources, there was only one possible line of march between the sea and the desert. The possibilities for strategic manoeuvre were non-existent, and those for tactical manoeuvre were extremely limited since all his divisions completely lacked baggage trains. In Rome, the general staff resubmitted the same appreciation they had originally made early in July. The estimates suggested that Graziani faced one armoured and four infantry divisions, 65,000 men in all, to which might be added up to three more divisions coming from Palestine. When the reinforcements that were en route arrived an offensive would be possible.[51]

If the attack on Sollum–Halfaya was to succeed the navy had to hold the Sicilian Channel* and keep the British naval forces at either end of the Mediterranean separate, and the air force had to degrade the ships anchored at Alexandria. The air force units on Rhodes and in Libya were ordered to intensify their bombing of the anchorage, and the navy to deploy light surface craft on either side of the Channel. Although not strong enough to face a naval battle, the sailors should be ready to intervene if the circumstances were favourable. At once problems appeared. Ideally the air force needed thirty German dive-bombers to base on Pantelleria and the Sicilian coast, but although promised they were unlikely on present schedules to arrive in time.[52] Then, at the end of July, Admiral Inigo Campioni reported that neither of the two new 35,000-ton battleships was ready for combat: the *Littorio* was at 70 per cent efficiency and the *Vittorio Veneto*'s guns were deficient. The *Caio Duilio* (rebuilt between 1937 and 1940) was also unfit for battle because its personnel were insufficiently trained. With three Italian battleships, all dating originally from the First World War, facing four British battleships at Alexandria, Campioni thought it imprudent to risk a battle at a distance from his bases.[53]

Badoglio had been counting on the two 35,000-ton warships in order to be able to set up a naval battle in which the Italian ships sailed from ports in Cyrenaica towards Alexandria. This now looked questionable. Nor was there much to hope for from the air force: the planes based in the Aegean would be operating at the extreme limits of their range and were unlikely to do much damage.[54] Graziani was going to have to rely on his own air units – 110 bombers, 135 fighters and 45 assault planes. Cavagnari put the final nail in the coffin. With two *Giulio Cesare*-type battleships, seven heavy and eleven light cruisers and forty destroyers, and with the navy's principal base at Taranto 760 miles away from Mersa Matruh, he did not think it advisable to employ 'the principal nucleus of our naval forces' to flank an army advance in North Africa. The best he could do was to deploy submarines to

* The *Canale di Sicilia* was the Italian term for the straits between Sicily and North Africa.

contest the movement of enemy surface units and sow mines on the routes to and from Alexandria.[55]

By the end of July the chief of the German general staff, General Franz Halder, had concluded that not much could be expected from the Italians, and during the first week of August the operations staff of the OKW produced a draft plan to send an armoured corps to North Africa. What the Italians wanted was German tanks and guns, not units of the Germany army. At the beginning of August the German high command ordered that Italian requests were to be satisfied from booty taken from the defeated French. The Italians got no tanks, and not much else.[56] A visit by a *Luftwaffe* team in mid-August concluded that a decisive result could be obtained in Egypt – the Italian soldiers in Cyrenaica made a good impression – but the Italians needed reinforcing with air power, tanks and artillery.[57]

In the first week of August Graziani was called urgently to Rome. He arrived armed with a detailed and unremittingly pessimistic appreciation. Reading from it, he told Mussolini and Badoglio that both the army general staff and the armed forces general staff had always held the action in Egypt to be 'unrealizable', that although the strategic correlation of forces was better now that France was out of the war the physical conditions were the same or worse, that the logistical problems were enormous, and that he needed substantial air superiority. The damage that would be done if his army were to be defeated in the desert would be 'total and irremediable'. But with a German attack on Great Britain apparently imminent Mussolini needed action of some kind in North Africa. Badoglio came up with a compromise: Graziani would eliminate British bases on the frontier, reach Sollum and the Halfaya ridge, and if things went well push on to Sidi-el-Barani. However, cordiality masked confusion and misunderstanding. Mussolini left the meeting with the impression that the offensive would begin within just a few days, whereas Graziani believed afterwards that he had made his position – that it could not – absolutely clear during the course of the discussion.[58]

Graziani's staffers were far from keen on attacking Sidi-el-Barani, a position 115 kilometres on from Bardia that they thought was of no tactical significance at all. All the enemy had to do was retreat, worsening the Italians' supply problems. Before the fighting had seriously begun the key operational problem that would afflict the plans of both sides was already apparent. To defeat the six or seven enemy divisions in Egypt would require nine fully motorized divisions, large numbers of 74mm and 149mm guns and 5,200 heavy lorries, 'without which we could be halted in front of the enemy's fortifications with 250 kilometres of desert at our backs'.[59] Returning to Tripoli, Graziani summoned his divisional, corps and army commanders. Their men, it appeared, were ready to fight and had complete faith in their commanders – but almost everything else was bad news. Climate, terrain and the fact that the army only had enough vehicles for its ordinary everyday needs and enough petrol for one month's fighting made a large-scale offensive impossible. The best that could be done would be to carry out small local actions. Pressed by Graziani, the generals admitted that by scratching together all the available materiel two fully motorized divisions and an armoured column could be put in the field. That would not solve the air-support problem: there were currently 108 fighters on strength and another 57 were needed, and much else besides.[60] Informing Rome that his senior generals – 'commanders with different temperaments but all in the top rank' – were against any idea of offensive action to a man, Graziani explained that this was not just because the enemy had moved from Sidi-el-Barani to Sollum but because of the 'persistently insufficient means of transport' that were available. Rome should send him orders that were within his means to carry out, or a superior who could assess whether the on-the-spot assessments were correct. In closing, he offered his resignation.[61]

As the North African campaign faltered, Yugoslavia and Greece moved back to centre stage. The day after Graziani's report on the state of his armies in North Africa, Mussolini was 'talk[ing] a lot about an Italian attack on Yugoslavia during the second half of September'.[62] Together the Italian forces in Venezia Giulia and in the one-time Austrian provinces of Carinthia and Styria would form the two arms of a military pincer. The aim was the conquest of Slovenia and Croatia. The planners assumed that Hungary would be an ally and a participant and Bulgaria would at least threaten Yugoslavia. Romania and Greece were expected to remain neutral, 'although the latter is untrustworthy as far as we are concerned'.[63] Mussolini ordered the army and the air force to be ready to act by 20 September.[64] Eleven days later he changed his mind.

At Palazzo Chigi, Ciano was pursuing a goal of his own. A visit to Albania while the Germans were sweeping across northern France had persuaded him that the mass of the local population was already won over to the Italian side, and he took note of their appetite for Kosovo and Ciamuria. In mid-June reports began to come in of Royal Navy ships in Suda Bay and a British battlecruiser in Navarino Bay – the latter turned out to be in fact an island with two skeletal palm trees. At the beginning of July the governor of the Aegean islands, Cesare De Vecchi, began stirring up trouble, reporting that English ships, and possibly planes too, were finding refuge and protection in Greece. Ciano left the Greek minister in Rome 'in no doubts about our intentions if Greece continues to make herself England's accomplice'.[65] Greece remonstrated, pointing out that Italian overflights were the only incursions and inviting Italian officials to see for themselves that Greek neutrality was not being violated by the British. Invitation and explanation alike were shrugged aside. A furious Mussolini announced that if 'this music' continued he would take action against Greece.[66] As Ciano piled on the pressure, encouraged by Hitler's readiness to support Italian operations to prevent the Ionian islands being converted into British bases, the Italians struck. On 12 July, Italian aircraft bombed the Greek auxiliary *Orion* and the Greek destroyer *Hydra*.

In the second week of August, Ciano reported to Mussolini on a 'very tricky situation' with respect to the Greek-Albanian border. It did not take much to reawaken Mussolini's wish to settle the Greeks' hash once and for all: his failure to take Corfu in 1923 remained a bitter defeat. He had an account to settle with Greece and, he told his son-in-law, the Greeks were deceiving themselves if they thought he had forgotten. Francesco Jacomoni, governor of Albania, and General Visconti Prasca, its military commander, were called to Rome, and Mussolini began to talk of a surprise attack on Greece at the end of September. The Fascist press raised the temperature with mendacious accounts of supposed Greek involvement in the murder of a notorious Albanian bandit. From Athens ambassador Grazzi reported that Greek ships were being hired out to England and Greek factories were making war materials for British troops.[67] Two days later, on De Vecchi's orders, an Italian submarine sank the Greek cruiser *Helli* in Tinos harbour. The Italians immediately blamed the British, but the Greek authorities recovered fragments of an Italian-made torpedo – though they did not make that public until after the Italian invasion had begun.

Jacomoni and Visconti Prasca met with Mussolini on 12 August. Afterwards none of the *Duce*'s lieutenants could agree on exactly what was said, or even when the meeting took place, but the essential lines of the conversation are fairly clear. The principals talked about an operation limited to Ciamuria, the coastal region of Epirus in western Greece, and probably also the island of Corfu – as had Guzzoni and Geloso in the draft plans they had drawn up previously. Visconti Prasca's analysis of the operational possibilities allowed his listeners to believe that a surprise operation would be possible provided that it took no more than a fortnight to move troops inside Albania from the Yugoslav to the Greek front and that the necessary additional troops were shipped across from Italy as individual battalions, not divisions, to get them in place more quickly. If surprise were not achieved then the occupation of the Epirus 'must from the outset assume the characteristics of an operation of force [i.e. in strength], needing large amounts of means and assuming quite a different character'. Mussolini, who at this point expected imminent Italian action in North Africa and was also attracted by the idea of attacking Yugoslavia, was minded to think that action against Greece should be put off until the end of September.[68]

When told of the new venture – the first he had heard of it – Badoglio refused to send a single extra man to Albania. There were lots of strategies for future operations and he had told the *Duce* that when 'the other, more important matters' had been sorted out 'we'll be able to get what we want from Greece without employing a single soldier there'. Having also been instructed by Mussolini to make contact with the German general staff to find out whether it was going to carry out an operation against Yugoslavia from Carinthia and Styria, or whether it would allow Italy to do so, General Roatta may have been relieved that at least one of the many operations ricocheting around the War Ministry corridors now seemed less likely to land heavily on his desk.[69]

One of the factors that contributed to Italy's readiness to attack Greece when the time came was a serious underestimation of the Greek army. It had shown itself a force to be reckoned with in the Balkan wars: in November 1912 it had taken Salonika after only twenty-three days and by the end of March 1913 it had driven the Turks out of Epirus. More recently, however, it had comprehensively lost the war of 1921–2 and been driven out of Turkey. On balance the Italian military were inclined to put this down more to Greek failures than Turkish successes. The Greeks had underestimated the difficulty of the enterprise, they had failed completely to counter-manoeuvre, their use of reserves had been poor and they had shown 'a lack of fighting spirit', especially in the final phase of the war.[70] Reports on the eve of the current war suggested that Greece was badly in need of light and medium guns, tanks, and anti-aircraft and anti-tank guns.[71] The arrest of a sub-chief of the Greek general staff for criticizing the government's defence spending, and the sympathy shown him by fellow officers, appeared to point to serious professional and political weaknesses in Greece's military machine.[72] The Italians were by no means alone in underrating their future enemy. A German military assessment concluded that 'the Greek army . . . will scarcely be able to mount military operations from its own strength let alone defend its own country without foreign help'.[73]

The Germans quickly made it plain that they would have nothing to do with the plans being cooked up in Rome to attack Yugoslavia. Halder dismissed Roatta's approach about collaborating in a strike through Carinthia and Styria as 'an incredible impertinence'. Nor was Hitler prepared to give Ciano's plans for an attack on Greece his backing – at least not until the war with Great Britain was over. In what must have been a stiff interview with the Italian ambassador, Dino Alfieri, Ribbentrop made it abundantly clear that England was the opponent on whom both partners should concentrate. Italian plans to attack Yugoslavia must be shelved, and Italian action against Greece was also unwelcome. 'It is a complete order to halt all along the line,' Ciano noted gloomily in his diary. 'Naturally we accept Berlin's point of view, even regarding Greece.'[74] When told that Germany would only collaborate in military action against Yugoslavia if and when the appropriate political agreements were in place, Badoglio clapped von Rintelen on the back 'full of enthusiasm' and remarked that this was a great help in his attempt to obstruct war in the Balkans.[75]

Once again, Mussolini's wandering gaze came to rest on North Africa. Two days after Ribbentrop's warning a telegram winged its way from Rome to Tripoli. A mixture of exhortation and exaggeration, it exemplified Mussolini's way with strategic decisions. The invasion of England could happen at any time. On '[t]he day the first German soldier touches British soil you will attack'. Italy had given Graziani everything it could and he now had 'an undoubted superiority in men, means and morale'. Five battleships were on hand to support him.

(As we have seen, they were not.) Graziani was to take Egypt, link up communications with Italian East Africa and give Great Britain 'the *coup de grâce*'.[76] But the *Duce* had not given up on either of his other victims of choice. The deployment against Yugoslavia was put back from 20 September to 20 October, and that against Greece from the end of August to the end of September. Once England was knocked out of the war, something Mussolini clearly expected to happen swiftly as a result of simultaneous offensives by the Germans against the United Kingdom and by Graziani in Egypt, those states that had 'more or less covertly sympathized with London' would fall in line with the decisions made by the Axis.[77]

'The orders will be executed,' Graziani told Mussolini, but there was little enthusiasm for doing so. The commander of 10th Army, General Mario Berti, who was to carry out the offensive, had no transport at all for one of his two corps and only 270 trucks for the two divisions in his second corps. Berti was ordered to be ready to move from 27 August – and Graziani made him countersign Mussolini's instructions, not something calculated to improve command relations. Then, a matter of days after ordering Graziani to launch his attack at the same time as the German landing in England, Mussolini jettisoned his precondition. After talking with Hitler at Berchtesgaden and being told that the *Luftwaffe* needed two weeks of good weather to get the necessary air superiority, Ciano came away with the impression that the assault on England had definitely been postponed and that no fixed date for it was in view.[78] Mussolini now wanted an offensive whether or not the Germans landed in England, in order not to be left out of discussions if Berlin and London struck an agreement. Graziani should be ready to attack between 8 and 10 September. 'By then,' Badoglio told him, 'you'll have received all the materiel you have asked for, and I'll alert Pricolo to send you the planes you need.'[79]

With Mussolini's attention now focused – at least temporarily – on Libya, war with Greece seemed no longer imminent: when Visconti Prasca pressed Rome for the two divisions he wanted for his attack he was told that the Epirus operation was now 'suspended' and that he would get no additional troops until new orders were issued.[80] But Greece was certainly not off the menu. 'Ciano wants his war,' Badoglio's deputy, General Quirino Armellini, noted at the end of August, 'and notwithstanding previous directives he will probably get it.'[81] War with Yugoslavia was still a distinct possibility too and the army carried on working up its plans. A lot turned on the Germans providing not just permission to transit their territory but also logistical support to enable Italian units to do so. The Germans were not prepared to co-operate. Keitel told Badoglio that the Italians should stop their studies for war with Yugoslavia so as not to upset the Balkans and give the British a reason to create bases in Greece. Badoglio replied soothingly that the Italians would not take the initiative against either Yugoslavia or Greece.[82] Mussolini assured Hitler that his political line was indeed the same as his partner's: to keep the Balkans out of the conflict. The military measures he was taking on the Greek and Yugoslav frontiers were simply precautionary given that both countries were profoundly hostile to the Axis 'and ready to stick the knife in its back if a favourable opportunity were to present itself'. The *Duce* was going to direct his forces against Egypt.[83]

In Libya, Graziani was heaping up obstacles. To carry out a double envelopment of British positions at Sidi-el-Barani he needed 600 motor vehicles, which would not arrive until the end of September at the earliest. Without them he could get no further than Sollum and Halfaya. If he did that he would lose the advantage of surprise and allow the enemy to bring forward forces presently within Egypt with which they could halt or destroy the advance, or at least claim that the Italians had run out of steam and had had to halt. From a strictly operational point of view, it would make sense to delay the operation at least until the start of October, when the hot season was coming to an end.[84] With the German invasion of England now on hold, the *Duce* was in no mood to wait. News arrived that Germany, now looking at the possibility of clearing the Mediterranean theatre over the coming winter, was ready to send one or two armoured divisions quickly to Egypt, annoying Badoglio, who had not asked for German help.[85] The idea that Germany might be thinking of taking an active role in operations in Mussolini's '*Mare Nostrum*' seems to have been the final straw. The day after Badoglio told Marras that he would put the German proposal to Mussolini a brief telegram left Rome for Tripoli, where it arrived two hours later. Graziani was to begin his attack in two days' time.

Mussolini was already looking ahead to fresh conquests. Having briefly been attracted by the possibility of occupying France as far as the River Rhône, made impossible by the agreements being reached with the Vichy government, he now lost interest in it. The armed forces must be prepared to act against Yugoslavia by the end of October. Albania must be reinforced as a prelude to the occupation of Ciamuria, the Epirus and Corfu, and after that Tripolitania too. Corsica could be occupied by troops presently stationed on Sardinia, and Tunisia by the 5th Army in Tripolitania.[86] Next day, Badoglio told the three chiefs of staff to crank up their plans for Yugoslavia, Greece and France and be prepared to have to move into Corsica and Tunisia.

When he got the order to attack the British in Egypt, Graziani changed his plans. Instead of attacking along two separate axes with his infantry divisions advancing along the coast and his motorized and armoured units moving inland, he massed five infantry divisions (only one of which was fully motorized) in two echelons and launched the whole force along the coastal route with a covering force operating on his inland flank. It took three days for his troops to move forward to their starting positions as units crossed each other's line of advance, got out of position, and used up fuel supplies. When they got going on 13 September the advance was slow, as operational intentions changed, contradictory orders were issued and units switched from one command to another. Inland, the *gruppo Maletti* ploughed its way across sand, slowing it down and increasing fuel consumption. Descending in zig-zags from Sollum ridge, Italian units were within range of British guns. Royal Air Force planes destroyed roads, and when they moved off-road the trucks sank into the sand.[87]

At 2.45 in the afternoon of 16 September Italian troops entered Sidi-el-Barani. They had advanced some fifty miles in three days. Casualties were not especially heavy – 120 dead and 410 wounded, one-third of them Libyans – largely because, rather than making a stand-up fight of it, the British had retired on Mersa Matruh. In the air both sides had been evenly matched, General Carlo Porro's *5a Squadra* of 300 planes facing about 300 British aircraft. Enemy opposition in the air cost it only four aircraft lost in combat and five destroyed on the ground. Afterwards Porro criticized the army: not understanding air power it had misused it, and the infantry had wanted constant protection.[88] Graziani explained away the slowness of the advance and his failure to take the British in the flank as due to his absolute inferiority in mechanized means, terrain and climate. In fact, the Italians had shown that they lacked training in moving in lorried columns and in the tactics of how to use motorized units (Berti had simply used his tanks to protect his infantry). General Annibale Bergonzoli complained that the troops of the 23 *Marzo* division – the only motorized division – only knew how to climb on and off lorries.

While Graziani's men trudged forward, Badoglio's staff went to work on General Jodl's proposal and concluded that it would be better to ask the Germans for 150 to 200 tanks, which could be in operation with Italian crews after two months, rather than accept a German armoured division which would take two months to transport to Libya and another month to acclimatize. Badoglio was prepared to agree that German tanks were to be preferred, but to his way of thinking Jodl had got hold of the wrong end of the stick – or rather, the wrong stick. What were needed were German dive-bombers that could make Alexandria untenable.[89] For the moment at least, Badoglio was confident – or so he had Marras (and therefore presumably the Germans) believe. Graziani's manoeuvre had succeeded completely, destroying more than half the tanks of the British armoured division facing him. Necessary road building would be completed by the end of October, when the Italian forces would be ready for another bound to Mersa Matruh. Italian airfields would then be only 250 kilometres from Alexandria. Then bombers, protected by fighters, would make it impossible for the British fleet to stay there. However, if the war lasted into the winter then as well as the armoured units the Germans had offered 'we shall have to count on a reinforcement of Stukas and fighters to work against Alexandria'.[90] The door to German intervention in Italy's war was not yet open – but it was now ajar.

With attention focused on Libya the planners might reasonably have hoped that Mussolini's other intentions had dwindled into the background. Not so. Ciano and his lieutenants were hard at work preparing the ground. Badoglio's office managed to block attempts by Jacomoni to get hold of French rifles and arm insurrectionary bands inside Greece, but, just as the orders to Graziani to get moving were going out, the head of the air force, General Pricolo, received the updated plan for Greece ('Emergenza G') and instructions from Ciano's office to get ready for an imminent attack on the country. It was, he complained, the first he knew about the Greek venture.[91] Incoming intelligence reports told of secret Greek mobilization on the Albanian frontier and of defensive works being thrown up at an increasing pace on the Yugoslav frontier. Badoglio tried to dissolve both the Yugoslav and the Greek designs.

Army-navy planning for Yugoslavia was uncoordinated and needed to be harmonized. In the circumstances, he advised Mussolini, it would be best to prepare for operations against France, which could not be done if the army was called on to fight Yugoslavia, and to reinforce Libya, which meant suspending sending troops to Albania. Corsica could be invaded at any moment with troops stationed in Sardinia. Mussolini had his own ideas. The armed forces should be ready to act against Yugoslavia at the end of October; three divisions were to be sent to Albania by the end of September, after which Tripolitania could be reinforced; and as far as France was concerned the Rhône operation was suspended now that unoccupied France was effectively under German guarantee. The army need only be 'ready for peace'. Pricolo was told that Greece was now 'off', and on the eve of Graziani's attack the three chiefs of staff were given their new directive.[92]

On 18 September Badoglio told Mussolini that by the end of the month there would be nine divisions in Albania and that they would be in place and ready to move against Epirus and Corfu ten to fifteen days later. The strike should begin with a surprise attack on Corfu and that would require at least twelve days' notice as some of the shipping needed was presently being used to transport men and supplies to Libya.[93] Arriving in Rome next day, Ribbentrop broke the news of the forthcoming Tripartite Pact with Japan, duly signed on 27 September. Yugoslavia and Greece, Ribbentrop said twice over, were exclusively of Italian interest. At the present time the main effort should be directed against England but Italy could adopt whatever policy she thought fit towards them 'with the full support of Germany'. Mussolini said nothing about Yugoslavia, though the army had begun slowly deploying the forces needed for an operation against her, now shorn of the flanking attack through Carinthia and Styria. To carry out the plan the soldiers would need 3,000 German motor vehicles – another sign that Italy was already slipping towards a subaltern position, even though Mussolini seemed quite unaware of the fact.[94] About Greece he was ominously forthcoming. The Greeks were to Italy what Norway had been to Germany before the previous April and it was therefore necessary to liquidate the country, 'all the more since, when our land forces have made further progress in Egypt, the English fleet will no longer be able to remain in Alexandria and will attempt to make for Greek ports'. If Ribbentrop intended his remarks to be a warning to Italy to focus on the British and steer clear of the Balkans at least for the moment, they were not taken that way.[95]

Currents which he did not control were now propelling Mussolini towards his war with Greece. As an afterthought, Ribbentrop told him at their meeting that Germany was planning to send a military mission to Romania to protect the oilfields – a sign that Mussolini's long-nurtured dream of Italian dominance of the Balkans south of the Danube was under threat. Then, only days after Hitler's and Ribbentrop's assurances that the war against England was already effectively over, Marras reported from Berlin first that in all probability a landing against England would be postponed until the following spring, and then that 'the sun had set' on it.[96]

A week after Ribbentrop's visit, Badoglio called the chiefs of staff together to inform them of Mussolini's current thinking. Intervention in Yugoslavia was for the present unlikely as it was neither in Germany's interest nor in Italy's to disturb the flow of raw materials they were getting from her. Three divisions were currently on their way to Visconti Prasca in Albania. When they arrived, bringing the total to nine, that would be sufficient to keep the Greeks in their place. Both the Greek and the Yugoslav problems would be resolved at the peace table – whether either power wanted it or not. The Mediterranean was a different matter. There the situation was 'as ever obscure and chaotic'. If the German invasion of England did not happen the 'barycentre' of the war would shift there. At that point there would have to be a joint meeting with the German general staff to decide what actions to undertake. Badoglio could see only one action that might succeed: a strike at Gibraltar and another by Italian and German aircraft at Alexandria after Graziani had pushed at least as far as Mersa Matruh to put the harbour in range. Together they could force the British out of the Mediterranean. Pricolo pointed out that German aircraft would not be needed since Alexandria would be in range of Italian planes. Badoglio's response – that they could anyway ask for eighty Stukas and a hundred Messerschmitts to replace the planes they would send down to Africa – exposed his attitude to his ally and his subordinates. Germany was a resource from which to fill the gaps in the Italian inventory, and the chiefs of staff were there not to debate strategy but only to design the requisite operations. The meeting was over in twenty-five minutes.[97]

Graziani was certainly not waging the kind of fast campaign that pre-war doctrine had promised. After visiting Pricolo in mid-September, a *Luftwaffe* liaison mission reported that Graziani seemed to have been following the kind of nineteenth-century operational methods used by Kitchener in the Sudan.[98] If anything, the comment was unfair to Kitchener – Graziani's soldiers had in fact moved into Egypt at the same average daily pace as Napoleon's armies. However, he was undoubtedly labouring under difficulties. For one thing, the port facilities at Tripoli, Benghazi (which was under constant bombardment) and Tobruk were very limited – as pre-war studies had shown all too clearly. In July, August and September the Libyan ports landed just over 50,000 tons of supplies a month. For another, he was in competition with Visconti Prasca. Between mid-July and 15 September 1,031 trucks were sent to Tripoli (200 of which were burned in port through enemy action) and 945 to Albania.[99]

At this moment General Soddu got his way on his long-gestating plans to cut back the army to 800,000 men, keeping only four classes (men aged between twenty and twenty-three) under arms. For the army the reduction threatened chaos: the younger recruits were often in less vital units such as frontier guards while the supply and service units were exclusively manned by the older conscripts, who would all leave.[100] Twenty of the seventy-one divisions would be reduced to three-quarters of their fully mobilized strength while another thirty were already at 'skeleton' strength. Mussolini weighed in: higher command organizations that were not immediately necessary could also be dissolved. With that 7th Army headquarters, responsible for covering the west, and 8th Army headquarters, which had been scheduled to oversee an attack on Yugoslavia, disappeared.[101] When Hitler had proposed demobilizing parts of the German army in July his generals had vigorously opposed the idea. In Italy the generals – with one exception – fell in line without a murmur. Roatta tried to get the decision reconsidered but failed. Badoglio accepted the reductions apparently without a qualm – as did Graziani – perhaps hoping that reducing the size of the army would make Mussolini less inclined to risky military adventures. If so, he was quickly going to be disillusioned.

The process of releasing the conscripts began on 10 October. Only in mid-December, when Badoglio had gone, would Roatta secure authorization to suspend the demobilization order.[102] Together, the demobilization of half the army, which numbered 1,700,000 men on 1 October 1940, and the German veto on operations from Carinthia and Styria spelt the end of the Yugoslav option. At the beginning of October the army general staff confirmed that 'Emergenza E' was now to be considered over. The original plan was shelved and units were sent back to their regional bases. A new plan, based on the occupation of part of Yugoslavia as a consequence of 'serious internal disturbances', would simply be a theoretical study. On 3 October Badoglio ordered that the Greek plans be updated, though their activation was deferred for the moment, and two days later revised plans for Greece, Albania and Yugoslavia were distributed.[103]

At the end of September Graziani came to Rome and announced that he was ready to restart his operations in mid-December. Mussolini wanted things to move much faster. October could get the Italians to Mersa Matruh, which would put Alexandria in bombing range, but for him Alexandria was no more than a name. What mattered was that Italy press forward. 'I never fix on territorial objectives,' the *Duce* declared. Badoglio proposed delaying the attack until October, and Graziani departed for Tripoli telling the pair that he would let them know his plans when he got back to his headquarters. Mussolini left the meeting irritated that Badoglio was backing Graziani's delaying tactics but confident that Graziani could score 'a success in Egypt which gives [Italy] the glory she has sought in vain for three centuries'.[104]

On 4 October Mussolini and Hitler met on the Brenner Pass. In a three-hour session Hitler rehearsed the difficulties he was having with Spain and suggested that Vichy France might possibly join a continental coalition against Great Britain. The spectre of a Franco-German partnership would shortly become one of the driving forces behind Mussolini's actions, but for the time being he simply reiterated Italy's demands for Nice, Corsica, Tunisia and Djibouti. Once they were obtained, Italy would have no conflicts with France. Sketching out his current strategy, he announced that the second phase of his Egyptian offensive would begin shortly and take Italian troops to Mersa Matruh. In the third phase his forces would get to the Nile Delta and occupy Alexandria. Hitler offered 'specialized forces', only to be told by Mussolini that they were not needed for the second phase. As for the third phase, what might be needed were trucks, some heavy tanks and some

Stukas.[105] After the conference the German high command appeared to view the occupation of the Suez Canal as 'military problem no.1 in the conduct of the war' and one which would both hit England in a vital part of her empire and clear up the situation in the Mediterranean. Hitler wanted to send an armoured division which would be able to live and fight autonomously. It could be readied, embarked and landed in eight weeks – by which time it was assumed that the Italians would have taken Mersa Matruh.[106]

Next day the order went down the wire to Tripoli: Graziani must start his offensive on Mersa Matruh between 10 and 15 October. German offers of aid had been turned down for the time being. Mussolini had no doubt that his commander had what he needed to carry out his instructions. He would get more if and when the moment came to start the great battle for the Nile Delta. In the meantime the only significant logistical problem was water. The *Duce* had the answer: men needed less water in October than in high summer, and in any case the Italians could stand the conditions better than the English. The enemy would only defend Mersa Matruh long enough to disentangle and extract their forces there. If Italy delayed during October in order to get reinforcements up, the enemy would do the same. Finally, there was the semblance of a real strategic idea. 'Once we have reached Marsa Matruh,' Mussolini told Graziani, 'we'll see which of the two pillars of England's Mediterranean defence should be knocked down: the Egyptian or the Greek.'[107]

One thing Graziani was not going to get was much direct help from the navy. It had abandoned the idea of using heavy cruisers to bombard the Egyptian coast, and had only five submarines ready to operate in the waters outside Alexandria.[108] Everyone except Mussolini agreed that since it was the weaker fleet the navy had to avoid a pitched battle unless it was the unavoidable consequence of one fleet trying to prevent the other from carrying out its primary mission. The best that the fleet could do in very adverse circumstances, Admiral Cavagnari believed, was to protect communications with Tripoli and Benghazi from a distance. If it could not solve the problems inherent in doing so with its own resources, then it would have to ask the Germans for help. To handle its task it wanted more dive-bombers on hand in Cyrenaica and more anti-aircraft guns to defend the coastal ports. Badoglio reminded Cavagnari that the navy's tasks were, as they had been from the start, to guarantee communications with Libya, protect the coasts of the mainland from enemy attack, and degrade enemy traffic using light surface craft and submarines.[109]

Already the Italians were slipping into German hands: the dive-bombers would have to come from the *Luftwaffe*, and the Germans would have to release some of the 500 aerial torpedoes they had on order from Fiume if Pricolo was to add to his current stock of ten. The chief of the air staff ordered his commanders to conserve their forces and avoid undue risk when selecting and carrying out operations as planes were difficult to replace. They were not to send aircraft against the enemy fleet if aircraft carriers were present and must prioritize using the limited supply of aerial torpedoes against enemy warships.[110] Mussolini weighed in. Too many warships were being used to escort merchantmen, using up reserves of fuel that would be difficult and perhaps impossible to replace. So escorts were to be abolished or reduced to the minimum in order to spin stocks out for another year.[111]

For a moment it looked as though Italy was going to focus her limited resources on a single task. Then, on 12 October, everything went awry. First, Badoglio handed Mussolini a letter from Graziani telling his superiors that he would not have the transport and the guns he needed to attack the fortified camp of Mersa Matruh until the end of October. Mussolini was angry. What made him more angry still was the news that the Germans had sent a military mission into Romania.[112] To cap it all, this was the day on which the invasion of England, Operation SEALION, was definitively postponed at least until 1941. When Badoglio was told, the normally calm generalissimo completely lost his temper. The British, far from fighting a desperate battle for the home islands, could now devote substantial forces to the Mediterranean and North African theatres. What seemed to concern him most was the probable loss in a lengthy war of Italian East Africa, which he had so recently conquered for Mussolini.[113]

ZEROING-IN ON GREECE

Hitler's move into Romania on 12 October 1940, which stung Mussolini into action, was not entirely a bolt from the blue. German interest in keeping Romanian oil flowing was a well-established fact, and the

Italian ambassador in Bucharest, Pellegrino Ghigi, had picked up as early as mid-September on the likelihood that a German mission would be arriving there.[114] There were, too, other stimuli to action for a mind as febrile as Mussolini's. Intelligence reports told him that German economic penetration of North Africa and Syria was increasing. From Berlin, General Marras offered the opinion that Germany was once again engaged in a *Drang nach Osten* ('drive to the east'), as she had done during the First World War. Her target was the Aegean at Salonika, and if Italy attacked Greece then Germany would probably get there first.[115] There was also the worrying possibility of a 'continental bloc' that included France. 'In the long run,' Ciano noted as events gathered speed, 'a rapprochement between Berlin and Paris could only work against us.'[116] Last but by no means least, there was the need to act militarily in order to show Germany that Italy was an ally worth having and one whose interests must therefore be taken into account. Action there must be, and quickly, but there seemed little hope of that now in North Africa, so Mussolini turned to the other British 'pillar' in the Mediterranean – Greece. 'I shall send in my resignation as an Italian if anyone objects to our fighting the Greeks,' he told his son-in-law.[117]

In mid-October SIM compiled a massive report on Italy's intended target. A nine-year programme of military reform and rearmament, begun in 1935 and accelerated a year later, had given the Greek forces 'new vigour and new order', and they now possessed new anti-aircraft and anti-tank guns. However, at least half their artillery was left over from the First World War (as indeed was Italy's), and even in respect of anti-aircraft defences 'Greece will not be able to do anything without the help of more organized powers'. The army did not appear to present much of an obstacle. The general level of the officer corps was 'not satisfactory'; most company, regimental and battalion commanders were unable to maintain the necessary 'cohesion of will and spirit' in combat; and the value of the non-commissioned officers was 'not very high'. Greece was vulnerable strategically: the defensive properties of the Greco-Albanian frontier were probably exaggerated, and only a single road across the Pindus mountains connected the Epirus with the rest of the country. She was also vulnerable operationally: her working concept was for a long war on First World War lines in which she would seek to manoeuvre and counter-attack, which meant that she could easily be surprised. However, a long war would expose another weakness: her munitions factories produced only ammunition and could not manufacture small arms or artillery. Finally, the Greeks were at a psychological disadvantage. Everyone was aware of 'the disadvantageous strategic situation of the land frontiers and . . . the deficiencies that still exist in their military organism'.[118] This appreciation did not quite square with reports from the military attaché in Athens, Colonel Luigi Mondini, that Greek officers were well trained and that the lack of artillery was compensated for by mortars.[119] But all in all Greece looked like a sitting duck for Fascist Italy's much-vaunted *guerra lampo*.

News of the German move into Romania arrived on 12 October. Next day Mussolini ordered Badoglio to prepare operations against Greece so that they could start in thirteen days' time. The navy was warned that it had twelve days to prepare for transporting troops to Corfu – one of the targets in the existing plans for a limited war against Greece.[120] General Roatta, who had just sent orders to Visconti Prasca to move the troops in Albania to their winter quarters, was given twenty-four hours' warning of a meeting with Mussolini and Badoglio. The plan currently in force was for an operation to occupy Ciamuria and the Epirus, push five divisions down to Prevesa, and land a division from Puglia on Corfu. When he got to the meeting, on 14 October, Roatta discovered that it was now to work up an operation to occupy the whole of Greece. 'This was the first time that I and the general staff had heard of this matter,' he complained afterwards. Roatta and Badoglio listened while Mussolini explained that Greece had to be occupied in order to deny the British fleet support and eliminate English influence in the country. What, Mussolini asked, was needed to do that? Twenty divisions all employed contemporaneously and three months, as long as the army was remobilized at once, Roatta told him. Badoglio agreed and Mussolini approved the design – but not for long.[121]

Next morning Roatta got a last-minute summons to another meeting at Palazzo Venezia. When he got there he found Mussolini, Ciano, Soddu, Jacomoni and Visconti Prasca discussing a war to occupy the whole of Greece. Jacomoni was upbeat – the Greek people appeared to be 'very profoundly depressed' – and so was Ciano, who claimed that apart from a very small minority of rich Anglophiles the rest of the population was 'indifferent to all events, including an invasion by us'. Visconti Prasca said he could take the Epirus and the port of Prevesa in ten to fifteen days, starting on 26 October. He had 70,000 men facing 30,000 Greeks, his troops were chock full of enthusiasm, and the Greeks had no stomach for fighting. Mussolini said he would line up Bulgarian support and wanted two divisions sent to Salonika, as this could be decisive in getting it. He also wanted the islands of Xante, Cefalonia and Corfu seized quickly.

Badoglio suggested that the action against Greece coincide with the attack on Mersa Matruh, which would make it difficult for the British to send planes to Greece. He then obliquely criticized the plan that was being cooked up. Taking the Epirus as the first step was not of itself enough. Twenty divisions would be needed to carry out the entire occupation, not the nine currently there, and it would take three months. Visconti Prasca assured everyone that getting from the Epirus to Athens, a 250-kilometre march across a mountain chain 2,000 metres high, would present no serious problems as there were plenty of mule, tracks; and everyone agreed that five or six divisions would be enough to take Athens. No one baulked at Visconti Prasca's solution to the problem of getting through the Pindus mountains, which involved landing three mountain divisions at the small port of Arta in a single night.

'Are we sure of victory?' Mussolini asked at one point. By the time that the meeting ended the more or less universal approval for a war with Greece had quelled any lingering doubts the *Duce* may have had. 'It seems to me,' he said summing up the ninety-minute meeting, 'that we have examined all aspects of the problem.' What had actually happened, with the connivance of the military representatives, was that all the many problems thrown up in the course of the discussion had been smoothed over or – like the suggestion made by Mussolini early in the meeting that he would line up Bulgaria to support the invasion – simply left unquestioned.[122]

The holes in the war plan began to show immediately. On the same day Graziani announced that it would take another two months to construct the roads and aqueducts and collect the trucks he would need before he could attack the British in North Africa. With no other choice, Mussolini agreed to give him more time.[123] Next day Admiral Cavagnari came to see Badoglio and told him that the navy could not carry out the troop landings at Prevesa or anywhere else in or near the Gulf of Arta. Access was too shallow, the time needed to transit the Adriatic would mean that there could be no hope of surprise, and in any case, because of the demands on shipping for North Africa and Albania, he had only enough to land two divisions not three. As far as he was concerned an Italian attack on Greece presented more dangers than opportunities: the British might establish naval and air bases there and that could make the major Italian naval base at Taranto untenable.[124]

With an attack on Greece now imminent Badoglio called the service chiefs together. When they met, two days after the Palazzo Venezia meeting, the navy immediately threw a spanner in the works. Admiral Odoardo Somigli, vice-chief of the naval staff, announced that the navy could land a division on Corfu and transport men and equipment to Albania but it could not simultaneously carry out the Prevesa landing and the Albanian transports. Shrugging that problem off, Roatta asked whether it could supply a column marching along the coast from Arta to Athens. 'No' was the answer, because British naval forces would prevent it. A key plank in Visconti Prasca's strategic construct had just collapsed. With no base at Prevesa, Badoglio believed that it would be useless to 'sink' into the Epirus without a strong backup force with which to carry out a breakthrough in depth. There was also the timing of Graziani's now delayed offensive – which Mussolini had wanted to precede the attack on Greece by a few days – to take into account. Five divisions could be shipped to Albania in the two months that Graziani now needed. Badoglio had an alternative strategy in mind. Time taken in preparation was never lost – he had shown as much in Ethiopia five years earlier. With time to mass sixteen divisions, the whole job could be done in a month. The chiefs were to gather next day at Palazzo Venezia where they and he would lay out the issues for the *Duce*.[125]

With more than double the number of aircraft available to the Greeks (355 Italian to 150 Greek planes) and with Roatta's assurance that by 27 October he would have all the materials he needed to complete the equipment of the local airfields, Pricolo was confident that he could put enough planes in the air to support the invasion. Next day he changed his mind. Given the time it would take to unload and distribute materiel, the air force would not be fully deployed until 3–4 November. If the Greek operation began before then he would be short of six fighter squadrons, which would mean that he could only defend the area around Tirana, Durazzo and Devoli. His bombers would have no escorts and the ground forces would have no fighter protection.[126]

When he turned up at the Palazzo Venezia the following morning, Badoglio found Mussolini in a raging temper both with Graziani and with him. Ciano had told his father-in-law that Badoglio had threatened to resign if the Greek operation went ahead – a move so out of character as far as Badoglio was concerned that it can only have been intended by Ciano to cut the ground from under the chief of the armed forces general staff. Not only did Badoglio not resign, but he apparently did not even repeat to Mussolini the doubts about the Greek plan that he had relayed to Ciano the previous day. All he got out of Mussolini was his agreement that Graziani could have his two months' delay, and a two-day delay in starting the Greek war, which would now begin on 28 October.[127] Now there was no stopping Mussolini. When General Favagrossa met him the day after his brief encounter with Badoglio and advised him not to add to the theatres of operations, Mussolini reassured him that the war would be over in a matter of days. After that Greece could be a source of supplies, especially minerals.[128]

Mussolini now agreed to a meeting between Badoglio and General Keitel – but only because Keitel had been the one to ask for it. The possibility of a German armoured division arriving in North Africa was on the table and the *Luftwaffe* wanted to send two bomber wings and a squadron of mine-laying aircraft to attack Alexandria. Mussolini did not want Germans taking part in his North African operation until after Mersa Matruh. The question would be handled at the forthcoming meeting but he wanted it delayed until mid-November, by which time he expected the Italian occupation of the Epirus to be done and dusted. Graziani did not want Germans on his patch. Playing skilfully on Badoglio's known dislike of their mutual partner, he acknowledged that a German armoured division would be of great advantage in the march on Mersa Matruh, but 'would it not be convenient to avoid this assemblage or at least limit it to the last phase of the campaign?' With a couple of hundred German armoured cars and enough transport to move three infantry battalions, he could put together an equivalent unit.[129]

On 19 October, with war now only nine days away, news arrived that King Boris III of Bulgaria had no intention of taking the bait and 'realizing some of his national aspirations' regarding Greece. With her rearmament delayed, and surrounded by neighbouring powers that obliged her to act 'with perspicacity and prudence', the king declared that his country must 'abstain from armed action'.[130] At the meeting of the council of ministers that morning Mussolini looked pale and tired. In North Africa, he complained, his generals were letting him down. The troops were aggressive and wanted to fight, but the generals did not. They expected him to resolve everything on the political level. Politics was his business, their job was to fight. Graziani was avoiding attacking but Mussolini was going to order him to do so. 'We need to win for our friends too,' he told his ministers at the end of his harangue, 'to have ever greater prestige.'[131] He told Hitler that he intended to settle the Greek question quickly. Operations in Egypt were on hold while logistical work was being carried out, but he hoped to act on both fronts simultaneously. After Mersa Matruh had been captured the decisive battle for the Delta would take place. That was the point at which German armour might be brought into play.[132]

One outcome of the Brenner Pass meeting between Mussolini and Hitler at the beginning of the month was the decision that detailed discussions ought to take place about the nuts and bolts of sending German armour to North Africa. General von Thoma came to Rome and detailed staff talks between 16 and 18 October thrashed out the issues that would have to be resolved if a reinforced German armoured brigade of 13,000 men with 200 tanks and armoured cars and 2,356 vehicles was going to be railed and then shipped to Libya. At least one German request proved too much for the Italian logisticians: they asked their ally to cut back on a ration of four lemons per man per day and a litre of lemon juice every ten days because of difficulties in supply.[133] The Italian staff had worked up some figures for supplying a full-sized motorized division, all too well aware of the difficulties. There were only twenty Italian merchant ships capable of carrying motor vehicles, and the ports of Benghazi and Tripoli could only unload ten ships and eighty vehicles a day between them. Moving an entire armoured division from Germany to North Africa would require 144 trains and sixty ship-voyages and would take two months. When the final agreement, which cut the time to forty-five days, landed on his desk, Badoglio put off making a decision until he had talked the matter over with Keitel.[134]

The OKW got wind of the forthcoming Italian attack on Greece ten days before it actually began when a colonel on the Italian Air Force headquarters staff leaked it to the *Luftwaffe* liaison staff. Its chief, General Oswald Pohl, was told on 23 October, but on the same day Badoglio led the German military attaché, General von Rintelen, to believe that Italy planned to take no action against Greece unless she was forced to do so because Greece or Great Britain had taken prior action against her. Roatta too denied that any action was planned, calling talk of an attack on Greece 'chatter'.[135] Busy trying to recruit both Vichy France and Francoist Spain for his 'continental bloc', a task which took him first to Montoire in the Loire Valley, then to Hendaye in south-western France, then back to Montoire between 22 and 24 October, Hitler was momentarily distracted. While his railway train was trundling around Europe, the Italian chiefs of staff met to discuss the landings on Corfu and Cefalonia. More holes appeared in the plans. The landing on Corfu might or might not work, depending on the weather and on whether the troops could land at two points on the island or only one – and it turned out that the navy and the army had not even discussed the practicability of landing 2,400 men on Cefalonia and leaving them with enough stores to hold out on their own for two weeks. Cefalonia was postponed, and Badoglio reassured everyone that the two-day delay to which Mussolini had agreed would aid Italy by 'demobilizing [the Greeks] a little' – a highly unlikely prospect. His main concern now that the war was close was 'not to wake up those [people] at Alexandria'.[136] The Corfu action would be postponed in its turn on 1 November. When Badoglio reported on his meeting with the chiefs, Mussolini told him that before starting the operation he intended to ask Greece to let Italy occupy several important strategic positions. If they refused he would proceed to a complete occupation of the country.[137]

On 25 October Mussolini was handed the orders for the attack on Greece: Corfu and the Epirus first, then a threat to Salonika and the march on Athens. Last-ditch moves were being made to try to unseat Visconti Prasca, who had never commanded anything of any consequence. Mussolini reassured the chosen one that he had every faith in him, adding somewhat ominously that it was up to Visconti Prasca to prove him right.[138] Next day poor weather prevented the Italian air force from taking to the skies. This was not the only bad omen. Four days before the war actually began the Italian army operations staff calculated that though at the start 150,000 Italians would face 120,000 Greeks, once both sides had completed their mobilization 175,000 Italians would be fighting 320,000 to 330,000 Greeks. The imbalance made Bulgarian co-operation all the more important.[139] Visconti Prasca's strategy, which depended on feeding extra divisions from mainland Italy into the fray faster than the Greeks could mobilize their reserves, was in difficulties even before the fighting had begun.[140]

Having confirmed Visconti Prasca in command of the Greek attack – a position he would hold for only thirteen days – Mussolini gave Graziani a jolt. It was time for him to ask himself whether he was going to continue in command. He had had sixteen months to get ready, he had been given all he had asked for, and with fifteen divisions all he had done was take Sidi-el-Barani.[141] Mussolini's letter hit Graziani like 'a bolt of lightning'. Defending himself from the charge of having wasted sixteen months (he had only been in command for four of them), Graziani repeated all his earlier arguments about the need for lengthy preparations. If he had made a wrong evaluation – 'something that I am unable to perceive' – then he had only one duty: 'to be recalled and replaced'.[142] The ball was back on Mussolini's side of the court.

In the brief interim between Mussolini's letter and Graziani's response Badoglio tried to put Mussolini off the idea that Egypt was ripe fruit waiting to fall and at the same time steer him away from the idea that von Thoma's armoured division might be just the answer to the problem. After subtracting the troops needed to guard the western frontier of Libya, 150,000 Italians were available for operations in Egypt against an estimated 250,000 to 300,000 enemy troops. A German armoured division, lightened in size, would not change the ratio of forces much. What was needed were 200,000 more men, and more heavy guns – but the ships to transport them did not exist, the light craft to escort the troop convoys also did not exist, and the port facilities were inadequate. So attacking the British on the Nile was now, as it had always been, beyond the Italians. The best they could hope to do in the circumstances was to occupy Mersa Matruh and turn it into a fortified base from which to resist a British counter-offensive. The best aid Germany could give them was Stuka dive-bombers and fighters to escort them.[143]

After failing to recruit either Pétain or Franco to his side, Hitler took his train to Florence. Whether he did so in order to try to persuade Mussolini not to attack Greece is still not entirely clear, but in any case he was too late. The Italian ambassador Emanuele Grazzi was holding a reception for Giacomo Puccini's son Antonio and the cast of *Madame Butterfly* at the Athens Embassy when, on 25 October, he was given the Italian ultimatum and strict instructions on what to do with it. On 27 October he hosted what was in the circumstances a low-key celebration of the anniversary of the Fascist revolution, and at 3 o'clock the following morning he handed the ultimatum to General Metaxas. Greece was accused of allowing the Royal Navy to use its territorial waters, coasts and ports for operations of war, and of terroristic acts against Albania. Italy demanded the right to occupy unspecified 'strategic points' in Greek territory and gave Greece only three hours to comply. At 6 o'clock that morning the Italian guns began firing. Antonio Puccini, who had left the previous afternoon, was detained at Salonika.[144]

If Hitler had intended to try to stop the Greek invasion at the last minute, he had abandoned the idea by the time he got to Florence. After filling in his partner on his frustrating talks with Pétain and Franco, and explaining that his collaboration with Russia was based purely on politics and that he distrusted Stalin as much as Stalin distrusted him, the Führer listened while his ally agreed with him on everything, including the prospect of a closer relationship between the Soviet Union and the Axis. Both parties were, it seemed, in perfect accord.[145] Hitler offered an air-transported division and a parachute division to help in Greece, particularly by defending Crete from the British. Nothing was said about sending German detachments to North Africa. With that, Mussolini went off to Puglia to establish the headquarters from which to oversee the Greek campaign. On the second day of the war, with good reports coming in from the airmen, Graziani got a reprieve. Just now, Greece was 'the principal front'. Mersa Matruh was – and remained – 'an object of exceptional importance' and Graziani would be helping the main front by completing his preparations to attack it. Like Visconti Prasca, Graziani was a general in whom the *Duce* still had faith – for the moment. 'To work, then,' he exhorted his lieutenant, 'for your new African victory.'[146]

THE NAVAL WAR

For Italy, the naval war had begun when French warships bombarded the Ligurian coast on 11 and 14 June 1940, and at more or less the same time the British Mediterranean Fleet attacked the coast of Cyrenaica. Admiral Cavagnari refused to detach any of his warships to either location. The lifeline to the Italian armies in Libya ran through the central Mediterranean and the Sicilian Channel, and if they were to fight the British then supplies must be kept flowing along it. At first the navy tried individual runs by motor boats, submarines and destroyers, but they could only carry small cargoes: in the last ten days of June they managed to transport only 1,397 men, 46 guns, 60 tons of munitions and 3,902 tons of materiel, fuel and frozen meat. Graziani needed more, in particular seventy medium tanks, if he was going to take the offensive. So it was decided to send the first convoy. To be sure that it got through, Badoglio ordered that it be escorted by the entire surface fleet. If the British chose to try to stop the convoy then he for one was ready for them, 'as I have complete confidence that in any encounter we shall soften them up'. Pricolo was instructed to have his bombers and reconnaissance aircraft ready to intervene and support the navy.[147] This was not going to be as easy as it sounded. Pricolo complained that when enemy ships were reported the navy was sending out both its own and his reconnaissance aircraft to look for them, thereby uselessly using up his aircraft and his men's energies.[148] The navy ordered its coastal commands to tell their air force opposite numbers what they were doing. The tortuous system for securing air support at sea, according to which the senior naval officer at sea had to make a request to the nearest shore-based naval command, which in turn passed it to the regional air force command (and then sometimes even to *Superaereo* in Rome), meant that co-operation was not going to be a straightforward matter.

General orders were issued on 3 July. The convoy of five steamships would make its way from Naples and Catania to Benghazi, turning for Tripoli if it could not get through. The navy would give the steamships direct and indirect protection by deploying a close escort of light cruisers and destroyers and a distant escort of heavy cruisers and destroyers to protect it against any threat from British warships coming from

Malta, while the main battle-fleet under Admiral Inigo Campioni, which included the battleships *Cavour* and *Giulio Cesare*, stood off at a distance. A screen of eleven submarines was spread out to help protect the surface ships and the convoy. 'If enemy forces are spotted,' Campioni told his subordinates, 'I intend to act with the greatest resolution against them.'[149]

The convoy set out on 6 July, and that same day the Italians learned that two British fleets were at sea. Very early that morning came news that Admiral Somerville's 'H' Force had left Gibraltar (it would return to port in the face of threats from Italian aircraft), and early in the evening Campioni learned that Admiral Cunningham's fleet, which included three battleships, was putting to sea to support two convoys heading to Alexandria from Malta. Signals intelligence was only of limited help to the Italian fleet: radio direction-finding told Campioni that significant enemy forces were at sea, but a signal from German intelligence misled him into thinking that the British fleet was steaming for Sicily in order to bombard the coastline there. His opponent was somewhat better off. The Royal Navy had taken a copy of the new Italian naval code book from a submarine at the end of June, and with its aid and that of radio direction finding and plain-language Italian transmissions Cunningham was able to work out what Campioni was trying to do.[150]

Sweeps by the Italian air force south of Sicily and east towards Navarino Bay in Greece still left a corridor of open sea along which Cunningham was able to move towards the Italian fleet unobserved. Finally his fleet was spotted by two seaplanes, and from 10 a.m. on 8 July the Italian air force tried to degrade the enemy fleet. Over the next eight and a half hours seventy-two aircraft dropped 531 bombs – and scored a single hit on the cruiser *Gloucester*. Italian seaplanes were more effective: one of them spotted the British battle-fleet and tailed it for most of the afternoon. As evening came on Campioni turned his fleet in the direction of the enemy. Then, at 6.45, an order came from *Supermarina*: 'Do not, repeat not, commit yourself against the enemy's battleships.' The instruction apparently came directly from Mussolini, who had ordered that his naval forces were not to engage.[151] *Supermarina* wanted Campioni to draw the enemy's fleet towards the coast and in reach of land-based air power, which could damage it and thus allow the navy to destroy it in detail. Five minutes before Campioni received the new order Italian bombers attacked his own cruiser and battleship divisions by mistake.

Campioni was ready for a fight, but feared that the British fleet might cut him off from his base at Taranto and then move in to destroy him. On the morning of 9 July he set a rendezvous at 2 o'clock that afternoon sixty miles east of Cape Spartivento for his divisions and signalled his plan to meet the enemy in four columns. On the surface the odds were finely balanced. He had only two battleships against the enemy's three (believed to be four) – Admiral Carlo Bergamini had asked to be allowed to take out the new battleships *Littorio* and *Vittorio Veneto*, but as their crews still needing training and the *Littorio* was out of action due to a fire in one of her gun turrets this was refused – and their 12.6-inch guns were out-ranged by the 15-inch guns of HMS *Warspite*. On the other hand his battleships were between two and five knots faster than the three British battleships, and he had more cruisers which were both faster and carried more firepower than their opposite numbers. Campioni thought that he had his forces in the ideal disposition when the battle began at 3.08 that afternoon.[152] In fact, his ships were out of position: the light division of destroyers and cruisers that was supposed to shield his battle-fleet was actually behind it and had to catch it up, and his heavy cruisers too were in the wrong place. They were also poorly disposed. Pre-war tactics dictated advancing to battle in echelon with light cruisers at the front, followed by a squadron of heavy cruisers, followed by the battleship division. Some of the light cruisers never caught up with the main fleet, others never got to the head of the formation but were between the Italian battleships and the *Warspite* when the battle began and had to get out of the way, and the heavy cruisers, which were supposed to join in bombarding the enemy's main battle-fleet, came under fire from the *Warspite*'s bigger guns and were then attacked by Swordfish aircraft and forced to take evasive action.

The sea battle did not last very long. The two sides' cruisers began firing at 3.08 p.m., but after twenty-four minutes the Italians broke off. Then at 3.53 the *Cesare* opened fire on the *Warspite*, while the *Cavour*, which should have joined in, mistakenly targeted a more distant British warship. After four minutes the *Cesare* was hit. With four of her eight boilers shut down and her speed down to 18 knots she obviously could not sustain further combat and nor could the Italians hope to get to

Taranto. Campioni turned his fleet south-west behind a smokescreen and headed for home. Knowing from intercepts that they were retreating into the zone protected by Italian submarines, Cunningham decided not to follow. As evening began to fall, 435 Italian aircraft bombed both fleets from 12,000 feet. Afterwards Pricolo denied that his planes had bombed their own ships – or if they had, only five aircraft had made what was in the circumstances an understandable mistake.[153]

The battle of Punta Stilo showed all too clearly that the Italian navy had serious functional, structural and institutional problems. Gunfire was poor – Italian salvoes were widely spread, due partly to variations in shell weight – and Italian destroyers launched torpedo attacks from too far away. Co-ordination between ships and aircraft was virtually non-existent, thanks in large part to the determination with which both services had held the other at arm's length before the war. Unable to identify its own ships, the Italian Air Force dropped its bombs from too great a height to be accurate. The need for dive-bombers was obvious and shortly the Germans would supply 100 Ju 87 Stukas. There were no torpedo-bombers because Cavagnari had cancelled experiments in January 1939, unwilling to spend any more money on them. Perhaps most importantly of all, Italy had no aircraft carriers, a shortcoming for which the admirals were prone to blame Mussolini, though in reality they were just as responsible. A plan to convert the liner *Roma* was revived towards the end of 1940 but then abandoned in January 1941. Revived again in July 1941 after the hard lessons learned at the battle of Cape Matapan, the project was again abandoned in June 1943 when the dockyard labour was switched to building escorts and submarines.[154]

The lack of co-ordination between Italian warships and Italian aircraft had obviously to be put right and Badoglio ordered that something be done about it. Pricolo's reaction was to blame the navy for everything that had gone wrong at Punta Stilo. The naval command had not oriented his fighters properly, the sailors had not made good use of their own seaplanes, the air force commands had received no requests for reconnaissance either before or after the battle, and the navy's requests for fighter cover had been vague and infrequent. If things were to improve then the way that the navy made those requests had to be changed. Using bombers in sea battles, as also in land battles, was in any case 'extremely hazardous' given the difficulties of high-altitude recognition. What they could do was strike at the enemy before and after battle and hit him in his bases. Pricolo intended to avoid frittering away his air force, no longer meeting frequent 'thoughtless requests' the purpose of which was never made clear and which made it seem that the *Regia Aeronautica* was no more than merely an arm of the navy – and the army. Badoglio should intervene to make all of this clear to the other two armed services.[155]

At the start of September intelligence suggested that two enemy fleets, with four battleships and a carrier in the vanguard, were planning to rendezvous at Malta and then steam eastward to Alexandria. With the odds stacked against them (three of Italy's five available battleships would be out-gunned by all four of the British battleships believed to be in the offing), *Supermarina* concluded that the Italian fleet should only consider engaging the enemy 'if the general situation of the war demands it and if the losses likely to result had therefore to be left out of account'.[156] Badoglio agreed. A chance encounter between the two fleets could occur if one tried to stop the other one from carrying out a mission, but seeking deliberately to destroy an element of the enemy's fleet was outside the range of possibilities 'because we are the weaker'. The conception of a naval battle as an end in itself was 'an absurdity'.[157] Mussolini read the reports of the numbers of ships involved in escorting convoys to Libya, the numbers of men (10,472), tanks (111) and motor vehicles (1,898) and the tonnage of goods (117,000 tons) carried in the first three months of the war – and immediately ordered that the escorts be drastically reduced in number and in certain cases abolished altogether. This kind of work was imposing excessive wear on the ships. Also, there was only enough fuel to run the navy for thirteen months. Re-stocking was 'very problematic' and so current reserves had to be made to last twice as long. That meant abolishing escort duties or reducing them to a minimum so that the fleet only used fuel 'for operations of war'.[158] The *Duce*'s naval strategy now directly contradicted Cavagnari's and Badoglio's, both of whom prioritized supporting the land campaign that the army was fighting in Libya.

Chapter 4
Defeat, Disaster, and Success

At 5.30 a.m. on 28 October 1940, Italian troops began crossing the Greek frontier. With that Italy's second major land campaign began. Over the next six months progress in Mussolini's war would be shaped not only by the military capacities of his enemies but also by the circumstances in which men fought. While Graziani assailed Rome with descriptions of the physical difficulties he faced in the desert and lists of the materiel he needed to overcome them, and Cavagnari's sailors saw their position in the central Mediterranean drastically weakened, Visconti Prasca's army advanced into a theatre in which nature and geography multiplied the challenges it faced. Roads were scarce – a single two-lane road connected Durazzo with Tirana and four roadways ran from Albania into Greece – and there were no railways. In the mountains the troops would be heavily dependent on mule-tracks and footpaths. Between them the ports of Durazzo and Valona could land only fifty trucks and 1,250 tons of materials a day. Narrow roads out into the mountains soon clogged up and it took motor columns on average three days to cover the 300 kilometres to the Greek frontier. Things were little better on the Greek side where a single road connected the Epirus, isolated from the rest of Greece by the Pindus mountains, with Albania. The Italians could not have chosen a worse time of year to invade, with the weather threatening what was in any event an over-optimistic timetable. In Albania, as elsewhere, supplying war was about to become as big a challenge for Fascist Italy as fighting it.

GREECE FIGHTS BACK

Expecting little in the way of initial resistance, Visconti Prasca launched three independent attack columns into the Epirus, intending them to join hands 'in front of the enemy' at Kalabaki. They were ordered to 'advance quickly and without worrying about the[ir] flanks'.[1] As soon as the first Italian soldier set foot in Greece things began to go wrong. Foul weather hampered movement and kept the air force on the ground, rivers flooded, and the Greeks predictably blew up the bridges. Units piled up and the few roadways were soon clogged with soldiers trying to get to the front. At the front the Italians found themselves facing strong Greek defensive lines. Greek 105mm guns, cleverly concealed and with longer ranges than the Italian guns, battered their opponents. Air support, when it arrived, was late and limited and the divisional artillery could not keep up even with the slow infantry advance. Five days after the fighting started the Italians began to run into serious opposition. Ciano, momentarily on the spot and aware that things were not going well, began shifting the responsibility for the campaign onto the soldiers, blaming Badoglio for 'a much weaker preparation than we were led to expect'.[2]

As the Italians advanced in the south-west, the Greeks pushed into Albania in the north-west. On 4 November an Albanian battalion broke under a Greek counter-attack and fled, firing on the *Carabinieri* who had been sent to stop them. After that no one trusted the Albanians. Visconti Prasca professed not to find the situation worrying but asked for more troops, trucks and mass air intervention. Then, ten days after it had begun, the Italian advance ground to a halt, stopped by stiff Greek resistance. It was useless to hope that they could reach their objective, Visconti Prasca told Rome, until more divisions had arrived. Mussolini sent General Pricolo across to Albania to assess the situation. The airman came back with bad news. Visconti Prasca, who seemed excessively sure of himself, was obviously way out of his depth.

For the generals in Rome, the rosy dawn in Greece had lasted only a week. On 3 November the chiefs of staff were called together to hear that the enemy was not just putting up serious resistance on the Epirus front but also threatening the left flank of Italian positions in the north. Five divisions were being emplaced to meet it, and Mussolini wanted a landing at Prevesa to get behind the enemy. He gave his legionaries forty-eight hours to carry it out. No one liked the idea. The soldiers thought that a single regiment of 1,300 *Bersaglieri*, which was all they could produce in that time, would be captured within days. Cavagnari was not prepared to send warships into Prevesa harbour, where they could easily be trapped, and did not think landing soldiers on an open beach was a good idea. Admiral Somigli pointed out that the weather was too bad to carry out the operation anyway. This was not what Badoglio needed to hear. The *Duce* demanded a plan, and the chiefs of staff were told to put it in Badoglio's hands in twenty-four hours.[3] The navy duly came up with an outline plan to transport 5,108 men, fifteen tanks, sixteen guns and assorted motorcycles and bicycles in sixteen hours – and reasons why they did not think it a good idea. The landing parties would be forty kilometres from the Italian front at Kalamas and that would mean resupplying them which, given the weather and the probable British reaction, could not be guaranteed.[4]

Mussolini now recognized that defeating Greece would take at least twenty divisions – twenty-five if the Greek islands were also to be occupied. Collecting such a force would take two and a half months, Mario Roatta, now managing the army, told him. The *Duce* was in no hurry. 'It is indispensable for us that the war lasts the whole winter,' he told his soldiers. 'When it comes to making peace we'll have more sacrifices and therefore more rights.'[5] He wanted the offensive resumed along the south-eastern part of the front, and he wanted a replacement for Visconti Prasca. General Soddu asked for the command and got it. On 9 November he took over as commander of the armed forces in Albania. Visconti Prasca, now on the steep slope to ignominy, was given command of 11th Army on the right of the line but kept it for only six days before being replaced by General Carlo Geloso, while General Mario Vercellini kept command of 9th Army on the left. On 30 November Visconti Prasca was put on permanent leave. The day after Soddu took over, the Greeks launched their counter-attack.

The debacle now brewing in Greece gave Graziani more time – but no more equipment. On 1 November, after hearing an encouraging report on the general situation in Albania, the chiefs of staff agreed to abandon the Corfu landing. Everything was now to go to Albania, which meant rerouting the ships transporting men and equipment to North Africa. Badoglio demoted Libya. 'Whether the advance on Mersa Matruh is made in December or in January doesn't matter much,' he told the chiefs. 'For the moment the most urgent and important problem is Greece.' With three times the number of divisions to support compared with the original plan, large amounts of munitions, food stuffs, fuel and much more besides would have to be shipped to a theatre with very limited port facilities. Soddu estimated that the air force could fly in 4,000 men a day. Transporting men was not the problem, Roatta pointed out, but transporting materials was. Sending men over without the means to support them was simply exporting disorder.[6]

On 7 November, as Visconti Prasca was reporting that his offensive in Ciamuria (Chameria), in the western Epirus, had been halted, Badoglio told Graziani what the new strategic line was going to be. The occupation of the whole of Greece would take twenty to twenty-five divisions and almost all the available warships and merchantmen. His task was to take Mersa Matruh with what he had. Requests must be kept to essentials.[7] Next day Mussolini decided to suspend the offensive in Greece for the moment and limit action to halting the Greek advance and accelerating the despatch of reinforcements. Roatta advised Soddu that seven infantry divisions, the *Trieste* motorized division and a *Celere* division were being sent out, and that when all was ready (a process expected to take four months) he was to launch 'an all-out (*totalitaria*) offensive'. In the meantime he should carry out local operations and prepare the ground for the big attack.[8] Badoglio ordered the air force to use all available resources in Albania and Italy in direct support of the troops under attack.[9] General Pricolo objected. His bombers should be used en masse against a small number of vital targets and not split into fragments to engage ground targets, which the troops should see to themselves.[10]

In North Africa, things appeared not to be as bad as they were painted. Taking into account the trucks in Libya and the ones Roatta had en route to him, Graziani had 5,254 vehicles, which was more than he had asked for. Graziani redid the numbers, calculated that he was in fact short, and asked for another 1,100 trucks. He could not do the impossible, he complained, because the means just were not there. His problems went far beyond trucks: among other things he lacked the specialized labour to build roads and aqueducts, and the people loading the ships at Naples were mixing up stuff intended for Tripoli and Cyrenaica.[11]

As yet it was not obvious that German help was going to be needed if Mussolini was to fight two wars simultaneously. The German high command believed that the Greek campaign, which had stalled because of Greek resistance, bad weather and poor organization, could only hope to succeed when reinforcements arrived, but was not prepared itself to attack Greece unless the British first threatened their Romanian oil supplies. It was, though, willing to consider sending German air power to North Africa. Still thinking that Graziani could pull off a victory on his own, and unwilling to weaken his standing with Hitler, Mussolini turned down the offer of a German armoured division.[12]

On 10 November 1940 the *Duce* called his military leaders together to shape the next stages of the war in Greece. He began with a lecture in Hitlerian style on the military realities and the operational steps that must now to be taken. It combined an apparent mastery of military facts with a complete disregard for detail. All had not gone as they had been led to believe it would. Visconti Prasca's calculation about the forces needed had not worked out, and the expected internal revolt had not taken place. General Soddu, who had shown himself from the very first the right man for the situation, would take over the direction of the war in the field. Vercellini's 9th Army would stand on the defensive at Korcia, and 11th Army would resume the offensive 'as the climate, albeit wintry, allows'. Six more divisions must be in place on the Greek front and ready for action by 5 December. Meantime the *Regia Aeronautica* would carry out 'the systematic destruction of Greece's urban centres', razing to the ground every city with more than 10,000 inhabitants. All looked promising because 'the Greek initiative against us is exhausted, or running out'. En route to this optimistic conclusion Mussolini declared that in some conditions lightning war was impossible – a fact he had disregarded only weeks earlier.

Then something happened that no one, least of all Mussolini, could have expected. Taking the floor, Badoglio reminded Mussolini that he had ignored the general staff's considered advice on the force strengths and 'time envelope' that would be needed if the campaign were to be undertaken. 'Therefore neither the armed forces' general staff nor the army general staff is responsible for what has happened,' he told the *Duce*. Mussolini's timetable could not be met. For one thing, the troops would need large amounts of additional artillery if they were going to break into what would be reinforced Greek defences. Badoglio asked for two days during which the army and navy staffs could work out what was logistically possible and therefore feasible. Roatta pointed out that altering the structure of the army to increase the two-regiment *binaria* divisions to three regiments, as Mussolini now wanted, would require another 100,000 men. Since the men who had just been sent home could not be recalled, Mussolini ordered that men from other classes be brought back, adding airily that there would always be some men who wanted to rejoin and fight.[13]

Next day Badoglio made a bid to be put in command in Greece – just as he had done five years before in Abyssinia.[14] Now Mussolini was in no mood to trust him. He would be allowed to go to Innsbruck to meet General Keitel, but Mussolini gave him strict instructions on what to say and what not to say. On no account was he to ask for German aid for Greece. All that Mussolini wanted was German action to prevent Yugoslavia intervening and if possible free passage for materiel, especially trucks, through that country. Ciano was instructed to find out 'what [Badoglio] really tells the Germans' at Innsbruck.[15]

When the two men met on 14 November, Keitel assured Badoglio that the war was won and gave an upbeat summary of the campaign against England, which the Germans thought would suffer a supply crisis in 1941. The Germans wanted the war in Greece localized and would only intervene militarily in the Balkans if the Romanian oil wells were attacked. As for North Africa, it had already been agreed that the Italians could make the next bound forward without German aid. The English, Keitel declared confidently, would never accept a great battle in the desert. Once the Italians had reached Mersa Matruh the Suez Canal would be in range and could be mined. In the third phase of the campaign the Italians would face an enemy whose numbers would have increased. For the moment, though, there was no need to send German tanks to North Africa.[16]

Next morning Badoglio began his response by reminding his hosts that in May 1939 Mussolini had sent Hitler a memorandum stating that Italy would not be ready for war until 1943. With no time to prepare, Italy had joined the war on 10 June 1940 'with the little that we had'. If Italy's actions since then had 'not been very brilliant' that was not due to lack of will. As far as North Africa was concerned Italy could get to Mersa Matruh on her own and so there was no need for a German armoured division. After listening to a good deal of verbiage, Keitel asked when the next bound forward would come. Badoglio hazarded that it might possibly be in December. The situation in Albania was stabilized, reinforcements were coming in, and 'as soon as we are able to do so we shall attack'. It was, he admitted, going to take three

months to get the necessary forces in place. Asked what Italy's 'programme for action' was, he replied that if the situation turned out
favourably she intended to occupy the whole of Greece.[17] Both men
agreed that now they were in the war together there should be no
secrets between them. Neither side had any intention of sticking to that
undertaking.

Keitel said nothing directly about Hitler's order to be prepared to
occupy the Greek mainland, signed three days earlier, but in further
talks that afternoon he raised the issue of the time and strength that
would be needed to occupy Thrace. He told Badoglio that it would take
ten to twelve weeks for the Germans to prepare for action and that
within a month or so they would have to agree details together unless
they had been forced to act earlier. The two men agreed that March or
April would be the best time to move.[18]

If the Italians thought that the conversations had gone reasonably
well they were deceiving themselves. In German eyes the attack on
Greece had been 'stupid' and because of Greece and Taranto (see
below, pp. 154–5) the mood, according to one observer, had been bad.
Unable to dissuade Italy from attacking Greece in the first place, the
Germans were now annoyed that the operation had come to 'a long
and foreseeable halt'. In future, operations there must be 'totalitarian'.
They also wanted assurances that despite being heavily engaged in
Greece the Italians still intended to push on from Mersa Matruh and
take Alexandria and the Suez Canal.[19] One immediate consequence of
the Italians' obvious shortcomings as an ally was that their military
attaché in Berlin, General Marras, lost any claim to special treatment.
Henceforth he was to be treated like any other foreign officer.[20]

Even by his standards Mussolini's speech to the provincial Fascist
party bosses in the Sala Regia of Palazzo Venezia on 18 November was
a masterpiece of lies, obfuscations and misrepresentations. After air-
brushing out of the picture the disaster at Taranto a week earlier with
the claim that the Italian navy had inflicted 'hard blows' on its enemy,
he turned to Greece. The Greeks were 'a subtle enemy' and every one
of them from the top of their society to the bottom hated Italy. Why
they did so was inexplicable, but it was at the root of their complicity
with Great Britain. Documents found at Vitry-la-Charité by the Germans after the fall of France proved that Greece had offered all its
naval and air bases to the British and the French. A stop had had to be

put to that, and so Italy had crossed the Graeco-Albanian frontier on 28 October. Things were not going to be easy, as the rugged Greek terrain did not lend itself to blitzkriegs, but 'no act or word of mine or of the government had forecast [that it would be]'. A lightning war was, of course, exactly what he and his myrmidons had initially taken for granted. However, all would be well. 'We shall break Greece's back. [Whether] in two months or twelve months matters little . . .'[21]

Meeting with Ciano on 18 November, Hitler announced that he proposed to march on Greece and would be ready to do so by mid-March. He advised the Italians to co-ordinate matters so that their advance was simultaneous. He also mentioned sending Stukas to Libya and mining the Suez Canal.[22] Pulling no punches, he told Mussolini that his 'threatening argument with Greece' had had 'very serious' psychological and military consequences. It had created obstacles in Hitler's dealings with Bulgaria, Russia and France, and exposed Germany's Romanian oil supplies and his own southern territory to air attack. Attacking the new British bases in Greece from Albania before the coming March was 'completely useless'. Strategically, the most important military measure now was to block the Mediterranean, which meant getting Spain into the war. Mussolini should concentrate on reaching Mersa Matruh as soon as possible – an attack on the Nile would be impossible before autumn 1941 – and the German and Italian air forces should then combine to attack Alexandria and mine the Suez Canal.[23]

Field Marshal Erhard Milch was despatched to Rome to make sure that the Italians held their ground in Albania, improved their supply lines and tied the Greeks down until the German army could intervene in the spring. The *Luftwaffe* was ordered to get ready to deploy bombers, mine-laying aircraft and long-range fighters to the Mediterranean to bomb Gibraltar, Alexandria and the Suez Canal.[24] Despite frequent protestations of comradeship on both sides, Milch's encounter with his opposite number did not go smoothly. Milch wanted the German air corps to concentrate on interrupting enemy traffic through the Sicilian Channel and attacking Alexandria. Pricolo thought that blocking the Sicilian Channel would have a minimal effect on the flow of enemy supplies and wanted the Germans to concentrate their efforts on the Aegean and the Red Sea. Milch held his ground, as he did too when Pricolo tried to get operational control of the German air corps. The

Italians were told in no uncertain terms that Goering commanded it and if for any reason an attack he ordered was not carried out because of impediments imposed by them then they would have to explain themselves to the *Reichsmarschall*.[25]

On 14 November, while Badoglio was talking with Keitel, the Greeks launched a counter-offensive against Vercellino's 9th Army all along the Korcia front. The Italian line gradually gave way under Greek pressure and after four days the enemy were within smallarms range of the town. Battalions were fed piecemeal into what quickly became individual battles. Amid the confusion, officers and men fought to the best of their ability. On 18 November, Colonel Luigi Zacco of the 84th Infantry regiment was killed in a bayonet counter-attack – one of ten regimental colonels killed during this war leading their men. Vercellino at first tried to stop the inroads but, with irreplaceable senior officers being killed or wounded, structural resilience disintegrating and the increasing likelihood that his army would be split off from its neighbour as the Greeks attacked his right flank, he prepared to retreat. Soddu told Rome he was going to win the defensive battle, or at least create a solid covering line from which to restart operations once his troops had fallen back to it.[26] Then, as Vercellino's men retired, he had no choice but to order a withdrawal. Abandoning much of their material, the troops retreated through deserted Albanian villages. According to Mario Cervi, who fought in the Greek campaign as an infantry officer, a 'wave of apprehension' began to spread through all ranks 'deriving from the feeling that they were inferior to the enemy even numerically'.[27]

Further south, 11th Army was already withdrawing in the face of a Greek drive aimed at Berat and Valona when Geloso arrived to take over command there on 16 November. Soddu wanted the army to hold its ground, but Geloso thought it so weakened that it must disengage and retire some distance to reorganize. The two generals began a brief conflict of their own. Geloso wanted to retreat to a line from Tepeleni to Klisura, but Soddu ordered him to hold an intermediate line protecting Argirokastro and Santa Quaranta. Facing continued Greek attacks, and with no fresh forces of his own to use in counter-attacks, Geloso again put the case for withdrawal to the shorter rearward line. As the month staggered towards its end Geloso tried to persuade Soddu to see things rationally. 'It will be easier to reconquer the position with organic units after a good [i.e. thorough] [re-]organization,' he argued, 'than to try to hold on to them with forces that have been reduced in numbers and tested to the extremes.' Soddu demurred: the military and political repercussions of withdrawing that far would be too great. Geloso must hold the Santa Quaranta–Argirokastro line.[28] While the two generals bickered Geloso's men were slowly forced back, some so exhausted that they did not even have the strength to light fires to keep themselves warm.

The soldiers in the front lines were now paying the price exacted as a consequence of haste, miscalculation and underpreparation. With too few divisions in place from the start there were no reserves with which to mount proper counter-attacks. The Italians had 160 light tanks – the Greeks had none – but these soon came to a halt in the face of skilfully sited Greek defences. Greek divisions, almost half as large again as Italian divisions, had only half as many mortars as an Italian division but more than twice as many machine guns and one and a half times the number of machine-pistols. The Blackshirt divisions were even less well armed, having little more than side-arms and 41mm mortars. Under-equipped for winter warfare in the mountains, Italian troops had no winter clothing and boots that were coming to pieces. On the eve of the Greek offensive, General Gualtiero Gabutti, commanding the *Siena* division, complained that his men did not even have the minimal comforts they had had in the First World War.[29]

Unlike in Abyssinia or in Spain, the *Regia Aeronautica* proved not to be a force multiplier. It allocated 194 bombers and 161 fighters to the campaign at the start and after further reinforcements had arrived lost 124 of them in aerial combat and another 322 to enemy anti-aircraft fire during the course of the war – an indication of Greek effectiveness. Air offensives were only 'sporadic' and, according to their own historian, 'gave no practical advantage'. Snow, high winds and mountains were not the only reasons. The airmen resented having to abandon strategic bombing – for which there were few worthwhile targets – to give the army tactical support. Resupplying units on the ground did not amount to much either: between the beginning of November 1940 and the end of February 1941 the airmen dropped only 200 tons of supplies. Lack of co-ordination contributed to the winter setbacks: according to the airmen observation of artillery fire was rarely requested by the army and equally rarely acted upon.[30]

While the logisticians struggled to get supplies forward along a single road, the commanders grappled with hopelessly inadequate communications systems. The army had only one permanent or semi-permanent telephone line, linking Tirana with Durazzo, and did not get a telephone network in place until the end of February 1941. The *Comando Aeronautica* had only a single phone line linking its headquarters with Tirana airport. Bureaucratic inertia made a difficult situation worse. Requests for air support had first to go to the local air commander in Tirana, who had then to pass on objectives, times and arrangements for fighter support to the 4th Air Wing in Brindisi via an officer flying every day between Brindisi and Tirana. At the front the few radios did not work, because of the weather and the mountains, and field commanders were reduced to using runners. Vercellini, trying to conduct the retreat of 9th Army from Korcia, exploded: 'We have no communications and almost no motor vehicles. Information comes only through couriers. How can you command an army in this manner?'[31]

With Graziani in Libya, Roatta was now effectively responsible for the army as a whole, though without full command authority. The state it was in caused him concern. Albania and North Africa were soaking up almost everything: homeland divisions were being stripped of motor vehicles, guns, engineers and rear services. If it was asked to carry out additional operations on the western front or in Corsica, that would mean remobilizing the entire army. The stores had only a quarter of the clothing they would need, planned munitions targets were not being met due to shortages of raw materials and would be insufficient if the entire army were fighting, tyres and fuel were in short supply, and there was not a single anti-aircraft gun on the mainland. The army could just about support the eighteen divisions allocated to defend the islands, guard the frontier with Yugoslavia, and occupy the armistice line in France. If more were required they could be raised 'with organizational acrobatics', but they would have little unity and not much training.[32] Mussolini's order on 19 November to remobilize the army was no help: gradual remobilization would take until the following spring.

Mussolini shrugged off the reverses. The setback in Greece was due to three factors, all of which he could claim were outside his control: bad weather, the almost total defection of Albanian army units, and

Bulgarian neutrality which had allowed the Greeks to bring eight more divisions to the fight. He had had his 'black week', but the worst was now over. Thirty divisions were being readied to 'annihilate' Greece.[33] Even he could see that the high command whose structure and personnel he carefully manipulated was now in need of repair. Somewhat belatedly, on 29 November he replaced the absent Soddu as undersecretary of state for war and deputy chief of the armed forces general staff with General Alfredo Guzzoni. Next day he began shedding all responsibility for the Greek imbroglio. 'The political side of the question was handled perfectly,' he told the council of ministers. The blame belonged to the military in general and to Badoglio in particular – 'he was the extremist'.[34]

Badoglio's days were numbered. According to Ciano, who hated him, he had told Keitel that he was opposed to the attack on Greece and took no responsibility for it, as it had been carried out against his opinion. Sensing his vulnerability the hyenas of the Fascist Party set about pulling down the now lame *generalissimo*. Alessandro Pavolini told Mussolini that Badoglio had said he, the *Duce*, was no longer fit to command the armed forces and should leave it to the professionals. The Fascist ideologue Roberto Farinacci attacked Badoglio in the pages of *Il Regime fascista* for a lack of foresight over Greece that had provided Winston Churchill with a handy diversion. Demanding an apology, Badoglio resigned on 26 November but took a week's leave to give Mussolini time to think it over. It was time the *Duce* did not need. Three days later the king, who had reservations about Badoglio's character – 'in any circumstances he thinks first of all of himself' – accepted the proposal to replace him with General Ugo Cavallero. Discovering that he was not indispensable, Badoglio rushed back to Rome and offered to withdraw his resignation. Mussolini toyed with him, offering to restore him to his former position if Cavallero preferred commanding in Albania to being chief of the armed forces general staff. For Badoglio, who detested Cavallero, accepting his rival's leftovers was a humiliation too far and on 4 December 1940 he confirmed his resignation. It was accepted immediately.[35]

At 8 a.m. that same day a desperate General Soddu called Badoglio's office and announced that military operations in Albania could not continue, that there could be a complete collapse at any moment and that it was time for a 'diplomatic intervention'. His troops were being forced to give ground metre by metre, 'lack of faith' was everywhere, and though there was no lack of desperate acts of heroic valour there were also cases in which detachments had dissolved 'in unexpected ways'.[36] 'Discouraged as never before', Mussolini told Ciano that they would have to ask for a truce through Hitler. Ciano, himself 'in a state of great alarm and anxiety', at first favoured an armistice but then decided to turn to Germany for help. In Berlin, Dino Alfieri was instructed to ask Hitler to get Yugoslavia into the Tripartite Pact, create a diversion with German troops in Romania or Bulgaria, and provide much-needed transport aircraft and artillery.[37] Only the aircraft were immediately forthcoming.

General Ugo Cavallero was sent to Albania with orders that ground must be held to the last. Arriving there, he told his son 'It's Caporetto all over again, and just like then I've got to put right Badoglio's mistakes.'[38] Four days after he arrived in Albania he replaced Badoglio as chief of the armed forces general staff. Fluent in German, with a degree in mathematics and a top student of the War School in Turin, Cavallero was essentially an 'office general'. A peacetime career with Ansaldo had ended ignominiously when the company was found to have been supplying the navy with steel plate not armour plate, earning him the nickname 'the profiteer general'. For two years (1937–9) he had commanded in Italian East Africa, making no impact on the rebellion that simmered there. The governor, Prince Amedeo d'Aosta, who sacked him, thought him a self-serving liar. However, he had at least one thing now in his favour: Badoglio detested him, and he detested Badoglio.

CONTEST AT SEA

At the start of October, after another abortive foray by the fleet during which it had been ordered not to move far beyond the Italian coast, Admiral Cavagnari went to the main naval base at Taranto to explain the general situation, the directives given by the *Comando Supremo* and the inadequacies of aerial reconnaissance. He wound up by telling the battleship commanders that permanent indirect protection of the communications with Libya 'is only possible because of the very existence of our principal naval forces, whose potential for action is in itself a brake on enemy initiative'.[39] It was the classic argument for a 'fleet in being', and it did not go down well with his listeners.

Admiral Angelo Iachino, commanding the 2nd battle squadron, believed that morale in the Italian battle-fleet, originally high, was falling and being replaced by a feeling of disappointment and perplexity. The impression in the fleet was that any offensive action beyond certain very restrictive limits was not to be undertaken whatever the strength of the enemy forces at sea. Both he and the battle-fleet commander, Admiral Inigo Campioni, thought that the British fleet at Gibraltar, whose duties were primarily in the Atlantic, should not be conflated with the fleet at Alexandria. The latter had never put more than four battleships to sea and more usually two or three. Italy, with five battleships and more cruisers, could not be considered inferior. The fact that Italy could not replace lost battleships while her enemy could do so 'should not be blown up to the point that we lose favourable occasions and prevent us from seeking certain success when we find ourselves in conditions of temporary and local superiority'. The speed advantage of the two *Littorio*-class battleships meant that they could chase enemy battleships faster than they could run away, open fire at a greater distance and were less vulnerable if caught by surprise. The battleship commanders were confident of success if and when the balance of forces was in their favour.[40] Cavagnari told Iachino that he had not read the directives properly, that the concept of using Italian ships only in a decisive encounter in conditions of superiority was nothing new and that, if there was a sense of unease deriving from 'an understandable lack of understanding of the situation as it actually is', then it was Iachino's job to put it right.[41]

The navy was already having difficulties carrying out its submarine war in the Mediterranean. By the end of October, forty-seven submarines had carried out fifty-five missions, attacking four enemy warships and eight enemy steamers. In fifty-two of those missions the submarines had been hunted by British aircraft or surface ships, in some cases for as many as five days. The meagre results, the submarine commander admitted, were out of proportion to the number of boats used. The problem, as the submariners saw it, was that unless they operated in waters where the Italians had naval and air control the possibilities of action were virtually nil thanks to the enemy's superior detection equipment and techniques. Things had to change. Cavagnari's response was to cut down the number of submarines used in the coming winter and to recommend that the boats stay deeply submerged during daylight hours and attack only at night and on the surface.[42]

On 11 November the battle-fleet was ordered to be ready to put to sea to bombard Suda Bay and Chania on the island of Crete. Shortly after nine that evening the alarms signalling an air attack sounded at the Taranto naval base. It was the second alarm of the evening. The first had been false but this one was not. Between 11 p.m. and midnight twenty-one Fairey Swordfish torpedo bombers launched in two successive waves from the carrier *Illustrious* struck the Italian battleships. The *Littorio* was hit by three torpedoes, the *Cavour* and the *Duilio* were each hit once, and the heavy cruiser *Trento* was struck by a 30-kilo bomb which went through two decks without exploding. The anti-aircraft guns claimed six aircraft shot down, though in fact only two Swordfish were lost in the action; afterwards it was said that the gunners' fire had been 'fairly well' directed but they had not been able to stop the attackers in time because of their 'great determination' and because of the manner in which they had attacked from close range.

The British success owed a little to chance, but rather more to the gallantry of the attackers – which the Italians acknowledged – and to the woeful shortcomings in the Italian defences. The searchlights, under a separate Territorial Anti-Aircraft Command, were never switched on, the aerial torpedoes were set to run just 60 centimetres below the 10-metre-deep anti-torpedo nets, and only a third of the 12,800 metres of nets were actually in place, thanks partly to the fact that the planned monthly output of 3,600 metres was only reached two months earlier and partly to the need to distribute what netting was available to a number of bases.[43] Admiral Campioni pointed out that his ships could only defend themselves at night if attacking aircraft had already been lit up by searchlights, and listed the multiple shortcomings in organization, co-ordination, communications and operational practice that had led to the debacle. Cavagnari's response was to list the eight directives and five official publications that covered all of Campioni's points. Ample regulations already existed, augmented by supplementary despatches, which left no doubt as to the great importance that the central authorities attached to the anti-aircraft defence of bases and ships.[44] The fact that they had not worked seemed not to trouble Cavagnari.

Taranto convinced the German navy that any possibility the Italians might achieve mastery of the Mediterranean had disappeared and with it any chance of a successful Italian offensive in Egypt. The material losses were one thing, the apparent lack of an Italian will for success was another. The Italian attack on Greece had been a grave strategic error which could have a detrimental effect on events in the eastern Mediterranean and Africa 'and therefore on the whole future of the war'. The German navy wanted economic control of the entire European-African bloc and the raw materials it could supply, including cotton, copper and petrol. To get it the Royal Navy had to be chased out of the Mediterranean. The Italian armed forces were neither efficient enough nor well enough commanded to bring the necessary operations in the Mediterranean to a speedy and successful conclusion. In future no substantial help or support from them should be expected. The whole of the Greek peninsula must be cleared of the enemy, preferably by a German offensive, Mersa Matruh occupied and the enemy chased out of the Mediterranean. The immediate next steps should be German and Italian air attacks on Alexandria to weaken the British fleet, for which the Italian air element currently bombing Great Britain should be withdrawn and put to use in North Africa.[45]

On 26 November, having picked up both that the British were attempting to run a convoy through the Mediterranean from Gibraltar and that Admiral Cunningham's battleships and carriers were out, *Supermarina* ordered Campioni to put to sea with two of the three remaining Italian battleships and supporting cruisers and destroyers. The remains of the Italian battle fleet had sortied some ten days earlier and stymied an attempt to deliver Hurricanes to Malta. Now two battleships (*Vittorio Veneto* and *Giulio Cesare*), six heavy cruisers and fourteen destroyers put to sea with orders to join battle if the situation was favourable.[46] On the morning of 27 November aerial sightings picked up the force coming from Gibraltar and Campioni turned to meet it, hoping to engage a force that he calculated was inferior to his own in waters close to Sicily, which would give him air cover. He knew that there was an unidentified group of six enemy ships at sea to the east closing on the fleet coming from Gibraltar and at midday he learned that it was closing fast on his force, as were British units coming from the west. This was in fact a group of four destroyers and three cruisers escorting the slow battleship *Ramillies* west from Alexandria to Malta. Aware that he could not now prevent the junction of the two forces, that the aircraft carrier *Ark Royal* was part of the force coming from Gibraltar, and that it and the enemy battleships could between them create 'an extremely serious situation', Campioni turned for home, disinclined on the basis of past experience to put much hope in an effective intervention by the *Regia Aeronautica*.[47]

While the Italian battleships headed for their Sardinian bases at a speed of 23 knots, the Italian and British cruisers got into a running fight. Both sides' ships came in and out of range as speeds were high – the Italian cruiser *Pola* reached a speed of 34 knots – and at about 1 p.m. as the British cruisers pursued the Italians they came within range of the *Vittorio Veneto*'s guns. After ten minutes under fire the British cruisers turned away. Campioni's fleet made its home ports next day, while Admiral Somerville shepherded his convoy safely to Malta, surviving two attacks by the *Regia Aeronautica* unscathed.

Despite the fact that the enemy convoy had got through to Malta, Cavagnari professed himself pleased at how the battle of Capo Teulada (Cape Spartivento to the British) had gone. Two British cruisers had been hit, the intervention of the Italian battleships had caused the enemy forces to withdraw, and the enemy's planes had done little damage thanks to skilful manoeuvring. It all went to demonstrate 'the high grade of efficiency of our ships'.[48] On a broader level, though, his strategy of controlling the Sicilian Channel, preventing enemy naval transit through it and seeking to hold down the enemy's centre of gravity was failing – as he recognized. The gradual entry into service of the two *Littorio*s and the *Duilio* had been counterbalanced by the arrival of a British battleship, an aircraft carrier and a number of escorts at Alexandria. The navy was losing reconnaissance aircraft to the British carrier-borne fighters, blinding it and reducing its offensive capacity and thereby allowing the enemy freedom to hunt down its submarines. The need to escort convoys to North Africa had further reduced its ability to control the central Mediterranean. The British were gradually realizing their aims – to gain more freedom of transit through the Sicilian Channel and cut mainland Italy off from North Africa – and this posed the gravest threat to the general conduct of the war. Cavagnari could only suggest that the three services jointly examine the situation, 'taking into account the methods and means to reduce, if not to eliminate, the concentric enemy pressure from east and west and give breathing space to our activity in the central Mediterranean'. Germany might be asked to help diminish the growing British naval and air pressure in the Mediterranean.[49]

Mussolini was far from pleased. The setback, for so he regarded it, at Taranto would take a couple of months to remedy, and Capo Teulada was at best a relative success and not what would have been expected. 'Fortune isn't found by staying at home. You have to go out and meet it,' he told Giuseppe Bottai.[50] On 7 December he fired Cavagnari, replacing him with Admiral Arturo Riccardi. Five days later, in a reshuffle at the top of the navy, Campioni became deputy chief of the naval staff and his subordinate in the recent sea battle, Admiral Angelo Iachino, succeeded him as commander-in-chief of the battle-fleet. Iachino was certainly politically acceptable: in 1938 he had supported Mussolini in print, backing the *Duce*'s view that the navy did not need carriers because Italy itself was a natural aircraft carrier.[51]

On the eve of Cavagnari's departure the naval staff pointed out that their ships were running on very limited reserves, which were limiting the fleet's actions. The enemy's naval forces at either end of the Mediterranean were superior to theirs. With no coastal objectives and no lines of communication to attack, the Italian surface fleet had sortied whenever the enemy fleet was known to be at sea but had never had the chance to make 'favourable contact'. Now it was up to 'the supreme Authorities' to decide whether the principal strategic objective was England and her naval power, in which case the western Mediterranean must be unblocked by allied action against Gibraltar so that the Italian navy could make a major contribution to the maritime war in the Atlantic, or rather the British Empire and its world power, which would require the Axis to reach the Red Sea and the Indian Ocean by way of the Balkans and Asia Minor on the one hand and Egypt on the other. While the powers that be made up their minds, the navy would go on co-operating with the army in the Mediterranean and with Germany by fixing a strong proportion of the Royal Navy in the Mediterranean and contributing to the submarine war in the Atlantic. For Riccardi, as for Cavagnari, the navy's essential task remained protecting the lines of communication to Albania and Libya, though it did begin to contemplate basing long-range submarines at Kisimaio on the Indian Ocean in mid-1941 and employing auxiliary cruisers there and outside the Straits of Gibraltar.[52] The dream of action in the Indian

Ocean would come briefly to life after the Japanese joined the war at the end of 1941.

Riccardi and Campioni had little room, if any, to develop a new strategy. With the Royal Navy now superior to their fleet in both the eastern and western Mediterranean basins, one of the planners' basic assumptions – that the Italian navy would be able to confront one or the other of the two fractions with superior forces – had gone overboard. Short winter days made it even more difficult to check on the movement of the enemy's fleet. Destroyers which were supposed to help guard the main battle-fleet were being pulled away to protect the transports crossing to Libya, and aircraft which the navy had expected to use to cover the fleet were being allocated to land theatres. Neither submarines nor aircraft could make much impact on the enemy's coastal traffic between Alexandria and Sollum. If the Italian navy had any hope of turning things around, the naval staff argued, it needed more air reconnaissance across the whole of the Mediterranean. As for winning control of the Sicilian Channel and the central Mediterranean, that depended very much on the German aircraft that were now arriving in Sicily. If their action, and sorties by the main Italian battle-fleet, could gradually reduce the size of the enemy's fleet then that could create the conditions in which the Italian battle-fleet could commit itself with a good chance of success. That in turn depended on developing and using better reconnaissance aircraft that could not be shot down by carrier-borne fighters – 'a purely aeronautical problem but [one] of vital interest to the navy'.[53]

The battle of Capo Teulada showed how much the Italian navy suffered from inadequate air power. As 1940 approached its end, battle was once more joined between the navy and the air force. Admiral Riccardi entered the lists, pointing out that the air command in Sardinia had failed to respond to two requests from the *Vittorio Veneto* for air cover because they supposed that the positions given were those of the Italian ships not the enemy ones. When two battle-fleets were engaged they were necessarily going to be close to one another, Riccardi pointed out. In any case, recognizing enemy ships in conditions of perfect visibility ought not to be too difficult. A somewhat weary-sounding Guzzoni pointed out that there was simply not enough air power completely to meet all needs. Air reconnaissance had to be based on the actual availability of aircraft and production capacity, and take into account the wear and tear on aircraft and the losses suffered. The two services should consult with one another and marry up what the *Regia Aeronautica* could do with what the *Regia Marina* wanted. The *Regia Aeronautica* hit back. The Sardinian air command had not been given warning of the likelihood and then the actuality of the battle-ships' engagement, but it had sent off bombers before the navy had asked for them. If the navy sent their requests for air support at the start of naval actions, the aircraft were unlikely to get there in time unless the fight lasted for some while. The Sardinian airmen had acted properly – what was needed in future was more, better and more timely information from the fleet.[54]

GRAZIANI LOSES AN ARMY

Graziani had been immobile for months and showed no immediate signs of moving. In mid-November, reinforced by SIM calculations which consistently overestimated the number of enemy troops facing him, he told Rome that if he was going to overcome the defences at Mersa Matruh he needed more guns to unleash 'an imposing mass of fire', an armoured brigade and at least one motorized division. To move, he needed trucks, caterpillar tractors, which appeared to be stuck on the quaysides in Naples, spare parts, repair shops and many more pipes for the aqueducts. Mixing somewhat histrionic pleading with vague threats, Graziani told Badoglio that if he found himself in the 'tragic position' of having with superhuman effort produced roads and water but then had to wait on the rest, he could certainly not be held responsible for the consequences.[55]

The Germans were not impressed by Graziani. The chief of staff of *Luftflotte V* reported that while earlier in the campaign he had been out and about with his troops he now never left his shelter in Cyrene for fear of British aircraft. He was 'a colonial war man' who up to now had only had to do with poorly armed peoples. Now that he was fighting a war that involved planes, trucks and all sorts of technical means, he was out of his depth. Nor was the Italian army what it had been in the earlier world war. Its morale was much weaker and it demanded constant assistance from the air force 'even when it could get along perfectly well with its own means'.[56]

At the start of October SIM believed that there were 200,000 Allied troops in theatre; in November it put the enemy's numbers at 250,000; and at the end of December they had climbed to 300,000 men organized in fifteen divisions – roughly twice the actual number. These estimates encouraged Graziani to keep asking Rome for more. From the end of October SIM began to warn him that the enemy was possibly preparing new offensive plans, that increasing numbers of men and weapons were being brought up and that they were being located in positions that were dangerous for the Italians. Ruled by the belief that the enemy would wait indefinitely on Italian initiative, and functioning more or less independently from Rome, Graziani's own intelligence section was disinclined to believe SIM. 'We have the sensation,' his office telegraphed on 28 October, 'that the enemy fears our offensive action and feels itself under pressure from us.'[57] A final warning on 6 December forecast that an enemy offensive was imminent. Graziani's chief of staff, General Giuseppe Tellera, took the SIM estimate to be accurate and expected the worst. 'Then what had to happen happened,' he wrote afterwards.[58]

On 9 December 1940 General Sir Richard O'Connor launched his attack on Graziani (Operation COMPASS). To meet it Graziani had 234,182 men, 2,301 guns, 417 tanks and 7,044 trucks in working order.[59] The three-day battle of Sidi-el-Barani (9–11 December) quickly overwhelmed the forward Italian defences. The troops were powerless against the Matilda II tanks, and with no shield to protect them the gunners manning the 47mm anti-tank guns died in droves. Bombing enemy tanks had little effect. The air force lost twenty-six of its ninety-seven efficient bombers in the first three days, and the odds against its 111 fighters became irreversible when the first Hurricanes appeared in the skies on 13 December. The British netted 38,000 Italian prisoners of war, 237 guns, 73 light and medium tanks and more than 1,000 motor vehicles.[60]

The day after the battle began Hitler ordered aircraft to southern Italy for a limited but unspecified period to join in attacking the Royal Navy at Alexandria and enemy traffic on the Suez Canal. There seemed little else that Germany would or could do immediately. The signals coming from Berlin were that she could not intervene in strength in the Mediterranean during the winter and that the fight would have to be carried on by Italy alone. General Jodl, who was evidently getting too much information about Albania for Italian tastes, lectured the Italian military attaché General Marras: the Italians had plenty of infantry and enough heavy artillery both in Albania and in North Africa and they should learn how to improvise.[61] That same day Hitler issued Directive 19 for Operation MARITA, to begin 'probably in March'.

As the remainder of 10th Army began retreating towards Solfaya and Sollum, Graziani announced that he was retiring to Tripoli to keep the Italian flag flying until the *madrepatria* gave him enough resources to continue operations. Everyone had done their best in the face of Rome's continued failure to give him what he needed, leaving his troops fighting 'the war of the flea against the elephant'. Mussolini fired off an immediate response. There were men and guns enough between Bardia and Tobruk to smash the enemy attack. They, and if necessary Benghazi too, were to be defended 'to the last'.[62] Graziani's response was entirely in character. Claiming the right to speak to Mussolini 'man to man', he accused the *Duce* of not listening to him. Others had deceived him and still were. Only he, Graziani, had the courage not to do so. Had Mussolini forgotten that Graziani had served him faithfully for twenty years? Had he forgotten that the victory in Ethiopia was solely the result of allowing Graziani to speak out? He had done his best with what he had been given. Now only Destiny would decide the outcome. Mussolini received the tirade calmly – 'Here is another man with whom I cannot get angry, because I despise him,' he told Ciano. Guzzoni ordered all trace of the telegram to be destroyed.[63] For the moment Graziani kept his command – perhaps because having just sacked one marshal Mussolini thought it better not to sack another just now or perhaps because there was at that moment no obvious successor to hand.

Badoglio's departure and the crises developing in Albania and Cyrenaica created an opening for the soldiers who believed that Italy could only win her war if she was more closely bound up with Germany. Mario Roatta was first into the lists, producing a comprehensive strategic survey of the kind that had been so wanting in the past. England was 'enemy Number 1' and the key to winning the war against her was not subduing the home islands, which the Germans might or might not manage to do, but defeating her at the 'hinge' of her empire in the Mediterranean. Italy could not break that hinge alone. What was needed now was not simply German help but common action en bloc.

Within that theatre the most important sectors were the Balkans, where German assistance would be essential if the British reinforced the Greeks, and North Africa, where Italy needed tanks that were the equal of the British and lots of anti-tank guns 'which – for now – we do not possess'. Third on Roatta's list of geographical priorities was a joint occupation of Vichy France, a power which could very well 'play a double game'. For all this to work, what was essential was a 'close, clear and on-going political understanding' with Germany, 'virtually a single direction' to co-ordinate both sides' strategic operations, and a pooling of materiel in common, 'it being inadmissible that one side fights with inadequate means while the other gives modern arms to third parties who are not all trustworthy'.[64]

A week after taking office, Cavallero set out his own assessment of the strategic situation. Remobilizing the army's seventy-three divisions, ordered by Mussolini some three weeks earlier, presented no problems as regarding manpower but there were serious difficulties as far as weapons, vehicles and horses were concerned. With German help the programme ought to be complete by April 1941. Even so, Cavallero was thirteen divisions short of the number needed to meet all the strategic requirements. New divisions could not be raised so there had to be cutbacks in the garrisons on the eastern and western frontiers, and any idea of occupying both Corsica and France up to the Rhône must be abandoned. The idea of a war of *rapido corso* must be abandoned too and the country must gear itself up for a war that would be hard and very likely long. The navy had temporarily lost three of its six battleships, one of twenty-two cruisers, nine of fifty-nine destroyers, five of sixty-nine torpedo boats and seventeen of 115 submarines. The calls on it were great, but all that Cavallero could suggest was recalling the Italian submarines from the Atlantic. Gross statistics suggested that the air force was in good shape: it had lost 297 planes since 10 June but had produced 1,204. However, when account was taken of accidents, wear and tear and aircraft under repair, the picture looked rather different. Not much more than a quarter of its tabled bomber strength (478 planes) and a third of its fighter strength (573 planes), its ground reconnaissance aircraft (226 planes) and its sea reconnaissance aircraft (125 planes) were fit for combat. Stocks of munitions were declining rapidly – in North Africa small and medium rounds had fallen from 708,387 tons at the start of June to 7,237 tons – and so were fuel stocks.

Cavallero had no remedies to suggest – but implicitly he was pointing to the importance of a German bailout.

Cavallero's suggestions for tackling a situation of 'extreme gravity' were as much political as operational. Like Roatta, he believed that there should be 'a complete understanding with Germany', concerting a common military and political action and leading to a single unified command. Secondly, there should be political action on Spain, Bulgaria, Yugoslavia and the Soviet Union to ease the pressure in Greece and open the way to operations in the western Mediterranean. Thirdly, there should be 'decisive and sweeping action' against Gibraltar (which meant prior accords with Spain), Greece and Egypt. Mussolini might know of other and better solutions, but what was beyond doubt was the need to act 'in perfect understanding with our allies' and not to lose any time in doing so.[65] Cavallero put the argument for 'absolute unity of command and effort' in the Mediterranean theatre to the German military representative Enno von Rintelen, and asked whether the Germans could provide an armoured division. In return, he was told that Hitler wanted to bring the German armed forces to their maximum potential, that even the French were working on German armaments, and that the Führer preferred to put Italian industry in a position to produce its own war materiel rather than give Italy finished goods.[66]

The situation was every bit as bad as Cavallero painted it – and statistical data piled up on Mussolini's desk to prove it. Although the numbers never seemed quite to match and sometimes oscillated quite dramatically – estimates of fuel supplies from Romania rose from 12,500 tons a month in mid-December to 30,000 tons a month sixteen days later – the overall situation was clear enough. Fuel stocks were steadily draining away, and by the end of December the army had only two months' supply left. The navy, itself running short of stocks, could spare no fuel at all for military transports.[67] Munitions production was 'notably inferior to consumption', due chiefly to a shortage of all metals except aluminium – the army was getting only 20 per cent of the 3,500 tons of copper it needed each month. Some of the forecasts were optimistic. One of the documents that went to Mussolini that month suggested that by working two ten-hour shifts a day the armaments factories could increase output from 70,000 to 110,000 rifles and from 26 to 255 artillery pieces a day by April 1941. Another, less comforting, forecast that production of the new M 13 tank would rise from sixty a

month in January 1941 to 100 a month in August.[68] Cavallero's gener-
alizations about the army veiled a situation in which only eight of the
forty-two divisions in metropolitan Italy were fully equipped.[69]

Guzzoni put the case for closer collaboration to Mussolini more or
less exactly as Roatta had made it to him the previous day. Mussolini
scrawled *esatto* ('exactly') on it. That was as far as he was prepared to
go. Guzzoni tried to persuade him to meet Hitler and hammer out an
agreed plan of operations, but the *Duce* was absolutely unwilling to
play the part of the poor relation.[70] Then he had an abrupt change of
mood. Three days later, a meeting in which Mussolini, Cavallero and
Soddu took part concluded that there was nothing left to do 'but put
everything in the hands of the Führer because we can do no more'.[71]
Having just rejected any idea of a full strategic partnership, the *Duce*
would now go cap in hand to Berlin for the wherewithal to fight the
wars he had started. On 20 December, Guzzoni met with von Rintelen
and asked, given the situation in Albania and Libya, for 'immediate
German intervention that would relieve us'.[72]

To stem the tide in Cyrenaica and prevent the British joining up with
French North Africa, about whose supposedly neutral status the Italians were always nervous, Cavallero asked for a German armoured
corps. Guzzoni told von Rintelen that the armoured division offered in
September would now be gratefully received – and two would be even
better. He also wanted enough gun batteries, munitions and instructors
to fit out ten Italian divisions. His need for 'immediate German intervention to ease our position in Libya and Albania' added up to 7,800
trucks (800 of which were needed 'at once'), 140 batteries of artillery
(560 guns) and 20 batteries of self-propelled guns, 1,600 37mm anti-
aircraft guns, 900 88mm anti-aircraft guns, 800 medium tanks and
300 armoured cars.[73] Ciano's list of Italy's main industrial needs
included 1,100,000 tons of coal a month, 100,000 tons of fuel and
mineral oils, and 70,000 tons of steel products.[74]

Mussolini's ally was about to prove much less bountiful than the
Italians hoped. General Keitel, who had received Hitler's Directive #21
for Operation BARBAROSSA and knew that preparations for the
attack on Russia had to be concluded by 15 May, made optimistic
noises about Italy's powers of resistance in Cyrenaica and poured cold
water on the idea of a German armoured corps coming to Graziani's
aid. The unit scheduled for the task had been dissolved after Mussolini

had rejected it on 9 November; existing units were either indispensable or were in the course of transformation to create new ones; a fresh corps could not be ready before March, by which time it would be getting too hot for German troops to operate in North Africa; and in any case armoured forces were not good for defensive work and not well suited to sandy terrains. The most that could be got out of him was an undertaking to increase German strength in Romania to ease Greek pressure, and an agreement to look again at the whole question.[75] Showing signs of desperation, Guzzoni ordered Marras to insist on increased German pressure in Thrace, and if not two armoured divisions in Libya then one, 'which will be used offensively in line with their characteristics'.[76]

Believing that the OKW had no idea of the efforts Italy was making to sustain the war, Roatta tried to get the discussions onto a proper footing. The question of material aid should be set in a broad strategic context in which both sides discussed how they were going to emerge victorious from the conflict, which theatres were important and in what order, and how the Germans could best contribute to operations in the Mediterranean.[77] With a master who was Hitler's ally but not his equal either in power or in status, this sensible idea was doomed to failure. Instead, a technical mission headed by General Favagrossa arrived in Berlin to be told by Keitel that the Germans had only enough raw materials to replace their own losses and equip new units, and that the Italians were going have to accept captured enemy weaponry. Jodl talked of a 'crisis of faith' between Italy and Germany in the past, and at one point asked whether the Italians were thinking of some other operations that they were keeping secret? No, was the indignant reply. More promisingly, he confirmed that German operations against Greece were scheduled to begin in the first fortnight of March, but warned that Albania must at all costs not be lost. In the interim the OKW was ready to offer a German mountain division. As far as Libya was concerned the Germans were now minded to think that an armoured corps of at least 250 tanks was going to be essential. The first detachments could be in Naples three weeks after a decision was made – and prolonged Italian resistance at Bardia could have a big influence in getting them.[78]

Words were one thing, weapons were quite another. General Georg Thomas, head of the Wehrmacht armaments office, was prepared to hand over twenty-one batteries of 88mm guns, ten batteries of 149mm howitzers with 120,000 rounds of ammunition, 100 37mm anti-tank guns with 100,000 rounds of ammunition, and 150 trucks. As far as German equipment went, that was all. There would be no self-propelled guns, no 149mm guns (the Italians were offered forty-eight French 155mm guns dating from 1917), no 47mm anti-tank guns (Belgian ones were offered instead), no German tanks (the Italians were offered 100 French medium and heavy tanks and 350 light Renault 35s), no armoured cars and no radio stations.[79]

As 1940 came to its end the services produced data on Italy's fighting capacity. Officially the navy had three of its six battleships and fourteen of its twenty cruisers fit for action, along with thirty-four out of thirty-eight destroyers and twenty-six out of fifty-three submarines. Actually only nine of its cruisers and thirty of its destroyers were in active service. Behind the statistics lay a dispiriting reality: thanks to a lack of raw materials, the navy was unable to replace its losses. Work on the battleship *Impero*, launched in November 1939, was suspended and never completed, and in December 1940 the *Capitani Romani* class of light cruisers were dismantled to build submarines and torpedo boats.[80] In metropolitan Italy 268 of the air force's 372 fighters were 'efficient' and 246 of 412 bombers. Overseas 177 fighters and 214 bombers were capable of action out of totals of 319 and 348 respectively. In North Africa, Graziani had sixty-five fighters fit for action (just over a third of his total of 165) and eighty-four bombers (out of 137).[81] Another set of figures – in Fascist Italy there was always more than one version of the numbers – suggested that in the Mediterranean theatre as a whole (Sardinia, Sicily and the Aegean), the air force could put 101 bombers, eighty-three fighters and forty-four naval reconnaissance planes into the air.[82] Mussolini was keen for German assistance. As well as accepting the offer of a German Alpine division for use in Albania, and a German armoured division in Libya, he now wanted the Germans to accelerate their attack on Greece.[83] Hitler, it seemed, was not going to be of much immediate help. German units were being moved by rail into Romania, but as far as future operations were concerned the Führer could for the time being tell his partner nothing – leaving Jodl's earlier confirmation that the Germans would attack Greece in March without Hitler's official imprimatur. What was immediately needed was the stabilization of the Albanian front so that at least the bulk of the Greek army and the Greco-British forces were committed there. As for North Africa, Hitler advised that there could be no major counter-attack there for three or four months, by which time the hot season would rule out any long-range action by German armoured units. In the immediate future, Mussolini should strip his other forces of anti-tank guns, and air power should weaken the British naval position and therefore prevent any improvement to the enemy's front-line situation.[84]

As the British and Commonwealth forces crossed the Italian frontier and advanced on Bardia, General Bergonzoli pulled back from Halfaya Pass and Capuzzo. In the Italian command fractiousness turned to friction. In July, Graziani had told Rome that both Bardia and Tobruk were in a state of 'full efficiency'. General Berti, commanding 10th Army, who was suffering from stomach and liver problems, returned from leave on 14 December and immediately gave Graziani a list of all Tobruk's defects. It needed more guns, a regiment of motorized infantry and at least two well-equipped and lorry-borne divisions as a mobile defence. Graziani reminded him that as commander in Cyrenaica he was partly responsible for the shortcomings. Berti professed loyalty and then suggested concentrating on Tobruk rather than deploying forces in depth to try to halt the enemy advance on successive lines of defence which could be easily outflanked. An awkward subordinate who, according to his successor, contested everything with Graziani, Berti had reached the end of his time.[85] Graziani sacked him and then adopted exactly the course he had advised against.

In the circumstances the loss of Bardia was inevitable – as von Rintelen had forecast a month earlier. Bergonzoli had a thirty-kilometre perimeter to defend with almost no anti-tank guns. Work on fortifications had stopped six weeks after the war began and only recommenced at the last minute. There was no time to build anti-tank obstacles so all that the garrison could do was sow what mines there were, clear an anti-tank ditch that had filled with sand, and repair the barbed-wire entanglements. When the battle began on 3 January 1941 the Italians were overwhelmed in the air and bombarded from the sea by three British battleships and seven destroyers. The defenders fought valiantly with what they had, believing thanks to SIM that they were under attack by two armoured divisions, three or four infantry divisions, 700 aircraft and the entire Mediterranean Fleet. Strongpoints fell rapidly to the Australians and by 1 p.m. on 5 January it was all over. The 10th Army lost 45,000 men, 430 guns, 13 medium and 177 light tanks and hundreds of trucks.[86] As the battle was raging, Guzzoni warned Mussolini that the disparity of force was such that he was going to lose Italian East Africa.[87]

The fall of Bardia prompted the Germans to ask how the Italians now saw the strategic situation on land, at sea and in the air. The navy and the air force were pessimistic. To them the abandonment of Tobruk would change the strategic situation in the Mediterranean to Italy's detriment.[88] In fact, what had been intended as a drive to push the British out of Egypt was now turning into the defence of a vulnerable colony. Guzzoni put the best slant on things that he could. Grossly overestimating the size of the British forces opposing Graziani in line with SIM estimates, he told the Germans that he believed the British advance into Cyrenaica could be slowed but would be difficult to stop. However, if the enemy did get to Benghazi they would have 600 kilometres of desert in front of them and another 650 kilometres behind them between Tobruk and Benghazi. There would have to be a long pause 'due to the nature of the terrain and the enormous logistical difficulties to be overcome'. The *Ariete* armoured division, which had only light tanks, was on its way to North Africa and the *Trento* motorized division could be there by the end of the third week in February. Overall, the situation on land was 'serious' but there was nevertheless both 'the will to confront it and the hope to overcome it'. Although Italy was clearly inferior at sea and would have to submit to British naval initiative, Italian and German air power could make things difficult for the enemy. Traffic across the Sicilian Strait would still be possible 'with some caution and limitation'. Things would take a turn for the better when the two damaged Italian battleships came back into service, and if Gibraltar could be seized that would at once turn the situation on its head. Viewed overall, Guzzoni told the Germans, the situation was 'serious but not desperate'.[89]

As Bardia fell, Graziani warned Mussolini there was little hope that Tobruk could hold out either. He planned to set up a defence line between Derna and Mechili but with only 20,000 men, 350 guns and sixty tanks facing what he described as 'an avalanche of steel', and eighty aircraft flying against what SIM estimated to be at least 1,100 enemy planes, there was not much to hope for. Tripoli was 'the final redoubt' because between it and Benghazi there were no further defences. The only thing that would change the fateful equation would be four or five fresh divisions with mobile artillery and tanks with which 'at the opportune moment' Graziani could perhaps get moving again and throw the enemy back across the frontier.[90] Mussolini ordered him to hold out at Tobruk for as long as possible, and his council of ministers voted an Order of the Day saluting the heroic troops of all arms. Standing on 'the brink of ruin', what the armed forces needed was not words of comfort and praise but 'an energetic surgical intervention', Badoglio's former deputy General Armellini noted gloomily in his diary.[91]

Hitler was now prepared to come to the rescue of his ally. Albania must not be allowed to fall, and he was ready to send a mountain division, a motorized division and part of a *Panzer* division there to buttress the Italians. Fearing 'the very detrimental psychological effect' that the loss of North Africa would have on the Italian people', he was also ready to send tanks, anti-tank and anti-aircraft units to defend Tripolitania, but limited port facilities meant they could not arrive until mid-February.[92] On 11 January, Hitler authorized the creation of a *Sperrverband* and three days later the plans were ready to embark a light motorized division from Naples on 15 February. Hitler asked whether Italy wanted Stukas, assault bombers and heavy fighters from the X *Fliegerkorps*, and General Marras was 'tactfully advised' that the German offers of help in Albania and North Africa should not be declined in favour of requests later renewed under even more demanding circumstances.[93]

The 5,307 men and 307 aircraft of X *Fliegerkorps* had arrived in Sicily and Reggio Calabria in mid-December 1940, initially to help out the Italian navy. Their commander, Lieutenant-General Hans Geisler, a specialist in anti-shipping warfare and a man the Italians found easy to get on with, had settled into the Hotel San Domenico at Taormina. The Italians and the Germans disagreed over command of the air expeditionary corps – Goering wanted to retain it – but settled for a German right to intervene. They were also at odds over air strategy: Geisler wanted to block the Sicilian Straits to enemy traffic and bomb Alexandria, but Pricolo thought it more important to mine the Suez Canal and attack the enemy's ships and their bases. A compromise solution incorporated both strategies. At the beginning of January the Italians turned down a German offer to transfer the entire *Fliegerkorps* to Tripoli. A month later, with Benghazi in British hands on 6 February 1941 and Graziani pleading for German aircraft, Mussolini would reverse this decision and demand at least 500 Italian and German aircraft in North Africa.

When the first Heinkel 111s arrived at Benghazi, on 15 January 1941, the Suez Canal was out of range. The Stukas, some piloted by Italians, made an immediate impact. On 9 January Cunningham's fleet of three battleships and seven destroyers joined up with a convoy from Gibraltar heading for Malta and Greece. The main Italian battle-fleet did not sortie to contest the move – a near miss had opened the *Cesare*'s plates, leaving the *Vittorio Veneto* the only undamaged battleship, and both ships were moved north to La Spezia – but attacks by German and Italian Stukas scored five hits on the carrier *Illustrious* and hit two cruisers, destroying one of them. Cunningham thereupon abandoned operations against Italian supply shipping.[94] Thanks to air power, Italian convoys arrived virtually unharmed through February and early March. The lesson was obvious: Italy's refusal throughout 1940 to seek and accept German help had had profound consequences.

While Cavallero and Guzzoni urged Mussolini to make common cause with his ally and organize a joint offensive against Greece – and Mussolini ordered his armed forces again to study the occupation of France up to the Rhône and of Corsica (an operation Admiral Riccardi said could not be done, not least because all the troop transports were being used for Libya and Albania) – Graziani added his voice to the chorus. Time was being wasted, and when the Germans arrived 'everything down here will be liquidated'.[95] With only twenty-seven fighters and twenty-four bombers the air force was limited to night-time bombing of ships, bases and airfields, and his fighters could only protect the area immediately around Benghazi. What Tellera called 'the notable disproportion of means between us and the enemy' was obvious to everybody.[96] Graziani was assured on 10 January that the arrival of the *Ariete* armoured division was close at hand, but it took another three weeks to get there.

As the British and Commonwealth forces advanced on Tobruk, and Cavallero prepared an ill-fated attempt to retake Klisura, Mussolini took the train for Salzburg and a long-postponed meeting with Hitler on 20 January 1941. Ciano went with him and so did General Guzzoni

– the first time that a senior military man had been allowed to accompany him. To Ciano's surprise the meeting between the two warlords was remarkably cordial. In preliminary talks with Keitel and Jodl, Guzzoni sketched out the position in the two active Italian theatres. The situation in Albania was not yet 'perfectly consolidated', but the Greeks certainly would not be able to take Berat and Valona. An offensive on Florina and Kastoria was being readied to concert with German action but would take at least two months to prepare. In North Africa an attack on Tobruk was imminent and Graziani was planning successive defensive lines at Derna–Mechili, Benghazi and Agedabia. Italian East Africa was more or less written off: although the Italians had 100,000 more men, the enemy dominated in tanks and aviation (see Chapter 5). Guzzoni acknowledged that Rome could only have minimal influence on operations there, where Italian forces were effectively cut off from Axis resupply. The Germans offered two mountain divisions (36,000 men) with 4,000 vehicles for Albania and the 5th Light Division, a force of 9,300 men, 111 anti-tank guns and 200 lorries specially created to fight tanks, for North Africa. Albania could at most absorb one of the mountain divisions, Guzzoni told his hosts. As far as North Africa was concerned what the Italians needed most were German air units actually stationed in Libya – something they had previously rejected.[97]

When the two warlords met next day Hitler, whose attention was chiefly focused on Spain and Gibraltar, was reluctant to send German forces to Albania – a move which would 'authorize' the British to attack the Romanian oil wells – but he was prepared to send anti-tank elements (*Sperrverbande*), which he thought more useful than proper armoured divisions, to North Africa as long as they were employed immediately and used offensively – but the Italians must do their share of the fighting.[98] German disdain for her ally was mounting. In December von Rintelen had warned that 'you there [in Berlin] with a justified feeling of strength don't want to see the weakness of the partner down here'.[99] No longer: only a few weeks after the Salzburg meetings he was told that 'the Italians have to get used slowly to the fact that they were not going to be treated as equals in all relations [between us].'[100]

As the Italians and the Germans talked at Salzburg, British and Commonwealth forces reached Tobruk, where General Bergonzoli's 22,000 men and 340 guns were strung out defending a fifty-four-kilometre perimeter. At 5.40 a.m. on 21 January the attack began. Helped by a wind which raised clouds of dust and blinded the defenders, Australian troops accompanied by heavy Matilda tanks quickly broke through the weak defensive ring. Poorly co-ordinated, blinded by the sand and with only 110 anti-tank guns, not all of which had perforating munitions, the Italian artillery was unable to protect the strongpoints. They fell one by one. At 4 p.m. next day the last one was lost and the one-sided battle was over. 'It was inevitable,' General Tellera said afterwards, 'and there was nothing we could do because we lack the means.'[101] Twenty-four thousand Italians were killed, wounded or taken prisoner.

British armoured forces pushed on west. The next line of Italian defence were the 14,000 men and 254 guns of XX Corps strung out west of Derna and above Mechili, and the fifty-seven M 13 tanks and twenty-five light tanks of General Valentino Babbini's armoured brigade. Babbini's forces fought a brief holding action at Mechili, after which Graziani followed the advice of General Tellera, now commanding what was left of 10th Army, and withdrew. On 30 January the Australians entered the abandoned town of Derna. Benghazi was 243 kilometres away along the via Balbia, and El Agheila another 280 kilometres beyond it along an asphalt road.

Graziani was aware that the enemy were going to try a wide long-range movement aiming at Benghazi to encircle what remained of 10th Army – not least because it had been announced in a radio bulletin from London. He was also aware that Gaullist forces were threatening the southern frontier of Libya. His plan now was to save as many troops as he could with which to defend Tripolitania, as Mussolini instructed him to do.[102] Tellera was given the task of directing the retreat from Cyrenaica. His troops began a staged withdrawal, 15,000 marching and a lucky 5,000 travelling in lorries, harried all the way by British aircraft. In Rome, Guzzoni's planners agreed on holding Sirte and shaped a plan of their own. The *Ariete* armoured division and the German 5th Light Division would be fed in as they arrived and the joint force should be able to start its counter-attack anytime from 1 March. In three months they could cover the 900 kilometres from Agedabia forward to Tobruk.

'Tell me how you intend to employ the German light division, which will start arriving at the beginning of February,' Mussolini asked

Graziani as Derna fell into the enemy's lap.[103] That unit alone, Hitler was told, was not going to be enough. On 1 February General Hans von Funck, sent to Libya in advance of the *Sperrverband* he was to command, told Hitler that he had no faith in the Italians' capacity to resist and that there was now a danger of losing Tripolitania as well as Cyrenaica. An elastic defence would need at least a full *Panzer* division and that could not arrive until the end of April, which might be too late unless the British advance could be slowed.[104] The Führer railed against his ally – the Italians wanted German weapons and equipment but showed an infantile jealousy of German aid and German soldiers. Unable to get a definite answer out of Guzzoni as to whether the Italians could stop the British advance before the Germans got there, he decided on 3 February to send the *Sperrverband* and a *Panzer* regiment for local attacks and to follow them up with the 2nd *Panzer* Division, flak artillery, and a German corps commander who would be in charge of all Italian armoured formations. General Erwin Rommel was selected to command what would become the *Deutsche Afrikakorps*.

As the news of Hitler's decision arrived in Rome, Graziani's 10th Army was in its death throes. Shortly after noon on 4 February British forces cut the via Balbia above Agedabia and next day they severed it again at Beda Fomm, creating a pocket ten kilometres long. A few Italian units fought their way through – Tellera was mortally wounded at this time – but for most the end came quickly. At dawn on 7 February Australian troops entered Benghazi and with that the campaign was over. Over 20,000 Italians were captured, and Graziani lost 100 tanks, 200 guns and 1,500 motor vehicles. Only 8,300 men got away to Tripolitania.

With German forces on their way to North Africa, Hitler advised his partner that his offer of a German armoured corps was being made on the presupposition that a strong armoured formation would be created and used offensively, and that the defence would not be pulled back to the zones around Tripoli. Such a defence would be 'impossible'.[105] Mussolini made the advice his own and passed it on to Graziani. Tripolitania was to be defended as far forward as possible to keep the British away from the port of Tripoli. The motorized and mechanized German and Italian units should be used to conduct a mobile defence of Sirte, delaying any enemy advance and always acting offensively.[106] Graziani showed no intention of doing as he was instructed. Sirte was too far forward and would be 'another Sidi-el-Barani'. Instead he proposed delaying the enemy as best he could and drawing him onto a defensive redoubt at Homs. With the *Ariete* division in its current state there was no hope of carrying out the flanking manoeuvre or counter-attack that would then be necessary. Until a full armoured corps was available only the air force could hold up the enemy, and that was presently in a state of 'maximum inefficiency'.[107]

This was certainly not the forward defence that Rome wanted, forcing the British to fight with the desert at their backs. Nor was Graziani the kind of commander that Mussolini wanted. On New Year's Day 1941, Mussolini had ordered that Graziani should get to the front and stay there until the action was over. 'Battles fought by modern armies are too complex to be directed from afar,' the *Duce* told Ugo Cavallero.[108] Perhaps with Soddu's fate in mind, Graziani pre-empted the possibility that Rome might fire him and asked on 8 February to be relieved of his command. Next day the *Duce* replaced him with General Italo Gariboldi. Two days later Graziani resigned again, this time from the position of army chief of staff, and was replaced by General Mario Roatta.

CAVALLERO'S GREEK WAR

Cavallero's immediate tasks were to prevent the Italian line from rupturing, halt the enemy advance, and then take the offensive as soon as possible and chase the enemy back into Greece. For the moment, with a 250-kilometre front being held by 100,000 men who had been in the line for fifty days, he commanded what was only a 'veil', he told Mussolini. He urgently needed four fresh divisions to consolidate his front and replace the most tested units: 'Only after that can we think of an offensive.'[109] To get the men, weapons and supplies he needed into action, the ports' efficiency had to be greatly enhanced. Cavallero got to work at once reorganizing labour and shipping so that by the end of December the three ports of San Giovanni di Medusa, Durazzo and Valona would be able between them to land 6,000 tons of supplies a day – though the army needed 10,000 tons a day.

Cavallero planned to launch an operation in the first half of February to reoccupy the Korcia basin and then establish a secure front behind which he could build up reserves for the next stage in the war.[110] The Greeks moved first. The Greek offensive, which began on 4 December 1940 and lasted until 3 January 1941, drove forward along three main axes, aiming at Elbasan in the north to cut off Tirana and northern Albania, at Berat in the centre to sever the junction between 9th and 11th Armies and take the oil wells at Devoli, and at Valona in the south-west. Cavallero plugged the holes in his fragile line with troops as and when they arrived, feeding them in battalion by battalion and demanding more divisions in the face of Rome's preference to prioritize shipping in food and munitions.[111] Afterwards Roatta painted a picture of complete disorder in which the transport plans put together by the general staff were continually upset by orders from Palazzo Venezia. Mario Cervi provided a front-line soldier's corrective: any Italian who had spent time in a military unit in war 'knows perfectly well that the picture of a rational and all-wise General Staff is a product of Roatta's retrospective imagination, and that the officers at the top level of the Italian military hierarchy calculated correctly only in such matters as the timing and allotment of promotion, jobs, and allowances'.[112]

Ordered to contest the ground inch by inch in order to win time for the reinforcements to arrive, the Italian army had to contend with the weather and the topography as well as the inadequacies of their own system – and of course the enemy. Units were strung out across long distances: the 3rd Grenadier regiment had to hold a six-kilometre front with only 350 men. Supplied with the wrong ammunition and without anti-freeze oil, machine guns stopped working. Artillery lacked rounds. Snow covered the mountains to a level of a metre and sometimes two. Units lost 30 per cent of their effectives to frostbite, and exhausted mules collapsed and died of cold and hunger, which only worsened the troops' situation: one *Alpini* battalion had only fifty mules to supply it instead of the 270 it was supposed to have. Men drove themselves to their limits to try to sustain the front lines. A party of thirty-five porters set out to carry food and ammunition to the *Bolzano* division but only twelve arrived, the rest collapsing from exhaustion on the way. Some enterprising engineers, copying the methods that had kept the army going in the Dolomites during the Great War, built *teleferiche* to get supplies up to the heights and wounded men back down.

As the enemy forces drove towards Bardia, Mussolini pressed Cavallero to take the offensive. The Italian retreat from Korcia and

Argirokastro and the fact that the Greeks had ordered flags to be flown
for three days when they took Himara, a major coastal staging post to
Valona, was more than he could stomach. Seven divisions, amounting to
between 120,000 and 140,000 men, had been sent across to Albania but
there was no sign of the defensive 'wall' that should have gone up as the
first positive consequence of the retreat. On Christmas Eve the *Duce*
asked for 'a full report including punitive arrangements' and told Cavallero it was time to reverse the situation.[113] With the enemy only fifty
kilometres away, Mussolini wanted an offensive to save Valona. Reassuring him that the enemy was making 'a desperate effort', Cavallero
ordered Geloso's 11th Army to launch an offensive operation on the
Valona front to ease the pressure there and on 9th Army's right flank.[114]
Soddu told Mussolini that Cavallero's counter-offensive south of
Valona, which he thought too much like one of Garibaldi's piecemeal
charges eighty years ago, could not and would not succeed because it
was too weak and lacked support.[115] His time, though, was also up.
On 29 December he was recalled to Rome, and next day Cavallero took
over command of the armed forces in Albania – adding the responsibility
for winning the Greek war to all the other tasks he now had to handle.

On New Year's Day instructions went out from the Palazzo Venezia
to tell the generals in Albania that the forthcoming offensive must end
'worldwide speculation on Italian military prestige'. Germany was
ready to send an Alpine division and was preparing an army to attack
Greece in March. Mussolini wanted the war to be won before direct
German aid was needed.[116] He even managed to find something positive in the North African debacle. When the Germans intervened in
Greece early in March the British would have to come to her aid with
troops that could only be brought in from Egypt. If Graziani kept up
the pressure around Tobruk, British plans to shift not only men but
also General Archibald Wavell's headquarters to Athens would be
stymied, or so SIM believed.[117]

Cavallero was struggling. Demoralized units, in continuous action
since 28 October, were retreating. In the mountains there were one and
a half metres of snow and the mule tracks by which the supplies went
forward were rivers of mud. The Fascist Blackshirts and two of the
army's divisions had no mules in any case. Dressed in inadequate
clothing, soldiers dug in with their bayonets because there were no
entrenching tools. Supplies were being landed at a fifth of the daily rate

the army needed. Fresh divisions were indeed coming in, as Mussolini frequently reminded Cavallero, but they were in no fit state to fight. On being told on 12 January that it was staying in Italy the *Cagliari* division shed many of its officers and much of its equipment, only to be instructed next day that it was going to Albania. Along with two other divisions, it was hastily reconstituted with recalled officers and men who had not done military service for a long time and were practically without training.[118] Orders came from Rome that the incoming divisions were on no account to be dismembered – but Greek pressure meant that there was no hope of obeying.

As the New Year began, Cavallero drafted three plans. The first, in case everything went wrong, was for two defensive redoubts to defend Valona and Tirana. The second was for a local advance to retake Himara and Porto Palermo. The third was to build a properly organized force with division-sized reserves for an offensive in the Korcia area starting on 20 February. With not much else other than optimism to fall back on, Guzzoni hoped that Cavallero's planned operation might spring 'a small surprise' which could produce 'considerable results', and that Bardia's resistance might so wear down the British that they had to pause.[119] Disappointment came immediately. In Albania the Greeks again moved first. At 7.30 a.m. on 8 January, after an hour's preliminary artillery bombardment, they launched an attack up the Vojussa valley towards Klisura. A counter-attack next day after a forced march of twenty miles by the *Lupi di Toscana* division, which arrived at the front with no mortars, no artillery, no radio transmitters and no supply transport, failed. Ordered to defend Klisura at all costs the local commander instead withdrew and the town fell two days later.

Things had not gone according to plan and Mussolini wanted to know why. If anyone had predicted on 15 October what had actually happened since then, he told Ciano, he would have had them shot. Using an analysis prepared by Cavallero's intelligence office, General Pricolo provided an explanation. Only five of the twenty-one divisions presently in Albania were in a state of 'full efficiency'. The troops arriving from Italy showed the effects of poor training: many had never even thrown a hand grenade and almost all arrived with no knowledge at all of automatic weapons. When in action they quickly fell victim to what was now being called 'the Greek obsession' – the danger of infiltration, fear of enemy mortars, and a preoccupation with being taken prisoner. Somewhat altering the tenor of the original report, which pointed out that commanders lacked reserves and that the deaths of the majority of regular company and battalion commanders meant that units were in the hands of reserve officers, some of whom were quite old, Pricolo told Mussolini that local commanders seemed to be in the grip of a 'moral paralysis'.[120]

Mussolini had no shortage of reasons for prodding the centurions who led his under-performing legions. Reports landing on his desk spoke of soldiers in Albania writing 'alarmingly defeatist' letters home, some of them threatening to 'chase away those responsible [for the setbacks and conditions] if they don't leave of their own accord'. The fact that displays of comradeship by the Fascist militia in Albania were apparently not being met with like spirit by the army was put down to anti-Fascist propaganda, and at the end of January undercover police agents were inserted into the ranks of men going to Albania to investigate and report on activity by 'subversive elements' there that seemed designed to provoke revolt. Much the same sort of thing was occurring in North Africa. At the ports many soldiers were refusing to embark for Libya and the *Carabinieri* were having to force them onto the ships. 'Sybelline whispers' of a possible military dictatorship under Badoglio were going the rounds in Libya, and troops who had been arriving 'full of enthusiasm' were being infected by it. In civilian circles, the fall of Bardia and then of Benghazi consolidated a now widely held public impression of Italy's lack of military preparedness. The British bombardment of Genoa in early February further depressed the public mood.[121]

Due to meet Hitler in Salzburg very shortly, Mussolini badly needed a success. 'We have to counter-attack and break this spell which for ninety days has made us lose ground position after position,' he told Cavallero's chief of staff, Colonel Salvatore Bartiromo. 'This way we shall find ourselves in the sea and there won't be any more positions!'[122] Counter-attacking was in fact impossible. The weather was partly responsible – flooding had carried away the bridges across the main rivers in 9th Army's sector – but so were the effects of the grinding attrition that was wearing away Italian divisions piecemeal. By mid-January the *Julia* Alpine division, on whose hardy mountain troops enormous burdens had been placed since the very beginning of the campaign, had lost 3,997 officers and men and was reduced to 1,000 men with fifteen serviceable machine guns and five mortars. Grim-faced and pessimistic, the *Duce* left for his meeting with Hitler. 'Greece,' he complained to his son-in-law, 'was a political masterpiece; we succeeded in isolating the country and making it fight us alone. It is the army that has completely failed.'[123]

As Italian soldiers struggled in Greece, pressure mounted on Rome to turn failure into success. The Germans were showing increasing interest in the Mediterranean as they began to develop their ideas of a 'New Order' in Europe. The submission of Romania appeared to be the first stage of a systematic expansion in the Balkans. From Berlin, General Marras reported that Salonika and an outlet onto the Aegean – presently one of the intended pillars of Mussolini's Roman empire – would be next, possibly followed in the future by an operation 'in grand style' through Anatolia and towards the Suez Canal. The alarm-ing spectre of Berlin controlling both Gibraltar and Suez began to loom. There looked, too, to be another, more immediate humiliation in store. When the Germans attacked Greece they would likely advance more quickly than the Italians, leaving them to take on the mass of the Greek army and thereby easing Germany's path to victory. The Italians would then lose 'the principal role they should have in beating Greece to re-establish their own prestige'.[124] Cavallero, Roatta and Favagrossa all wanted closer co-ordination with Italy's ally, but the *Duce* was dead set against it.

Before he left for Salzburg, Mussolini summoned Cavallero and his senior generals to Foggia, a major air base north-east of Naples and close to the Adriatic coast. German interest in the Greek campaign was becoming more apparent. A visit by General Jodl, who had offered two mountain divisions, left Cavallero with the impression that Germany intended to take a dominant role in the future. At Foggia, Cavallero told Mussolini that the *Alpini* could be ready for action by the end of February but the other divisions would need more time. Presently Italy did not have the 'marked superiority in efficiency and preparation' necessary for a rapid offensive of the kind that pre-war military doctrine had proposed. If the Germans did act in Macedonia then they would surely gain the swift and extensive successes that were beyond Italy's reach. Italy needed political and military accords to co-ordinate future operations in Greece. '[The] disadvantages if we don't have [them] will be all Italy's.'[125] On 26 January 1941, Cavallero tried to retake Klisura. 'Tell [your men] that now is the moment to end the sad speculation in the world about our soldiers' valour,' Mussolini told General Francesco Rossi. 'The Greeks are not rabbits, but they are not lions either.'[126] In freezing temperatures and hammering rain the Italian columns formed up. The *Alpini* attacked the heights on either side of the road into the town, taking one but not the other. Italian tanks got into the outskirts of Klisura but were held up there. The Greeks counter-attacked and on 30 January the battle fizzled out with Klisura still in Greek hands.

In Rome, Guzzoni summoned two army commanders, twelve corps commanders and fifteen territorial defence commanders, and after briefly giving them a chance to report on army morale (generally good) and training (generally wanting), he launched into a biting critique of his soldiery. On the Albanian front officers were allowing themselves to be captured without firing a shot, and at home too many were reporting sick when posted abroad. They would be sent anyway. Excessive bureaucracy and over-zealous adherence to peacetime routines were matched by disciplinary slackness. There had been individual acts of heroism, but generally officers were showing little enthusiasm for the war. The reserve officers who now dominated the lower levels of the officer corps had been 'a complete failure' and senior officers too were failing in their duty. There had been 'inexplicable losses' and an enemy who was 'worth nothing' had humiliated Italy and cost her all her military prestige. The army was suffering from 'moral flabbiness'. Matters had to be taken in hand. 'Too few are shot,' Guzzoni concluded, showing a punitive streak worthy of General Luigi Cadorna.[127]

The first bloc of the promised divisions had now arrived – though, as General Camillo Mercalli of IV Corps noted, with a very reduced offensive spirit. No doubt wanting to tell the *Duce* what he hoped to hear, the local Fascist Party boss Piero Parini reported a decisive improvement in troop morale over recent weeks. Thanks to improved logistics, the arrival of 'copious artillery' and the 'generous and continuous action of the air force', there was a tangible sense of superiority in the air.[128] Back in Rome, Guzzoni ordered that the immediate and remote causes of the war be explained to the troops who were being recalled to fill the ranks of the units destined for Greece. The themes he selected – that the war was being fought because of the 'continued and deceitful' acts of hostility by the British against Italy and the need to engage them in Greece in order to draw them away from other fronts – were strategic abstractions that had little or no traction with the men being rounded up for the war.[129]

On 13 February the Greeks launched another offensive, to bite off the Tepeleni 'bulge' and then drive on Valona. While Cavallero reassured Mussolini that the turning movement had been arrested, and Geloso ordered General Rossi's XXV Corps to hold out to the last man, the Italian infantrymen fought off the attackers. In temperatures that fell to –15 °C, with deep snow wiping out the trackways and winds ripping tents and groundsheets away, the struggle swayed back and forth from summit to summit in the mountains east and south of Tepeleni as positions were lost, retaken and lost again. After a brief pause in late February, when the weather was so bad that nobody could fight, the Greeks attacked again on the last day of the month. Now Cavallero had entire divisions to feed into the combat. The reconstituted *Julia* division, some 10,500 officers and men, came into line just before the second and final Greek pulse, and the fresh *Lupi di Toscana* division helped halt the final Greek push, stimulated by the news that the Germans had entered Bulgaria, now allied with the Axis, on 1 March.

Cavallero told Mussolini on 22 February that he thought the Greek action against Tepeleni had failed. Next afternoon Mussolini arrived – apparently unexpectedly – at the Teatro Adriano, where the heads of the Fascist Party in Rome were convening. Acknowledging the loss of Benghazi and the defeat of 10th Army three weeks earlier, Mussolini told the enthusiastic audience that Greece was Britain's last point of support on the continent. There was praise for the Italian soldiers who had fought superbly in Albania, and a tangential accusation that the generals were responsible for setbacks there because it had been their plan, but no real explanation of what had happened or what was going to happen. Instead the *Duce* reassured them that, although things had been 'adverse' since Taranto, Britain could not win the war. Italy was marching arm in arm with her German partner, Axis morale was infinitely superior, and Italy's war potential was improving daily 'in quality and quantity'. Winding up his peroration, Mussolini assured his audience that 'the Fascist people deserve victory and they will have it'.[130] Press reports spoke of an immense ovation exploding in the hall when he finished.

Cavallero had told Mussolini that he expected the newly arrived divisions to be ready for action by the end of February, but on the day after Mussolini's speech he was told that they would not be properly equipped and ready until mid-March. Supplies were being landed at a rate of 3,000 tons a day but the army was consuming 2,700 tons a day, so that even by mid-March there would only be enough reserves to sustain five divisions for four days.[131] Cavallero now had 400,000 men under his command in Albania, facing what SIM calculated to be 300,000 Greeks. His planned next step was an attack down the Desnizza valley to recapture Klisura. Guzzoni disagreed and tried to persuade Mussolini that taking Koritsa was a better choice. Strategically, his was the better option: the Klisura attack led to nowhere of any importance whereas the Koritsa line, where the enemy was less dense, offered the opportunity to combine with the German offensive from Bulgaria that everyone now knew was coming shortly. Cavallero got his way, and Mussolini flew into Tirana on 2 March to watch the progress of what he clearly expected to be a much-needed military success. After listening while the commanders of five of the six divisions slated for the offensive listed all their deficiencies, he told them that 'great tactical success and probably also some strategic success' were in the offing. Greece could hope for nothing – 'It can only succumb.' Afterwards he telephoned the absent commander, General Giovanni Esposito: 'I've held a meeting which you didn't attend, but you haven't missed anything.'[132]

The attack, entrusted to General Gastone Gambara, who had recently arrived to command VIII Corps, which would make the central thrust in the drive south, began with an artillery barrage at 7 a.m. on 9 March. It was soon in trouble. High-level bombing had little effect and the low-level dive-bombers scheduled to participate did not turn up. After five hours the advance was at maximum range of the 149mm medium field guns and beyond the range of all the other guns. A simple deception plan, which involved heavy gunfire in sectors not involved in the offensive to confuse the enemy, failed, partly because the preparatory movements of the attacking corps had been observed by the Greeks and partly because they had captured an Italian officer who was carrying all the orders for the offensive. On the south-western flank, XXV Corps' guns took part – the *Cagliari* division's men carrying 250 tons of ammunition along eight kilometres of muddy mule tracks on their backs – but were themselves attacked by the Greeks and could do little to help. Greek artillery fired down on the attackers from higher ground, and well-sited mortars took a heavy toll. Within hours Gambara's attack had come to a complete standstill. Mussolini returned to his headquarters that night in an ill-humour. 'Don't you think that these generals show little spirit, little élan, and above all have little initiative?' he asked Pricolo, who was accompanying him. 'Look at Rommel, who is restoring the situation in Libya with a single division and a reconnaissance group.'[133]

Mussolini stayed until 21 March, inspecting troops, visiting the wounded, opening bridges, and insisting when it quickly stalled that the attack must continue. His visits to hospital were greeted with frenzied enthusiasm by the inmates. 'You find the same sort of thing in villages, especially in the South of Italy if there's been an earthquake or some other menace,' General Giovanni Messe, who accompanied him, remembered later. '[T]hey turn to the Madonna, or to some saint, and wait for a miracle to happen when they realize they can expect no help.'[134] Two days after the offensive began Roatta warned that Italy was running out of artillery ammunition. After a second attempt at breaking through the Greek positions failed, Cavallero proposed breaking off the action for a while and then resuming it and simultaneously launching a second attack from Tepeleni. Without troops capable of using infiltration tactics and without enough officers, he explained, he was having to resort to applying weight and wearing the enemy down. Are we wearing the enemy down? Mussolini asked. Cavallero thought the news that the King of Greece wanted to negotiate an end to the war proved that they were.[135] Orders went out on 16 March to halt the Klisura offensive, and five days later Mussolini flew back to Rome.

Before he left, Mussolini called Cavallero, Geloso and the 11th Army corps commanders together. After analysing what had gone wrong with the offensive – deficiencies in artillery fire, deficient training, 'particular techniques', and the difficulties of the ground – he laid down the law about what his generals must now do. The Germans were going to start their operation against Greece on 6 April and it looked as though Yugoslavia would join the Axis powers on 23 March. Italian forces must get back into action first and the Greeks must be thrown back and defeated. It was 'inadmissible' that the Italians were incapable of giving them a thrashing. The military honour of the nation was in play. If the generals got moving by 1 April there should be time to do just that.[136] Cavallero reassured him that the action on Klisura and the offensive from Tepeleni could begin at the end of the month. With that Mussolini flew off, 'disgusted' by the environment he had been in, profoundly contemptuous of the generals he had just been praising to their faces and convinced that 'they have been deceiving me to this very day'.[137]

On 25 March Yugoslavia joined the Tripartite Pact and two days later the pro-German regent Prince Paul was deposed in a coup d'état. Hitler wrote immediately to Mussolini appealing to him not to begin operations in Albania in the next few days, so that the Albanian-Yugoslav frontier could be reinforced. Mussolini did as he was asked and Cavallero duly shifted five divisions north and east to protect Tirana, Scutari and the Yugoslav frontier. At 5.30 a.m. on Sunday, 6 April, the Germans struck Greece and Yugoslavia, and Rome declared war on Belgrade. The Germans wanted to link up their forces in Bulgaria with the Italians in Albania, cut the Yugoslav forces in two and then annihilate the Yugoslav army by concentric attacks. After that, common preparations could be made for the war on Greece.[138]

The Yugoslavs attacked Albania, aiming at Scutari, on 13 April and were driven off by the *Centauro* armoured division with heavy losses. Obeying Mussolini's injunctions to press forward against an obviously demoralized and dispirited army, Cavallero's troops occupied Cattaro, Cetinje and Ragusa on 17 April. Deception had a hand in their success: SIM, which possessed the Yugoslav military cipher, sent out two fake telegrams on 13 April over the name of General Simović, ordering the Yugoslav divisions to retreat. It took forty-eight hours for the Yugoslav Army Command in Sarajevo to issue a correction, during which time the Cetinje division ceased its attack on Scutari and began withdrawing north.[139] On the northern border with Italy, General Vittorio Ambrosio's 2nd Army, ordered by Mussolini to advance its start date and attack on 11 April, occupied Ljubljana.[140] In the south, 9th Army's advance into western Yugoslavia was slowed by snow and thick fog, but it took Struga and then met the Germans at Lake Okrida. On 18 April Yugoslavia surrendered.

While the Germans sliced through eastern Greece, reaching Salonika three days after the war began and then Florina before turning south, the Greek forces in the Epirus launched their last offensive towards Elbasan and Tirana, hoping for assistance from Yugoslavia.

None was forthcoming, and on 12 April they began to retreat. At long last 9th and 11th Armies could advance on all fronts – but only on foot: an army now numbering 491,731 officers and men had only 13,000 motor vehicles. The Greeks put up a dogged resistance, blowing up bridges, sowing minefields and blocking roads: on one twenty-kilometre stretch in front of Klisura the Italians had to break through eighteen separate barriers. Koritsa fell to the men of the *Venezia* division on 14 April, and Argirokastro on 18 April. On 22 April Italian units reached Ponte Perati just inside the Greek-Albanian border. The Germans were already there. Next day the war ended, less than three weeks after the Germans had crossed the border, but only after Mussolini, infuriated when he learned that Field Marshal Wilhelm List had accepted the Greek surrender the previous day, insisted that they formally surrender to the Italians too. At 2.45 p.m. on 23 April 1941 all three parties signed the definitive armistice agreement. The Greek war in total had cost the Italians 13,755 dead, 25,067 missing, and 50,974 wounded, along with 52,108 sick and 12,368 cases of frostbite. Greek casualties amounted to 13,408 dead, 42,485 wounded and 4,253 missing.[141] For Yugoslavia and Greece nightmarish years of occupation and terror now began.

Chapter 5
Sea, Sand, and Endless Steppes

Mussolini cancelled the annual meeting of the Supreme Defence Commission scheduled for February 1941 (it never reconvened), so there was no opportunity for a general discussion of the economic situation. The numbers were far from encouraging. Italy's raw materials needs were, as everyone knew, gigantic. Production of cast iron inched upward from 1,036,106 tons in 1939–40 to 1,090,330 tons in 1940–1, due to a lack of fuel for coke ovens and a lack of electrical energy during winter. Fuel shortages were exacerbated by the complex bureaucracy that enveloped distribution.[1] No proper system of rationing fuel for civilian use existed until March 1941. The War Ministry told Mussolini that there were one hundred times as many civilian motor vehicles as military ones in Italy, and that Rome and Milan each consumed as much petrol in a month as all the military vehicles in the country put together. Mussolini then agreed to restrict the civilian circulation of traffic from 1 April 1941.[2]

One number perhaps mattered above all others: steel production. By 1941 all the services were feeling the effects of shortages. The merchant navy's allocation, halved at the end of 1939, had stopped altogether in June 1940. In all, it had received 37,000 tons for the entire year instead of 144,000 tons. Another 38,000 tons had been scraped together from various sources (including 8,000 tons of scrap imported from the United States), but the pre-war programme was running behind. If regular allocations could be kept up the Communications Ministry expected to be able to build thirty-two merchantmen during 1941.[3] This was not going to keep pace with losses. The chief of the naval staff Arturo Riccardi had only forty destroyer escorts to screen his battlefleet and shepherd convoys to North Africa. In May 1941 the army in Libya wanted 200 ships' worth of supplies a month in order to build up reserves for an offensive, but because of the shortage of escorts the navy could only manage thirty, which was just enough to keep up with everyday needs. Riccardi's 1942 'minimum' build programme included eight destroyers and twelve *torpedinieri*. To get them, he was ready to abandon the merchant navy build completely.[4]

Shortages of raw materials did not stop the services putting forward ambitious construction and manufacturing programmes. At the end of June 1941 the navy presented a new naval programme that required 43,250 tons of iron and 3,870 tons of copper, as well as smaller amounts of other metals, on top of their current year's allocation of 265,000 tons of iron and 5,600 tons of copper.[5] This amounted to almost a quarter of total iron-ore production that year (1,340,000 tons) and half the total copper production (16,000 tons). Bigger programmes were yet to come – as they had to if the navy was to have any chance of making up the losses it was suffering. The air force planned to increase production from 300 aircraft a month in June 1940 to 500 aircraft and 800 aero-engines a month in 1941 and 660 aircraft and 980 aero-engines a month in 1942. These numbers, which depended on expanding volumes of German raw materials and were probably constructed partly to justify getting them, proved wildly optimistic. Italy produced 292 aircraft a month in 1941 and 235 aircraft a month in 1942.[6] Over-ambitious programmes to double and even triple output of rifles and light and medium machine guns between 1941 and 1942, dependent on redistributing the limited stock of machine tools, could not be met. Breda was scheduled to produce 1,500 model-30 light machine guns – an over-complicated weapon which the troops did not like – every month by June 1942. It managed to produce 1,100 a month during the first three months of 1943.[7]

The services saw the problem as one of relative shortage to be solved by shuffling steel allocations. In reality, it was an absolute problem. Fabbriguerra* estimated that the United States, with an annual output of 80 million tons at the start of 1940, would increase that figure to 91 million tons by the end of 1941. Italy produced 2,258,000 tons of steel in 1940 and 2,063,000 tons in 1941.[8] Like his ally, Mussolini discounted

---

* The shorthand name given to the former General Commissariat for War Production (COGEFAG) after its head, General Favagrossa, was made an under-secretary of state on 23 May 1940.

America. Announcing his invasion of Russia, Hitler told Mussolini that it was a matter of indifference to him whether the United States entered the war or not, as it had already mobilized all the strength it could to help Great Britain. Mussolini quickly agreed: even if he formally declared war, President Roosevelt 'could not do us greater harm than he has already done so far'. It was, he thought, 'dramatic' that the destiny of the Anglo-Saxon world was in the hands of a man who had had infantile paralysis for forty-four years and 'a notorious alcoholic'.[9]

ITALIAN EAST AFRICA FALLS

When, back in April 1940, Mussolini had told the incoming chief of staff of the army in Italian East Africa, General Claudio Trezzani, that once the war began there would be no help from Italy, he was expecting a short war. As France collapsed, the viceroy, Amedeo III Duke of Aosta, asked for permission to attack Kassala in eastern Sudan, one of the two East African targets mentioned in Mussolini's war directive of 31 March. General Badoglio thought that, in a prolonged war, intervention by the *madrepatria* in Italian East Africa would be next to impossible except by air or by restocking from the Red Sea using neutral states. All that Italy could do, he advised Mussolini, was to organize things there using the maximum economy of means, make the most of local resources, put internal security first, and undertake operations beyond the borders of the empire only if they increased its 'autonomy' or produced 'a real and certain improvement in the internal situation'.[10] On the eve of the war, the order went out from Rome to stand strictly on the defensive until told otherwise.

The forces defending East Africa, which included two Italian divisions (*Granatieri di Savoia* and *Africa*), looked strong on paper: 75,000 Italians were supported by 182,000 native troops. In fact, there were serious weaknesses. There were only forty-eight tanks (when in 1938 General Gariboldi, then chief of staff at Addis Ababa, had asked for an armoured and mechanized contingent, Rome had merely 'guffawed'), the artillery was almost all small-calibre pack-guns, the few motor vehicles were soon worn out by bad roads and shortages of tyres and fuel, and the native 'volunteers', many of whom were mobilized hastily in 1940, were mostly men over thirty. The 183 front-line aircraft that could fly in defence of the colony were obsolescent.[11] The war they were about to fight was entirely separate from everything that was going on elsewhere and would have no effect on the campaign in North Africa. Almost none of the factors that had so recently led to the successful invasion of Abyssinia now applied. British neutrality had facilitated that campaign. British hostility now made Italian East Africa a prey to events elsewhere.

The fighting began with some small-scale skirmishing on the Kenyan frontier. The Italians' first move came on 4 July 1940 when their troops took possession of Kassala, thirty kilometres beyond the frontier, blocking the main route into Eritrea. Then, to prevent the possibility of a British landing and ensure that Djibouti (in French Somalia) remained neutral, General Guglielmo Nasi led 35,000 troops into British Somaliland on 3 August. With a substantial superiority in troops and local command of the air – the British territory was defended by a single battery of light artillery and 4,500 troops – it took him only sixteen days to conquer the country. Mussolini lauded the viceroy and General Nasi, but appearance and reality were miles apart. Italian estimates put the number of defenders at 11,000, of whom 10,000 had, they believed, embarked from Berbera under the Italian guns, pulling off what Nasi afterwards described as 'a little Dunkirk'. Nasi, whose troops had been slow in pursuing their enemy, consoled himself with the thought that the British had done the same thing under the noses of the mighty German Wehrmacht.[12] The native *ascari*, who made up six-sevenths of his force, fought bravely but were unprepared and temperamentally unsuited to handle complex tactical problems. Trezzani blamed their officers, who were gravely wanting in professional skills. As long as it was a case of risking their necks they were admirable, but when it came to reconnaissance, making contact with the enemy, fire preparation, co-ordination of movement and the like 'they are almost illiterate'.[13]

Badoglio now made what has been described as his first and last attempt at a co-ordinated Middle Eastern strategy. Tying together the forthcoming move by Marshal Graziani into Egypt that would be a jumping-off point for deeper advances with the German air offensive against Great Britain, which he expected to fall by the end of September or early October, he ordered Aosta to be ready to seize a buffer zone in the Sudan and prepare an offensive towards Egypt. By the end of August, with German victory against England either in the air or on land now postponed, Badoglio's strategic window had closed. Aosta was instructed to get used to the idea that the war would last beyond the early autumn and to subordinate planning to resources – which in his case were exiguous. The concerted offensive against Egypt was consigned to the *Comando Supremo*'s wastepaper basket.[14]

While the Italians debated what to do next, the British built up their forces in Kenya and the Sudan, able to draw on the extensive resources available to them around the Indian Ocean. Italian garrisons at Kassala and Gallabat held off British attacks in the first week of November, thanks largely to mass intervention by the air force. The outlook, though, was grim. The delicate internal situation, especially in the province of Amhara, was 'a slow-fuse which could set off the mine of revolution' and bring the enemy forces into the country. It was all the more worrying because there was effectively no defence against enemy bombing. The colony was short of weapons and munitions, rubber and fuel. If they did not arrive, Aosta warned Rome in September, all that could be done was to prolong resistance as long as possible.[15] A month later the Bletchley Park outstation at Cairo broke the *Comando Supremo*'s ciphers, after which everything that passed between Aosta and Rome was known to his opponents. More Italian ciphers came into their enemy's hands when the South Africans overwhelmed a local outpost at El Wak in mid-December. By the end of 1940 General Wavell and his staff had in their hands near real-time decrypts of Italian messages.[16] As the year came to a close at least one senior Italian commander seems to have realized that the game was up. In December 1940, General Gustavo Pesenti, commanding the Giuba sector facing Kenya (which included the key port of Kisimaio), suggested starting armistice talks. Aosta sacked the 'madman' immediately, replacing him with General Carlo De Simone.[17]

Once the British had completed Operation COMPASS it was evident in Addis Ababa that they would likely focus their air power and a large portion of their armoured forces against Italian East Africa. Trezzani discounted the threat to the colony from Somalia, because of logistical difficulties, and thought the serious danger lay in the north.[18] A deception plan intended to persuade the Italians that the main British attack would come in the form of coastal landings failed to convince. Instead the Italians concentrated the majority of their strength along the Sudan frontier, expecting that the main attack would be against

Agordat or Gondar. If this could be stopped then the expected attack on Kisimaio might be halted and with luck the rainy season would come to the rescue. If the worst came to the worst, rather than attempt a gradual withdrawal to a single central redoubt, during which time the native *ascari* units would surely disband and which would have to shelter the white population that could not be fed, each region was to create its own redoubt where it would resist to the last as best it could. The command headquarters would retire to its own central stronghold at Addis Ababa.

Not everyone was convinced. General Pietro Gazzera, commanding the southern sector, who Trezzani thought exaggerated the threat there in order to get more materiel, proposed creating two large masses of troops, one in the north and the other in the south, and giving battle in the open field. No region, even his own, which was the richest in resources, could fight it out on its own, Gazzera pointed out. In the north, General Luigi Frusci went his own way. Abandoning the idea of a frontier battle, he withdrew the garrisons at Kassala and Gallabat and prepared to make his stand on the *altopiano*. Aosta reconfirmed his original directive and referred Frusci's actions to Mussolini. The *Duce* let Frusci's plan stand. 'Don't forget', he told Aosta, 'that the destiny of Africa will be decided by what happens in Europe.'[19]

As the Italian position in North Africa teetered on the brink of collapse SIM warned that the British would probably start their attack on Italian East Africa at the end of January or the beginning of February. The main effort would come from the Sudan and Kenya, while diversionary landings would probably be launched on the Red Sea coast near Assab or on Djibouti from Aden to encourage internal disturbances.[20] Two days after the intelligence forecast, Frusci's foot-bound infantry began their retirement. Momentarily taken by surprise, Major-General William Platt's tanks, armoured cars and lorry-borne infantry swiftly followed up and in some cases overtook the retreating Italians. Kassala, by now largely deserted, fell on 19 January 1941 and Agordat, whose defenders were virtually helpless in the face of British armour, twelve days later. Fighting delaying actions, Frusci retired to Keren, 'one of the best natural defensive positions available to any commander throughout the entire Second World War', which guarded the port of Massawa.[21] Tough troops, relatively well armed and well led by General Nicolangelo Carnimeo, put up stiff resistance and held off a first attack (2–13 February), but after a pause during which the encirclement tightened the final battle was joined on 15 March. With uncontested air superiority, British bombers dropped over 120 tons of bombs before and during the assault. After eleven days' fighting the town fell. The Italians lost some 3,000 dead and 4,500 wounded, along with some 9,000 *ascari* dead and perhaps double that number wounded. British losses numbered 536 dead and 3,229 wounded. After that, Asmara and Massawa fell quickly.

In the south, General Sir Alan Cunningham's attack on Italian Somaliland began on 11 February. Kisimaio was abandoned that day and Nigerian troops took the town three days later, along with valuable guns and ammunition and 200,000 gallons of petrol.[22] The native units began to disintegrate. Mogadishu was taken without a fight on 25 February and the remnants of the Italian forces fell back to Harrar. Enthused by the prospect of German aid against Greece and in Libya, Mussolini believed that the British were only interested in getting possession of Massawa and Mogadishu in order to prevent any aid reaching the embattled forces in Abyssinia. The rest he thought the British would leave to Emperor Haile Selassie, who had arrived in Khartoum early in July and had been raising troops among Ethiopian exiles, supplying him with money, weapons and officers. Pointing out that all his forces could do was parry the enemy's attacks and that he was facing an internal situation that was growing ever more serious, Aosta told Mussolini that he would hold Addis Ababa until the enemy got within tactical range of the city and then take what remained of his forces and fight to the last in the mountains.[23]

On 16 March a landing by Punjabi units took the Italian-occupied port of Berbera in the Gulf of Aden, the defenders offering little resistance. Next, Harrar and Diredawa were abandoned as the Italians withdrew yet further into the interior. By the end of March they had lost the whole of Eritrea and Somaliland, and with them all their main logistical bases and supply dumps. Addis Ababa was abandoned on 6 April for a defensive redoubt around Amba Alagi in the heart of the country. It fell to Indian and South African troops on 19 May. A few determined units held out in pockets of resistance. General Gazzera surrendered on 3 July. Gondar on the Ethiopian plateau, where General Nasi held on for another four months, was the last to fall. Italy and the world were watching them, he told his officers, and their resistance would have great moral value in a hostile world that had always denigrated the Italian soldier.[24] On 27 November, after a short but bitter last-ditch fight, he surrendered and the last embers of Italian resistance in East Africa were extinguished.

The East African campaign cost the Italians 3,896 dead, 6,432 wounded and 45,857 missing or prisoners of war.[25] Afterwards the Italians put their defeat down to *ascari* defections, the enemy's enormous material superiority, and British flooding of the Abyssinian market with local currency which had reduced the value of the *lira*. On the ground, poorly equipped Italian infantry had been overwhelmed by the combined action of air power, artillery and armour. With 336,000 men and precious little else the generals on the spot faced an enemy 254,000 strong, better armed and equipped, and well led – though they might perhaps have made their enemy's job harder.[26] Even before the campaign was finally over, planning began to reconquer the lost colony. That, General Guzzoni thought, would require fifteen divisions, five from the 'Army of Egypt' that would have reached the Nile and ten new ones from Italy. Since the entire output of trucks in 1941 was being absorbed by the army in North Africa, the 'Army of Africa' could not be ready until the autumn of 1942 – but that, his staff warned, could be delayed yet further by the new commitment to Russia.[27]

MALTA AND NAVAL STRATEGY

Before the European war began, the navy had wanted the air force to help ensure its control of the central Mediterranean by making Malta and the French port of Bizerta in Tunisia unusable by significant enemy naval forces. The air force chief of staff General Pricolo was confident that he had enough bombers, fighters and ground-attack aircraft in Libya, Sicily and Sardinia to do that.[28] In June 1940 the navy examined the task of taking Malta and concluded that it would have to be weakened by protracted air action and submarine blockade, after which a force of at least 20,000 men would effect a landing, helped by parachute troops. The navy would bombard the defences – not risking the two *Littorio*s – but doubted whether it would be able to dominate the eighty-odd batteries of guns, most of which were sited in caverns. It would, the sailors concluded, be a very arduous undertaking. Luckily, however, the British had for some time given up using the island as a main operational base, preferring Gibraltar and Alexandria. Therefore the threat that it posed to Italy's naval communications and bases was thought to be 'of secondary importance'.[29] That was indeed the case – for the moment. Italy shipped 304,467 tons of supplies to North Africa between June and December 1940 and lost only 2.3 per cent of them.[30]

On 7 February 1941, learning that Force H with the battleships *Malaya* and *Renown* and the aircraft carrier *Ark Royal* had put to sea – supposedly to support another convoy to Malta – the *Vittorio Veneto*, *Andrea Doria* and *Giulio Cesare* left La Spezia and steamed down the west coast of Corsica looking for it. Admiral Somerville was in fact off Genoa, which his ships bombarded next day, sinking four merchantmen, damaging eighteen others and killing 144 people. The commander-in-chief of the battle-fleet Admiral Iachino turned his ships north to try to cut off the enemy, but a combination of poor weather and inadequate air reconnaissance deprived him of the chance to match his ships against those of his foe. Afterwards the navy complained that if the air force had done its job properly the battle-fleet would have been certain to have met with the enemy with a clear superiority. How the navy might in fact have got on would shortly be demonstrated all too clearly. In the meantime, Pricolo found that bomber and fighter groups which should have been fully prepared for swift action had in fact been unprepared despite advance warning. If anything like it happened again, he told all his senior commanders, 'those directly responsible will be removed'.[31] The navy, it seemed, had at least a partial case.

Malta was on the agenda when Admiral Riccardi met Grand Admiral Erich Raeder at Merano on 13–14 February 1941 to concert Axis naval strategy in the Mediterranean. The Italian navy thought that everything was against them. The strategic balance had changed now that the British were present on Crete, which they had garrisoned in October 1940, and in Greece, where British forces began to arrive on 2 March 1941. Now the enemy controlled all the entrances to the Mediterranean, had the eastern and western basins in its grip, and could also control the crucial central Mediterranean. The base at Tobruk had gone and use of the port of Benghazi would soon be lost too. Then the enemy could occupy Tripolitania. Heaping spectre upon spectre, the naval staff envisaged the enemy taking the whole of Libya, the French navy coming in on their side, and serious new threats developing in the Gulf of Genoa and the Tyrrhenian Sea which would draw already slender escort forces away from the Sicilian Channel. Outnumbered – by its reckoning the combined Mediterranean fleets had six battleships, four carriers, seventeen cruisers and forty-seven destroyers – the Italian battle-fleet had no obvious targets in the shape of major seaborne traffic lines, unlike its enemy, and could only act when it knew for certain the enemy's position, strength and movements, 'which in the present state of things is not obtainable'.[32] British ships sailing round the Cape of Good Hope or from the numerous African bases were entirely out of reach.

Riccardi came to Merano with a shopping list. He wanted anti-aircraft guns, fifty long-range seaplanes, and especially fuel. If Italy did not get more from Romania, he told Raeder, then his fleet would have to cease all surface activity in June, when stocks would be down to 52,000 tons. The Germans wanted more action and Riccardi had to listen to what he afterwards described as a lesson in naval education as Rear-Admiral Kurt Fricke explained at length the success the *Reichs-marine* ~~Kriegsmarine~~ was securing by acting offensively wherever and whenever it could. Nothing of substance came out of the talks. Both sides reaffirmed the absolute need to keep Malta under continuous attack, and the Germans talked the Italians out of launching a surprise assault on Corsica, which, as Rear-Admiral Fricke pointed out, was part of Unoccupied France and therefore out of play. The Germans did succeed in inserting the head of their naval liaison command into the *Supermarina*'s staff, in the hope that the Italians might adopt German operational concepts. Vice-Admiral Eberhard Weichold was sceptical. All Italian fleet actions were conceived entirely from a defensive standpoint, he told Berlin a month later.[33]

Admiral Iachino was looking for action and suggested attacking the convoys from Benghazi that were supplying the British forces now fighting in Greece (Operation LUSTRE). After at first refusing, a reluctant Riccardi finally agreed as long as the *Luftwaffe* and the *Regia Aeronautica* provided 'exploratory, protective and offensive support in the field'. It would not appear: the Italian air units on Rhodes that were supposed to provide most of the air cover never took off, due supposedly to adverse weather conditions. Then, in the first of a series of intelligence failures, Weichold wrongly informed the Italians that the carrier *Formidable* had left the eastern Mediterranean, which it had not, and that the Germans had damaged two British battleships in Alexandria, so leaving only the *Valiant* capable of action – which they had not. Under German pressure and ready to give Iachino's battle-fleet the action it wanted, *Supermarina* was also keen 'to give the world the impression that England has not precluded our initiative in zones far from our bases'.[34] Iachino put to sea with the *Vittorio Veneto*, eight cruisers and fourteen destroyers on the evening of 27 March 1941 – totally unaware that ENIGMA decrypts had given Admiral Cunningham many key details, including the exact date of the operation, in advance.[35] Cunningham stopped the convoy and sent out a destroyer division ahead of his battle-fleet.

The battle of Cape Matapan, which would last on and off the whole day, began at 8.12 a.m. on 28 March 1941 when Vice-Admiral Luigi Sansonetti's 3rd cruiser division attacked a group of eight enemy cruisers and destroyers spotted at 6.35 a.m. by an Italian plane. After a short engagement he retired, drawing the British ships onto the main Italian battle fleet. At 10.56 the *Vittorio Veneto* opened fire on the enemy formation. Over the next twenty minutes the Italian cruisers fired 542 rounds from their 203mm guns and the *Vittorio Veneto* fired 94 rounds from her 381mm guns. None hit the target. Faced with the threat of attack by torpedo bombers, Iachino then broke off the action – and learned twenty minutes later that he was not going to get the promised air support from Rhodes. Ten German fighters did eventually turn up. A series of British aerial attacks followed during the afternoon. One damaged the *Vittorio Veneto*, forcing Iachino to pull his cruisers and destroyers together around her. As twilight fell another attack immobilized the cruiser *Pola*. Misled by reports which suggested that the British battle fleet was at least twenty miles further away than was actually the case, Iachino ordered Vice-Admiral Carlo Cattaneo to take the rest of his 1st cruiser division and go to *Pola*'s rescue. It ran straight into Cunningham's three battleships and in four and a half minutes it was smashed to pieces. When the long night came to an end, the Italian battle fleet had lost three cruisers (*Fiume*, *Zara* and *Pola*), two destroyers (*Vittorio Alfieri* and *Carducci*), and 2,200 men, including Vice-Admiral Cattaneo, who for a long time afterwards was blamed for the defeat and wrongly accused of disobeying orders in going to *Pola*'s help.[36] The battle put the *Vittorio Veneto* out of action until August 1941. She would be out of action again four months later:

torpedoed by a British submarine on 14 December 1941, she would not be fit to go to sea again until June 1942. It also revealed to the Italians for the first time that British warships were using radar and so could carry on fighting throughout the hours of darkness.

A week after he arrived in Rome, Cavallero called the head of the air force in to discuss smashing the British fleet in the Mediterranean. Directives went out next day to the heads of the navy and air force to study a 'mass aero-naval action' against the Mediterranean Fleet. The sailors, straining to support the Libyan convoys and acutely aware of the difficulties involved in improvising an action, and no doubt shaken by the disaster at Matapan, were decidedly unenthusiastic. Other than Malta, there was no obvious objective for them to attack; the navy's numerical inferiority meant that it could only provoke the enemy into action in conditions of local superiority; and a year's war experience proved that it could not fight outside the 110-mile maximum range of land-based air power. Mussolini wanted action and so on 14 June Cavallero ordered the chiefs of the naval and air staffs as a matter of urgency to make the necessary bases ready, deploy their forces so that they could be used against fractions of the English fleet under air cover, and carry out as quickly as possible the exercises needed to ensure effective air to sea co-ordination.[37]

Operational planning then proceeded at a leisurely pace and after two months Cavallero had to send Riccardi an order to concert with Pricolo and come up with a final design. The battleship admirals were smarting at lost opportunities. They had missed intercepting three convoys to Malta (Operation TIGER) in early May, after which Admiral Iachino complained to Riccardi that if the navy was absent every time the enemy tried to pass through the Sicilian Straits it would be said that it was no longer even capable of carrying out its role in the central Mediterranean and should be kept exclusively to convoy protection.[38] Very aware of the cost of not having aircraft carriers like his opponent, Iachino wanted 'real' air force detachments set up and practice begun in simultaneous co-ordinated action by ships and planes. He was still complaining a month later that nothing of the kind was happening.[39]

The admirals caught an enemy convoy on 15 June (Operation HARPOON), sinking three freighters and a tanker thanks to combined air and surface action and winning what has been described as 'the only squadron-sized surface naval victory of the war for Italy', but then missed another convoy (Operation SUBSTANCE) at the end of July.[40] Then intelligence arrived that a British convoy had left Gibraltar and that a part at least of the Mediterranean fleet at Alexandria was also at sea. On 22 August the heads of the navy and air force met to choreograph the action. It would take place within range of Italian fighter cover: the air force had twenty-five planes ready on Sardinia and Sicily, and thirty-nine torpedoes. The *Littorio*, back in action at the end of March after Taranto, and the *Vittorio Veneto* would be at sea in the central Tyrrhenian Sea supported by four heavy cruisers and twenty-three destroyers. Cavallero, who intended to render the Mediterranean inaccessible to the enemy 'with all the means we have available', told Mussolini about the plan at Riccione on 23 August before the two men left for their meeting with Hitler at Rastenburg.[41] Iachino put to sea the same day, deploying between Sicily and Sardinia and able for the first time to make use of a direct radio link with the *Regia Aeronautica*. But this time there was no convoy. Force H from Gibraltar had been guarding a minelayer at work off Livorno (Leghorn) and three days later it was back at its base. Afterwards Iachino said the abortive exercise had been invaluable for morale and for testing the links with the air force. It had certainly used up yet more of the navy's fast-disappearing stocks of diesel fuel. On 26–27 September he tried again, this time unaware that the fast convoy that was his target was escorted by three British battleships, but the two fleets never caught sight of one another.

Despite its lack of success in combat, the Italian battle fleet was by its mere existence performing a strategic task. In April 1941 Royal Navy planners calculated that they needed to keep five battleships, two carriers and twelve cruisers at Alexandria and Gibraltar to mask it, and in the autumn they dropped a planned invasion of Sicily because of its presence.[42] But only if the British were obliged for reasons outside Italian control to remove several units from the theatre could that imbalance be diminished and Iachino have any hope at all of altering the course of the naval war in the Mediterranean.

ROMMEL COMES TO NORTH AFRICA

Erwin Rommel arrived at Tripoli on 12 February 1941 determined to test what he quickly realized were weak British defences in Cyrenaica, first by grabbing El Agheila and then by mounting a major offensive in early summer that would recapture Cyrenaica and then go on into Egypt and up to the Suez Canal. General Gariboldi's immediate task was to win three or four weeks during which Italian and German armour could be shipped in. Conscious that his infantry, 'static and without the necessary arms', was at the mercy of a mechanized enemy – believed to have two armoured divisions and seven or eight motorized divisions – Gariboldi was assured that his five infantry divisions would be rebuilt, the *Ariete* armoured division re-equipped, and the *Trento* motorized division would be coming, together with two more divisions. As far as the Italians were concerned, an offensive might be launched in September.[43]

In Rome, Rommel's 'dynamic and daring' temperament rang alarm bells. Until the 5th Light division was complete and the 15th *Panzer* division and the *Ariete* armoured division had been brought up to strength, any offensive could play into the enemy's hands. The presence of German troops in North Africa, and their imminent arrival in Greece, was making the Italians feel distinctly uneasy. It appeared that their ally's next move might well be into Palestine and Syria, which would put them rather than Rome in possession of the 'hinge' of three continents. That made it all the more necessary that Italian forces in North Africa first reconquer Cyrenaica and then proceed east.[44] For the time being Rome determined to 'throw a little water on the fire'. SIM would compute what would be available at the start of May, which would give the attackers a month before the hot season began, after which everything would have to stop until September. The move of choice was to retake Benghazi. Failure had to be avoided at all costs.[45]

Rommel flew to Berlin. There, with Operation BARBAROSSA imminent, he was told that for the moment he would get no further reinforcements. When 15th *Panzer* division arrived at the end of May he could attack British outposts at Agedabia and even retake Benghazi, but no more. Returning to Tripoli, he told Gariboldi that his plans for a much more ambitious offensive had been accepted. His lightning reconquest of Cyrenaica, using the 5th Light division, the *Ariete* and three Italian infantry divisions, began with the taking of El Agheila on 24 March 1941. The watchword in Rome was caution and Gariboldi was reminded that his first obligation was to ensure that the defensive deployment of his forces was 'securely solid'.[46] The German invasion of

Yugoslavia and Greece on 6 April, and an abortive pro-German coup in Iraq, put unexpected cards in Rommel's hand as General Wavell moved troops out of theatre. One after another Agedabia, Benghazi, Bardia and Sollum fell into Axis hands and on 11 April Tobruk was invested. Four days later Rommel was at the border with Egypt. Believing that the Axis forces had gone about as far as they could go, Guzzoni persuaded Mussolini to sign a directive telling Gariboldi that it would be 'very dangerous' to advance beyond Sollum until there was 'sufficient preparation'.[47]

With Cyrenaica once again in Axis hands Rommel opted for an offensive defence of the Egyptian border and began to batter Tobruk's now robust defences. When his first attempt to take the fortress (14–17 April 1941) failed, he put his lack of success down 'above all to the Italian's bad training and armament'. When, two days later, an offensive push by the Tobruk garrison unexpectedly met with local success, he exploded. Again it was the Italians' fault. There had been 'displeasing cases of lack of discipline in combat and [lack of a] strong resistance'. If this happened again he would not hesitate to put soldiers, officers and their commanders in front of military tribunals. Gariboldi enquired into the events of the night and was forced to tell his divisional commanders that there was indeed some merit in Rommel's charges. Their job, he told his generals, was to restore morale and put the detachments in the best possible position to do their duty.[48] At more or less the same time Mussolini was being told that morale in the army was generally good, though in the case of the rank and file this was due 'more to discipline than to enthusiasm for [the] war'.[49]

With Rommel on the march, the planners in Rome looked into the future. Operations in Egypt would need ten divisions, three or four of them armoured and all the rest motorized. Once the Delta had been reached, the army would then face the reconquest of Italian East Africa. That would need another ten fresh divisions, all 'appropriately equipped'.[50] The notion of using Egypt as a springboard to recapture Italian East Africa was nonsensical, not least because of the shortage of motor vehicles simply to cover all existing demands. Even Mussolini, who talked of Ethiopia as 'the Pearl of the Regime', had to recognize the risks and difficulties involved in trying to reconquer it.[51] As a target it made little or no strategic sense as long as Britain was still unbeaten in North Africa – but Mussolini would surely want it back. So the staff in Rome worked up plans for an ambitious three-phase operation beginning at the end of September 1941 and lasting until the end of December. First would come an advance to Mersa Matruh, the elusive goal of the previous year, provided that Tobruk had already been destroyed or captured, then on to El Alamein, and finally the Nile. This would entail shipping across five more divisions, including the *Littorio*, *Trieste* and *Frecce* mechanized divisions, in stages.[52] Although there were still problems finding the necessary transport, collecting together everything needed would be easier because with Greece's defeat all available means could be sent to North Africa.[53] But within days, Mussolini would decide that the army was going to Russia too.

Arriving in North Africa at the end of May to take up the post of chief of staff to Gariboldi, General Gastone Gambara found plenty to complain about. Too much authority had been abdicated to Rommel, whose most recent attack on Tobruk, carried out 'somewhat *lightly*', had cost plenty of casualties but had had no significant effect on the defences. '[V]olcanic, agitated, always on the move', the German was prone to give orders on the spot from his command vehicle that contradicted ones he had given earlier. Morale among Italian soldiers was 'very high'. Organically, though, things were bad. The three Italian divisions in line (*Ariete, Trento* and *Brescia*) were reduced to almost nothing, the M 13 tanks could do no more than eight kilometres an hour because their diesel engines were under-powered, and spare parts were in very short supply. With the Germans now on Crete and things apparently going the way of the Axis in Iraq and Syria, Gambara's advice was to let Tobruk wither on the vine, rebuild the *Ariete* and *Trento* divisions, send across the *Trieste* and the thousands of trucks that had been requested, and be ready within four to six weeks to launch a strong Italian corps against the Nile alongside the Germans.[54] Then, after a British attempt to take Halfaya Pass and attack Sollum on 15 June (Operation BATTLEAXE) failed, activities came to a halt.

On 17 May 1941 Cavallero returned to Rome and immediately made a bid for more power. Merely being able to 'co-ordinate' the service chiefs was equivalent to almost nothing, he told Mussolini. Though they were his subordinates, as under-secretaries of state (which all three also were) they were not only independent of him but outranked him. They also had direct access to Mussolini. Cavallero wanted full authority over them. Mussolini agreed immediately, but the new powers he gave Cavallero were more apparent than real. Cavallero could not give the chiefs of staff orders, only transmit the *Duce*'s directives. Although they were now formally below him in the hierarchy of office, the heads of the navy and the air force still had direct access to Mussolini – who could in any case call them in whenever he wanted.[55] Cavallero's vigorous shake-up alarmed the Air Ministry, afraid that he was thinking of reorganizing them too, but he left them more or less to their own devices. He did bring the War Ministry, which he thought had been a 'clandestine general staff', to heel, replacing its under-secretary General Antonio Sorice with his own man, General Antonio Scuero. To make sure that he sat at the top of the new pyramid Cavallero jettisoned the post of deputy chief of staff, and with it Guzzoni. As head of the *Comando Supremo*, a title he chose to replace the much less impressive sounding one he had inherited from Badoglio, he also took control of the military intelligence bureau (SIM), hitherto part of the War Ministry. 'I must be kept informed of everything,' he told its head.[56]

Two weeks after taking up his new office Cavallero travelled with Foreign Minister Ciano to the Brenner Pass, and on 2 June he met his opposite number, Field Marshal Keitel. After a short strategic *tour d'horizon* which took in Iraq, Syria and Cyprus, the two focused on Libya. Cavallero raised the issue of supplying Libya through the French port of Bizerta. Keitel agreed that the port was 'an essential necessity', but made it clear that Germany was not going to put a gun to France's head to get access to it. Moving on, Keitel promised German heavy artillery and howitzers to bombard Tobruk and suggested that two German *Panzer* divisions, the *Ariete* and *Trento* divisions when brought up to full strength, and two or three motorized divisions would be 'the indispensable minimum' with which to launch the march on the Suez Canal. Cavallero undertook to send the *Littorio* armoured division (which would not actually arrive until 1942) along with the *Trieste* motorized and *Pavia* auto-transportable divisions and 14,000 motor vehicles. What he wanted most urgently was a transport plan which could be carried out using Bizerta. The matter was left floating in mid-air.

Towards the close of the meeting, Cavallero produced what was becoming the usual wish list: fuel – 'at the end of June we shan't be able to sail'; coal – Italian industries were 'paralysed' for lack of it; and rubber – 'an absolutely vital problem'. Coal stocks had in fact fallen slightly during the first half of 1941 and in June the Italian railways had 1,100,533 tons, which they estimated would last three months. The navy's fuel stocks were falling fast – from 754,700 tons in January to 280,200 tons in June. By December 1941 it had only 53,300 tons of fuel in its storage tanks – less than a month's average consumption.[57] Cavallero was assured that efforts were being made to bring coal deliveries, interrupted by the effects of the Balkan war, back up to a million tons a month, and that Italy would get all the fuel it needed from Romania. Rubber was more of a problem: 'it all depends on what we can get from Japan' was Keitel's response to that.[58]

Hitler was having further thoughts about the conduct of the war in North Africa, and after the Brenner Pass meeting they were passed to the *Comando Supremo* in Rome. Tobruk must fall as the essential precursor to the offensive against Alexandria. Supply was of the greatest importance: munitions, food, fuel and spare parts should go via Benghazi and Derna, while reinforcements, guns and vehicles went to Tripoli and Bizerta.[59] Limited port capacity, the scarcity of anti-aircraft guns and the vulnerability of ships in harbour to attack from the air meant that the Italian navy could only transport enough for the everyday needs of the two armies and the civilian population. To get ready for the offensive that the planners had in mind the army wanted another 97,000 men and 9,800 motor vehicles shipped across to North Africa by 1 September. The navy reckoned that by sending alternate four- and six-ship convoys across every four days it could transport all the men and vehicles the army wanted in four months.[60] The *Comando Supremo* calculated that with eight convoys a month, not five, as hitherto, the job could be done in thirteen months and using twelve convoys a month it could be done in six.[61]

The navy's plan strained shipping resources almost to the limit. It used all the thirty-one merchantmen requisitioned for North Africa more or less continuously, and the five fast troop carriers would be steaming to and fro non-stop. Moreover, when the plan was examined in detail the navy declared that unless unloading facilities were improved it could only send across four convoys a month and not five.[62] There was a way round the problem. Using the French ports of Bizerta and Tunis would halve the distance the convoys had to travel and so double the deliverable load, making it possible to ship six divisions across by September.[63] Bizerta would remain an Italian chimera almost up to the end, but Hitler was never willing either to force the Vichy government's hand or make concessions to get Italy full access to the port.

With the departure of the German X *Fliegerkorps* for Russia at the end of May, the air force too was facing problems. Left on its own to protect the convoys, it could only do so in daylight and could only provide fighter cover up to a maximum of 100 miles from land. Up to 100 planes a day were being used and that, Pricolo warned, could lead to a rapid wearing out of materiel which would make it impossible for him to provide the same level of convoy protection in the future. His solution was to retime and reroute the convoys.[64] In North Africa, General Ajmone Cat, commanding *5a Squadra Aerea*, was finding the Germans uncooperative. When they asked for Italian help they got it, but when the Italians in their turn asked for support they were almost always met with evasive answers or refusals. Ajmone Cat wanted an effective command system that would divide up tasks according to capabilities. Me 110s with their long range and speed could do daylight reconnaissance, long-range escort duty and attack tanks, Ju 87s could hit tanks, and Ju 88s could do long-range daylight bombing. Italian S 79s could do daylight reconnaissance inland and out at sea.[65] It was a logical idea – but one that spoke more to Italian weaknesses than anything else.

Gariboldi wanted the promised reinforcements, especially motor vehicles, as quickly as possible. If the enemy got reinforcements faster than he did, the Axis forces would have to abandon the siege of Tobruk and retreat to a defensive line he was preparing at Ain-el-Gazala.[66] Rome needed a clear idea of the situation on the ground, and the army chief of staff Mario Roatta was despatched to Libya to observe and report. What he found was less than encouraging. Gariboldi did not trust Rommel, who, if freed of responsibility for Tobruk, would use his troops as he thought fit and only along the Egyptian frontier. Grandiose plans to march on Cairo and the Suez Canal were in the air, but that would require between thirteen and fifteen armoured and motorized divisions, four infantry divisions, and all the air power currently in Sicily, Greece, Crete and Libya. At current rates of transport, amassing this huge force would take until the autumn of 1942. Tobruk could not for the moment be taken and any offensive against Alexandria was a distant prospect. There was, moreover, the immediate threat of an enemy offensive. Therefore what mattered now was the defensive. Gariboldi, who appeared to be suffering from an inferiority complex as far as the Germans were concerned, must be replaced. If Gambara was not senior enough to take his place, then the post should be given to someone who would give him freedom of action. That man was General Ettore Bastico.[67] On 12 July Cavallero relieved Gariboldi and put Bastico in his place.

Bastico's orders were to ensure that Cyrenaica's defences were in as strong a position as possible, create a strong mobile force, prepare to 'expunge' Tobruk, take steps to defend Tripolitania against enemy landings, try to improve the port facilities and continue organizing rear positions in case of need. Rommel made his views of his ally's fighting capabilities clear. Italian troops were good in defence but lacked the drive needed to attack. Many actions failed because of poor co-ordination between the artillery and the infantry. Training was inadequate, and reserves could not intervene in a timely fashion because of the lack of transport. What his troops lacked, Bastico pointed out, was not aggression but adequate firepower and transport – only 20 per cent of the *Trento*'s motor vehicles were presently working. There was no hiding the fact that the troops, as well as being tired, were showing evident signs of unease. This was due to the contrast between 'the abundance of means of every type that the German units have – including food – and the parsimony that is forced on them'. Fundamentally, everything depended on transport, both to North Africa and within it. The navy and the air force must do more, no matter what the cost.[68]

A defensive mindset was developing in Rome. The strategic environment had changed, as Cavallero pointed out to Mussolini. What he regarded as slow progress in Russia, where the German campaign was in its second week, meant that the prospect of a joint attack on Egypt was now far off in the future, there was no sign that the French would concede the use of Bizerta, and after losing Syria to the British and facing intensified Gaullist propaganda the threat that Vichy France posed to Tripolitania had increased.[69] All this, and the fact that the heavy artillery scheduled for the attack on Tobruk was now at the bottom of the sea after the convoy carrying it had been sunk, meant that for the time being there could be no question either of knocking out Tobruk or of attacking the British in Egypt. Intelligence suggested that an enemy attack in September was likely. Now the priority was to decide on and prepare for the move to a rearward defensive.[70] Cavallero wanted the move worked out in full agreement with Rommel, but Rommel was confident that he would soon have the means to take Tobruk and equally confident that he could contain an enemy attack from the east or a sortie from Tobruk by counter-manoeuvring. *Mentalità carrista!* ('A tank man's thinking!') was Cavallero's reaction.[71]

First Cavallero reassured Keitel that taking Tobruk was 'the fundamental objective of our action in Cyrenaica'.[72] Then he met Bastico and Gambara in Cyrenaica and tried squaring some operational circles. Defensive positions at Ain-el-Gazara (Rommel's preference) and Derna–Mechili (his own) must both be considered. To avoid the spectre of Rommel controlling all the mobile forces in Cyrenaica, a mobile corps should be created comprising the *Trento* and *Ariete* divisions along with the *Trieste*, which would arrive by early September. This would function as a mobile 'rearward position' able to act in all directions and support the front-line infantry. Gambara would be in command. As far as Tobruk was concerned, Cavallero was sure the British would attack before it could be taken. Given the state of transportation it would take at least three months to ship across the three extra divisions that Rommel and Bastico agreed would be necessary, so operations against Tobruk could not begin until January or February 1942.[73] Next day, General von Rintelen and the German liaison officer with *Superasi* (North African High Command), Lieutenant-Colonel Heggenreiner, bought into the Italians' ideas. With everyone in agreement, Cavallero thought they now had a good chance of facing whatever happened in Cyrenaica 'even if things did not go well on the Sollum front'.[74]

When he met Keitel on 25 August, Cavallero was guarded about what Italy could and could not hope to do. Keitel, who believed that there was no immediate danger of a British attack, wanted Tobruk taken by the end of September. That, Cavallero told him, would not be possible – but he kept to himself the timelines that he had established earlier. Keitel was reassured that orders had been given to prepare a defensive line at Ain-el-Gazara, as he wanted, and that it would be integrated with the mobile force. What should be next? Keitel thought a further advance on Suez after Tobruk fell was impossible for the moment: 'With every step forward, the [supply] lines get longer and the situation gets worse.' Everything now depended on port capacity and convoy protection. For the moment there was no chance of using Bizerta. Cavallero was advised that, because of the distance between Tripoli and Benghazi, as much transport as possible should be directed to Benghazi, Bardia and Derna – and he assured Keitel that Italy was already doing everything possible in that regard and would try to do even more. An Italian request for the loan of some German fighters for four or five weeks to help with convoy protection met with an abrupt refusal. The Germans were, however, prepared to send some submarines into the Mediterranean.[75] Admiral Raeder had already made this suggestion, and on 17 September Hitler ordered six U-boats into the Mediterranean (eventually there would be twenty-seven).

German submarines were needed in the Mediterranean because the Italian submarines were not performing well. At the time and afterwards people blamed the clear waters but in reality the problems lay at least as much in the submarines themselves. Italian submarines had been built on the basis of the lessons drawn from the First World War and the Spanish Civil War – that they would be in action during daylight, would fire their torpedoes while submerged and would not be chased by an enemy able to locate them with echo-sounders. Their defects – among them high conning towers, long periscopes and noisy machinery – contrasted dramatically with the German boats, which were faster on the surface, submerged more rapidly, ran more quietly, were more manoeuvrable and fired electric torpedoes which ran without a wake or give-away bubbles – all of which the Italians recognized far too late.[76] In June 1942 the British captured the submarine *Perla*. When they got inside, its captors were bemused: the mechanical conditions were 'deplorable' and it was 'a mystery how the Italians succeeded in operating the ship'.[77]

Malta was starting to look like an insoluble problem. Guzzoni asked in mid-April that the island be subjected to intense and continuous daily bombardment from the air, and Pricolo replied that he was doing as much as he could but could not prevent the enemy from interdicting Italian traffic. Eliminating or at least seriously damaging the island, Raeder told Riccardi, was a job for the Italian navy and air force. While Germany fought Russia, he could expect very little help in the way of materiel or personnel.[78] Naval planners looked at the problem and concluded that with the resources Italy had to hand the operation was not at the moment practicable, that preparing it would take at least a year and that the timetable could only be speeded up with some help from the German navy and more from the German air force, 'given the crisis of insufficiency that the Italian air force is going through'.[79] Riccardi offloaded the problem of neutralizing what he called 'this terrible wasps' nest' onto the air force. The navy would contribute 'indirectly' by participating in attacks on the traffic resupplying the island.[80]

The Italian surface fleet missed another opportunity to engage the enemy at the end of September when the British ran a convoy of nine merchantmen to Malta escorted by a force which included three battle-ships and a carrier (Operation HALBERD). Ordered not to engage the enemy unless he enjoyed 'decisive superiority of force' which could be verified by air action, Admiral Iachino first thought his opponent's aim was to attack Sardinia or the Genoese coast. Receiving intelligence that the enemy was shepherding a convoy he turned south-west to meet it, thinking he was facing a lone battleship and a carrier. At 2.35 p.m. on 27 September, while torpedo bombers of the Italian air force were attacking the main British fleet (hitting the battleship *Nelson*), Iachino was told that there were two enemy battleships at sea, not one. Believing he no longer had the decisive superiority that Riccardi had laid down as essential, and without the air cover he both expected and needed (it turned up almost an hour later), Iachino turned his fleet away. News of the damage the air force had done to the enemy caused him to turn around yet again, but by then he was too far away to meet up with his quarry and with visibility worsening as dusk came on he was ordered to stay put. During the night the convoy steamed on beyond his reach, delivering 50,000 tons of badly needed supplies to Malta, and Admiral Somerville's battle-fleet turned for home.[81]

Supply was crucial to the fortunes of Italians and Germans alike, and the problems involved in giving Bastico and Rommel what they asked for were many. Italian output was limited – asked for 130 search-lights to defend the North African ports, Cavallero could only scrape together seventeen – and increasingly outclassed. Inter-service co-operation was weak, potentially multiplying losses that had somehow to be made good. But the most pressing issue was getting what materiel was available to Tripoli and Benghazi safely. Traffic management was poor. Ships left with on average between 25 and 50 per cent of their potential loads, which was justified by the need to meet urgent demands from the front and split loads up to reduce the impact of losses. Sending small convoys of five or six ships at a time increased the wear and tear on escorts and used up shrinking supplies of fuel, but port capacity was limited: Tripoli and Benghazi could handle roughly 3,000 tons a day between them and in 1941 were working more or less flat out.[82] The navy's August transport plan envisaged running five normal convoys, together with one fast convoy of Italian and German troops. All this did was replace normal losses and refill existing gaps. There was nothing for expansion, though the navy did hope to be able to start shipping the *Trieste* division across at the end of the month.[83]

By mid-October the convoy system was experiencing serious difficulties. Daylight escort by Italian fighters seemed to be working, but the slow convoys were being caught during moonlit nights by enemy torpedo bombers. Cavallero asked Pricolo to sort the matter out, and at the same time to keep bombing the air bases at Malta.[84] Pricolo could be of no help when, on the night of 8–9 November, the 'Duisburg' convoy, composed of seven ships and carrying 389 vehicles, 34,473 tons of munitions, 17,821 tons of fuel, 223 Italian and German soldiers and twenty-one civilians, was ambushed by a force of two light cruisers and two destroyers from Malta. The British ships arrived out of the blue on a direct collision course with the convoy. 'It was as if they knew the position, route and speed exactly,' Admiral Riccardi noted afterwards.[85] They did, thanks to ENIGMA. The brief defence of the convoy was spectacularly mishandled. Some of the six destroyers in the close escort at first drew away and then returned, only to be chased off. Rear-Admiral Bruno Brivonesi's distant escort, too far away and travelling too slowly, turned in the wrong direction so that when it spotted the attacking force the distance between the two was increasing not diminishing. His ships fired 289 rounds of 8-inch and 4-inch shells and thought they had scored two hits. Brivonesi then departed the scene. The entire convoy went to the bottom.[86] Brivonesi was accused of 'errors of tactical appreciation' and court-martialled, and all convoys to Tripoli were temporarily suspended.

By early November the evidence that the British were planning a major land offensive was compelling: advanced supply dumps were being created and air activity intensified, columns of motor vehicles were moving towards advance bases and a fresh armoured brigade had appeared.[87] When Operation CRUSADER began on 18 November 1941, 100,000 Italians and 70,000 Germans were spread out around and in front of Tobruk and guarding the ground above Sollum and the Halfaya Pass, supported by 395 working tanks, 10,000 trucks and 220 aircraft. While one arm of the attack swung round to cut off the Italian garrisons at Sollum and Bardia, another pushed on towards Sidi Rezegh to link up with the Tobruk garrison. General Claude Auchinleck's plans met with an immediate setback. Fore-warned by intercepted enemy radio messages, the tanks of the *Ariete* division supported by *Bersaglieri* and by truck-mounted 102mm naval guns defeated the 22nd Armoured Brigade at Bir-el-Gobi. Italian weaponry was still comparatively poor, but leadership was stronger and tactics had improved. Commonwealth forces pushed forward to Sidi Rezegh and Tobruk. Twice the garrison tried to break out, and twice it was held by the *Pavia* and *Bologna* divisions. Below Tobruk, General Ludwig Crüwell's *Panzers* and the *Ariete*'s tanks fought a two-day battle for Sidi Rezegh and by 23 November the main Commonwealth drive towards Tobruk from the south-east had been halted.

After a brief contest with Bastico over who now had operational command of the battle, Rommel launched his armoured divisions in a 'dash to the wire' to cut off the retiring British armour. But Common-wealth forces were regrouping south of Bir-el-Gobi, and New Zealanders were advancing from the east in an effort to link up with the Tobruk garrison. On 26–27 November they reoccupied Sidi Rezegh after a bitter battle in which troops of the 9th *Bersaglieri* fought to the end. Reversing his thrust, Rommel pulled the *Panzers* and the *Ariete* back west. On 1 December Sidi Rezegh was in Axis hands again. To continue the battle, Rommel needed fuel and munitions. Facing what he thought would be a campaign of attrition in which the enemy would seek to wear down Axis forces, Bastico wanted tanks, guns, armoured cars and motor vehicles. Fuel and guns would be brought across on warships, Cavallero told them both, and Italian and German tanks would leave for Tripoli when that was possible. For the moment they must make use of what they had. With Sidi Omar now in enemy hands, both Sollum and Bardia invested and Bir el Gobi under attack again, the twenty-day battle drew to an end.[88]

Faced with fresh Commonwealth forces, aware that no reinforce-ments were on their way to him, and unable to break the enemy's attack, Rommel decided to retreat into Tripolitania. The garrisons at

Sollum and Bardia must be left to their own devices – nothing could be done to save them. He could not hold Agedabia, because after five weeks of continuous fighting the Italian troops were no longer strong enough for him to do so without running the risk that his forces would be completely destroyed. If that happened he could not carry out Mussolini's order to defend Tripolitania to the last.[89] Cavallero went to see Mussolini and came away with a line in the sand. Cyrenaica must be held and with it the port of Benghazi, otherwise Tripoli would be the only point through which Italy could route supplies. So, to prevent the enemy 'turning' Cyrenaica with a long-range move, Rommel must hold Agedabia. Rome was in an optimistic mood. Mussolini and Cavallero both thought that Japan's entry into the war in December 1941 meant that the war potential Great Britain could maintain in the Mediterranean must decrease, while Italy's was increasing.[90]

Reinforcing Cyrenaica was now pressing. German anti-tank units were airlifted in and more fighter cover was on the way. Mussolini told Cavallero that he wanted 'energetic action' that would break 'the hypnotic state' into which the services would otherwise lapse, and Cavallero fell back on a four-ship convoy escorted by five cruisers and eleven destroyers. The convoy duly left Naples on 20 November but turned back to Taranto in the small hours of 22 November after two cruisers were torpedoed that night. Having offered Mussolini extra *Luftwaffe* strength at the end of October to protect Italian convoys, Hitler ordered the squadrons that would become the basis of Field Marshal Albert Kesselring's *Luftflotte II* away from Russia on 10 November. Kesselring arrived in Rome on 28 November, and six days later joined the heads of all three services to examine the problem. The top brass were able to identify their needs – more fuel for the merchant ships, an increase in air transport and speeding up the arrival of the German air units – but had no immediate solutions to offer.[91]

Given the urgency of the situation in Libya the navy tried again, this time planning to run five ships to Tripoli and three to Benghazi, escorted by four battleships, a dozen cruisers and twenty-six destroyers. While the convoy was being readied an attempt to run aviation fuel to Tripoli ended in disaster when the two cruisers involved, the *Alberico da Barbiano* and the *Alberto da Giussano*, were ambushed on 13 December by British destroyers and sunk. Once again, a combination of ENIGMA and radar was responsible, and once again the Italians put their loss down to aerial reconnaissance and radio direction finding. The following day the *Vittorio Veneto* was torpedoed, putting her out of action for six months.

On 16 December Iachino took three battleships and two cruisers to sea to escort convoy M 42 across to Libya. Facing only a single battleship and with no enemy carrier to disrupt his aerial reconnaissance and threaten his main fleet for once, he was able to fulfil his mission. A brief encounter with the enemy fleet at a distance was all he could manage – his two older battleships lacked the necessary range – but his destroyers did carry out a counter-attack as twilight fell. 'It was', he recorded enthusiastically afterwards in a report read by Mussolini, 'an unforgettable spectacle replete with power and warrior beauty.'[92] The first battle of Sirte Gulf was over. On 20 December news arrived in Rome that the convoy of four ships had arrived in Tripoli.

At the front, Rommel and Bastico were at sixes and sevens. Rommel thought he could resist the enemy but Bastico believed he intended in fact to withdraw quickly and feared for his infantrymen, who could only retreat slowly on foot. On 16 December Cavallero flew to North Africa to persuade his generals to accept Rommel's strategy. Bastico and Gambara wanted to make a stand at Ain-el-Gazala. Gambara was convinced that they should play their last card there in defence of the whole of Libya. Over the next three days Cavallero argued against them. Gambara's readiness to die like a soldier at his post was admirable in itself, he remarked, but it was not going to be enough to defend Tripolitania. That would require mobile units and since there were none there those in Cyrenaica must be pulled back. Rommel reassured the Italians: he was ready to defend first Derna and then Benghazi, to withdraw slowly, and to protect the two Italian corps. Benghazi could not be held indefinitely but Agedabia would be held. Cavallero returned to Rome happy that the dispute had been resolved and that Rommel's strategy was the order of the day.[93]

Using the ports of Tunis and Bizerta and thereby allowing convoys to be routed west of Malta and out of reach of enemy air attack was the only way Cavallero could see of resolving the supply dilemma. Thus would victory be assured. There would then be no need to keep Italian forces on the western frontier of Tripolitania, and with four divisions well supplied with reinforcements 'we shall be able to go where we like'. Italian East Africa could even be recovered, though that could be picked up along with other things in the peace treaty that would end the war. If the Axis could plant its foot in Tunisia 'Egypt is ours', and if it had possession of Tunis 'the war in the Mediterranean is won'.[94] Mussolini put the argument for the Tunisian ports to Hitler, adding that if Vichy France rejected accords 'I would prefer to send my tanks into Tunisia rather than see them disappear to the bottom of the sea on the route to Tripoli.'[95] Hitler gave him detailed advice on how to distribute shipping loads to North Africa and suggested that the 'final goal' should be the elimination of Malta. As far as Tunisia was concerned, there was little or nothing to hope for. The Führer did not think that France could be induced to give the Axis effective aid.[96]

Twelve months' fighting in North Africa had, Mussolini was told, cost the Italian army 2,594 dead, 2,983 wounded and 123,676 missing or prisoners of war. Casualty figures were being kept from the public.[97] However, the year in North Africa ended with a major intelligence coup for the Italians. On 23 December 1941 army intelligence reported the interception of a report sent by 'an official American observer' to the War Ministry in Washington. The source was almost certainly the American colonel Bonner Fellers, whose intercepted reports gave Rommel a helping hand during the year to come. The intercepted report contained the explosive news that the English were intercepting Rommel's messages and thus reading his orders.[98] Told the previous day, Cavallero instructed General Cesare Amé, the head of SIM, to tell Rommel urgently that all his communications were being intercepted.[99] Italian naval intelligence (SIS), which had been using ten commercial ENIGMA machines originally supplied by the Germans in 1936, stopped all use of them on 30 December 1941.[100]

WAR IN THE EAST

Mussolini's decision to commit his soldiers to a third campaign, less than two months after the Greek war, turned out to be one of his greatest mistakes, but in ideological and political terms it fitted squarely into the frame of Italian-Soviet relations. In the 1920s and early 1930s relations between the two powers had been relatively amicable. It seemed then that they had more in common than not, especially their hostility towards capitalist-imperialist powers. 'Corporativist' Fascists claimed that Fascism and bolshevism stood side by side against the bourgeois plutocracies, and Fascist ideologues argued that both movements agreed on the necessity of a centralized and unitary state underpinned by strict discipline, differing only over the means to achieve it.[101] Moscow's support for League of Nations sanctions against Italy during the Abyssinian war, and her support for the Republicans during the Spanish Civil War, changed all that. Thereafter, as far as Fascist Italy was concerned, the two 'popular' revolutionary polities were fundamentally in conflict. Mussolini said as much when, in August 1938, he praised the Fascist Blackshirts who were fighting bolshevism in Spain in 'the first encounter between the two revolutions, that of the last century . . . and ours'.[102]

In January 1940 Mussolini told Hitler that together they had to demolish bolshevism. When they had done that 'we shall have kept faith with our two revolutions'.[103] The threat that Russia posed to his expansionist aims was made clear six months later. In October 1939 the Russians told the Italian navy that they could no longer export oil on the previously agreed terms. Then, in July 1940, the Soviet commissar for foreign trade Anastas Mikoyan announced that any further development of commercial exchanges depended on 'a complete clarification of relations between the two powers'. Translated into plain language, this meant agreeing terms with Russia over the Danube-Balkans region and the Straits.[104] Mussolini's expansionist goals in the Balkans and the Eastern Mediterranean meant he could never reach an accommodation with Moscow on either front.

The anti-Russian strain in Nazi political and strategic thinking became increasingly apparent during the autumn of 1940 and Hitler confirmed it when, in January 1941, he told an audience at Salzburg that 'Without the Russian factor all the problems in Europe would be easily solvable.'[105] For the moment a German attack on Russia seemed unlikely, as German military thinking appeared to be focused on defeating England, on Greece, on helping Italy, and possibly on war with Turkey.[106] But as the Greek campaign came to its conclusion the intelligence picture began to change. In March, SIM reported that substantial German forces were being moved into Poland and towards Bessarabia, where the Soviets had themselves been building up troops since the end of January.[107] By the middle of April, with German troops now in Finland and some seventy divisions in East Prussia and Poland, there were unmistakable signs that something was in the wind. The German general staff was envisaging a campaign lasting two and a half months, which would begin between July and September in order to capture the Ukrainian harvest before it had been distributed across Russia.[108] Russia, too, was taking exceptional measures. Units along the western and south-western fronts were being brought up to full strength, troops and equipment shifted from central Russia to the west and forces moved across from the Far East.[109]

On 13 May 1941 the head of SIM, General Amé, returned from a meeting with the head of the Hungarian intelligence service. Next day Amé told Ciano that the German war on Russia would begin on 15 June.[110] Two weeks later Mussolini told Cavallero that in the event of a Russo-German conflict Italy could not stay on the sidelines, because 'it would be a question of the fight against communism'. Cavallero was ordered to station an armoured division, a motorized division and the Sardinian *Granatieri* infantry division between Ljubljana and Zagreb in Yugoslavia ready to take part in the upcoming crusade.[111]

When Cavallero met Keitel at the Brenner Pass on 2 June the head of the OKW said nothing about Operation BARBAROSSA. Mussolini was told in general terms of German intentions but Ciano came away with the impression that the Germans did not intend to attack, even though both they and the Russians were concentrating forces on their common frontier.[112] On 5 June, shortly after the pair arrived back in Rome, news arrived that three-quarters of the German armed forces were more or less ready to engage in operations against the Soviet Union. Four days later Cavallero had his first discussions with his staff about the eventuality of Italian action against Russia, the most convenient routes by which Italian troops could get to the front, and the make-up of the special army corps that would be sent there.[113] On 13 June came the news that the German military authorities were now admitting that action against Russia was 'very close' and would take place sometime between 20 June and the first days of July. Mussolini and Cavallero discussed the inevitability of a Russo-German war next day.[114] In the final week of peace the Italian military attaché in Berlin, General Marras, reported that discussions between the Germans and the Russians had collapsed and that the only solution now was force.[115] The offer of an Italian army corps for Russia was in Hitler's hands on the eve of the attack.

Cavallero told Mussolini that he was preparing to send an army corps composed of two 'auto-transportable' infantry divisions (a term which meant that they were trained as lorry-borne troops, but not that they actually possessed the lorries they needed) and a *Celere* division comprising cavalry and *Bersaglieri* light infantry into the fray, a commitment of some 40,000 to 50,000 men. Mussolini approved.[116] The *Duce* might expect another fast war of the kind that had already overwhelmed Poland and France, but sceptics were not so sure. The word went round Rome that Hitler was writing a book to be entitled *Ten Years of Blitzkrieg*. On 21 June Mussolini left Rome – perhaps, it has been suggested, to avoid 'the affront of having for the umpteenth time to receive from a German messenger news of a *fatto compiuto* (fait accompli)'.[117] Next day, as the Wehrmacht drove into Russia, he was in a gloomy frame of mind. 'The curve has begun to descend,' he told his mistress, Claretta Petacci. The Germans would make the same mistakes as they had between 1914 and 1918, winning lots of battles but losing the war. He was sending a small expeditionary force to insure Italy against an uncertain future, but 'I think this is the beginning of the end.'[118]

Mussolini had many reasons for going into Russia on the Wehrmacht's heels. At that moment one of the most powerful was the issue of Fascist Italy's military prestige and credibility, much diminished after defeat in Libya and an inglorious campaign in Greece that had cost her at least 270,000 men – the equivalent of twenty divisions or a quarter of her army. At the council of ministers Mussolini spoke of a problem of 'proportions' between what the Germans had achieved and what his forces had done and would do in the war. Political repercussions would inevitably follow. Therefore it was not enough for Fascist Italy simply to keep the enemy committed. He must be engaged and defeated – and Italian forces must not be beaten.[119] In fact, Mussolini was in more perilous waters than he realized. Hitler intended to make Germany the only power in Europe. After what he thought would be a rapid success against Russia he expected not to need to take any further account of Italy.[120]

Although the *Comando Supremo* exuded confidence, not everyone believed that knocking out Russia was going to be a walkover. The former military attaché in Moscow, Colonel Valfré di Bonzo, warned that the Red Army was a tougher enemy than some supposed. It had weaknesses – the artillery was not as effective as it could be because the guns were used individually or in batteries, and air power was poorly organized and employed, apparently because the Red Air Force had no war doctrine – but it had made intelligent use of its experience in the Finnish war. The rank and file were solid and the senior commanders were reacting to the German *Blitzkrieg* 'more agilely and rationally than might have been foreseen'. The Soviet military machine might collapse, as some people were forecasting, but after a month of combat Valfré did not think such an occurrence was imminent.[121]

As the first Italian soldiers began entraining for Hungary, Mussolini set out his ideas about Italy's strategic priorities. She was currently fighting on two fronts: Cyrenaica and Russia. For the time being offensive action in Cyrenaica was impossible: Italy was too weak and the enemy too strong. Only a change in Turkey's attitude 'or some other unforeseeable events' would permit her to take the offensive. To do so she would need twelve divisions, two of them armoured, two motorized, and two German. Considerations of prestige required that a second army corps, 'more or less motorized, according to what the possibilities allow', be sent to Russia: 'we cannot be less present than Slovakia and we must pay our debts to our ally'. Then there was Vichy France, whose hostile and ambiguous attitude presented Italy with a third front made up of the Alps, Corsica and Tunisia. That would require another seventeen divisions, one armoured and two motorized. In Croatia – the fourth front – Italy must be ready for anything. That added another ten divisions, two armoured and two motorized, to the list. Next Mussolini tacked on a fifth front, Sicily and Sardinia, which would require seven more divisions. Finally, there were no available reserves in the Po valley. Filling that gap would require at least twenty divisions. Adding up his sums, Mussolini told his generals that the army must have at least eighty divisions, five of them armoured and six motorized, by the following spring.[122] At current rates of production the munitions could be ready in between six and eighteen months. To produce 55,000 machine guns would take twenty-one months, and to put 1,620 M 13 tanks and 47,000 motor vehicles into the army's hands would take twenty and twenty-one months respectively. The draft production programme ran on until December 1943.[123]

Even as the first Italian army corps was being readied for the Russian war, Roatta and his staff were working to prepare a second. When he learned about the plan to add another three infantry divisions to his command, the man selected to command the Italian contribution to the war in the East, General Giovanni Messe, protested. Sending more marching divisions was 'absurd': all units sent to the Russian front needed to be lorry-borne.[124] Finding the necessary lorries proved impossible. In mid-July the army calculated that the new army corps for Russia needed 4,000 of them – but the entire output for the next three months had to go to Libya. The soldiers scratched around but were still 3,000 vehicles short. These they thought they could get by August using repaired vehicles, but only by abolishing the workers' summer holidays. Mussolini agreed to do this, but by early August it was evident that this was a pipe dream. Only the artillery and support services could be motorized, and two of the three new divisions would be marching through Russia.[125]

Mussolini had some reason to think that the public were with him in his Russian venture. At the end of June 1941 the crime figures recorded an increase in the monthly cases of 'subversion' (from fifty-eight to eighty-six), mostly in Rome, which the *Carabinieri* put down to the attack on Russia. However, the declaration of war went down well in Fascist circles in Rome, and public opinion at large, after first being taken by surprise, accepted 'the ineluctability of the new campaign'. Whether, as the *Carabinieri* claimed, the public had been galvanized at least in part by 'the adhesion of the European population to the anti-Bolshevik struggle' and the swiftness with which Great Britain and the United States had joined hands with 'their implacable enemy' is open to doubt – but this was certainly the kind of thing that Mussolini wanted to hear.[126]

On 10 July the first Italian soldiers began to move. Over twenty-six days 216 trains carried the 62,000 men of the *Corpo di spedizione italiano in Russia* (CSIR) into Hungary, after which they marched 300 kilometres along a single narrow road through the Carpathians to their assembly point in Romania. Once through the bottleneck they had to catch up with the Germans on the southern end of the advance. There were only enough trucks for one of the two infantry divisions and the *Pasubio* got them, leaving the *Torino* division to cover 1,300 kilometres on foot before it got to the Donbas and joined in the action. The other division, 3rd *Celere*, which was partly cavalry and had divisional transport, moved forward under its own power. All three divisions were complete – many in the Italian army were not – and all had been through the latter part of the Balkan campaign, but only a single *Bersaglieri* regiment could claim to be battle-hardened. None had fought against a modern European army, unlike many of the German divisions which accompanied them.[127]

By Italian standards the CSIR was relatively well equipped. Along with 5,500 lorries and 4,600 animals, it had 220 guns (among them sixty-four 20mm anti-aircraft guns and eighty-eight 75mm field guns, seventy-two of which were pre-1915 models), one hundred and fifty-three 81mm mortars, ninety-two 47mm anti-tank guns (three times as many as three normal Italian infantry divisions), sixty light 3-ton L-3 tanks and eighty-three aircraft.[128] The standard of equipment impressed at least one of its members. 'This expeditionary force is marvellous,' one of the drivers wrote. '[It is] enormously rich in motor vehicles and some of the best weapons which are marvelled at by the [local] populations and by the troops of our allies. Everything is organized and directed to perfection, it must certainly put the Bolshevik wave to rout.'[129] Behind the facade, though, there were weaknesses. To get the Russian-bound divisions up to full strength had meant robbing other divisions in Italy of transport and guns – one of its three anti-tank companies was taken away from the *Centauro* armoured division which was destined for North Africa. The 105mm guns had a maximum range of 14,000 metres, which meant that when the campaign moved fast their firepower was left behind, and the 47mm anti-tank guns could not penetrate the T-34 tank's 45mm armour. Logistical arrangements were soon under pressure. The Italian deployment zone was some 250 to 300 kilometres ahead of the supply centres, twice the usual distance, and therefore needed twice the number of motor vehicles.

The Italian soldiers who walked – or if they were lucky rode – into Russia were borne along on a wave of propaganda. Before the war, Fascist media had drenched the public with anti-Semitic material designed to convince it that Russia was a Jewish-Bolshevik conspiracy. Once it began, the war on Russia was depicted as an ideological crusade against the Jewish-Masonic-Bolshevik alliance. As the troops marched into the country the Turin newspapers described for their readers the chaos of bolshevism under 'the Bear in the Kremlin'. Building on a rhetoric established at the time of the Spanish Civil War,

Fascist Party propaganda told them that Communist Russia was now as much an enemy as 'plutocratic' Great Britain. However, for the vast majority of the Italian soldiers who deployed to Russia, Fascist ideology seems to have played at most a minor role.[130]

The Catholic Church told the soldiers and their families that in fighting atheistic bolshevism they were on a crusade. The new prince-archbishop of Trento, Carlo Da Ferrari, spoke openly in favour of the Axis war, drawing 'warm support in response', according to the *Carabinieri* report to Mussolini.[131] 'Catholics must not forget', the Vatican newspaper thundered in September 1941, 'that among the most pressing objects of their prayers is this: the salvation of 180 million souls ruled by a few militant atheists.' Divisional chaplains reinforced the message. As their first winter on the Eastern Front began to bite, the men of the *Pasubio* division were told by their priest that they were returning religion to a thirsting population in a country where icons had been hidden and churches used as cinemas and brothels.[132]

As they marched into Russia many Italians were struck both by the rich black soil of the Ukraine and by the generosity and the poverty of the peasants who worked it. The villagers seemed happy to shelter the occupiers in their homes and share the little food they had. Afterwards General Giovanni Zanghieri, II Corps commander, put this down to physical similarities ('the faces, especially of the women and children, could have been ours'), to common sentiments, which included a love of music and religious sensibilities – and to the fact that both the Bolsheviks and the Germans were regarded by the Ukrainians as much worse than the Italians.[133] The uninvited guests were seemingly oblivious of the fact that their hosts, some of whose sons had probably already been killed by the Axis invaders, had little or no choice but to get along as best they could with the occupying forces. Behind this seemingly amicable relationship between conquered and conquerors there was always the implicit threat of violence. A gunner of the *Sforzesca* division, writing home in December 1942, made no bones about it: 'We send our laundry to be washed and ironed; if they resist, we claim the service with force. They have to do everything we want, otherwise we'll kill them one by one.'[134]

On 20 July Hitler wrote to Mussolini telling him that the collapse of the Red Army was imminent and that the war was already won. Mussolini replied that he was preparing a second corps for Russia and could prepare a third, adding 'It is not the men we lack.'[135] In fact, Italy was already heading towards a crisis over everything including manpower. By April 1941 she had lost at least twenty of the seventy-two divisions with which she had begun the war and 270,000 of the 1,400,000 men making them up. With all twenty-six divisions stationed in metropolitan Italy committed to frontier defences or slated for potential operations there was no reserve. When the army began creating sixteen new divisions in August it had to find 9,000 officers and 11,000 non-commissioned officers, both already in woefully short supply, and 200,000 men, which meant calling up reservists aged between thirty-one and forty-three. There were not enough motor vehicles or horses to equip them, and the staff worked out that it would take between six and ten months to produce the weapons they needed. Even if half the divisions in the army were left incomplete, the programme could not be completed before the end of 1942. By December 1941 they had raised seventy-seven under-equipped divisions totalling 2,500,000 men.[136] The operational capacity of Italian units was on a downward curve while that of their enemies was inexorably increasing.

A month into the Russian campaign, the air war seemed to be going in the Axis favour. The *Luftwaffe* estimated that at the start of the campaign they had faced 8,000 Russian war planes of all types, and by mid-July they had destroyed 7,450 of them. Now they faced an effective force of only 270 fighters and 255 bombers.[137] Russian airmen, the Germans reported, were nothing much to worry about. Uneducated and with a 'very limited spiritual level', they did not even understand the need to use maps and photographs to prepare routes and targets.[138] Already, though, the Italian airmen were having difficulty keeping up with the rapid advance of the troops, which was affecting their ability to intervene on the battlefield. General Messe asked for temporary forward airstrips, civil planes to fly forward replacement officers, and transport aircraft to bring up supplies. General Giuseppe Santoro, vice-chief of the air staff, was uncooperative, offering only some modified S 81 planes with limited carrying capacity.[139] On-the-spot inspection for *Superaereo* in October backed Messe. Single-track railway lines ran as far as Romania, but from there onwards everything had to be brought forward by road, which required a superhuman effort of will, or by air. Given the distances between supply centres and forward operating bases, air transport was the most convenient means of getting urgent materiel and replacements forward and the only way the airmen could keep up with the rapid advances and get into action immediately. The available logistical means were not sufficient to ensure transportation in the current circumstances. When winter arrived 'one can foresee that air will not always be able to effect the necessary connections and resupply'.[140]

The first Italian fighting came as part of the great encircling movement by generals Heinz Guderian and Ewald von Kleist, which ended with the taking of Kiev in September. Marching into action through a violent storm, the *Pasubio* division went into action on 11–12 August, blocking a line of retreat of Soviet units that were being encircled between the Dniester and Bug rivers. Leading his 3rd *Bersaglieri* towards the Bug river, Colonel Aminto Caretto saw 'rich plains brimful of wheat and maize, rolling ground covered in meadow, thickets of trees, woods, neat little houses surrounded by flowers'. It all looked pretty enough as he and his men raced across it, he thought, but nothing to compare with Italy.[141] After some brief fighting the division pushed further east to the Dnieper river. The motorized elements of the *Celere* division joined them and by 3 September both divisions were on the Dnieper. Colonel Caretto set up his regimental headquarters on a bluff overlooking the city of Dniepropetrovsk. Spread out below him he saw 'an immense stretch of factories, workshops, houses, [and] *palazzi*'. The inhabitants were bustling to and fro, and traffic seemed to be moving as normal.[142]

Behind the advancing troops, spread out over 350 kilometres, were their field hospitals, ovens, munitions dumps, magazines and workshops. Also strung out behind them were the infantrymen of the *Torino* division slogging forward on foot. They reached the Dnieper on 15 September. For two weeks the Italian divisions held bridgeheads on the river and blocked Soviet attempts to reach it. Then, in their first major operation alone, the two infantry divisions fought the battle of Petrikovka (28–30 September 1941), blocking the Russians' escape route west of the city and taking 10,000 prisoners for a loss of 87 dead, 190 wounded and 14 missing.

As the CSIR got its first taste of combat in Russia, the question hanging in the air was how big the Italian contribution was going to be. At the beginning of August, Hitler thanked Mussolini for the offer of a second corps – but that was all. In the middle of the month came the unsettling news that Germany might be going to ask for twenty-six Italian divisions in Russia, though the request never actually transpired.[143] On 24 August Mussolini and Cavallero left for Munich. When Cavallero met General Keitel next morning, Russia was the first topic on the agenda. Thanking his Italian opposite number for the offer of a second army corps, Keitel announced that because of the serious transport situation in Russia no German trucks were on offer. It would, he advised Cavallero, be 'imprudent' to equip a second Italian corps with trucks destined for Libya. Admitting that a second Italian corps could not be given as many motor vehicles as the first, Cavallero undertook to refer the matter to the *Duce*.[144] At the second of two meetings that day Mussolini offered 'another six, nine or even more divisions' for Russia. When Hitler pointed out that logistical problems would make transporting and sustaining huge military forces a matter 'of no small difficulty', Mussolini merely pressed to be able to make a larger contribution.

In the afternoon Cavellero set out the armed forces' economic requirements. The Italian navy needed 100,000 tons of fuel a month, but during the year so far it had only received 50,000 tons and was having to use up its reserves. If the flow of supplies were not increased it would come to a standstill. The navy's construction programme was stalling and it needed 21,000 tons of raw materials that had been promised but not yet delivered. The air force was in difficulties over fuel too. Tank and truck production needed raw materials, and munitions production was running at between 12 and 60 per cent of monthly consumption. Lots of materials had been promised but not yet delivered. Would Keitel please lend his personal help in getting this done? Keitel offered the Italians 500 new trucks from French production and 600 German trucks – 400 of which would have no tyres. Using tracks instead of wheels on rear axles saved tyres, he told his Italian counterpart. Discussion then tailed off.[145]

Leaving Munich, Mussolini and Hitler took themselves off to see the Russian front. Mussolini, as both Italian and German generals afterwards remarked, had no real idea of how to assess the efficiency of the troops he inspected. A special unit, including a motorized battalion, was spatchcocked together from the *Torino* division for him to review. When he arrived, the *Duce* looked tired and worn. General Messe took the opportunity to lay out the logistical difficulties he was having

because of a lack of vehicles and fuel shortages. Mussolini said nothing. 'It was as if he wasn't there,' Messe said afterwards, though at the
time the *Duce* left a much more positive impression.[146] Watching the
drive-past of requisitioned trucks still carrying the names of the commercial companies they had come from, one of Mussolini's diplomatic
entourage saw 'a gypsy-like improvisation' when compared with the
highly organized German war machine.[147]

As the Italians prepared for the next big drive forward to the Donets
Basin, the shape of the campaign in Russia was becoming clear.
Armoured spearheads were pushing far ahead of the marching infantry
to create 'sacs' of Russian units, tactical groups were pushing forward
up to 120 kilometres ahead of the bulk of the armies to contact the
enemy and identify weak points, and the offensive drives were causing
enormous wear and tear on the motor vehicles. Italians and Germans
were using their infantry in frequent attacks against defensive fieldworks, utilizing First World War-style methods involving brief
twenty- or thirty-minute preliminary bombardments. The Germans had
210mm mortars to do this; the Italians had no heavy artillery of their
own. Thanks to their better training, the Germans were evidently
adapting more quickly to this style of fighting than the Italians.[148]

It was also becoming clear that the Germans had seriously underestimated the strength of the enemy they had taken on. At the start of
the campaign they had estimated Soviet tank strength at 12,000 but
by early September that number had doubled. In August it had been
thought that the Russians could produce 400 tanks a month; now there
was talk of the Soviet war-machine being able to produce 1,000 tanks
a month. There were signs that the campaign's goals – Moscow, the
neutralization of Leningrad and the capture of the Don Basin – were
not going to be achieved in a single sweep. What the Germans – and
therefore the Italians – were now fighting to achieve seemed to be control over the larger part of the enemy's mining and industrial zones,
reducing his industrial capacity to a quarter of what it had been so that
his remaining war potential would not allow him to undertake major
operations in 1942. If they were going to achieve their goals before the
winter set in, General Marras advised Rome, they would have to speed
up the pace of operations.[149] Back in Rome the *Carabinieri* reported
'a certain perplexity' in the public mind about the war in Russia and
doubts that it would be brought to a swift conclusion.[150]

Having already marched and driven 1,000 kilometres to the Dnieper river, the CSIR now got ready for another 300-kilometre advance, to the Don Basin. The zone through which the Italian troops had been moving was agriculturally rich and able to supply most of their needs for foodstuffs.[151] The winter harvest had not yet been gathered and there was grain, potatoes and sunflower seeds in the fields and lots of cattle – 'very useful for the troops', Messe recalled later.[152] In the Donbas, where the communists had to import grain, things would get harder. As winter approached supply problems began to mount. With the restored Russian railway system only just beginning to come into service, the supply dumps nearest to the front-line troops were almost 400 kilometres from the railhead. Supplies were beginning to shrink as the Germans tightened their control and lorries were wearing out due to the lack of repair shops and spare parts. As the three Italian divisions began their advance, rain turned the roads into a sea of mud. The first snows of winter arrived on 7 October and shortly afterwards the temperatures fell below freezing point.

Unlike the Germans, the Italians were not caught out. The *Aeronautica* had begun ordering winter clothing for its airmen on 2 August, and Cavallero's staff, drawing on their experience in Greece, had started organizing winter clothing for the troops in Russia shortly afterwards.[153] Drawing up tables of clothing and equipment was one thing, but getting it to the men at the front was another. In October 1941, having experienced at first hand the lack of winter clothing in Greece and exasperated by Rome's dilatoriness, Messe had sent his interpreter off to Bucharest and Budapest, where he bought winter clothing and boots.[154] Despite Messe's requests for Russian-style felt *valenki* boots, Rome would go no further than allowing him to buy a few thousand pairs of locally made quilted cloth boots.

Von Kleist's main objectives were Taganrog on the Sea of Azov and Rostov-on-Don. Covering the northern flank of the German advance, and strung out along a 150-kilometre front, the *Celere* and *Pasubio* divisions set out on 5 October for their first objective, the railhead of Stalino (now Donetzk). The infantry trudged forward through rain, wind and snow, marching at two kilometres an hour from dawn to dusk and often beyond. The *Bersaglieri* and the *Novara* cavalry regiment took the railway station on 20 October in what Messe described as 'implacable' rain. His next objective was the industrial town of

Gorlovka. The *Torino* division caught up with him on 30 October, having marched 1,400 kilometres from their starting point in Romania and his troops took the town on 2 November after house-to-house fighting. Messe now learned that the Germans' objectives were Stalingrad and the oil wells of Maikop. Going any further, he told Rome, needed massive logistical support: more trains, more fuel, temporary resupply from German stores, and a pause to get his forces into some order and supply his troops with food, warm clothing and boots.[155] Messe got no answer. His problems would soon be solved – by the Russians. Shortly, the whole front would come to a standstill.

The Italians had almost reached the limit of their advance. Forward units took the town of Nikitovka and were immediately counter-attacked by three Russian divisions. After holding them off for five days with little or no artillery support, because the guns were stuck in the rear, and after four relief attempts had failed, the Italian units finally broke out and made it back to Gorlovka, losing 130 dead and 569 wounded. Fighting in or near villages and towns, as the Italians were doing in the more densely populated Don Basin, had one advantage: the troops always had a roof over their heads. 'We occupy a village, the Russians maybe another in front of us, more or less near,' Colonel Caretto wrote to his wife, 'but there's not the continuous worry of the last war, when there were often only a few metres between the trenches and you had to be on your guard day and night . . .'[156]

General Messe settled down for the winter, launching one final offensive on 5 December to improve and solidify his line by filling in a 20-kilometre hole to his left and provide his troops with some shelter for the winter in Russian *izbes* (peasant shacks). The battle, fought by the relatively inexperienced men of the *Torino* division in chest-deep snow and temperatures of −30 °C, lasted ten days. Hot drinks froze immediately, food congealed as soon as it was taken out of containers, the cold froze up the working parts of the 45mm mortars and almost all the automatic weapons, and men's hands froze to firing levers and gun barrels. The Russians launched a violent counter-attack, and the battle came to a halt on 14 December. It had cost the Italians 135 dead, 523 wounded and 10 missing. As outside temperatures dropped to −47° the troops settled into their winter positions and Messe bombarded his superiors with requests for materials to build trenches, shelters and barracks. His Intendance staff and their opposite numbers back in

Rome performed minor miracles and by mid-December all Italian soldiers in line and in the rear echelons had full winter kit – which was more than the Germans had.[157] Everything seemed to be settling down for a pause – but the Russians had other ideas.

Italian military intelligence in Russia had performed poorly during the early months of the campaign. The central intelligence office failed to compile situation reports, exchange information with divisional intelligence sections, or make contact with the various German intelligence sections in the field.[158] General Amé was forced to intervene early in September and tell the head of intelligence with CSIR, Lieutenant-Colonel Clemente Giorelli, what he should be doing. What was missing were clear assessments of the strength, deployment, command posts, fortifications, armament, lines of communication, support services, troop morale and physical condition – in a word everything about the Russian divisions facing the Italians.[159] Giorelli was labouring under difficulties – he had no radio intercept units of his own and had to rely on divisional intercepts, and the Germans never really trusted the Italians – but he was clearly not up to the task. Amé replaced him and gradually things improved so that two days before the Russian Christmas offensive military intelligence was able to indicate exactly when and where it was going to happen.[160]

At 6.40 a.m. on 25 December, after a ten-minute preliminary bombardment, two Soviet cavalry divisions and a rifle division hit the *Celere* division, whose five battalions were holding a twenty-kilometre front at the junction point with the German XLIX Alpine Corps. Air reconnaissance had tracked the Russian build-up over the previous five days, so that the attack was no surprise. 'We were waiting for them,' 2nd Lieutenant Amedeo Rainaldi of the 3rd *Bersaglieri* wrote later. 'And on they came, by the thousand . . . a frontal attack by those faithless people.'[161] The Italian defences were spread out in a loose line of strongpoints. The Russians bit into the Italian positions, taking the outliers. Italian defenders fought hard: one company of the *Tagliamento* beat off two Russian infantry battalions, losing all its officers in the fight, and one of 3rd *Bersaglieri*'s regiments threw back two Russian infantry regiments. Behind the *Celere* were two German regiments and seventy-five tanks. The Germans launched a counter-attack at midday – an hour and a half after Messe had requested it – which helped contain the Russian offensive. Further counter-attacks and then a counter-offensive over the next two days stabilized the front, and the battle came to an end on 31 December 1941. It had cost the Italians 168 dead, 715 wounded and 207 missing.

Two days before the year ended, Hitler wrote to his ally. If the war in Russia had not been brought to a decisive conclusion then that was due to the weather. Tired generals had been put out to grass and replaced with talented new ones. They and the new divisions that were being created would be ready early in the spring for the 'definitive annihilation' of the enemy. Hitler now needed men. An offer of two Italian army corps made by Ciano at Berlin on 29 November was accepted with thanks. They should be moved to the front before the snows began to melt, when movement would be impossible for four to six weeks. As far as Italy's main enemy was concerned, Japan's entry into the war meant that Great Britain could not fight successfully on two or three fronts. The time was coming when Churchill would get his comeuppance.[162]

Summing up German military operations in 1941 from his vantage point in Berlin, General Marras pointed out that the Russians had been underestimated from the start and were still being underestimated, just as England had been in September 1940. Hitler's armies had won great victories but had not achieved the decisive success his high command had been expecting. Instead, the Soviets had broken the myth of German invincibility. In focusing on Russia and England, the Germans had lost sight of the importance of the Mediterranean – and would continue to do so. German strategic and tactical methods, which had won such rapid and imposing successes in Poland, Belgium and France, were progressively losing their effectiveness. The Germans and the Soviets were fighting for their existence in what had become a war of annihilation – in which, it went without saying, the Italians were now caught up. The fighting had reached 'levels of ferocity and destruction that have not happened in European wars for centuries'.[163]

Italy's war in Russia would never reach the levels of barbarism plumbed by the Germans, but Fascist propaganda did its best, depicting the Red Army as a well-equipped but mindless horde prone to barbaric violence and fuelled by alcohol. By the end of 1941, censors were reporting soldiers' stories of Russians eating the hearts and kidneys of their own dead, and Mongolians horribly mutilating prisoners. Some of the invaders acknowledged that the Russian soldier, though often ill-fed and poorly outfitted, was a brave opponent who frequently fought to the last. Others faced a different enemy. 'We've had absolute proof of their wickedness,' one soldier wrote home. '[W]e've had the honour of seeing the naked corpses of our brothers who died as heroes. On their bodies were the signs of the tortures inflicted by these bandits.'[164]

Chapter 6
Terror in the Balkans

When Mussolini and his entourage had met Hitler at Munich on 18 June 1940 to discuss the terms of France's capitulation, Foreign Minister Ciano had asked a question about Italian gains in the Balkans. 'You need to be moderate,' Hitler told the Italians, 'you must not have eyes bigger than your stomach – let's hope that you don't want Croatia.'[1] In fact, Mussolini's eye had been on the region for some time. In his 'New Order' in the Mediterranean, Croatia and Albania were to be Rome's two outposts dominating the Balkans. The occupation of Albania in April 1939 had laid a foundation for the new construction, and Ante Pavelić's Croatian *Ustaŝa* were intended to help complete it.

Pavelić had first arrived in Italy in May 1929, and three years later he was allowed to form a small émigré militarized force. After attempting to assassinate King Zog of Albania, and actually assassinating King Alexander of Yugoslavia in October 1934 – quite likely acting on behalf of Italian military intelligence – the *Ustaŝa* were disarmed and Pavelić was sent to prison in Turin, where he served a comfortable two-year sentence. For several years he and his gang were kept on ice, but then at the start of 1940 Ciano renewed contact with them in the belief that they could start an internal insurrection which would legitimize Italian intervention. At that moment Mussolini was interested in a possible alignment with Yugoslavia which would put limits on German expansion in the Balkans and speed up the collapse of Greece, so for the moment Pavelić was not part of the Fascist design for the region. His time came with the Yugoslav coup on 26–27 March 1941 which unseated the pro-Axis administration. His assertion that the Croat population was eagerly anticipating the collapse of the last bulwark of the Versailles system and the end of a mongrel state 'created to oppress the Croat nation and perpetually trouble the Italian nation' was just what Mussolini wanted to hear.[2]

INTO THE WHIRLPOOL

Hitler immediately opted for revenge and German military planning was revised to attack Belgrade. Mussolini now had his eye on Dalmatia and Croatia, and Pavelić was his instrument to get them. While Roatta was advising General Ambrosio, whose 2nd Army would attack the target, immediately to shoot Serbian *Četniks* or any other civilians 'coming from beyond the frontier who commit acts of hostility, sabotage or rebellion', Mussolini called in Pavelić. In return for being set up in Zagreb as master there, he promised to prepare the local populace for Italy's demands to rule Dalmatia. With that 250 *Ustaša* were released from confinement, given uniforms, arms and equipment, and sent into Croatia via Fiume when the invasion of Yugoslavia began.[3] On 6 April, as German bombers hit Belgrade and German ground forces began their swift land campaign, Italian bombers struck at Dalmatia. Five days later units of Ambrosio's 2nd Army began advancing into Slovenia and along the Dalmatian coast. They met little resistance and six days after that the Yugoslav government surrendered unconditionally. The swift campaign cost the Italians forty-nine dead, wounded and missing.

In talks at Vienna on 21–22 April, Ciano and Ribbentrop dismembered the former kingdom of Yugoslavia. Italy annexed southern Slovenia, Dalmatia, which contained almost half a million Croats and where she installed a civilian governor, Giuseppe Bastianini, who was soon fighting with the Italian military authorities over control, and Cattaro on the coast, established a protectorate over Montenegro, and incorporated Kosovo, Ciamuria (in western Greece) and parts of Macedonia in an expanded Albania. The Germans took control of northern Slovenia and Serbia. Croatia-Slovenia, Bosnia-Herzegovina and part of Dalmatia, including the coastline between Spalato and Cattaro, became the Independent State of Croatia. The Germans and Italians split responsibility for the new state between them, the Germans controlling the northern half and the Italians the southern. The division was far from equal: the Germans controlled the large urban

centres, including the capital Zagreb, and levered economic concessions in the Italian zone including the rich bauxite mines. To make an
immediately fragile situation even more complex, the Italians' share of
southern Croatia was divided into three: a coastal zone in their hands;
a demilitarized inland zone behind it where they could conduct military operations but where civil power was in Croat hands; and a third
zone under civil and military control by the Croats but which German
and Italian troops could enter if necessity required.

The Italian army now began a headlong plunge into wartime Balkan
politics. The monarchist and nationalist Draža Mihailović and his Serbian *Četniks* retreated into the mountains of western Serbia, where they
began their fight to restore the monarchy after the Allies won the war.
Pavelić arrived in Zagreb to find the Germans already established there.
Trouble began brewing at once. The Croats fell on the Yugoslav army's
weapons stores and began unofficially recruiting in the Italian occupation zones. Ambrosio's occupying troops were greeted with 'tepid
sympathy' in the countryside. In the towns, where *Ustaša* propaganda
was active, they were looked upon as 'a necessary but transitory evil'.[4]
In northern Croatia, Italian military intelligence believed that the
Gestapo were activating a prearranged plan to take control of Croatian
mineral and industrial resources in partnership with Croat financiers
and industrialists.[5] The Croats, meanwhile, were making no secret of
their territorial ambitions: the annexation of Dalmatia, Bosnia and the
whole of Herzegovina, to which, SIM reported, *Ustaša* detachments
had been sent, 'ostensibly to safeguard Croat nationals, but in reality
to support the Muslim movement [there]'.[6]

In late May Mussolini decreed that Montenegrin affairs were the
responsibility of the Foreign Ministry.[7] Having lost slices of their territory to Albania, Montenegrins now found themselves the targets of
Croat claims to the former Sanjak of Novi-Bazar. Armed clashes broke
out between the two sides in the latter part of June and the *Marche*
division found itself in the middle of the dispute, losing some soldiers
killed and wounded by *Ustaša* fighters. In Albania, 9th Army faced
what the military authorities regarded as traditional local banditry,
devoid of political significance but encouraged by the cloudy political
situation, 'which lets them think [they can act] for some time with relative impunity'.[8] This was an underestimation of the problems. The
Muslim-dominated population of Kosovo, which was handed over to

Albania, itched to get their revenge on the Serbs who had persecuted them for decades. Terrified Serbs fled into Montenegro. So did Serbs from the Croatian borderlands escaping from the *Ustaša*. Currents of ethnic, nationalist and religious tension washed in all directions as Catholic Croats, Orthodox Serbs and Muslims began the bloody process of settling long-standing historic accounts.

Surveying the situation at the start of June 1941, SIM claimed that the Italians had been well received in Slovenia, chiefly because of the spoliations being carried out by the Germans in their own part of the country. The dangers to Italy appeared to come from two sources: German pressures on the local population to join the Reich, and the increasingly desperate economic situation of Slovene former officers and non-commissioned officers of the Yugoslav army who were getting no financial assistance. Dalmatia seemed to be settling down to rule by the Italians, helped by the existence of substantial numbers of Italian speakers, though not all were sympathetic to Fascism. In Croatia, Pavelić was under pressure from the Croat National Socialist Party. This and the pro-German leanings of some members of his administration was leading many to hope for help and assistance from the Italians. In the Croat-occupied parts of Dalmatia *Ustaša* reprisals and vendettas were making Orthodox Serbs look to Italy for protection. In SIM's view, the contrast between Italian occupation and the military occupations of the Serbs, Germans and Croats was 'to our clear advantage'.[9]

The German invasion of Russia on 22 June 1941 brought yet another combatant into the field: Tito and the Yugoslav Communist Party (KPJ). SIM believed communism was widely diffused among the Serbian intellectual class but that it was counting above all on the workers and sailors. Dalmatia was thought to be a particularly fertile ground because it contained most of the former sailors of the Yugoslav navy.[10] Communism now presented a greater threat everywhere, but particularly in the Balkans. Facing occupation forces that were both the expression of Fascist ideology and the fact of foreigners in arms on national soil, communists and nationalists were joining forces. This was especially true, SIM believed, in the former Yugoslavia, where the two were joining forces under the banner of pan-Slavism.[11] In fact, any unity between the two groupings was only skin-deep, because the communist partisans were seen by Mihailović and the Yugoslav government-in-exile as their main enemy. 'We are at war with the occupiers, but we don't want the Communist Party as our guide' became the stance for many who were resisters, and in independent Croatia, Dalmatia, Bosnia and Herzegovina rebel commanders made common cause with the Italians. The first fighting between communists and *Četniks* occurred at the end of October. A process of collaboration now began as Italian commanders made accords with *Četnik* bands and they in turn co-operated with Germans and Italians against the partisans.[12]

With no unified plan for its Balkan acquisitions, no rights to any of them, and facing problems that were soon beyond its administrative capacities, Fascism was going to have to rely on military force to hold onto its gains – and to hold them down. While civilians haggled and manoeuvred, the soldiers juggled with numbers. Ambrosio's 2nd Army, slated to hold Dalmatia, Slovenia and the Croat zone, lost its mobile divisions and by mid-July had shrunk from fourteen divisions to nine. The planners in Rome intended to pack the majority of them into Dalmatia and the zones close to it: Cavallero told Ambrosio on 6 July that he wanted Croatia 'confronted by troops'. Ninth Army, responsible for Albania, Montenegro and Kosovo, put in a bid for seven divisions; 11th Army, slated for Greece (which Guzzoni thought the Germans might abandon completely, extending Italy's military obligations even further), claimed another sixteen divisions. Logistics alone made it impossible to sustain thirty-two divisions in the Balkans, and the army general staff reduced the total to between twenty-three and twenty-eight divisions. After the losses in Greece, the army had a total of sixty-four divisions. Keeping more than a third of them in Greece and the Balkans would put enormous pressure on an army that was fighting in North Africa and Russia and at the same time facing the possibility of having at any moment to occupy Corsica, Tunisia and parts of metropolitan France. By July, Rome had been able to pull two of its thirteen divisions out of Greece, but because of the trouble brewing in Montenegro it was only able to pull out one of the twelve divisions stationed there.[13]

As soon as the Croats occupied Bosnia and Herzegovina the *Ustaša* set about butchering their Serbian, Jewish and gypsy inhabitants. In all, as many as 530,000 Orthodox Serbs, 30,000 Jews and some 27,000 gypsies died between 1941 and 1945.[14] When Russia and Germany went to war the *Ustaša* outrages accelerated. The Italian army soon discovered what was going on. When the Italian military command took over the garrison at Knin it found the corpses of fourteen people, some of them women whose breasts had been sliced off, in the cellars. On the island of Pago, which had been turned into a concentration camp for Serbs and Jews, the Croats were known to be killing fifty people a day and throwing their corpses into the sea. Things were now happening that were beyond belief. In one village, the *Marche* division reported, *Ustaša* officers offered starving mothers in prison a meal composed of their own children, roasted on a spit. At another, the children of Orthodox Serbs who had managed to escape were killed, their hearts and livers removed and draped on the door handles of abandoned houses.[15] Desperate Orthodox Serbs, Muslims and dissident Catholics appealed to the Italians for help. Ordered to stay at their posts and not to interfere in local affairs, the Italians looked on as the *Ustaša* committed rapes and bestial murders with impunity. 'Any feeling of sympathy for the Croat nation ceased when forced to witness these excesses,' General Furio Monticelli, commanding the *Sassari* division, reported.[16]

Analysing the Croatian situation, Ambrosio believed that the masses were democratically minded but that Italy's annexation of Dalmatia had stirred up nationalist feeling. The 'excesses into which the regime has fallen in confronting and resolving the racial problem' were due to the rise to power of men who were unprepared for it and executive organs that were 'blinded by . . . the desire for vendetta'. The result was an explosion of excesses that at times descended into 'medieval barbarities'. The *Ustaša* were infiltrating men into the Italian-occupied ports of Spalato and Sebenico to fan the flames of local irredentism, and they and the uniformed remnants of the Yugoslav army regarded the Italians with 'an ill-concealed sense of mistrust, if not outright hostility'. His conclusions were far from comforting. Apart from Pavelić, who was likely gradually but inexorably to fall under the influence of his extremist collaborators, the country and almost all the heads of the *Ustaša* movement 'are against us'. The situation was likely to get worse and not better, and unless something happened which reversed all the negative currents, close and cordial collaboration with the nascent Croat state would never happen.[17]

Ambrosio's analysis went down badly in the Foreign Ministry. What the military commanders did not appear to understand was that any sympathy shown towards Serbs and Jews was a 'negative involvement' in an internal struggle which created 'a state of mind of loathing for us'. What went on inside Croatia was a matter for the Party and the Croat government. The army should come into line with official policy and stop doing anything that secretly favoured Jews or Serbs.[18] Following his ministry's lead, the Italian ambassador in Zagreb, Raffaele Casertano, proposed that the Italian army withdraw from the occupied territories and leave the Croats a free hand, thereby demonstrating that Italy respected the independence and the sovereignty of her ally. A gulf was opening up between the army and the Fascist political authorities in Zagreb and in Rome that would only widen.

In every one of Italy's new Balkan fiefdoms the Italian army found itself standing on highly unstable ground. On 12 July 1941 Montenegro was declared an independent sovereign state by a handful of carefully chosen deputies who were each then given 3,000 lire by the Italian civil commissioner, Serafino Mazzolini. Becoming a protectorate under Fascist Italy was not what even 'collaborationist' Montenegrins expected.[19] A local revolt broke out at once and within days the Italian army was pinned to a handful of the major towns as pan-Slavism married up with local communism, the insurrection spread inland from the coast, and the villages fell into the hands of a mixture of communist-led and local resistance.[20] General Pirzio Biroli, 9th Army commander in Albania, instructed General Luigi Mentasti to put down the revolt. His troops were ordered to act with 'extreme rigour' but to avoid reprisals and 'useless cruelty'. In the focal points of the rebellion, people and habitations were to be destroyed, and hostages taken in the operational zones were to be frequently exchanged for others, so that 'the whole population runs the risk of eventual repression'.[21] Pirzio Piroli told his troops that they faced a 'presumptuous, untrustworthy and vengeful' enemy who bore all the marks of 'the ancient Asiatic hordes' and hated Italy's 'racial superiority'.[22] Afterwards he would admit to following a racial policy but paint himself as the defender of the Slavs against the Croat Ustaša, the Germans and Tito's communists.[23]

Cavallero wanted the revolt repressed in such a way as to provide an example to the neighbouring territories. Moving out from Podgorice, their operational centre, Italian troops lifted the siege of Cetinje and started sweeping the coastal zone. Mentasti demanded 'maximum aggression' in order 'always to maintain moral superiority', and

General Gino Pedrazzoli ordered the men of the *Taro* division to act 'in the most pitiless manner' as they moved out from Cattaro and cleared the surrounding zone of rebels.[24] Reprisals began at once as both sides shot captives. A mass popular uprising which they could not control was the last thing the communists wanted. Following instructions from Tito, they abandoned attacking towns, sent the insurgents back to their homes and switched to guerrilla tactics. As they did so, Pirzio Biroli began the second stage of his action. Aided by local tribes and nationalist groups who were eager to fight the communists, his troops first cleared the coastal zone and then spread inland. By the middle of August the military reoccupation of Montenegro was complete and strong garrisons had been established across the country. The whole operation cost the Italians 1,079 dead and wounded. The civilian population felt the weight of the insurrection: 5,000 died, 7,000 were wounded and 10,000 were deported.[25]

Given full civil and military powers by Mussolini on 25 July, Pirzio Biroli was made governor of Montenegro in October. To run his new fiefdom, he drew on his colonial experience. As governor of the Amhara region in the immediate aftermath of the Abyssinian war he had been bombarded with instructions from Marshal Graziani to show 'refractory' tribesmen no mercy, to hang rebel chiefs, shoot their most important lieutenants and raze villages to the ground. He had also been told that repression to disarm rebels should never get out of hand, and that propaganda and persuasion should be used as well as force. He had obeyed orders, but had criticized the 'wave of terror' Graziani had unleashed in Abyssinia after the attempt on his life in 1937.[26] From that experience he forged the policy he would now apply to Montenegro. Civilians must be brought to abandon vain hopes of a successful revolt against the Italians and see that a new life was possible if they collaborated. Translating this into practical terms meant addressing the economic problems the country was suffering, but first and foremost it meant maintaining order. The Balkan peoples only respected the strong and thought goodness was weakness. They had to be treated justly but toughly 'like all rough and primitive peoples'.[27] 'Arming in order to disarm', he recruited trustworthy local chiefs and doled out carefully recorded weapons to their followers. This, he believed, was 'the only way to get positive results and guarantee the populations of the villages that are most far away from us which have declared their allegiance to us (and which we cannot garrison) from reprisals by a few bandits'.[28]

With autumn approaching, Pirzio Biroli was confident that his strategy was working. Snow and cold would force the rebels out of the mountains and into the villages to find supplies. His troops now had to deal with the final phase of the rebel movement – brigandage. For this they needed the right attitude. A feeling of hatred towards communist partisans and anyone who helped them was a necessary part of a counter-guerrilla strategy. Without it, it was impossible to fight an enemy who was 'unscrupulous, determined, violent, and bloodthirsty'.[29] The troops also needed a new methodology. The 'garrison mentality' which tied soldiers to their barracks had to go: barracks were for resting in, not for living in. Units must get thoroughly familiar with the terrain, relying less and less on locals, so that they could react quickly and go anywhere. Light units, well supplied with automatic weapons, would be the main instruments. Once the main communication routes were secure, the soldiers of XV Corps' four divisions (*Messina*, *Venezia*, *Taro* and *Pusteria*) would seize the initiative from the enemy, taking them by surprise in the villages where they took refuge and vying with them 'in method, audacity, [and] readiness'.[30] The idea was sound enough – but it was way beyond the capacity of a poorly equipped army of unenthusiastic conscripts, undertrained junior officers, and senior officers who often showed signs of over-promotion and incompetence. Instead, the Italians exerted their control by burning villages and executing partisans, and the partisans fought back. On one occasion a group of over 200 attacked the head and tail of an Italian motorized column with machine guns and grenades, burning trucks, killing or wounding nineteen soldiers and capturing forty. An *Alpini* battalion which came to their aid lost three dead and eight wounded.[31]

As thick snow began falling on the mountains Italian garrisons were withdrawn from exposed posts in the central highlands. The partisans now busied themselves liquidating so-called 'collaborationists', spies and Muslim militiamen. The Fascist civilian authorities complained that Pirzio Biroli was showing the rebels too much clemency and turning Montenegro into a 'hospital' for partisans, and the local *Carabinieri* thought there were too many proclamations and too few shootings, but Pirzio Biroli saw an opportunity to isolate the hard-line partisan chiefs who were executing 'deviationists' from their supporters and the population at large. On 31 October 1941 the repressive policy of the previous three months was ended. Controls were put on military action: suspects could no longer be interned directly, and the soldiers were ordered to stop carrying out arbitrary actions that damaged Italian prestige. A special commission scrutinized the grounds on which every single internee was being held and at the end of the year 3,000 were pardoned and allowed home. In an effort to make them propagandists for a soldiery that was both 'gentle' and 'solicitous', the hostages that the army did take were well treated. The new policy did not go down well with the local Foreign Ministry representative, who criticized Pirzio Biroli for being too soft.[32]

The guerrilla war continued – roads and railway lines were particular targets – and the partisans showed no signs of taking up Pirzio Biroli's offer of a thirty-day amnesty during which they could give up their arms and return home. Italian columns were ambushed and on 1 December, against Tito's orders, 2,500 partisans attacked the city of Pljevlja, garrisoned by 1,800 *Alpini*. The attack was beaten off and some ninety rebels, *francs-tireurs* and suspects were shot. In return, after ambushing a relief column the partisans shot twelve wounded *Alpini* on the spot and another forty-four captives three weeks later. With that Pirzio Biroli abandoned his attempt to win over a population he had believed to be at least malleable. His soldiers were ordered to raze to the ground villages suspected of harbouring rebels and confiscate their livestock. Next day an order from Mussolini, enthusiastically backed up by Cavallero, instructed him to stop co-operating with native auxiliaries no matter how anti-partisan they might appear to be.[33] Pirzio Biroli ignored it, encouraging the Montenegrin people to take arms against the 'bandits' if they did not want to open themselves up to Italian reprisals, while at the same time giving the Četniks the space to take over fighting the communists.[34]

If the military problem was temporarily solved – Pljevlja had been a major setback for the communists and Montenegro would stay fairly quiet until spring 1943 as the Italians conducted a 'pacification' programme against local partisans with the help of Montenegrin Četniks – the Italians faced considerable economic problems. Before the war Belgrade had milked Montenegro, keeping it just afloat with an annual subsidy which had now disappeared. The public finances now had to be reorganized, commerce generated, public hygiene implemented, roads built, wages raised from 'derisory' levels, and food and fuel provided before winter began. If the country was going to get back on its feet there was everything still to do, Pirzio Biroli told Rome.[35] He suggested that the solution to the problem was annexation by Italy – but Mussolini would have none of it, and the military were left to govern the country on their own.

While Pirzio Biroli went about 'pacifying' Montenegro, Mussolini grew worried about the increasingly close alignment between the Croats and the Germans. The 'fluidity' of the situation required 'maximum vigilance', and on 24 July 1941 he demanded that the nine divisions stationed along the Dalmatian border with Croatia be increased to ten, two of them armoured and two motorized. The fact that the Wehrmacht was at that moment carving its way deep into Russia, confident that its war with bolshevism would shortly be over, probably had something to do with his decision.[36] Three days later Serbs in the demilitarized zone rose up against the hated *Ustaša*. The Italians still had a foothold in the area at Knin, where elements of the *Sassari* division were garrisoning the town. The military and civilian Croat authorities were cleared out and the garrison commander took full control. Accepting the Serbs' assertions that they had nothing to do with the communist partisans and that they were only fighting the *Ustaša*, whom he saw as the real troublemakers, the local commander, General Monticelli, allowed them to take over the town.

Ambrosio told Rome that after a period of relative restraint during which they had only killed 'valid men' the *Ustaša* were on the rampage again, committing 'unheard-of atrocities' on women and children whose menfolk had fled to the mountains, and shipping the Jews of Zagreb off to a concentration camp. If the revolt grew, was he to use all available troops to carry out an in-depth pacification of the region or to leave that to Croat units and only occupy locations of major interest to the Italians?[37] Cavallero proposed that the army occupy the entire demilitarized zone, eject all the Croat troops there and assume full civilian as well as military powers. Mussolini consented and on 7 September 1941 Ambrosio assumed full power there. His troops were ordered to follow a policy of 'equidistance' between Serbs and Croats. By mediating impartially between the two he hoped to win both over to collaboration with Italy, and by safeguarding both their interests and their persons he hoped to prevent the Serbs from joining the communist partisans.

The appearance of communist resistance alarmed the upper reaches of an occupying army in which anti-Slav feeling was already deeply rooted. The local inhabitants began showing their feelings, spitting on the ground when officers passed them, ostentatiously leaving public places frequented by Italians, and disappearing at the sound of Italian military music.[38] At the start of August, General Mario Robotti, XI Corps commander in Slovenia, warned his officers to remember that 'we are in an enemy country, surrounded by people who only apparently behave properly'. During that month local resisters tried to sabotage railways and telephone lines and ambushed and killed an officer and a soldier. Robotti asked Ambrosio for the powers to take hostages, hold the local population accountable for any attacks, and shoot suspects immediately 'on the very site of the crime and without following long judicial procedures'. The deaths of two more Italian soldiers shortly afterwards made Robotti even more determined to make 'some of these communist elements pay, even if they are not openly or completely guilty'. On 13 September the civilian high commissioner, Emilio Grazioli, introduced the death penalty for those responsible for attacks, for anyone taking part in subversive gatherings and for anyone found in possession of anti-Italian propaganda material. As the month went on Robotti manoeuvred to take power away from the civilian authorities, whom he regarded as weak and indecisive, and Grazioli attempted to stop him. A raid by Grazioli's *Carabinieri*, police, *Guardia di Finanza* and border guards on a resistance stronghold in the mountains south of Ljubljana at the end of the month brought the contest between the soldiers and the Fascist civil authorities to a head. On 3 October a royal decree extended the state of war to Italian-controlled Slovenia.

As the violence intensified, Ambrosio grew increasingly angry with the civilian authorities in Slovenia. Harsh sanctions announced by the high commissioner had been immediately suspended because they coincided with the Ljubljana Fair. That had made Italy look weak. Then Rome had commuted the death penalty imposed on three resisters, leaving an 'enormous and entirely negative' impression. People were saying that the Italians were afraid to apply laws they had been noisily trumpeting. Things were different in Dalmatia. There Bastianini was handing down death sentences and carrying them out quickly. That was the model to follow. Ambrosio had fourteen captured rebels awaiting sentence. 'I hope,' he told the army general staff in Rome, 'that no intervention will alter the exemplary sentence that I am expecting.'[39] A week later he sent out orders that captured rebels were 'immediately to be shot' and towns where they were based burned to the ground.[40]

Robotti's men were now responsible for policing and protecting a vast area covered with mountains and forests. In the central Ljubljana province the *Granatieri di Sardegna* division spread its troops across the area in over a hundred small garrisons. Railways had to be patrolled, fortifications guarded, suspects watched and raids carried out. A long and increasingly bloody tit-for-tat war began. In October the *Granatieri* carried out a series of raids on Mount Krim, south of Ljubljana, killing or capturing sixty-five rebels. Some captives were shot soon afterwards. The resistance struck back, attacking a small outpost close to the southern border of Slovenia and then ambushing a truckload of Italians sent to help. Next they blew up a magazine in a nearby town. Robotti ordered his commanders to react energetically to attacks and if necessary destroy inhabited areas, and General Taddeo Orlando told the *Granatieri* division to respond to offensives in towns 'without any hesitation or false mercy'.[41]

Robotti had no time for the 'enlightened' notion of Grazioli that the Slovenes could be assimilated into the Italian community through a process of Italianization. The cost was too high. 'Not a single day passed,' he said afterwards, 'that Balkan soil was not bathed with the blood of an Italian soldier.'[42] The Slovenes were enemies of Fascist Italy who could only be constrained by savage repression. At the beginning of November, Grazioli, Robotti and his divisional commanders met in Ljubljana and agreed that if and when raids were to be carried out the soldiers had 'maximum autonomy'. Propaganda was ramped up and much was made of atrocities committed by partisans against civilians and captured Italian soldiers. Partisan attacks continued throughout December as railways lines were hit, Italian soldiers killed and bombs exploded in public places. As the year ended, Robotti ordered his soldiers to react 'with the same violence and decisiveness' to 'every violent and bloody attack', and gave them a free rein to raze or burn civilians' houses in retaliation. On 19 January 1942, as General Mario Roatta took over 2nd Army from Ambrosio, Mussolini, who wanted every suspected communist in Yugoslavia to be shot, handed the army complete responsibility for the defence of public order in Slovenia.[43]

On 15 December 1941 Hitler ordered that as many troops as possible be sent to the Eastern Front. Four of the six German divisions in the Balkans (but not the two divisions in Greece) must be withdrawn. The Italians must assume occupation duties in Croatia and the Bulgarians in Serbia. If the Germans withdrew their forces from Croatia in order to employ them elsewhere, would Italy be willing to take on the task of providing and maintaining order there?[44] Mussolini was in favour of the idea, and so too were Ciano and Ambrosio.[45] Roatta tried to persuade Mussolini against it, arguing that the Germans were only making the suggestion because they needed to withdraw troops to deal with the situation in Serbia (which, Hitler's intention notwithstanding, was still very much in their control), that Germany would not give up its stake in Croatia regardless of what Hitler and Ribbentrop said about its being the *spazio vitale dell'Italia*, and that if Italy did take on the obligation they would be in difficulties finding troops for other tasks. Mussolini cut him off: the troop problem would not occur. Asked how he would close down the situation in Croatia, Ambrosio proposed two concentric actions – 'not just sweeps' – the first around Sarajevo and the second north of the Sava. For that he would need an extra five divisions. Mussolini and Roatta approved the idea, and ambassador Casertano was instructed to prepare the Croats diplomatically for what was to come.[46]

When he returned to Rome next day and learned what was in the wind, Cavallero had reservations. If the current British offensive in North Africa threatened Italy's hold on Tripolitania she would need the five divisions slated for Croatia to defend her own territory.[47] The Germans on the ground doubted that the Italians could hold down Croatia, and so, given the Italians' situation in North Africa, did the OKW in Berlin. While Cavallero and Roatta modified their plan, cutting the Italian contribution down to just a handful of battalions, the Germans changed their minds. New German forces would put down trouble in Croatia and conduct deep actions across the demarcation line in co-operation with the Italians while Bulgarians policed Serbia under German command. Ambrosio blamed the German general Glaise von Horstenau for having leaked the original proposal to the Croats and made it out to be an Italian idea, and also made a veiled attack on Cavallero and Roatta, who he believed had sabotaged the plan. In fact, Italy was very ill-placed to undertake a major operation in the Balkans. In the process of propping up North Africa, she was at the same time scheduling units for the expanded Italian contribution to the Russian campaign in 1942. On the other hand, the Balkan situation might get worse. As Ciano put it, 'next spring Bosnia, Serbia and Montenegro will be big cats to skin.'[48]

By the end of 1941, Cavallero and Ambrosio were no longer in tune on Balkan policy. Ambrosio believed the situation in Croatia was good, save for the communists; to suppress them he needed more men. As the New Year began, he worried that 'weak and indecisive' policing was permitting rebel bands to gather anew. For that he blamed Grazioli.[49] He opposed the policy of deporting Jews from Mostar in the 'second' zone: 'preconceptions' against groups who had not caused verified 'inconveniences' must in no circumstances be tolerated.[50] Cavallero thought that 2nd Army should keep out of politics altogether, that there were too many small, isolated outposts and that instead of scattering his forces Ambrosio should concentrate on defending the most important centres and lines of communication using strong columns, not small detachments. Cavallero too was drawing on the lessons of colonial warfare: as military governor of Italian East Africa, Marshal Graziani had told his subordinates that territory was held by using mobile columns, not by scattering small detachments through it.[51] Roatta and Cavallero agreed that if 'a Balkan battle' in Croatia was to be avoided the military authorities must be given full powers over public order and the region must be declared a war zone.[52]

ROATTA TAKES COMMAND

Early in January 1942, General Roatta visited the theatre of war. His assessment of the situation was bleak but accurate. The rebellions in Slovenia, Croatia, Montenegro and Serbia were not a single phenomenon but they shared a single ideal: all were 'anti-Axis'. The revolt was now a common struggle against the occupation regime and as such it would only grow. Unless other factors intervened, it would be extinguished 'only when – with Russia definitively crushed – the rebels will have lost every hope'. Occupying the whole of Croatia would need five more divisions, but if Tripolitania fell every division would then be needed to defend the Italian coasts from British and now potentially American attack. There were three options. Italy could join with the Germans, Croats and Bulgarians in a combined operation to hunt the most important nuclei of the rebellion out of their hiding places; or she could construct strongly fortified positions in the second and third zones she already occupied and send out fast, strongly armed columns to seize the initiative from the enemy; or she could restrict herself to the second zone, fortify the line of the Dinaric Alps which marked its boundary, and clear out the hostile elements within.[53] Mussolini preferred the first alternative.[54] Roatta recommended the third, in conjunction with a combined anti-partisan action. Cavallero preferred the third option too, and wanted Roatta to carry it out: a new man for a new policy and one, moreover, whose lengthy absences from Rome were slowing down general staff work.[55] On 19 January 1942 Roatta took command of 2nd Army and Ambrosio became army chief of staff. Ambrosio now had direct command over Roatta – but not for long. On 7 May 1942 Cavallero created a new joint Balkan command, christened *Supersloda* (covering Slovenia and Dalmatia), and took control of it himself.

Cavallero was not the man to recoil at the thought of more Balkan violence. During his time as military commander in Italian East Africa in 1938–9 he had abandoned the viceroy's policy of attempting political negotiations and overseen several cycles of harsh, repressive action, culminating in an action at the Cave of Zeret in April 1939 when insurgents had been gassed and 924 'bandits' shot.[56] Because the partisans were attacking small columns and isolated garrisons, Cavallero proposed that the Italians should concentrate their troops to defend important centres and essential communications – as Roatta had suggested at the time of his inspection visit. But first the partisans had to be dealt with. The idea of a co-ordinated action to clean up Italian-occupied Croatia and eastern Bosnia had been batted to and fro over the turn of the year. Timing an operation depended on moving extra divisions into the Balkans and this was complicated as second-class 'occupation divisions' had to be exchanged for regular divisions which would then go off to Russia as part of the new 8th Army. They could not be in place before the end of February. So the Germans went ahead on their own on 15 January, sweeping the Sarajevo–Tuzla area. The operation, which ended on 31 January, killed 521 partisans and took 1,400 prisoners at a cost of 156 Germans and 50 Croats dead and wounded. The zone of operations was swept, but the partisans were able to retreat into Italian-held territory – as Ambrosio warned that they would.[57] As the action ended, the Italian air force bombed the Germans in Mostar by mistake. They immediately abandoned asking for further Italian air support.

The heads of the army were all broadly in favour of a joint Italian-German operation, and the German civil military authorities in Zagreb wanted more Italian action. On 4 February General Keitel offered German troops for a co-ordinated three-way action with the Croats to clean up the region and eradicate the insurrectional movement. There must, though, be no friendly accord with the rebels. 'Any passive toleration whatever of the intrigues of the Orthodox [Serbs], Četniks, communists etc.' simply strengthened them and could lead to a dangerous situation throughout the Balkans. The Italians were far from happy with the idea that they would be chasing the rebels out of eastern Bosnia only to hand it back to the Germans. Cavallero, Ambrosio and Pietromarchi all wanted to use the opportunity to push the demarcation line out to the Drina river and have complete military control over Croatia, 'the indispensable premise from which to make it our true *spazio vitale*'. Italy was in the process of carving out for herself a major new area of territory which would at the war's end be integrated into the new Fascist *patria*. Arguments over it with other Axis allies at the war's end must be avoided. Should the question of who controlled Croatia be discussed now in Rome or left until the Italians, Germans and Croats met on the spot? Ciano washed his hands of the decision and let Cavallero do as he thought fit. Because the rebels tended to operate on either side of the Drina river, shifting from western Serbia to eastern Bosnia in response to Axis operations, Cavallero wanted the main Italian effort to be made in Bosnia, which was the bulwark for Montenegro and the pillar of the military situation in Croatia, while the Germans acted from Serbia. He also assured the Germans that the Italian troops occupying Croatia had always turned down any proposal to collaborate with the Četniks – which was untrue.[58]

With Roatta's arrival, Axis military operations in Croatia and southern Slovenia made a qualitative leap, changing from repressive policing intended to establish order and quiescence to large-scale operations of war.[59] As he arrived, a battalion of the *Re* division in the town of Korenica in the second zone was holding out in a siege which lasted three months. Four other isolated Italian garrisons were also under siege. The troops at Korenica were only rescued at the very end of March after two relieving columns had been thrown back by the partisans and over a thousand men lost. In Italian Slovenia a detachment of *Granatieri* defending a railway station south-west of Ljubljana was attacked in early February by a well-armed group of communist partisans. In follow-up operations, four captured members of the resistance were shot on the spot and houses and barns were burned down.

On the night of 23 February, in a vain attempt to decapitate the resistance, Robotti threw a ring of barbed wire, machine guns and searchlights around Ljubljana. The entire city was swept by soldiers and police, thousands were stopped and searched, and some 900 inhabitants were arrested. The haul included the secretary of the central committee of the Slovenian Communist Party, Tone Tomšič, who was shot three months later. Those caught up by the sweep were packed off to the first of several concentration camps. The numbers thus imprisoned grew rapidly – by the end of December official figures showed that almost 20,000 people were at or about to be sent to the camps, where living conditions were appalling.[60]

Mandated to apply a new strategy, Roatta faced serious obstacles – and not just those posed by his enemies. To cover a vast theatre that was largely mountains and forests (the three occupied zones of Croatia and Montenegro together covered some 45,000 square kilometres), he had twelve divisions only one of which had a full complement of men and transport. Eight had only half the motor vehicles they were supposed to have, and nine had only three-quarters of the required number of pack animals. As well as lacking mobility, his troops were underarmed: with only one light machine gun for every forty men, one machine gun for every seventy to eighty men, one mortar for every 100 to 150 men, one light gun for every 500 men and one medium gun for every 1,000 men, the occupying army was basically dependent on foot soldiers with rifles.[61] With only eight aircraft allocated to aerial resupply because of the transport needs in Libya, neither the punitive columns nor the isolated garrisons could count on much succour from the air.[62]

The army regrouped into large garrisons, which meant that the Italian military writ ran only in the towns and along the roads. The *Ustaša* carried on with their reign of terror; the Serbs took to guerrilla action to defend themselves against the Croats and also began to settle old scores with Serbian 'apostates' who had converted and become Muslims under the Turks; the Četniks fought the Ustaša; and the communist partisans began to move into the troubled region. While the army tried to control the uncontrollable, the diplomats in Palazzo Chigi pursued their daydream: full possession of Croatia, 'one of the most pleasant, fertile and rich countries of Europe', which could, Count Pietromarchi was sure, provide Italy with 'important reserves of farm animals, cereals, wood and minerals'.[63]

On 20 January 1942 Mussolini decreed that Dalmatia, Slovenia and occupied Croatia were now 'zones of operations'. Bastianini protested immediately and the military's right to intervene in issues of public order on its own initiative was removed. Military units could now intervene if and when the civil authorities ceded them control but all operations against armed rebel formations were strictly army business. Then, on 1 March 1942, to ensure that the army recovered its offensive spirit and fought to win, Roatta expanded Ambrosio's earlier instructions.[64] The environment favoured the enemy because, 'willingly or unwillingly, directly or indirectly', the population gave away information about the army's location and its movements. So soldiers must be ready to be attacked at any moment, and when they were they must be imbued with 'the iron determination to react blow for blow, with one hundred per cent interest'. The rule was not a tooth for a tooth 'but rather "a head for a tooth"'. In operational zones entire families, lacking adult males without good reason were to be interned. Hostages should be taken, and if there were 'treacherous attacks' against soldiers in those zones they were to be shot unless the aggressors had been identified within forty-eight hours. 'Excessive reactions' undertaken in good faith would never be prosecuted. As befitted a conquering army, general behaviour must at all times and in all circumstances be that of 'a great victorious Nation'.[65]

A 'clarification' issued on 7 April 1942 ordered that captured rebels, or any unarmed male in a combat zone who could be a rebel, be shot on the spot. Further instructions licensed commanders to seize livestock and raze the villages of those aiding insurgents and to intern anyone living near areas where sabotage had occurred. Finally, in January 1943 as part of the preparations for Operation WEISS, Roatta would order that all males found in areas where military operations were taking place should be shot at once.[66]

On 2–3 March 1942, Italians, Germans and Croats met at Abbazia to co-ordinate the anti-partisan action. Not far below the surface there were tensions and suspicions. The Germans thought that the Italians were trying to encroach on their economic interests in Croatia. The OKW was determined that German troops should not come under Italian command. The Croats thought the Italians were trying to get a foothold in eastern Bosnia. Ambrosio, armed with evidence that the Croats did not stick to their agreements, thought their real aims were to regain control of the Italian-occupied zones and recover their sovereignty over Dalmatia. With some difficulty, the three parties agreed that the forthcoming joint action would focus on the Drina area east and north-east of Sarajevo and, at the Italians' suggestion, would occur in two phases in April and May. Three Italian divisions and one German division would take part, while a dozen Croat divisions closed off the escape route to the north-west. Roatta would have overall command while General Paul Bader commanded the German troops. Any 'rebels' caught carrying arms, or who were found alongside men who were armed, would be shot out of hand.

The Croats immediately threw a couple of political spokes in the wheel: they wanted Serb bands to be included in the 'rebel' category, and they refused to allow the use of *Četniks* in the operation – a precondition Cavallero had actually accepted in his reply to Keitel.[67] Ambrosio was convinced that the Germans and the Croats had tried to keep the Italians out of eastern Bosnia. The Abbazia meeting had finally agreed that Italian troops could stay there after the operation until the region was pacified – which meant for an indeterminate time. Now it was up to Italy's diplomats to make sure that 'the famous *spazio vitale* becomes, for this region, an effective reality'.[68] Roatta wanted to make limited use of *Četnik* formations against the communists (whom the *Četniks* regarded for the moment as a greater threat to their post-war goal of a Greater Serbia than the Germans or the Italians), something that had been expressly ruled out in the agreement.[69]

When the three sides met for the second time, at Zagreb on 28–29 March, ethnic politics moved into the foreground. Roatta argued that logically they should first take on the communists and then the *Četniks* but not both at the same time: 'one cannot initiate operations by beginning to shoot people who do not oppose us and in part are fighting our enemies at our side.' He wanted an assurance from the Croats that if the *Četniks* gave proof of loyal collaboration they would not be attacked and that the Serb-Orthodox population would be left in peace. The Croat representative, General Vladimir Laxa, did not reject the proposal to use *Četnik* forces, and the Germans had little choice but to agree. When he heard about this, Eugen Kvaternik, the minister in charge of the Croat armed forces, flatly refused to arm Serbian *Četniks* of any stripe. Messages about whether or not to deal with the *Četniks* sped to and fro. Hitler wanted them left out. Cavallero toed the German line and told Roatta to do so too. Roatta, who had been ordered by Ambrosio to ensure that the operations were carried out 'as rapidly as possible and with maximum energy', played for time. He was starting to see the *Četniks* as a valuable pawn in the game, win or lose. If the Axis won, then the Italians and Serbs together could form a common front against German hegemony, and, if it lost, Serbs who had been saved from the *Ustaša* and the Germans might be the only help Italy would have in extricating herself from the inevitable chaos that would then follow.[70]

The first phase of Operation TRIO began on 17 April 1942 – without the Italians. Told to get going, they temporized, suspecting that the Germans and the Croats had reached an agreement behind their backs. Now they were told that, thanks to the Croats, German troops had been able to start moving, that the *Četniks* had been assured that if they returned home they would not be harmed, and that the Italians were not now needed. Three days later, General Bader told his superiors that the operation had miscarried 'due to the absence of the Italians'.[71] The second part of Operation TRIO began on 7 May 1942 and lasted only eight days. German and Croat forces cleared the partisans out of eastern Bosnia, advancing up to the demarcation line, while the Italians cleared Herzegovina using *Četniks* and Montenegrin nationalists as the spearheads of their attacks, supported by Italian guns, tanks and aircraft. The official record put Italian casualties at 220 dead, 556 wounded and 173 missing; the Germans lost 27 dead, wounded and missing; the Croats and *Četniks* lost 352 and 179 men respectively. A total of 1,646 rebels were killed, 719 wounded and 2,626 captured.[72] The Germans put Italian losses at seven dead and twenty-three wounded.[73] On 10

May, *Alpini* entered the town of Foča, Tito's headquarters – but the partisans had slipped the trap.

The operation had done what the Germans wanted it to do – clear the communication lines feeding supplies to their air and naval forces in the eastern Mediterranean along the Zagreb–Belgrade–Salonika–Athens railway line. It had not, though, wiped out the partisans. Tito moved into central Montenegro, but the partisans there were too weak to stay. Under pressure from the Italians and the *Četniks*, short of ammunition, short of food and having squeezed the local population mercilessly – 'we even took the dirt from under their fingernails' – they had turned a previously sympathetic region against them.[74] An order from Tito on 22 May moved the partisan units out of Montenegro into southern Herzegovina and towards western Bosnia. As they moved out, *Alpini* from the *Pusteria* division cleared the Sanjak in the north, while elements of three other divisions and *Četniks* swept the partisans out of central Montenegro. Pirzio Biroli's strategy – of steadily pushing the partisans into the inhospitable mountains of northern and central Montenegro, encircling them and annihilating them – had worked. Abandoning frontal warfare fought by large units to take or keep control of substantial areas, the partisans who stayed behind split into small groups and turned to what Tito labelled 'intelligent partisan warfare'. The main bands would not return until April 1943.

Facing increasing trouble in Dalmatia and Slovenia, where garrisons had been reduced, the Italians were starting to outrun their strength. On 17 May the chiefs of staff agreed that 2nd Army would have to relinquish two divisions before the end of the year. Deeply suspicious of both the Germans and the Croats, who he thought were using the Italian army as a kind of 'armed guard', and aware of the pressures on the army as a whole, Ambrosio thought that rather than be drawn deeper into Croatia, where it would be worn down yet further, the army should protect the vital Adriatic 'fascia'. There the local authorities in Dalmatia were worried that an 'extremely serious' situation was developing as increasing numbers of young people, impelled by growing nationalist feeling, were joining the rebel bands that 'swarmed' up and down the zone.[75] Ambrosio worried that the troubles on the Yugoslavian side of the pre-war frontier might leach into the Italian provinces of Udine and Gorizia, and military intelligence confirmed that rebel bands were indeed operating in the province of Venezia Giulia with some local support.[76] He now recommended withdrawal to the Dinaric Alps – the 'natural frontier' of Dalmatia. In a series of meetings during the second and third weeks of May, Cavallero, Roatta, Grazioli and Pietromarchi agreed to withdraw all garrisons in the third zone, except for the one in Karlovac, and many in the second zone, concentrate the troops and increase their forces in Slovenia, where the situation had worsened. In an effort to seal off the Italian possessions, Roatta proposed clearing the border with Croatia to a depth of three or four kilometres, covering it with patrols ordered to shoot on sight, and interning 20,000 to 30,000 people. The process began in June.[77]

In Slovenia the partisans had started their spring campaign by successfully ambushing the car of the *Carabinieri* general Giovanni Battista Oxilia on 13 March. They followed this up with several attacks on trains, and in April they attacked a Blackshirt unit, killing four and wounding six. The machinery of repression immediately cranked into gear. Robotti complained that 'too many guilty men' were being 'arrested and transported . . . Let them be shot by all means.' General Taddeo Orlando ordered the men of the *Granatieri* division to shoot 'healthy men' if they were found within the operational area and were 'recognized as rebels'.[78] Raids became the order of the day, villages were burned and suspected partisans were shot. On 7 May partisans ambushed a column of *Granatieri*, killing Colonel Latini and thirty-two of his men and wounding another seventy-eight. The *Granatieri* took their revenge, shooting twenty-six 'rebels' in the next few days and fourteen more men, selected at random from a group of seventy captured in and around a local village, a week later. The black hole of violence deepened. Trains were attacked, Italian soldiers were attacked and killed, and at least one raid turned into a pitched battle, after which the Italians carpet-bombed the area and killed about a hundred 'rebels'.

From the soldier's point of view, this was a war in which the niceties of 'civilized' conflict no longer applied. 'There's nothing here,' an *Alpino* wrote home in January 1942, 'nothing to smoke, nothing to eat, and the rations they give us are poor with a little bread and that's supposed to last us all day.' 'While we were on a night march we burned all the houses and carried off the animals, just like the Germans taught us,' another soldier reported. 'The peasants tried to stop us, but we sorted them out.' Women and girl partisans who were captured and put before firing squads – despite wearing uniforms – died smiling, shouting 'Long live communism and death to the Italians', and spitting at their executioners. Children of twelve shot at the soldiers and when they were captured shouted 'Cowardly stinking Italians.' 'These people have a great [self-]belief and a great hatred of us,' another soldier wrote, 'so we'll never get the better of them.'[79]

Back in Italy the propaganda machine strove to convince the population that all was going well in the Balkans. In the cinemas newsreels put together by the *Istituto Luce* showed confident soldiers being greeted with Fascist salutes by enthusiastic flag-waving locals. Letters home, though guarded in what they revealed, told a different story. Very cold, often hungry, the soldiers were stuck in snow-covered mountains. '[The] rebels hide in these mountains and we have to go and find them and we kill them all because they're foul treacherous people,' one soldier wrote home at the beginning of 1943. The enemy seemed impervious even to death. 'A few days ago we shot 6 communists we had captured,' another soldier wrote home in July 1942; 'they sang all the way to the spot where we killed them . . . dying or living is all the same to them.' 'I'd rather be in Russia, where at least you know the enemy is in front of you, unlike here,' wrote another.[80]

As the Italian soldiers set about the repressive campaign, some believed that there was much to be learned from the way the Germans were fighting their anti-partisan war. Italian losses were due to the softness and weakness of their commanders. Violence seemed to be effective. Men returning to Italy from the Balkans were enthusiastic about the German methods, not least the shooting of hostages. As one soldier from the *Sassari* division remarked, the Germans shot people ruthlessly and were feared and respected, 'while the Slavs say to us "bravi italiani, bravi italiani" and then shoot us in the back'.[81] In May 1942 soldiers returning from Croatia openly admitted that they were following German methods and were now 'competing with the Germans in killing'. Some were critical of violence, which they believed was counter-productive – but they seem to have been in the minority.[82]

Through the spring and summer of 1942 the violence intensified. In May eight captured *Carabinieri* were stripped and shot by partisans; two survived and made it back to their garrison. In June partisans stopped a train carrying 600 Slovenians to a concentration camp, freed the prisoners and then sent it on its way empty. It was the signal for the start of a partisan offensive which lasted until mid-September. The generals grew irate, and so did Mussolini. Meeting Roatta in Fiume on 23 May, the *Duce* demanded extreme measures. The best situation was 'when the enemy is dead'. The army needed to take plenty of hostages and shoot them 'every time that may be necessary'.[83] The partisans got hold of the Italian plans at the start of operations, and as a result sweeps drew blanks and encirclements failed.[84] As the partisans grew stronger, the army's weaknesses were exposed: guard posts were poorly defended, raids were carried out sloppily or inadequately, and round-ups quickly turned into exercises in pillaging and theft. Troops slipped their leash and went on the rampage, stealing goods, and raping and torturing women. Robotti told his officers that there were 'still too many thefts and acts of sabotage committed by soldiers', which 'had to stop' – but Roatta had enjoined his army to be ferocious.[85]

A key component in the strategy now being pursued by Italian military and civilian authorities was the recruitment of local military auxiliaries and the mobilization of actual or potential anti-communist elements. Altogether, the auxiliaries in Slovenia, Dalmatia, Cattaro, independent Croatia and Montenegro, together with assorted gendarmerie, Muslim and other local bands and 'free' *Četnik* formations operating alongside the Italians amounted to perhaps 100,000 men, at least as many as the partisan forces. These attempts to enrol dissident locals to fight other dissident locals met with mixed success. In one region, however, the strategy seemed to work.[86] In Montenegro, Pirzio Biroli sought to mobilize the hostility and war-weariness of 'the many healthy elements' in Montenegrin society by giving them a voice in the management of their country's affairs. His purpose in doing this was to 'nationalize' the irregular Montenegrin bands he had hitherto used only sparingly, who could get into regions his regular soldiers could not reach.[87] Between February and June 1942 the military did deals with 'white' nationalists and *Četniks*, and in July Pirzio Biroli reached an 'omni-comprehensive' accord with General Blažo Djukanović, who emerged as head of the Montenegrin Nationalist Committee. Montenegrins took over control of most of the country while the Italians garrisoned the towns and guarded the communications. Armed by the Italians, Djukanović's 'flying detachments', which by the year's end numbered 35,500 men, roamed the countryside rounding up and interning thousands of communists and suspected fellow travellers. The 'omni-comprehensive' accord, described by one historian as Pirzio Biroli's 'masterpiece', allowed the Italians to keep control of Montenegro throughout 1942 and for a part of 1943.[88]

Operation TRIO had been only a limited success: Mussolini told Roatta that since he had taken over command the situation had 'not stabilized but deteriorated'.[89] Roatta's 2nd Army was clearly overstretched, so Cavallero and Pietromarchi agreed that the moment had come to let the Croats do more of the heavy lifting. Accordingly, on 19 June 1942 Roatta signed an agreement with Pavelić under which the Italians would withdraw their garrisons from the third zone, leaving the Croats to man the forts, and give them policing and public order powers in the second zone, where the Italians would maintain some garrisons. Roatta reserved the right to reoccupy territory if there were renewed outbreaks of violence. Within days, reports arrived that weak Croat control was allowing the rebels in.[90] The Croats had recovered sovereignty in the second and third zones but lacked the military force needed to take over guarding the railways and policing the countryside. The Germans intervened, asking the Italians only to withdraw at a rate that the Croats could cope with.[91] A couple of weeks after the agreement was signed a Croat document pre-dating it and signed by the chief of the Croat police fell into Italian hands. In it, he ordered his subordinates not to start persecuting Jews and Serbs in the second zone 'during the first days'.[92]

Roatta's withdrawal from the third zone created a power vacuum. Soon he was complaining that the Croats had not fulfilled their part of the agreement, forcing him to delay or give up altogether withdrawing Italian garrisons and to continue guarding railway lines, and making it impossible for him to redeploy Italian troops in mobile offensive actions.[93] Wrangling dragged on through the summer and into the autumn, the Croats asking for weapons, ammunition and equipment and the Italians delaying giving them an answer. One reason – among many – to be wary of arming the Croats was intelligence suggesting that they intended to form *Četnik*-type bands and fight a guerrilla war against the Italians in Dalmatia.[94] Even though the *Četniks* were growing more undisciplined, and his generals were commenting on their unrestrained violence, Roatta had no choice but to rely on them since arming his only other potential cat's paw, the Muslim *domobrani* (semi-regular troops), had failed. So as his troops left he handed over what had once been Italian outposts to the *Četniks*.

In Slovenia, where Grazioli estimated that the army controlled fewer than half of the ninety-five provincial communes and less than 10 per cent of the ground, the crisis grew more intense.[95] At the beginning of June, two Italians, one a woman, were killed by partisans. Twenty-two communists were shot in reprisal. Robotti drew up a plan to sweep the entire province. Orders went out reminding the troops that rebels or anyone caught with a handgun was to be shot on the spot unless they were wounded, women, or young men under eighteen, in which case they should be handed over to military tribunals. The population was told that anyone carrying out hostile acts against Italian troops, anyone caught in possession of weapons or explosives, anyone who assisted the rebels, and any healthy males caught near the combat zones without a valid explanation would be shot. Operation VELEBIT began on 16 July 1942. Next day, visiting the generals on the spot, Roatta gave their men the authority to check on anyone simply found outdoors during the operation and 'immediately shoot any civilian found at fault'.[96] When the first three cycles of the operation ended on 26 August, the Italians had killed 1,053 partisans, taken 1,381 prisoners and shot another 1,236 people.

At the end of July Mussolini met Cavallero, Ambrosio, Roatta, Robotti (XI Corps) and General Renato Coturri (V Corps) at Gorizia to review the situation in Slovenia and the adjacent territories. Roatta and Robotti were at odds. Roatta criticized Robotti for failing to clear large areas of rebel formations and Robotti argued that against a fluid enemy 'classic annihilation operations' were impossible. What he had planned for and was carrying out was 'episodic fight[s] against small groups found while scouring the terrain'.[97] Mussolini believed that, because of the invasion of Russia, the war had entered a new phase, in which the Slav population no longer felt that the Italian flag was the least possible evil. The Italians must now show themselves ready to do anything 'for the good of the country and the prestige of the armed forces'. There was to be an end to the traditional 'easygoing softness'. The rhythm of operations must be speeded up and partisan 'terror' must be met with 'iron and fire'. Behind the bombast, the *Duce* was at last becoming aware of military overstretch. 'We cannot hold so many divisions in the Balkans,' he told the generals. 'We need to increase our forces on the western frontier and in Tripolitania.'[98] The number of regular army divisions in Dalmatia and Slovenia gradually diminished in the months that followed – from sixteen in June to thirteen in August and eleven by the end of October 1942. *Četnik* militia filled the gap.

As terrorism in Slovenia increased, Robotti announced that ten hostages would be shot for every victim of the partisans. More operations followed during September and by the time they ended Slovenia was 'on its knees'.[99] The enemy, however, was not. Partisans ambushed an Italian force, leading to more local sweeps during October and November which they were increasingly able to evade. Nor were the Italians able to halt an in-flow of partisan reinforcements. Robotti blamed the civil authorities who had 'hindered, obstructed, [and] hampered' the army in a myriad of ways.[100] In Ljubljana curfews were imposed and there were mass round-ups of suspects. Sweeping through the countryside, Italian soldiers destroyed villages, burned houses and seized property and livestock.

On 16 December 1942 General Gastone Gambara, arriving fresh from limbo after an inquiry into charges that he had mismanaged army funds for personal gain, took over command of XI Corps in Slovenia from Robotti. At first he followed a more tempered policy, relaxing the restrictions on Ljubljana and avoiding large-scale search-and-destroy operations. Reprisals were carried out more sparingly, and Gambara made more use of local militias in repression. During the early months of 1943 the official figures recorded a drop in insurgency. However, the partisans continued to move relatively freely through the countryside and on at least one occasion a poorly co-ordinated attempt by three separate Italian columns to intercept them came badly to grief. Then, in April and May 1943, the brief interlude was brought to an end as the partisans renewed their attacks on the railways. Reprisals were once again the order of the day, though Gambara warned his subordinates not to 'strike out blindly', and the order went out that all captured 'rebels' were to be shot. The fall of Mussolini would produce no let-up in the policy of repression: military sweeps continued up to 10 August 1943. In all, the counter-insurgency campaigns in Italian Slovenia cost the army 1,200 dead, 1,974 wounded and 285 missing. Some 25,000 Slovenes were interned, another 2,000 died in the Italian concentration camps, and 1,620 were shot by the Italians.[101]

While the Italian sweeps through Slovenia were taking place, Tito set off with his communist partisans on their 250-kilometre 'long march' from Montenegro to Bihać in western Bosnia. On 4 November 1942 they reached their goal and three weeks later the Bihać Congress announced the formation of the People's Liberation Movement. Uniquely, the communists disregarded religion and as a result recruited Orthodox Serbs, Catholic Croats who were nauseated by the *Ustaša*'s bestial violence, and Muslims alike. Although they remained very much a communist organization – political commissars educated and led the newly formed proletarian brigades and shock troops – the new forces were coalescing under the banner of patriotism.[102]

As the Italians drew back towards the coastal zones, the German-Croat campaign to destroy the Jews moved into overdrive. In mid-August the German ambassador, Prince Bismarck, asked for the delivery of all Jews in Croatia, 'to destroy them'. The Italian authorities knew from mid-1942 that the Jews were being exterminated. Mussolini agreed that all Jews in Italian-occupied territories should be handed over to the Germans, and at the end of the month Pietromarchi and Castellani agreed on the ways in which this should be done. Roatta demurred. The Jews in the Italian zones could not be given to the Germans, because 'they were placed under our authority'. Handing them over would damage Italian prestige and would have repercussions on the *Četniks*, who would think that they too would in due course be handed over to the Croats. In the light of Mussolini's order the civil and military authorities could not refuse outright to hand over 'their' Jews, so they gave the Germans evasive responses.[103] In early December Roatta persuaded Mussolini that there would be negative repercussions if the Jews in occupied Croatia were handed over to the Germans and Mussolini agreed that they should be interned instead. The Germans kept up the pressure, and when Ribbentrop met Mussolini in Rome in late February 1943 the *Duce* appeared to accept the idea of deportation but then told Robotti to 'invent all the excuses necessary, but not consign a single Jew to the Germans'. The Italians interned 2,261 Jews – but turned away others who arrived at their borders seeking refuge. In so doing they adopted a policy similar to the one applied in the Italian zone of Occupied France, taken over by the Axis powers in November 1942 after the Anglo-American landings in North Africa

(Operation TORCH), which was driven chiefly by a determination to resist German interference.[104]

'IF THE BALKANS ARE IN DANGER SO IS ITALY'

The defeat of the Axis forces at El Alamein in October 1942 and the Anglo-American landings in North Africa on 8 November changed Italian and German strategy in the Balkans. Italy now faced a potentially ruinous situation as new threats magnified her already fragile hold on her Mediterranean rim. For Rome, Balkan strategy now turned on two questions: what should be done to meet the threats both internal and now external, and could units be withdrawn to reinforce North Africa? The outcome, to which Mussolini gave his approval, was a proposal to withdraw a single division from 2nd Army (and another from Montenegro), to pull back yet further towards the Adriatic coasts giving up more garrison posts, and to create a mobile force to counter partisan actions in less vital areas. To defend the islands and the coasts against possible Anglo-American incursions, and protect the border with Croatia, Roatta ordered that maximum effort be put into building fortifications. There were to be no major new anti-partisan actions before the coming spring.[105] The new strategy was partly a reflection too of weakness in the air. Short of aircraft and lacking fuel, the *Regia Aeronautica* wanted fewer small spread-out garrisons and those only where they could be reached by road in the snow.[106]

Although he agreed with Pavelić in mid-October not to arm any new *Četnik* formations and to keep them under tighter control, Roatta intended to continue using them in the fight against the partisans. With partisan activity increasing and the spectre of an Allied landing in the Balkans now starting to haunt Hitler, the Germans regarded the *Četniks*, whose long-term goal was to rid the Balkans of Germans and Italians alike and recreate a federal Yugoslavia, as a potential enemy in the Axis nest. They estimated that there were 70,000 *Četniks* and 35,000 communist partisans. If the Allies landed in the Balkans, the two forces would act as a joint 'liberating force'. They wanted the partisans crushed during the winter to avoid the danger that the two groups would coalesce in the spring and cause the occupying forces serious embarrassment.[107]

The news that the Italians planned to pull back to three enclaves along the coast (Slovenia–Fiume, Spalato and Cattaro–Ragusa–Herzegovina), and hand over seven garrison posts in the second zone to the Croats and eleven to *Četniks* in order to create the mobile force, did not go down well with the Germans, who thought that would allow the partisans, already a major threat in the third zone, to penetrate even further into the second zone. On 12 December the *Comando Supremo* announced that they were indeed withdrawing into the first zone in order to concentrate their forces for an anti-partisan action. Four days later Hitler ordered General Alexander Löhr to start preparations for Operation WEISS to restabilize the region.

Mussolini was too ill to attend the meeting with Hitler on 18 December 1942, so Ciano went in his place and took Cavallero with him. Hitler spoke at length. To meet the threat of an Allied attack, the Axis needed to control 'key points' – Dalmatia, Albania, Greece, Crete and Rhodes – and it also needed to pacify the interior in order to guarantee the railway supply lines. 'Brutal action' would be needed. He, like Mussolini, thought that there should be a joint command. The question who should get it was left unresolved. Then there was the matter of what to do about the *Četniks*. In the event of an Allied attack Mihailović and his forces would certainly move against the Axis forces. Hitler told the Italians that Roatta had to stop using them in support of Italian anti-partisan operations, and they and their pan-Slavist ideals must be annihilated. The Italians must not withdraw from the second zone; instead they should get ready to reoccupy the third zone. To do that would require more men. Cavallero told the Germans that he could do this by sending the next class of recruits to be called up (the class of 1923, who would be called to arms the following spring), from which he would create special combat groups that would be suited for the kind of operations they would be carrying out – which was patently absurd. The Germans were ready to fight in the winter, something the Italians were much less keen on doing. During the course of the meeting, which was filled with gloom because of the situation at Stalingrad, General Keitel admitted that the Germans had in fact already decided on war with Poland and set the date before Cavallero arrived in June 1939 with the request for a three-year period of grace.[108]

The broad design for the forthcoming Operation WEISS was shaped during the first week of January 1943. It would cover a wide swathe of territory from south of Zagreb to the Montenegrin border. In the first phase the Germans would act in their zone while the Italians moved up from the coast and made contact with them; in the second phase the Germans would complete the encirclement and annihilation of the partisans alone; and in the third the *Četniks* would be disarmed and destroyed. In fact, the Italian generals had no intention of doing away with the *Četniks* just now. Roatta called them the only 'white ball' they had in the Croat region (an allusion to billiards).[109] Mussolini, who was trying to persuade Hitler to reach a separate peace with Russia and shift the 'barycentre' of the war to the Mediterranean and therefore wanted the soldiers to reconsider their *Četnik* policy, was persuaded by Cavallero to hold the issue over while waiting for clearance from the Germans to use them in Operation WEISS. On 10 January 1943 Cavallero issued his operational orders. Roatta was to deploy three divisions along a front stretching from Karlovac to Mostar and up to the Montenegrin border. Shortly afterwards the Germans agreed to using the *Četniks*.[110]

Operation WEISS I began on 20 January 1943, at temperatures of −25 °C, with a two-pronged drive by five German and one Croat divisions on Bihać from the north-east and south. According to General Paolo Berardi of the *Sassari* division (writing after the war), all the local commanders were against it, not least he himself.[111] Bad weather and stiff partisan resistance slowed the German advance, which only reached the former Titoist headquarters on 29 January. Partisan bands moved away south-east towards Herzegovina pursued by the Germans. At one point during their escape the Titoists' route was blocked by *Četniks* who were then themselves attacked from the rear by the Germans, allowing them to escape.[112] In the course of their retreat the partisans ran into and over the *Murge* division, taking two key garrisons on 16–17 and 22–23 February. By 10 March the *Murge* was almost completely destroyed. Before the operation was over Mussolini reconfigured the Italian high command, firing Cavallero and replacing him as *Capo di stato maggiore generale* with Ambrosio. On 5 February Roatta was sent to command 6th Army in Sicily and replaced by Robotti.

Ambrosio was far from convinced that Operation WEISS was a good investment of effort. The first stage of the operation was not going

as the Germans had foreseen, they now wanted to compress the original timetable and start phase two at once, and the question of who was
going to occupy the territories once cleared of partisans had not been
properly settled either by Cavallero or by Roatta.[113] General Walter
Warlimont arrived from the OKW and demanded that the cleared
zones be garrisoned immediately by the Italians. Ambrosio flatly
refused. On the contrary, he told Warlimont, it was Italy's intention to
withdraw troops from Croatia. Warlimont explained that Hitler's idea
was to have Italy occupy the cleared area by June so that all German
forces would be available in case there was an enemy action in the Balkans in the summer. Was this discussed at the meeting between Ciano,
Cavallero and Hitler, Ambrosio asked. 'No' was the reply from one of
the Italian generals who had also been present. The only thing on which
the two men agreed was that the Četniks would be disarmed – but not
until Operation WEISS was over, and then only 'with great tact and
not in a short period of time', Ambrosio warned.[114]

This was not good enough for Hitler, and soon afterwards Ribbentrop arrived in Rome with a letter from the Führer. If the Allies tried a
landing in the Balkans, which he thought they might, then the Greeks,
the communists and Mihailović's Četniks would all join in. The Italians should co-operate with General Löhr to hit the communists while
there was still time, consider Mihailović an enemy, and help disarm
both communists and Četniks.[115] Mussolini called all parties to Palazzo
Venezia. A determined Ambrosio stood his ground: the Četniks had
fought well, they should be allowed to continue, and in any case 'annihilating' them would not be easy. Then he went onto the attack. There
was little imminent danger of a landing in Greece as long as the Axis
held Tunisia. As for the strategy behind WEISS, it was not working
and would not work. WEISS I was over and the supply columns were
being attacked exactly as they had been before it started. Sweeps could
not pacify a country – after two weeks you were back to square one. It
was 'a Utopia' to think that the WEISS operations would produce a
solid outcome, and if they did not 'we must not persist'. There were
'many needs' in Italy. Mussolini wound up the meeting with the observation that pacification came first, after which the Četniks could be
disarmed.[116]

When Warlimont and Ambrosio met next day to resolve the unresolved details, the German demanded that the Četniks be disarmed

quickly. Ambrosio played the *Duce* card: Mussolini had said that the matter would be resolved after the partisan problem had been overcome. The Italians would complete the current operations but would not commit to any others, because they had to think first of themselves: 'If the Balkans are in danger so is Italy.' Warlimont told him that the Germans intended to complete their operations against Mihailović, who, unlike the Italians, they had always distrusted as a monarchist and a Serbian nationalist and whose forces were now centred in Montenegro – which was Italian territory.[117]

The Italians never expected much to come from Operation WEISS. General Ezio Rosi, chief of the army general staff, believed that the rebels would evade encirclement once more, and he was proved right: the first phase failed to net the partisans, who reappeared behind the Axis lines in the 'cleared' zones.[118] Now, though, the Balkans were part of a much larger picture. As the Anglo-American armies pursued the retreating Axis forces in North Africa, the prospect of enemy landings on Italian territory or in Greece began to loom large. Ambrosio thought he had until May or June before the enemy could land somewhere in Europe and reckoned that he needed to find nine more divisions just to defend Italy itself. That meant releasing divisions from Croatia, which the army general staff now regarded as a sterile guerrilla war that was wearing down Italian strength and prestige alike with no concrete result. Pulling back to the coast could save four divisions, and reducing dispersion in other theatres to a minimum could make further savings. Greece had also to be defended and that meant sending divisions there to guard Salonika, the danger point.[119]

As he sought to rationalize Italian deployments and focus strategy on the absolute essentials, Ambrosio had to fend off yet more demands for troops in the Balkans. The governor of Albania, Francesco Jacomoni, reported that communist propaganda was gaining ground there and asked for the equivalent of three more divisions.[120] In Slovenia, General Gambara, with 24,000 infantry, was facing 10,000 to 12,000 partisans and needed reinforcements to eliminate them. None were forthcoming, only replacements to fill existing gaps in the ranks.[121] As far as WEISS II was concerned, the Italians would support the right flank of an SS division as it swept down the eastern side of the Dinaric Alps towards Livno and Herzegovina. The operation began on 25 February. The Germans took the major role,

encircling Tito's bands and forcing them to retreat east into Montenegro, while four Italian divisions with *Četnik* support defended
Mostar, thereby keeping the Germans out of it, and harried the
retreating partisans. Robotti had wanted to continue to keep the Germans out of Herzegovina but in mid-March the Italians were forced
to allow Löhr and his two German divisions permission to enter the
region temporarily. In a skilfully managed retreat the communist
bands overcame the *Alpi Graie* division. In the aftermath of
WEISS II the Italians stuck to the letter of their vague undertaking to
disarm the *Četniks* after the partisan problem had been sorted out.
Mussolini backed them, telling Pirzio Biroli to keep the slow-moving
Italian troops in barracks and train what he called Italian *Četniks* 'to
fight in the woods and off well-worn tracks'. Ambrosio toyed with the
idea of creating a force of 100,000 irregular 'guerrillas' in order to
free eight or ten divisions from the Balkans.[122]

The possibility that the Axis might have to fight off an Allied landing in Greece brought the problem of co-ordinated command in the
Balkans back to the top of the German agenda. The local German commander in the south-east, General Löhr, wanted tactical command of
all Italian and German forces in the region, and Field Marshal
Kesselring, as the ranking German commander in the southern theatre,
wanted overall command in the Balkans on the grounds that they were
the right flank of the Russian theatre. Cavallero had refused to put
Geloso under Löhr, and now so did Ambrosio. That was a matter of
pride and national prestige. The immediate practical problem was how
best to equip Geloso to defend Greece. With 4,000 kilometres of coast
to defend and seven divisions to do it, only one of which (the *Brennero*)
was reasonably well armed and then only with antiquated weapons,
Geloso thought he could successfully handle limited landings directed
on a few objectives. Offered one extra division, he made a bid for
another two: not only could he then 'guarantee' Greece against an
attack in force, but the Italians with more troops than their ally could
claim complete responsibility for the defence of the country. Seeing off
an enemy landing would raise the prestige of the army. He had his own
solution to the manpower issue: reduce the occupation of the rest of the
Balkans to the most strategically important zones and lines of communication. How he proposed to handle the 'influx' of rebels he then
expected from the surrounding regions, and the 25,000 rebels he

already had to deal with, he did not say.[123] His case, argued with staff college logic, collapsed in the face of the other demands on Ambrosio's diminishing resources.

The Foreign Ministry was concerned that Italy's prestige and her 'pre-eminent rights' in Croatia would suffer as troops were withdrawn, and so was the army. As the Italians prepared for the upcoming conference at Klessheim (7–10 April 1943), Ambrosio alerted Mussolini to the need to ensure that the Germans accepted the terms of the original agreement with the Croats in May 1941 – in other words prevent the Germans from encroaching yet further into what was left of Italy's Balkan sphere of influence. He ruled out major operations against Mihailović, and also suggested that Mussolini raise the question of a single command for Greece and the Aegean.[124] At Klessheim the political conversations were dominated by the war in Russia. The question of imposing a single unified command on the Balkans was fudged, both sides settling for a formula under which it would be confirmed only when there was an actual emergency. Formally, both sides agreed that Italian garrisons would gradually withdraw from parts of the second zone and be replaced either by German or by Croat troops but remain under Italian control. Ambrosio was determined that the Adriatic coast be held by Italian garrisons which were strong enough not to be 'submersed'. That meant pushing into stretches of coastline hitherto under Croatian control. 'If we cannot prevent Croats getting to the coasts,' Ambrosio told Robotti and General Ezio Rosi, currently chief of the army general staff but shortly to be put in command of all the Italians in the Balkans as commander of Army Group East, 'that must absolutely be forbidden to the Germans.'[125]

On 15 May the Germans launched their third attempt to mop up the partisans – Operation SCHWARZ. Tito, wounded at the battle of River Sutjeska (5–10 June 1943), fled into eastern Bosnia, along with 3,000 to 4,000 of his partisans. Mihailović, also the Germans' target, escaped to western Serbia. The Germans disarmed 4,000 of his Četniks and took them prisoner but believed that the majority had escaped their grasp thanks to help from the Italians.[126] Taking part in SCHWARZ cost the Italians 2,106 dead, wounded and missing, and exhausted what was left of Italian military capacity. The troops of 2nd Army, many of whom had been fighting in the Balkans since the start, were reportedly at the end of their strength. Now exposed to both partisan reprisals and *ustaša* onslaughts as the Italians withdrew from the second and third zones, and running short of weapons, the *Četniks* were ceasing to exist as a fighting force, and Pavelić, who had lost control of large parts of Croatia, was surviving only thanks to the Germans, who were now in control there and acting, as the *Carabinieri* general Giuseppe Pièche reported, 'as if they were in their own homes' and consulting neither Italian nor Croat authorities.[127] Having had to give up two divisions (*Sassari* and 1st *Celere*), and having lost a third (*Murge*) to enemy action, Robotti could no longer hold his ground. On 28 May General Giuseppe Amico of the *Marche* division formally handed Mostar over to the Germans, and in very short order the Italians withdrew almost all their remaining garrisons in the third and second zones. The Germans moved in. Although the Italians were at last incrementing their '15 January' plan, the troop savings Ambrosio was looking for did not occur. Only one division – the *Sassari* – left the Balkans and the size of 2nd Army and the Italian forces in Montenegro actually increased slightly between January and May 1943 to 234,000 and 74,000 men respectively.[128]

Worried by the continuing build-up of Allied forces in the Mediterranean, which he thought pointed to 'vast operational projects' in the western Mediterranean, and preoccupied with the need to defend the French Mediterranean coast, Sardinia, Corsica and the Italian peninsula against potential attack, Ambrosio ordered the generals in the Balkans to give no more ground and to take the offensive against the partisans in Herzegovina and Montenegro. But, he warned them, there were no additional troops to assist them. Instead they must collaborate, using forces in one another's zones and such allied units as were capable of intervening. This did not include *Četniks*, who were being urged by London to collaborate with the partisans. They must be watched closely, and doubtful units disarmed as soon as they showed 'the first symptoms of infidelity'.[129] The army, too, now needed careful monitoring. The impressionable, the uncertain, the unaggressive were to be looked after and 'regenerated', Roatta (newly restored to his former post as army chief of staff) ordered, but anyone showing signs of 'indiscipline, weakness, defeatism, or disorder' was to be put up against a wall and shot.[130] Six weeks later twenty-eight *Alpini* were indeed shot for having surrendered to partisans without a fight.

By the beginning of June, 2nd Army had pulled its three corps back to the coast, where they took up positions around Senj, in the Zara–Spalato zone, and between Ragusa and Cattaro. A month later, after the *Comando Supremo* had sanctioned an agreement between Pirzio Biroli and Löhr, the Italians began somewhat half-heartedly disarming the *Četniks*. Pirzio Biroli, who like a number of his subordinate commanders felt deeply unhappy at leaving his former allies in the lurch, left on 1 July 1943, replaced by General Curio Barbasetti di Prun. By now it was obvious to the generals – as it had been obvious to their troops for some time – that the partisans were controlling the war. '[T]hese partisans have manoeuvred magnificently,' General Gambara acknowledged bitterly, 'and they have known how to "unhook" themselves from our battalions whenever they wanted to do so.'[131] The Allied landings in Sicily on 10 July forced Ambrosio to speed up the Italian retreat from the Balkans, and in August he decided that he must pull three divisions out of the region and allow the Germans to relieve Italian troops on the margins of the first zone. The *Četniks* were to enjoy another lease of life: on the eve of the armistice the general staff planned to get their co-operation against the communists and to use them on a 'case-by-case' basis to help with security in specific zones.[132] Before they could do that the interim Badoglio government fled Rome and the Germans took control of the Balkans.

When, on 8 September 1943, news of the Italian armistice was announced, the soldiers in the Balkans, who were given no warning, were left to work out their own fate. Some generals behaved admirably, others did not. In Spalato, Umberto Spigo abandoned his men to the mercies of the Germans. In Dubrovnik, Giuseppe Amico and his men fought to the last; he and a number of his officers were shot by the Germans on 13 September. Guido Cerruti, commander of the *Isonzo* division, who had been in contact with the partisans since August, joined up with them as an ordinary soldier; Rosi went into a German prisoner-of-war camp; and Gambara joined Mussolini's Salò Republic. The entire *Venezia* division joined the partisans, as did the remains of the *Taurinense* and *Italia* divisions, along with other small groups. In all, an estimated 7,000 Italian soldiers died fighting with the Yugoslav partisans after 8 September 1943.[133]

A GREEK ODYSSEY

Once the Greek army had been defeated, the Germans were ready to leave most of the rest of the country to their allies. 'Whether the Italian occupation forces are masters of the Greek government or not isn't our affair,' Jodl remarked.[134] Dividing up the defeated enemy territory, the Germans took control of Athens and Piraeus, Salonika, the islands of Lesbos, Lemnos and Chios, and western Crete, leaving the rest to the Italians and the Bulgarians, who took over most of Thrace and part of eastern Macedonia. Everything to do with the defence and administration of the rest of the country was left to the Italians to sort out, and the German authorities were ordered 'in particular, [to] refuse any Greek requests for mediation'.[135] By the end of July 1941, eleven Italian divisions were garrisoning Greece: three in Epirus, three in the Peloponnese, three in Thessalonica east of the Pindus mountains, and two on the Ionian islands and the Greek Aegean islands. Two months later revolts broke out in Thrace and Greek Macedonia. SIM reported that 'a violent irredentist campaign' was under way designed to establish Bulgaria's rights over the neighbouring regions and especially Salonika. In the repression that followed 15,000 died and somewhere between 70,000 and 200,000 were deported. Greeks fled to the Italian and German occupied zones.[136] In northern Epirus, where the Albanians were pursuing their dream of a Greater Albania, a Fascist militia composed of Albanian Muslims busied itself carrying out pogroms against Greeks and Jews.

The Italian army of occupation in Greece was expected from the outset to behave as implacable conquerors, just like the soldiers in Dalmatia, Slovenia and Montenegro. Relations between conqueror and conquered were not helped when, shortly after the end of the Italo-Greek war, an Italian commission inquired into Greek treatment of Italian prisoners of war. It found that captured Italians had been subject to theft, inhumane treatment – lightly wounded prisoners and those suffering from frostbite had been forced to march to prison camps and when no longer able to move some had been shot on the spot – beatings, food deprivation and forced labour. Former prisoners complained that they had been forced to march through the streets of Athens and other major cities 'allowing the inhabitants to give vent to their feelings in the vilest ways'.[137] Soldiers, whose behaviour had to be 'irreprehensible in every respect', were ordered not to fraternize with the locals and always to act as befitted the victors. Any hostile actions against military camps, stores or public utilities were to be met, where necessary, with force.

Within weeks the German invasion of Russia raised the prospect of externally provoked insurrection. General Carlo Geloso warned his subordinates not to scatter their men in small, local garrisons but to concentrate their forces near the major centres of population so that they could dominate them with artillery fire and move infantry in quickly when and where necessary.[138] As 'V for Victory' signs and hammers and sickles began to appear on the walls, the invaders faced a population which was anti-Italian, many of whom (especially Cretans) were unemployed, and which was controlled by a police force whose co-operation with the occupiers looked more apparent than real. Geloso was prepared to take some steps to ameliorate the situation, starting a small public-works programme of road building for the Cretans and asking Rome to ship in flour. But absolute firmness was to be the bedrock of order. Anyone caught leading acts of 'disorder' or sabotage was to be shot on the spot.[139] General Giuseppe Pafundi reminded the divisional commanders of VIII Corps of the need to stamp on their men's minds 'the concept of being always ready to parry any hostile act with an <u>immediate and violent reaction</u>'. The population must be '<u>controlled and dominated</u>'.[140]

In 1941, as national resistance groups large and small formed in mainland Greece, the Peloponnese and the islands, the Italian army in Greece enjoyed a relatively quiet life while the majority of Greeks struggled simply to survive. Until 1942, when the security situation began to deteriorate, Italian soldiers had mostly to acclimatize themselves to what some saw as a very foreign country. 'The inhabitants (borghesi) are like Abyssinians,' Ferdinando Armando (later to go missing in Russia) wrote home in February 1942, 'they have homes like wolves and who knows what they eat.' To a Venetian officer Greece was 'a desert of white stones'. To a Neapolitan it was 'cold . . . very thin air, [and] woods, woods, woods'. In the vast coastal zones malaria was so bad that 'malarial battalions' were established that were unfit for combat.[141]

While everything was as yet comparatively quiet, Geloso was well aware that he faced a situation which was 'complex and difficult'. The

Greek government was inert and incapable; the police, the local administrations and the Greek Orthodox clergy were all to varying degrees
hostile, the intellectual class were mostly 'our irreducible enemies', and
the former officers of the Greek army were secretly reuniting in their
former units. So far the mass of the population had not shown signs of
overt hostility, but Geloso suspected that if they had the means they
would then openly demonstrate their hatred of the Italians. Hunger
was the key issue. If the authorities could do something to solve the
food problems, then a population that was not ideologically disposed
to communism might be brought round.[142] Greece was not yet a pow-
der keg – but there was plenty of combustible material lying around.

The war and the occupation had exactly the effects that Geloso
feared. As the Italian occupation took root, the Greek economy, already
weak as a consequence of the European war, shrank rapidly. A merchant fleet of 1,200,000 tons was reduced in a few months to 60,000
tons; agricultural production in 1941 fell by 25 per cent compared to
1939; and industrial production fell by two-thirds during 1941 due to
a shortage of raw materials. National income halved and occupation
costs took 40 per cent of what was left. As winter loomed, occupation policies made things worse. German and Italian wheat imports,
which were in any case only enough to feed Athens and Piraeus, were
soon in arrears, and on 1 November the Germans handed responsibility for provisioning all of Greece – including the parts they controlled
– over to the Italians, 'since Greece lies in Italy's sphere of influence'.[143]
The Germans refused to allow the export of wheat from Macedonia,
the only region which produced an excess of supply over demand and,
according to Geloso, ate up the potatoes on which the Greeks depended
in lieu of wheat.[144]

For a country which even in peacetime depended on imported foodstuffs to supplement domestic production, the effects were catastrophic.
The cost of living rocketed – in December 1942 it was 156.5 times what
it had been in April 1941 – the black market went into overdrive, and
in October 1941 the first deaths from starvation occurred in Athens
and Piraeus. The Italian Red Cross and the Catholic Church in the
person of Cardinal Roncalli (the future Pope John XXIII) took what
steps they could to alleviate the famine, and at least one Italian regiment arriving in Athens shared its food with the starving inhabitants.
Nevertheless, deaths mounted: in the twelve months from October

1941 to September 1942 recorded deaths in Athens and Piraeus more than tripled, reaching 49,188. Italy gave direct aid to the islanders of Lesbos and Samos, particularly hard hit because of a ban on fishing, especially at night. In all, perhaps 250,000 people died as the direct or indirect consequences of famine in Greece between 1941 and 1943. In 1943, when it was far too late, it was agreed that the Italians and Germans had to compensate the Greeks for the food they had previously sequestered.[145]

In March 1942 an agreement between Germans, Italians and Greeks set the occupation costs at 1,500,000,000 drachmae a month, split evenly between the two occupying powers. In practice the Germans squeezed Greece harder and the level of their exactions became a worry for the Italians. Stopping off in Athens in late July 1942 on his way back from North Africa, Mussolini saw for himself the human price the Greeks were paying: during the previous winter 24,000 people had died from starvation. The country, which had hitherto been tranquil, might cease to be ordered and calm. That would not be in the interests of the Axis. There was only one way to avoid the danger, he told Hitler: 'to lighten the occupation costs'. The Germans, who were taking 30,000,000,000 drachmae a month in 'military expenses' to the Italians' 6,000,000,000 a month (plus another 15,000,000,000 drachmae to pay for Axis occupation troops), had no intention of reducing the charges. To avoid the danger of being left on their own to contain a revolt, the Italians briefly contemplated making up the money by giving the Germans the balance after the Greeks had paid what they could.[146] To ameliorate the situation Mussolini was prepared to encourage the involvement of the International Red Cross in Greece and in October 1942 a mission arrived in Athens. Thereafter condensed and fresh milk was distributed to small children, grain was shipped in – regular supplies of Canadian wheat arrived from August 1942 – and medicines were also brought in.

Italian and German economists and financiers tinkered with the problem, for example by closing the border with Thrace to stop Greeks leaving Bulgarian-controlled territory, but then in January 1943 loaded another 20,000,000,000 drachmae of debt onto Greece in order to build fortifications all over the country to meet the threat of a British attack. In all, between August 1941 and March 1943 the Germans took 187,917,000,000 drachmae from the Greek national bank and the

Italians took 71,970,000,000 drachmae. By June 1943 the special chargé for economic affairs, Vincenzo Fagiuoli, suspected that the Greeks were handing over whatever sums the occupiers asked for and inflating the currency by printing ever more bank notes simply in order to create financial chaos.[147]

During 1942 the forces of Greek resistance gradually cohered. There were protests in Athens in January and March organized by the National Liberation Front (EAM), and rural strikes in the Peloponnese in June. Confident that together his troops and the gendarmerie were containing 'brigandage' within normal levels, Geloso told Rome that in line with Ciano's opposition to 'excessive rigour' he was trying to avoid reprisals, shooting hostages, and 'similar barbarities'.[148] At the same time, he took steps to try to prevent individual soldiers from taking the law into their own hands and stealing from the local inhabitants – not least because they were liable to get killed in the attempt – and warned his subordinates that they were not to overdo the burning down of habitations suspected of harbouring rebels.[149] The first *andartes* (partisans) gathered in the Epirus in the late summer, and on 9 September they attacked and annihilated an Italian garrison at Rika in central Greece. More attacks on Italian garrisons followed – in central Greece, then in Thessaly, then in Epirus. In response, the army turned to the kind of tactics that were now being used in the Balkans. 'Serene but inexorable firmness' was the watchword as far as the population was concerned, and the army was to show 'no pity, no hesitation towards bandits and their supporters'.[150] Captured 'brigands' and anyone taken carrying arms illegally were to be shot on the spot, villages within a thirteen-kilometre radius of attacks destroyed, hostages taken (including women and children where there were no males over eighteen), civilians interned in concentration camps, and 'bandits' warned that for every Italian soldier killed or wounded ten hostages would be shot.

The Italian army was now breaking its own laws: legally, hostages had the right to be treated as prisoners of war and could not be executed, Geloso's chief of staff informed the three corps commanders in mid-August.[151] The policy now was one of semi-qualified brutality: burning villages where rebels had sheltered or been supplied was to be regarded as 'wholly exceptional' and generally to be avoided because, Geloso pointed out, it could encourage men to join the rebel bands and generate 'a spirit of hatred and revolt' against the occupying forces. That 'would be to the advantage of the enemy'.[152] Between October 1942 and August 1943 eighty-two villages were totally or partially razed and 14,888 homes were destroyed. From December 1942 until the end of September 1943 the Italians killed 1,526 civilians in the course of carrying out twenty-nine reprisal operations. In nine villages in the Trikkala region all the men were killed. On the island of Mytilene during the summer of 1942 dozens of civilians were machine-gunned to death and then thrown into the sea in sacks.[153]

On 25 November 1942 the communist-led ELAS and nationalist-republican EDES groups, together with the first British military mission, attacked the railway viaduct at Gorgopotamus on the Athens–Salonika line. Next month, disregarding Italian protests, the Germans took over guarding the railway line, and orders went out to clear ground within ten kilometres of any important railway installation and to shoot anyone found within it.[154] As the year ended and partisan activity increased, hostility towards the Italian occupiers grew. Public opinion was turning against the Italians – as well as the Germans. Locally this was explained as due partly to Allied propaganda and partly to the Axis retreats in North Africa. Mass arrests, poor discipline among the troops, and the spectacle of senior officers dedicating themselves to an easy life in which women and sport figured large were also playing their part. The requisition of private houses which were then used by officers for 'irregular *ménage[s]*' was particularly resented by hitherto loyal Athenians.[155] Allied broadcasts spoke disdainfully of the Italians as the *corpo erotico di occupazione*.

Facing not just increasing insurrection by the *andartes* but also the possibility of Allied landings, Geloso put in bids to use Italian forces in Albania as a reserve for Greece, which was refused, and for more supplies and especially more fuel. As spring arrived, rebel bands began to spread down from the mountains of northern and central Greece, conscripting ever larger numbers of Greeks and arming them with weapons taken from Italian outposts or dropped by the Allies. Italian army detachments were attacked – in one case by a band of 800 men – and large motor convoys ambushed and their passengers captured. Small posts manned by *Carabinieri* and *Guardia di Finanza* were overwhelmed, rail and road transport links were attacked, and the *andartes* broke into prisons four times during March and early April and freed inmates. By mid-April 1943 they had got as far south as the Gulf of Corinth and were threatening the Peloponnese.[156]

On 3 February 1943 Geloso issued a directive establishing the principle of collective responsibility for partisan acts. Now formally authorized to terrorize the population at large, Italian units reacted violently to the growing partisan activity. One of the worst massacres occurred at and near the village of Domeniko on 16 February. After an attempted ambush had been fought off, twenty hostages were shot immediately, another 135 were shot soon afterwards and the village was razed to the ground.[157] Under increased pressure from the *andartes*, whom the military authorities estimated to number 20,000, the army pulled back garrisons from the central regions of Greece and resorted to 'energetic actions of repression'. On 13 June 1943, General Cesare Benelli of the *Pinerolo* division issued an order that if there was any sabotage of the Larissa–Volo railway line or of trains on it then fifty Greeks would be shot. While the Italians shot combatants and burned villages, the partisan bands swelled and extended their control over large parts of Epirus, the Pindus and the Peloponnese. Greece was slipping out of Geloso's control.

On 3 May 1943 he was removed from command after refusing to collaborate with General Löhr, commanding the south-east theatre, and hand over Jews, and replaced by General Carlo Vecchiarelli. Two weeks later Ambrosio sent a blistering memorandum to the theatre commanders in Greece, the Aegean and Montenegro. Senior officers in command headquarters were living way beyond their means and engaging in financial speculation, smuggling and currency trafficking. They were to put a stop to this at once, starting at the very top of the ladder.[158] Stories of the Italians' sexual laxness abounded. One unnamed general was notorious for ordering the management of his Athens hotel to provide him with a ceaseless supply of young women – 'every evening another one, to present herself in the room punctually at the appointed time'.[159]

An inquiry into Geloso's failure to keep a grip on his senior officers got under way amid reports of officers diverting rations intended for the troops, giving jewellery and other valuables to Greek women, and trafficking in currency. Geloso himself was accused of protecting a Greek woman who was a known agent of British intelligence, entertaining and being entertained 'to a suspicious degree' by Greeks, and sending home jewels, works of art, carpets and other valuable items obtained with the help of Greek women. A *Carabinieri* report on the wholesale mismanagement of every aspect of Greek policy spoke of 'Inertia, decay, [and] moral disorder of our leaders and [their] associates; [a] life of indolence and pleasure; intrigues by women and businessmen; plots by spies and adventurers; an entire world at odds with the demands and imperatives of the war which has led to decomposition and scandal.'[160] When it concluded, the inquiry recommended that four generals and twenty-six other senior officers be sacked for a variety of misdemeanours which included taking bribes, illegal financial dealings, dishonest conduct and 'notorious relations with Greek women'.[161] Mussolini held Geloso ultimately responsible for 'a wholly deplorable state of affairs' which had undermined the prestige of the armed forces, and when Geloso pleaded ignorance of the exact charges against him and asked for formal recognition of his 'blamelessness' the *Duce* ignored him.[162]

At the beginning of July *Carabiniere* general Pièche advised Rome that the whole of Greece was now in a state of open or potential revolt and was only waiting for a propitious moment to rise up against the occupying regime. Recent shooting of hostages as a reprisal for the sabotage of an Italian ship anchored in the Bosphorus had roused the Athenians. The communists were stirring people up and a fifteen-day strike by the banks had been followed a series of demonstrations that were apparently economically motivated but actually political. The communists were working to extend a general strike in Athens to the rest of Greece. The whole country was preparing for the coming uprising. Shooting hostages, interning without discriminating and razing villages were helping to 'exasperate minds and create martyrs to the national idea'. Force was necessary to dominate the people, but it should not be 'separated from that sense of justice which is at the basis of our heritage of civilization'.[163]

If Pièche hoped to trigger a rethink of Italian counter-insurgency policy, he failed. The rhythm of anti-insurgency operations increased so that between June and August they were happening virtually every day. The navy and the air force joined in the bombing of villages, and the *Carabinieri* did their share of destruction. The actions even increased in intensity after Mussolini fell on 25 July 1943. Villages were destroyed, livestock seized and fines levied, but the Italians appear to have left Greek girls and young women alone.[164] With Mussolini gone, partisan propaganda intensified. Leaflets were distributed around Athens urging Italian soldiers to demand repatriation and peace. When captured by partisans, they were frequently released after a few days – emphasizing the distinction the partisans wanted to make and were making between Italians and Germans.

In the first days of September, while Badoglio's administration was attempting to back out of the Axis, the Italian Foreign Ministry tried to reset policy in Greece. If the military were to take over full powers from the Greek civilian government, then as much territory as possible should be left in German, not Italian hands. Italian troops should withdraw close to the Albanian border and the sea. The civilian population should be treated according to 'legal principles' and 'humanitarian norms'. If partisans were taken with arms in their hands then it was up to the military to decide whether or not they should be shot, but 'the use of reprisals and the treatment of hostages in ways contrary to International Law' were to be 'absolutely' excluded.[165] Perhaps this was the Foreign Ministry's attempt to turn its back on Fascism – or perhaps it was simply another example of how easy it seems to have been for many Fascist functionaries to live with their heads in the clouds and their feet in the mire.

Three days after Mussolini's fall General Löhr took command of the 172,000 Italian soldiers on mainland Greece. Anticipating their ally's next move, the Germans began tightening the screw. A Wehrmacht order forbade Italian soldiers to go about in groups of more than two. More ominously, an Italian garrison of a hundred men at Corinth were killed by the Germans after announcing that they wanted to go home. On 9 September, when the news of the Italian armistice arrived, the Germans moved swiftly according to a prearranged plan, taking over stores and munitions dumps and putting down any attempts at resistance. Löhr told Vecchiarelli that his men must either fight as part of the German Army Group East or surrender unconditionally. Ambrosio left the commanders of the 63,000 men of the Aegean command to decide for themselves what to do, but to disarm the Germans if it looked as though there would be conflict. General Vecchiarelli told the troops on Cefalonia not to use force against the Germans if they did not do so themselves and not – 'I repeat not' – to make common cause either with the 'rebels' or with Anglo-American troops if they landed.[166] On

Cefalonia, officers and men of the *Acqui* division decided to fight, along with some *Carabinieri, Guardia di Finanza* and sailors. Hopelessly outnumbered, the Italians fought until 24 September, after which the Germans shot 155 officers and 4,750 men. A few hundred escaped to join the partisans. After two days' fighting Rhodes fell to the Germans, aided by the local Fascist Blackshirts, and 40,000 Italians became prisoners of war. Cos fell too; Simi and Leros held out, with British help, until November; Samos and Icaria were quickly occupied by the British. The ignominious departure of the Badoglio government from Rome was the *andartes* gain. Large stocks of weapons fell into their hands and some Italians – among them an entire division – went over to the partisans. Eight months after the Germans took over Greece there were perhaps 10,000 Italians in the hills fighting with the *andartes* against their former Axis partner.[167]

Chapter 7

Year of Destiny

America's entry into the war would within the year help bring Fascist Italy to the edge of the precipice. On the day that the Japanese attacked Pearl Harbor (7 December 1941) Italian military intelligence forecast that it would take between six months and a year before the American army was sufficiently well trained and equipped to face a war.[1] Four days later, Mussolini announced that together Italy, Germany and Japan had 250 million men under their banner – a sure guarantor of victory. According to the official record the assembled crowd in Piazza Venezia applauded and whistled its approval. But Ciano, who was there, thought the demonstration 'not very enthusiastic'.[2]

Japan's entry into the war seemed to promise good things. The rapid loss of Malaya's rubber supplies looked likely to upset the entire war preparations of both Great Britain and America. The tide of Japanese victories in the Pacific encouraged the idea that the British would now have to divert some of their effort from the European theatre to defend Australia and India. And it seemed that the United States would surely concentrate its attention on the Pacific. The Italian navy was especially enthused, seeing the prospect of a reduction of British naval pressure in the Mediterranean, joint operations with the Japanese in the Indian Ocean and access to the oil resources that would eventually fall into Axis hands – all hopes that would come to naught.[3]

Three weeks before the United States entered the war, SIM forecast that with a budget of $66,000,000,000 America would be able to equip an army of 1,750,000 men with three million reserves during 1942 and launch two 8,000-ton merchant ships a day, and that during 1943 it would produce 50,000 aeroplanes and 25,000 tanks. When President Roosevelt announced in his State of the Union Address on 6 January 1942 that the war production programme for the coming year would

amount to $56,000,000,000 – more than half the country's estimated annual income – this was dismissed as pure propaganda, 'being much greater than the real possibilities of the American war industry'.[4] Following German appreciations, Italian military intelligence also believed that the British would have to repatriate the three Australian divisions currently in the Mediterranean theatre, and now needed to defend their own country, and would therefore be able to make no net gains there. The successes that General Erwin Rommel was starting to notch up would deny the British any possibility of starting a new offensive 'for a long period'.

What the Americans would and could do was a matter of guesswork. An intercepted report of a conversation between the Turkish military attaché in Washington and the head of American military intelligence suggested that they intended to build up a stockpile of supplies and a large troop concentration in Egypt, Palestine and Iraq so as to be able to support the Soviet front, the North African front and possibly 'the Turkish front.'[5] German assessments of American air power, passed on to Italian air intelligence (SIA) in July 1942, predicted that the United States would fall some way short of the targets set in the Roosevelt programme. American factories would produce 20,500 front-line war planes not 45,000 in 1942, and 42,000 not 100,000 in 1943.[6] In March 1943 the German estimate of total American air production remained 42,000 for the year.[7] The Germans misread the Roosevelt plan and underestimated American production. In 1942 the United States forces took delivery of 47,836 planes, 23,396 of which were fighters and bombers, and in 1943 they received 85,898 planes of which 53,344 were fighters and bombers.[8]

On 11 June 1942 some of the uncertainty about Anglo-American strategy disappeared when the British, American and Soviet governments issued a joint communiqué announcing that a full understanding had been reached between all three Allies regarding a second front in 1942. Analysing its strategic significance, Italian military intelligence expected that it would result in a Russian declaration of war on Japan and the opening of a second front in Europe. The necessary conditions for an Allied landing, including possessing decisive air supremacy, could not be achieved before the winter and spring of 1942–3. The most likely targets were northern France, northern Norway, or the Atlantic coast.[9] New theatres of operations now had to be incorporated into military planning. In the coming year Italy was going to have to make a bigger contribution to the Russian war, be ready to man a possible Atlantic front in France and face increased American action, which would likely come particularly from the air. Italy's coasts would have to be defended, her industrial plants protected, and her anti-aircraft defences (which were exiguous) increased.[10] The parameters of the war, already far too widely drawn for Italy, now widened yet further. To stand any chance at all of coping with them Italy would need more help from Germany.[11]

DEFEAT IN RUSSIA

In the last week of January 1942 Cavallero and Ambrosio discussed sending the new 8th Army to Russia and concluded that it would take at least three months to transport the six divisions and the command headquarters there.[12] At the front, exhausted men of the *Celere* division lost the town of Voroshilovgrad on 23 January and were unable to retake it two days later. For the first time there were signs of falling morale. General Messe, whose three-division CSIR was shortly to be transformed into XXXV Corps of the new 8th Army (ARMIR), warned the *Comando Supremo*: without fresh divisions to replace exhausted ones and more guns and tanks he would not be able to participate in the coming spring operations with enough strength and operational capability 'to safeguard and hopefully increase the heritage of great prestige' his men had built up.[13] In April he told Rome that he commanded 'a mass of tired veterans' who were in no condition to face a second winter campaign and in May he reported 'a widespread, persistent, [and] unusual feeling of weariness'. Among the many reasons for this was awareness that, while fresh personnel and the most modern weapons were starting to flood in to the Germans, the Italians were without heavy guns, tanks, self-propelled guns and bombers.[14]

A more senior general was needed to command what was now no longer a Corps but an Army, and after some time the choice settled on General Italo Gariboldi, who was duly nominated on 1 April 1942. Messe was outraged at having been superseded by a general he thought old and stupid. Others too thought Gariboldi was second-rate.[15] General Giacomo Zanussi, visiting Cyrenaica in June 1941, saw a

1. Marshal Pietro Badoglio.

2. General Alfredo Guzzoni.

4. General Mario Roatta, Spain,
1937.

3. General Vittorio Ambrosio (centre) and General Efisio
Marras (left).

5. North Africa: M 13/40 tanks moving up to the front line, October 1940.

6. North Africa: *Bersaglieri* advancing on Tobruk.

7. North Africa: Assault engineers attacking north of El Alamein, November 1942.

8. North Africa: Rommel and Cavallero (centre right) visit the front, November 1942.

9. North Africa: *Bersaglieri* manning a 47 mm anti-tank gun, Tunisia, March 1943.

10. Greece/Albania: Mussolini leads the advance on Greece.

11. Greece/Albania: Italian artillery on the front line.

12. Greece/Albania: Supplying the front was often a hand-to-mouth business.

13. Greece/Albania: Tapping a phone line; communications were a perpetual problem.

14. Greece/Albania: Front-line propaganda – the headline reads 'Hate the English'.

15. Croatia: A *Četnik* militiaman.

16. Croatia: Captured rebels.

17. Croatia: In action – a burning village.

18. Russia: An Italian snapshot taken during the invasion of the Donets Basin 1941.

19. Russia: Italian cavalry charging on the Don.

20. Russia: Italian infantry attacking a factory.

21: Russia: Old artillery in action – a 1911 model 75 mm gun.

22. Russia: General Giovanni Messe inspecting *Bersaglieri*, 1942.

23: Russia: Christmas Day, 1941.

24. Admiral Domenico Cavagnari.

25. Admiral Arturo Riccardi.

26. Admiral
Angelo
Iachino.

27. The battleship *Vittorio Veneto*, 1940.

28. The Italian heavy cruiser squadron heading into the Battle of Punta Stilo, 9 July 1940.

29. Taranto, 12 November 1940. The rear turret of the battleship *Cavour*, with the *Doria* in the background.

30. An Italian merchantman burning in Tripoli harbour, 1942.

31. Mussolini inspects a squadron of Savoia-Marchetti SM.79 bombers.

32. Known to Italian airmen as the *gobbo maledetto* ('damned hunchback'), the SM.79 was the multi-role workhorse of the *Regia Aeronautica*.

33. An airfield in Russia.

34. A Macchi MC.200 fighter on the Russian front.

35. Wrecked Italian CR.42 and G.50 aircraft, Tripoli, 1943.

commander who might once have been intelligent and capable but who was now 'in evident decline'.[16] The head of Gariboldi's operations staff thought him brusque, crabby and conceited.[17] To General Maximilian von Weichs, commanding Army Group B, who thought all Italian generals were too puffed up with self-importance and too vain, Gariboldi was a nice old man, 'extraordinarily modest for an Italian', whose military capacity was 'insignificant'.[18]

At the end of May, Messe went to Rome to try to persuade Cavallero and Mussolini that tripling the size of the army in Russia from 60,000 to 200,000 would simply multiply all the difficulties his force already faced and that sending out two fresh divisions (25,000 to 30,000 men) would be the better course of action. Mussolini was immovable. The Germans would stick to their agreement to help the Italians in any way possible, and in any case he had to be at Hitler's side as Hitler had been at his in Greece and was still in North Africa.[19]

At the Salzburg summit on 29 April, Hitler told Mussolini that he intended to use the *Alpini* to help force a way through the Caucasus mountains to the Caspian Sea. Cavallero met Field Marshal Keitel and General Jodl at Klessheim that day and heard that the Wehrmacht planned to complete the encirclement of Leningrad, 'clean up' the central front, and 'act decisively' in the direction of the Caucasus.[20] Gariboldi went to Germany in May and heard Hitler sketch out German strategy for the coming year. In the first stages he planned to use the Italian army along with the other allies to hold the Don front. ARMIR would operate between the Hungarian and Romanian armies. Everyone on the German side was supremely confident of success.[21] They were not alone. 'There were times,' Messe said afterwards, 'when you could see the collapse of Russia was imminent, you saw that during the campaign of 1941 to 1942. It looked as if they might pack up at any moment.'[22]

As Cavallero and his subordinates began the task of preparing the new army, Italian army intelligence produced some statistics about the enemy. Although the Soviet Union had lost two-thirds of its coal and approximately 50 per cent of its industrial potential, it still had the equivalent of its total pre-war production of aluminium, petrol, copper and manganese, and enough synthetic rubber to meet civilian and military needs. Russian factories could produce 1,500 aircraft, 1,500 tanks and 10,000 trucks a month. There was sufficient capacity in the Soviet system to equip the new armies being created in the Volga region, estimated to number seventy infantry divisions, twenty-one cavalry divisions and six armoured divisions. The needs of the twenty-three divisions and four armoured brigades of the Siberian armies were being met locally.[23]

German estimates, passed along to the *Regia Aeronautica*, painted a more encouraging picture. The *Luftwaffe* believed that the Russians could produce 650 fighters and 176 bombers a month and calculated that when the campaigning season began at the start of May the Axis would face some 2,000 Russian warplanes – fewer than the number it had faced in June 1941. That in turn meant that the air force would only be able to support the Red Army in force 'at its centres of gravity'.[24] Both the Italian and the German figures were underestimates, but the Italian numbers were closer to the mark: during 1942 Soviet factories produced 24,500 tanks and self-propelled guns and 21,342 combat aircraft. None of the projections gave any indication of the capacity of the Soviet economy to expand output still further.[25]

Between February and May the units slated for the Russian front trained in the dense agricultural land of the Po valley. Preparing for a war of movement, they went on prolonged marches. This paid off: marching to the Don, divisions covered thirty kilometres and more a day. They were, though, seriously under-armed. The army which would face its final battle on the Don that winter numbered 229,000 men with 16,700 vehicles, thirty-one L-6 tanks and sixty-four aircraft. Together with 850 guns and 278 obsolescent 47mm anti-tank guns (plus fifty-four German 75mm guns), it had 423 81mm mortars and fifty-two anti-aircraft guns. To defend themselves against Russian aircraft, the three army corps had to rely on 20mm machine guns. The *Alpini* had a handful of good French 105mm pack howitzers, but only seventy-two 81mm mortars. Mostly they had to depend on Austrian 75mm howitzers captured by the Italians during the First World War. The entire force had some 550 81mm mortars.[26]

The three infantry divisions of II Corps (*Ravenna*, *Cosseria* and *Sforzesca*) entrained at Bologna and rode 2,800 kilometres to Kharkov, where they joined the old CSIR, now XXXV Corps. The motorized troops were carried as far as Troppau and then drove the remaining 1,500 kilometres to the front. The troops were still arriving when the army headquarters reached Voroshilovgrad on 21–22 June.[27] On 23

July the Italians were ordered to move forward and take up position on the right bank of the River Don to protect the advance on Stalingrad and the Caucasus. That same day Hitler ordered the *Alpini* corps to take part in Army Group A's drive towards the oil wells at Maikop and Baku. Cavallero concurred: to employ the *Alpini* on the plains would be 'absurd'.[28]

On 12 July, two weeks after Operation BLAU began, Messe's XXXV Corps, along with two German corps, began an offensive designed to take the mining basin of Krasnyi Luch in an encircling manoeuvre. After a week's fighting in which all three Italian divisions took part, one of Russia's richest coal basins was in Axis hands. As the Italians moved forward to the Don river pursuing the retreating Russians, the motorized *Celere* was diverted to help the Germans eliminate a Russian bridgehead at Serafimovich on the Don. Covering 400 kilometres in four days, the division came into line on 29 July. Over the next eight days (30 July–6 August) the Italians fought off a heavy Soviet attack, took the town, swept the woods and swamps around it, and fought off infiltrations and counter-attacks, destroying an enemy armoured brigade, knocking out thirty-five Soviet tanks and taking 1,600 prisoners. The battle cost the division 2,989 dead and wounded – a third of ARMIR's total losses before December 1942. When they moved across to the Italian front on the Don, now reduced to one-third strength and leaving behind half their guns, the *Celere* were put in reserve. After they left, the Soviet forces reoccupied the Serafimovich bend, from where they would subsequently launch a major counter-attack.[29]

The five Italian and two German divisions in Army Group B had to defend a 282-kilometre front along the right bank of the Don. Higher than the opposite bank, it often fell steeply to the river, creating dead ground. The Russian bank, lower and flatter, was thickly wooded opposite their centre but there were few trees or none on either flank. The river, between 100 and 400 metres wide, was fordable in the summer. Messe's corps was stationed on the right-hand of the front, and to his right there was a thirty-kilometre gap held only by a handful of Germans equipped with a few anti-tank guns. Warning his men that they were likely to be there for a long time, Gariboldi ordered them to construct a 'systematic' defensive system and organize shelters, which would have to be dug out of the ground. Given the length of the front

– the Italian divisions had fronts averaging thirty-four kilometres – and the scarcity of means, there could be no continuous line of fieldworks, so they would have to depend on a spread of strongpoints. Although there was not much transportation, the troops must be prepared to be as mobile as possible and to counter-attack.[30] Army Group B promised help if the Italians were attacked. The commander of II Corps, General Giovanni Zanghieri, warned his men that as troops new to combat they could expect to be tested by the enemy immediately and promised them mines, barbed wire, 47mm anti-tank guns, flamethrowers and machine-gun companies, most of which never arrived.[31]

As the 1942 campaign got under way, soldiers wrote home proudly that they were bringing religion and Roman civilization to a people who, under Stalin's rule, were godless, savage and inhuman.[32] 'We're fighting the greatest battle there may ever have been between peoples and nations,' one officer wrote home to his mother, 'the crusade by a new world against the darkness of the godless.' The Russian peasants were receiving them as liberators.[33] The army's newspaper *Dovunque* ('Everywhere') rammed home the message that the struggle was against bolshevism. Men believed that they were on a mission. 'You must be proud that you have a husband fighting people who do not know the Catholic religion,' Corporal-Major Donato Briscese, in civilian life a poor stone-breaker, told his wife. 'We are here not to fight against Russia, but against bolshevism which seeks to dominate the world.'[34] Red Army intelligence, reading captured letters from home or from the front, claimed to see in them no genuine conviction in the causes of the war and the need for victory. Prayers for the soldiers' safe return and injunctions to try to keep out of harm's way were, it thought, likely to be having a demoralizing effect on soldiers who were plainly tired of the war. This helped fuel the communist propagandists' assertion that *Italianci ne hotiat voevat* ('The Italians don't want to make war').[35] In fact, the army's morale remained sound right up to the last cataclysmic battles at the end of 1942.

On 12 August a week-long series of Soviet attacks began probing the Italian front and the Hungarian lines on their left. Then at 2.30 a.m. on 20 August, after a brief artillery bombardment, the six divisions of the Soviet 63rd Army smashed into Messe's two divisions on the right of the Italian front. They had been in their new positions for only a week, during which time intensive enemy activity during the day had made it all but impossible to do much in the way of building defences. Afterwards, Italian intelligence calculated that over six days the Russians had thrown twenty-five infantry battalions against the six battalions of the *Sforzesca*. Air support was called in but by 4 o'clock that afternoon it had not arrived. Some units were quickly surrounded – one battalion of the *Sforzesca* lost 608 of its 680 men cutting its way out of an encirclement. Attempted counter-attacks were either beaten to the draw when the Russians, ferrying fresh battalions across the river, attacked first or were fought off. By the evening of the second day the *Ravenna* division to the north was also under attack. The *Sforzesca*'s reserves were now gone and it began to pull back. Messe set up two strongpoints in the rear of his retreating troops to stem the assault. Both came under fierce Russian attack. The only available reserve, the 3rd *Celere*, joined in the battle after a 155-kilometre truck ride and counter-attacked together with a Croat battalion and 400 German infantrymen. Cavalry charges slowed down the enemy's advance. At Izbushenski on 24 August, 650 men of the *Savoia Cavalleria* charged a Siberian regiment of 2,000, killing 250 and taking 300 prisoners, and temporarily staving off the threat to the smaller of the two strongpoints at Tschebotarevski.[36] Next day the Russians drove into it. A scratch force of muleteers, drivers, cooks and despatch riders fought the enemy house to house. Overwhelmed, the defenders fell back covered by the *Novara* cavalry regiment. Gunners defended their pieces with hand grenades and dragged them by hand to safer positions when fuel ran out.

In the evening of 25 August the Germans took over the defence of the *Sforzesca* sector. Passing on German instructions, Gariboldi ordered the division to stop withdrawing 'at all costs' and warned that anyone ordering a retreat would be subject to 'grave sanctions'.[37] Messe obeyed under protest, objecting to Gariboldi's 'ungenerous evaluation' of a division that had fought the enemy non-stop for six days with no help and to an action that made Italian generalship look inadequate.[38] Over the next week the Italians and Germans halted the Russian offensive. Aircraft now played a major part in the battle, bombing the enemy, airlifting the wounded and carrying out reconnaissance flights. On 1 September the Germans and Italians launched a counter-offensive, which the Soviets fought off. A promised German tank attack never happened, explained afterwards as due to a last-minute lack of fuel.

With that, the battle came to a halt. It cost the Italians 883 dead and 4,212 wounded. The *Celere* lost 50 per cent of its effectives, and the *Sforzesca* had practically to be rebuilt.

The battle was the swan-song of Messe's veterans of the old CSIR, most of whom were now repatriated after having served over twelve months in Russia.[39] At the end of August, Messe asked Mussolini to relieve him of his command. No advantage was being taken of his experience, and there was now nothing left of his old expeditionary force save 'its glorious name and its memory'. Three weeks later he wrote to Gariboldi telling him bluntly that effective collaboration between the two generals was impossible.[40] On 1 November 1942 he flew back to Rome.

For 8th Army the first battle of the Don was a qualified success. The Soviets had failed to achieve their strategic objectives – diverting as many enemy forces as possible from Stalingrad and cutting off General Friedrich Paulus's 6th Army from its bases west of the Don – but they had won a significant operational victory, expanding a small pocket on the southern bank of the Don into a bridgehead which would become a jumping-off point for their attack on the Romanians and their encirclement of Stalingrad at the end of November. For the Italians, the coming months looked grim. Their thinly spread defensive strongpoints could not hold an enemy attack, and with only a handful of feeble L-13 light tanks and 175mm guns (their longest-range corps artillery), which could not cover a whole corps sector, they lacked the mobility and the firepower to carry out effective counter-attacks.

The three divisions of the *Alpini* Corps (*Tridentina*, *Cuneense* and *Julia*) began their move to Russia early in July, arriving at their assembly points for the planned attack on Maikop in the last fortnight of August. There were no trucks, so the first units to arrive set out on a 330-kilometre march on 16 August. Three days later they were told they were now to join 8th Army on the Don. German military intelligence thought it likely that the Russians would attempt to attack the weak points in Army Group B's front as it drove forward to Stalingrad and the Volga. The *Alpini*, who the Germans thought among the best of the Italian troops, were shifted across from Army Group C to von Weichs's Army Group B to shore up a vulnerable stretch of the line. Two days after receiving their new orders the *Alpini* divisions set out on foot for the Don. The *Julia* and *Cuneense* slotted into line between

20 and 25 September, and the *Tridentina*, whose advance units had made it to the Don in time to help shore up Messe's fragile line, were all in place on 31 October.[41]

Meanwhile the Italians prepared for a second winter campaign. Now, learning both from German experience, some of which came from the Finns, and their own, they began shipping in the clothing and equipment they would need, including two-piece white camouflage clothing, fur-lined overcoats, multiple pairs of woollen and leather gloves, wooden-soled, fur-lined boots to replace the nailed boots which collected snow and absorbed damp, and, most desirable of all, Russian-style felt boots. By August 1942 a good deal of winter equipment had reached Russia, including 900,000 pairs of woollen socks and 244,000 pairs of gloves, but the army was still short among other things of 127,000 fur coats and 450,000 field blankets. The troops continued to complain about poor boots (a problem that was never resolved), inadequate rations and the lack of winter clothing.

The immediate problems were due partly to the considerable distances over which supplies had to be carried forward, but were also the consequence of General Gariboldi's conception of commanding troops and of the parsimony of 8th Army's Intendance. On Gariboldi's orders chocolate, Parmesan cheese and cognac stayed in the stores. Woollen clothing was not issued to the troops on the Don until November, when temperatures were down to −23 °C at night, and by the end of that month the advanced stores had issued only 110,000 winter overcoats. Quartermasters had an excuse for keeping large stocks out of the hands of the men who needed them as they contemplated another winter-long campaign. The result, though, was that vast amounts of clothing and equipment were either burned or abandoned when the Red Army rolled over the Italians at the end of the year. In November 1944 the Intendant General of 8th Army would be accused of failing to make the appropriate logistical arrangements for the coming of winter and instead 'preoccupying himself with transferring to Italy for his personal use a Russian woman, foodstuffs, and various objects of uncertain provenance'.[42]

Partisan activity in the Italian sectors of the front, although it increased during the final months of the campaign when the Russians parachuted men in, was never as fierce as elsewhere in the theatre. In the first year of the war the Red Army had been retreating and many of the local inhabitants had welcomed the disappearance of the communists. When the Italians moved up to the Don in 1942 they had behind them an area of open plains with no vast forests, swamps or mountains in which guerrillas could shelter. The nature of the country made it impossible to create large partisan formations of the kind that were able to operate in the Ukraine or White Russia, so resistance mainly took the form of propaganda, sabotage and infiltrating collaborationist groupings. The partisans failed to achieve their main strategic objective, the systematic disruption of rail traffic behind the front.[43] As winter ended the Russians changed their tactics, sending fewer better-quality 'informers' across the line dressed in uniform so that if caught they could claim to be deserters. If they escaped detection, they became partisans.

Messe thought the Germans, who lacked political sensibility, were far too prone to shoot any suspects whether innocent or guilty, fuelling Soviet propaganda and increasing hatred of the invaders. The 'softer' policy the Italians followed, which included reactivating hospitals, pharmacies and schools, restoring churches and holding religious services, partly explains why the war behind the fighting front was less barbarous in the Italian sector than elsewhere.[44] On 'the other side of the hill' the Soviets were taken by surprise by the rapidity of the enemy advance up to the Don. Partisans were ill-prepared, disputes between the various Soviet authorities over who should direct the guerrilla war were not resolved until the autumn of 1942, local Party leaders were sometimes inactive and sometimes deserted their posts, and some groups were small (the Rossosh group, only four strong, carried out no military activity at all). Once the Italians established their defensive lines along the Don it proved almost impossible to infiltrate spies and saboteurs overland, and the Red Army was very reluctant to allocate any planes – for which fuel was in any case very short – to airdrop men and women into occupied territory.[45]

In what was a relatively low intensity anti-partisan campaign, Italian units hunted down and hanged or shot 'spies', partisans and 'suspect bandits', including women. Following orders to collaborate with the Germans, the Italians handed over Jews to the *Sonderkommandos* and captured partisans were generally handed over to the *Feldpolizei*, the *SS* or the *SD*.[46] Well-armed volunteer 'bandit hunter' groups guided by local informers – eight were set up in the summer of 1942 – were the most successful at running down partisans. The men of the *Vicenza* division, sharing responsibility with the *Carabinieri* for security behind the lines, went out on nightly patrols rounding up men suspected of being members of Red Army units sent to hunt out and kill Italian officers. 'After three or four days,' one of their number recorded casually in a letter home, 'they generally shoot them.'[47]

As the summer campaigning season opened, 8th Army received a boost to its intelligence capabilities. SIM cryptographers were able to read some of the Russian army's field-grade ciphers with help from the Hungarian Cryptographic Service, though frequent changes made this difficult. Until June 1942, though, interception and decryption of enemy signals traffic were kept separate from one another. In that month Lieutenant-Colonel Guido Emer arrived at Stalino with a sixteen-strong decryption section which was quickly combined with the 300-man intercept force working on the spot. In practice what the cryptographers could do was severely limited by the lack of experienced personnel and by the fact that most of them had no Russian, so that instead of carrying out proper cryptography they worked mainly on identifying Russian units and formations.[48]

In Rome, where during the summer minds were increasingly focusing on the events in North Africa, the campaign in Russia seemed likely to stretch at least into the following year. In July, after having held the Italians at arm's length on economic matters ever since the campaign began, the Germans indicated that they were prepared to share the resources captured in Russia with their ally. The Italians needed scrap iron, minerals, coal, petroleum and grain, and on the eve of the great Don battle the Ministry of Agriculture had plans to run up to 14,000 collective farms in the occupied territories, overseen by up to 14,000 Italian specialist personnel.[49] As August ended, the *Comando Supremo* was expecting to have to make a bigger contribution to the Russian campaign during 1943. Cavallero calculated that reserves would not be needed there until the spring of 1943, so that the class of 1943 need not be called to the colours until 1 December 1942. Mussolini was told that the situation in Russia was 'much improved', and after a brief visit to the front in early October, Aldo Vidussoni, secretary of the Fascist Party, assured the *Duce* that the troops' spirits were 'very high'.[50]

During September and early October the Italian front was reconfigured. The *Alpini* came into the line on the left, a German infantry division was put into the second line and the 22nd German *Panzer* division was emplaced behind 8th Army. Small enemy attacks were fought off. Visiting the front at the end of September, General Marras reported that the defensive work was not getting very far due to a shortage of materials, the length of front that the Italians were guarding, and the shortage of anti-tank guns and automatic weapons.[51] Von Weichs reassured him: the Italians would be given weaponry that would fall into the Germans' hands after they had captured Stalingrad. On 14 October Hitler ordered Army Group B to prepare for the coming winter campaign. The line on which the Axis forces now stood was to be defended at all costs, defence must be active not passive, and because rivers, lakes and swamps were no obstacle in winter the armies must establish an uninterrupted line of resistance. The weaknesses in the Italian line were now worrying the Germans. The liaison officer, General von Tippelskirch, thought the whole set-up alarmingly weak and wanted German units stationed behind the Italians, and von Weichs complained to Gariboldi that almost half of his forces were deployed not on the front line but behind it.[52] The Italians believed that German insistence on a continuous line of invulnerable defences along the Don was depriving them of depth both in front of and behind their main line.[53]

On 18 September Gariboldi ordered his troops to organize winter positions along their current defensive lines. As daytime temperatures fell precipitously and the nights began to freeze he passed on detailed German instructions about how to build and fortify a defensive line. In difficult circumstances – roads were poor, railheads were up to 130 kilometres from the front line, and after the third battle of El Alamein the lion's share of limited supplies was being funnelled to Cyrenaica and Tunisia – the *Comando Supremo* sent up maintenance specialists, huts, clothing and other items. The Italian units did what they could. Minefields were laid, but only in limited numbers. Short of barbed wire, the infantry units set primed hand grenades on wires to give warning of an attack. In October, as enemy activity increased, patrolling was improved and the construction of defences speeded up.[54]

The Soviet Operation URANUS began on 19 November and four days later Stalingrad was surrounded. The two German infantry divisions and the 200 tanks of 22nd *Panzer* division which backed up the Italians were withdrawn to help the Germans and Romanians. As the Italians dug their trenches and put together prefabricated winter shelters, and partisan activity increased, air observation and the

interrogation of Russian deserters and prisoners of war produced growing evidence that a Soviet attack was coming. Troops were being moved
into position in daytime, bridges built, guns brought up, and Soviet
aircraft overflying Italian command posts, railway nodes and artillery
positions. Italian intelligence was able to make fairly accurate estimates
of the enemy's frontline troops, but not of second-line forces and
reserves which were unobservable by air and unknown to interrogated
Soviet soldiers. Facing the two Italian corps (II and XXXV) and the
twelve battalions of the *Cosseria* and *Ravenna* divisions, each on average 300 to 400 men strong, that were their immediate targets were
ninety Red Army rifle battalions backed by twenty-five battalions of
motorized infantry and 754 tanks supported by 810 guns and 1,255
mortars, 300 anti-tank guns and 200 rocket launchers. To fight them
off, General Zanghieri's II Corps had 47 tanks, 132 guns, 108 mortars
and 114 anti-tank guns, ninety of them the ineffective 47mm version.
The troops had no sub-machine guns; only the *Carabinieri* were issued
with the Beretta 38/A. 'We very much felt the lack of individual automatic and semi-automatic weapons facing an enemy well-supplied with
them,' a veteran of the Russian campaign commented after the war.[55]

On 11 December 1942 units of two Russian armies struck Zanghieri's divisions. The first phase of Operation LITTLE SATURN had
begun. The *Ravenna* division was attacked from either end of the
'pocket' below the Don river held by the Soviets since their August
offensive. The division's commander, General Francesco Dupont, asked
for a diversionary attack by the nearest *Alpini* division. Gariboldi
refused because he thought the enemy facing it was too strong and
there was too little time. Nor did he deploy the German 27th *Panzers*,
which had been put under his command two days earlier. The *Ravenna*
destroyed seventy of the 200 Soviet tanks that attacked it, and its commander was awarded an Iron Cross First Class in the field by the
Germans.[56]

Next day the pressure intensified and spread west and east as the
Cosseria and *Pasubio* divisions were attacked in turn. Local counter-
attacks over the next two days worked when better-equipped German
troops took part, but not when they were absent. The *Cosseria* division
was now fighting three Soviet divisions on its own without any tanks to
support it. His division almost exhausted, Zanghieri again asked for a
diversionary attack and for some *Alpini* battalions to strengthen his

line. Again Gariboldi refused. As what was only the preliminary 'wearing down' phase of the battle drew to its close von Weichs intervened, giving the commander of the 27th *Panzers* the authority to decide for himself the time and strength of a counter-attack.[57]

At dawn on 16 December, 2,500 Russian guns opened up on II Corps and the main attack began. Heavy fog prevented the airmen of either side from taking a hand in the battle. On the first day Soviet infantry and tanks bit into the Italian front to a depth of five kilometres. Next day the front widened as the Red Army struck at three more Italian divisions (*Pasubio*, *Torino* and 3rd *Celere*). Convinced that Gariboldi was not directing the battle, Von Weichs ordered the *Julia* Alpine division to move and put a German colonel in charge of II Corps after its headquarters retreated. Over the next three days Red Army units smashed the Italian front wide open, creating a gap 150 kilometres wide and driving 55 kilometres south to Kantemirovka, cutting the railway between Millerovo and the *Alpini* corps headquarters at Rossosh. When Soviet tanks appeared on the hill above Kantemirovka railway station they were thought to be German – until they started firing. Some 300 motor vehicles were standing with their motors running because of the cold. There was chaos as the Italians rushed to escape, some driving off overloaded, others empty.[58] As the Soviet attack drove west along the Don, elements of the *Julia* Alpine division finally moved into place behind the *Cosseria*.

Ordered by Army Group B not to retire to the line of the Rossosh-Millerovo railway, Gariboldi was still trying to hold his positions by feeding units into the line. Had Messe been in command he would likely have refused to do so and would instead have pulled back south and west – as indeed Zanghieri suggested. But the centre and right of the 8th Army's front had been stove in. On 19 December the order to retire was given. A desperate race now began to get away from the advancing Red Army. While the *Cosseria* division moved west to join the *Alpini* at Rossosh, the remains of five divisions (*Torino*, *Ravenna*, *Pasubio*, *Sforzesca* and 3rd *Celere*) began an odyssey that would be burnt into the memories of those who survived it – and shape the national myths that developed out of the final act of the Russian war.

Shredded divisions – the *Pasubio* was down to 600 men and four guns, the *Torino* had three 75mm guns and four trucks – fell back, fighting continuously to defend their backs and break free of encircling

Soviet units which surrounded them whenever they paused. The men of the *Torino* division were saved from total annihilation, according to their infantry commander, only by the surviving German armoured forces, which were able to provide them with just enough food to keep going.[59] Chaotic conditions – the *Torino*'s commander described them as like being in a burning theatre or on a sinking ship – were made worse by inept command.[60] The *Sforzesca* division was first ordered to destroy everything that could not be carried the 200 kilometres to safety on its remaining trucks and retreat and then, when it had done so, the order was countermanded and the division was ordered to retrace its steps and help protect the flank of a retreating German unit. Contradictory orders resulted in the loss of the *Sforzesca*'s artillery and vehicles.[61]

In desperate circumstances the retreat began to look like a rout as men who were very near the end of their tether threw away their weapons, plundered German stores of cognac, and drank the anti-freeze from Russian lorries in the belief that it was alcohol. The *kolkhozy* (collective farms) were stripped of livestock, and civilians were killed. As the men staggered on, Russian women collected abandoned clothing from the fields on either side of the columns. Nuto Revelli, who escaped with the remnants of the *Tridentina* division and who spoke for many of the survivors of the retreat, catalogued multiple examples of German arrogance and disdain for their allies during the retreat, denying Italian wounded places on lorries and throwing Italians out of the *izbes* (Russian peasant huts) in which they tried to find shelter. He recorded only a single friendly action by a German.[62] By contrast Eugenio Corti, retreating with the *Pasubio* division, recognized that he and others owed their lives to the German units who fought off Russian tanks and spearheaded breakouts. 'What would have become of us without the Germans . . .' he wrote afterwards; 'had we been alone, we Italians would have ended up in enemy hands.'[63] General Francesco Zingales thought the cause of the Germans' hostile behaviour towards their allies was their 'gratuitous belief' that the Italians' failure to resist the Russians was entirely responsible for the reversal.[64] At times the Italians threatened to use their arms on Germans or actually did so. The German general Karl Eibl died during the retreat after an explosion in his half-track. German eyewitnesses were sure he was the victim of an Italian grenade.

Staggering southward in temperatures of −35/40 °C, battered by strong winds, attacked by partisans and regular Soviet units and on one occasion accidentally bombed by German aircraft, one bloc reached the safety of German positions at midnight on 28 December. The other large bloc, moving south-west, broke out of a Soviet attempt at encirclement and after walking for almost forty-eight hours without pause and without food reached the settlement of Tcherkovo on Christmas night, thanks in large part to the work of a German armoured group commanded by a Major Hoffman which held Red Army soldiers and partisans at bay.[65] There some 14,000 Germans and Italians were surrounded. Stores were full of food but munitions were in very short supply, forcing the Italian defenders to rely on capturing their own guns and ammunition from the enemy during counter-attacks.[66] Incendiaries destroyed clothing and equipment stores and an airdrop failed when the containers drifted into the enemy's lines. The head of the air force contingent, General Mario Pezzi, flew in to assess the situation but was shot down and killed on the return flight. A German attempt to break through to the besieged column was halted fourteen kilometres short of its goal.

On 15 January 1943 German units led a last attempt by the column, now only some 6,500 strong, to break out. Two lorries and a few sledges carried a hundred wounded. The remaining 3,850 wounded and the thousand-odd men unable to walk were left behind. Fighting off sporadic attacks with the aid of German anti-tank guns and Stukas, the survivors reached the safety of German lines at Belovodsk on 16 January 1943.[67] Of the 11,000 men of the *Torino* division who began the retreat from the Don, only 1,200 made it to safety. The 12,500-strong *Pasubio* division lost 7,500 missing, dead, wounded or frostbitten in the battles on the Don and another 1,800 in the retreat that followed. The *Ravenna* division, which came into line on the Don in August, lost 8,040 men to all causes over the following five months.

While the centre and right of Gariboldi's army fell away, the *Alpini* still stood in their positions on the left, guarding the Don where it turned north and protecting the southern flank of the Hungarian army which was deployed next to it. In the last weeks before the Russian attack their engineers used some of their 15,000 Russian prisoners of war as well as workers and women to improve the front-line defences. They also found ways to feed their starving workforce against orders, which saved some *Alpini* lives when the Rossosh strongpoint fell to the Russians.[68] On 12 January 1943 the Red Army attacked the Hungarians, who quickly broke. Two days later they overwhelmed the German XXIV *Panzer* Corps to the south of the *Alpini*'s positions, and on 15 January they attacked its headquarters at Rossosh but were driven off. With Soviet pincers now choking off their escape route from both sides, the 70,000 men of the *Alpini* were trapped. Under direct orders from Hitler, Army Group B refused Gariboldi's request for authorization to withdraw. Gariboldi duly forbade the commander of the *Alpini*, General Nasci, from leaving the Don without precise orders from him. Next day, von Weichs ordered the *Julia* division to join in an attack by the German XXIV Corps but told the rest of the corps to stay where it was 'until the dislocation of the Don [front] is approved by the Führer'.[69]

On the afternoon of 17 January 1943 the order came to retire. The *Alpini* were given what remained of the German XXIV *Panzers* – four tanks, two self-propelled guns and five artillery pieces. The three *Alpini* divisions and the *Vicenza* division formed into individual columns, and Nasci ordered his troops to act from now on as if they were 'operating in a high mountain zone'. All motor vehicles were to be abandoned and as many supplies and munitions as possible were to be carried on sledges and pack animals. The only exceptions to this call for the troops to return to their traditional ways were anti-tank guns and munitions, to be towed by tractors.[70] While the command posts and the hospital were being evacuated thirty-one civilians were removed from the prison and shot, among them a boy of twelve and another of fifteen.

The German lines were 100 kilometres away at Nikolaevka, but the *Alpini* walked at least another hundred kilometres as they wound their way past or through Soviet obstacles. The *Tridentina* made good progress, so Nasci made it the advance guard. Under its commander, General Luigi Revèberi, it maintained its cohesion and fought 'brilliantly'.[71] As it marched out of the trap the inhabitants of the villages it passed gave the starving soldiers food. On 26 January, led in person by Reverberi, the *Tridentina* broke the last Soviet barrier at Nikolaevka, after which it reached the River Oskol and the safety of the German lines.[72] It was the only division to escape encirclement. On 26 January the *Vicenza*'s commander accepted terms but before they could be put into force his column was captured by the Soviets. Next day what remained of the *Vicenza*, *Cuneense* and *Julia* divisions and their generals were captured at Valujki after being overwhelmed by the Cossack Cavalry Corps.[73]

By 31 January 1943, when the Italian 8th Army was officially dissolved, the human remnants of Mussolini's Russian gamble were safe. On the eve of the second battle of the Don, ARMIR had numbered 229,888 men. During the battle and the retreat that followed it lost 114,520 men, 26,690 of whom were wounded or frostbitten and 84,830 dead or missing. During the previous seventeen months it had suffered 18,600 losses, of whom 5,008 were dead or missing. Total losses amounted to half the entire army, and 37 per cent of the force were dead or missing.[74] Virtually all 8th Army's guns and four-fifths of its vehicles were lost too. The upper ranks of the *Alpini* paid a particularly high price: eight out of twelve regimental commanders were killed or captured, one general died in battle, three were captured and the remaining two led their troops to safety.[75] The Russians took some 70,000 Italians prisoner. These unfortunates then set out on the long march to incarceration: 22,000 men died on the way, and another 38,000 died in the prisoner-of-war camps.[76] Eventually, in 1946, 10,032 men were released and returned home. They, and the men who never returned, endured almost indescribable conditions which were in due course set down in print and shaped much of the public memory of the campaign for the next half century.[77]

In the days and months that followed, relations between the Italians and the Germans deteriorated, both parties blaming each other for the debacle on the Don. The Germans thought the Italians insufficiently trained and poorly led, and pointed to command failures, among which one of the most critical was the misuse of reserves in attempts to block up the holes that began appearing in their front line instead of using them in organized counter-attacks. They also highlighted panic and chaos in the retreat. Von Tippelskirch was prepared to make an exception for the *Bersaglieri* and the *Alpini*, but otherwise he had little faith in the Italian troops or their generals. Zanghieri and Zingales he thought 'completely incapable' and the others not much better.[78] The Italians thought that the Germans were too influenced by the disorders they had seen during the retreat and that the real reasons for the collapse were the over-extension of the Italian front, the shortage of anti-tank guns, the failure of the Germans to provide the resources they had obviously needed and been promised, especially petrol for the artillery tractors, and the weakness of the German divisions that had been assigned to ARMIR's sector.[79] Hitler thought Mussolini should disband his 'pathetic army divisions' and replace them with Fascist militia divisions.[80]

MALTA AND THE MEDITERRANEAN

Malta had become a thorn in the Italians' side during 1941, thanks to the presence there of the light cruisers and destroyers of Force K and the 10th Submarine Flotilla. Admiral Raeder was convinced that it should be eliminated, and in February Hitler agreed to plan for the capture of the island – but only after the defeat of Russia. The German *Luftflotte II* flew 1,465 bombing sorties against the island between January and May 1941 with results that the air force chief, General Santoro, thought 'do not correspond to the number of planes employed'. In May 1941, General Guzzoni ordered the heads of the three services to study the problem (Operation C3) anew. The navy was very interested – 'no one more so' – in taking Malta but reckoned that it would take them until the end of the year to gather the necessary means and train the men needed for an invasion – if a start was made immediately. Taking the island would require protracted air action to create maximum devastation. Events in Africa and Greece pushed Malta to one side, and for the rest of the year action was left to the *Regia Aeronautica*, which flew over 1,900 sorties against the island between June and November. The effect was minimal. Between June and November 1941 ships and aircraft from Malta sank or damaged 197,500 tons of Italian shipping, and average convoy losses rose from 7 per cent in June to 77 per cent in November.[81]

The immediate need was to get supplies through to North Africa. Rommel wanted to attack and Mussolini wanted him to do so, but that required food, fuel and munitions, which in turn meant neutralizing Malta. German help was needed. On 17 September 1941 Hitler ordered the first of twenty-seven U-boats to the Mediterranean. They soon showed results. On 13 November U-81 sank the carrier *Ark Royal* and twelve days later U-331 sank the battleship *Barham*. To Hitler, it was the *Regia Aeronautica*'s job to take the lead in weakening Malta and securing air and sea supremacy. He was, though, prepared to make planes of the *X CAT*, currently guarding the Aegean, available from time to time as necessary.[82] At the end of the month Field Marshal Kesselring arrived in Rome with *Luftflotte II*, switched from Russia over the winter. It was soon in action, tasked by Hitler to assure communications with Libya, paralyse enemy traffic in the Mediterranean, and prevent the provisioning of Tobruk and Malta. The neutralization of Malta was, Hitler emphasized, 'particularly urgent'.[83]

On 4 December Admiral Riccardi admitted that the enemy had aero-naval supremacy in the central Mediterranean. Five days later the cruisers and destroyers of Force K sank all seven ships of the Duisburg convoy, which was carrying 35,000 tons of stores including 17,000 tons of fuel and almost 400 vehicles, and three of the seven escorting destroyers. Already short of fuel, and without the ship-building capacity to replace its losses, the Italian navy now concentrated its efforts on its so-called 'battleship' convoys. The first of these, M 41, an eight-ship convoy escorted by the entire Italian battle fleet, including four battleships, which set out on 13 December 1941, was not a success: the *Vittorio Veneto* was torpedoed and put out of action for four months, two merchantmen were sunk, and the entire convoy was recalled. Then the wheel of fortune turned in Italy's favour with the first battle of the Sirte Gulf (16–17 December 1941). Admiral Iachino's battleships fought a short and indecisive gun-battle towards evening, but during the following night a group of three light cruisers and four destroyers from Force K at Malta ran into an Italian minefield. A light cruiser and one of the destroyers were sunk and the other two cruisers damaged. The following night three Italian human-torpedo crews slipped through the defences at Alexandria and planted explosive on the battleships *Queen Elizabeth* and *Valiant*, putting them out of action for months. Now there were no British battleships in the eastern Mediterranean and no aircraft carrier either.[84] Admiral Cunningham was forced to resort to land-based air power, and for a few months the Italian convoys could get through.

With Kesselring's newly arrived *Luftflotte II* attacking Malta and providing air cover, the threat to the North African convoys from Malta was for the moment at an end. At the beginning of January 1942 three separate convoys all got through to Tripoli. Another convoy of five ships later in January landed 97 tanks and 271 motor vehicles at

Tripoli despite losing one ship to British torpedo bombers and another to engine trouble, bringing the total number of tanks arriving in North Africa during the month to 205. Thanks to that, to the use of submarines to carry munitions and petrol across to North Africa, and to Rommel, a commander who conducted operations 'with prudence and boldness', Mussolini was sure that the battle in Africa was now won.[85] In all, the Italians took delivery of 474 tanks and 4,772 trucks, and the Germans 331 tanks, between January and June 1942.[86]

The question for the Axis now was against which of the two key points – Malta or Egypt – to act. On this the Italian and German navies seemingly saw eye to eye. When Admiral Riccardi met Raeder at Garmisch (14–15 January 1942) they agreed that maintaining and reinforcing the Axis position in North Africa was their primary objective and that to do it they had to neutralize or possibly occupy Malta. With the supplies they brought, Rommel would be able to launch his counter-offensive before the enemy could reorganize and beat him to it. On 15 January Rommel warned the new commander of the *corpo armata di manovra*, General Francesco Zingales (who had replaced Gambara on 31 December 1941), of what at first he painted as a defensive battle. Next day he told the Italians that he intended to launch an offensive operation.

The first six months of 1942 would be good ones for the Axis war in North Africa: one naval historian has labelled them 'the best period of our entire war'.[87] Between January and May 1942 the navy embarked 427,989 tons of materiel for North Africa and landed 409,551 tons of it, a loss rate of 4.3 per cent. During the same period it employed 1,132,560 tons of shipping and lost 61,318 tons of it, a loss rate of 5.5 per cent.[88] In reality, the good times were not securely based. As Admiral Iachino afterwards acknowledged, from a strategic point of view using the entire battle-fleet and huge amounts of fuel to get four ships across to Tripoli was 'totally out of proportion to the objective'.[89] It was, though, only one dimension of a complex, many-sided problem. Italian convoys were small, generally no more than half a dozen ships and sometimes only one or two vessels. Only forty-nine out of a total of approximately 1,000 convoys were bigger. Italian merchantmen carried average loads of 1,200 to 1,500 tons. They could have carried 5,500 tons but were generally under-loaded, either to meet urgent demands from the front or because loads were split to reduce the risk of loss. In 1941 Tripoli and Benghazi between them could in theory unload 180,000 tons of war materiel a month. Rome calculated the true figure to be 120,000 tons a month, but problems at the ports meant that even this figure could not be assured. With better unloading facilities the total could rise to 140,000 tons a month.[90] Whether in 1942 they could have handled bigger convoys is very doubtful, but this was never really tried.[91] Shuttling smaller convoys across the Mediterranean at faster rates would have required more ships than the Italians possessed and put more strain on escorts and fuel supplies. Unless something was done to increase and then maintain the flow of supplies across the Sicilian Channel, or the enemy's capacity to interrupt them was significantly degraded, the North African campaign was sooner or later going to come to a standstill.

Malta seemed to be the key to the conundrum, and during the early months of 1942 Cavallero kept the planners working on Operation C3. Unless it was neutralized there appeared to be little hope of preventing the transfer of enemy materiel to a theatre in which the *Duce* was determined to triumph. Planning threw up a multitude of problems, from practical issues such as getting hold of flamethrowers or how long parachute rip cords should be to the strategic decisions of when and where to land. This was an issue upon which the general and the admiral assigned to command and the Japanese, who were brought in to offer advice on the basis of their experience in the Philippines and at Singapore, could not agree. As the preparations went ahead, it became increasingly obvious that without a large German contribution the whole operation was impossible. The navy needed 40,000 tons of fuel from the German-controlled Romanian oilfields, and the *Regia Aeronautica* needed another 10,000 tons of fuel and over 200 Ju 52s to airlift attacking troops. Without German gliders sabotage units could not land and destroy the anti-aircraft defences in advance of the main assault. The army wanted a German parachute division and German tanks.

In April, as the likelihood that *Luftflotte II* would shortly be withdrawn and returned to Russia increased, Cavallero turned to the idea of a *coup de main* carried out by German and Italian paratroops. Kesselring pressed the case with Hitler, who seemed generally in favour and inclined to provide the necessary means.[92] Within weeks he changed his mind. When Cavallero met Keitel at Klessheim at the end of April he tried to persuade his German opposite number of the need to carry out the Malta operation 'as soon as possible'. Unmoved, Keitel told him that it was 'indispensable' to give priority to the annihilation of mobile British forces in front of Tobruk.[93] Next day, at Berchtesgaden, Hitler confirmed that Rommel's offensive in North Africa must come first.

For the next five or six weeks, while Cavallero kept the Malta option in the air as a possible *coup de main*, the services finally produced detailed plans for a fully fledged invasion. To take the island the army proposed to deploy two parachute divisions and six infantry divisions, covered by 400 attack planes and carried by 300 transport aircraft. The navy, producing serious plans for the first time, proposed to commit five battleships, four heavy cruisers and eight light cruisers – virtually the entire battle-fleet – to the operation.[94] At the end of June the services held a major exercise at Livorno in the presence of the king – a sign of how seriously they took the plan. In one vital respect they were already living on dreams. By April the *Luftwaffe* had won command of the air, but after it was withdrawn the *Regia Aeronautica* lost it. Realistically, any hope of eliminating Malta had now gone.

Mussolini still wanted the Malta operation and was ready to wait until August for it. The island was recovering its offensive capacity and making movement across to Libya difficult once again. If Malta were taken, he told Hitler, fuel consumption would be reduced – but to do it Italy would need 70,000 tons of fuel, 40,000 tons of which must arrive at least a week before the end of July. Rommel's recapture of Tobruk on 21 June, the day after Mussolini's letter, torpedoed the idea. Hitler was determined that the Axis not make the same mistake as the British did when they halted just short of Tobruk to send troops to Greece. The Axis forces must now push on as far as possible into the heart of Egypt without distraction. The loss of Egypt and the coming offensive in Russia would together contribute to bringing about the fall of 'the eastern pillar of the British Empire'.[95] The priority now was to keep supplies flowing to Rommel. Told the same day that the Germans were no longer going to support the Malta option, Cavallero said that he intended to keep the plan 'under full consideration and preparation' so that it could be put into action should the opportunity arise.[96] Mussolini, on the other hand, was in a state of high excitement about the idea of an immediate attack on Egypt and the taking of Cairo and Alexandria that would inevitably follow.[97] On 29 June he left for Libya, preparing to ride into Alexandria on a white horse as its conqueror. Eight days later Cavallero converted C3 into C4 – a plan for the occupation of Tunisia – and three weeks after that he told the chiefs of staff that C3 was off for the current year.

FORWARD INTO EGYPT!

Reports from North Africa at the end of 1941 were upbeat – morale was 'high', ground was being contested yard by yard, and the enemy was being worn down – but there were also clear warnings that things were not going well. Troops who would have won had they had 'the swift resupply of new units' enjoyed by the enemy had been fighting ceaselessly, crossing dozens of kilometres of desert on foot dragging their guns by hand, collapsing with exhaustion and drinking their own urine to quench their thirst.[98] As 1942 began, Cavallero needed to rebuild his forces. The enemy would be prodded with limited land and air offensives, but the big decisions would be taken after the reorganization was complete. The *Ariete* armoured division, the advance guard of fresh reinforcements, received sixteen new 75mm self-propelled guns in January. The XXI Corps (*Pavia*, *Trento*, and *Sabratha* divisions) screened the regrouping German motorized units; a new X Corps (*Bologna* and *Brescia* divisions) was created; and the Italians reconfigured their divisions. Machine guns, anti-aircraft and anti-tank guns were parcelled out, infantry regiments were reduced in size, and artillery regiments were scheduled to have 88mm German or 90mm Italian anti-aircraft/anti-tank guns and armoured cars – though enough of these never arrived and the Italians had to use captured British armoured cars.

Attrition was steadily taking its toll on the Italian merchant fleet. In June 1940, having lost one-third of her merchant fleet (including forty-six tankers) trapped in enemy or neutral ports or on the wrong side of the Suez Canal, Italy put 574 ships to work in the Mediterranean. In 1940 she lost 44 ships there, in 1941 another 134, and in 1942 150 more. Between January and September 1943 she would lose a further 168 ships making the crossing. In all, losses sustaining the Mediterranean war at sea added up to 496 ships.[99] Sinkings were to a degree compensated for by putting into service new, captured or repaired ships: between 1940 and 1942, 140 ships were added to the Mediterranean fleet in this way, and between January and September 1943 another seventy.[100] However, the true scale of Italian weakness is perhaps best illustrated in the new-build statistics. From 1941 to September 1943 Italy sent only fifty-eight new merchantmen down the slipways, and between 1 January 1939 and 1 September 1943 only four new tankers were added to her fleet. And it was tankers that were the prize targets of the ENIGMA-informed attacks by British submarines and aircraft.

The arrival of a convoy carrying fifty-five tanks and twenty armoured cars gave Rommel the impetus to think about attacking again. Italian intelligence estimated the enemy's strength at between 330 and 350 tanks and 200 to 220 armoured cars. His own intelligence service put the numbers at approximately 180 tanks and 180 armoured cars, encouraging him to move before the balance of forces shifted again in his opponent's favour.[101] Rommel kept his cards close to his chest, telling General Bastico that he intended to launch an attack to dislocate the enemy's deployment around Mersa Brega. The Italian agreed, not aware that something bigger was imminent. Rome was told nothing at all. The counter-attack began on 21 January and within eight days the Axis forces had retaken Benghazi. This would be the start of what has been described as 'Rommel's most brilliant offensive'.[102]

Rommel's intention to retake Benghazi alarmed Cavallero. Worried about convoying – to the extent of asking about the safe arrival of individual merchant ships – and therefore about the resilience of the Italian forces in North Africa, he flew to Misrata on 22 January. On arrival, he was told that Bastico had at first approved Rommel's plans for a limited offensive, which would delay the likelihood of an enemy offensive and improve Italian combative spirits, but that both he and Gambara now thought the offensive should be halted. Otherwise it might turn into a 'rush forward' which they did not have the means to support and which could create a new situation 'much weaker than the previous one'. Next day Cavallero gave Rommel his orders – or tried to. For the moment the Mediterranean situation did not allow of thoughts of an advance and so Rommel was to stay put at Mersa Brega.

Cavallero had his reasons. Pushing the enemy back towards his own bases would increase the permanent transport crisis for the Axis. The navy's fuel supplies might run so short that after the middle of February convoys might have to be suspended. Indeed, next day Admiral Riccardi told him that the navy was suspending convoys along its eastern route and only running fuel convoys along the western route on moonless nights because of enemy air action. He also thought that the British or the Gaullists might try a landing in Libya or Tunisia, unlikely though that was.[103] To his way of thinking, the principal task of the Italian forces in Libya was to assure the defence of Tripolitania. Mussolini overruled him. Rommel was to be given 'a certain latitude for further movement'.[104]

Benghazi fell on 28 January and on 3 February Derna followed. By now, both the Italians and Kesselring expected that Rommel would be running out of fuel. Cavallero was determined to exert his – and Italy's – authority. Lieutenant-Colonel Montezemolo was sent over to determine exactly where the Italian line of resistance should be. Rommel was to be told – by Kesselring 'with great tact' – that if he went any further forward he was absolutely forbidden to use Italian infantry, only mobile forces. Rommel wanted the five Italian infantry divisions pushed forward to occupy defensive positions while the German and Italian armour was held behind it as a manoeuvre force. Gambara agreed, and so did Bastico. Sensitive as always about Italy's status as a military ally, Mussolini disapproved: the Germans were being allowed 'a rest home'.[105] On 16 February minefields were laid from the coast to Mechili. The British 8th Army pulled back to Ain-el-Gazala west of Tobruk, and there things came to rest for the next three and a half months.

Bastico was concerned about the state of his army. It had first retreated and then taken the offensive, largely on foot, testing the physical resistance of officers and men. The army now needed a pause. It also needed leave – 30,000 men were due to go home – and replacements. Men were being airlifted in at a rate of 5,000 a month but at least 6,000 to 7,000 were needed every month simply to keep pace with normal attrition. Only by flying in 10,000 men a month could the backlog be dealt with, but that would mean suspending the airlifting of essential materiel. Officer replacements were another problem. What Bastico needed were 'young, fit and able' regular officers able to support the hardships of the colony. What he was getting were reserve officers, many of whom were old, whose military preparation amounted only to 'some vague remembrance of earlier times'.[106] Leave was fundamentally a question of maritime transport. It appeared insoluble.

In agreeing to Rommel's scheme Gambara had crossed one of Cavallero's red lines. The *Capo di stato maggiore generale* was the man in charge of running the war – he ordered the other service chiefs not to report directly to Mussolini but always to go through him – and Bastico's chief of staff had gone against one of his directives. Bastico wanted Gambara to stay in post because he and Rommel got along well. Cavallero, ready to crush 'any act of indiscipline whoever commits it', was determined to replace him, possibly for the same reason. A case was already being built against him in the War Ministry. Shortly his successor, General Curio Barbasetti di Prun, would discover that 4,000,000 lire had gone missing from the quartermaster's department.[107] (Misbehaviour in the higher reaches of the army was by no means unknown: General Roatta was hauled over the coals while in command in the Balkans for buying a yacht and maintaining a staff of forty to run it, and Geloso's army of occupation in Greece would become a byword for laxness.)

Cavallero's attention now focused on the need to build up strength in Libya in order then to advance east towards the Black Sea. That meant reconstructing the port of Benghazi so that it could offload 3,500 tons of supplies a day, but more importantly gaining and then maintaining mastery of Malta. Bastico was ordered to ensure the defence of Tripolitania, make sure that Benghazi and the main airports in Cyrenaica were available for use, and 'facilitate preparations for a successive action on Tobruk'.[108] The Italian divisions were not to move until they had been reorganized and more trucks sent to Libya: 'the *Duce* does not want the infantry walking on foot in the desert'.[109] Bastico's staff calculated that turning the army in North Africa from a 'static' into a 'dynamic' one would require 6,650 motor vehicles. Bringing it up to its full complement would require an additional 55,000 men. Shipping 1,200 trucks a month (and allowing 300 for wastage) and 10,000 men a month, it would take seven months to get the army in North Africa up to full strength.[110] The authorities in Rome juggled the numbers, but after subtracting new and repaired vehicles they still had to find 4,000 trucks – this when according to the latest calculations the CSIR in Russia needed 700 trucks a month and North Africa 600, the equivalent of total monthly production, just to cover wastage and the new ARMIR in Russia was scheduled to have 16,700 motor vehicles. The tank problem was equally serious: Italy could only produce 30 L 16s, 60 M 14s and a dozen self-propelled guns a month.[111]

Until April, when the port of Benghazi reopened, all Italian traffic had to come into Tripoli, from where it had to be moved forward 700 kilometres to El Agheila, where units were being rebuilt, and another 500 kilometres to the new front line. Travelling across the desert presented problems all its own; not for nothing was it labelled a paradise for tacticians and a hell for logisticians. The centralized Italian supply system, in which the Intendance controlled the transport and distributed supplies and munitions to individual formations, contrasted with the more flexible, devolved German system in which divisions and even smaller detachments had their own motor transport and could draw their needs directly from supply dumps and stores. It worked well in normal times when demand could be forecast, but not when improvisation and fast reactions were necessary. The Italian high command in North Africa (*Superasi*) was unwilling to loosen its control over the motor transport in case Rommel got his hands on Italian trucks and fuel.[112]

On 30 April Rommel unveiled his plan first to attack Tobruk and then push on towards Bardia and Sollum. The *Comando Supremo*, which had been reckoning on having the Italian and German divisions 'perfectly set-up' by the autumn, found its timetable being pushed aside. The Italian units were not yet fully ready: the *Ariete* and *Trieste* were almost complete, but the infantry divisions lacked trucks. Given that the longer-term intention was to be in a position to launch decisive operations in Egypt, Cavallero was prepared to allow Rommel to try his luck – but only within limits. The operation offered the chance to erode the enemy's strength and get into good positions from which to launch the planned attack into Egypt, but it must 'absolutely avoid seriously wearing down our forces [and] compromising the laborious work of rebuilding and strengthening our units'. Nor must it compromise the preparations for the attack on Malta. Bastico was ordered to support the attack on Tobruk but not to get himself into 'unfavourable positions'. If Tobruk fell he could advance to the Sollum–Halfaya–Sidi Omar line but no farther; if it did not, he was not to go beyond Ain-el-Gazala. And he was warned not to allow the operation to continue beyond 20 June, after which date the air force units loaned from Sicily would be brought home.[113] Bastico's chief of staff doubted whether Rommel's plan to encircle the enemy was going to work and warned that moving straight from it to attacking Tobruk without a pause to ensure 'continuity' presented possibly insuperable logistical difficulties.[114]

On paper the British 8th Army defending the Gazala line fifty-nine kilometres west of Tobruk looked the stronger force: 100,000 men, 849 tanks (including the newly arrived M3 Grant, which could outmatch most of Rommel's *Panzer* IIIs and IVs and all the Italian tanks) and 604 aircraft were protected by a network of minefields. The Italians had some of the new 90mm guns, more 75mm anti-tank guns, a handful of self-propelled 75mm guns and a few armoured cars – their first, sent to the desert without compasses. They also had hollow-charge anti-tank ammunition.[115] Both sides could take advantage of intelligence breakthroughs, ENIGMA decrypts from Bletchley Park in General Neil Ritchie's case and decrypts of reports on 8th Army's plans and dispositions by the American military attaché in Cairo, Colonel Bonner Fellers, available to Rommel after SIM got hold of the American Black Code. Rommel also profited – not for the first time or the last – from the tendency of British generals to discuss their plans with one another over radio-telephones.[116] The British system of self-defending 'boxes' played into the Axis' hands and so did the imperfections in the British chain of command, still working its way towards devolving command to divisions, which all too often dislocated British fighting power.[117] As the moment for the attack drew near the *Ariete* and *Trieste* took up their position on the right of the front line and an infantry division (*Sabratha*) took its place in the centre.

Operation VENEZIA was intended to encircle and destroy the enemy forces manning the advanced defence of Tobruk. At the start of the Gazala battles (26 May–15 June 1942) the four infantry divisions of X and XXI Corps 'fixed' the front while the *Ariete* armoured division and the *Trieste* motorized division, together with two *Panzer* divisions, took part in a sweeping 'right hook'. One *Ariete* battalion tried to charge into the Free French 'box' at Bir Hacheim unsupported either by artillery or infantry, its commander 'revert[ing] 25 years back to his young Lieutenancy and the Bayonet charges of World War I', but was stopped in its tracks by mines and anti-tank fire, losing thirty-one tanks in the process.[118] Meanwhile the *Trieste* struggled through a minefield north of the strongpoint. Joining up, the two Italian divisions and the Germans fought off poorly co-ordinated British attempts to encircle them in their turn, the *Ariete*'s artillery giving a particularly good account of itself.

So far, the battle appeared to be going more or less according to Cavallero's design: not going off into the distance looking for the enemy but provoking him into action and then counter-attacking. To keep it within bounds Bastico was told to keep wastage to a minimum, to bring about the fall of the Ain-el-Gazala line and to take Bir Hacheim but not to do anything which threatened the main action and brought his forces up against the time limit (20 June), which was what Cavallero believed his opponent wanted him to do.[119] Even so, Cavallero was worried that his army in North Africa was in danger of going beyond the limits he had imposed. With the incomplete *Littorio* armoured division its only reserve, there looked to be a real danger of its wearing out its armour and swiftly finding itself again inferior to its enemy. With his favoured Malta operation in mind, he advised Mussolini not to go beyond the predetermined time limit.[120]

Presented with a German timetable for ongoing operations culminating in an attack on Tobruk between 18 and 25 June, Cavallero would not commit the Italians to it but made Tobruk conditional on taking Bir Hacheim and Ain-el-Gazala.[121] Over the next four days that was exactly what happened. In the closing days of the battle the *Trieste* took part in a German attack on Bir Hacheim, which the Free French surrendered on 11 June after a heavy bombardment, and the *Ariete* fought off a heavy British counter-attack with the help of the *Afrikakorps*. With the Germans at El Adem, south of Tobruk, by 12 June the British lines of retreat from Gazala were all but cut. Two days later the order went out for them to retreat to the Egyptian frontier.

While Rommel was closing in on Tobruk the Italian navy fought the battles of *Mezzo Giugno* – 'the closest thing to a major naval victory in the whole war'.[122] While one Malta-bound convoy from Gibraltar was degraded by Italian torpedo bombers and then by Admiral Da Zara's cruiser squadron at the battle of Pantelleria (15 June 1942) before running into a minefield off Valletta, Admiral Iachino led the *Littorio*, the *Vittorio Veneto*, four cruisers and twelve destroyers to intercept a second Malta convoy coming from Haifa and Port Said. The presence of the Italian battle-fleet was enough to force the convoy commander, Admiral

Vian, to give up and turn back. The Italian fleet lost a heavy cruiser (*Trento*) and the *Littorio* was hit by a B24 bomber and put out of action until August, but the British lost a cruiser and five destroyers and only two of the seventeen merchantmen in the convoys reached Malta.

On 20 June 1942, Italian and German armoured and motorized formations attacked Tobruk from the south-east, while the *Trento* and the *Sabratha* infantry division masked the south and west side of the fifty-four-kilometre long defences. After the defences had been hammered from the air, 21st *Panzer* opened a path through the defending minefields and rapidly knocked out half a dozen of the defence's fortlets. The *Trieste* was supposed to do likewise but because of 'the lesser attitude of our units to manoeuvre' (as the Italian liaison officer with the *Panzers* put it afterwards) its arrival 'suffered a slight delay'.[123] The *Trieste*'s engineers, arriving too late, were hit by defending artillery and were unable to clear their section of the minefield. Rommel halted the division and sent the *Ariete* through the breach made by the Germans. The fortress was swiftly split in two and the defence collapsed. Next day the garrison surrendered. German front-line recovery units, something the Italians did not have, swept up the lion's share of the Tobruk booty – 2,000 vehicles, 5,000 tons of food and 2,000 tons of fuel. With that to hand Rommel was ready to push forward at once to Mersa Matruh and then on to Cairo, the Canal and 'eventually' the Persian Gulf. Their orders being not to go beyond Sollum–Halfaya, Bastico and his chief of staff put up every objection in their arsenal. Rommel knocked them down one by one. 'I'm going [to Mersa Matruh],' he finally told Bastico. 'If the Italians want to follow us, let them come, otherwise they can stay put. It's a matter of indifference to me.' Then, smiling at Bastico, he invited him to lunch – in Cairo.[124]

At 11.10 a.m. on 23 June von Rintelen arrived in Cavallero's office with the news that Rommel had taken enough booty at Tobruk to continue his advance. During that day Hitler's letter backing Rommel arrived, followed soon afterwards by an intercept from Bonner Fellers reporting that the 8th Army had only 127 tanks left, that half of its artillery was lost, that morale was low, and that if Rommel intended to take the Delta then this was the best moment to do it. Mussolini was convinced. The problem now was transporting supplies to sustain the advance and that, Cavallero told von Rintelen, was not Rommel's – 'it's ours'. The extent of the problem had been starkly illustrated four days earlier. At a meeting of the chiefs of staff on 19 June, Vice-Admiral Luigi Sansonetti, deputy chief of the naval staff, announced that if he was faced with a big British convoy he could only put up a few submarines against it because 'our ships are absolutely empty [of fuel]', and General Santoro admitted that the air force now possessed only seven aerial torpedoes.[125] June would indeed take the record as the worst month for supplying Libya since the beginning of the war, only 41,519 tons being despatched, of which 32,327 reached the North African ports.

In the course of a hectic day of meetings Admiral Riccardi told Cavallero that the navy could only meet its fuel problems by raiding stocks intended for the submarines, that because Tobruk was nearer to Alexandria and therefore to the British fleet there than to Benghazi, ships sent there would need a heavier escort, that all but one of Tobruk's wharves had been destroyed, and that moving cargo up the coast from Benghazi would expose ships to prolonged dangers from enemy torpedo bombers. Asked what cover the *Regia Aeronautica* could offer, General Rino Corso Fougier, Pricolo's successor as chief of the air staff, replied that the matter was under examination.[126] That evening Cavallero told Mussolini that with the elimination of Malta no longer on the cards the problem now was neutralizing the island. There were others: the fuel problem, the problem of Tobruk, which in normal circumstances could only handle 800 tons of goods a day, and the problem of Tripolitania (by which he meant its defence against a possible attack by Vichy France) posed by the advance into Egypt. As for Operation C3, 'we'll see what can be done'.[127]

It was not Cavallero but Kesselring who decided what would be done. Meeting Cavallero and Bastico at Derna, he told the Italians that there was not enough air power to fight a holding action on the Egyptian frontier before attacking and at the same time suppress Malta. As long as the Axis advance continued, nothing could be done about Malta. North Africa must have priority. There, on the land front the Axis could put 120 to 140 fighters in the air against 600 enemy aircraft, and only about half of them would be able to back up Rommel's advance, because of transport problems. Going after further objectives beyond El Alamein with anything more than light units would be impossible. It was not just a question of fuel or of bombs, but of strength in relation to objectives. On that basis Rommel's advance could continue for eight to ten days but he could not go beyond El Alamein.

Admiral Weichold weighed in: the Italians should take over shipping supplies along the coast from Benghazi to Tobruk, where in his view they ought to be able to unload 1,000 tons of supplies a day.

With no other choice Cavallero first subsided into acquiescence and then, working towards what he thought the *Duce* would want, re-emerged as an enthusiast for the German design.[128] First Bastico was ordered to eliminate the enemy's position at Mersa Matruh. Then, after hearing Rommel assert next day that he could get through the El Alamein pass and be in Cairo by 30 June, Cavallero told Bastico his objectives were now Suez, Ismailia and Port Said, and Cairo.[129] Bastico believed the better course would be to occupy Mersa Matruh and Jarabub oasis and then wait until his forces had been completely reorganized before investing El Alamein. 'But', he told Cavallero after Rommel's monologue, 'it's too late now to change the programme . . . Let's put our hope in God!'[130]

On 26 June Rommel attacked Mersa Matruh. Italian military intelligence calculated that he was facing roughly 100 efficient tanks, 150 armoured cars and 500 planes. Behind them in the Delta were one or two English divisions, much reduced in size, a couple of Indian divisions that were not worth much, and a handful of Greek, Polish and Czech units.[131] Three Italian divisions (*Trento*, *Pavia* and *Brescia*) attacked the target from the west and south while the German and Italian armoured and motorized forces pushed forward to defeat scattered Commonwealth troops south of the town and cut the garrison's line of retreat. In three days of confused fighting the Axis forces profited from overestimation of their strength and from uncoordinated counterattacks launched by an opponent who was ready to abandon Mersa Matruh and live to fight another day. On 28 June an attempt by the *Trento* division and the 7th *Bersaglieri* to break into the town, along with the German 90th Light division, was halted by a combination of artillery fire, minefields and air attacks. The town fell next day to X Corps, which netted 5,000 prisoners and a considerable amount of booty.

At 7.45 that same evening Mussolini landed in Derna with a large entourage, promoted Cavallero to *Maresciallo d'Italia* in anticipation of a great victory and waited for the moment when he could ride into Cairo in triumph. A chase now developed as the Commonwealth forces retreated eastwards. Stiff resistance, however, eroded the Italian units' strength. With supply precarious and forward movement slow due to the deficiencies of Italian materiel – German armoured columns had cruising speeds of twenty kilometres an hour whereas Italian columns could only manage seven to eight kilometres an hour – and also to a huge traffic jam that built up along the coastal road, Rommel had to pause for twenty-four hours before launching his battle for El Alamein.[132]

Back in Rome, General Ambrosio contemplated the future. Success would mean finding an army of occupation to defend Egypt against the counter-offensive from the east and south that would certainly follow. That would require more divisions and they could only come from Greece. The Italian divisions there were below strength and had few motor vehicles – but there was no other choice. The logistics would have to run through the Balkans, Greece and Crete – but Greece did not have anything like the structural framework to feed an occupied Egypt. That would have to be built up. Moreover, success in Egypt could have 'unfavourable repercussions' in other sectors. The army had to be ready to send an expeditionary force into Tunisia, an ongoing Italian concern. That needed an eight- or ten-division reserve in addition to the three divisions already slated to take part in the operation. Then there was the western frontier with France; Ambrosio wanted at least six divisions for that scenario. To get them, one division would have to be pulled back from Montenegro and another from Slovenia. Finally, operations in Tunisia would require more munitions 'and we already do not have enough'.[133]

Opening the first battle of El Alamein (1–3 July), Rommel pitched 8,000 Italian infantrymen and 2,000 Germans equipped with 125 tanks (seventy of them the lightweight Italian L and M models), fifteen armoured cars and 530 guns against 15,000 Commonwealth infantry, 150 tanks, a hundred armoured cars and 400 guns. From the very first encounter it was clear that the enemy's defences were too strong and the Axis armies too tired and too thinly spread to get through relying on speed alone.[134] The *Panzers* failed to make any inroads and the weakened *Ariete* division (it had only eight working M 13 tanks and forty guns), ordered forward into a basin and surrounded on three sides, suffered heavily, losing thirty-six of its guns, fifty-five motor vehicles and 531 men. Afterwards Rommel blamed the *Ariete* as a key factor in his failure to win the battle.[135] Forced to pause for what he expected to be ten to fourteen days and fight a defensive battle (10–27 July), Rommel requested another 12,000 to 15,000 German troops and more men for the two Italian infantry corps, complaining that the Germans were not getting an appropriate share of the reduced tonnage available and that Kesselring was taking the lion's share for the *Luftwaffe*.

During the pause the enemy launched a series of local actions against weak-looking sectors of the Axis line. The Italians proved especially vulnerable. On 7 July the *Sabratha* infantry division gave way when attacked by a couple of Australian battalions, temporarily opening up a gap in the lines; on 10 July the *Trieste* motorized division and some of the *Afrikakorps* were brought to their knees by low-level air attacks; and on 15 July the junction of the *Brescia* and *Pavia* infantry divisions gave way. Next day an infantry battalion of the *Trieste* was overrun and another breakthrough occurred that night at the junction of the *Trento* and *Trieste* divisions. Italian units were, Brigadier-General Giuseppe Mancinelli acknowledged, showing 'unjustifiable apprehensiveness' when faced with a few advancing tanks, 'hypersensitivity' when surrounded in strongholds, and a tendency to retire when not directly engaged 'transforming what would [otherwise] be an unfavourable incident into [a] retreat'. Rommel brusquely demanded that corps commanders intervene immediately, using the death sentence when necessary.[136]

The *Sabratha* division now had no complete battalions and no guns left, the *Brescia* had one battalion and no guns, the *Ariete* armoured division had one *Bersaglieri* battalion and fifteen tanks, and the *Littorio* armoured division had one *Bersaglieri* battalion, twenty tanks and one gun. Four Italian divisions had been virtually annihilated in the battle and the 'pause' that had followed. As a result, Rommel announced, further offensive action against the enemy was now impossible. Mussolini, sitting in Berta waiting to celebrate victory, called in Cavallero, Kesselring and Bastico. The meeting produced a telegram telling Rommel that the *Duce* 'feels it necessary at this point . . . to abstain from initiatives that submit our troops . . . to further wear, which would otherwise render their recovery for further tasks difficult'. Measures were under way, Mussolini added, to bring Rommel the reinforcements he needed to reach his objectives.[137] Rommel told Cavallero that if reinforcements did not arrive within the week he would have to retreat. Asked when they would arrive, Bastico could only reply somewhat lamely that there were so many small elements to take into account that he could not give a date, but that everything would come as quickly as possible.[138] Two days later, after again listening to Rommel badgering him for reinforcements and drumming his fingers nervously on the table the while, Cavallero assured him that three infantry divisions and a Blackshirt division would be made available immediately. In fact, only two divisions – one of them the *Folgore* airborne division – were being readied to go to North Africa.[139]

Prompted partly by Russia's 'desperate' call for a second front in June 1942, which he seized upon as a sign that the war was turning in the Axis's favour, Mussolini now set out his thoughts on the military situation. The battle of Tobruk had come to an end. Tomorrow's battle would be for the Delta. The time for preparation must be numbered in weeks and not a minute must be lost. The first charge was to make the jumping-off lines safe. To do that, the soldiers should sow broad minefields, gather together as much artillery as they could find in Libya and in Italy, deploy air power as efficiently as possible, increase the numbers of self-propelled guns in the armoured divisions 'given that our M 14 has been superseded in the contest between armour and gun', get the infantry divisions up to establishment, bring up new divisions, making sure that they had at least a minimum of mobility, and get rid of men who were worn out 'and whose presence constitutes a danger'. Turning to the possibility of an Allied second front, Mussolini declared that it would come in Egypt, Palestine, Syria and Iraq – 'that is, in countries where men and equipment can be landed without fighting, in countries which constitute the great crossroads of the British Empire'. The aim would be to prevent the Tripartite forces coming from the north, east and west from meeting up. To be ready for whatever might transpire, the defences of Cyrenaica and Tripolitania must be strengthened and both garrisoned.[140]

Next day Mussolini flew back to Rome. At first he was optimistic, thinking that the Axis offensive could restart in two or three weeks, but that soon wore off. Three days after getting back to Palazzo Venezia, he was furious. He had flown to Libya expecting that after his armies had won a decisive victory in the field he would be able to enter Egypt as its conqueror – not just another Napoleon but another Octavian. Now for the second time (Greece had been the first) the soldiers had made him look a fool by arriving at the front 'at unfortunate moments'.[141]

As Mussolini returned to Rome, the army general staff contemplated the likely consequences of the Allied declaration that there would be a second front in Europe in 1942. The Italian navy had expected that its new ally, Japan, would be able to attack Allied convoys routed round the Cape and through the western Indian Ocean and so reduce, if not cut, the flow of men and materiel going to the British 8th Army. In reality the Japanese threat to the western Indian Ocean had already disappeared during the summer, partly through the Allied invasion of Madagascar but mainly because of the Japanese defeats in the Coral Sea (4–8 May) and at Midway (4–7 June 1942). Rome, though, was unaware of the Japanese defeats and was assured by the Japanese that occupying Ceylon and operating in the Indian Ocean remained their top priority.[142]

Misleading intelligence from Tokyo meant that the Italian navy lacked accurate information about their Far Eastern ally's naval balance sheet. Such information as was available from the Japanese about the number of enemy ships sunk in the Indian Ocean now suggested that within a short time their foe would have 'a crushing superiority in Egypt'. That made the prospect of Allied landings even more threatening. Admiral Riccardi thought Dakar a possible target, and Ambrosio added Casablanca. Oran and Algiers were also put on the list. Riccardi did not think a second European front was probable 'at this moment' but if it happened Italian troops might be called on to help. By late August Ambrosio was also facing the possibility of Allied landings west of the Rhône striking for Toulon and Marseilles. For that, and for the defence of French North Africa, mobile armoured divisions would be needed – armoured divisions that Ambrosio did not have.[143]

After fighting off a two-day enemy offensive (the Second Battle of Ruweisat, 21–22 July), Rommel warned that if the enemy broke through his defensive front he would have to recommend pulling back to positions nearer his supply base, thereby saving the bulk of the army and therefore also North Africa. Bastico agreed, and Cavallero allowed that in such circumstances the commanders on the spot would have to make their own decisions. But, he added, the loss of North Africa could in no circumstances be contemplated. After another attempt by Commonwealth troops to break the Axis lines on 27 July had failed, the first battle of El Alamein came to an end.

In the brief pause that followed, the *Ariete* and *Littorio* armoured divisions, the *Trieste* motorized division, X Corps and the *Pavia* and *Brescia* infantry divisions all got new commanders. Adhering to a practice of making bureaucracies as complicated as possible, Cavallero reconfigured the command system. To underline the fact that Italy was in the lead in North Africa, Bastico, newly promoted *Maresciallo d'Italia*, was made supreme commander of the armed forces in Libya (*Superlibia*) and Rommel's *Panzer* army was formally put under the *Comando Supremo* in Rome. Bastico had reported disorder behind the lines, with corps, divisions, regiments and even battalions creating multiple rear and forward bases cluttered with men, vehicles and equipment 'in remarkable quantities'. Instead of leaving him to clear matters up, which he had begun to do, Cavallero made Barbasetti (still Bastico's chief of staff) head of a direct 'Delegation' of the *Comando Supremo* tasked with organizing the logistics for the Italo-German forces. He was also put in charge of the rear areas and given command of the Italian aircraft in Libya. Bastico's 'unified command' was gone. The changes were necessary, Cavallero told Mussolini, because not enough energy was being applied to the organization and management of affairs behind the front lines. Italian prestige was being degraded, and lack of action was allowing 'incessant German penetration'. The new system would allow the *Comando Supremo* to intervene directly when necessary.[144] Cavallero had overlooked the law of unintended consequences. Taking full advantage of the complex chain of command that he had created, Rommel could now simply ignore Bastico and go directly to von Rintelen in Rome whenever he felt inclined. Bastico always suspected that Cavallero reduced his status in order not to have to share the glory for the forthcoming capture of Alexandria with anyone else – save, of course, Mussolini.

The decision to start the second battle of El Alamein was Rommel's alone.* Aware that reinforcements were on their way to General Auchinleck and that they would probably start arriving at the end of August, he told Barbasetti on 10 August that he intended to attack about 26 August, using his armour against the extreme left of his enemy's positions where the minefields were thinner and less effective. Thanks to

---

* The battle of Alam-el-Halfa in anglophone histories – Italian historians number El Alamein the third battle.

ULTRA, Rommel's decision was known to the British a week after he told Barbasetti. Cavallero approved the plan in Mussolini's name – but with characteristic qualifications. Within 'a few days' the Axis would have enough force to beat the enemy, but the start date would depend on the supply programme, especially fuel, not being interrupted. In practice, programmes were not being met. The army needed 75,000 tons of materials a month, but in the first half of August it received only 15,000 tons. It was now getting half the food and munitions it required – some guns had less than 150 rounds left – and only just over a quarter of the fuel. The Germans were not much better off: on the eve of their attack the *Panzer* units had only enough fuel to drive for 150 kilometres.[145] Morale was being increasingly affected by the inability of Italian units to rotate men home. In September 1942, attempting to ameliorate the problem, the Italians increased the weekly rate of rotation out of theatre to 100 men per regiment.[146]

As Rommel prepared for battle, an Axis attempt to strangle Malta failed. Operation PEDESTAL (11–15 August 1942) was a fourteen-ship convoy with a massive 'double escort', including three carriers, two battleships, nine cruisers, twenty-four destroyers and eight submarines. The Italian admirals were unwilling to risk their heavy ships, which were in any case short of fuel, without sufficient air escorts. Kesselring, who distrusted the Italian navy after the second battle of Sirte, was not willing to provide air cover, and Fougier could only offer twenty-four aircraft. In the circumstances Admiral Riccardi thought using his fleet was not worth the risk. The battle was fought by Italian and German submarines, aircraft and torpedo boats. The U-73 sank the carrier *Eagle* on 11 August, and over the next three days Axis forces sank two cruisers, one destroyer and nine large steamships, damaging eight more warships and steamers. However, the victory was a limited one: 32,000 tons of supplies and 11,100 tons of fuel got through to Malta nonetheless, allowing the island to live for another day and recommence attacking Axis traffic.

For the battle of Alam-el-Halfa (30 August–5 September), the Axis forces amounted to sixty-six infantry battalions (thirty-nine Italian), 536 guns, 447 medium tanks (244 Italian), seventy-eight armoured cars, 365 fighter aircraft (215 Italian) and 335 assault aircraft and bombers (165 Italian). Estimates suggested that on the ground the two sides were evenly balanced – but they were wrong: Axis intelligence put the enemy's tank strength at 400 to 450, whereas in fact 8th Army had 700 tanks. In the air, the enemy was thought to be able to deploy 1,100 bombers and fighters. The design for the battle, in which the Italian infantry divisions held a 'defensive wall' on the left while the *Littorio* and *Ariete* armoured divisions and the *Trento* motorized divisions formed the inside and the two *Panzer* divisions of the *Afrikorps* the outside of a wheeling manoeuvre aiming for the Alam Halfa ridge, went awry from the start. The advancing Germans were hammered from the air, losing their corps commander and two divisional commanders; the Italian mobile divisions got held up in minefields; and the Germans, crossing unexpectedly sandy ground which slowed them down and used up valuable fuel, ran into well-prepared defences and then attacks by concentrated British armour. Then, on 1 September, news arrived that two Italian tankers had been sunk and a third seriously damaged. Half the 5,000 tons of fuel the army needed had gone to the bottom. With little air cover and no more fuel scheduled to arrive until 7 September at best, Rommel had no choice but to abandon his offensive and retreat. The battle cost the Axis 2,855 dead, wounded and missing, forty-seven tanks, 324 motor vehicles, fifty-three guns and forty-one aircraft. The vast majority of the Italian losses were suffered by the three armoured and motorized divisions. Italian mobile units had to leave two-thirds of their men and one-third of their guns behind for want of motor vehicles.[147]

On 22 September Rommel called his Italian and German divisional commanders together and told them that until they had enough fuel and means of all kinds he could not risk another offensive. Disregarding the enemy's air superiority, he told the generals that the problem was 'only a question of resupply' – thereby loading all the responsibility for the operational failure onto the one factor for which the *Afrikakorps* staff had absolutely no responsibility.[148] The supply situation did indeed look parlous. In Egypt, the Axis forces had enough fuel and munitions to fight on the defensive for eight days. The weakness of Axis naval forces and the British destruction of much of the Italian merchant fleet (between June and August 1942 the Italians lost fourteen merchantmen, totalling 43,761 tons) now effectively doomed any attempt to reach Alexandria, let alone the Suez Canal. In Rome, the army staff calculated that it needed 30,000 tons of fuel a month to cover its own and German consumption merely to stand still. Taking the offensive would require another 16,000 tons of fuel. Its own figures suggested that there were only 2,587 tons of petrol and diesel in stock. By the end of the month there were enough munitions for one major action, after which the army would no longer be able to operate.[149]

Preparing for the enemy attack he was confident he could fight off, Rommel set up a line of interconnecting strongpoints fronted by mine-fields intersected by 'devil's gardens' sown with explosive charges. The Italian infantry divisions and the *Trieste* motorized division held the northern and central parts of the line, the two Italian armoured divisions and the *Folgore* held the southern stretch, and the *Panzer* divisions formed a mobile reserve behind the Italian armour. German and Italian units were intermixed in the line of strongpoints, evidence that Rommel's doubts about Italian fighting power persisted. When it came to taking the offensive, Italian and German armour would form joint mobile groups. Unhappy about this arrangement, the *Comando Supremo* in Rome sent orders that the Italian units must be under the authority of their own higher commands during mobile operations when the difference in speed between German and Italian units would make it impossible to maintain the intermixing that could be achieved in static defensive situations. *Superlibia* passed on the orders but failed to name anyone as in command of the combined mobile groups. That in turn meant that when they went into action Italian and German divisions would each be operating on their own account. Later Mancinelli would describe this arrangement an 'insane organic *pasticcio* (muddle)'.[150]

En route back to Germany for a brief period of leave, Rommel assured Mussolini that if the enemy attacked, which he thought unlikely, he could hold them off with limited counter-attacks and announced that for a renewed offensive he needed at least thirty days' reserves and two fresh divisions, one Italian and the other German. Cavallero assured Mussolini that the *Centauro* armoured division and the *Piave* motorized division would be shipped across from their pre-sent stations on the French frontier as soon as pressure on Malta was renewed and they could be moved by the more direct western route.[151] As well as a direct frontal attack, both Rommel and his temporary replacement, General Georg Stumme, foresaw the possibility of a wide enemy 'turning' attack through the desert and coastal landings. Ideally the Axis should pre-empt the enemy move with an attack aimed at destroying the 8th Army. That required supplies and reinforcements.

Finding them and getting them across was now almost beyond Italy: to run convoys, destroyer escorts were taking fuel from cruisers. As the coming battle drew nearer, the supply situation grew steadily worse. Food was a particular problem: in September, the army in North Africa consumed 5,200 tons but only received 1,800 tons. It had been living on captured enemy supplies, but early in October the situation was becoming 'insupportable'.[152] In Rome arguments about convoying simmered. Admirals Sansonetti and Riccardi agreed that they could not send convoys to both Tripoli and Benghazi, as the Germans wanted, because they had too few ships whose speeds in any case differed. Port capacity – or rather incapacity – in Libya was another problem.

Before the Alamein battles began Kesselring had demanded that the Italians send a few large convoys across to North Africa instead of lots of small ones. The navy's response had been that the only defence against night attacks by enemy torpedo-bombers was fog and manoeuvre, and for the latter to work convoys must be manageable and therefore small.[153] Now it planned to send ten ships across, mostly in ones and twos, during the middle third of the month, carrying 24,000 tons of supplies and 13,000 tons of fuel. After that, there was not enough tonnage to meet requests.[154] Kesselring complained about the Italian policy of sending lone ships across, and when told that the navy planned to do exactly that with the *Amsterdam*, the largest ship making the Tripoli run, he called it 'a race with death'. Admiral Sansonetti remarked that ships which set out un-timetabled were not attacked. That, he believed, pointed to espionage based in Italian ports as the cause of the sinkings. The Italians would go on hunting for spies, completely unaware that the enemy was getting vital intelligence directly via ENIGMA decrypts.[155]

As the climactic battle approached, the Axis forces were instructed to face in all directions. The Germans told Cavallero that it was absolutely necessary to defend the western frontier of Libya and be ready to land in Tunisia to stave off any potential enemy landing there. Mussolini forecast 'large, intense and simultaneous' enemy attacks on the Egyptian front, and from Kufra in the south and from the Sahara into Libya, as well as attacks in the Aegean, after which the Tunisian frontier too could come into play. To meet the threats 'the entire Mediterranean sector' should be reinforced. For Cavallero, who thought Italy might soon face threats from Nigeria and Dakar too,

Malta was still the key. Hitler had decided that the air attacks on the island to cover transports to Libya were too costly and could not be continued. Depending on how that problem was resolved, Cavallero told the *Duce* on the day that the third battle of El Alamein began, Italy 'could win or resoundingly lose the war'.[156]

On 10 October a calm descended on the front as for ten days heavy sandstorms reduced visibility in Egypt almost to nothing. General Stumme, Rommel's temporary replacement, exuded confidence. The British did not feel themselves strong enough for a major offensive and with their front reorganized and minefields laid the Axis forces could await future events 'with maximum calm'.[157] The Italian generals were less sanguine. Troop morale was high – but fissures were starting to appear. War in the desert with all its attendant hardships was wearing the men down, and with rotation out of theatre only possible after four years, for most of them no end was in sight. The sensation that the soldiers were simply being 'consumed' was spreading. Fascist propaganda was not helping. Far more coverage was being given to the troops in Russia, who were also receiving more parcels from home, and the rank and file were getting the sense that their sacrifice was not appreciated.[158]

When the sandstorms ended, intense enemy air activity began. Then, at 8.40 p.m. on 23 October, a violent air and artillery bombardment heralded the start of the third – and last – battle of El Alamein. It opened with a double attack on the Axis positions in the north and the south. In the north the attack hit the *Trento* division, one of whose regiments was destroyed in what Rommel later called a barrage of First World War proportions. Over the next two days counter-attacks by Italian and German armour held the line in the north and pushed back the attackers. Fuel was running out: when Rommel, recalled from Germany after the death of General Stumme, landed at Ciampino airport outside Rome on 25 October, he was told that there was only enough left for 300 kilometres' movement. Next day a tanker carrying 2,500 tons of fuel and a merchant ship with 3,000 tons of ammunition went to the bottom. Gradually, intense artillery fire, enemy air superiority and sheer exhaustion wore down the capacity of the defenders. By 27 October a dangerous gap had opened up at the lower end of the northern sector.[159] In the south the *Folgore*, three-quarters of whose 108 anti-tank guns were effective only at ranges of 300 feet or less, used skilful tactics to force British armour to a halt and then beat back an attack by two battalions of the French Foreign Legion.[160] Over the following three days fighting in that sector sputtered but did not burst into a blaze.

Rommel asked Cavallero to come over and discuss the supply situation. Cavallero declined. 'I would truly like to come to you as soon as possible,' he told Rommel. 'But my personal presence is needed here to make supplies arrive and I am confident they soon will.' It was 'necessary to insist a lot' to get what was wanted from the navy and so 'the situation is to be solved here.'[161] Cavallero did indeed spend a great deal of time discussing shipping questions in considerable detail – 242 of the 300 meetings of the chiefs of staff over which he presided in 1942 dealt with transports, convoys and escorts. His prioritizing of supply spoke to the need to eke out Italy's increasingly meagre economic resources.

For two days (29–30 October) General Bernard Montgomery paused. On the first day Rommel could see little hope of resisting another major attack, or of withdrawing, because of the lack of motor transport and fuel. Next day he changed his mind: with 1,500 motor vehicles and the necessary fuel, he could pull his line back 100 kilometres to Fuka, close to Mersa Matruh. Rome turned him down flat. All available motor vehicles were being used to ferry supplies up to the front. If they were taken away and used to move troops instead, then the army would not be able to fight at all. 'If we give him the vehicles he'll retreat without a doubt,' General Barbasetti told Mancinelli as he left Rommel's command vehicle.[162] Next day the battle began again.

The fighting which now took place on the northern section of the front has been described as 'the most ferocious of all the engagements in the El Alamein battles'.[163] Rommel began the battle with only sixty-five Italian M 13 tanks and 102 *Panzers* left. At the north end of the front, elements of the *Littorio*, the only whole battalion of the *Trieste* that still existed, and two *Panzer* divisions battled 1st Armoured Division. Outgunned by the enemy's Grant and Sherman tanks, and with no effective anti-tank guns of their own, the Italian tanks were shot to pieces one by one.[164] As the Axis forces were ground down, Rommel and his staff prepared to retreat. Far away in Rome, Cavallero, who believed quite wrongly that Rommel had started the battle with at least 250 tanks, refused to face unpleasant facts. Our men were tired, he told Kesselring, 'but the English must be at the end of their strength'. 'It's his battle' was his reaction when told that Rommel had thrown all his reserves into the fight; 'he has petrol and munitions. The enemy thinks he has exhausted his reserves and is making his ultimate effort.'[165]

When they learned of the impending withdrawal, Hitler and Mussolini both ordered Rommel to stand where he was. As the order arrived, the withdrawal was beginning. Two of the Italian infantry divisions (*Pavia* and *Brescia*) had enough vehicles to disengage and shuttle back fifteen kilometres. They then began to walk across the desert towards Fuka. With next to no transport, moving its mortars and guns by hand, and carrying its ammunition, as there was no hope of resupply, the *Folgore* too retired through the desert, covering 126 kilometres in two nights. Finally, on 6 November, the remnants of all three divisions – with no vehicles, food or water – were surrounded by British armour. After a brief last fight which used up all the ammunition they had left, the 400 men left of the *Folgore* destroyed their weapons and they and the survivors of the *Pavia* and *Brescia* surrendered.[166] With no transport at all, the *Trento* and the *Bologna* infantry division dragged their 47mm guns by hand and carried their weapons on their backs as they tried to join up with the remains of the Italian and German armour.

Moving north to support the now collapsing front, the *Ariete* armoured division was struck by a large force of tanks and almost destroyed. The remnants fought their way to the *Afrikakorps* positions, where they joined what was left of the *Littorio* and *Trieste* divisions. On 4 November, the final day of the battle, *Trento* fought for four hours until it ran out of ammunition and was overpowered; the *Bologna* division, retreating exhausted on foot, was rounded up by New Zealand armoured cars and light tanks; and the *Ariete*, after fighting for five and a half hours against an enemy whose Sherman tanks greatly outranged their M 13s, was finally overrun. At 3.30 p.m., with three holes punched in his fragile defensive position and the *Ariete* gone, Rommel ordered the retreat.[167] Five and a quarter hours later he received Hitler's and Mussolini's permission to do what he had already done. Somehow the *Ariete* managed to disengage and save 200 men, 31 tanks and 17 guns (only half of them still working).

The Axis forces probably lost 11,000 to 12,000 dead and wounded and 17,000 prisoners of war in the battle and left over a thousand guns and more than 400 tanks (out of an initial 500) on the field. Over the next eighteen days the remnants of the German and Italian units fell back along the coast past Tobruk, Ain-el-Gazala and Benghazi to Agedabia, where they came to rest for just short of a month (22 November–19 December 1942). As the Axis forces began their long fighting retreat westwards, a peremptory request arrived in Rome. Field Marshal Keitel wanted six more Italian divisions ready to send to the Russian front in May and June 1943.

Chapter 8
Overstretched and Overcome

As the Axis forces withdrew to El Agheila and the armies in the East faced the coming Russian onslaught, Mussolini brimmed with confidence. The war was going well, he told Hitler. 'While 1942 is registering successes for the Tripartite [Alliance], the so-called United Nations have registered nothing but failures and catastrophes, especially the United States.'[1] A week later the Allied landings in French North Africa signalled the beginning of the end for Mussolini's war. At the year's end, ambassador Dino Alfieri warned that Germany would demand that Italy take more responsibility for the war and make more sacrifices for it if she wanted to have more influence on its development and direction.[2] That was a path Italy could not take. Instead, with a war machine that was already overstretched militarily and underpowered economically, her generals demanded yet more from Germany. Meanwhile their *Duce* pursued his personal chimera of a compromise peace with Russia, encouraged by misleading reports from Berlin that Hitler had given up the idea of forcing Russia's capitulation.[3]

PLANNING FOR A FUTURE

At the end of August 1942, on Mussolini's instruction, the armed forces began crafting a production programme for the coming year. The strategic brief stretched from Russia via Libya and the Tunisian frontier to unoccupied France and the French Atlantic coast, and included the need to confront new and greater offensives by the Anglo-Americans. Problems abounded – and not just with the now well-known shortage of raw materials. Series production of new aircraft, General Fougier told the chiefs, would take at least two years, by which time the planes would be out of date due to the speed of air-craft evolution. A major expansion of output was only possible for certain types of plane 'which aren't much use'.[4] When General Pietro Ago proposed concentrating all available labour and cement to build two new hydroelectric plants, Cavallero told him that that would cause 'bureaucratic difficulties' with the various ministries which nursed the interests of smaller factories.[5] After all the preliminary dis-cussions were done, Cavallero gave the chiefs the bottom line. There was 'only one circumstance in which you get nothing, and that's when you don't ask for anything'.[6]

The army planned to bring thirty divisions up to full efficiency (twenty abroad and ten in Italy), increase tank production so as to put four armoured divisions in the line during the first half of 1943 and a fifth in the second half of the year when the new P 40 tank would be available, provide the replenishments and supplies to keep thirty divi-sions in operation, and increase the levels of industrial output. The programme required an extra 27,000 tons of metals a month. To achieve the core targets – tanks, motor vehicles and guns – the army was prepared to cut back on items such as barbed wire and gas masks. However, even if it got all the extra raw materials it was asking for the factories could not produce enough ammunition and it would be short of 10,000 trucks.[7] The navy, anxious to replace at least some of its losses and build cargo-carrying submarines, tabled a programme to build 156 ships, including sixteen destroyers, eighteen submarines and a second aircraft carrier (the first remained incomplete) by December 1944, and a request for an extra 5,500 tons of steel a month throughout 1943, without which the first year of the programme could not be achieved. The numbers revealed how fast Italy was losing the war at sea: submarine losses were currently running at twenty to twenty-four boats a year, and simply to complete the current merchant navy build of 129 ships would need an extra 25,000 tons of steel (equivalent to five months' normal allocation) and without more labour they would not be finished until February 1944.[8]

On 1 October, facing what looked (wrongly) to be a coming winter of stasis on both the Russian and North African fronts, Mussolini called his military men together. First he defined the roles played by the Egyptian, Russian and Balkan fronts in his war. The Egyptian front was 'the most interesting from the political and strategical point of view' and the Russian front 'principally the task of our allies'. Then he added in the Western Front with France, Corsica and North Africa. France's 'ambiguous attitude' might necessitate the occupation of the rest of the country, so the army must be ready to move into southern France and Corsica. The generals must be ready to take on 'the difficult task' of attacking the cities of Toulon and Marseilles and move in quickly to 'places where there are collections of Italian populations who would run the risk of being massacred'. Finally, Mussolini wanted three divisions, one armoured and another motorized, in Tripolitania in case the Vichy regime moved to Algeria and gave up the pretence of defending potential Allied landing zones. To do all this he wanted a minimum of at least thirty-four divisions, five of them armoured.[9] Three weeks earlier Cavallero had said that he did not have the means even to meet the current target of thirty divisions. Now he told the *Duce* that though the necessary raw materials were 'somewhat scarce' they could be made to suffice.

Mussolini turned to the other two services. Italy had six battleships and would soon have eight. Shortly the fuel problem would be solved: 'I am confident that operations in the Caucasus will improve the situation.' Italy needed more cruisers and destroyers, new types of day and night fighters, torpedo bombers, dive-bombers and transport aircraft. She must produce 500 aircraft a month. As for the raw materials problems, 'If we had sufficient metals, coal and electrical energy, worries about raw materials would largely be overcome.'[10] Fougier thought Italy could produce 350 planes a month at best. When he added that the air force was experimenting with making planes out of wood and iron, Mussolini enthused. If the war lasted a long time, as everything suggested it would, all the belligerents would be short of raw materials 'and we would find ourselves in the vanguard if we use more rustic materials'.[11] General Ago promised to increase tank production to 150 a month – on condition that he was assured of raw materials, fuel and labour. Italy was short of almost everything, General Favagrossa pointed out, even wood. Key raw materials, especially iron and steel, were going to have to come from Germany. Describing the situation as 'not brilliant, but relatively calm', the *Duce* had an answer for almost every shortage. Coal could be substituted with lignite, copper could be recovered from electric wires, and artificial rubber could be made from buna. By intensifying effort, getting something from Germany, especially coal and steel, and making better use of raw materials the country could produce a large part of the 1943 programme, if not all of it.[12]

By the closing months of 1942, simply supplying Mussolini's divisions with the manpower they needed was becoming problematic. In order to provide industry with labour and not impact too heavily on civilian life, particularly agriculture, the army reduced its planned intake for 1943 from 778,000 to 590,000 men – thereby halving the number of men scheduled for North Africa and Russia from 330,000 to 170,000. At the end of November, Cavallero ordered the immediate call-up of the conscript class of 1923, which could only be given two months' training, to be followed by the call-up of the class of 1924 in May 1943.

As the year ended the logistics services sat down to consider the tasks they had to fulfil during the coming year. The army would increase by 830,000 men, bringing it up to 135,000 officers and 3,780,000 men. Stocks in Tunisia, presently one month's rations and forty to fifty days' worth of munitions, should be kept up 'if everything whose despatch has been pre-arranged [actually] arrives'. In Russia, where stocks must be able to meet 'any eventuality', blankets, winter clothing, eating utensils, spare parts for motor vehicles, radio sets and thirty field hospitals were needed. In Montenegro, Albania and Greece levels of self-sufficiency must be more or less doubled from six to eight weeks to two months. New units were being created for coastal defence. They would need munitions, guns (particularly self-propelled guns) and tanks. A 'significant' output of guns was to be expected from the factories but, General Rossi warned, the programme that had been devised must not experience delays. Needs were easy to identify, but there was no clear idea of what could actually be produced from the amounts of raw materials to be allocated to industry.[13]

By January 1943 the army's plan for thirty fully-equipped active divisions was under threat. Some of the raw materials needed to carry it out were available, but not all; production cycles meant that turning what was available into finished items would take six to seven months; and while enemy air action was delaying the output of some items, for others such as motor vehicles and the guns being manufactured by Ansaldo the damage done could not be made up. Priorities had changed too. There were now only thirteen divisions to be supported overseas, not twenty. Home defence had moved to the top of the agenda and for that the army wanted to upgrade the sixteen divisions and other smaller units in the homeland, complete the other fourteen divisions, and reconstitute an armoured division for homeland defence. This would mean reconsidering the allocation of raw materials – how much in all it could not yet say. When it came down to the details, the picture was grim. Only half the necessary coastal defence units could be created *if* the clothing and equipment situation would allow it. Plans to have 324 M 40 tanks by August were going awry: sixty came out of the factories in January but only twenty-two in February. Production of self-propelled guns, which should have begun in December 1942, would not now start until March 1943. But for the army the glass was not half empty (and emptying fast), it was half full. In the second half of 1943, production would increase: more raw materials would be available, and industrial capacity would come into its own.[14]

The navy too revised its plans. It had started the war with fifty-nine destroyers and now had only thirty-seven, most of which were ageing. Up until December 1942 it had lost on average one or two destroyers and torpedo boats a month; then, in two months, five destroyers and three torpedo boats had been lost and another four destroyers and four torpedo boats seriously damaged. The joint occupation of Vichy France by Germany and Italy in November had done little to help. So far only nine French navy vessels, including one obsolescent destroyer, had been forthcoming, while another thirty-two were on the bottom at Toulon, having been scuttled to prevent their falling into Axis hands. By slowing down or suspending other construction and concentrating on light escorts, the navy estimated that it could launch three destroyers, ten corvettes and fourteen torpedo boats during 1943. In 1944 it expected to be able to send twelve destroyers, twenty corvettes and eight torpedo boats down the slip-ways. More needed to be done but that depended (as ever) on a radical improvement in supplies of raw materials and on solving the problem of the shortage of skilled labour.[15]

The *Regia Aeronautica*'s plans had been affected by the bombing of Turin and the subsequent decentralization of the aircraft industry: in December 1942, 215 aircraft had been produced out of a planned 250. By simplifying production, gradually reducing the types of planes to only six and the types of engines to three or four, and reorganizing production facilities into groups of companies, it planned to be able to produce 3,557 aircraft during 1943 and 400 aircraft a month by the end of 1944. To do that would require the necessary raw materials – and a lot more besides. More German machine tools would be needed, and a larger share must go to the war industries. The aeronautical industries must have precedence on the railways. Six thousand skilled workers must be released from the armed services, the working week increased to seventy-two hours, and the labour force put under military law to end the 20 per cent absentee rate. The airmen were also contemplating using prisoners of war as forced labour.[16]

On 28 January 1943 Mussolini called everyone to Palazzo Venezia for another look at the armaments programmes. Two admirals and fourteen generals sat beside Ugo Cavallero – now at the end of his time as chief of the armed forces general staff. The *Duce* surveyed the strategic scene. The situation was 'negative' in that the enemy had 'set foot' in North Africa and had the initiative in the air, though that would be 'contained and overcome', and positive in respect of the damage being done to enemy shipping by German and Italian submarines. If the enemy wanted to launch a second front, Sicily was not the logical place – it was 'certainly not the door that leads to Germany' – but Greece was. If the Anglo-Americans landed, 'all the Greeks would make common cause with them'. Montenegro was for the moment calm, the situation in Croatia was 'confused', and in Slovenia a Slav crusade was in the making. The Germans had suffered a strategic check in Russia. They would not hold in the Caucasus, but would stabilize the situation. Corsica was not a worry, because the population at large 'has some sympathy for us', but southern France was, 'because there the population detest us, almost [as much] as they detest the Germans'.[17]

Turning to the armed forces, Mussolini wanted above all to bring the manpower in the army's divisions up to full strength. As far as armaments were concerned, Italy needed lots more anti-aircraft guns to defend itself against the bombing which was now happening and which he had forecast last October, more and better tanks, and better artillery pieces. If the sea route to Tunisia was to be protected, possible landings in Greece prevented and national territory defended, Italy needed an 'aerial umbrella' composed of a 'mass' of at least 500 of the new Macchi 202 fighters (there were presently 402) and they must be armed with cannon, not machine guns, 'as I foresaw years ago'.[18] German success in doubling and even tripling aircraft output seemed difficult to emulate, but Mussolini had the answer. Shortage of raw materials was not the problem: General Favagrossa, about to be raised from under-secretary of state to minister for war production, was providing enough of them to produce 350 aircraft a month, but the aircraft industry was only producing 300. The explanation was to be found in poor organization of the industry and a mania for continual modifications to every component. The time taken from prototype to serial production must be drastically reduced from the present sixteen to eighteen months. Fougier told him bluntly that this was simply impossible. Charging on, Mussolini told the airmen to think about day and night bombers, dive-bombers, torpedo bombers and transport aircraft. The navy's proposals for submarines and destroyers were endorsed.

When it came to finding the resources to fulfil the services' programmes, Mussolini again had the remedy: if necessary, the navy and the air force must 'switch over raw materials from one sector to another and suspend certain less urgent production'.[19] Germany was unable to provide any raw materials, Cavallero told him. If II Army Corps in Russia had to be reconstituted that would require a quantity of equipment, including motor vehicles, which 'it is completely and absolutely impossible for us to provide' other than by 'abandoning [that part of] the programme which relates to our [national] territory'. Mussolini's answer: that would have to be provided by Germany, 'I see no other solution'.[20] General Ambrosio pointed out that Favagrossa had not been able to provide all the raw materials the army needed and that the benefits of the extra quotas he had found would take six or seven months to work their way through the manufacturing processes, during which time bombing would certainly shrink industrial capacity. Now it was time to put the defence of the country first. At the present moment there were no fixed or mobile guns for coastal defence, no anti-tank weapons, only 40 to 50 per cent of the munitions needed for automatic weapons and light guns, and no tanks. The new P 40 tanks could not be in service before the beginning of 1944.

The meeting soldiered on. Admiral Riccardi glossed the navy's programme, and General Fougier reassured Mussolini that the air force was indeed experimenting with new types of fighters and high-altitude bombers and would do its best to cut back manufacture of older planes. When he asked for a seventy-two-hour working week the *Duce* sprang to life. There was a mass of evidence from France, Great

Britain, the United States and Italy to show that once it went beyond seventy hours productivity shrank. That was his limit. Favagrossa raised uncomfortable questions about the armaments programmes. Could the quantities of raw materials allocated actually be achieved? And, if they could, then for how long? He was confident that he could deliver the promised raw materials for the first six months of 1943, but thereafter steel production would contract. A lengthy discussion of the labour problem ended with Mussolini laying down the law. Only men who were 'absolutely indispensable' should be exempt from call-up and there should be no exemptions at all for the classes of 1923, 1924 and 1925 (which would all be called up by October). Drawing things to a close, Mussolini announced that it was evident that the raw materials needed by the chiefs of staff to fulfil their October programmes were to hand. The provisions were not without a certain recklessness but 'sometimes it's necessary for courage to surpass recklessness'.[21] Two weeks later he was asking Hitler for submarines, planes and artillery 'because the English have very modern guns, while ours are very antiquated'.[22]

While the planners in Rome built their paper arsenals, the men at the sharp end struggled to keep the war in North Africa alive. Supply became ever more difficult as Allied aircraft, the three cruisers and four destroyers of the reconstituted Force K operating from Malta, and the four cruisers and eight destroyers of Force Q now operating out of the former French port of Bône attacked the transports. Surface protection was down to a minimum. After American Liberator bombers hit Naples on 4 December, destroying or damaging three cruisers, the *Vittorio Veneto* and the *Littorio* were pulled back to La Spezia and a second cruiser division to La Maddalena. With only a single cruiser division left at Messina and the *Doria* and *Duilio* at Taranto, the *Regia Marina*'s heavy surface fleet had effectively abandoned the central Mediterranean. By the beginning of February 1943 Admiral Riccardi had only twenty functioning destroyers (some of which he was having to divert to ferrying German troops across to Tunisia), thirty torpedo boats and thirty submarines. His ships were using 65,000–80,000 tons of fuel a month and getting 42,000–44,000 tons from Romania and Germany. There was, he said, very little he could do by way of offensive action to interrupt the Allied supplies now coming in to Tripoli, lost to the Axis twelve days earlier.[23]

THE LOSS OF NORTH AFRICA

On 8 November 1942 British and American troops landed in Morocco and Algeria and began to push towards Bizerta and Tunis. Hitler's response was immediate. Vichy France was occupied, the Italians took over Corsica, and the 10th *Panzer* division landed at Tunis and Bizerta, followed by the Italian *Superga* division. Two weeks later the remains of the Italo-German armies reached El Agheila after covering a thousand kilometres in eighteen days. Four days after the Anglo-American landings Cavallero flew into Libya, put General Bastico in command of everything, and ordered him to resist to the last on the Mersa Brega-Agheila position but also to make 'every effort' to keep hold of Tripolitania. He did not accept Bastico's suggestion that Rommel, now a field marshal, whom Bastico judged to be 'morally beaten', be removed from his command. When Bastico then demanded German armour, artillery and powerful anti-tank guns, 'copious air reinforcements', motor vehicles, fuel and other supplies, he was assured that the *Comando Supremo* would provide it all 'in the shortest time possible'.[24] These 'indispensable' reinforcements never arrived.

Bastico reorganized his depleted army. Seven divisions disappeared from the lists, among them the *Folgore*, *Ariete* and *Littorio*. The remaining units were organized into an armoured corps comprising the *Centauro* and *Giovani Fascisti* divisions (the latter little more than a partially motorized infantry division) and a three-division infantry corps (*La Spezia*, *Pistoia* and *Trieste*). Rather than stay to fight, defend a 160-kilometre long front and risk losing the Italian marching infantry for a second time, Rommel sent General Giuseppe de Stefanis to Rome to persuade Cavallero and Mussolini that it would be better to pull back closer to the Axis supply base at Tripoli and force the enemy to extend his supply lines. His Italian liaison, General Mancinelli, thought that Rommel was underestimating the time it would take the enemy – at least a month – to prepare and launch a major attack. A proper operational decision could not be reached, he suggested to Rome, until 'broadly approximate' calculations had been made of how strong the Axis forces might be at the end of that period.[25] Neither Cavallero nor General Kesselring thought withdrawal to Buerat was acceptable. Nor at first did Bastico. Then, after a talk with Rommel left him in no doubt that if the combined army made a stand at Mersa el

Brega it would be destroyed, Bastico changed his mind: withdrawal would put off the coming battle for at least three weeks, which would give time for reinforcements and supplies to arrive.

Supplying North Africa, particularly with motor vehicles, was now more pressing than ever. If this battle could be won then Africa would be saved and so would Italy itself, or so Mussolini believed. With the loss of Africa, Italy would be obliged simply to wait passively for an Allied invasion, which could fall on any part of the coast between southern France and Greece. The eastern route to Tripoli was under threat not just from Malta but also from Algeria. The Italian navy only had five fast merchantmen left; slower ships were useless. Nights were longer and at night the enemy's attacks were 'stronger and incontestable'. Finally, there were very few escorts left.[26] When Kesselring asked for two fast supply ships to be sent to Tripoli, Admiral Riccardi replied that to get them there would need an escort of ten destroyers, that all traffic to Tunisia would have to be halted for four or five days, and that to judge by past experience one of the two merchantmen and half the escorting force would be lost. If one of the two merchantmen were lost that would mean a crisis for Tunisia. Admiral Sansonetti chimed in: if five destroyers were lost then the fleet would be lost. The upshot was that for the time being North Africa would be resupplied by air and an attempt would be made to run a single ship through when the weather was bad. As Sansonetti pointed out drily, a single ship would not resolve the situation.[27]

On 24 November, Cavallero and Kesselring flew across to Libya to discuss the situation with Bastico, Rommel and his chief of staff, General Siegfried Westphal. The meeting went badly. Neither Cavallero, who thought too rapid a retreat to Tunisia would simply mean locking the troops up in a 'surrender citadel', nor Kesselring, whose priority was fighting the air war in the Mediterranean, would agree to the evacuation of Libya.[28] The outcome was, as so often, a compromise. The pause on the Mersa el Brega line would be prolonged for as long as possible, and Bastico could withdraw to Buerat only in the face of a 'preponderant enemy attack'. Meanwhile the withdrawal was to be studied and organized. Its timing should be by common agreement between the Italian and German commanders. Bastico instructed Rommel that no withdrawal was to take place without his explicit advance orders. Rommel protested: he would obey Hitler's and Mussolini's orders to stand and fight until he was forced to abandon the Mersa el Brega position by the enemy or ordered to do so because of the situation in Tunisia.

With decision-making in North Africa temporarily at an impasse, and Bastico unsure whether to obey orders and stay put or pull back to save what remained of his army, Rommel took matters into his own hands. On 28 November he first flew to Germany to see Hitler and afterwards travelled on by train to Rome. At Rastenburg, Hitler treated his proposal to withdraw to Gabès in Tunisia with blistering contempt. Rommel would get more supplies. Rommel must fight. When Rommel reached Rome on 30 November, Kesselring also flatly rejected the Gabès plan. Later that day Rommel, Goering and Kesselring met with Mussolini, Cavallero and Admiral Riccardi. Rommel's future as a commander was now hanging in the balance. Two days earlier Mancinelli had told Rome that Rommel plainly did not believe effective resistance in North Africa was possible given the Axis' material inferiority and the vast masses of modern equipment in his enemy's hands. The question now was whether he could remain in command of an army 'where he will certainly do his duty like the great soldier he is but not wholeheartedly and not with belief'.[29] Angered by Rommel's insubordination in going over his head to Hitler, Bastico told Cavallero that if an Italian general had done such a thing 'he would be put in front of a military tribunal for abandoning his post in the face of the enemy'. It was a tetchy session. Rommel clashed with Goering, who had agreed to the Gabès plan until he learned that his Führer insisted on holding the Mers el Brega line and then smartly reversed, and Goering clashed with Mussolini when the *Duce* gave permission to begin building defences at Buerat.

On 1 December, facing the possible loss of the foot-bound Italian infantry divisions, the *Comando Supremo* authorized a retreat and sixteen days later, after marching along the coastline of the Gulf of Sirte, the Axis forces came to rest at Buerat. While Cavallero and Kesselring skirmished with one another over who should have first call on the shipping taken from Vichy France and who should be in command of the ports at Bizerta and Tunis, reinforcements were not getting through to Libya and fuel was in desperately short supply – Sansonetti ruled out using aircraft to fly it in and could only offer a lone submarine carrying 178 tons of aviation petrol which, when mixed with diesel, would do to run motor vehicles (or so he said). Bastico warned Cavallero that his forces could not hold out for long against the 8th Army and that the likelihood that the Germans would withdraw to Tunisia was increasing by the hour. If they did so, Italy would lose almost all its troops in Tripolitania and the Sahara and all its stocks. Bastico needed orders. Was he to start the logistical move back to Tunisia, or to sacrifice everything and defend Tripolitania to the last?[30]

Mussolini wanted the Axis powers to turn their full attention to the Mediterranean. Britain was the number-one enemy and the industrial strength of the United States – to which he had very belatedly woken up – was such that the enemy was bound to achieve air superiority. One way or another, he told Goering, the war with Russia must be concluded. Either a deal should be done – another Brest-Litovsk – or if that was impossible a defensive line should be set up that would break any enemy initiative while using the minimum possible Axis forces. That, Goering assured him, was Hitler's idea too – which, as the Italians would shortly discover, was not exactly true.[31] Mussolini had characteristically gran-diose – and characteristically unrealistic – plans to boost Italy's military effort during 1943 to new levels. In his instructions for the Rastenburg meeting (18–20 December) to which Hitler had invited him, Foreign Minister Ciano was told that the *Duce* intended to recall two classes of recruits in January 1943 (one of them thirty-six-year-olds, the other twenty-year-olds), a third class of nineteen-year-olds in March, and then a fourth class of eighteen-year-olds, making a million men in all, along with equipment and arms.[32] The men certainly existed – but the rest did not.

Too ill to travel himself, Mussolini sent Cavallero and Ciano to Rastenburg in his place. Ciano, who disliked the boredom of barracks life and the dismal surroundings, found the atmosphere at Hitler's headquarters in the forest 'heavy' and hostile.[33] The accounts he sent back to Mussolini, sometimes less than complete, painted a more agree-able picture than the discussions and the general atmosphere warranted. He detected 'a very high evaluation' of the Italian contribution to the struggle and a 'much more prudent' judgement about the future than had been customary in the past. In private his entourage saw a very different Ciano, who gave the impression of having completely lost his nerve. The Germans had lost the war, he told them. 'There's nothing to do but wait for the collapse.'[34]

The Italians were treated to a typical Hitler performance. They were, Hitler told them, fighting not for the existence of their regimes but for the existence of their nations and for world civilization. After a brief excursion to the situation on the Russian front, where the key to success lay in greater collaboration and the recognition that the Germans had the necessary experience, and the Balkans, where all the necessary dispositions must be made to resist an attempt at a landing, the Führer turned to North Africa. With Tunis now in Axis hands, the 'dominant problem' was transportation. If that could be solved he would send 'the best German divisions' to French North Africa. Algeria would then be theirs; Axis troops would get to Melilla, which would force Spain to change its attitude; and the British would be forced to use the Cape Town route, wasting tonnage and laying themselves open to even greater losses from German U-boats. Otherwise nothing could be done.[35] Ciano presented Mussolini's ideas on Russia and Hitler explained at length that a deal with Russia was impossible. For one thing, Italy and the other satellite nations needed Russian foodstuffs, raw materials and petrol, and for another, even if Germany were not fighting Russia, Rommel would not get a single extra soldier, because the problem was essentially one of transport. Once the first Stuka attacks began he was sure that 'many things [in North Africa] will change'.

Cavallero fared no better when it came to Italy's immediate military needs than Mussolini did with his Russian scheme. Everyone agreed that the Axis forces in North Africa could now only be supplied via Tunisia. That meant organizing accurate anti-submarine warfare and providing suitable air escorts. Also, the enemy must be hit at his weakest point – his embarkation ports. To do all this Cavallero wanted at least 500 German aircraft. For the moment none were forthcoming. The best that he could get was a promise to bring the German units in the Mediterranean up to full efficiency as soon as possible. The Italians were told to stop making 90mm guns, which were slow to build and uneconomical, and instead produce 88mm guns like the Germans – something which, Cavallero pointed out, they could only do if they were given German manufacturing equipment. As far as weaponry was concerned, with German forces now heavily engaged on the eastern and south-eastern fronts all the Italians could expect was war booty such as old French 75s, which German workshops could turn into effective anti-tank guns in a couple of weeks. The Germans expected their allies to step up to the plate. 'The decision of the war depends on the *Regia Marina Italiana*,' Field Marshal Keitel remarked at one point.[36]

Rome now confirmed that Bastico was to make a stand at Buerat. Worried that it might be turned from the Sahara, Rommel pressed his case for retreat. Bastico was for staying put. On New Year's Day 1943 Cavallero and Kesselring resolved the dispute. There was to be no final all-out defensive battle at Buerat. Instead the forces would be withdrawn in stages over six weeks while offensive action weakened the enemy, finally coming to rest on the eastern front of 'the fortified camp of Tripoli'. During that time Rommel should have freedom of action but would also be responsible for fulfilling the timetable.[37] The withdrawal, which began three days later, was intended to delay the enemy for long enough to build up sufficient supplies in Tunisia. The decision had been taken to abandon Libya, Cavallero told Rommel, 'because of the impossibility of re-supply'.[38] The retirement was made no easier (said Bastico) by Rommel's continually changing his orders according to his on-the-spot inspections and taking no account of the complexities of the movement schedules.

By 18 January the Axis forces were at Beni Ulid–Tarhuna. Bastico expected a few days' rest there, but Rommel thought otherwise. Fearing that the enemy was about to turn his flank – a danger which Bastico thought was neither serious nor imminent – he began the second stage of the retreat on his own authority.[39] On 23 January, Tripoli was no longer Italian. All the guns were pulled out of Tripolitania, but most of the munitions were left behind for want of transport. The Italians had abandoned any idea of a last-ditch defence of the city à la Stalingrad or Tobruk two weeks earlier.[40] Next day the first Axis detachments reached the Mareth Line, and by 28 January all the Italian divisions had come to rest there. Organizing three successive lines of 'final' resistance when the army command, favouring withdrawal, seemed to regard them as only temporary halts caused the logistical services considerable problems, though they were somewhat eased when a supply line was set up running from Tunis to Gabès and then to Tripoli.[41]

As the Allies entered Tripoli, and Colonel-General Hans-Jürgen von Arnim fought off Anglo-American attacks on the central sector of the Tunisian enclave, Mussolini called General Messe to Rome and told him that he was going to Tunisia to take over command from Rommel.

Afterwards Messe was convinced that Cavallero sent him to North Africa 'on a job which was bound to end disastrously . . . so that he could get me out of the way'.[42] In fact, Cavallero had wanted Rommel to command 1st Army in southern Tunisia while von Arnim commanded 5th Army in northern Tunisia, but dividing the responsibilities presented difficulties on the ground and in Rome, so when Ambrosio took over the reins he resolved the problem by giving Rommel command of an Army Group comprising both armies.[43] 'You are taking over an army that is in good order,' Mussolini told Messe, 'it is still well armed; it has 700 guns and some 7,000 motor vehicles . . . the men are well clad.' His task was above all to check the enemy advance coming from the west and south which was threatening to crush the Axis forces in Tunisia in a vice. 'In the summer,' Mussolini promised, 'we'll retake the initiative with a great offensive push towards Algeria [and] Morocco and to reconquer Libya.' The most Messe was prepared to promise was that the forces under his command would resist to the last.[44]

A wide-ranging changing of the guard took place as Messe was recalled to service. Ciano was sacked (Mussolini took over the reins as Foreign Minister) and so too was Cavallero, replaced as chief of the armed forces' general staff by the army chief of staff, general Vittorio Ambrosio. Ambrosio came into office with three objectives: to slim down the organization of the *Comando Supremo* and make it essentially an operational headquarters ('Do it,' Mussolini told him); to recall as many divisions as possible to Italy (Mussolini said nothing); and to 'put [our] foot down' as far as the Germans were concerned ('excellent', said the *Duce*).[45] The Germans had to understand that the Russian front was not the be-all and end-all of the Axis' war, and that it was just as important to hold firm in Sicily and the Peloponnese as on the Dnieper. If they did not change their attitude and help Italy, he shortly told Mussolini, then 'we shall no longer be obliged to follow them in their mistaken conduct of the war'.[46] As Messe was about to take over command in North Africa, an outgoing Cavallero argued that only more German aircraft could save Tunisia. Kesselring was having none of it: there were few airfields there and flying from Sicily and Sardinia was not the solution, because when the weather was good at one end it was often bad at the other.[47]

Messe's 1st Army comprised four Italian infantry divisions (*Trieste, Pistoia, Spezia* and *Giovani Fascisti*), two German infantry divisions and what remained of the *Deutsche Afrikakorps*, consisting of the 15th *Panzer* division, the Sahara group, which amounted to a weak division and various artillery and engineer units, and the skeletal remains of the *Centauro* armoured division – in all some 77,000 men. Tanks, guns and ammunition were in short supply: the entire force had 400 field and heavy field guns, eighty-seven armoured cars and eighty tanks, fourteen of which were Italian.[48] So was air support. When he took over, Messe had only eighteen operational Macchi 202 fighters and fourteen Macchi 200s without pilots. The men, who had retreated for over 2,500 kilometres since El Alamein, were tired and depressed. Everyone, Messe told Rome, down to the last soldier was convinced that the struggle could not be decided by individual valour alone – 'if that were so we would already have won the war' – but by possessing weapons and equipment that were 'not inferior or almost [equal] to the enemy's: guns, tanks, planes.'[49]

Over time the difficulties of life in the desert had begun to erode army morale. Heat, brackish water and the lack of fresh vegetables discouraged the soldiers and, according to the commander of XXI Corps, General Enea Navarini, made them feel 'abandoned like a being which had been badly treated by fate'. This easily degenerated into 'a Muslim-type fatalism'.[50] On 23 December a private soldier was shot for desertion. Bastico ordered that the fact be made known throughout the army so everyone understood that there would be no pardon for anyone who voluntarily abandoned their post in the face of the enemy.[51] As the army retreated to and then beyond Tripoli, General Calvi di Bergolo demanded that discipline be properly understood and enforced. Lots of soldiers were going about 'in disordered uniforms', few were saluting their superior officers and then badly. Officers were setting a bad example. No soldier was to leave barracks unless his hair was cut, his beard shaved and he was in uniform, and patrols must sweep up soldiers found 'arbitrarily wandering around'.[52] Other generals reprimanded their subordinates in similar terms. Mussolini believed troop morale to be high. Kesselring, who went to and fro frequently, demurred. He had heard that some Italian units had retired from Libya 'somewhat shaken'. What was needed were new units, strongly armed and with their spirits high.[53]

As things went awry on the various battle fronts, Rome grew increasingly concerned about morale and discipline. The under-secretary at the War Office, General Antonio Scuero, worried about growing signs of indiscipline in the army. An unacceptably laissez-faire attitude was evident from top to bottom of the officer corps, but particularly in the younger officers. Orders went out to give the men more physical exercise, exercise greater vigilance over them, and punish backsliders quickly and severely.[54] As part of a programme to bring discipline up to the levels required by the current circumstances, Scuero ordered all corps commanders to circulate 'punishment bulletins' setting out the details of punishments that were either noteworthy or 'particularly significant', together with the charges and sentences. Names were to be omitted.[55]

As the position in Tunisia grew increasingly precarious, general morale began to show signs of weakening. In March, *Carabinieri* reports spoke of 'very cautious' forecasts, public awareness that the enemy's materiel was better than that of their own troops, and a fear that the Axis forces could not hold out there for long. Limited German successes on the Eastern Front were giving grounds for modest hope but fears of Allied landings in Calabria and on Sardinia and Sicily were evident, and the increasingly frequent Allied bombing raids of southern Italian cities were causing 'grave preoccupation' because of the lack of safe shelters. A month later, with the end in Tunisia obviously very near, the public mood was one of 'strong apprehension', not least because of the likely intensification of the enemy's air offensive on home territory that would be bound to follow. In the main, army morale still appeared to be holding up well, or so the *Carabinieri* reported. Officers and non-commissioned officers were complaining about their pay, and the troops were grumbling about inadequate rations, worn-out boots and delays in getting mail, but there seemed to be no serious cause for anxiety. In Corsica (occupied by the Italians on 11 November 1942), things were not going well. Communist agitation was growing and the reinforcement of the island's defences was badly behind schedule due chiefly to a lack of labour. Not a single barracks had yet been built to shelter the troops and everyone was convinced that in the event of Allied bombing the command system would cease to function. With masterly understatement General Azolino Hazon, commanding the *Carabinieri*, reported that this was creating 'a state of perplexity'.[56]

Messe's army settled in behind a minefield, barbed wire and an anti-tank ditch and awaited the enemy. Having studied the battle of El

Alamein closely, its commander had a fair idea of what to expect. His subordinates were told to counter-attack quickly to prevent the enemy from consolidating his initial gains. On 31 January 1943 *Superlibia* was dissolved and on 5 February a new 1st Army was created in its place, though it did not actually begin to function operationally for another two weeks. Rommel was determined to hold on to command of 1st Army at least for the time being and on 14 February, with Ambrosio's support, he launched a brief series of offensives designed to protect the western shoulder of the Axis position behind the Mareth Line, culminating in the initially successful battle of the Kasserine Pass (19–22 February). Strong counter-attacks, difficult terrain and heavy rain, and pressure by General Montgomery on the Libya-Tunisia border, forced the Germans to halt the attack.[57] Afterwards Rommel paid tribute to the 7th *Bersagliere* and the *Centauro* division for the part they played in the operation.

Rommel's attack at Medenine (6 March 1943), which was intended to disrupt the inevitable enemy attack, was delayed by the need to reorganize the armoured divisions and repair as many tanks as possible. This gave Montgomery time to regroup, and air reconnaissance told him what to expect and where to expect it. The battle, in which Rommel's 141 tanks and 160 aircraft took on Lieutenant-General Oliver Leese's 350 field guns, 460 anti-tank guns and 300 tanks, began at 6 a.m. and ended some eleven hours later. The three *Panzer* divisions and the *Trieste* and *Spezia* divisions were stopped dead by artillery and anti-tank fire. Even before it began, Rommel's future was settled. On 4 March Hitler received his evaluation of the situation in Tunisia. Since his troops were receiving only some two-thirds of the monthly supplies they needed, the army should withdraw to Enfidaville, which effectively meant abandoning everything bar a small zone around Tunis itself. Furious, Hitler refused and ordered the army to launch containing attacks against the enemy to create a state of 'equilibrium' while supplies were doubled and then tripled.

His time now up, Rommel left for Rome on 9 March 1943. His place as army group commander was taken by Colonel-General von Arnim. In Rome, Rommel gave the *Duce* a fairly downbeat assessment of the situation. A week earlier, Kesselring had told Mussolini that negative assessments of the situation in Tunisia were wrong. The Axis might be outnumbered in the air by between three and four to one but qualitatively 'our aviation is better by a long way'. The advantage in terms of getting men and equipment there lay with the Axis and not the enemy. All in all, the situation was 'in our favour'.[58] This was nonsense. Rome had the men but not much else, and what it had could not be shipped over until April. Getting stuff across to Messe was little short of nightmarish. Tunisia needed at least 90,000 tons of materials and fuel every month, but thirty-two ship-voyages (the maximum possible in a month) meant that only 60,000–70,000 tons could leave Italy, 30 to 40 per cent of which might be lost en route. Together the Italians and the Germans needed 30,000 tons of petrol and diesel a month. With only three tankers available each doing two voyages a month, only 17,000 tons could be carried across. Notwithstanding the difficulties Mussolini was optimistic. He knew that the British and Americans had difficulties, of their own – though he did not say what they were. 'For us,' he told Rommel, 'it is essentially a problem of will and no one has truly lost a battle who does not recognize that they have lost it.'[59]

Mussolini was determined that Tunisia must be held for as long as possible in order to disrupt the Anglo-American plans agreed at Casablanca. That meant expanding the Axis bridgehead and not reducing it as Rommel had suggested. To get the necessary guns, tanks and fuel across the Sicilian Channel transport must be 'guaranteed'. That meant having Axis air power at least equal to the enemy's air strength. If this 'fundamental requirement' were not met, Tunisia would fall. Then, northern and central Italy would suffer 'massive' enemy aerial bombardments while the Allies tried commando and parachute landings on Sicily and Sardinia 'to improve their naval position'. Of one thing he was confident. A 'real and proper' landing on the Italian peninsula was something that the Allies 'cannot seriously plan [for]'. Italy was at last getting the modern weapons she needed to defend herself and so any attempt at a landing on Italy's islands was destined to fail – 'excluding surprise'.[60]

Hitler agreed: transport was 'the decisive factor' and only its 'maximum development' could resolve the supply problems that had caused Rommel, a commander of 'exceptional gifts', to fail. There was no reason that he could see why 150,000 or even 200,000 tons of supplies could not be got over to Tunisia every month. All it needed was a proper organization of the escorts. There was no offer of German planes. Instead, Hitler sent Grand-Admiral Dönitz to advise the *Comando Supremo* on how to do things better.[61] Something of Rommel's pessimism about the chances of holding the Mareth Line had, however, penetrated Hitler's thoughts, preoccupied as they were with the defeat at Stalingrad. Von Arnim was advised to pull parts of two Italian divisions back to the Wadi Akarit to create a safe reserve. On the night before the battle for the Mareth Line began, the *Spezia* and *Pistoia* divisions were taken out of line and sent north.

In Rome the Italians and the Germans argued. The Italian navy was unwilling to continue transporting men to North Africa and losing them but was prepared to keep trying to get materiel across. Air transport could ferry only 1,500 men a day, so Kesselring wanted the Italian navy to reconsider using destroyers to get men to Tunisia. Admiral Riccardi declined: if the Allies tried to land in Sicily, Sardinia or Greece then inevitably there would be an all-out naval battle, and for that he would need his destroyers to protect his battleships. Citing Hitler, Kesselring then argued that the Chott–Akarit line must be the final position and could be held if more men and materiel were sent in. With that Ambrosio went on the attack. The Axis armies had only come to rest at Akarit at all because Rommel had retreated so fast. Kesselring needed to recognize that it was not just Tunisia that was under threat – so was Italy, in particular Sardinia. Responding, Kesselring complained that the Italian navy was not collaborating with their ally. Then, on 15 March, as Messe was preparing to defend the Mareth Line, Grand-Admiral Dönitz arrived in Rome. 'If we could get one more tanker a month [across] we could declare ourselves satisfied,' he told Mussolini. His solution to the problem was to put Admiral Friedrich Ruge in charge of a special traffic protection staff in Rome answerable directly to Berlin and to put German naval officers on Italian ships. Riccardi was non-committal about the details, and Mussolini simply asked for more fuel.[62] Ruge's insertion into an already overcomplicated command system soon produced tensions, not least with Kesselring's own staff.

The Mareth Line, adopted for the defence of south-eastern Tunisia, was the old French defensive line against Italian invasion. The 'Maginot of the desert' consisted of a belt of reinforced concrete casemates on the flat coastal ground and fieldworks in the mountains at its right-hand end. The fieldworks had practically disappeared thanks to the actions of the weather and the locals but the twenty-seven permanent works were still standing. The decision to stand there had been taken before Messe arrived, though Rommel had wanted to make a stand further west on a position less open to outflanking and Messe would have preferred to do so too. The battle for the Mareth Line (16–30 March) began with a massive enemy artillery barrage along El Alamein lines. Out-ranged, inferior in numbers and short of munitions, the Italian guns could not engage the enemy with counter-battery fire and had to measure out the number of rounds fired against the threat to their troops. Though contested ferociously by both sides, it was a one-sided match from the start. Slightly outnumbered in manpower, Messe's 1st Army was heavily outnumbered by Montgomery's 8th Army in every category of weaponry but one (mortars): 580 guns against 706, 66 armoured cars against 192, 94 tanks against 620. Qualitatively, the differences were even greater than the raw numbers suggest.[63]

In the first phase of the battle, thanks to vigorous counter-attacks, effective use of their limited artillery and skilful deployment of his forces by Messe, 1st Army fought off a frontal attack and an attempt to turn his position from the western flank. As he did so, von Arnim ordered him to prepare to retreat to the Akarit line if it looked as though his army risked destruction. In the second phase, Italian and German troops held off an attempt at a wide encirclement for long enough to enable the defenders to extract themselves from the looming trap and withdraw in obedience to von Arnim's orders. The troops defending the Mareth Line got away successfully, taking everything with them 'down to the last round'. Those defending El Hamma were less lucky: the lack of motor vehicles meant that they suffered heavy losses in men and guns.[64]

As Messe was fighting the battle, Mussolini produced another of his strategic 'solutions' to current dilemmas. The Anglo-American position in North Africa and their planned invasion could both be turned into a 'catastrophe' for the Allies, he told Hitler. What the Axis had to do was to put up 'extreme resistance' in North Africa, fall on the enemy's rear via Spain and Morocco, and occupy the Balearics so as to control the Straits of Gibraltar and the Atlantic ports that were serving the Americans.[65] Like so many of his proposals, it was an abstract counsel of perfection that bore little or no relationship to real possibilities.

When Messe's official account of the battle of Mareth arrived on his desk Mussolini was so taken with it that he handed it straight to the press – but not before cutting several passages. Out went a table of enemy strength that 'clearly demonstrated the enemy's power', which in turn was the result 'not just of quantity but of quality and morale factors'. Out, too, went references to the fact that Rommel was no longer there. Enough remained for readers to realize that Messe's army had had to fight against a superior opponent – British armoured units were described as 'on a level with the best armoured forces in all modern armies' – and had had to jettison outdated tactics to survive. A shortage of air power had left Messe unable to hit and weaken the enemy columns as they had advanced for the attack. At the start of his report, Messe declared that the 1st Army had inflicted 'a resounding check' on the enemy. At its conclusion he warned that, though it had given of its best and would continue to do so, its combat potential, in respect of both men and weapons, had been 'seriously diminished'.[66]

Ambrosio's immediate concern as the battle played out was that von Arnim should not sacrifice the whole of Messe's army. More broadly, there were two strategic questions to be considered. Should the Axis continue to pour resources into 'the Tunisian furnace', thereby playing the enemy's game? And when the end came in Tunisia, how should Italy best prepare to defend Sicily, Sardinia, Corsica, Albania, Greece and the Aegean? One thing she could not afford to do was lose shipping, which would then be under even greater pressure. Therefore if at the last Germany asked for ships to get materiel out, Italy must refuse.[67] There would be no Dunkirk for Messe and his men. Their job was now simply to hold out for as long as possible and buy Ambrosio time to organize the defence of Italy's sprawling possessions. Aware of the great imbalance between Messe's army and Montgomery's – 'the enemy has a strong prevalence in tanks' – and the losses his navy was suffering, Mussolini sent an urgent telegram to Hitler asking for 500 fighters and bombers. If the *Luftwaffe* did not have the crews, the Italian air force could make use of 300 planes. (How he imagined the crews could be trained in time is a mystery.) If he did not get aerial reinforcements with which to protect the sea transports then the same thing would happen as had happened at El Alamein: 'the battle will be lost at sea before it is on land.' Another telegram, telling Hitler that Russia was too big to annihilate and that the only viable solutions in the East were either peace if possible or else a 'systematized defence', followed hard on the heels of the first one. Yet another desperate request for help in the air went down the wires to Hitler two weeks before the final collapse.[68]

Von Arnim knew that 1st Army's new position was weak. 'If I don't get anything on the new line within two days, I'll be dead,' he told General Siegfried Westphal at the end of March. The Akarit position was 'nothing special', and with only ninety-three working tanks available and 410 planes his forces were badly outnumbered.[69] A further retirement was inevitable, and while Messe's troops pulled back to the Chott–Akarit line a rearward position at Mansour–Enfidaville was prepared. Worried that if the troops in the line got to hear about it they would lose confidence, Ambrosio ordered Messe and von Arnim to prevent the idea that the current position was just a delaying one from gaining hold at all costs. The present position must be defended tenaciously. It was better to run the risk of losing some materiel than 'dangerously to influence the spirit of the units by premature withdrawals', he told them both.[70]

The new position was stronger than the Mareth Line, being shorter and anchored on one side by the sea and on the other by salt marshes, but the defending army was weaker – 15th *Panzer* could now field only sixteen tanks against the enemy's 460 – and had no time to build defences. The way the attack was mounted gave the Italians even less to hope for: instead of developing a battle of attrition over several days, Montgomery concentrated almost all his resources in time and space. The battle of Wadi Akarit (6 April 1943) lasted barely twenty-four hours. As it came to an end, and after delaying making up his mind for several hours, von Arnim ordered a staged retreat back to Enfidaville. Messe, annoyed at the delay, wanted a strategic withdrawal and not a tactical retreat.[71] Manoeuvring simultaneously around his nominal commander and away from his enemy, Messe sent what remained of the *Trieste* and *Spezia* divisions straight back to Enfidaville. Over the following week 1st Army followed suit, pulling back 250 kilometres.

Mussolini was now nursing hopes that a last-ditch resistance of the kind that the Russians had put up at Stalingrad could create 'new strategic situations'.[72] As the last Axis troops in North Africa prepared for their final battle, he gave his orders. The zone was to be defended to the utmost. Every opportunity must be taken to improve it whenever possible. *Supermarina* was responsible for ensuring and continuing sea-borne supply. The navy must take every opportunity to attack enemy convoys. *Superaereo* and the German 2nd Air Fleet would give 'maximum support', operating 'with great intensity' against land and sea targets and exerting maximum pressure on the enemy's land and sea lines of communication.[73] They were pipe dreams – as Ambrosio, who was fast losing the last ounce of belief in the *Duce* as warlord, surely knew. In Tunisia, Messe argued with von Arnim over the best defensive positions. The result was an unsatisfactory compromise. Kesselring flew over on 16 April to tell him that there was no question of carrying away 300,000 men and that they would undoubtedly prefer to fight even if they were then captured. 'The First Army will do its duty to the last,' was Messe's response.[74] Afterwards, in captivity, he would describe the *Oberbefehlshaber Süd* as 'a Party man, absolutely unscrupulous and capable of anything'.[75]

For Messe's army, and for von Arnim, supply by sea was fast disappearing. Now operating freely, Allied air and sea units sank half the 175 Italian ships and 40 per cent of the 169 additional merchantmen (mostly requisitioned French ships) trying to reach Messe's army, and reduced the unloading capacity of the ports of Tunis, Bizerta, Susa, Sfax and Gabès from 7,500 tons a day to 2,200 tons. Although in all 71 per cent of traffic sent to Tunisia arrived there (306,500 tons between November 1942 and May 1943), losses were mounting exponentially: 16 per cent in March, 31 per cent in April and 72 per cent in May. Air supply was rapidly giving way too: between 18 and 22 April, 100 transport aircraft were shot down by the Allies.[76] While it battled to the last on land, Messe's 1st Army was being steadily and inexorably throttled at sea and in the air. 'All the time we were fighting we knew just how it would end,' General Paolo Berardi, one of Messe's two corps commanders, said afterwards. 'All the same everybody kept marvellously calm.'[77]

The first battle of Enfidaville began on 19 April. To defend the southern end of the Axis perimeter, Messe had 70,000 Italian troops and 43,000 Germans, 250 guns (many short range) and one and a half days' ammunition. Another 36,000 Italians fought with von Arnim's 5th Army and the *Afrikakorps* in the centre and north. Fifty Italian and 328 German aircraft made up the air defences. Remorselessly, the Allied 8th Army pushed back the perimeter. The defenders held on for almost a month, counter-attacking to slow down the enemy's advance, but the end was never in any doubt. On the third day of the battle, with the army running out of ammunition, General Mancinelli sent an urgent request – which he afterwards acknowledged 'perhaps wasn't strictly accurate' – for more. The Allies then momentarily broke off the battle. Had it continued into a fourth day, Mancinelli would have had nothing left.[78] The arrival of 280 tons of petrol on 24 April gave 1st Army a little breathing space, but not much. A signal from von Arnim on 2 May told its own story: there was only half a day's fuel left and the stocks of gun ammunition were exhausted.

As the end drew near, discussion in Rome went round in circles. Mussolini and Kesselring argued over whether destroyers should be used to ferry urgently needed supplies to Tunisia, as Kesselring wanted but Mussolini and his admirals did not, and whether they should go at night as Kesselring urged or in daylight as Mussolini preferred. Mussolini thought the enemy could try a landing in Italy but could not invade her. Kesselring pointed out that there was already enough shipping in North Africa to land two infantry divisions and two and a half armoured divisions.[79] Mussolini thought there was only one way to resolve the situation in North Africa, by attacking Gibraltar, but in the next breath admitted that was impossible. Disregarding Ambrosio's advice, he wanted more men sent to Tunisia 'in order to give the feeling that we are not abandoning the men down there'.

Switching attention to another topic – a characteristic of these meetings (this one had twenty topics on the agenda) – Mussolini believed that a landing from the sea somewhere in the western Mediterranean would be very difficult 'but surprise could come from the air'. General Rossi, Ambrosio's deputy chief of staff, chipped in: a landing by air could be fought off 'because it would be a fight of man against man', but Italy did not have the means to resist a landing by tanks even if half of them were destroyed. The initial defence against an attempted landing, Mussolini declared, would be in the air, followed by naval defence and finally by land troops. Rossi again corrected the *Duce*. Aerial resistance was 'lacking', the navy could do nothing to defend Sicily and the army did not have the tanks to mount a mobile defence. By way of reassurance, an ever-optimistic Kesselring pointed out that General Roatta, in charge of the defence of Sicily, was 'a man of extraordinary energy', and General Westphal added that there were already forty German tanks in Sicily and another thirty to forty ready to replace them if they were sent to Tunisia.[80]

On 7 May the Allies entered Tunis and four days later, as von Arnim was taken prisoner, Indian troops reached Cape Bon. With the northern front gone and with no fuel left, Messe ordered what remained of his army, which included two German divisions, to retreat to a final perimeter and defend it to the last. The remnants of the once-mighty *Afrikakorps*, now reduced to two tanks and with no ammunition, surrendered on 12 May. Messe held on, refusing to surrender uncondi-tionally as telegrams sped to and from Rome. Mancinelli was sent to explore 8th Army's terms. Waylaid by the French, he was taken to a French general who, he said later, 'received him in pyjamas and was intoxicated'. Under pressure to surrender to the French, Mancinelli stuck it out and was eventually taken to Montgomery's headquarters.[81] At 7.35 that evening a last message arrived from the *Duce*: 'Cease fight-ing. You are created [a] Marshal of Italy. Honour to You and to Your brave men.'[82] At 12.30 next day Messe accepted the surrender terms and told Rome that all resistance in Africa had ended. At the last, the remaining Italian artillery batteries were lined up and as Messe walked between the lines their muzzles were lowered in respect.[83]

No definitive figures exist for the human cost to the Italians of the Tunisian campaign, but when it was over the Allies had 89,442 Italian prisoners of war. In the period of time stretching from the start of the third battle of El Alamein to the surrender, Allied calculations suggest that the Italian losses amounted to 34,100 dead and wounded and 113,500 prisoners of war.[84] In all, the Italian merchant fleet shipped 262,000 men to Libya and Tunisia – and almost four times as many (982,000) to the Balkans – and lost 955,644 tons of shipping doing so.[85] The overall cost of the North and East African campaigns in terms of dead, missing and prisoners of war has proved impossible to calculate. The best current estimate is that 19,882 Italians died in North Africa and 8,550 in East Africa.[86] Prisoner-of-war totals are no less problem-atical, but by August 1941 almost 200,000 Italians were in British hands. The total number of Italian prisoners of war taken in North Africa would therefore appear to be somewhere in the region of 400,000.

AMBROSIO TAKES CHARGE

Ambitious forecasts of weapons production had been made during 1942, but the economy was too weak – and now too vulnerable to

Allied bombers – to maintain them. A German offer of the plans of the PzKw IV tank had to be refused because of a lack of raw materials. The hopes of Italian industrialists that they would profit from a close relationship with German arms manufacturers collapsed as the military situation worsened with the defeats in Russia and North Africa. Arms production fell during September, October and November due to shortages of coal and electrical energy. Allied carpet-bombing proved the final straw. Large parts of FIAT's Mirafiori plant were put out of action after two bombing attacks on 18 and 20 November 1942; production of the P 40, Italy's first heavy tank, had to be put back to May 1943; and more bombing of Turin on 28 November and 8–9 December hit innumerable smaller sub-contractors and suppliers of parts. At the end of December, FIAT's head, Giovanni Agnelli, reported that more than fifty firms had been totally or partially damaged and production by the Ansaldo steel works was down by 54 per cent. What worried him most was that workers, technicians and small and medium firms were disappearing.[87] Tank output for the year was set at the start of 1943 at 1,345 M 3s and 380 of the new P 40s. By late March, Ambrosio had to report that output had fallen by 30 per cent due to enemy air action, and in April he told the king that it was now set at 100 units a month – for the second half of the year. In May all he could say was that a new production programme was being studied.[88]

As the bombing began, Mussolini complained that alarms were being sounded in Turin, Milan and other northern cities between 1 and 2 p.m. every day. He did not want the population alarmed and nor did he want it habituating itself to air-raid warnings and taking no notice.[89] There was little popular enthusiasm for joining in the air defence of the mainland. The army looked for 40,000 volunteers from the militia to man anti-aircraft guns but got only 3,000 and had to make up the shortfall. Anti-aircraft defences at night still depended on searchlights, but German help was on hand: 400 88mm guns had been installed at Milan, Turin, Genoa and Savona, and the first tranche of an expected gift of sixty-five radar sets had arrived.[90]

Allied air power was now having devastating effects on what remained of the Italian navy. A raid on Naples in December 1942 sank the cruiser *Attendolo*, and in April 1943 B-17 bombers knocked out Italy's last two heavy cruisers, the *Trieste* and the *Gorizia*. The battleships, pulled back to La Spezia, were not out of harm's way either: in early June, B-17s hit the *Vittorio Veneto* and the *Roma*. Italy's night-fighter defences were particularly weak and there was no prospect of any direct help from Germany: at the end of 1942 all Germany's night-fighters were defending the western reaches of Hitler's Reich.[91] To help with the defence of the industrial region in northern Italy, Goering ordered an extension of Josef Kammhuber's night-fighter zone, which covered western Europe from Denmark to the Upper Rhône, down as far as Marseilles. Though Allied bombers would now have to fly through the protected zone, the Germans did not expect to have it fully operational before June 1943.

To improve air defence of the *madrepatria* Mussolini wanted an air-field built at Aspromonte in southern Italy. The problem, General Fougier explained, was not that there were not enough advanced air-fields: without radar the fighters got very little warning of incoming bomber raids. A lack of ready spare parts was also making it difficult to keep enough fighters in action. The air force chief was, though, upbeat. In the next six months a number of 'new and very modern planes' would be introduced and by 1944 'everything will be in place'.[92] Mussolini's insistence on dispersing the operational headquarters of the three services made running the war no easier: Fougier spent his mornings at the air force headquarters twenty-eight kilometres outside Rome and his afternoons in the air ministry back in the city. On the front line his airmen had little reason for optimism, being all too well aware of how inferior their own aircraft were in comparison to those of their enemy. Brigadier-General Boschi was overwhelmed by what he saw when his men captured a Liberator that had crash-landed near Gabès. '[Y]ou should see what a Liberator carries,' he told Messe after-wards in captivity. 'It's marvellous . . . there was not a single instrument, even the smallest and most insignificant, which wasn't ten times better than anything we've got. Everything electric . . . all different from ours, ten years ahead of us.'[93]

Vittorio Ambrosio, who replaced Cavallero as chief of the armed forces general staff on 30 January 1943, was regarded by contemporar-ies as cool and somewhat austere, but also as a man who had 'character and to spare'. He was also recognized by at least one of his subor-dinates as having 'a clear, panoramic and synthetic view of our war problems'.[94] Asked to prepare a statement for a forthcoming visit by Foreign Minister Ribbentrop, he handed Mussolini an unambiguous strategic assessment which chimed with the line that the Foreign Ministry wanted taken.[95] The Germans should adopt a defensive strategy in Russia, which if well conducted promised to reduce Russia's 'residual potential' to zero. Economizing on means in the East would be to the advantage of the Mediterranean theatre, which was as much in Germany's interest as in Italy's. There the Axis should do likewise, holding out in Tunisia for as long as possible for the obvious reason that Algeria and Tunisia were going to be the Allies' springboard for future operations against Europe.[96] A couple of weeks later the heads of the navy and the air force produced top-secret surveys of the situation, reserved for Ambrosio's eyes only.

To Riccardi, keeping possession of Tunisia was 'extremely important'. Without it, sealing the Sicilian Straits, one of the only two effective strategic operations the Axis could undertake in the Mediterranean (the other being submarine warfare), would be impossible. As long as it was sealed the enemy was forced to use three times as much tonnage to supply his forces as would otherwise be necessary, thereby exposing his ships to greater losses from the submarines operating in the Atlantic. While the Italians held Bizerta, enemy landings in Provence, on Sicily and Sardinia, in Greece and in the Aegean were 'improbable'. If it was lost the enemy might drive on Crete, the Dodecanese islands and the Balkan mainland and threaten the supplies of Romanian petrol – which were essential if the armed forces were going to be able to fight at all. The lines of communication with Tunisia were the easiest to defend because they were the shortest. Keeping supplies flowing depended on having enough escorts. That in turn could only be achieved if work on destroyers and torpedo boats that were presently being repaired or were in an advanced state of construction was accelerated – something which did not require more raw materials but did need labour and organization. Admiral Riccardi also wanted more air support, more fuel (he had sufficient, he said, for a single mission by the *Littorio* and four destroyers, after which there would not be enough left to refill their tanks), and technical equipment such as radar and echo-finders, which would have to come from Germany.[97] Ambrosio's terse response was that the *Comando Supremo* took exactly the same view of Tunisia's importance as the navy secretary did.

Looking at the strategic situation from the air force's point of view, Fougier concluded that the enemy was building up to a direct attack on the European continent. That attack might be delayed so that Germany and Russia could wear one another out, or it might be launched to speed up Russian progress, in which case it could come soon – probably next month. Weighing up the advantages and disadvantages to the Allies of landing in the Balkans, in Italy itself or in France, Fougier concluded that France was the most likely choice. The initial targets might be Marseilles or Narbonne, with a cross-Channel operation to follow, or they might be elsewhere – it was difficult to foresee. Whenever and wherever a landing came, it would be big. One thing was certain: once Tunisia was lost, Italy would be exposed to the full weight of Allied air power. Fougier did his sums: 747 Axis fighters faced 2,270 Allied fighters, and 1,116 Axis bombers, dive-bombers and torpedo bombers would be matched against an estimated 2,000 Anglo-American equivalents. The Axis was heavily outnumbered and as far as Italy was concerned there was no hope of reducing the imbalance. Over the next six months the factories would produce on average 115 to 120 fighters, bombers and torpedo bombers a month, barely enough to keep up with normal losses. There was only one way to get some kind of balance into the equations: immediate German help, for which Fougier had a precise figure – 360 fighters and 144 bombers.[98]

Goering came to Rome on 8 March to tell the Italians how to use their sea and air power – advice which included suspending defensive air operations to protect sea-borne traffic in favour of offensive operations against Malta. It was no use, he told Ambrosio, for the Italians to say they wanted to hold on to Tunisia if they did not do 'everything that was humanly possible in every minute detail to achieve that'. Pointing out, among many other things, that Italy had to defend a coastline stretching from Toulon to Rhodes and that the Allies put up twenty escorts for a convoy of six to eight merchantmen while he could only find seven at best, Ambrosio ended a long exposition of Italy's difficulties with a bleak forecast. Fresh systems and methods, if indeed there were any, were not going to solve the real situation, which must be gauged according to 'the inexorable numbers'.[99]

The advice Ambrosio now gave Mussolini was uncompromising. The Axis forces in Tunisia were overwhelmingly outnumbered in tanks and aircraft, Italy could not get across even half the monthly supply of fuel Hitler deemed essential, and continuing to throw men and weapons into 'the Tunisian furnace' risked playing the enemy's game. Italy, he told the *Duce*, needed to husband her shipping because she was going to need it to resupply Sicily, Sardinia, Corsica, Albania, Greece and the Aegean when the expected assault across the Mediterranean came. To defend herself against the bombers that would hammer her ports and airports, she needed German air power. Without it the country's air defences, already weak, would be unable to resist a big air offensive. Divisions were being pulled back from the Balkans, but without German planes and guns of all types (and other supplies too, including boots), the *madrepatria* could not be defended. Ambrosio wanted a frank discussion of all this as the necessary preliminary to agreed lines for the future joint conduct of the war. '[V]ery serious' developments in the war were probably going to happen very shortly, he warned Mussolini. '[W]ith our forces alone we cannot in any way avoid [them].'[100] Responding to Ambrosio's warnings, Mussolini asked Hitler for German air power – and got it in the shape of three squadrons of FW 190 fighters, three squadrons of Me 110s, and three of Ju 88 bombers. Immediate use was out of the question though, as training the Italian crews would take a couple of months.[101]

WEAPONS, PLANS AND THE DEFENCE OF THE *MADREPATRIA*

Italy, now hard-pressed, needed to maximize efficient production of war materiel and Cavallero's departure created an opening to restructure her over-complex war machinery. A brief attempt to co-ordinate war production had been made in 1940 when Mussolini appointed General Caracciolo di Feroleto to the new post of higher inspector of technical services, but it had quickly been strangled by the technical branches of the armed services, none of whom were ready to allow inroads on their independence.[102] The two key players now sat down to work out how to overcome the obstructions that were hobbling weapons development and production. Ambrosio proposed devolving everything to do with war production to the three service ministries and the Ministry for War Production. The technical directorates of the three services would work to a joint technical committee for arms and munitions within the Ministry for War Production. General Favagrossa intended that his ministry take an overview of the issues while the services' technical directorates worked out the details. It should have the authority to approve new weapons types because of their possible impact on overall arms production. It should also have the ability to advise increased production of one type of weapon to compensate for reduced production of another. The problem as he saw it was one of discrimination between the needs of the army, the navy and the air force. In that case, Ambrosio retorted, he wanted the *Comando Supremo* and the joint technical committee to be involved. It took a couple of months to implement the project, but by the end of March the technical directorates of the army and navy had moved across to Favagrossa's ministry and the air force was about to follow suit.[103]

A lot hinged on increasing weapons production. A shortage of coal was delaying production of the P 40 tank until July, and at present rates at least two of the four armoured divisions the army was trying either to create or rebuild would not be fully equipped until the latter part of 1943.[104] To maximize Italy's chances Ambrosio ordered the services and the armaments procurement organizations to stop their continuous modification of existing weaponry, improve the repair process, limit the number of types so as to facilitate series production, and focus their efforts on a range of weapons – high-altitude anti-aircraft guns, anti-tank guns, anti-tank mines, radar, perforating munitions, P 40 tanks and self-propelled guns – that were obviously going to be essential.[105]

Somewhat belatedly, Mussolini now called leading ministers together to co-ordinate the financial side of the economy. The Minister for Foreign Exchange told them a tale of woe. Foreign currency was being spent unnecessarily on the tourist industry; ministries and the service attachés of all three services were competing individually overseas for imports of raw materials and thereby jacking up the prices; exports were declining, which meant either that imports had to be paid for with foreign currency that Italy did not have, or they had to be reduced; and politics was adversely interfering with commerce, as when Rome undertook to give Romania 500,000,000 lire's worth of goods without securing an equal reduction in her 1,000,000,000 lire of indebtedness. What was now needed was centralized control of such transactions through his ministry. Some of his colleagues were far from happy at the prospect of giving up their direct contacts with foreign partners, and losing power to a rival, but Mussolini backed him. The various ministries would prepare their plans and pass them to the Ministry for Foreign Exchange and it would balance things out. 'The important thing,' Mussolini told the assembled group, 'is to ensure that no one trespasses onto someone else's field of activity' – which was not quite what he had just agreed to.[106]

Early in March Admiral Canaris told General Amé that he no longer believed the German U-boat campaign could achieve decisive results.[107] Soon afterwards Admiral Riccardi warned that he was going to have to reduce the activity of his submarine fleet. Only twenty submarines had been built since the war began, and of the total of 141 boats sixty-seven had been lost and eight decommissioned. Balancing the rhythm of losses against expected new construction, he expected to have only thirty submarines operating in June and twenty-five in December. Experience showed that submarines were most effective when acting in groups of ten and twelve, and that meant he was going to have to reduce the number of organized traps. By the end of the month he had only thirty-eight operational destroyers and torpedo boats left, far too few to protect seven different sea supply routes to say nothing of coastal traffic. Much though the Germans might want to increase protection for the convoys travelling to Tunisia, they were already getting the lion's share and there was simply nothing more to spare. The Allies protected convoys of six to eight merchantmen with up to twenty war-ships. (This made them difficult to attack: in the Mediterranean Italian submarines sank only twenty-one merchant ships and thirteen enemy warships, totalling approximately 100,000 tons; in the Atlantic thirty-two Italian submarines sank 109 Allied merchant ships, totalling 593,864 tons.) The most Riccardi could manage, he told Ambrosio, was three to seven escorts.[108]

By now the merchant fleet was in terribly bad shape. Having begun the war with 574 merchantmen it had lost 178 ships in 1941 and another 148 in 1942, launching only thirty-one replacements. In March, during the last three weeks of which she lost forty-one mer-chantmen, Italy had 595,000 tons of usable shipping (and 174,000 tons of tankers) and was losing them at a rate of 70,000 tons a month. At that rate, by the end of 1943 none would be left. Rational utilization could improve things, Mussolini was told, but it would not fundamen-tally change them. The *Duce* had an answer – transform slower passenger liners into freighters – and when told that doing so was not straightforward he had an answer to that too – technical experts always gave you a negative response at first and then changed their minds. After the experts had chewed over the many problems around shipping repair – everyone agreed that ships constructed out of concrete were not going to be of any use – and come up with a range of answers which included massive increases in the dockyard labour force to speed up construction, Mussolini told them that forecasts were often wrong, that no one could be exact about future loss rates, and that the essential thing was 'to protect what we have and fill in the gaps as far as possible'.[109]

As 1943 began, SIM picked up Allied interest in Sicily and Sardinia – apparently indirectly from General Archibald Nye, vice-chief of the Imperial General Staff.[110] With the Axis hold on North Africa weakening, attention turned to the defence of Italy's now vulnerable islands. In mid-January the Minister for Communications warned that the everyday needs of the civilian population and the military units currently stationed on Sicily could not be met and that the situation would get worse when Messina and the ports on the mainland were put entirely to military use.[111] Messina was a choke-point and by mid-February it was so engorged with materiel that it was taking weeks to get anti-aircraft units onto the island and ready for action, partly because men, guns, munitions and equipment were being shipped across separately.[112] Now in command of 6th Army and responsible for its defence, General Roatta wanted the power to use the large number of unemployed men in Sicily to improve its defences. Mussolini would not give it. The most he was prepared to do was to put in 'a personality' whose orders the civilian prefects on the island would have to obey. Roatta bridled: the new commissioner, equal in rank to him, would become 'a kind of governor of the island' and his difficulties would increase. Commissioners were installed – on Sicily and on Sardinia – but were put under the authority of the local military commander.[113]

Defending the islands was starting to concern Hitler too and at the end of February, in response to an Italian request, he agreed to release 124 coastal guns and forty-two Russian field guns. The Germans were ready, General Walter Warlimont reported, to strengthen the anti-aircraft and anti-tank defences in the Aegean. The Italians' response was to ask for more. To fight on in Tunisia, they needed submarines, radar sets, echo-finders and fuel, which must arrive at twice the current rate.[114] The Germans sent commissions to Greece, the Dodecanese, Sicily, Sardinia, Corsica and Calabria to report on the state of the defences. Determined to keep a greater distance between himself and the Germans than his predecessor had done, Ambrosio made it clear that they were there only to advise and not to act, and only for as long as the local army commanders thought useful.

With 50,000 men, forty-eight anti-aircraft guns, 251 coastal and mobile guns and twelve aircraft, and with more weapons on the way from domestic production and from Germany, the *Comando Supremo* expected Corsica to be ready to face Dieppe-style incursions by the end of March.[115] How the islanders would react was an open question. After visiting the island in January, General Caracciolo di Feroleto was convinced that the hostility of the local population would break out openly as soon as an enemy landing looked probable, as it would also if Italy said anything to indicate that she intended to remain there permanently and exercise sovereignty over the island.[116] Mussolini thought that Sardinia was the most threatened of all the Italian islands, and planned to throw a strong submarine screen around it as a first line of defence.[117] Defending the islands touched on delicate service susceptibilities. To co-ordinate the defences, Ambrosio wanted the army to take charge of defending naval establishments and airfields on Sicily and Sardinia right away. Riccardi agreed in principle but did not want the practice to occur until an enemy attack was actually foreseeable. Ambrosio instructed him to do as he was told.

On 5 April, now expecting major landings on Sardinia, Corsica or Sicily, Rome ordered the armed forces to ensure that everything was made ready, including preparations to clear the civilian population away from the coastal zones along with magazines and stores. In the early stages, Ambrosio warned, defence would rest with the forces actually on the ground.[118] Soon afterwards the Germans began to feed in troops to defend Sicily. Clearing the island's coasts posed a major problem for the military because there was no possibility of the inland regions absorbing the coastal population. Nor was the civilian population self-sufficient in food – though the military there were expected to be so by the end of the month.[119]

In mid-April a SIM report suggested that the Allied massing of materiel in North Africa, clearly intended for landings, pointed not to the Balkans but more probably Sicily, Sardinia and southern France as the potential targets.[120] At the end of the month, Ambrosio called all the service chiefs together. First, they explored defending Sardinia. SIM estimated that the enemy had on hand ten infantry divisions, an armoured division, three armoured brigades, 5,000 aircraft (of which 3,500 were west of Sirte) and 900 landing craft. A cautious calculation suggested that with that lift 30,000 men and 2,000 motor vehicles (half of them tanks) could be carried to landing grounds. General Fougier thought that the enemy would need to deploy 500 fighters to cover a landing, which could only be done if they possessed airfields at Bizerta and Tunis. He had twenty-seven bombers, thirty-three torpedo planes and forty-seven fighters on the island and could bring in support within a day, including a fighter wing from Rome – 'my last reserve'.

Riccardi reckoned that the landing would be supported by four battleships, at least two aircraft carriers, an anti-aircraft cruiser and a mass of corvettes for anti-submarine work. Against that he could put up three battleships, a solitary cruiser and a handful of destroyers which were not fully trained for battle-fleet work – 'in sum, an important battle group with . . . minimum protection'. Two more cruisers and twenty-four motor torpedo boats could arrive within thirty-two hours. Neither man could counter any enemy preparations. Fougier did not have enough bombers to hit enemy air bases at Oran, and Riccardi admitted that in that respect the navy could do 'very little'. The three Italian divisions stationed on Sardinia had very limited mobility, leading Ambrosio to conclude that they could not wait for the enemy to secure a bridgehead but must attack at once 'to prevent him setting foot on land'. Eighty thousand women, children and invalids would have to be moved away from the coasts by the civilian authorities. Having established the parameters of the enormous task it faced, the group adjourned, leaving the separate commanders to work up their individual plans and await final directives from the *Comando Supremo*.[121]

Three days later the same group met to do the same thing for Sicily. Roatta spoke at length. The general staff had told him in mid-April that the forces available to defend the island were what they were and would remain substantially the same. There were no mobile anti-aircraft guns, no 'proper' anti-ship guns (other than those at the ports and the naval *piazze*), only one soldier to defend every thirty-four kilometres and one anti-tank gun for every 2.2 kilometres, and the island's fixed defences were in a poor state. The list of shortcomings was almost endless: coastal defence works were mostly only earthworks, routes inland had not been properly blocked, anti-tank ditches were not wide enough or deep enough, coastal defence units lacked the motor vehicles to be able to support one another and depended on telephones for communication as radios were reserved mainly for regimental and divisional commands, and defences against aerial attack were primitive or non-existent.[122] To make the best of what he had, Roatta needed 3,000 kilometres of barbed wire, 250 million kilos of cement, 400,000 anti-tank mines and an extra labour force of 15,000 men. If that looked a lot, it was the very minimum he needed for an adequate defence of the island.

His likely enemy, 8th Army, was, he declared, a force of 'exceptional capacity'. To defend Sicily he had a total of 247 Italian and 381 German aircraft, though not all the Italian aircraft were usable and the German aircraft (some of which were on Sardinia) were moved about more than the Italian aircraft and could thus not all be counted on. His airfields were vulnerable, being well within range of North Africa and Malta, so he would depend on support from mainland airfields. Since the enemy could now throw tanks, armoured cars, self-propelled guns and infantry onto any beach, landings were much less easy to parry. To do so the defence needed to contain the enemy by means of defensive works and local forces and then hit him with high-quality mobile forces. If enemy armour broke through the defensive crust – which was thin everywhere – then it would have to be met inland where the ground and prepared defences could compensate for the defenders' lack of armour and anti-tank guns. Then, with tank reinforcements, a counter-offensive 'big style' could be launched.[123]

Ambrosio congratulated Roatta on the clarity of his exposition – but told him that the lion's share of his requests could not be met. All he could suggest was more training and more preparation. Riccardi found small comfort in the fact that the enemy would probably not use his battleships, but did not intend to employ his own battle-fleet as long as there was a possible threat to Sardinia. His battleships, and his destroyers, would be at the mercy of an enemy who would enjoy 'complete dominance in the air'. So there was no possibility of using the surface fleet to oppose a landing. Fougier could not say exactly how many planes would be available to defend Sicily – that would depend on what was happening elsewhere – but did not think an enemy attempt on the island likely as long as Italy held Tunisia and Sardinia. As for Sicily itself, he was confident of the possibility of 'effectively resisting' a landing – apparently solely on the basis of the fact that the possibility of massing his planes was 'considerable'. Roatta turned to the Axis. Since the best that Italy could do on her own if faced with a major landing was put up 'an honourable resistance', why was her ally not thinking of giving her the means to strengthen the island's defences? Little or nothing could be expected from that quarter, Ambrosio explained. The matter had been discussed at the Salzburg meeting 'within the framework of the euphoria which makes [the Germans] think the Russian offensive will yet be rewarding' – with no outcome. Whatever could be done to improve the island's defences must be done quickly.[124]

As General Messe's army was dying in Tunisia, Ambrosio set out his orders for his force commanders. The first charge on the Italian armed forces was to keep the fight going in North Africa for as long as possible. The enemy's air supremacy was making supply extremely costly, but every sacrifice was fully justifiable because it delayed the possibility of a direct attack on Italian soil. The massive build-up of enemy troops in North Africa pointed to the likelihood of landings in the western Mediterranean, possibly even before the Axis position in Tunisia fell. If Sardinia fell Corsica would inexorably follow, and that would put the entire Italian peninsula in danger. On the other hand, the enemy might try to occupy Sicily as a transit point to the Aegean and the Balkans. The second charge on the armed forces was therefore to prepare to defend Italy's coasts: success there could change the course of the war. Last, but by no mean least, came the Balkans. A landing there appeared to be less imminent, but the fragile internal situation in Herzegovina, Montenegro and Greece might make the region a more attractive target. No more troops could be spared for the Balkans, but neither could the 'enormous mass of men and equipment' presently in theatre be reduced. The Balkan targets must be defended, and it was up to the men on the spot to do it with the means they had to hand.[125]

Mussolini turned his attention to the defence of Italy. On 13 May an urgent telegram went down the wires to Hitler asking for three German divisions, six tank battalions, 200 anti-aircraft guns and fifty squadrons of fighters and bombers (though it quickly became apparent that he had no idea how many planes there were in a German air squadron).[126] As there would not be time to train Italians to man the tanks, guns and planes, they must all come with German personnel. That same day Mussolini told Admiral Dönitz blandly that he had been sure since the previous August that the battle at sea was lost. He was also aware that Italy was now greatly inferior in the air. Nevertheless, with the reinforcements he had asked for an enemy landing could be faced 'calmly'. So could enemy bombing. Domestic morale was good and hatred of the enemy was rising.[127] Mussolini got his answer next day. Hitler would not send him three divisions. He was prepared to build up the *Hermann Goering* division, part of which was already on the island, and consider sending a parachute division. Otherwise Mussolini would have to make do with the scratch German units already in Sicily and Sardinia. They would be backed up by others destined for Tunisia and currently being massed in northern Italy. Eighteen squadrons of combat aircraft were on their way, as well as 120 88mm anti-aircraft guns and various lighter weapons.[128]

While his generals and admirals struggled to fight his war, Mussolini was on a mission of his own. At Görlitz in December he had floated the idea of a compromise peace with Russia, or at least a defensive deployment that would release forces for use elsewhere. His views about the likely success or otherwise of the Russian war could veer wildly from one extreme to the other – in November 1942 he told Giuseppe Bastianini, under-secretary of state at the Foreign Ministry, that Russia had not yet used her full force, and in December that 'Russia is beaten', but by the beginning of 1943 he regarded the Führer's determination to defeat the Russians as a hopeless task.[129] After the final collapse at Stalingrad he tried to 'Mediterraneanize' the war, repeating his case for a settlement of the conflict in the East and hoping to persuade General Franco to allow the Axis to move troops through Spanish Morocco to attack the Allies in Tunisia. As far as Russia was concerned, Mussolini's plan stood no chance of succeeding: on 27 February, Foreign Minister Ribbentrop told the king that there was no possibility of accords with Russia and announced what would be the forthcoming Kursk offensive.[130] As for the Spanish option, Hitler simply ignored it.

Ambrosio's analysis of the war was very different. At the beginning of March 1943 he warned Mussolini that if Germany could not help Italy then she must 'concentrate on avoiding the consequences of errors that are not hers'. Ten days later he told the *Duce* that it was time to evaluate 'whether our sacrifice will contribute to final victory'. If not, the *Patria* could not ask its sons to commit suicide. And three days after that he told Mussolini that 'if it is agreed that the near future is thick with dangers, we must take a long-term look at the situation and draw the necessary conclusions.'[131] Tunisia was already lost: 'it's only a matter of time,' he told the king. The moment had come for Mussolini, who was now completely in German hands, to give way to new men. His choice would be Badoglio.[132] The king kept his own counsel and for the time being Mussolini went unchallenged. But the forces that would topple him were gathering.

Mussolini had been far from well during the early months of the year and meetings had been cancelled, sometimes at short notice.[133] A meeting with Hitler was at last arranged for 7 April. Ambrosio tried to steer his warlord. What mattered most was to establish a single vision of how to conduct the war whose general lines must be fixed in common agreement with their ally. The importance for Germany of defending Italy must be got across to the Germans, and so too must Italy's need for weapons and munitions that were 'absolutely indispensable for the defence of our coasts'. Details of strategy and policy in the Balkans and Greece needed discussion, as did the needs of the navy (fuel came top of the list) and the air force (day and night fighters, fuel and lubricants). Among half a dozen random items tacked on the end of the list, one read simply 'German behaviour in Italy'.[134]

Mussolini was in no condition to press Hitler on Ambrosio's behalf. When he arrived at Klessheim near Salzburg he looked pale and emaciated and had to be helped down from the train, and over the next three days he spent a considerable part of the time in bed. When active he pursued will-o'-the-wisps of his own. One was the idea of shaping a political 'New Order' in Europe as a counterblast to the Atlantic Charter, a blind alley he was encouraged to go down by his ambassador in Berlin, Dino Alfieri, who told him that only the *Duce* possessed 'the acuteness, the profound psychological awareness of the needs of other peoples, and the political sense' to be able to activate such a programme. A declaration duly emerged and Mussolini was very pleased with it, though in practice it meant absolutely nothing.[135] Another was his scheme for falling on the rear of the Anglo-American armies in French North Africa by way of Spain and the Straits. Hitler brushed the idea aside but Mussolini tried to play the Spanish card up to his last day in office, concocting a convoluted plan to use Franco's Catholicism to persuade Hitler to end the war with Russia.[136]

The diplomatic discussions at Klessheim were uncompromising. Ribbentrop told Bastianini that the Russian problem could only be solved militarily and not politically and that Germany intended to pursue 'the progressive systematic annihilation of the Bolshevik army'. With the Russians 'three-quarters beaten', the English beaten everywhere else and the Americans 'counting for little', the Reich could not be preoccupied with 'set-backs in Africa'.[137] The military discussions fared no better as far as Italy was concerned. Ambrosio came away convinced that for the Germans the Mediterranean was 'a war theatre of secondary importance' and that while they feared an Allied landing in Sardinia and Sicily they were not prepared to send the weapons they had available to any sector that was not actually an existing combat zone. Guns and anti-tank mines would be forthcoming, but no tanks and no trucks. Nor would Italy get the extra 70,000 tons of fuel oil the navy needed in addition to the 58,480 tons it would receive in April. Of the 500 aircraft Mussolini had begged, some 100 would be forthcoming by July or August – but Italian crews would have to be trained to fly them. Nor, unless pressure on Romania increased her oil production, would the air force get any extra aviation fuel.[138]

As the strategic position went from bad to worse, centripetal forces began to gather within Italy. Food prices were rising everywhere, though faster in the south than in the north, and black-market prices were beyond most people's reach: in Rome by June 1943 black-market butter cost five times the official price, bread eight times as much, and milk ten times. The value of money had collapsed, thanks partly to the state printing money to cover the huge deficits created by missing tax revenues.[139] Strikes began to spread through the industrial plants in Milan, Turin and Genoa from early March. Organized by the Communist Party, they took the authorities completely by surprise. Triggered chiefly by the high cost of living, they were rooted in a widespread desire to end the war. Strict censorship kept the press silent, but news spread by word of mouth.[140] Giuseppe Volpi, head of the General Confederation of Italian Industry, believed the disturbances were economic and not socio-political. General Hazon, head of the *Carabinieri* and now one of the men preparing Mussolini's overthrow, thought exactly the reverse and lamented the fact that Mussolini appeared unable to recognize how averse the population now was to Fascism.[141] Whatever his perception of its causes, Mussolini could not but be aware that his hold on the populace was weakening. When his train stopped overnight at Udine on its way back from Klessheim it needed a 400-man guard because of the danger of infiltration by 'rebels'.

A week after the Klessheim meeting, Bastianini called the heads of the armed forces together to assess its outcome. Ambrosio enumerated the shortcomings. The army's request for 1,250 tanks had produced practically nothing, less than half the coastal guns and three-fifths of the anti-tank guns previously requested had arrived, and a request for 7,400 trucks had been met with a negative. Kesselring replied that after Stalingrad the OKW was having to use all its reserves to hold back the Soviets and listed the armaments that had in fact made it to Italy, which included 512 88mm anti-aircraft guns and 180 searchlights. The underlying temper of the meeting was exposed when Bastianini, exercising his diplomat's skills, announced that it appeared from Kesselring's list that they were close to achieving their requests. 'No,' Ambrosio interjected, 'we are very far away.' The size of Ambrosio's requests were enough to kill the strongest man, Kesselring shot back.

Ambrosio blamed Cavallero, who had allowed the army's requests to mount up over time, and agreed to spread out his own. Riccardi made his by now customary request for fuel (50,000 tons a month), adding that his three battleships had enough for only six hours' combat. As far as raw materials for shipbuilding were concerned, everything was going well. Fougier acknowledged Kesselring's efforts, but the air force needed at least double the 9,000 tons of fuel it was getting each month from Germany. Goering, he was told, would not contemplate any increase. What of Mussolini's request for 300 bombers and fighters, he asked. Between 120 and 150 were on their way to Sardinia, Sicily and Tunisia was the reply. More would follow when the Germans could manage it. The Italian shopping list lengthened: 20mm machine guns and urgently needed radar sets for the air force, more trains for the Balkans, more steamships for the Aegean, a share in the output of the French aircraft industry. Winding up, Bastianini claimed that the direct contacts between the Italian navy and air force and the Germans were working effectively and hoped that the army would be able to establish similar arrangements.[142] Summarizing the outcome for Mussolini, he reported Kesselring's undertaking 'to support with all his authority the *Comando Supremo*'s requests' as soon as he could get to Germany – something Kesselring never quite said. Ambrosio did not think they had made a single step forward.[143]

No doubt encouraged by a particularly fawning report from Alfieri in Berlin about the impact he had had on the Germans, Mussolini told the king that when he had met Hitler at Klessheim he had found him to be 'very understanding'.[144] Vittorio Emanuele III had been 'profoundly annoyed' by the defeat at El Alamein, and as winter drew on a succession of high-ranking retired soldiers came to the Quirinale urging him to intervene and 'end the madness'.[145] Not yet ready to consider taking active steps himself to replace Mussolini, he told Cavallero early in the New Year that Italy's efforts must be prolonged as long as possible because she would have nothing to gain from a compromise peace.[146] Ambrosio came back from Klessheim convinced that if Germany did not do more to help Italy then she must review her policy, and convinced too that Mussolini would never separate himself from Hitler. On his return he ordered his military assistant, General Giuseppe Castellano, to prepare a plan for Mussolini's arrest.[147] With the *madrepatria* itself now squarely in the enemy's sights the army was gradually readying itself to move against the leader it had obeyed in peace and in war for the previous twenty years.

The military shape of the war was not the only thing worrying Ambrosio. The previous autumn he had been concerned about what the Catholic Church was up to and about popular vulnerability to peace propaganda, from which it was 'only a short step to pacifism and peace of whatever sort'.[148] Now he had another thing to worry about. Communist propaganda had increased over the winter, especially in the industrial centres and military establishments where it was aimed at both workers and soldiers. By March the army believed that a massive propaganda offensive was under way aimed at securing a secret peace with the Anglo-Americans and the Soviet Union. Demands for improvements in economic conditions were believed to be the first step in a strategy that would develop into stoppages in workplaces and demonstrations outside factory gates and then into major demonstrations in city centres which would demand immediate peace.[149]

On the day that Messe surrendered, Ambrosio took to the airwaves to explain to the Italian people what had happened. The withdrawal after El Alamein had been 'one of the most perfect manoeuvres of retreat in [all] military history'. The Anglo-American landings had increased the unfavourable balance of forces facing the Axis troops. From then on the 'great function' that Tunisia had fulfilled had been a delaying one. The navy and the air force had 'valorously' protected the supply convoys in the face of massive enemy superiority. The 1st Italian Army had only fallen back from the Mareth Line after setbacks in the centre of the defensive perimeter. Faced with overwhelming enemy superiority on land – twenty to one in tanks, seven to one in armoured cars, three to one in artillery – and in the air, no force could hold out for ever no matter how great its human energy and will. At the last, the Germans had acknowledged the Italians' fighting contribution. Messe's determination to fight until given the honour of surrendering under arms had been 'the ultimate expression of manly courage', but because further sacrifice was useless the *Duce* had ordered that fighting cease. Ambrosio's closing encomium contained an implicit warning of what was to come. The lesson to be drawn from the 'conscious [self-]sacrifice of our soldiers in Africa' was to fight with the same faith that they had shown in the 'heroic fulfilment of their duty'.[150] Clearly, it was going to be Italy's turn next.

Chapter 9
Endgame

While the Anglo-American armies fought their way towards Tunis the Italian intelligence services tried to work out where they would go next. To General Amé and Italian military intelligence the logical steps to unblocking the Mediterranean were for the Allies first to conquer Tunisia and then push on to Sicily. However, making sense of the flood of hints, tips, fabrications and guesses that were now arriving was almost impossible. At the end of January 1943 an agent with access to the British Embassy in Madrid reported that a force of 600,000 to 800,000 men was being readied for an attack on the Balkans as soon as operations in North Africa were concluded.[1] Sources in Vichy France (now under total German and Italian control) with connections in North Africa believed that the Allies might be planning to attack Sardinia and Corsica as stepping stones to northern Italy, or they might be planning to attack Spain, or even repeat a First World War ploy and attack Salonika. The vast range of strategic options available to the Allies paralysed Italian planning. General Ambrosio read them as confirming the need to ensure that the defences of both the western and the eastern Alps were kept up to scratch.[2]

At the end of April, Italian military intelligence estimated that out of a total of thirty-two or thirty-three infantry divisions, six armoured divisions and six or seven armoured brigades in the western Mediterranean basin the enemy had nine or ten infantry divisions, an armoured division and two or three armoured brigades immediately available, together with seven or eight divisions and four armoured brigades in the eastern Mediterranean and some 5,000 planes. There was already enough sealift in the Algerian ports to carry 30,000 men and 2,000 vehicles, half of them tanks and armoured cars. Landing craft were moving by a process of 'osmosis' to ports in eastern Algeria, which suggested that their targets were Sardinia and Sicily. What was happening in the eastern Mediterranean was more difficult to estimate, chiefly because there was no Gibraltar from which spies could pass on detailed intelligence, but there seemed to be enough lift for one motorized division, a single tank brigade and some commandos. Their most likely objectives appeared to be Crete and Rhodes. On a broader level, the Allies might be aiming at operations against southern France in concert with a much larger cross-Channel invasion of western France.[3]

As the Axis position in North Africa collapsed, Mussolini too turned his attention to what might happen next. Once again his strategic 'intuition' was off beam. Reading English newspapers, he believed that the Allies wanted to invade France, not Italy, because from there they could attack Germany directly. They could also try to invade the Balkans where at least part of the population was sympathetic. Field Marshal Kesselring pointed out to him that the enemy was massing in the western Mediterranean. Mussolini thought that possessing Sicily and Sardinia was 'not of primary importance' to the enemy. Kesselring told him that the two large islands must be reinforced. Infantry, armoured divisions and landing craft were being massed around Oran. Sicily and Sardinia were the targets. 'It would be a crime to allow ourselves to be surprised,' he told the *Duce*. Abandoning his strategic musing, Mussolini asked what was going to happen to the generals in Tunisia. 'They will stay at their posts,' Kesselring told him.[4]

In the weeks following the fall of Tunisia, Italian air reconnaissance tracked the arrival of increasing numbers of landing craft, pontoons and ships in the Mediterranean. As lift capacity increased so did the size of the probable landing. By early June, SIM calculated that the enemy could land five or six divisions (100,000 men) not two, along with up to 6,000 vehicles, half of them tanks and armoured cars. It did not think there was the capacity for more than one major landing operation. By far the largest number of landing ships was in the ports of eastern Algeria.[5] During the same period air intelligence identified Sicily, Sardinia, Corsica, the French Mediterranean coast, the Aegean (this from Spanish military intelligence), and (according to chatter picked up at Allied Headquarters in Cairo) the Atlantic coast of France and three unspecified points in southern Europe as possible targets for Allied invasion.[6] Days before the Tunisian bridgehead collapsed, German air intelligence expected that a landing in southern France or against Sicily or Sardinia was imminent. At the end of May it believed that Allied propaganda was deliberately trying to make the defenders think that landings would take place in Sicily and southern Italy when the real target was Sardinia, that the enemy would have the forces in place to carry this out by the end of June and that they might be accompanied more or less simultaneously by landings in southern France and Norway.[7]

The Italians were, as they well knew, being subjected to an intensified campaign by the enemy 'to disorientate the Axis intelligence services on what could be the directions chosen by the Anglo-Saxons for their imminent offensive actions'.[8] One thing they did not fall for was the 'plant' in Operation MINCEMEAT on 30 April intended to persuade the Axis that the Allies planned to land in Greece. General Amé thought that the circumstances in which the document had been discovered were 'somewhat suspect' and could see no other evidence that might back up the idea. 'The means available and their location do not seem such as to support the hypothesis of imminent operations in that area [i.e. Greece and the Dodecanese],' he told the *Comando Supremo*.[9] In early June the Italian Foreign Ministry chipped in with its own list of hypotheses collected from embassies, legations and consulates across Europe. Collectively they identified enemy landings at points all around the continent from Norway to Salonika. In some cases their reports were suspiciously exact: the Italian consul in Tangier reported that the landings would take place on 17 June, and the consulate in Tetuán that they would occur on 22 June. 'Every direction [possible] is in it, so that they don't make a mistake,' Ambrosio's deputy, General Francesco Rossi, commented drily.[10]

Despite the 'noise' that was fogging the picture, two things were now becoming increasingly clear: that the enemy was most likely aiming at Sicily or Sardinia, and that when it came the landing would be in considerable force. After the fall of the small islands of Pantelleria and Lampedusa, which would happen on 11 and 12 June, Italian naval intelligence, which had forecast the attacks on the islands on 23 May, believed that Sardinia was next. At the very end of June it settled on Sicily as the enemy's immediate target. General Amé complained that though it was certain that the enemy would unleash 'the violence of his preponderant means' somewhere, his outstations and his statistical section could give him no exact appreciation of where, when and with how much force the enemy would strike.[11] He was perhaps preparing his excuses. The movement of ships did in fact provide ever clearer indications of where the enemy were likely to appear. At the very end of June the *Comando Supremo* concluded that enemy landing craft were being concentrated against Sicily and that the attack could come at any moment.[12] Amé and Ambrosio both thought so, though Admiral Sansonetti and Field Marshal Kesselring favoured Sardinia.[13]

THE DEFENCE OF SICILY

With Tunisia gone the Germans were prepared to consider reinforcing Sicily with mines, barbed wire, a German division (*Hermann Goering*) and *Tiger* tanks. Mario Roatta thought that the island's defences would be ready by July or August. He wanted the German tanks concentrated in the centre of the island, but Kesselring advised that they be split into two groups because while powerful the *Tigers* were slow. Mussolini believed that the principal attack would come from Malta. Kesselring told him it would not: aerial photography showed that there was only one troop transport there. Mussolini thought the attack would come against the centre of the island. Kesselring told him that was unlikely. The Allies could protect a coastal landing with fighter cover from Tunisia and Malta but lacked the necessary aircraft carriers to support a landing in the middle of the island.[14] The *Duce*'s grasp of strategy, never strong, was looking even shakier.

At the end of May, Roatta returned to Rome as chief of the army general staff. His place as commander of 6th Army was taken by General Guzzoni, who had been languishing in retirement for two years and who now found himself responsible for defending Sicily. Guzzoni arrived in a very upbeat mood: the story had it that Mussolini had promised him promotion to *Maresciallo d'Italia* and Ambrosio's job as chief of the armed forces general staff if things went well.[15] A rapid inspection tour persuaded Guzzoni that in some parts of the island his subordinates were disguising the slowness with which defences were being prepared from a mistaken sense of pride and *esprit de corps*. The overall defensive situation was 'inadequate', the mobile land forces and the air force's 'reactive capacity' were insufficient, and the population's spirits were 'depressed'. For the latter he blamed the local clergy who had exacerbated local apathy and resignation by telling them to put their faith in God. He needed another German armoured division, an Italian motorized division, and more aviation.[16] Nobody could agree on whereabouts on the island the Allies would invade, leaving the commander of XVI Corps, General Carlo Rossi, to conclude that the defenders had to be ready to meet the enemy wherever he appeared. Kesselring was convinced that it was most likely to happen on the western side of the island, while Guzzoni thought it would come in the east or south-east. The navy thought the Trapani–Marsala coast, Cagliari and Siracusa might all be possible enemy objectives.

On 10 April, Allied planes slipped past weak air defences and hit the port of La Maddalena on Sardinia, damaging the *Gorizia*, killing eighty and wounding 217. La Maddalena's defences were obviously too vulnerable – the closest airfield hosted only six Macchi fighters – so Admiral Riccardi pulled his cruisers and forty-eight 88mm guns destined for its defence back to La Spezia. On 5 June and again on 23 June, Allied planes hit the battleships *Vittorio Veneto* and *Roma* at La Spezia, holing them both and causing internal explosions. Ambrosio thought they would need at least two months to repair, but Mussolini told Kesselring the work might be done in a few weeks. Both men were being over-optimistic about fending off an attack on Sicily, or so Ambrosio thought. Kesselring put his faith in dispersing planes on the ground and in the arrival of seven German radar outfits, with which they would be able to claim more enemy fighters and bombers.[17] Ambrosio wanted the enemy's ships attacked. Riccardi told him that his light surface craft had been sacrificed to the needs of North Africa and his torpedo boats and MAS boats (fast torpedo-armed motorboats) were effectively all exhausted. The naval situation could only be 'restabilized' if the air situation was stabilized first. All the navy could do was ready itself to react against 'the probable coming invasion'.[18]

As the Italian high command readied Sicily for the assault to come the smaller islands fell to the Allies. In the last week of May the *Comando Supremo* warned, apparently on the basis of a source in Malta, that preparations were being made for simultaneous attacks on Pantelleria and Lampedusa. They would start with aero-naval attacks, which would then be followed up by landings.[19] Pantelleria was defended by 11,650 soldiers with 165 guns, 13 tanks and 653 machine guns, and 60 fighters – of which by 3 June only three remained, the rest having been hit by bombers or withdrawn. It was completely dependent on resupply by sea. The island was prepared to resist a landing – though permanent works were few and it relied on fieldworks – but not prepared for the aerial bombardment that began on 18 May. Over the next three weeks Allied bombing intensified until eventually it went on day and night without pause. By the time the island surrendered on 11 June the enemy had dropped 6,400 tons of bombs on it and shot down forty-seven Axis planes, losing only fifteen of their own in the process.[20]

The garrison could do little to defend themselves or the population, who abandoned their homes and lived in caves, against bombardment from the sea and the air. The navy refused even to deploy submarines, leaving the island's commander, Vice-Admiral Gino Pavesi, with only fourteen motor torpedo boats to contest the sea. On land his guns lacked fire-control equipment and telephone connections, batteries were out in the open and therefore vulnerable, and radio sets arrived dismantled and with accumulator batteries that would not work. 'In the early days,' Pavesi said later, 'when our communications were working, we were given a warning [of incoming raids] . . . then they smashed up our radio-location centre and we didn't even get that.' Distribution of water was – or, some thought, was afterwards made to seem – a perpetual problem, made worse when the island's three aqueducts were destroyed. After that, some 11,650 soldiers and 12,000 civilians relied for water on three wells. For Pavesi, during the last few days, the water question was 'an absolute torment to me'.[21] When he surrendered the island, two hours before Mussolini's order to do so reached him, he had by his own account only three days' supply of water left. For the last month he lived in a cave bombed so heavily he could not leave it even to go to the latrine.[22] After a short but violent bombardment from the air and the sea, the island of Lampedusa surrendered the day after Pantelleria gave up. Pavesi blamed its loss on the lack of fighter cover: 'I sent the same signal every day: "There are no aircraft whatever."' Later, after a game of tennis as a prisoner of war in England, he was heard to say (much to the disgust of some of his fellow captives) 'If I had not surrendered the men would have killed me.'[23]

The apparent ease with which Pantelleria fell into enemy hands greatly displeased the Fascist Party. The commander of 5th Army, General Caracciolo di Feroleto, who had overall responsibility for defending the islands of Corsica and Sardinia as well as the northern mainland, was summoned by the party secretary, Carlo Scorza, and told that the party expected more of the army.[24] He may have had a point. An inquiry carried out by Admiral Iachino concluded that only a very small part of the island's defences had in fact been hit at the moment of surrender. Ambrosio was concerned that the example of Pantelleria might generate the 'unjustified feeling' among the troops that 'a few days' aerial bombardment, even if intense', might be enough to break down the resistance of defenders. Everyone must know that the *patria* would be defended to the death and all ranks must personally believe in final victory. The heads of all three armed services were ordered to redouble their efforts to reactivate a declining offensive spirit. The army must inculcate the *arditi* spirit. The air force and the navy could carry out actions 'even of limited range' which would show the enemy that Italy had teeth.[25]

Preparations to defend the mainland and the larger islands were not moving forward smoothly. Inspections of Puglia and Calabria revealed that defensive works were behind schedule and going slowly. Increasing the numbers of troops in Sicily and Sardinia was causing supply problems and stocks were low. In Sardinia, Roatta saw 'the finest defensive works we've got in the whole of Italy'. The local commanders were fully up to the job, and the Germans on the island were being co-operative. In Corsica, where the local military commander and the commissioner were tussling over their respective rights and authority, both regular units and coastal defence battalions were short of men (some coastal defence regiments had less than half their effectives), units were being robbed of specialist manpower, and four of the five coastal defence regiments had no commanding colonel. Another problem, though Roatta did not as yet think it serious, was the 300 to 400 'unreliables' who had taken to the *maquis* and another 200 to 300 'bandits' in the south of the island. According to the local prefect, the troops could in the future find that they had an enemy at their backs as well as their front.[26] The apparent ease with which the enemy appeared to have taken Pantelleria raised doubts about whether, when called upon, Italian troops would defend their coastal positions to the last and carry out energetic counter-attacks as they were being instructed to do (and which would expose them to the overwhelming firepower that the Allies could now bring to bear to support coastal landings). Guzzoni warned his subordinate commanders not to put 'blind faith' in their men but to be 'very vigilant'. When and where necessary, they must not hesitate to take action and shoot men if necessary.[27]

Meeting the Japanese admiral Hiroake Abe on 15 June, the *Duce* was in an optimistic frame of mind. The news that the Japanese did not expect to deploy submarines in the Indian Ocean and intensify the war on Allied shipping there until mid-November did not put him out of countenance. Italian morale was good and everyone was convinced that the war must be fought to the bitter end. The enemy was in difficulties. The food situation in Russia was 'catastrophic', Great Britain was showing signs of 'uneasiness and tiredness', and the United States would shortly face 'a serious politico-social crisis'. The American population had believed that the war would be short. It was used to a very high standard of living but now 'goods were disappearing and . . . discontent is serious'. The Senate was 'somewhat hostile' to President Roosevelt's policy and a failed invasion would have 'grave consequences'. Hope was to be found in the Japanese theatre of war too. If the Japanese appeared at the Indian frontier in force with Indian troops a revolution could break out. The Japanese too believed that the Allies were suffering 'enormous' losses in planes and aircrews and that America would soon reach the extreme limit of its war production capabilities – which is perhaps where Mussolini got his strange ideas from.[28] However, the Japanese had problems of their own – a shortage of petrol, difficulties with food supplies, and a shortage of iron (they were having to tear up secondary railway lines). The two parties agreed on the need for greater co-operation in the strategic field and also in propaganda – and that was all.[29]

Ambrosio's most pressing need was for more air power. Allied aircraft outnumbered Italian and German aircraft by more than three to one. If that was not remedied the enemy would use his permanent predominance in the skies to destroy or paralyse the nation's military and civil facilities and then invade. The Germans were asked for another 2,000 aircraft.[30] The army, navy and air staffs were instructed to revise their armaments programmes for 1944 to prioritize production of fighters, anti-aircraft and anti-tank guns, P 40 tanks, and motorized rafts and transport submarines (to reinforce the islands and units overseas). Truck production should be recalculated now that Italy no longer had a presence in Libya or Russia. The services were told that they could expect more or less the same amount of raw materials in 1944 as they had during 1943 – but also told to provide realistic figures for the raw materials they would need to meet the new targets (which included 500 aircraft a month) 'regardless of previous allocations'.[31] The air force chose this moment to attempt to accelerate its planning for the post-war world. By March 1943 a process that had begun eight months earlier had not got much further than a list of seventy-five issues which had to be addressed. It included the need for a body of trained general staff officers such as the army had but the navy did not, and the need to eliminate 'the technical and administrative superstructures' that were obstructing supply. The deputy chief of the air staff handed out the tasks on 21 April. Two months later he was still awaiting responses.[32]

Mussolini was in confident mood when, on 24 June, he addressed the national directors of the Fascist Party. The enemy had often proclaimed the necessity of invading the continent and he would have to try it – but he would fail. If he got past the dry-water mark, the reserves would throw themselves on him and annihilate him. Then he could indeed say he had occupied a stretch of enemy territory – but only in a horizontal position and not a vertical one. And once he failed, he would have 'no other card to play to defeat the Tripartite [Alliance]'. It was the Party's task to spread this idea 'not as a hope but as an absolute certainty'.[33] As he spoke the two corps commanders on Sicily were telling Guzzoni that their guns lacked munitions, fuses, spare barrels, telescopic sights and personnel.

A false alarm on 7 July led the defenders to think that the Allies were about to land near Marsala. Bad weather made an immediate attack seem unlikely. Then at 7.30 p.m. on 9 July came the news that convoys of enemy ships were approaching. A state of alarm was declared, and converted to a state of emergency at 1.10 the next morning following news that enemy paratroops had landed. When they learned that the Allies had landed on Sicily, the Italian generals who had just gone into captivity were reported by their captors to be optimistic. The English were 'not too keen on attacking mountains', and the Canadians and Americans were not trained for it. The outflanking movements that had worked in the desert were not going to work in Sicily. Sixth Army intelligence likewise undervalued their opponent, partly on the basis of the fact that it had taken the Americans three weeks to conquer Attu in the Aleutians in May and overcome 2,630 defenders, and partly on the basis of racial prejudices.

They expected that the Americans might use coloured troops who would be incapable of resisting a rapid reaction by the defenders and believed that all Americans, regardless of race, were incapable of manoeuvring at night or of fighting at close quarters.[34]

To defend the island, Guzzoni had two German divisions in place (*Hermann Goering* and 15th *Panzergrenadier*) and a third which arrived in the week following the attack (29th *Panzergrenadier*), two regiments of German parachutists and assorted flak, mortar and pioneer units – in all 28,000 Germans with 149 tanks (seventeen *Tigers*). Alongside them stood 175,000 Italians with 100 tanks and 490 field guns together with another 57,000 Italians and Germans in the service and support units. The *Regia Aeronautica* had 449 combat-worthy aircraft and the German *Luftflotte II* 563 to defend the skies against the enemy's 2,510 operational combat aircraft. On land, Sicily's defences were strung out: a single reinforced battalion with sixteen guns faced Lieutenant-General Leese's entire invading XXX Corps on the southeast corner of the island. The Americans, landing near Gela and Licata, faced stronger opposition in the shape of the 207th Italian coastal division and the *Hermann Goering* division. Thanks mainly to supporting fire from American warships standing off the coast, German and Italian counter-attacks failed. Siracusa fell on the first day and the port of Augusta fell to a small British landing party three days later – all too easily according to the Germans and to the local *Carabinieri* commander, who concluded that the port's main defences had been blown up prematurely and that a state of great confusion had prevailed from the outset. Signs of weakening Italian morale quickly began to appear. Sailors manning an armoured train tore up railway tracks to ensure that it could not get into position, and the crews of four ships at Messina abandoned them, making resupply from the mainland even more difficult.

As the Allied 7th and 8th Armies began pushing inland from the southern coast, Mussolini sent an urgent request to Hitler for air reinforcements. He got an immediate response. Hitler promised him 250 fighters and bombers in addition to 220 fighters already offered plus more by the end of July.[35] The battle of Kursk had begun a week earlier. Five days later General Jodl told Ambrosio that though Germany was ready to defend peninsular Italy 'as well as the north-east extremity of Sicily', he was unable to say when the promised air reinforcements would be made available, because of a production crisis in the German aeronautical manufacturing industry which would not be resolved for several months yet.[36] The number of planes allocated to the defence of the island fell precipitously over the week following the landings – from 198 Italian and 283 German planes on 11 July to seventy-six Italian and eighty-five German planes four days later. Lack of a single unified command and poor co-operation between the Italian and German air forces meant that the Axis airmen took to the skies in small and un-coordinated packets. The German and Italian bombers flew from bases on the mainland, leaving the island airfields mainly to the fighters and assault planes.[37] The battle-fleet did not sortie to help the island's defenders – as indeed Riccardi had said it would not. It was now being kept in reserve for a final desperate action when the moment came to defend the Italian peninsula, much to German displeasure. The idea that an armistice was probably nearing and that keeping a 'fleet in being' would give Italy a card to play in those negotiations may also have been in *Supermarina*'s mind.[38]

While the Allies were securing their first foothold on Sicily, Musso-lini met with Kesselring. The *Duce* was, as ever, free with strategic platitudes. There were three phases to the enemy action: landing, pene-tration, and occupation 'or invasion'. They were now in the second phase. The situation was 'delicate' but not 'desperate' and could be improved, but no time must be lost. When it came to actually grappling with what could be done Guzzoni was pessimistic, reporting that he could not hold western Sicily with the forces he had and doubting the value of sending more troops to the island. Kesselring thought the enemy had a two-to-one superiority in bombers and a two- or three-to-one superiority in fighters. Forty Axis fighters had just been destroyed in one strike at Trapani. Two days earlier he had visited the front in Sicily and come away with the impression that the Italian divisions were at sixes and sevens and the Italian commanders not up to the task. Now he was more upbeat: German planes had sunk or damaged 100,000 tons of enemy shipping in a single night, making the total lost so far 460,000 tons. Two days later he hoisted the figure to 740,000 tons. (In reality the Allies lost a total of 85,000 tons, including ships sunk while transferring from the Atlantic.) Both men were agreed that everything possible must be done to hold on to at least part of the island.[39] Mussolini ordered the navy and air force to deploy *en masse* to obstruct the enemy's reinforcements – something the navy had no intention of doing.

Ambrosio thought that the island's future would be decided very shortly thanks to the complete absence of any naval opposition, weak resistance in the air, inadequate weaponry, the scarcity and weakness of defensive works and the low-efficiency levels of the reserve divisions, and told Mussolini as much. Alarmed by what he was hearing, and already doubtful about the resilience of local units, Mussolini ordered Guzzoni to apply 'the most severe sanctions' to anyone no matter what their rank who was not 'completely fulfilling their duty as a soldier'. The Sicilian was a great fighter, he told a gathering of his top brass next day, 'but he must attack; on the defensive he's different.'[40] Some units were certainly fighting heroically and suffering heavy casualties in the process, but others were not. Shortly after Brigadier-General Gino Ficalbi took over the 202nd coastal division almost all his staff deserted, put on civilian clothes, and joined the local population to welcome the Allies. Later he told fellow captives that when it looked obvious that the Fascist hold on Sicily was over, the local population began breaking into the stores to steal things 'and when they saw we had been made prisoners, they all came along with sacks to see if they could get into our rooms and carry off something or other'. As they had all suffered a great deal he was inclined to be non-judgemental. Rear-Admiral Priamo Leonardi had gone around the countryside rounding up officers and men with his revolver but afterwards he felt that the task had been hopeless from the start. The Sicilian troops had been unreliable, the weapons and ammunition of poor quality, and 'in fact, everything was an absolute fiasco'.[41]

In Rome, Mussolini, Kesselring, Ambrosio and von Rintelen argued over whether or not to pull the Axis forces back to the north-east corner of the island. While they did so, further inroads were made into the island's defences. Catania was abandoned by its prefect when a naval bombardment began on 14 July, and the personnel of an entire militia battery deserted. Its commander was subsequently shot. Agrigento fell on 16 July, and so too did Porto Empedocle after a heavy naval bombardment. Guzzoni wanted to pull his forces back but the Germans were determined not to give ground unless forced to do so by the enemy. At the same time, and contradictorily, the two divisions of Lieutenant-General Francesco Zingales's XII Corps (*Assietta* and *Aosta*) were shuffled north-west to protect Palermo, isolating them and leaving them to their fate. Ambrosio intervened, and Guzzoni was ordered not to pull his forces back as he wanted to do. Shortly afterwards a personal envoy sent by Roatta arrived at Guzzoni's headquarters with a letter telling him that the *Duce* thought it essential to preserve a larger space for manoeuvre than Guzzoni had in mind. Disregarding this instruction, Guzzoni first ordered the three divisions of XVI Corps to pull back towards the north-east corner of the island and then reversed his decision two hours later.[42] The counter-order never reached two of his divisions, which now pulled back towards the centre of the island, and the third (the German *Sizilien* division) was also forced backwards thirty-six hours later after trying to stand its ground and fight.

With Guzzoni's capacity to conduct the defence of the island now evidently in doubt – he next countermanded his order to the *Assietta* division to defend the north-west and ordered it to the north-east – Roatta's envoy, General Gorlier, took over direction and set up a defensive arc in the mountains above Cefalù. Over the next few days, as the Allied air forces ground down the German and Italian air forces and unloaded avalanches of propaganda leaflets on the island's inhabitants, General George Patton's 7th Army drove north-west towards Palermo while General Montgomery's 8th Army and the 1st US division pushed north-east past Catania and towards Mount Etna. No less displeased with Guzzoni than Rome evidently was, the Germans took over direct command of all their forces in Sicily at midnight on 18 July. Next day, Hitler met Mussolini and treated him to an angry monologue in which he accused the Italians of ineptitude in allowing so many of their aircraft to be destroyed on the ground and the army of lacking any real will to fight. The former accusation at least had some basis in fact.[43]

As their masters conferred, the defenders of the island gave way – some with more alacrity than others. Palermo was abandoned by the prefect, the local party boss and most of the local Fascist hierarchy on 20 July and fell to the Americans two days later, its port still more or less intact. Guzzoni and Roatta called repeatedly for more air action to chase the enemy fighters out of captured Sicilian airfields, to strike at the resupply convoys, and to counter the bombing and machine-gunning of the rear, but both air forces were being relentlessly shot out of the skies. On 21 July the Italian air force withdrew to Sardinia and by 27 July not a single air detachment was left on the island and the squadron stationed in Puglia had more or less ceased offensive action. By 31 July the air force had only forty-one modern fighters fit for combat, together with eighty-three bombers and twenty-two torpedo aircraft.[44] Sicily cost both air forces dear. The *Regia Aeronautica* lost fifty planes destroyed on the ground and another 115 in combat, and *Luftflotte II* lost 118 aircraft on the ground and 273 in combat. Another 125 aircraft fell into American hands when they took Comiso.[45]

By 24 July the whole of western Sicily was in enemy hands. In the east of the island, a mainly German line reinforced by the newly arrived 29th *Panzergrenadier* division resisted pressure by Allied forces that were swinging west and north around the Catania plain and Mount Etna. The Italian forces in the central area of the island tried to pull back towards the north-east corner and Messina. Orders arrived late (one of Guzzoni's orders to Zingales took twenty-eight hours to reach him), and retreating battalions marched for up to forty kilometres under continuous attack from enemy aircraft and armoured units that had infiltrated their positions. Men began to desert. As the Italian and German forces were pressed back, the planners in Rome calculated that they could still ferry enough supplies – 1,900 tons of materials and 700 trucks a day – across the Straits of Messina to keep the bridgehead going. With the *Luftwaffe* concentrating on the ports the enemy was using, appeals to do something about enemy naval gunfire and mass bombing and machine-gunning at and behind the fronts lines went unanswered. General Fougier, his attention now focused more on possible enemy landings in Calabria, Sardinia and Corsica than on Sicily, could only offer the view that reinforcement of Sicily by air would always be possible 'but at great risk, with the certainty of serious losses, and in any case in less than necessary amounts'. The island's resistance, he predicted, would eventually be exhausted through insufficient supplies.[46]

When Hitler heard the news of Mussolini's fall on 25 July, his initial reaction was to abandon not just Sicily but the whole of southern and central Italy and pull back to the Pisa–Rimini line. He quickly changed his mind. Resistance on Sicily must be prolonged for as long as possible. Six days later, on orders from Rome, Guzzoni handed over command of the entire land front to General Hans-Valentin Hube, whose task was now to fight a delaying campaign. On the north side of the island the *Assietta* and *Aosta* divisions were crumbling as they fell back: on 3 August the *Assietta* was missing over 9,000 men and the *Aosta* almost 2,700 men. The *Aosta*'s divisional command and the *Assietta*'s infantry command left the island for Calabria that day – the Germans were not informed – and Guzzoni's 6th Army command followed three days later, along with all the surviving Italian units not necessary for the defence of the island. Over fourteen days (3–16 August), some 62,000 men, 45 guns, 227 motor vehicles and twelve mules were ferried across to the mainland. German units were now holding the entire front line. Determined counter-attacks could not hold back the tide. Catania fell on 5 August and so did Bronte, seat of Nelson's dukedom, three days later. Taormina was taken on 15 August and Messina fell the following night. Over the preceding six days the Germans ferried 39,569 men, 9,605 motor vehicles, 47 tanks, 94 field guns and 17,770 tons of munitions, fuel and other supplies across to safety on the mainland.[47]

The Sicilian campaign cost the Italians some 40,800 dead and missing and 116,681 prisoners of war. German losses added up to 8,900 dead and missing and 5,523 prisoners of war. The Allied armies suffered much less: 4,299 dead and 13,083 wounded. On the mainland, the troops and the population at large had watched the fighting anxiously, doubtful about whether the ill-equipped Italian armed forces could chase the invaders off the island and hopeful that the Germans might intervene more effectively. *Carabinieri* reports suggested that though the troops were grumbling about rations and boots, and were concerned about how their families at home were getting on, generally morale in the army as a whole still looked good.[48] What was happening on the island worried Roatta more than a little. Retreating civilians had blocked the roads, individual soldiers and even entire detachments had abandoned their positions, and Sicilian recruits brought in to defend their homeland had simply gone back to their families. The resulting disorders had been an 'indecorous spectacle' which had had a 'pernicious effect' on the mass of the troops. Order had only been restored by shooting soldiers and even officers. The same thing was not going to happen again. From now on, energetic action must be taken at the first signs of disorder, and, where soldiers or civilians did not obey all orders and instructions, they were to be 'shot on the spot'.[49]

MUSSOLINI'S FALL

Alarmed by what was happening in Sicily, Hitler had sent an urgent invitation to Mussolini on 17 July to meet him at a summit conference somewhere in Italy. Ambrosio armed himself with a list of eight specific requests for German help he had sent since 25 March, and the day before the meeting he asked Field Marshal Keitel how far he was going to be able to meet them. In reinforcing the Italians in southern Italy, he pointed out, the OKW was indirectly defending Germany, southern France and especially the Balkans.[50] The two warlords met at the Villa Gaggia near Feltre on 19 July. Neither man was at his best. Hitler, pallid and bent, looked a shadow of his former self and seemed to one observer to be living in the clouds.[51] Apart from interrupting briefly when he was brought the news that the Allies were bombing Rome, Mussolini sat silently in a deep armchair, shifting at times to rub his back, occasionally sighing deeply, and passing a handkerchief across his face. In a strident monotone that could be heard by underlings outside the room, Hitler subjected the *Duce* to a rambling, two-hour monologue which touched on the quality, or lack of it, of future generations, on weaponry ('perfection doesn't exist . . . one can never attain absolute superiority in everything'), on the importance of the Eastern Front, on aircraft ('We too need lots of aviation . . .'), and on the 'enormous importance' of decentralizing planes on the ground and protecting them there. The Italians came in for a good deal of criticism for their general 'casualness' and for not making up their minds whether they wanted to defend north, central or southern Italy or Sicily. The failed Allied attack on Dieppe had shown that it was best to snuff out attempted landings before the enemy had set foot on shore. Sicily must be defended, but to do so meant ensuring that the Straits of Messina and the ports being used to supply the island were protected against enemy action. Calabria and Puglia must also be defended. When it came down to details, however, it became apparent that Hitler was not going to provide the resources Ambrosio thought Italy had good reason to be given. Sending 2,000 aircraft was impossible. Italy was not going to get Stukas or special air formations. As for anti-aircraft and anti-tank guns, they were 'of vital importance for us'. Mussolini was advised to manufacture these modern weapons and new types of tank for himself, and to make sure that there was 'lots of organization and lots of order', especially behind the fighting lines.[52]

Ambrosio knew more or less what to expect. Travelling by train from Treviso to Feltre with Keitel, he was told that German strategy was to wear down and weaken the enemy in Russia while preparing fresh forces which would allow of active operations on the southern front, in Italy and in the Balkans next winter. When he objected that this would be to abandon the operational initiative he was told that Germany could not give more aircraft than Hitler had already promised, that she had no armoured division to spare, and that Italy would have to defend herself for the next two months by shifting her own divisions from the north and the centre to the south. German divisions could fill the gap as and when they arrived.[53] Learning before the invasion of Sicily that the Germans were quietly printing large numbers of maps of northern Italy despite having been given 'millions' of Italian maps, Ambrosio was already suspicious about his ally's intentions.[54] Having Germans crawling all over northern Italy while his own troops fought in the south was something he was not prepared to accept.

During the midday break Ambrosio did his best to make Mussolini look the situation in the face. Using blunt language, he told his master that there could be a military collapse within a fortnight. Mussolini must talk to Hitler and find a way out, otherwise what was presently a military crisis could be become an institutional and social crisis. If there was to be a political break-up, it was better that it happen while the state structure was still intact and the *Carabinieri* were still in control. After lunch, during which (according to his own account) Mussolini told Hitler that Italy's air defences must be strengthened, the two dictators passed a few moments in the garden and then spent another hour together in the train from Feltre to Treviso before taking to their respective aircraft. Exactly what was said during that train journey is not clear, but according to Mussolini he was promised more planes and fresh divisions as long as Italian requests were 'reasonable and not astronomic'. Ambrosio was incandescent. Mussolini had once again asked for reinforcements that the Germans would simply never send. The man was mad.[55]

Travelling back to Treviso in the train with Ambrosio, Keitel set out the conditions under which the Germans were prepared to make their support available. Southern Italy must be reinforced – it was 'the most delicate area and in the greatest danger' – and the OKW was prepared to provide two infantry divisions but Italy must do the same. Ambrosio, who was 'unforthcoming and monosyllabic', demurred: his divisions were needed to defend the coasts and counter a possible enemy attack in Lazio. Keitel laid down three essential conditions for the defence of Sicily: strong forward and rear defensive positions, secure resupply and strong defences in Calabria and Puglia, and a free hand for the military authorities in southern Italy to do whatever was necessary. Unless they were agreed, he would not ask Hitler for the two additional divisions. Ambrosio thought the question of divisions for southern Italy was 'a distant issue'. What Italy needed was urgent support. Showing some signs of controlled irritation, Keitel retorted that it all came down to whether they were going to fight all-out for Sicily and then possibly take the offensive – or not, in which case there was no point in sending further reinforcements there. Ambrosio stonewalled: he would re-examine the availability of Italian forces and the *Duce* would decide the bigger issues.[56] Mussolini flew back to Rome. Circling the city he saw the effects of the Allied bombing that day. The Littorio station was out of action, hundreds of railway wagons were burning, the engine depot and the entire district of San Lorenzo was a mass of flames and destruction. The damage seemed to him immense.

By the time of the Feltre meeting the army was ready to ditch Mussolini if given the right lead. In mid-March Ambrosio told Vittorio Emanuele that the dictator was simply a pawn in Hitler's hands and must be replaced by Badoglio. At the end of March the one-time head of SIM, Giacomo Carboni, recalled from command of an army corps in Sicily, arrived in Rome convinced (by his own account) of the need 'to fight an open and all-out battle against the military errors of the Fascist government, to save Italy'. Badoglio was manoeuvring to take up the opening: from May 1942 he was in contact with an SOE agent in Berne, and six months later he sent an agent to North Africa to negotiate his acceptance as Mussolini's successor at the head of an 'anti-Fascist Italian army'. Soon after Ambrosio took over as chief of the armed forces general staff, he and Badoglio opened direct contact with one another.[57] At first Ambrosio hoped that Mussolini would divorce Italy from her ally and then conclude an armistice with the Anglo-Americans. Then after Klessheim, convinced that Mussolini would never separate himself from Hitler, he ordered that plans be prepared for Mussolini's arrest. Temporarily set aside, they were revived as the Allies closed up on Sicily and Sardinia.[58]

As the fall of Sicily became ever more likely, the fate overhanging Italy began to appear inescapable. Everyone – including the wife of Crown Prince Umberto – seemed to be plotting but no one could come up with a clear path to a brighter future. To the conservative circle around the king a Badoglio government was one possible solution, but as one of them remarked that would only solve half the problem: 'The day that Mussolini is removed, the Germans will be on top of us.'[59] A small group of staff officers gathered around General Carboni and began to discuss whether they were obliged to become German cannon fodder simply because that was the *Duce*'s pleasure and whether there was not a way to free Italy of her erstwhile partner. Roatta was told of these mutterings by his chief of staff, but though he agreed that Italy must change direction if defeat was to be avoided he did not as yet see a way in which this could be done. Indeed, far from wanting the Germans out Roatta wanted more of them to come in. To defend the Italian peninsula, he needed more two or three more German armoured divisions to add to the three already in Italy, the lone Italian motorized division (*Piave*) and the two Italian armoured divisions that were being built up (*Ariete* and '*M*'). Together they would form three manoeuvre groups which he proposed to locate between Salerno and Puglia, in Campania and Lazio, and in Tuscany.[60]

After Feltre all the cards seemed to be up in the air but no one had any clear idea where or how they would land. Ambrosio offered his resignation and Mussolini rejected it. For a moment everything seemed to depend on the *Duce*, who was 'nailed to his position' by the Germans. The king seemed unwilling to take any initiative and was waiting for Mussolini to resign. The army, under Ambrosio's leadership, was waiting on the king. Preparing for the invasion that was surely coming – and perhaps also for a strike against the *Duce* – Ambrosio did some complicated juggling, building up a central reserve of regular units in mainland Italy and moving Blackshirt militia units away from Rome and other key locations. To make matters more complicated than they already were, on 21 July a motorized armoured division '*M*' was formed out of Fascist militia units and placed under the command of General Carboni, who announced that he knew of the plans to move against Mussolini and the Fascist regime and stood ready to scotch them.[61] The issue for the armed forces leadership and many in government was how to get Italy out of the war more or less in one piece and not split into two zones, one occupied by the Germans and the other by the Allies. That at least was how ambassador Luca Pietromarchi saw things three days before Mussolini fell.[62]

Finally Vittorio Emanuele III, who by his own later account had decided to end Mussolini's regime in January, was propelled into action. Faced with a kaleidoscope of unpalatable possibilities which included a revolt by the generals, the offer of the crown to his son Prince Umberto, Mussolini's assassination, and the outbreak of civil war, and stimulated by the bombing of Rome on 19 July, he summoned Mussolini and tried to persuade him to go of his own accord, telling him that he was an obstacle to internal renewal and to a 'resolution' of the military situation. 'It was as if I had talked to the wind,' he told his aide-de-camp.[63] That settled matters. Mussolini would be dismissed when he came for his regular audience on Monday 26 July and replaced by Marshal Badoglio. As it turned out, the Fascist Party moved first. The Fascist Grand Council met on 24–25 July and passed a motion removing the *Duce* from office. On Sunday 25 July Mussolini went to the king's personal residence, Villa Savoia, where he was arrested by loyal *Carabinieri* as he left the building. At 10.45 that evening a radio announcement in the king's name declared Marshal Badoglio the new head of government, and another in Badoglio's name promised that Italy would keep to its word and carry on fighting the Allies.

Badoglio sent General Enrico Ferone to Mussolini in the *Carabinieri* barracks in Prati to tell him that he had been arrested for his own safety and ask him where he would like to be taken. Although it was nearly midnight the streets were thronged with people applauding the king, Badoglio and the army, and cursing Mussolini and Fascism. Mussolini asked to be taken to his home at Rocca delle Caminate and expressed 'contentment' that the war would continue. The war, he told Ferone, was not lost: 'If Germany succeeds in stopping the haemorrhage it's suffering in the fields of Russia so that it can bring all its weight [across] to the West . . .'[64] Carmine Senise, appointed chief of police that very day, ruled out sending the former *Duce* to Rocca delle Caminate on the grounds that 'he would not be safe from the fury of the people'.[65] Mussolini began a forty-five-day odyssey that took him first to exile on the island of Ponza, then to La Maddalena and finally to Gran Sasso in the Apennines.

At 9.30 that night Hitler was told what had happened in Rome. He was enraged. Mussolini's removal was a 'betrayal', Badoglio's assertion that Italy would continue to fight alongside Germany was 'untruthful nonsense' – 'If only I could catch this filthy pig!' But though caught by surprise the Führer was not caught unprepared. Several months earlier he had ordered Keitel to prepare an operation, code-named ALARIC, to take control of northern Italy in the event of an Italian volte-face. Faced with a coup like that which had overthrown King Paul in April 1941, Hitler was 'determined to strike like lightning . . . just as I did in Yugoslavia'. Orders went out immediately to take control of the northern passes into Italy, two divisions (26th *Panzer* and 4th Parachute) were on the move within hours, and over the next two weeks eight German divisions were funnelled into northern Italy.[66]

Mussolini's sudden removal from office presented the army, the king and Badoglio with an almost impossible complex of problems. Incidents between the army and the Fascist Blackshirt militia were one. That was quickly solved by replacing the head of the MVSN, General Enzo Galbiati, with Badoglio's former deputy General Quirino Armellini, though the loyalty of some at least of the Blackshirt units remained doubtful. Public order was another. There was trouble in Milan which the local commanding general seemed unable to cope with, and also in Rome at the Ostiense and Trastevere railway stations and in the via Salaria district. Demonstrations in the major cities and towns of northern Italy calling for peace threatened to open a third front just when the army was facing the Allies on home territory and at the same time having to handle increasingly fraught relations with the Germans – according to some sources there was a fifth column of some 6,000 well-armed Germans already inside Rome itself. The new War Minister, General Antonio Sorice, was sure that the demonstrators were acting under orders coming from 'a single directing centre' and the chief of police pointed the finger at the communists.[67] Roatta ordered a crackdown, telling his commanders that 'A little blood spilled at the outset will save rivers of blood later.' When faced with disorder, troops were not to fire into the air but must also shoot to hit 'as in combat'.[68] All available divisions were deployed and by the end of July the army was in control of the domestic arena again – but only momentarily.

As far as handling relations with the Germans was concerned, force was not an option. Reports from Berlin that Hitler felt himself even more closely bound to Mussolini, and intelligence that the Germans were readying a parachute division for immediate despatch to Italy, led the king to approve precautionary measures against the Germans on 28 July, but, as everyone knew, the army was in no position to start fighting its ally. The situation for public order looked serious; there appeared to be a real possibility that the Germans might try to seize the new authorities; and only half a dozen of the divisions in metropolitan Italy were capable of fighting at all, only one of which – the *Piave* motorized division – was ready to face a modern, well-armed enemy.[69]

General von Rintelen put the critical question to Ambrosio the day after Mussolini's fall: what line was the new administration going to follow regarding the war? Ambrosio relayed this to the king, and, on 30 July, Vittorio Emanuele backed Badoglio's line: the new regime would continue the fight alongside its ally.[70] Tasked with relaying Badoglio's assurance that Italy would stay in the war to Hitler, the Italian military attaché Efisio Marras had a difficult interview in which the Führer did not disguise his distrust and resentment, followed by another in which ambassador Walther Hewel told him bluntly that the Germans believed the Italian army had shown itself to be unreliable.[71] There was good reason to fear a German reaction. Four days after Mussolini was seized General Amé, the head of Italian military intelligence, met the head of the *Abwehr*, Admiral Canaris, for lunch at the Hotel Danieli in Venice. At that meeting Amé, who was a fervent monarchist and a Badoglio supporter, learned that the German *Sicherheitsdienst* was planning to rescue Mussolini and kill Vittorio Emanuele and Pope Pius XII. The two intelligence chiefs agreed that Canaris would tell Hitler that the Badoglio government remained completely loyal to Hitler.[72]

MARSHAL BADOGLIO'S FORTY-FIVE DAYS

Some of the heads of the armed forces fell with Mussolini. Admiral Raffaele de Courten became the new Navy Minister (replacing Mussolini) and chief of the naval staff (replacing Admiral Riccardi); General Renato Sandalli became Air Minister (replacing Mussolini) and chief of the air staff (replacing Fougier); and Brigadier-General Antonio Sorice became War Minister (replacing Mussolini). Badoglio left Ambrosio and Roatta in post. As chief of the army general staff, Roatta had two immediate concerns. Although the OKW did not believe there was a threat to central Italy, there was mounting evidence that the Germans had stopped sending troops to southern Italy and were building up a growing force north and south of Rome while at the same time moving four infantry and four armoured divisions into Liguria, Emilia and Romagna to protect their lines of communications. This suggested to him that the Germans were planning to hold the Po valley and defend it along the line of the Apennines. This was contrary to Italian interests. The army wanted the defences in Calabria, Puglia and Liguria reinforced and the reserves distributed between southern Italy, Campania–Lazio and Tuscany–Liguria. But there could be more to it than that. Among other things, the Germans were moving an entire SS corps – 'troops [who are] extremist by definition, and of a specifically political colouring' – into Italy. There were also indications from Athens that the Germans had a plan to disarm Italian forces in Greece. The obvious conclusion was that they intended either to restore Fascism or to install a puppet government, in which case Italy would become another Norway or Denmark. Setting aside 'possible political solutions', the high command needed to concentrate its own troops so as to be able to fend off 'future intolerable German interference', and also decide whether to defend the entire peninsula to the last or follow German ideas and concentrate all available forces in the north.[73] Ambrosio was in no doubt: the whole of peninsular Italy must be defended, and Italian divisions must predominate in central and northern Italy. The behaviour of the Germans presently in Italy, which they were now treating as an occupied country, 'must be totally changed'.[74]

On 5 August Badoglio and Ambrosio advised the king that the Germans be told that it was impossible for Italy to continue the war. Fearing immediate German reprisals which would have 'very serious repercussions on internal order', Vittorio Emanuele refused his consent.[75] Badoglio wanted a meeting with Hitler to 'clarify' matters, but the Führer turned him down. Instead, on 6 August, Ambrosio and the new Foreign Minister, Raffaele Guariglia, met Foreign Minister Ribbentrop and Field Marshal Keitel at Tarvisio. Ambrosio went armed with a long list of strategic complaints and a warning. The Germans, who had never had 'a realistic and panoramic view of the Axis's war', had fought 'the German war'. Economically they had forced the Italians to compete for the resources of occupied countries, thus indirectly weakening the military possibilities in the Mediterranean, and they even appeared to be deliberately despoiling Italy by buying up scarce goods there with money provided by the Italians. Their 'incomprehension' of the importance of the Mediterranean theatre was explicable during the first three years of the war, but no longer. It was obvious now that the Anglo-Americans were going to break into fortress Europe in the Mediterranean and that almost certainly meant the military defeat of the Axis.[76]

Ribbentrop began by telling the Italians that the 'disappearance' of the *Duce* suggested that the Italians might be intending to change their foreign policy, that the internal situation and the threat posed by the communists were 'preoccupying' his government, and that German faith in them needed to be restored. As for the general strategic picture, the Soviet Union was on the point of defeat and following that up with the defeat of Great Britain and the United States was nothing to worry about. Guariglia assured the Germans that Italy would continue the war, that she recognized she could not pursue an autonomous policy, because her armed forces were 'interlinked' with those of the Germans, and that a communist victory would be 'fatal to all'. Ambrosio told them that the military had had nothing to do with the overthrow of Mussolini. Then he raised the matter of German forces in Italy. The *Comando Supremo* had been 'more than a little surprised' at the speed with which German divisions had been sent into Italy. The positions they were taking up, which were 'not in accord with the common interest', gave him the impression that they had abandoned the forces in southern Italy. Ribbentrop and Keitel batted away the accusation that their troops seemed to be more concerned with public order than fighting the Allies, blaming the state of Italian railways for Ambrosio's sense that he was not the military master of his own house. Ambrosio in turn dismissed Keitel's suggestion that the Allies might attack northern Italy and announced he was pulling the entire 4th Army back from France and three divisions from 2nd Army in the Balkans on the grounds that it was 'not acceptable that the majority of units defending the peninsula are German not Italian'. His main problem, though, was not land power but air power. Finally, he told Keitel that Italy was not occupied territory and that the Germans should adjust their behaviour accordingly.[77] His orders withdrawing troops from beyond Italy went out two days later.[78]

Both sides left Tarvisio distrusting the other. The Germans flatly rejected an Italian move to put the German division guarding the Brenner Pass under their authority, something that had not been agreed at Tarvisio, and accused the Italians of masking their intentions behind a 'lack of clarity'.[79] Italian opinions about what to do next were divided as both immediate and longer-term political considerations became bound up with strategic and operational issues. Castellano believed that Hitler would likely decide to act against his one-time ally. If he did so Italian forces in the centre of Italy would face a two-front internal war against German units in northern and southern Italy. Italy was in no condition to take on such a struggle and needed aid. She should tell the Allies that she was willing to come over to their side 'if they will give us the assurance of their immediate aid'.[80] Pietromarchi too believed that the Italians should abandon the German alliance and take sides with the Allies. Lieutenant-General Giacomo Zanussi thought that Italy should break with the Germans without necessarily making a prior agreement with the Allies. Ambrosio's deputy, General Francesco Rossi, thought the first move should be to clarify the situation with the United Nations.

Ambrosio now took a practical step towards the separation that he had been trying for some months to engineer. Three days after the Tarvisio meeting he ordered Castellano to draw up a plan for severing relations with Germany. Castellano assumed that it was out of the question to try to concentrate Italian troops in any one region of Italy and that the struggle would 'necessarily assume a fragmentary character'. Italian divisions would therefore be shifted into key positions in northern Italy, around Rome, and in defence of La Spezia, Gaeta and Taranto. In the Balkans hostilities against the partisans would end, the Italians would make common cause with the Četniks, and Dalmatia would be evacuated, as would Corsica, which would free two crack divisions. The government and the *Comando Supremo* would remain in Rome 'for very important morale reasons' and the king would put to sea in a battleship to await developments or go to Sardinia.[81] When shown the scheme, Roatta said that he would only put the military elements of the plan into operation when he had the king's express approval to do so.[82]

On 10 August the king agreed that contacts should be opened with the Allies but refused to allow the envoy any official accreditation. Castellano left for Portugal two days later. His instructions were to explain Italy's military situation, find out the Allies' intentions and get their help in detaching Italy from Germany, preferably in the form of landings north of Rome and north of Rimini.[83] He was not empowered to discuss the terms of an armistice between the two sides, which quickly became the core issue in the discussions in Lisbon. Nobody seems to have given any serious thought as to whether the Allies were capable of carrying out either landing at any time in the immediate future. Intelligence forwarded by SIM as Castellano left indicated only that an enemy attack on the mainland was imminent, and that it might be accompanied by attacks on Sardinia and Corsica. Ambrosio moved two Italian divisions to the south and ordered Roatta to arrange for more German units to move there too.[84]

Italian actions were grating with the German high command. At Bologna on 15 August Jodl and Rommel took Roatta and Rossi to task. First they challenged the decision to withdraw the 4th Army from France. When Roatta explained that even leaving two coastal divisions there represented a considerable sacrifice as there were parts of the Italian coast where a single battalion was covering a front of 175 kilometres, Rommel merely laughed. Then they challenged the distribution of Italian units in the peninsula. Their troops, who were moving down it to help the Italians defend their country, were 'stupefied' when they saw Italian units travelling up it to the northern valleys. Roatta countered: two incomplete Italian divisions were being moved into the area to protect the Brenner railways as had been agreed at Tarvisio, and that was all. The Germans were sending troops across the frontier by train and on foot without prior notice and German officers had forced Italian railwaymen to send their trains onward at gunpoint. The first German units to cross the frontier had marched in combat formation. If the Italians had chosen to judge by appearances, they would have had reason to believe that the movements 'were not of a friendly character'. And there was more – much more. Among other things, a German general had demanded the keys to all the Italian fortifications on the frontier.[85]

Eventually Roatta stopped rehearsing Italian complaints and suggested a compromise. Both sides should clear their troops out of the

frontier, leaving only anti-aircraft defences. General Jodl was not prepared to sign up to that. The defence of the lines of communication was
a matter of interest to the Germans '[in view of] the variety of solutions
that Italian policy might adopt'. There had been, as he put it, a 'special
[kind of] revolution, put down by force'. Whether you called it a
'revolution' or, as Roatta preferred, 'manifestations of a revolutionary
character' (which Roatta claimed had now been suppressed), Italy had
not, he pointed out to Jodl, always been a friend of Germany – except
under Fascism. Jodl wanted an agreed joint role for the Germans on
seven railway lines running into Italy right along the arc of the northern frontier. Roatta was determined that the area should not fall under
German control. 'Why do you think we can't guarantee the security
of the [railway] communications?' he asked. 'I could ask you why you
need German troops fighting in Italy,' Jodl countered. A regime that
had lasted twenty years had disappeared in a moment. Who could
guarantee that the new government would not shortly be replaced in its
turn? If that happened, Jodl continued, the Italian troops might abandon their posts and then the job of defending the railway communications
would anyway fall to the Germans.[86]

Parking the issue of who should defend Italian communications, the
Germans moved on to the strategic justification for their force dispositions. The OKW did not think that the Allies would try to invade Italy
'piece by piece' starting with Calabria and Puglia. They wanted a
'robust' concentration of force in northern Italy ready to act against
possible landings in Liguria and Tuscany, to protect central Italy, and
to form a general reserve for whatever other action in the peninsula
might be necessary. The Italians wanted the spread of their own and
German forces to defend not just northern Italy but the centre 'and
above all the south'. If they were lost not only would there be moral,
material and political repercussions but also the Axis occupation of the
Balkans, Greece and the Aegean islands would be in serious danger.
And Italians must be in command. The Germans intended that Rommel should command all the Italian and German troops in northern
Italy. That, and the question of whether there was to be a unified command in Italy, was left for future resolution by those higher up the
chain of command. Closing the meeting, Jodl told the Italians that the
Russians had lost heavily in the battle of Kursk, the Germans less so –
and their losses were easily replaceable. Now the Russians could only

carry out actions at a limited range, which they were doing. Their current efforts would preclude them launching a winter offensive. The German intentions were simple: 'the Russians must exhaust themselves.'[87]

The news that Rommel would be in command of the German troops in northern Italy, and the obvious intention to put him in command if units in the north were funnelled south to meet an Allied invasion, did not go down well. Ambrosio saw it as 'unequivocal evidence' of the Germans' 'complete lack of faith' in their ally and lodged a formal protest: Rommel was 'associated with all the events in North Africa and Tunisia', whence he had been recalled, and was also senior in rank to both himself and Roatta.[88] Then more alarming news arrived. Rommel's Army Group B in northern Italy would comprise seven German divisions, including an entire SS corps of three divisions – not the single SS division Jodl had alluded to at Bologna.[89] Next the Germans tabled proposals for joint command arrangements which would give Army Group B – and therefore Rommel – effective command over all troops in northern Italy, including the Italian 4th and 8th Armies, and asked for approval for Rommel to exchange ideas with their commanders for the defence of the region. Doubtless all too well aware of what giving Rommel command would mean, and probably alarmed too at losing control over Italian troops in northern Italy just as tensions between the two allies were mounting, Ambrosio refused permission for Rommel to contact the Italian army commanders and reserved his position on the command arrangements – which included German command over all the Italian units in the Balkans and the Aegean.[90]

As the arrival of Allied armies on the shores of mainland Italy grew ever nearer the strategic dispute and the political tensions that were intimately bound up with it intensified. At the Bologna meeting Roatta had asked for six additional German divisions to defend the south. The Germans served notice that the four reconstituted divisions withdrawn from Sicily would form part of the six-division force. That was all the Italians were going to get, and if their resupply could not be guaranteed then some of them would be pulled back north of Rome. The German deployment in central Italy was essential because of the 'total uncertainty about enemy plans for a landing', and the 2nd Parachute division was located there so that it could move rapidly in whatever direction was required. The German forces in northern Italy formed a reserve in case the enemy, moving across Sardinia, threatened the coasts of Liguria and southern France, and would also be in place if the situation in the Balkans grew more menacing.[91] The balance of Axis forces inside Italy was steadily tipping against the Italians: in mid-August twenty-six regular Italian divisions shared the peninsula with sixteen German divisions, two of the latter armoured.[92]

At this moment the short-lived domestic order enforced by the army at the end of July collapsed as strikes and demonstrations began in Lombardy and Piedmont. Heavy bombing raids on the northern industrial cities during the spring, which left Genoa 'little more than a heap of rubble', triggered mounting popular protest.[93] Ambrosio was worried that the defence of continental Italy was being made increasingly hazardous because of the number of troops being diverted from national defence to maintain public order.[94] To reinforce the ranks, he planned to recall to service all available men aged between twenty-one and thirty-six not currently serving.[95] On 19 August, after ten days of Allied bombing which killed 510 people and caused heavy damage, 35,000 workers in Turin went on strike. The army high command drew up defensive instructions (OP 44), ready next day but not released until the first days of September, to safeguard vital installations against attempts by the Germans, the Fascists or communists to restore the old regime or topple the new one.[96] The disorders calmed down momentarily when Leopoldo Piccardi, the Minister of Corporations, told the strikers' leaders that the government had started peace talks with the Allies, but by the beginning of September at least 3,500 people had been arrested in twenty major cities and sentenced to between six months and eighteen years in prison.[97] Public order duties were taking up too many divisions and Ambrosio ordered that they be disentangled from that task and made available for action as quickly as possible. A third of his tanks and armoured cars were in vehicle parks, reserve units and training centres. They were to be used 'as much as possible' to maintain public order.[98]

As August ended, German troops continued to pour into Italy, turning the coast between Livorno and Viareggio into something resembling a foreign tourist resort according to the local Italian commander: 'between the sea and the pinewoods, naked bathing, sun, and all the comforts – a true paradise on earth!'[99] Minor incidents exacerbated an increasingly tense situation. In Verona the *Luftwaffe* filched 45,000 bottles of wine belonging to the Italian air force. At Castel Porziano three German parachutists broke through the wire surrounding the royal estate one night and shot one of the king's deer. The *Carabinieri* reported widespread and mounting public deprecation of a hopeless and destructive war and increasing hostility towards the Germans.[100] The *Comando Supremo* complained: Italy was not an occupied country and therefore no military steps should be taken without common agreement first. German troops were advancing beyond the agreed positions on the frontier. What, Rossi asked von Rintelen, were the OKW's intentions with regard to making and adhering to common regulations? The German response was immediate and brusque. The protection of the sixteen German divisions in Italy was more important than the prestige of the Italian army. If the Italian army was ordered to use force against its ally, then 'incalculable consequences' would follow.[101] Ambrosio warned Badoglio about German behaviour and asked him to act. The Germans were using the Italian railway system to speed their troops down the country while at the same time sending in only one-third of the agreed coal deliveries and less than a fifth of the fuels promised. It looked to him like 'a premeditated plan progressively to deprive Italy of the means [that are] indispensable to [our] life and [our] defence', which would in turn allow Germany to become 'the arbiter of our decisions' and put her in 'undisturbed command'.[102]

While Ambrosio and Roatta tussled with the Germans, Castellano was in Lisbon trying to persuade the Allies that when they landed in Italy the Italian government would be ready to join them and that in these circumstances Italy should become a partner in a military alliance. He was told bluntly that the Italian government had a choice: accept the proposed armistice terms or reject them. There was no question, for the time being at least, of Italy being regarded by the British and American governments as an ally. The terms included the immediate cessation of hostilities by the Italian armed forces, their withdrawal from all participation in the current war, the immediate handing over of the Italian fleet and Italian aircraft and the surrender of all Italian territory to the Allies for them to use as they thought fit. Other political, economic and financial conditions, with which Italy must comply, would follow at a later date. With no mandate to discuss an armistice, and having tried – and failed – to tease out something about the Allied plans for a landing in Italy, Castellano returned to Rome with the terms in his hand and the demand for an answer by 30 August.[103]

Castellano reached Rome on 27 August to discover that Ambrosio was on leave – 'lucky fellow!' Accompanied by Rossi and Guariglia, he saw Badoglio, gave an account of his trip, and read out the armistice terms. Badoglio, who gave Castellano 'the impression of an imbecile', said nothing other than to ask for copies of the original documents.[104] Guariglia thought that if the Italians asked for an armistice 'the Germans would butcher us'. He wanted the Anglo-Americans to invade first, with the Italians putting up no resistance, and only after they were firmly established would Italy lay down its arms. He also wanted to take over the negotiations so that he could put minimizing the damage the Germans could do to Italy front and centre. Castellano thought the Foreign Minister's plan 'simply childish'.[105] Ambrosio was minded to accept the Allies' terms immediately and he and Castellano convinced the king's chief adviser, the Duke of Acquarone. What happened next is best told in Castellano's own words:

> At eleven [a.m. on 29 August], I accompanied Ambrosio to the Quirinale Palace. The King, through Acquarone, states that the head of government will decide and then he will give the last word. Badoglio, Ambrosio and Guariglia hold a meeting in a private room. A few minutes later they go to see the King. Upon coming out, Ambrosio made a sign to the effect that the answer had been negative.

The meeting had been ill-tempered. Badoglio emerged from it in a very bad mood, and Guariglia accused Ambrosio of insulting him in front of the king by saying that decisions were being affected by personal fear.[106]

Castellano was instructed neither to accept nor refuse the Allied terms. Instead he was to obtain what the powers-that-be believed was indispensable: that the Allies would land first and then the armistice would be officially proclaimed. As he was preparing to leave, news arrived that fresh terms were on their way from Lisbon. General Carboni, now Badoglio's intelligence co-ordinator as well as commanding the 'M' division, had been kept at arm's length from Castellano's mission but had been tasked by Badoglio with organizing a follow-up mission by Lieutenant-General Zanussi.[107] In fact, no new terms arrived. Accordingly, Castellano was sent back to meet the Allies in Sicily with Badoglio's gloss on the conditions discussed the previous day with the king. Before the Italian government could announce that it was accepting the armistice conditions, the Allies must land at least fifteen divisions on the mainland, most of them between Civitavecchia and La Spezia. Italian airfields would be put at their disposal.

In the swirling discussions that were now going on the four men at the head of the cast list in Rome were pursuing separate agendas. Some converged, others did not. The king, seen by many as the only secure point in a collapsing world, hovered in the wings, undecided and inactive, with no political ideas of his own but determined to guard his dynasty's position. As far as he was concerned, royal interests and national interests were one and the same thing.[108] Badoglio wanted to stage-manage events in such a way as to stop the Germans from taking reprisals against the high command, the government and the king (and, no doubt, himself) if Italy changed sides without firm Allied protection. That required the utmost secrecy. To achieve that he was ready to sacrifice what remained of Italy's army overseas. There was, he told Ambrosio in the last week of August, 'plenty of time to issue orders and that, in keeping [the armistice secret] he expected to lose half a million men in the Balkans'.[109] Before, during and after the Feltre meeting Ambrosio had wanted to sever relations with Germany. Now, according to Castellano, his 'unstable will power' was waning and he lacked the courage to act, 'fearful of putting the country to fire and sword'.[110] Roatta intended to continue the war in alliance with Germany until policy changed. In the meantime there must be no incident with the German troops now flooding into the country. His immediate preoccupation was the maintenance of public order, actively challenged by the increasing public demonstrations and potentially threatened by the Fascist Blackshirt militia whose present inactivity gave no indication of whether or not they were still loyal to Mussolini.

At Cassibile on 30 August Castellano told the Allies what the Italian government wanted: landings north and south of Rome (the bulk of them to the north), which the Italians would initially oppose for a short time, after which they would announce the armistice. He was turned down flat. The armistice must be accepted or declined by midnight on 2 September. Castellano asked whether he could indeed assume that fifteen Allied divisions would land, most of them north of Rome. General Walter Bedell Smith told him that with a bridgehead of fifteen divisions the Allies would not need an armistice. Twice Castellano asked Bedell Smith if the Allies intended to land north of Rome and twice Bedell Smith declined to give him an answer. The most he would say was that landings would be made 'as far north as possible taking into consideration the range of fighter support'. In discussion it was made clear to Castellano that if the armistice terms were accepted there would be two landings: a 'secondary' landing of five or six divisions against Italian opposition, followed after a week or two by a second 'principal' landing of nine or ten divisions south of Rome.[111] Bedell Smith was prepared to consider landing a parachute division near Rome on the night of the armistice declaration. Castellano asked for a simultaneous landing by an armoured force at Ostia, but got no definite answer.[112]

Roatta was worrying about the state of army morale. In July, Ambrosio had reassured the king that discipline in the army was 'always improving'.[113] Now, soldiers returning from Sicily knew that the local population had behaved in a 'wholly unpatriotic way', that some units, including an entire battalion of Blackshirt militia 'with its commander at its head', had surrendered, that some Sicilian officers had put on civilian clothes and gone home, and that parts of the civilian population had welcomed the invaders with open arms. The official encomiums for the island's defenders were having a counter-productive effect, and soldiers were asking themselves whether doing their duty was worth it. On top of this, labour unrest, with its demands for immediate peace and the ejection of the Germans, was 'leaking' into the junior officer corps. Apparently contemplating a re-enactment in Italy of the first Russian revolution, Roatta sketched a scenario in which the 'consent' which underpinned army morale dissolved and the soldiers demanded that the war and the politics connected with it be discussed with them. The reports of instability appearing in the press could only increase German distrust of its ally 'and confirm [them] in their possible intention to do us harm'. His solutions: the military tribunals should be stiffened and soldiers who took part in demonstrations and the officers who allowed them to do so should be threatened with the most severe punishment.[114]

Ambrosio warned Badoglio on the day Castellano got back to Rome that army morale, 'already not excessively brilliant as a result of military events', had been weakened by the conviction that the fall of Mussolini and the change of government would automatically lead to peace, and by reports of how parts of the Sicilian population had behaved. The rapid collapse of some Sicilian units even before the enemy attacked them was in striking contrast with the way official propaganda had talked up the population. Unable, unlike the 'cultivated classes', to understand the reasons that had led the authorities to keep silent about how the islanders had behaved, the troops had concluded that it was not worth doing their duty 'if those people who don't are praised [anyway]'. But the reverberations of the Sicilian battles were not the only, and certainly not the chief, problem. The soldiers, far from home, deprived of leave, poorly paid, and never praised for their discipline ('considered a natural phenomenon'), could only draw negative conclusions from the fact that the factory workers, who lived at home and were better paid, could abandon their work, discuss military problems with the authorities, be listened to, and then be publicly praised for their discipline. At the present time this was 'the most serious danger' for the armed forces, and could lead to the creation of workers' and soldiers' councils 'as elsewhere in the past'. Moreover, the government's current practice and the news it was generating 'increased German distrust' and strengthened German intentions 'to "occupy us" and control all our national activities'. Harking back to norms that had been established in the last years of the previous century, Ambrosio warned the head of the government that the armed forces were the only bulwark against forces that threatened to split the country apart. All 'exaltations' of the discipline of the working class 'just when it is giving evidence of the opposite' had to cease.[115]

Castellano returned to Rome on 31 August. Next day Badoglio summoned the principals. Ambrosio and Guariglia were for accepting the terms. Carboni was against doing so: for one thing the Allies' word could not be trusted, and for another as the man responsible for the defence of Rome he claimed that his troops did not have the fuel and munitions they would need to fight the Germans. The Duke of Acquarone somewhat half-heartedly agreed with the majority. The king then agreed to accept the Allies' conditions, and Castellano was sent back to sign the armistice, which he did on 3 September. The main military dimensions of the agreement were clear. There would be an Allied landing in force south of Rome, an Allied parachute action near Rome, and the simultaneous announcement of the armistice. Castellano had done what he was required to do and secured concrete armistice terms

– though the suspicion remains that by using a relatively junior general with no official authorization as their emissary some or all of the powers-that-be in Rome were keeping open the opportunity to hang him out to dry if that became necessary. The issue now was how the switch-over was to be handled. Here there were unresolved loose ends. The Italians wanted their declaration to follow an Allied landing, but the Allies insisted that the two be simultaneous. In that case the timing would be in the Allies' hands: the best Castellano could say was that it would be on or around 12 September. As the landings were going to be in the south the Italians would have to save Rome themselves, which the Allies thought they should be able to do, though General Eisenhower was prepared to send an airborne division to Rome.

Calling his three service ministers, Ambrosio and Acquarone together in the afternoon of 3 September, Badoglio told them that the armistice negotiations were under way – but did not apparently tell them that the decision had been taken to accept them, or indeed that they had been signed. He then gave them specific details of the forthcoming Allied operations: small-scale landings in Calabria, then a six-division landing near Naples, then a paratroop landing near Rome. In the meantime Carboni's six divisions and the Italian 4th Army, which had been occupying part of Vichy France and was presently trickling back, would be concentrated around Rome. How he knew in such detail about the Allied landing is something of a mystery: Bedell Smith had resolutely refused to reveal any details, and in his report to the principals on 1 September Castellano had said only that it would take place 'in an unspecified location'.[116] It would appear that Badoglio made no mention of Carboni's intervention two days earlier, which undermined the entire scheme, and certainly no orders were issued.

After calling the three chiefs of staff together, putting them in the picture, and ordering them to prepare the operations needed to support the Allied landings that might begin as soon as 12 September, Ambrosio left Rome on 6 September on a mysterious two-day trip to Turin, ostensibly to retrieve documents that he did not want to fall into German hands. In his absence the deal that Castellano had constructed on the government's behalf started to collapse as the doubts about whether the Italian army could resist the Germans resurfaced. Taking his stand on the lack of fuel and ammunition, and showing signs of what some would afterwards interpret as a preference for fighting with them and not against them, Carboni told anyone who would listen that fighting the Germans would be suicidal. When General Rossi, formerly Intendant of the Army, found him supplies of both, Carboni simply ignored him. He would shortly tell the American envoy, Brigadier-General Maxwell Taylor, that there was no fuel, even though there was in fact a large depot on the Rome–Ostia road still in Italian hands.[117]

The planned Allied landing was too far from Rome, so the *Comando Supremo* wanted the Italian request for an armistice to follow several days later. Whenever it was made, Italy should not initiate hostilities against the Germans immediately, because Rome would quickly be crushed by the two German divisions stationed nearby and others that would swiftly follow from the north. Carboni claimed, and Roatta apparently concurred, that there was no question of the Italian army resisting the Germans for several days unless the Germans were simultaneously fighting the Americans. So the planned parachute landing (Operation GIANT) should not take place, as in current circumstances it was almost certain to lead to failure. A letter went off to Castellano setting out Rome's reservations and its new conditions.[118]

On 2 September Ambrosio reported to the king that there were now nineteen German divisions in or en route to Italy, twelve of them in or heading for northern and central Italy.[119] Faced with both internal and external threats to the new regime, the *Comando Supremo* issued OP 44 the same day. Exactly what it said is impossible to establish – all twelve copies were burned on the morning of 9 September – but it appears to have given instructions about defending command centres, barracks, supply dumps, electrical plant, railways and ports in case force was being used to remove Badoglio and bring Mussolini back to power. Commanders were told that they would get a telephone order to activate it, or they should do so on their own initiative according to the local situation. Some generals only saw it at the eleventh hour and others seemingly never did.[120] Three days later General Caracciolo di Feroleto went to the army general staff headquarters at Monterotondo outside Rome for instructions. He found the general staff there 'in great agitation'. Intelligence from secure sources indicated that the Germans were organizing a *coup de main* to seize the leading personalities of the *Comando Supremo*, the Badoglio government and the Royal Household. Roatta, who confirmed the news, was now returning to Rome every night and sleeping at a secret location.[121]

In a situation that was fast becoming chaotic, the *Comando Supremo* issued two follow-up orders on 6 September. The first (PM 1) went to armed forces' staffs and told them that if the Germans began hostilities against the government or themselves they must take steps to defend Rome and especially the roads leading to it, assure fuel supplies, interrupt German telephone communications and defend power stations. The Germans were expected to destroy everything 'along the line of their retreat (presumably Naples–Rome–Florence–Bologna–Brenner Pass)'. The navy was to capture or sink German warships and merchantmen, scuttling their own ships if necessary to avoid their falling into enemy hands. The air force was to occupy airports in German hands, capturing the personnel and destroying stocks of fuel and munitions; if they could not be held they must be made unusable. The second memorandum (PM 2) gave commanders in Greece and the Aegean the freedom to act as they thought best, and instructed them to tell the Germans 'frankly' that if they did not use their weapons against the Italians then the Italians would not take up arms against them or make common cause with the 'rebels' or Anglo-American troops 'who may land in the future'.[122] Many units never received these orders before the sudden, final collapse two days later.

In the evening of 7 September, after secretly landing in Gaeta and driving up the Appian Way, General Maxwell Taylor arrived in Rome to organize the landing of American airborne troops at the airfields around Rome (Operation GIANT TWO). First he met General Carboni. Displaying what Taylor later described as 'alarming pessimism', Carboni rehearsed the reasons why he could not fight. There were 36,000 heavily armed Germans north and south of Rome. The Germans had cut off the Italian gasoline supply, his mobile units could only move eighty kilometres before becoming immobile, and his forces were short of ammunition. It was impossible for him to protect the airfields, he told Taylor. The expected force was too small. If the Americans brought gasoline and ammunition with them he would be glad to fight 'but he could do nothing now'. He could only suggest that the Allies 'make a large landing north of Rome'. At Taylor's request, he was then taken to Badoglio. The head of government, who was in his pyjamas (it was about midnight), cut an unimpressive figure: according to Carboni he looked like 'a strange bird, its feathers plucked ready to be cooked'. Once dressed, Badoglio confirmed Carboni's analysis, and when asked if he realized how deeply his government was committed by the Castellano conversations he could only reply that 'the situation had changed and that General Castellano had not known all the facts'. Taylor returned to Tunis armed only with a note from Badoglio saying that because of the disposition and strength of the German forces in the Rome area it was no longer possible to accept an immediate armistice, relieved that his visit had 'brought matters to a head and stopped an operation (GIANT TWO) which was near being launched into a situation which invited disaster'.[123]

As Taylor left, a message arrived from Eisenhower: if the Italians did not stick to the agreement they had signed five days earlier, he would tell the world. A Crown council was hastily summoned. The military men were not, as Guariglia (who took part) afterwards put it with masterly understatement, 'of one mind'.[124] Carboni was for ditching the armistice – and with it Castellano and Badoglio too – which in practice meant continuing to fight alongside the Germans. Guariglia agreed. The War Minister, General Sorice, sidled in their direction, claiming that no one could deny Italy's right to delay the armistice. After telling everyone that the armistice was coming sooner than they had expected and that Italy was unprepared militarily to deal with that fact, Ambrosio stayed silent. External forces now took a hand. In the middle of the discussion news arrived that Radio Algiers had just reported the armistice, and Ambrosio's assistant, Colonel Marchesi, returned after a brief absence with the third part of a telegram sent by Eisenhower earlier. Badoglio's request for a postponement was summarily rejected. The armistice would be announced at 6.30 p.m. that day, and if the Italian armed forces did not co-operate as they had undertaken to do then Eisenhower would publish the entire record of the negotiations and 'serious consequences' would follow. When Carboni pressed on with his case regardless, Colonel Marchesi – by far the most junior member of the group but the only person to come out of it with his honour wholly intact – commandeered the floor. Italy could not now turn back, he told his masters. Only military collaboration could reduce the harshness of the armistice clauses. The idea of postponement was illusory, because there would certainly be a violent Allied reaction. Vittorio Emanuele left the meeting, perhaps turning over in his mind another consideration: if the masses, who wanted peace at all costs, were to be told that even though Mussolini had gone the war was going on, the monarchy would be held responsible. After spending ten minutes alone he called Badoglio in and told him to accept the armistice.[125]

On the night of 8–9 September 1943 the curtain came down on the Badoglio regime – and, effectively, on the Italian monarchy too. The actions that the army's leaders took, and the ones they failed to take, damaged the reputations of many of them beyond repair. Carboni, who at first thought that the Germans would simply retire to the north and who would subsequently be charged along with Roatta and others with the crime of failing to defend Rome, excused his own shortcomings and everybody else's with the remark that there were a hundred people in command but no one understood the situation.[126]

As midnight approached, news arrived that the German Embassy was burning documents, giving away bottles and saying its goodbyes. Hopes that the Germans had 'lost their heads' were quickly put to bed. Within minutes news arrived of fighting in Milan and around the Lido di Roma, quickly followed by a telephone intercept confirming that the Germans intended to disarm Italian troops – and were confident of succeeding. The fighting spread rapidly as the 3rd *Panzergrenadier* division marched on Rome and the 2nd Parachute division attacked an Italian division stationed between the Tiber and Anzio. Roatta declined to activate OP 44 without explicit instructions from Ambrosio. At the time he thought that it was unnecessary, because Badoglio's announcement that the army should react with force to any attack no matter from whichever direction it came did in fact put the 'reactive-defensive' part of OP 44 into effect. Later he justified his inaction on the grounds that the only 'true hostilities' going on at the time were the attacks by the German Parachute division on the outskirts of Rome.[127] Neither Badoglio nor Ambrosio was prepared to authorize OP 44, the latter apparently on the grounds that Italy was not in a state of war with Germany but was instead in a state of 'non-belligerence' towards all parties. Absent the authority he needed, and aware that PM 2 had not reached commanders, Roatta sent them two instructions shortly after midnight. The first ordered them not to take the initiative in 'hostile acts against the Germans', and the second told them to 'react to acts of force with acts of force'. A radio despatch soon afterwards told the army 'not to obstruct the operations of the Anglo-Americans' and to 'avoid incidents with the German troops'.[128] These 'orders' effectively disarmed those of his soldiers who were not already fighting for their country.

Roatta now argued that Rome could not hold out against the Germans for long, that the capital should not be exposed to 'the horrors of combat', and that the king and the government could not be captured and must escape while there was still one route out – the Tivoli–Pescara road. Ambrosio had at first thought that the king should stay in Rome, but now he and Badoglio both agreed.[129] Determined not to fall into Hitler's hands and become a marionette, Vittorio Emanuele had been thinking about leaving Rome for over a month.[130] Having accepted the armistice, he now decided that it was his duty to guarantee the continued collaboration of his government with the Allies. That meant leaving Rome, which he did. A convoy of five cars, including the king's FIAT 2800 emblazoned with the royal insignia, left Rome at 5.10 a.m. on 9 September and after passing through a number of German roadblocks and being stopped at least once – a circumstance so odd as to persuade Carboni that Ambrosio and Kesselring, both Freemasons, had done a deal to swap Rome for the king's escape – it arrived at Ortona on the Adriatic coast at midnight. Shortly afterwards the king, Badoglio, Ambrosio, Admiral de Courten and General Sandalli boarded an Italian corvette and sailed for Brindisi, leaving the civilian members of the government in Rome unaware that the principals had beaten a hasty retreat and that they were now in charge – a burden they immediately refused to shoulder.

The other two services were caught as much by surprise by the sudden surrender as the army. Under new leadership, the navy had been chafing at inaction and at the beginning of August Admiral de Courten had proposed using two cruisers in a raid on Palermo, where there were believed to be two or three enemy cruisers and a dozen destroyers, in the hope of sinking two or three of the smaller craft. It was a risky venture but Ambrosio agreed to it mainly because of the effect it would have on crew morale.[131] Now, the battle-fleet was preparing to fight off the imminent enemy offensive according to two sets of orders. One envisaged possible enemy action to occupy the ports of Naples or Taranto, with secondary objectives of Salerno, Gaeta and Brindisi, and the other landings on the coasts of Albania and Greece. In both cases the central directive was the same: to oppose the enemy's landings by attacking his convoys, avoiding night actions and (if possible) actions against equal forces en route.[132] De Courten, told about the armistice negotiations on 6 September, instructed his admirals to react 'with maximum force' if the Germans attacked.

In accordance with his orders the commander in chief of the battle-fleet, Admiral Carlo Bergamini, was preparing to lead a raid on Salerno when he learned in the afternoon of 8 September that they were annulled. Rather than surrender the fleet, as stipulated in the armistice terms, he would have preferred to scuttle it, but de Courten overrode him: the king's orders were to obey the surrender terms. After receiving orders from *Supermarina* just before midnight, Bergamini assembled his fleet – three battleships (*Roma*, *Vittorio Veneto* and *Italia*, formerly the *Littorio*), six cruisers, eight destroyers and five escorts – at 3 a.m. on 9 September and set out for La Maddalena on Sardinia. Learning en route that it was already in German hands, he changed course. A squadron of Dornier DO 217s armed with radio-guided bombs caught him in mid-afternoon, hitting the *Italia* and sinking the *Roma*. Bergamini went down with his ship, together with two-thirds of his crew. The Germans subsequently picked up 124 of the 319 ships the navy had left. What remained of the Italian fleet gathered in Malta, where on 11 September it surrendered.[133]

The head of the air force, General Sandalli, was told by Badoglio on 3 September that armistice negotiations were under way. He passed the news on to his two immediate subordinates – apparently the only service chief to do so – three days later. When they received PM 1, his orders were to pull planes back from Sardinia and concentrate fighters on the airfields around Rome. He also gave broad general directions about moving planes to Allied airfields at the moment the armistice was announced. That same evening thirteen telegrams went out to units around Italy and to one close to Rome and the air ministry itself to have planes ready next morning 'for the transport of materiel and personnel' that would be 'in transfer'.[134] The air force was preparing to escort the battle-fleet, which was sortieing against the Allied invasion, when the Allied announcement of the armistice was intercepted. A little after midnight on 8–9 September *Superaereo* received Ambrosio's formal announcement of the armistice and his instructions to act decisively against offensives from any direction (a telegram it took almost two and a half hours to decipher). An hour later Ambrosio's order was passed on to all major air units.[135] Told that the government was on the move to southern Italy, the planes were ordered to Puglia and Sardinia, then still in Italian hands. Only a third of the air force was able to escape the Germans.[136]

On 8 September, as Badoglio surrendered, a German plane flew over Gran Sasso. Over the next three days the German rescue plan was finalized and on 12 September a party led by Colonel Otto Skorzeny freed Mussolini. The former *Duce* apparently asked to be allowed to go into retirement at his home at Rocca delle Caminate, but Hitler thought otherwise and he was flown to Munich. His task for the next six hundred days was to head the puppet Salò Republic in northern Italy as Hitler's catspaw. In November 1939 he had told his mistress, Claretta Petacci, 'I shall get to eighty – if they don't shoot me first.'[137] He did not – and eventually, on 28 April 1945, they did.

Afterword

After the war, Field Marshal Keitel and General Jodl both bore witness to Hitler's apparently boundless knowledge of all things military, from classical theory and historical campaigns to the technical minutiae of modern weaponry. Mussolini's generals and admirals could not say the same – nor did they. Admiral Leonardi, scooped up by the British after the fall of Pantelleria, believed that Mussolini had been 'mad for four years' and so did General Berardi.[1] As his under-secretary at the war ministry in 1939–40, General Ubaldo Soddu saw Mussolini at first hand. To his mind the *Duce* was not 'mad' – he just reasoned in a different way, working through intuition with results that were 'sometimes brilliant, sometimes catastrophic'. Unlike Napoleon 'he did not ground his plans on what was possible' and so was not a true strategist.[2] General Giuseppe Castellano was less forgiving. In his judgement 'The errors were essentially of a political nature and many times the military were thrust into more dangerous adventures through the incompetence and intemperance of the man who ran the government.'[3]

Taddeo Orlando, another of the captive generals, believed that the military blunders committed by Italy would not have been made 'if the technical experts had been able to speak their minds and prepare thoroughly for war. Instead of which that journalist Mussolini insisted on making the preparations on his own account. That's why things have turned out as they have.' Marshal Messe, a defeated commander but an able one, thought on similar lines: Mussolini's 'great mistake' was in thinking that 'a delicate instrument like the army could be led by men whom he appointed arbitrarily or for political reasons'.[4] The questions these opinions raise are fundamental ones. Were Mussolini's generals right? How far was Italy's defeat due to misrule by 'one man, and one man alone', as Winston Churchill later put it? Did Italy go to war in

1940 with one hand metaphorically strapped behind her back because of her weaknesses, material or otherwise? How well did Mussolini's generals manage the war and did they make the best use of the resources they had to hand? And what determined how well the Fascist armed forces performed during that war?

Mussolini had little if any comprehension of military strategy and none at all of grand strategy. First an apparently enthusiastic conscript in the *Bersaglieri* in 1905 and 1906 and then a front-line soldier between September 1915 and February 1917, his understanding of war and matters military was extremely limited. So it is not surprising that his grasp of the wider dimensions of war, which was formed from experience and untutored observation, was equally limited. His ruminations on the world war, published as commentaries in his newspaper *Il Popolo d'Italia*, ranked *spirito* (morale) and willpower above everything else. His perception of what really mattered was summed up in a simple phrase – 'he wins who wants to win'. Italian morale had defeated Austrian morale, as Italy's recovery from the near-disastrous defeat at Caporetto in October 1917 had clearly demonstrated. That victory had in turn been possible because the government of the day had imposed 'the necessary discipline of war' on society at large.

For Mussolini victories would be won by mass armies that had been mobilized morally as well as physically for war – the *massa cosciente*. Fascism would discipline society at large and would at the same time raise the armed forces to a state of 'formidable spiritual efficiency'.[5] Putting form above substance in this way was one of Mussolini's most marked, and most damaging, traits. Thus in the summer of 1940 he wanted to nominate youths in the *Giovani Fascisti* as second lieutenants in the army even though some were illiterate and none had anything more than elementary school education, on the grounds that 'culture' was not necessary for an officer. All that was needed was 'a strong Fascist spirit'.[6]

Mussolini's working methods speak to his priorities – and his shortcomings. When in Rome he saw the chiefs of the armed forces general staff twice every day – but only after he had been briefed by police and Party representatives on the state of the public mood. Exactly what passed between him and his military chiefs is mostly unknown. His frequent telephone calls, as often about matters of detail as about general progress, give the impression of someone chivvying and directing his subordinates but not truly leading and certainly not interested in their thoughts on the war. About the state of his armed forces he was well informed but seemingly none the wiser. Sheaves of data about the three services, the raw materials situation, the rate of armaments manufacture and much more besides passed across his desk. He read – or at least skimmed – much of it. On the face of things he was a hard-working warlord. In reality his working methods were disorganized and inefficient.

We can get some idea of what his subordinates thought Mussolini had to be told, and of the trivia with which he was ready to concern himself, from the contents of his personal office files for the month of October 1940. During those thirty-one days, as well as handling the more heavyweight business of the war and making time for extra-mural activities, he adjudicated on whether an individual (and fairly junior) officer should or should not go to North Africa, fixed a general's pay level, pronounced on whether a particular hotel (the *Albergo Valentini* at Salsomaggiore) could go on the list of hotels approved for military use by the Ministry of Popular Culture, noted that a bomb had gone off in Civitavecchia without hurting anyone or doing any damage to property, was told that pecorino cheese could not be substituted for Parmesan, because the soldiers did not like it, and absorbed a report about the distribution of lemons to the troops in North Africa. Winston Churchill could at times plunge into similar minutiae – but he could also rise far above it.

Under Mussolini, Fascist Italy proved incapable of the kind of structural mobilization developed by her enemies as they fought him and his ally. From the Great War he took the lesson that state and society must be readied for combat, but his reading of that experience was superficial. Between 1915 and 1918 the civil population had contributed to the war effort not only by bearing arms but by producing the materiel needed by the front-line armies and by cutting its own consumption. The conditions in which a future war would be fought would be 'aggravated' because Italy could not be sure of access to resources overseas or external financial support, both of which she had enjoyed during the Great War. Therefore, according to the *Duce*'s formula, industrial effort would have to be greater and would need to be matched by a similar effort in agriculture and minerals, along with substantial limits to consumption.[7] It was a simplistic recipe and one he stuck to through thick and thin.

Mussolini's loose conception of what modern war required was only one of the reasons why Fascist Italy never fully mobilized to make the best use of the limited resources she possessed. For one thing, there was never a clear and consistent set of war aims that could then be married up to a national strategy. Mussolini first went after colonial conquests, then Mediterranean predominance, then a Balkan fiefdom – all the while ambitious also to push Italy out into the wider waters of the Atlantic and the Indian Ocean, goals that his navy nursed too. He also wanted to rule alongside Hitler over a conquered Europe. With no clear focus to his war, he could not impart a clear strategic direction to his armed forces. The three armed services lived in institutional 'silos' and stayed inside them thanks to a combination of personal and professional rivalries and bureaucratic inertia. Conflictual Fascist politics made co-ordinating military effort across the spectrum all the harder. In January 1942, discussing with Goering the need to co-ordinate anti-aircraft defence, presently handled by the Fascist militia, the navy and the air force, Mussolini had to admit that it had been under study 'for a long time' with no result and would now have to wait for a solution until after the war was over.[8]

The British and American war machines worked on the basis of programming, correlating strategic priorities with industrial capacity and balancing the manpower needs of the armed forces with those of the war industries and the domestic economy. This proved to be beyond Fascist Italy. In February 1940 Favagrossa made the 'sudden discovery' that there was no general plan for the annual workforce requirements of the factories. Thanks in part to Mussolini's obsession with 'boots on the ground', no one then sat down and worked out the optimal distribution of the labour force between the fighting arms and the civilian economy. As late as September 1942, Cavallero had to ask for an estimate of the amount of labour needed for industry.[9] The result was a continual shortage of skilled labour in the factories, a large reserve of unused agricultural labour in central and southern Italy and a lack of it in the north, and only a marginal increase in the low proportion of women employed in the total industrial workforce. In 1943, only 10 per cent of the workforce at Ansaldo Meccanico was female. At Olivetti the ratio between the genders stayed the same throughout the war, and at Pirelli the proportion of women in the labour force actually fell.[10]

Prioritizing production was an ad hoc affair from start to finish. On 27 December 1941, Mussolini told the council of ministers that the war Italy was now fighting would last longer than the First World War. Logically, that meant a war of four years' duration or more. Fascist Italy had been fighting for eighteen months and if the *Duce* was right (which, unusually, turned out on this occasion to be the case) she had at least twice as far to go. If there was any single moment at which to confront the future head on and set about repositioning the country for a long, hard struggle then this was it. No one took it. Instead, Fascist Italy continued on its chosen path towards defeat.

The meeting called by Mussolini on 1 October 1942 to examine the strength of his 'war-making apparatus' is a microcosm of much that was wrong with the direction and management of Italy's war. The armed forces' programmes that Cavallero put in front of Mussolini started by calculating the armaments they needed and then translated the result into the raw materials it would take to produce them. This was how they had operated in peacetime and it was how they continued to operate in wartime. Everyone was willing to shuffle numbers around in order to satisfy the agenda. Ambrosio's last-minute attempts to impose priorities in armaments manufacture were well intentioned but came much too late. In 1943 all the previous errors, mistakes and short-comings – the strategic 'overstretch' created by Mussolini's political decisions and exacerbated by the Allied decision to launch a second front that year, the consequences of what has been called Italy's *mobilitazione sotto tono* ('toned-down mobilization'), and the inability of the soldiers to field enough efficient divisions and the sailors to deploy enough warships to fight the war – came home to roost.

Although occasionally a favourite could pop up, usually only for a brief moment, Mussolini did not care very much for generals – or admirals. The First World War generals had shown a dismal inability to manoeuvre on the battlefield. In the second half of the 1930s Federico Baistrocchi and Alberto Pariani offered him a new kind of Napoleonic warfare – a new model army composed of a mix of mechanized units and motorized infantry, the whole thing articulated by a doctrine of 'lightning war' and inspired by ideals of boldness and action. When Mussolini went to war in 1940 their 'revolution in warfare' was far from complete. Indeed, it may well have been beyond Fascist Italy ever to bring it to completion. So when it came to fighting the war things did not work out in the way they had intended, or that the *Duce* expected they would. As European war turned into world war there was only one way in which Fascist Italy's military could keep fighting – by getting ever more in hock to Nazi Germany. Historians have dated Mussolini's 'subaltern war' to the moment when Rommel arrived in North Africa in February 1941, but from a longer perspective it was on the cards from the very start.

Handed full authority by King Vittorio Emanuele III, Mussolini ran the war exactly as he wished. At the start it was in the hands of two men neither of whom, in very different ways, measured up to the new Fascist ideals. His chief lieutenant, Pietro Badoglio, held that position partly because he was the figurehead of the Piedmontese military caste and so able to make it appear to the king, the army and conservative circles that a safe pair of hands was helping to guide Italy's military destiny, and partly because after the Abyssinian war he was without question Italy's leading general. A quintessential military conservative, Badoglio spent his time as chief of the armed forces general staff attempting to damp down Mussolini's enthusiasm for action while at the same time focusing the minds of the chiefs of staff on the nuts and bolts of military planning. The one never worked and the other perhaps worked too well, smothering anything resembling true strategic debate and reducing men he regarded as his underlings to little more than professional ciphers. This accidentally made it easier for Mussolini to exert unexamined control over the war.

The risks attached to the invasion of Egypt were considerable and so were the potential gains. Rodolfo Graziani, chosen to steer the attack, was no longer the man he had been in Libya in the 1920s or in Somalia in 1936. An attempt on his life while in Abyssinia in 1937 seems to have made him acutely risk-averse – not a facet of his personality apparent before. Like other Fascist generals, he was ready to encourage his warlord. 'Everything will automatically fall into place,' he declared confidently on the eve of Italian entry into the war. Three months later 'the belief that everything will gradually resolve itself' still had widespread traction, much to the concern of his deputy, Mario Roatta.[11] When it came to action, though, Graziani turned out to be as conservative a practitioner as Badoglio. Whether a Baistrocchi or a Pariani could have done any better than he did with what he had is debatable, but the suspicion remains that something more might perhaps have been achieved in North Africa in the summer of 1940. As it was, Graziani failed. So too did Visconti Prasca, who certainly had no excuses. Neither did Domenico Cavagnari, head of a navy caught napping at Taranto and lacking the justification of an undeclared war that caught Admiral Kimmel by surprise at Pearl Harbor a year later. The reverses in 1940 were not uniquely Mussolini's fault.

Almost everyone seems to have disliked, distrusted or despised Mussolini's next choice as chief of the armed forces general staff, Ugo Cavallero. Messe called him 'a scoundrel' and worse. Cavallero had managerial experience in both the military and civilian spheres and some organizational talent. That was enough to keep things going – but not enough to change them. His signature underscored the strategic directives that went out from Rome to the various theatres of war. Exactly how far they reflected and reproduced the *Duce*'s own ideas is not easy to measure, but it is reasonable to suppose that Cavallero never went beyond his master's wishes. His management style, as evidenced by his efforts to pull parts of the war machinery together and give it some overall cohesion, was one of centralization – in himself. His day-to-day involvement in organizing the North African convoys, a role which in other wartime polities was delegated to subordinates, all too often took him down into depths of detail that submerged the bigger picture. But that probably made no real difference, because, like everyone else, Cavallero gave Mussolini no real strategic alternatives, something he regarded as pointless. Mussolini took his decisions on the basis of political considerations and discussing them was useless.[12]

His successor, Vittorio Ambrosio, a tougher-minded professional and a very practical strategist, was certainly not his master's voice, as the events leading up to Mussolini's fall show. His time as *Capo di stato maggiore generale* had a complexity all its own. Defending the *madrepatria* was a thankless task, not least because after so many of his generals had been captured in North Africa there was no one with any recent experience of fighting the British and Americans to whom he felt able to confide the defence of Sicily. Ending a war in any circumstances, but especially those in which Italy found herself in the summer of 1943, is very much harder than getting into one in the first place. In the circumstances Ambrosio managed an unenviable task as well as anyone could reasonably be expected to do.

No one counselled Mussolini. The striking absence of any genuine strategic discussion, and the fact that no one gave him any real alternatives or options until things were too far gone to change course, was partly the consequence of the way he structured the defence machinery so as to leave himself alone and aloof at the top. So when Cavallero was made the intermediary between the *Duce* and the armed forces he was given 'direction' of the co-ordination and preparation of military activity but not empowered to make proposals. It was also partly due to the way the general staffs functioned. Two things were conspicuously lacking in the way they managed the war: strategic position papers (what they produced, as they were tasked to do, was operational options) and combined inter-service planning advice.

Messe, Fascist Italy's most competent general, thought the army general staff's 'principal, fundamental, essential, irremediable defect' was that its members knew nothing about war.[13] This was, of course, unfair: failure has complex causes, not simple ones. With hindsight, though, some of the planners' ideas can look a little odd. In March 1942, just as Cavallero was seeking to build up Italian strength in North Africa and Rommel was preparing for his next bound forward, they recommended examining the possibility of reducing the number of tanks going to Libya in order to give a larger portion of production to the new units being built up in Italy.[14] But perhaps we should remember that like planners everywhere they were working to the directions, actual or presumed, of their seniors.

When Mussolini went to war in June 1940 his generals had already scored notable victories, but in both cases circumstances had been in their favour. In Abyssinia they had applied overwhelming force against an ill-armed and inferior enemy with no external support. In Spain they had shown themselves able to fight a successful war of movement – alongside two other armed forces and against an opponent who was only able to hold out against them when outside support was on hand. In Russia and in North Africa the tables were turned. As the three main Allied powers supported and sustained one another, Italy grew ever more dependent for the resources she needed on an ally whose military and economic strength was also not equal to the task. In these circumstances the absence of any real strategic collaboration between the two Axis powers, despite the efforts of one or two Italian generals to encourage it, could be described as a 'weakness multiplier'.

In the field, Italian generals lacked modern weaponry and transport. What they also lacked – and what some of their British opponents in the western desert had and would use against them – was experience of combined-arms warfare against a skilled and well-led modern army. Italy had no equivalent of the '100 Days' which ended the First World War and her generals were at a severe disadvantage as a consequence. Structural weaknesses exacerbated the difficulties of learning on the job. Admirals too lacked equivalent experience, though in some areas such as submarine and anti-submarine warfare the First World War had seen considerable activity of which better use might have been made. Handicapped as much by a perceived sense of material and numerical inferiority as by the actuality, they handled their fleets poorly on occasion and were thought little of by their ally. Airmen too often wedded to theories of strategic bombing and too little practised in ground-air support and long-range reconnaissance over the sea parcelled out their increasingly obsolescent planes in ways which often clashed with the needs and wishes of the other two services.

Catastrophes happen in war and the Italians suffered their share, notably in North Africa at the end of 1940 and in Russia in the winter of 1942–3. But suffering massive defeat is not the prerogative of the losers alone. The humiliation of Operation COMPASS was more than matched by Britain's humiliation in the battle of France in 1940, which ended the only serious attempt to stop the Third Reich from running amok in Europe, and again when she proved unable to halt the Japanese invasion of South-East Asia in 1941–2. In both cases the British, like the Italians, were outmanoeuvred and outfought. Britain survived in 1940 because she could retreat behind the Channel, buying herself time in which to petition the United States for help. She recovered her Far Eastern possessions thanks in considerable part to that same American power which came to her support. The United Kingdom had the resources to fight back, and the political and organizational framework necessary to make best use of them. Fascist Italy had neither.

The men who commanded and led Mussolini's army and navy (it is more difficult to generalize about the air force, not least because the image it cultivated was that of a youthful and iconoclastic fighting arm), and who fought Mussolini's war, grew to military maturity in systems and cultures that were rigidly hierarchical, highly conservative in their attitudes, and traditionally somewhat at odds with civilian authority. Fascism laid a canopy over these foundations. Some generals – many perhaps – thought that Fascism was by no means a bad thing. Berardi thought Mussolini had 'done a lot of good' for Italy, and Orlando believed Fascism had things to its credit: it had quelled a communist revolt, improved the moral and material conditions of the country through public works, maternity and child welfare organizations and sport, and through the corporate state had ensured that workers were well paid.[15]

Belief in Fascism alone was not the glue that held the armed forces together, much though Mussolini would have wanted it to be. The upper ranks of all three services, and at least some of the rank and file who served under them, shared beliefs and attitudes that seem to have made fighting for Fascist Italy easier and perhaps more fulfilling too. Among them was the idea that bolshevism and communism were the greatest dangers facing Europe. Men fighting in Russia could see themselves on a crusade that was either religious, or ideological, or a mixture of both. As a couple of the captured generals agreed, 'Fascism represents everything Christian, and communism everything anti-Christian.'[16] More generally, men of all ranks fought for Fascist Italy for a mixture of reasons: careerism, belief in the regime's broad goals, recognition of its achievements during the pre-war years, support for its intention to raise Italy up to Great Power status, and straightforward patriotism. Professionalism too had its part to play. To win – or at least do their best to win – the war that political authority had decreed must be fought was what the *Forze Armate* existed to do. Against that must be set the fact that the conscripts who filled the ranks of all three services had no choice in the matter.

The Italian formula for military success as set down in the 1928 regulations required 'well-trained troops nourished by a strong combative spirit'. To bring that about, as Mussolini expected, was the task of both the military and the Fascist Party. For different reasons neither succeeded. Fascist propaganda, capable of stirring up passing enthusiasms, became increasingly ineffective as the war went on and the obvious setbacks mounted. 'Affective mobilization' of the population, never especially strong during the war, grew ever weaker, its consequences multiplied by weak structural mobilization.[17] Generals and admirals had to fight with partially trained reservists and undertrained conscripts. Time and opportunity to bring raw recruits up to professional levels were luxuries the heads of the Fascist armed services did not have – but although they were ready enough to complain about them they never paid enough attention to raising the standard of junior officers. Nevertheless, and despite their multiple handicaps, Italian units often fought hard until they could fight no longer.

On the front lines in North Africa the Italian army fought a 'clean' war. Behind the lines, though, brutal policies and practices that had been encouraged and legitimated during Italy's colonial wars were in evidence.[18] There and elsewhere attitudes born of imperialist conquests went hand in hand with other unwholesome beliefs. Anti-Semitism, albeit in a moderated form, is evident among the highest ranks: General Berardi thought the Jewish problem had become acute 'after GERMANY had brought it to light' and that the Jews were 'an international organization acting in their own interests', and General Mancinelli believed that the Jews had proved they were 'incapable of fitting in with any European social structure' and thought the problem would have to be faced but 'was not in favour of the German method of solving it'.[19] In the Balkans, anti-Semitic attitudes among the middle-level corps commanders and officers on Roatta's staff married up with anti-Slavism. There, under the pressure of counter-insurgency warfare and ordered by their generals to act mercilessly, the army went far outside the laws of war. Generals who had directed the violence in the Balkans afterwards flatly denied any wrong-doing. They and their subordinates escaped post-war indictments for war crimes when the Cold War cut Yugoslavia off from the West and turned Italy into a bulwark against communism.

On 2 December 1942 Mussolini addressed the Fascist Chamber. In the course of a somewhat rambling speech which was mainly directed against Churchill, who had accused him of being the man who had taken Italy into the war, he announced that the conflict had now become 'cosmic'. So far 40,219 Italians had lost their lives in the fighting, and the Allied bombing that had started only recently had already caused severe damage to Milan, Turin, Savona and Genoa – for which he gave exact statistics. The implication was unmistakable: more were going to die. Winding up, he told his audience that Italy had no choice but to fight on. Otherwise the sacrifice of the dead would be in vain.[20]

Now that the war was directly hitting home, the *Duce*'s rhetoric no longer chloroformed the public as it had when he was in his heyday. 'You don't know, dearest mother,' one anonymous correspondent wrote from Milan that same day, 'what a tense life we lead. Now today the Duce's speech has properly demoralized me.' 'We've lived through nights of terror,' wrote another from Turin two days before Christmas, 'listening for hours on end to the thud of bombs dropped by endless waves of bombers on all parts of the city . . . there are countless dead.'[21]

More was to come. As the year ended, a piece of intelligence arrived that was especially ominous for a combatant whose air force would soon be in tatters. Sources inside American aeronautical testing centres reported that studies were being completed for the construction of 'a new bomber of enormous dimensions' which could carry a 10-ton bomb load and had a range of 10,000 miles.[22] The first prototype B-29 had in fact flown three months earlier and by the year's end 1,500 were on order. It would never be used against Italy – but it was one more brick in the 'wall of money' that was the productive power of the United States and its allies. The year 1943 was the coda to a story whose likely ending had become all too apparent during the twelve months that preceded it.

In June 1940 Mussolini threw his military cards – such as they were – on the table, telling his service chiefs, 'We shall do what we can.' He knew all about Italy's economic weaknesses, over which he and his subordinates had pored for the previous fifteen years. He knew, too, that his army was in no condition to do more than undertake a single, limited campaign. Graziani told him only weeks before that if he wanted to attack a Yugoslavia which was already in a state of internal collapse, the optimal scenario, then putting together the fifteen divisions to do it would mean robbing the rest of the army, as, 'for the time being, and for some time to come, the supply of clothing and equipment on hand is not sufficient for the needs of the whole mobilized army.'[23]

Clear-headed calculation might have led to the conclusion that waiting until the professionals were ready would be worth considering – but Mussolini never believed in experts unless they agreed with him. Could he stand aside from war in June 1940 and wait for two or three years? With France sinking to its knees and the world of his more conservative generals, with Badoglio at their head, apparently turned upside down by the virtuosity of the Wehrmacht, it is not difficult to see why he thought he could not. Add the compelling need to avoid the diplomatic 'mistakes' of the First World War, when belated entry seemingly lost Liberal Italy the chance to make her presence count and a junior role in the Allies' military partnership resulted in the 'mutilated peace' of 1919, and the pressure to gamble becomes yet stronger. Mussolini succumbed and in so doing embraced his own fate. Whether he understood the lessons of the First World War well enough to realize that he would do well to avoid a long, capital-intensive conflict, or poorly enough to believe that he could do so, the result in the end was the same.

Abbreviations

ACS	Archivio Centrale di Stato, Rome
All.	*Allegato/Allegati* (attachment/s)
AMR	Archivio dei Musei del Risorgimento e di Storia Contemporanea, Comune di Milano
App	Appendix
ARMIR	*Armata Italiana in Russia* (Italian Army in Russia)
ASAM	Archivio Storico dell'Aeronautica Militare
ASI	*Africa Settentrionale Italiana* (Italian North Africa)
ASMAE	Archivio Storico del Ministero degli Affari Esteri
ASV	Archivio di Stato di Venezia
AUSMM	Archivio dell'Ufficio Storico della Marina Militare
AUSSME	Archivio dell'Ufficio Storico dello Stato Maggiore dell'Esercito
b.	*busta*
BA-MA	Bundesarchiv-Militärarchiv
CCRR	*Carabinieri Reali*
COGEFAG	*Commissariato Generale per Fabbricazione di Guerra* (General Commissariat for War Production)
CSD	*Commissione Suprema di Difesa* (Supreme Defence Commission)
CSIR	*Corpo spedizione italiano in Russia* (Italian expeditionary corps in Russia)
CTV	*Corpo Truppe Volontarie* (Corps of volunteer troops [in Spain])
DDI	*I Documenti Diplomatici Italiani* (series/volume number)
DGFP	Documents on German Foreign Policy (series/volume number)
doc.	document
DSCS	*Diario Storico del Comando Supremo*
EDS	Enemy Documents Section
fasc.	fascicolo
FFAA	*Forze Armate* (armed forces)
FLE	Fondazione Luigi Einaudi

fr./ff.	frame/s
GFM	German Foreign Ministry records
IWM(D)	Imperial War Museum, Duxford
MMIS	*Missione Militare Italiana in Spagna*
MVSN	*Milizia Volontaria per la Sicurezza Nazionale* (Voluntary Militia for National Security)
NARS	National Archives and Records Service
NDU	National Defense University
n./no.	number
OKW	*Oberkommando der Wehrmacht* (German Armed Forces High Command)
OO	*Opera Omnia di Benito Mussolini*
PR	*Piano di Radunata* (deployment plan)
RRCC	*Carabinieri Reali*
SIA	*Servizio Informazioni Aeronautica* (Italian Air Force Intelligence)
SIE	*Servizio Informazioni Esercito* (Italian Army Intelligence)
SIM	*Servizio Informazioni Militari* (Italian Military Intelligence)
SIS	*Servizio Informazioni Segreto* (Italian Naval Intelligence)
SOE	Special Operations Executive
SUA	*Stati Uniti Americani* (USA)
TNA	The National Archives
T./Ts.	telegram/s
USAMHI	United States Army Military History Institute
WO	War Office

List of Illustrations

1. Marshal Pietro Badoglio.
2. General Alfredo Guzzoni.
3. General Vittorio Ambrosio (centre) and General Efisio Marras (left).
4. General Mario Roatta, Spain, 1937.
5. North Africa. M 13/40 tanks moving up to the front line, October 1940.
6. North Africa. *Bersaglieri* advancing on Tobruk.
7. North Africa. Assault engineers attacking north of El Alamein, November 1942.
8. North Africa. Rommel and Cavallero (centre right) visit the front, November 1942.
9. North Africa. *Bersaglieri* manning a 47mm anti-tank gun, Tunisia, March 1943.
10. Greece/Albania. Mussolini leads the advance on Greece.
11. Greece/Albania. Italian artillery on the front line.
12. Greece/Albania. Supplying the front was often a hand-to-mouth business.
13. Greece/Albania. Tapping a phone line; communications were a perpetual problem.
14. Greece/Albania. Front-line propaganda – the headline reads 'Hate the English'.
15. Croatia. A *Četnik* militiaman.
16. Croatia. Captured rebels.
17. Croatia. In action – a burning village.
18. Russia. Capturing the Donets Basin, 1941.
19. Russia. Italian cavalry charging on the Don.
20. Russia. Italian infantry attacking a factory.
21. Russia. Old artillery in action – a 1911 model 75mm gun.
22. Russia. Christmas Day 1941.
23. Russia. General Giovanni Messe inspecting *Bersaglieri*, 1942.
24. Admiral Domenico Cavagnari.
25. Admiral Arturo Riccardi.
26. Admiral Angelo Iachino.

Nos. 1–23 and 33 are reproduced with permission from the Archivio Fotografico dell'Ufficio Storico dello Stato Maggiore dell'Esercito.

Nos. 24–30 are reproduced with permission from the Archivio Storico della Marina Militare.

Nos. 31–2 and 34–5 from Wikimedia Commons (public domain, out of copyright).

Notes

INTRODUCTION

1 Raymond Jonas, *The Battle of Adwa: African Victory in the Age of Empire* (Cambridge, MA: Belknap/Harvard University Press, 2011).

2 John Gooch, *The Italian Army and the First World War* (Cambridge: Cambridge University Press, 2014), p. 310.

3 'Governo e nazione', 7 September 1917; 'Dopo un mese', 24 November 1917; 'I nostri postulati. Per la storia di una settimana', 27 November 1917; 'Trincerocrazia', 15 December 1917: *Opera Omnia di Benito Mussolini* (Florence/Rome: La Fenice, 1983), vol. IX, p. 166; vol. X, pp. 75–7, 86–8, 140–2. On Mussolini's wartime career, see Paul O'Brien, *Mussolini in the First World War: The Journalist, the Soldier, the Fascist* (Oxford: Berg, 2005).

4 Italy's record in this respect has come in for some stiff criticism, but the pendulum is now swinging the other way: see Richard Carrier, 'Some Reflections on the Fighting Power of the Italian Army in North Africa, 1940–1943', *War in History*, vol. 22, no. 4, November 2015, pp. 503–28, and Bastian Matteo Scianna, *The Italian War on the Eastern Front, 1941–1943: Operations, Myths and Memories* (Cham, Switzerland: Springer Nature; London: Palgrave Macmillan, 2019), pp 79–85.

CHAPTER 1

1 Ivan Panebianco, 'Gli Arditi. Dalla guerra di trincea alla guerra fratricida (1917–1921)', tesi di laurea Università degli Studi Pisa, 2007–8, pp. 72–3, 88; Marco Mondini, *La politica delle armi. Il ruolo dell'esercito nell'avvento del fascismo* (Rome-Bari: Laterza, 2006), p. 25.

2 *L'esercito italiano tra la 1a e la 2a guerra mondiale* (Rome: Ufficio Storico dello Stato Maggiore dell'Esercito, 1954), pp. 66–80; Lucio Ceva, 'L'Alto Comando delle Forze Armate in Italia durante il regime fascista 1925–1943', in *idem., Teatri di guerra. Comandi, soldati e scrittori nei conflitti europei* (Milan: Franco Angeli, 2005), pp. 68–71.

3 Vincenzo Gallinari, *L'esercito italiano nel primo dopoguerra 1918–1920* (Rome: Ufficio Storico dello Stato Maggiore dell'Esercito, 1980), pp. 227–9; [Anon.], *L'esercito italiano tra la 1a e la 2a guerra mondiale*, pp. 55–9, 87–90; Filippo Stefani, *La storia della dottrina e degli ordinamenti dell'esercito italiano. Da Vittorio Veneto alla 2a Guerra Mondiale* (Rome: Ufficio Storico dello Stato Maggiore dell'Esercito, 1985), vol. II, tomo 1, pp. 113–36.

4 Giorgio Rochat, *Guerre italiane in Libia e Etiopia. Studi militari 1921– 1939* (Treviso: Pagus, 1991), pp. 81–5.

5 Mussolini to Lanza di Scalea, 10 July 1925: Renzo De Felice, *Mussolini il Duce* I: *Gli anni del consenso 1929–1936* (Turin: Einaudi, 1974), p. 603.

6 Dino Grandi, *La politica estera dell'Italia dal 1929 al 1932* (Rome: Bonacci, 1985), vol. I, p. 285.

7 Guariglia to Grandi, 19 February 1932; memorandum, 27 August 1932: Raffaele Guariglia, *Ricordi 1922–1946* (Naples: Edizioni Scientifiche Italiane, 1950), pp. 168, 170–1, 769.

8 Franco Fucci, *Emilio De Bono – Il maresciallo fucilato* (Milan: Mursia, 1989), p. 184.

9 Badoglio to De Bono, 17 December 1932: Piero Pieri and Giorgio Rochat, *Badoglio* (Turin: UTET, 1974), p. 635.

10 Mussolini to De Bono, 23 February 1934: Fortunato Minniti, 'Oltre Adua. Lo sviluppo e la scelta della strategia operativa per la guerra contro l'Etiopia', *Società di storia militare*, Quaderno, 1993, p. 104.

11 De Felice, *Gli anni del consenso*, pp. 508–9; Fucci, *Emilio De Bono*, p. 190.

12 Badoglio to De Bono and Valle, 12 May 1934: Giorgio Rochat, *Militari e politici nella preparazione della campagna d'Etiopia. Studio e documenti 1932–1936* (Milan: Franco Angeli, 1971), no. 16, p. 325.

13 Seduta del 31 maggio 1934: Antonello Biagini and Alessandro Gionfrida, *Lo Stato Maggiore Generale tra le due guerre (Verbali delle riunioni presedute da Badoglio dal 1925 al 1937)* (Rome: Ufficio Storico dello Stato Maggiore dell'Esercito, 1997), no. 34, p. 295.

14 Rochat, *Militari e politici*, no. 21, pp. 356–7, 10 August 1934.

15 Promemoria per SE il Capo di stato maggiore generale, 30 December 1934: Luigi Emilio Longo, *La campagna italo-etiopica (1935–1936)* (Rome: Ufficio Storico dello Stato Maggiore dell'Esercito, 2005), tomo II, pp. 130–31.

16 Promemoria, Directorate of the Military Chemical Service, 11 February 1935; Note by Baistrocchi, 15 February 1935: Longo, *La campagna italo-etiopica*, tomo I, pp. 470–1.

17 See Eric Lehmann, *Le ali del potere. La propaganda aeronautica nell'Italia fascista* (Turin: UTET, 2010); Thomas Hippler, *Bombing the People: Giulio Douhet and the Foundations of Air Power Strategy, 1884–1939* (Cambridge: Cambridge University Press, 2013).

18 Valle to Badoglio, 12 January 1935: Rochat, *Militari e politici*, p. 381 (emphasis in original).

19 Badoglio to Mussolini, 19 January 1935: Longo, *La campagna italo-etiopica*, tomo II, pp. 132-40.

20 Alessandro Lessona, *Memorie* (Rome: Edizione Lessona, 1963), p. 172.

21 Badoglio to Mussolini, 6 March 1935: Rochat, *Militari e politici*, pp. 403-4.

22 Mussolini to De Bono, 8 March 1935: Pieri and Rochat, *Badoglio*, p. 654.

23 Lessona, *Memorie*, pp. 131, 135-6, 267; Giuseppe Bottai, *Diario 1935-1944* (Milan: Rizzoli, 2001), pp. 73-4 (5 January 1936); Alexander De Grand, 'Mussolini's Follies: Fascism in its Imperial and Racist Phase, 1935-1940', *Contemporary European History*, vol. 13, no. 2, May 2004, pp. 136-8.

24 'La vertenza italo-etiopica e la politica estera italiana alla Camera dei Deputati', 25 May 1935; 'Il discorso di Cagliari', 8 June 1935; 'Il "Dato" irrefutabile', 31 July 1935: O O XXVII, pp. 76-80, 84-5, 110-11.

25 John Gooch, *Mussolini and his Generals: The Armed Forces and Fascist Foreign Policy, 1922-1940* (Cambridge: Cambridge University Press, 2007), pp. 287-92.

26 Badoglio to Mussolini, 14 August 1935: Pieri and Rochat, *Badoglio*, pp. 662-4.

27 Grandi to Mussolini, 15 August 1935; Mussolini to De Bono, 21 August 1935; De Bono to Mussolini, 7 September 1935; Mussolini to De Bono, 9 and 13 September 1935: De Felice, *Gli anni del consenso*, pp. 674 fn. 1, 675-6 fn. 3.

28 Badoglio to Mussolini, 14 August 1935; Badoglio to Mussolini, [?] September 1935; Badoglio to Mussolini, 17 September 1935: Rochat, *Militari e politici*, pp. 226-30.

29 Emilia Chiaravelli, *L'Opera della marina italiana nella guerra italo-etiopica* (Milan: Giuffrè, 1969), pp. 20-21, 24, 30-44; Giorgio Rochat, 'L'aeronautica italiana nella guerra d'Etiopia (1935-1936)', *Studi Piacentini* no. 7, September 1990, pp. 102-3; Ezio Cecchini, 'Organizzazione, preparazione e supporto logistico della campagna 1935-1936 in Africa Orientale', *Memorie Storiche Militari*, 1979, pp. 9-38.

30 De Felice, *Gli anni del consenso*, pp. 624-5, 761-2.

31 Mario Montanari, *Politica e strategia in cento anni di guerre italiane*, vol. III, tomo 1: *Le guerre degli anni trenta* (Rome: Ufficio Storico dello Stato Maggiore dell'Esercito, 2005), p. 292.

32 Badoglio to Mussolini, 3 November 1935: Longo, *La campagna italo-etiopica*, tomo II, pp. 245-66.

33 Pietro Badoglio, *La guerra d'Etiopia* (Milan: Mondadori, 1936), pp. 9, 29-30, 33.

34 Baistrocchi to Mussolini, 1 December 1935: Longo, *La campagna italo-etiopica*, tomo II, pp. 746-51.

35 Baistrocchi to Mussolini, 24 December 1935: Emilio Canevari, *La guerra italiana. Retroscena della disfatta* (Rome: Tosi, 1948), vol. I, p. 404 (original emphasis).

36 Badoglio to army corps commanders, 10 December 1935: Badoglio, *La guerra d'Etiopia*, p. 39.

37 'Rapporto sul combattimento del giorno 15 dicembre 1935 XIV di Dembeguinà', 15 December 1935; 'Decapitazione e tortura di prigionieri italiani' [30 December 1935]: Longo, *La campagna italo-etiopico*, tomo II, pp. 351–3, 803–4.

38 Badoglio to Mussolini, 30 December 1935: Longo, *La campagna italo-etiopica*, tomo II, p. 357.

39 Mussolini to Badoglio, 1 January 1936: *ibid.*, p. 419.

40 Mussolini to Badoglio, 14 January 1936: OO XXVII, p. 308.

41 Rochat, 'L'aeronautica italiana nella guerra d'Etiopia (1935–1936)', p. 108.

42 Badoglio, *La guerra d'Etiopia*, pp. 71, 75–7, 80, 83.

43 *Ibid.*, p. 87.

44 Pieri and Rochat, *Badoglio*, p. 693.

45 Longo, *La campagna italo-etiopica*, tomo I, pp. 268–79.

46 'Norme per le prossime operazioni', 21 February 1936: Longo, *La campagna italo-etiopica*, tomo II, p. 515.

47 Longo, *La campagna italo-etiopica*, tomo I, pp. 288–92.

48 'Offensive nello Scirè', 16 February 1936: Longo, *La campagna italo-etiopica*, tomo II, pp. 530–8.

49 Longo, *La campagna italo-etiopica*, tomo I, p. 296 fn. 292.

50 *Ibid.*, pp. 300–1.

51 Badoglio, *La guerra d'Etiopia*, pp. 173, 176.

52 Montanari, *Le guerre degli anni trenta*, p. 346.

53 T. Badoglio to Mussolini, 18 March 1936: Longo, *La guerra italo-etiopica*, tomo II, pp. 568–9.

54 Longo, *La guerra italo-etiopica*, tomo I, p. 325; Badoglio, *La guerra d'Etiopia*, p. 182.

55 Badoglio, *La guerra d'Etiopia*, p. 185.

56 Emilio Canevari, *Graziani mi ha detto* (Rome: Magi-Spinetti, 1947), p. 17.

57 For numbers, which vary, see Lucio Ceva, *Le forze armate* (Turin: UTET, 1981), p. 236; Longo, *La campagna italo-etiopica*, tomo I, p. 379.

58 Giorgio Rochat, 'L'impiego dei gas nella guerra d'Etiopia', in Angelo Del Boca, ed., *I gas di Mussolini* (Rome: Riuniti, 1996), pp. 64, 73–4, 179 fn. 71.

59 Giuseppe Maione, 'I costi delle imprese coloniali', in Angelo Del Boca, ed., *Le guerre coloniali del fascismo* (Bari: Laterza, 1991), pp. 401, 414–16.

60 Ferdinando Pedriali, 'Le armi chimiche in Africa Orientale. Storia, tecnica, obiettivi, efficacia', in Del Boca, ed., *I gas di Mussolini*, pp. 99, 100–3.

61 Badoglio, *La guerra d'Etiopia*, p. 213; Montanari, *Le guerre degli anni trenta*, p. 393.

62 Baistrocchi to Mussolini, 18 September 1936: Canevari, *La guerra italiana*, vol. I, pp. 381–3.

63 Nicola Labanca, 'Chi ha studiato il "consenso" alla guerra d'Etiopia?', in *Le forze armate e la nazione d'Italia (1915–1943). Atti del convegno di*

studi tenuto a Roma nei giorni 22–24 ottobre 2003 (Rome: Commissione italiana di storia militare, 2004), pp. 220–2, 225–6.

64 De Felice, *Gli anni del consenso*, p. 696 fn. 1.

65 John F. Coverdale, *Italian Intervention in the Spanish Civil War* (Princeton, NJ: Princeton University Press, 1975), pp. 70–84; Lucio Ceva, *Spagne 1936–1939. Politica e guerra civile* (Milan: Franco Angeli, 2010), pp. 268–70.

66 Enzo Collotti, *Fascismo e politica di Potenza. Politica estera 1922–1939* (Milan: RCS, 2000), pp. 293–6, 299, 308; 'Discorso di Milano', 1 November 1936: OO, XXVIII, p. 70.

67 'Intervista a un giornalista americano', 24 May 1937: OO, XXVIII, p. 184.

68 Lucio Ceva, 'L'opinione pubblica in Italia sulla guerra civile di Spagna (1936–1939)', in *Le forze armate e la nazione italiana (1915–1943)*, pp. 227–50; Renzo De Felice, *Mussolini il Duce* II: *Lo stato totalitario 1936–1940* (Turin: Einaudi, 1981), pp. 159–64, 177–8.

69 Sandro Attanasio, *Gli italiani e la guerra di Spagna* (Milan: Mursia, 1974), p. 77.

70 Ferdinando Pedriali, *Guerra di Spagna e aviazione italiana* (Pinerolo: Società storica pinerolese, 1989), pp. 132, 140–1.

71 Roatta to War Ministry etc., 8 November 1936: Alberto Rovighi and Filippo Stefani, *La partecipazione italiana alla guerra civile spagnola (1936–1939)* (Rome: Ufficio Storico dello Stato Maggiore dell'Esercito, 1992), vol. I, All. no. 13, p. 66.

72 AUSSME, Attività germanica [SIM], n.d. [c.15 October 1936]: F-18/1/33.

73 AUSSME, Roatta to SIM, 31 October 1936: F-18/1/5.

74 AUSSME, Roatta to SIM, 17 November 1936: F-18/5/12.

75 Pariani to Ciano, 28 November 1937: Rovighi and Stefani, *La partecipazione italiana*, vol. I, All. no. 20, pp. 135–6.

76 Marras to SIM, 2 December 1936: Rovighi and Stefani, *La partecipazione italiana*, vol. I, All. no. 22/a, pp. 143–4.

77 Verbale della riunione tenutasi a Palazzo Venezia presso il Capo del governo, 6 December 1936: Rovighi and Stefani, *La partecipazione italiana*, vol. I, All. no. 21, pp. 137–42.

78 Coverdale, *Italian Intervention*, p. 167.

79 Verbale della riunione a Palazzo Venezia, 14 January 1937: Rovighi and Stefani, *La partecipazione italiana*, vol. I, All. no. 27, pp. 156–69.

80 Direttive 'S', Pariani to MMIS, 18 January 1937: *ibid.*, pp. 198–200.

81 Rovighi and Stefani, *La partecipazione italiana*, vol. I, ch. IX; Coverdale, *Italian Intervention*, pp. 207–12.

82 Coverdale, *Italian Intervention*, pp. 215–16.

83 TNA, MMIS to Franco, 13 February 1937: Azione di Guadalajara, p. 1: GFM 36/254/048603.

84 Montanari, *Le guerre degli anni trenta*, pp. 504–6.

85 Pedriali, *Guerra di Spagna*, p. 184.

86 For the debate on numbers see Coverdale, *Italian Intervention*, p. 249 fn. 86.

87 'Colli' [Roatta] to U[fficio].S[pagna]., 19 March 1937, 'Colli' to Ciano, 20 March 1937: Ismael Saz and Javier Tusell, *Fascistas en España. La intervención italiana en la Guerra Civil a través de los telegramas del 'Missione Militare Italiana in Spagna' 15 Diciembre 1936–31 Marzo 1937* (Rome: Escuela Española de Historia y Arqueología en Roma, 1981), pp. 179–80, 181–3.

88 TNA, Azioni di Guadalajara, p. 77: GFM 36/254/048680.

89 Leonardo Sciascia, 'L'antimonio', in *Gli zii di Sicilia* (Turin: Einaudi, 1963), p. 212, quoted in Lucio Ceva, 'Ripensare Guadalajara', *Italia Contemporanea* no. 192, September 1993, p. 478.

90 TNA, Relazione dei RRCC sulla presa di Guadalajara, 21 March 1937, p. 5: GFM 36/254/048693.

91 AUSSME, To.01298, Ufficio Spagna to War Ministry, 15 April 1937: F-18/2/17; TNA, Bastico to Giuseppe Gaetano, 8 December 1944, p. 3: WO 204/12853.

92 Educazione alla guerra, 27 May 1937; La lotta contro i carri armati, 20 April 1937: Rovighi and Stefani, *La partecipazione italiana*, vol. I, All., pp. 360–9, 356–8.

93 AUSSME, Promemoria, 13 April 1937: F-18/5/9.

94 AUSSME, 'Doria' [Bastico] to Pariani, 28 May 1937, All., 'Sui danni della modestia': F-18/2/19.

95 AUSSME, Ciano to 'Doria', 2 May 1937: F-18/4/9.

96 Bastico to Ciano and Pariani, 31 May 1937: Canevari, *La guerra italiana*, vol. I, pp. 490–4.

97 Bastico to Ciano and Pariani, 18 June 1937: *ibid.*, vol. I, pp. 494–7.

98 AUSSME, Diario storico della Delegazione italiana presso il Cuartel General del Generalissimo, 30 February 1938, pp. 17–23: F-18/6/1.

99 Franco Bargoni, *L'impegno navale italiano durante la guerra civile spagnola (1936–1939)* (Rome: Ufficio Storico della Marina Militare, 1992), pp. 266–70, 314, 317–18.

100 AUSSME, Mussolini to 'Doria', 20 July 1937: F-18/4/9; Viola to [?Pariani], 22 July 1937: F-18/4/11.

101 AUSSME, Mussolini to 'Doria', 4 August 1937: F-18/4/9.

102 Rovighi and Stefani, *La partecipazione italiana*, vol. I, pp. 420–4, 430–63.

103 'Stralcio dalla "Relazione sulla battaglia di Santander", 14–26 agosto 1937': *ibid.*, vol. I, All. doc. 131, p. 562.

104 AUSSME, Diario storico della Delegazione italiano presso il Cuartel General del Generalisimo, p. 33: F-18/6/1.

105 AUSSME, N.32, Bastico to Ciano and Pariani, 10 September 1937, p. 4: F-18/4/25; Viaggio compiuto in Spagna dal 21 al 31 agosto u.s., 2 September 1937: F-18/5/4.

106 ASV, Diario, 25 August and 2 October 1937: Archivio Pariani b.7.

107 Galeazzo Ciano, *Diario 1937–1943* (Milan: Rizzoli, 1980), p. 43 (6 October 1937).

108 AUSSME, N.4, Berti to Ciano, 6 November 1937: F-18/4/7; N.6, Pr, Berti to Pariani, 16 November 1937: F-18/4/25.

109 AUSSME, N.9, Berti to Ciano, 1 December 1937: F-18/4/27.

110 AUSSME, N.025949, Pariani to Ciano, 5 December 1937: F-18/4/26; N.3088, Mussolini to Berti, 14 December 1937: F-18/4/25.

111 ASV, Diario, 27 December 1937: Archivio Pariani b.7.

112 Coverdale, *Italian Intervention*, p. 338.

113 AUSSME, N.39, Ciano to Berti, 6 January 1938: F-18/5/28.

114 Lucio Ceva, 'L'ultima vittoria del Fascismo Spagna 1938–1939', *Italia Contemporanea* no. 196, September 1994, p. 521.

115 Rovighi and Stefani, *La partecipazione italiana*, vol. II, pp. 88–90.

116 *Ibid.*, pp. 155–8; Coverdale, *Italian Intervention*, pp. 350–1.

117 Ciano, *Diario*, p. 131 (30 April 1938).

118 Muti to Ciano, 6 June 1938: Rovighi and Stefani, *La partecipazione italiana*, vol. II, All, p. 170.

119 AUSSME, Situazione politico-militare nella Spagna rossa, 28 June 1938: F-18/3/19.

120 Rovighi and Stefani, *La partecipazione italiana*, vol. II, pp. 244–7.

121 AUSSME, Berri to Ciano, 9 August 1938: F-18/4/28; Consulate General Marseilles to Foreign Ministry, 10 August 1938: F-18/4/10.

122 AUSSME, Margottini to Marina Roma, 30 August 1938: F-18/3/19.

123 Ciano, *Diario*, pp. 164–5, 167, 169 (12, 21 and 29 August 1938); Rovighi and Stefani, *La partecipazione italiana*, vol. II, pp. 276–9.

124 AUSSME, Gambara to Pietromarchi, 13 November 1938, p. 5: F-18/6/7.

125 Gastone Gambara, 'L'ultima parola sulla guerra di Spagna', *Tempo*, 22 August 1957, quoted in Ceva, 'L'ultima vittoria del Fascismo', pp. 524–5.

126 Ciano, *Diario*, p. 273 (28 March 1939).

127 AUSSME, Appunto per il ministro Pietromarchi, n.d., pp. 1–5, 6–8: F-18/1/33.

128 Dati numerici dalla 'Relazione finale sulle attività dello "Ufficio Spagna"', Rovighi and Stefani, *La partecipazione italiana*, vol. II, All. no. 115, pp. 454–7.

129 Materiali del Ministero della Guerra forniti alla Spagna Nazionale, in *ibid.*, no. 116, pp. 462–4.

130 Rovighi and Stefani, *La partecipazione italiana*, vol. II, All., p. 482.

131 NARS, Osservazioni e constatazioni fatte nella guerra di Spagna, 1 February 1939, p. 1: T-821/231/5701.

132 Montanari, *Le guerre degli anni trenta*, p. 641.

133 Ciano, *Diario*, pp. 95–6 (8 February 1938); Claudia Baldoli, 'L'Italia meridionale sotto le bombe, 1940–44', *Meridiana* no. 82, 2015, pp. 46–50.

134 Osservazioni e constatazioni fatte nella guerra di Spagna, p. 4.

135 Dati d'esperienza relativi ai reparti specializzati e desunti dalle recenti operazioni, 31 March 1937; Raggruppamento reparti specializzati-Comando, 15 September 1937; Raggruppamento carristi – relazione sulle operazioni da Rudilla (19 marzo) a Tortosa (19 aprile 1938); Note sull'impiego delle minori unità di fanteria e artiglieria nella guerra di Spagna, 20 May 1938: Rovighi and Stefani, *La partecipazione italiana*, vol. II, All. nos. 123, 124, 125, 127, pp. 474–7, 478–87, 488–507, 511–27.

136 Promemoria relativo alla sostituzione della divisione ternaria, n.d.: *ibid.*, no. 113, pp. 449–52.

137 AUSSME, Contributo dell'esercito alla guerra in Spagna, n.d., p. 3: F-18/1/31.

138 Quirino Armellini, *Diario di guerra. Nove mesi al Comando Supremo* (Milan: Garzanti, 1946), pp. 9–10 (24 May 1940).

CHAPTER 2

1 AUSSME, Cadorna to Zupelli, 26 November 1914: F-3/85/6.

2 Emilio Canevari, *La guerra italiana. Retroscena della disfatta* (Rome: Tosi, 1948), vol. I, p. 127.

3 Il problema della motorizzazione e della meccanizzazione nei riguardi dello sviluppo degli eserciti moderni, n.d.: Paolo Matucci, *Federico Baistrocchi, Sottosegretaria (1933–1936)* (Florence: Pagnini, 2006), pp. 89–94.

4 *L'esercito italiano tra la 1a e la 2a guerra mondiale* (Rome: Ufficio Storico dello Stato Maggiore dell'Esercito, 1954), pp. 124–9.

5 Filippo Stefani, *La storia della dottrina e degli ordinamenti dell'esercito italiano*, vol. II, tomo 1: *Da Vittorio Veneto alla 2a Guerra Mondiale* (Rome: Ufficio Storico dello Stato Maggiore dell'Esercito, 1985), pp. 331–2 fn. 58.

6 BA-MA, Von Rintelen to von Tippelskirch, 18 June 1937: RH 2/2936.

7 AMR, Visita in Germania, 4–11 July 1938. Quaderni Pariani XXVIII.

8 Appunti sulla visita in Germania (7–12 July) [1938]: [Mario Montanari], *L'esercito italiano alla vigilia della 2a guerra mondiale* (Rome: Ufficio Storico dello Stato Maggiore dell'Esercito, 1982), pp. 374–6.

9 AUSSME, Carlo Geloso, 'Con la Ia Armata nella guerra contro la Grecia' (unpubl. mss.), ch. 1, p. 2: L-13/105/8.

10 Notes for Wehrmacht Discussions with Italy, 26 November 1938: *DGFP* D/IV no. 412 enc., pp. 530–1.

11 ASMAE, Ciano to Attolico, 23 February and 23 March 1939: UC4 #1120/3/4; UC6 #1122/5/2.

12 BA-MA, Von Rintelen to von Tippelskirch, 21 March 1939: RH 2/2936.

13 AUSSME, N.608, 'Futuri obiettivi dell'azione politico-militare della Germania', 18 March 1939; N.674, 'Germania e Polonia', 25 March 1939: L-13/47/3.

14 Record of the Keitel–Pariani conversation 4 [5] April 1939: *DGFP* D/VI App. I/III, p. 111; Verbale riassuntivo del colloquio tra il generale Pariani ed il Generale Keitel del 5 aprile 1935: [Montanari], *L'esercito italiano alla vigilia della 2a guerra mondiale*, pp. 379–80; Mario Toscano, 'Le conversazioni militari italo-tedesche alla vigilia della seconda guerra mondiale', *Rivista Storica Italiana* anno LXIV, fasc. 3, December 1952, p. 350.

15 Promemoria per SE il Sottosegretario alla guerra, Pariani, 5 April 1939: [Montanari], *L'esercito italiano alla vigilia della 2a guerra mondiale*, p. 383.

16 AUSSME, Dati forniti a SE Pariani per le sue conversazioni con la missione militare italiana: Materiale da richiedere (n.d.); Preventivo sommario del fabbisogno principali materie per alimentazione esercito e funzionamento industria bellica per esercito durante primo anno di guerra [6 May 1939]: L-13/44/5.

17 ASMAE, Stralcio della relazione della R. Legazione d'Italia in Atene per l'anno 1937; Boscarelli to Ciano, 29 November 1938: Affari Politici: Grecia 1941–45 b.18.

18 ASMAE, To.3085/468, Athens to Ministero degli Esteri, 3 May 1939: Affari Politici: Grecia 1941–45 b.18.

19 Giordano Bruno Guerri, *Galeazzo Ciano. Una vita 1903/1944* (Milan: Bompiani, 1979), pp. 374–5; G. Bruce Strang, *On the Fiery March: Mussolini Prepares for War* (Westport, CT: Praeger, 2003), pp. 242–3.

20 *Le truppe italiane in Albania (Anni 1914–20 e 1939)* (Rome: Ufficio Storico dello Stato Maggiore dell'Esercito, 1978), pp. 255–6, 261, 273–5.

21 AUSSME, Germania. Eventualità di operazioni contro la Polonia, 6 May 1939: F-9/2/39.

22 Mussolini to Cavagnari, 27 May 1939: Francesco Mattesini, *Corrispondenza e direttive tecnico-operative di Supermarina*, vol. I, tomo 1: *Maggio 1939–Luglio 1940* (Rome: Ufficio Storico dello Stato Maggiore della Marina Militare, 2000), pp. 65–6 (original emphasis).

23 Criteri base per la collaborazione in campo operative navale, 12 June 1939; Convegno italo-tedesco di Friedrichshafen Resoconto sulla riunione del 20.6.39; Riunione del 21.6.1939: Mattesini, *Corrispondenza di Supermarina* I/1, pp. 72–9, 95–100, 100–5; Toscano, 'Le conversazioni militari', pp. 368–7, 377.

24 Relazione sui colloqui di Friederichshafen, 20–21 June 1939: Mattesini, *Corrispondenza di Supermarina* I/1, p. 92; Record of the conversation at Friedrichshafen on 20–21 June 1939; Conversation between the Italian Admirals Sansonetti and de Courten and Rear-Admiral Schniewind and Captain Frick, 21 June 1939: *DGFP* D/VI App I/XIII, pp. 1,121, 1,125.

25 Relazione sul viaggio in Germania: Lucio Ceva, 'Altre notizie sulle conversazioni militari italo-tedesche alla vigilia della seconda guerra mondiale (aprile–giugno 1939)', *Il Risorgimento* anno XXX, no. 3, October 1978, pp. 175–8.

26 Mussolini to Ciano, 7 July 1939: *DDI* 8/XII, no. 505, pp. 381–2.

27 Enzo Collotti, *Fascismo e politica di potenza. Politica estera 1922–1939* (Milan: RCS, 2000), p. 450.

28 Galeazzo Ciano, *Diario 1937–1943* (Milan: Rizzoli, 1980), p. 325 (6 August 1939).

29 Malcolm Muggeridge, ed., *Ciano's Diplomatic Papers* (London: Odhams, 1948), pp. 299, 301, 302.

30 Secondo appunto per il Ministro degli esteri, Ciano, 21 August 1939: [Montanari], *L'esercito italiano alla vigilia della 2a guerra mondiale*, pp. 437–8.

31 AUSSME, Badoglio to Valle, Cavagnari and Pariani, 17 August 1939: I-4/7/7.

32 Badoglio to Mussolini, 17 August 1939: *DSCS* 1/2, p. 103.

33 AUSSME, Badoglio to Valle, Cavagnari and Pariani, 27 August 1939: I-4/7/7.

34 Studi operative (Gandin), n.d.; Pariani memorandum, 27 August 1939: *DSCS* 1/2, pp. 104–5, 106–9.

35 Roatta Diary, 15 August 1939. AUSSME, Intenzioni germaniche (Roatta), 16 August 1939: F-18/2/39.

36 'Berlino 1939' (unpubl. mss), Roatta, p. 15. Sergio Pelagalli, *Il generale Efisio Marras addetto militare a Berlino (1936–1943)* (Rome: Ufficio Storico dello Stato Maggiore dell'Esercito, 1994), pp. 86–7.

37 Roatta Diary, 25 August 1939. AUSSME, Notizie sui proposti germanici (Roatta), 26 August 1939: F-18/2/39.

38 Mussolini to Badoglio, 23 August 1939, Badoglio to Mussolini, 31 August 1939: *DSCS* 1/2, pp. 145, 150.

39 Marco Cuzzi, 'L'opinione pubblica italiana e lo scoppio della guerra', in *Le forze armate e la nazione italiana (1915–1943). Atti del Convegno di Studi tenuto a Roma nei giorni 22–24 ottobre 2003* (Rome: Commissione italiana di storia militare, 2004), pp. 326–34.

40 Ciano, *Diario*, p. 341 (2 September 1939).

41 'Alla "Decima legio"', 23 September 1939: *OO* XXIX, p. 312.

42 'Rapporto ai gerarchi di Genova', 30 September 1939: *OO* XXIX, p. 316.

43 AMR, Pariani to Bancale, 25 August 1939: Quaderni Pariani XXXXIII.

44 AMR, Pariani to Bancale and Soddu, 2 September 1939, Riunione Libia, 26 September 1939, Pariani to Bancale, 28 September 1939: Quaderni Pariani XXXXI, XXXXIII; *L'esercito italiano tra la 1a e la 2a guerra mondiale*, pp. 183–4; Mario Caracciolo di Feroleto, *Memorie di un Generale d'Armata. Mezzo secolo nel Regio Esercito* (Padua: Nova Charta, 2006), pp. 263–7.

45 Fortunato Minniti, *Fino alla guerra. Strategia e conflitto nella politica di potenza di Mussolini 1923–1940* (Naples: Edizioni Scientifiche Italiane, 2000), pp. 200–1.

46 Mario Cervi, *The Hollow Legions: Mussolini's Blunder in Greece 1940–41* (London: Chatto & Windus, 1972), p. 9.

47 ASMAE, To.6053/957, Politica estera greca, 6 August 1939; Rapporti italo-greci, 6 September 1939: Affari Politici: Grecia 1941–45 b.18.

48 ASMAE, Accordo italo-greco sul ritiro truppe frontiera Greco-albanese: Affari Politici: Grecia 1941–45, b. 18.

49 Rapporti, 11 September 1939 (Genoa), 13 September 1939 (Rome), 16 September 1939 (Milan), 27 September 1939 (Tripoli): [Montanari], *L'esercito italiano alla vigilia della 2a guerra mondiale*, pp. 509–14.

50 Mussolini to Vittorio Emanuele III, 27 October 1939: Dorello Ferrari, 'La mobilitazione dell'esercito nella seconda guerra mondiale', *Storia contemporanea* anno XIII, no. 6, December 1992, p. 1,015.

51 Situazione delle forze armate alla data del 1o novembre 1939 [Badoglio]: *DSCS* I/II, pp. 157–9. Efficienza delle forze armate, 2 November 1939 [Pariani]: [Montanari], *L'esercito italiano alla vigilia della 2a guerra mondiale*, pp. 367–70.

52 Ezio Ferrante, *Il pensiero strategico navale in Italia* (Rome: Rivista Marittima, 1988), pp. 42–56.

53 Esame del problema strategico in caso di conflitto, nella attuale situazione politica, 20 August 1939: Mattesini, ed., *Corrispondenza di Supermarina* I/1, pp. 138–41.

54 Giovanni Ansaldo, *Il giornalista di Ciano. Diari 1932–1943* (Bologna: Il Mulino, 2000), p. 196: quoted in Enrico Cernuschi, *Domenico Cavagnari: Storia di un Ammiraglio* (Rome: Rivista Marittima, 2001), p. 181.

55 Ferrante, *Il pensiero strategico navale in Italia*, pp. 57–8.

56 Deficienze di personale, mezzi ed apprestamenti vari della Regia Marina, 21 February 1940: Mattesini, *Corrispondenza di Supermarina* I/1, pp. 233–41.

57 Magistrati to Ciano, 17 September 1939: *DDI* 9/I, no. 295, p. 177. The assistant air attaché in Berlin, Lieutenant-Colonel Roero di Cortanze, thought the same: James J. Sadkovich, 'Some Considerations Regarding Italian Armoured Doctrine Prior to June 1940', *Global War Studies*, vol. 9, no. 1, 2012, p. 56.

58 AUSSME, La campagna polacca secondo la propaganda germanica (SIM), 21 November 1939: H-5/2a/2.

59 IWM(D), N.2258/S, Notizie circa l'azione dell'aviazione tedesca su Varsavia, 27 September 1939; Relazione su di una visita al fronte orientale, 30 September 1939, pp. 2–3, 8: E.2542.

60 IWM(D), Relazione riassuntiva del grande stato maggiore Tedesco sulla campagna in Polonia, 4 October 1939, p. 7: E.2542.

61 IWM(D), N.18974, Teucci to General Eraldo Ilari, 9 October 1939: E.2542.

62 IWM(D), Considerazione sulla guerra di Polonia, 8 October 1939: E.2542.

63 Teucci to Valle, 13 October 1939: *DDI* 9/I, no. 755 All. 1, pp. 471–2.

64 AUSSME, Argomenti da trattare alla riunione dei Capi di SM del 16 novembre [1939], p. 1: H-10/1/f. 4.

65 Seduta del 18 novembre 1939: [Carlo Mazzaccara and Antonello Biagini, eds.,] *Verbali delle riunioni tenute dal Capo di SM Generale*, vol. I: *26 gennaio 1939–29 dicembre 1940* (Rome: Ufficio Storico dello Stato Maggiore dell'Esercito, 1983), p. 18.

66 AUSSME, Promemoria per il Duce: Comunicazioni dell'addetto militare germanico, 3 April 1940: H-9/8/1.

67 Sadkovich, 'Some Considerations Regarding Italian Armoured Doctrine Prior to June 1940', pp. 58, 60.

68 BA-MA, Von Rintelen to von Tippelskirch, 5 September 1939: RH 2/2936.

69 Muggeridge, ed., *Ciano's Diplomatic Papers*, p. 314 (1 October 1939); Renzo De Felice, *Mussolini il Duce* II: *Lo stato totalitario 1936–1940* (Turin: Einaudi, 1981), p. 677 (7 October 1939).

70 BA-MA, Von Rintelen to von Tippelskirch, 14 November 1939: RH 2/2936.

71 Seduta del 18 Novembre 1939: *Verbali delle riunioni tenute dal Capo di SM Generale* I, pp. 16–31.

72 Mario Montanari, *Politica e strategia in cento anni di guerre italiane*, vol. III, tomo 2: *La seconda guerra mondiale* (Rome: Ufficio Storico dello Stato Maggiore dell'Esercito, 2007), p. 226.

73 AUSSME, Punto fermo sull'ordinamento, 19 December 1939: L-14/121.

74 Mussolini to Hitler, 5 January 1940: *DDI* 9/III, no. 33, pp. 19–22.

75 Ciano, *Diario*, pp. 389–90 (23 January 1940); Giuseppe Bottai, *Diario 1935–1944* (Milan: Rizzoli, 2001), pp. 174–5 (23 January 1940).

76 AUSSME, Sintesi degli argomenti trattati dal sottocapo di SM nella riunione del 18 gennaio 1940: H-10/8/3.

77 Programmi delle Forze Armate, 11 December 1939: [Montanari], *L'esercito italiano alla vigilia della 2a guerra mondiale*, pp. 515–21; Carlo Favagrossa, *Perché perdemmo la guerra* (Milan: Rizzoli, 1946), pp. 112, 114, 115, 116, 118.

78 FLE, Pietromarchi Diary, 12 January 1940.

79 Programmi, 16 February 1940; Situazione in caso di conflitto, 13 May 1940; Munizionamento, 1 June 1940: Favagrossa, *Perché perdemmo la guerra*, pp. 258–61, 263–6, 267–8.

80 Fondazione Wilsoniana, Riccardi *Memoriale* [mss., 1946], pp. 78, 87–8: Fondo Riccardi.

81 AUSSME, Relazione di SE il Ministro della Marina: Scorte, February 1940: F-9/60/1.

82 AUSSME, Relazione di SE il Sottosegretario di guerra: Scorte, February 1940: F-9/60/1.

83 AUSSME, Promemoria per il Duce: Programma nuova artiglieria, 22 December 1939: H-9/3/5.

84 AUSSME, Commissione Suprema di Difesa Verbali della XVII Sessione (8–14 febbraio 1940), 1a seduta, 8 February 1940, pp. 9–15: F-9/57/2.

85 Commissione Suprema di Difesa, 1a seduta, 8 February 1940, pp. 24–5.

86 Commissione Suprema di Difesa, 2a seduta, 9 February 1940, pp. 37–40.

87 Commissione Suprema di Difesa, 3a seduta, 10 February 1940, pp. 51–3, 59.

88 *Ibid.*, pp. 75–7.

89 AUSSME, Preparazione bellica in Africa Settentrionale, January 1940: F-9/62/1.

90 Commissione Suprema di Difesa, 5a seduta, 13 February 1940, pp. 116, 117–18.

91 Cristiano Andrea Ristuccia, 'The Italian Economy under Fascism: 1934–1943. The Rearmament Paradox', D. Phil. University of Oxford, 2008, pp. 68–81, 94, 98, 296–7.

92 AUSSME, Organizzazione militare delle terre italiane d'Oltremare, n.d.: F-9/62/1.

93 Bottai, *Diario 1935–1944*, p. 176 (4 February 1940).

94 AUSSME, Verbale della riunione del 21 febbraio 1940, p. 5: H-10/1/5.

95 Favagrossa to Mussolini, 16 February 1940: Favagrossa, *Perché perdemmo la guerra*, pp. 258–61.

96 AUSSME, Verbale della riunione del 21 febbraio 1940, p. 8: H-10/1/5.

97 IWM(D), Fabriguerra: Reports and drafts Italian war production and essential war materials position, 1939–40, n.d [apparently prepared in late 1941], Part 2, pp. 11–13: Speer Collection FD 1940/44; [Montanari], *L'esercito italiano alla vigilia della 2a guerra mondiale*, pp. 293–6; Nicola Pignato and Filippo Cappellano, *Le armi della fanteria italiana (1919–1945)* (Parma: Albertelli Edizioni Speciali, 2008), pp. 71–3, 99, 100.

98 AUSSME, N.54A, Marras to War Ministry, 16 January 1940; Dalla conversazione con H[alder], 31 January 1940; N.72A, Marras to War Ministry, 20 January 1940: L-13/45/2.

99 AUSSME, N.184A, Marras to War Ministry, 16 February 1940; N.151A, Marras to War Ministry, 10 February 1940: L-13/45/2.

100 AUSSME, N.345/A, Situazione politico-militare, 9 March 1940: L-13/45/2.

101 BA-MA, Conversation with Roatta, 16 March 1940: RH 2/2936.

102 BA-MA, Matzky to von Rintelen, 14 March 1940: RH 2/2936.

103 Hitler to Mussolini, 8 March 1940: *DDI* 9/III, no. 492, pp. 415–23.

104 Colloquio del Capo del Governo, Mussolini, con il cancelliere del Reich, Hitler, 18 March 1940: *DDI* 9/III, no, 578, pp. 503–7; MacGregor Knox, *Mussolini Unleashed 1939–1941: Politics and Strategy in Fascist Italy's Last War* (Cambridge: Cambridge University Press, 1982), p. 87. Gin suggests that Mussolini's attitude at this conference was 'instrumental' and not wholehearted: Emilio Gin, *L'ora segnata del destino. Gli Alleati e Mussolini da Monaco all'intervento settembre 1938–giugno 1940* (Rome: Nuova Cultura, 2012), p. 287.

105 Mussolini to Vittorio Emanuele III, Ciano, Badoglio, Graziani, Cavagnari and Pricolo, 31 March 1940: *DDI* 9'III, no. 669, pp. 576–9.

106 Marras to SIM, 7 April 1940: *DSCS* I/2, pp. 202–3.

107 Seduta del 9 aprile 1940: *Verbali delle riunioni tenute dal Capo di SM Generale* I, pp. 32–42.

108 Badoglio to Mussolini, 11 April 1940: Mattesini, *Corrispondenza di Supermarina* I/1, pp. 270–1.

109 Claretta Petacci, *Verso il disastro. Mussolini in guerra. Diari 1939–40* (Milan: Rizzoli, 2011), p. 313 (11 April 1940); Ugo Guspini, *L'orecchio del regime. Le intercettazioni telefoniche al tempo del fascismo* (Milan: Mursia, 1973), p. 168 (10 May 1940).

110 Promemoria [Graziani], 11 April 1939: *DSCS* I/2, pp. 194–6.

111 Seduta del 9 aprile 1940: *Verbali delle riunioni tenute dal Capo di SM Generale* I, p. 41; Promemoria consegnata al Capo del Governo dal CSM della Marina il 14 aprile 1940: Cernuschi, *Cavagnari*, pp. 301–2.

112 Ciano, *Diario*, p. 418 (11 April 1940).

113 Badoglio to Mussolini, 15 April 1940: *DSCS* I/2, p. 205.

114 AUSSME, N.546A, Marras to Head of SIM, 4 May 1940: L-13/45/4.

115 Seduta del 6 maggio 1940: *Verbali delle riunioni tenute dal Capo di SM Generale* I, pp. 43–7; Balbo to Mussolini, 11 May 1940: Giorgio Rochat, *Italo Balbo* (Turin: UTET, 1986), pp. 288–9.

116 AUSSME, N.578/A, Offensiva alla fronte occidentale, 8 May 1940: L-13/45/3.

117 Ciano, *Diario*, pp. 427–9 (10 May 1940).

118 Gobbi to Ciano, 8 May 1940; Pavolini to Attolico, 11 May 1940; Ciano to Talamo, 12 May 1940; Bonfatti to Soddu, 11 May 1940: *DDI* 9/IV, nos. 335, 371, 395, 397 All., pp. 267–8, 301, 328, 329–30.

119 Ciano, *Diario*, pp. 430 (13 May 1940).

120 Favagrossa to Mussolini, 13 May 1940: Favagrossa, *Perché perdemmo la guerra*, pp. 263–6.

121 'Alle gerarchie trentine', 16 May 1940: OO XXIX, pp. 393–5.

122 Mussolini to Roosevelt, 18 May 1940; Mussolini to Churchill, 18 May 1940: *DDI* 9/IV, nos. 486, 487, pp. 389–90.

123 NARS, Geloso to Soddu and Graziani, 25 May 1940: T-821/127/fr. 172–4.

124 AUSSME, Efficienza dell'esercito, 25 May 1940: H-9/6/2. Original emphasis.

125 Ugoberto Alfassio Grimaldi and Gherardo Bozzetti, *Dieci giugno 1940. Il giorno della follia* (Bari: Laterza, 1974), p. 747.

126 Riunione, 29 May 1940: *DDI* 9/IV, no. 642, pp. 495–7. Exactly when Mussolini made his decision is a matter of some dispute. After the war Badoglio claimed in his memoirs that he learned on 26 May of Mussolini's

decision to enter the war on 5 June. De Felice, who believes the decision was taken two days later, demolishes the claim: De Felice, *Lo stato totalitario*, pp. 823–4, 832–3. On the basis of different evidence Gin opts for 27 May: Gin, *L'ora segnata del destino*, p. 388.

127 Cuzzi, 'L'opinione pubblica italiana e lo scoppio della guerra', pp. 338–50; Lucio Ceva, 'Voci dai vari "fronti"', in Anna Lisa Carlotti, ed., *Italia 1939–1945. Storia e memoria* (Milan: Vita e Pensiero, 1996), p. 179.

128 Di.Na.Zero-Concetti Generali di azione in Mediterraneo nella ipotesi di conflitto Alfa Uno, 29 May 1940: Mattesini, *Corrispondenza de Supermarina* I/1, pp. 317–19.

129 Mussolini to Hitler, 30 May 1940; Hitler to Mussolini, 31 May 1940: *DDI* 9/IV, nos. 646, 680, pp. 500, 519–21; Gin, *L'ora segnata del destino*, pp. 400–1 fn. 206.

130 Seduta del 30 maggio 1940: *Verbali delle riunioni tenute dal Capo di SM Generale* I, pp. 48–53.

131 Minniti, *Fino alla guerra*, pp. 213–14 (31 May 1940).

132 AUSSME, Stato d'efficienza dell'esercito al Io giugno 1940: M-3/3.

133 Badoglio to Mussolini, 1 June 1940: *DDI* 9/IV, no. 694, pp. 536–7; Quirino Armellini, *Diario di guerra. Nove mesi al Comando Supremo* (Milan: Garzanti, 1946), pp. 14–15 (1 June 1940).

134 Favagrossa to Mussolini, 1 June 1940: Favagrossa, *Perché perdemmo la guerra*, pp. 267–8.

135 Mussolini to Hitler, 2 June 1940: *DDI* 9/IV, no. 706, pp. 541–2.

136 AUSSME, Invio di truppe in Germania, 3 June 1940: H-9/8/1; DSCS I/1, p. 6 (11 June 1940).

137 Undated note written shortly before 10 June 1940: Grimaldi and Bozzetti, *Dieci giugno 1940*, pp. 398–9.

138 De Felice, *Lo stato totalitario*, pp. 839 fn. 133, 840.

139 Costituzione e funzionamento del Comando Supremo delle FF.AA. in caso di guerra, 4 June 1940; Costituzione dello Stato Maggiore Generale, 6 June 1940: Mattesini, *Corrispondenza di Supermarina* I/1, pp. 350–2, 353–4. The staffs changed their names: the army general staff became *Superesercito*, the navy general staff *Supermarina* and the air force general staff *Superaereo*.

140 Costituzione dell'organo operativo dello Stato Maggiore della R. Marina, n.d.: *ibid.*, pp. 313–14.

141 Seduta del 5 giugno 1940: *Verbali delle riunioni tenute dal Capo di SM Generale* I, pp. 54–8; François-Poncet to Ciano, 3 June 1940: *DDI* 9/IV, no. 728, p. 557.

142 PR 12, Direttive operative, 8 June 1940 [Stato Maggiore della R. Aeronautica]: Mattesini, *Corrispondenza di Supermarina* I/1, pp. 360–3.

CHAPTER 3

1 AUSSME, Istituto superiore di guerra, 'Appunti per lo studio degli Scac-chieri di Operazioni: Gli Scacchieri italo-germanici/Lo scacchiero alpino italo-francese', anno 1938–9, fasc. XII, pp. 3–13, 43: I-3/211/1.

2 AUSSME, Roatta to Carboni, 30 December 1939: H-3/35/2; Carboni to Roatta, 20 January 1940: H-3/35/4.

3 AUSSME, Francia-Sforzo Massimo di mobilitazione e preventive intend-imenti operative, 7 February 1940: H-3/35/4.

4 AUSSME, SIM to Under-Secretary of War, [25?] March, 27 March, 30 March, 1 April, 23 April, 4 June 1940: H-3/35/4.

5 AUSSME, SIM–FRANCIA–Le nuove forme di lotta e la dottrina tattica francese, 27 May 1940: H-3/35/4.

6 AUSSME, Graziani to Army Group West, 30 May 1940; N.70, Graziani to 1st Army, 4th Army, AG West, 1 June 1940; Lavori di fortificazione alla frontiera alpina, 7 June 1940; Graziani to Army Group West, 7 June 1940: N-9/2072/1.

7 [Vincenzo Gallinari], *Le operazioni del giugno 1940 sulle Alpi occidentali* (Rome: Ufficio Storico dello Stato Maggiore dell'Esercito, 1994), pp. 30, 105–6.

8 AUSSME, Graziani to Army Group West, 14 June 1940: N-9/2071/1.

9 *DSCS* I/1, p. 22.

10 AUSSME, N.1875, Graziani to Army Group West, 6th and 7th Armies, 16 June 1940: N-9/2071/1. Original emphasis.

11 *DSCS* I/1, p. 31 (17 June 1940); AUSSME, N.1926, Operazioni offensive, 17 June 1940: N-9/2071/1.

12 [Gallinari], *Le operazioni sulle Alpi occidentali*, p. 116.

13 USAMHI, 'Personal Notes on the Franco-Italian Armistice' [Roatta], n.d., p. 2: William Donovan Collection, Box 74B.

14 AUSSME, Graziani to Badoglio, 19 June 1940, encl. Memoriale 18–19 June (Roatta): I-4/7/11. See MacGregor Knox, *Mussolini Unleashed 1939–1941: Politics and Strategy in Fascist Italy's Last War* (Cambridge: Cambridge University Press, 1982), pp. 126–9.

15 'Personal Notes on the Franco-Italian Armistice', p. 1; Galeazzo Ciano, *Diario 1937–1943* (Milan: Rizzoli, 1980), pp. 443–4 (18–19 June 1940).

16 AUSSME, 'In viaggio, 19 June 1940' (Roatta), enclosed with Graziani to Badoglio, 19 June 1940: I-4/7/11.

17 [Gallinari], *Le operazione sulle Alpi occidentali*, p. 116.

18 Ciano, *Diario*, p. 444 (20 June 1940).

19 *DSCS* I/1, p. 47 (20 June 1940); [Gallinari], *Le operazioni sulle Alpi occi-dentali*, pp. 130–1, 134–6; Quirino Armellini, *Diario di guerra. Nove mesi al Comando Supremo* (Milan: Garzanti, 1946), pp. 32–5 (20–21 June 1940).

20 Klaus Meier *et al.*, *Germany and the Second World War,* vol.II: *Germany's Initial Conquests in Europe* (Oxford: Clarendon Press, 1991, p. 303.

21 *DSCS* I/1, p. 53, 21 June 1940.

22 'Personal Notes on the Franco-Italian Armistice', p. 8.

23 *DSCS* I/1, p. 60, 22 June 1940.

24 Ugo Guspini, *L'orecchio del regime. Le intercettazioni telefoniche al tempo del fascismo* (Milan: Mursia, 1973), p. 177, 23 June 1924.

25 *DSCS* I/1, p. 147, 7 July 1940.

26 [Gallinari], *Le operazioni sulle Alpi occidentali*, pp. 205–6.

27 Claretta Petacci, *Verso il disastro. Mussolini in guerra. Diari 1939–1940* (Milan: Rizzoli, 2011), pp. 342–3, 28 June 1940.

28 AUSSME, Carlo Geloso, 'Con la Ia Armata nella guerra contro la Grecia', ch. 1, pp. 14–15: L-13/105/8.

29 See Nir Arielli, *Fascist Italy and the Middle East, 1933–1940* (Basingstoke: Palgrave Macmillan, 2010); Massimiliano Fiore, 'The Clash of Empires: Anglo-Italian Relations in the Middle East and the Origins of the Second World War, 1935–1940', PhD University of London, 2008.

30 AUSSME, La suddivisione del territorio Africano in zone d'influenza, n.d. [? June 1940]: I-4/32; Pier Paolo Battistelli, 'La "guerra dell'Asse". Condotta bellica e collaborazione militare italo-tedesca 1939–1943', Tesi di dottorato Università degli Studi Padova, 2000, p. 124.

31 ACS, Roatta to Graziani, 12 July 1940; Roatta to Graziani, 27 September 1940: Carte Graziani 58/47/ 9.

32 Seduta del 25 giugno 1940: *Verbali delle riunioni tenute dal Capo di SM Generale*, vol. I: *26 gennaio 1939–29 dicembre 1940* (Rome: Ufficio Storico dello Stato Maggiore dell'Esercito, 1983), pp. 62–6.

33 Badoglio to Balbo, 25 June 1940; Badoglio to Balbo, 26 June 1940: Ministero della Difesa, *In Africa settentrionale: La preparazione al conflitto. L'avanzata su Sidi el Barrani (ottobre 1935–settembre 1940)* (Rome: Ufficio Storico dello Stato Maggiore dell'Esercito, 1955), pp. 94–5.

34 Bastian Matteo Scianna, 'Myths and Memories: The Italian Operations on the Eastern Front (1941–1943) and Their Contested Legacies during the Cold War', D.Phil University of Potsdam, 2017, p. 92.

35 *DSCS* I/1, pp. 61, 83, 22 and 26 June 1940.

36 Alfieri to Ciano, 1 July 1940: *DDI* 9/V, no. 161, pp. 148–9.

37 Ciano, *Diario*, p. 45 (17 July 1940); 'Conversation with the Feuhrer [*sic*]', 7 July 1940: Malcolm Muggeridge, ed., *Ciano's Diplomatic Papers* (London: Odhams, 1948), pp. 375–9; Knox, *Mussolini Unleashed*, pp. 140–2.

38 Geloso, 'Con la Ia Armata nella guerra contro la Grecia', ch. 1, p. 13.

39 AUSSME, Eventuale azione contro la Jugoslavia, 9 July 1940: N-9/ 2072/2.

40 Battistelli, 'La "guerra dell'Asse"', p. 130 fn. 285.

41 AUSSME, Marras to Carboni, 1 July 1940: L-13/46/5.

42 AUSSME, Offensiva contro l'Inghilterra, 25 July 1940; Marras to War Ministry, 7 August 1940; Marras to War Ministry, 13 August 1940; Marras to War Ministry, 18 August 1940: L-13/45/3.

43 *DSCS* I/1, p. 118 (3 July 1940).

44 Direttive strategiche, 11 July 1940: *In Africa settentrionale*, pp. 205–6.

45 Badoglio to Graziani, 13 and 14 July 1940: *ibid.*, pp. 206–7; Emilio Faldella, *L'Italia e la seconda guerra mondiale: Revisione di giudizi* (Bologna: Cappelli, 1960), p. 212.

46 Hitler to Mussolini, 13 July 1940: *DDI* 9/V, no. 242, pp. 227–30.

47 Richard L. DiNardo, *Germany and the Axis Powers: From Coalition to Collapse* (Lawrence, KS: University Press of Kansas, 2005), pp. 39–43.

48 Soddu to Mussolini, 2 July 1940: Mario Montanari, *Politica e strategia in cento anni di guerre italiane*, vol. III, tomo 2: *La seconda guerra mondiale* (Rome: Ufficio Storico dello Stato Maggiore dell'Esercito, 2007), p. 245; Soddu to Army General Staff, 19 July 1940: Mario Montanari, *L'esercito italiano nella campagna di Grecia* (Rome: Ufficio Storico dello Stato Maggiore dell'Esercito, 1999), p. 54.

49 Armellini, *Diario di guerra* p. 61 (20 August 1940).

50 Mussolini to Hitler, 17 July 1940: *DDI* 9/V, no. 264, p. 248.

51 Mario Montanari, *Le operazioni in Africa settentrionale*, vol. I: *Sidi el Barrani (Giugno 1940–Febbraio 1941)* (Rome: Ufficio Storico dello Stato Maggiore dell'Esercito, 2000), pp. 82, 86–7; Graziani to Badoglio, 29 July 1940: *In Africa settentrionale*, pp. 102–3.

52 Promemoria, 24 July 1940; Promemoria, 25 July 1940; Promemoria, 30 July 1940 [Armellini]: Francesco Mattesini, *Corrispondenza e direttive tecnico-operative di Supermarina*, vol. I, tomo 1: *Maggio 1939–Luglio 1940* (Rome: Ufficio Storico della Marina Militare, 2000), pp. 533–4, 535–6, 537–8.

53 The *Conte di Cavour* and the *Giulio Cesare* had been rebuilt between 1933 and 1937; the *Andrea Doria*, like the *Caio Duilio*, was rebuilt between 1937 and 1940.

54 Annotation by Badoglio, 30 July 1940: Mattesini, *Corrispondenza di Supermarina*, I/1, p. 539.

55 Cavagnari to Badoglio, 1 August 1940: Francesco Mattesini, *Corrispondenza e direttive tecnico-strategiche di Supermarina*, vol. I, tomo 2: *Agosto 1940–Dicembre 1940* (Rome: Ufficio Storico della Marina Militare, 2000), p. 561.

56 Enno von Rintelen, *Mussolini l'Alleato. Ricordi dell'addetto militare tedesco a Roma (1936–1943)* (Rome: Corso, 1952), p. 89.

57 Battistelli, 'La "guerra dell'Asse"', p. 119 fn. 223.

58 *In Africa settentrionale*, pp. 103–4 (5 August 1940); Faldella, *L'Italia e la seconda guerra mondiale*, p. 212; Montanari, *La seconda guerra mondiale*, p. 248; Rodolfo Graziani, *Ho difeso la patria* (Milan: Garzanti, 1948), pp. 253–4.

59 Montanari, *Le operazioni in Africa settentrionale* I, p. 90 (5 August 1940) (original emphasis).

60 Verbale della riunione . . . per l'esame delle possibilità operative, 18 August 1940: *In Africa settentrionale*, pp. 216–21.

61 Graziani to Badoglio, 18 August 1940 [but written next day]: *ibid.*, pp. 221–2.

62 Ciano, *Diario*, p. 456 (6 August 1940).

63 AUSSME, Eventuale azione contro la Jugoslavia, 9 July 1940; Predisposizioni, 1 August 1940; Predisposizioni, 9 August 1940; Emergenza Est, 22 August 1940: N-9/2072/1, 2.

64 Appunto, 11 August 1940: Francesco Mattesini and Mario Cermelli, *Le direttive tecnico-operative di Superaereo* (Rome: Stato Maggiore Aeronautica Ufficio Storico, n.d.), vol. I: *Aprile 1940–Dicembre 1940*, tomo 1, p. 235.

65 Ciano to Grazzi, 4 July 1940: *DDI* 9/V, no. 177, p. 167.

66 Ciano, *Diario*, pp. 433–4, 450 (22 and 23 May, 3 July 1940).

67 Grazzi to Ciano, 13 August 1940: *DDI* 9/V, no. 409, pp. 392–4.

68 Renzo De Felice, *Mussolini l'alleato*, vol. I: *L'Italia in guerra 1940–1943*, tomo 1: *Dalla guerra 'breve' alla guerra lunga* (Turin: Einaudi, 1990), pp. 192–3; Montanari, *L'esercito italiano nella campagna di Grecia*, p. 31 fn. 33.

69 ACS, Roatta to Graziani, 13 August 1940: Fondo Graziani 58/47/9.

70 AUSSME, La guerra italo-turca [n.d. but sent to Mussolini 6 December 1940], p. 4: H-9/9/2.

71 Luigi Emilio Longo, *L'attività degli addetti militari italiani all'estero fra le due guerre mondiali (1919–1939)* (Rome: Ufficio Storico dello Stato Maggiore dell'Esercito, 1999), pp. 365–7.

72 Grazzi to Ciano, 23 July 1940: *DDI* 9/V, no. 293, pp. 267–8.

73 Craig Stockings and Eleanor Hancock, *Swastika over the Acropolis: Reinterpreting the Nazi Invasion of Greece in World War II* (Leiden: Brill, 2013), p. 41.

74 Ciano, *Diario*, p. 458 (17 August 1940).

75 Von Rintelen, *Mussolini l'Alleato*, p. 101.

76 Mussolini to Graziani, 19 August 1940: *In Africa settentrionale*, pp. 105–6.

77 Direttive, 22 August 1940: *DDI* 9/V, no. 467, pp. 452–3.

78 Ciano to Mussolini, 29 August 1940: *DDI* 9/V, no. 516, pp. 505–6; Ciano, *Diario*, p. 460 (28 August 1940).

79 Badoglio to Graziani, 29 August 1940: *In Africa settentrionale*, p. 230.

80 Visconti Prasca to Roatta, 13 August 1940; Roatta to Visconti Prasca, 23 August 1940: Montanari, *L'esercito italiano nella campagna di Grecia*, pp. 38, 42.

81 Armellini, *Diario di guerra*, p. 66 (28 August 1940).

82 Keitel to Badoglio, 21 August 1940; Badoglio to Keitel, 23 August 1940: *DSCS* I/1, pp. 416, 427.

83 Mussolini to Hitler, 24 August 1940: *DDI* 9/V, no. 484, pp. 469–70.

84 Graziani to Badoglio, 5 September 1940: *DSCS* II/2, doc. 7, pp. 12–13.

85 AUSSME, Marras to Badoglio, 3 September 1940: I-4/7/11; Badoglio to Marras, 6 September 1940: *DSCS* II/2, p. 5.

86 *DSCS* II/1, p. 59 (11 September 1940); Badoglio to Superesercito, Supermarina, Superaereo, 12 September 1940: Mattesini, *Corrispondenza di Supermarina* I/2, pp. 669–70.

87 Montanari, *Le operazioni in Africa settentrionale* I, pp. 102–15.

88 Giuseppe Santoro, *L'aeronautica italiana nella seconda guerra mondiale* (Rome: Esse, 1957), vol. I, pp. 281–3.

89 AUSSME, Proposte generale Jodl, 17 September 1940, with undated mss. note by Badoglio: I-4/7/11.

90 AUSSME, Badoglio to Marras, 19 September 1940: I-4/7/11.

91 Armellino, *Diario di guerra*, pp. 77–8 (8 September 1940); Pricolo to Stamage [Badoglio], 9 September 1940: *DSCS* II/2, p. 15.

92 Emergenza 'E' (Badoglio), 10 September 1940: Mattesini, *Corrispondenza di Supermarina* I/2, p. 623; *DSCS* II/1, pp. 59, 63 (11 and 12 September 1940).

93 Badoglio to Mussolini, 18 September 1940: Mattesini, *Corrispondenza di Supermarina* I/2, p. 667.

94 AUSSME, 'Emergenza E', 25 September 1940: N-9/2073/1.

95 Colloquio tra il Capo del governo, Mussolini, ed il Ministro degli Esteri del Reich, Ribbentrop, 19 September 1940: *DDI* 9/V, no. 617, pp. 598–601.

96 *DSCS* II/1, pp. 151, 156 (28 and 29 September 1940).

97 Seduta del 15 [*sic* – 25] settembre 1940: *Verbali delle riunioni tenute dal Capo di SM Generale* I, pp. 80–6.

98 Battistelli, 'La "guerra dell'Asse"', p. 139 fn. 330.

99 Montanari, *Le operazioni in Africa settentrionale* I, pp. 128, 130.

100 AUSSME, Riduzione forze alle armi, 8 September 1940: H-10/8/3.

101 AUSSME, Adeguamento della struttura e della forza dell'Esercito alla situazione in atto, 1 October 1940: N-9/2073/3.

102 Dorello Ferrari, 'La mobilitazione dell'esercito nella seconda guerra mondiale', *Storia Contemporanea* anno XIII, no. 6, December 1992, pp. 1,016–19.

103 AUSSME, Emergenza E, 4 October 1940: N-9/2073/3; Graziani to Comando Gruppo Armate, 4 October 1940: *DSCS* II/2, p. 70; *DSCS* II/1, pp. 174, 183 (3 and 5 October 1940).

104 Montanari, *Le operazioni in Africa settentrionale* I, p. 131; Ciano, *Diario*, p. 467 (30 September 1940).

105 Colloquio tra il Capo del governo, Mussolini, ed il Cancelliere del Reich, Hitler, 4 October 1940: *DDI* 9/V, no. 677, pp. 655–8.

106 AUSSME, Conversazione col Maresciallo Keitel e col Generale Jodl, 11 October 1940: L-13/45/4.

107 Badoglio to Graziani, 5 October 1940, encl. Nota sullo sviluppo delle operazioni in Egitto [Mussolini], *DSCS* II/2, pp. 71–2.

108 Collaborazione della R.M. alle operazioni in Egitto, 17 September [1940]: Mattesini, *Corrispondenza di Supermarina* I/2, p. 680.

109 Badoglio to Cavagnari, 16 September 1940; Considerazioni sulla situazione strategica in relazione alle operazioni in Egitto, 22 September 1940; Badoglio to Cavagnari, 28 September 1940: *ibid.*, pp. 678–9, 681–4, 685–6.

110 Direttive d'impiego (Superaereo), 28 September 1940: *ibid.*, pp. 698–9.

111 Nota per lo Stato Maggiore della Marina (Mussolini), 2 October 1940: *ibid.*, pp. 753–4.

112 Montanari, *Le operazioni in Africa settentrionale* I, p. 136; Ciano, *Diario*, p. 470 (12 October 1940).

113 Von Rintelen, *Mussolini l'Alleato*, p. 98.

114 Ghigi to Ciano, 15, 16, 18, 19, 20 September 1940: *DDI* 9/V nos. 590, 596, 603, 615, 618, pp. 576, 579, 588, 596–7, 601–2.

115 AUSSME, Marras to War Ministry, 12 October 1940: L-13/45/3.

116 Ciano, *Diario*, p. 472 (20 October 1940).

117 *Ibid.*, p. 470 (12 October 1940).

118 AUSSME, #566S Grecia [SIM], October 1940, pp. 61–4, 87–8, 106–7, 180, 183–4: H-3/46/6.

119 Cesare Amé, *Guerra segreta in Italia 1940–1943* (Milan: Bietti, 2011), p. 46; Giuseppe Conti, *Una guerra segreta. Il Sim nel secondo conflitto mondiale* (Bologna: Il Mulino, 2009), pp. 178–9.

120 Badoglio to Superaereo, Superesercito and Supermarina, 13 October 1940: *DSCS* II/2, p. 82; Armellini, *Diario di guerra*, p. 111 (13 October 1940).

121 Mario Roatta, "*Otto milioni di baionette*" (Milan: Mondadori, 1946), pp. 119–22; *DSCS* II/1, p. 229 (14 October 1940).

122 Riunione presso il Capo del governo, Mussolini, 15 October 1940: *DDI* 9/V, no. 728, pp. 699–705; Roatta, "*Otto milioni di baionette*", pp. 122–7

123 Graziani to Badoglio, 15 October 1940; Badoglio to Graziani, 18 October 1940: *DSCS* II/2, pp. 97–9, 100.

124 Operazioni contro la Grecia (versante occidentale), 15 October 1940: Mattesini, *Corrispondenza di Supermarina* I/2, pp. 792–3; *DSCS* II/1, p. 242 (16 October 1940).

125 Seduta del 17 ottobre 1940: *Verbali delle riunioni tenute dal Capo di SM Generale* I, pp. 97–102.

126 Pricolo to Badoglio, 18 October 1940: Mattesini and Cermelli, *Le direttive tecnico–operative di Superaereo* I/1, pp. 306–7.

127 Ciano, *Diario*, p. 471 (17 and 18 October 1940); *DSCS* II/1, pp. 246, 250 (17 and 18 October 1940).

128 Carlo Favagrossa, *Perché perdemmo la guerra* (Milan: Rizzoli, 1946), pp. 146–7.

129 Graziani to Badoglio, 24 October 1940: Romano Canosa, *Graziani. Il maresciallo d'Italia dalla guerra d'Etiopia alla Repubblica di Salò* (Milan: Mondadori, 2005), pp. 251–2.

130 Mussolini to Boris III, 16 October 1940; Boris III to Mussolini, 18 October 1940: *DDI* 9/V, nos. 738, 746, pp. 712–13, 716–17.

131 Giuseppe Bottai, *Diario 1935–1944* (Milan: Rizzoli, 2001), pp. 227–8 (19 October 1940).

132 Mussolini to Hitler, 19 October 1940: *DDI* 9/V, no. 753, pp. 719–21.

133 AUSSME, Marras to War Ministry, 6 October 1940; T. Marras to War Ministry, 12 October 1940; Sorice to Army General Staff, 14 October 1940; Riunione plenaria, 16 October 1940; Riunione sotto commissione motorizzazione, 16–17 October 1940; Accordi presi dalla sotto commissione mista, 17–18 October 1940: I-4/7/11.

134 AUSSME, Trasporto in Libia di una grande unità motorizzata germanica, 25 September 1940; Trasferimento di unità corazzate germaniche in Libia, 23 October 1940 (with marginal pencil note by Badoglio): I-4/7/11.

135 Battistelli, 'La "guerra dell'Asse"', p. 179.

136 Seduta del 24 ottobre 1940: *Verbali delle riunioni tenute dal Capo di SM Generale* I, pp. 103–6.

137 *DSCS* II/1, p. 280 (24 October 1940).

138 Mussolini to Visconti Prasca, 25 October 1940: S. Visconti Prasca, *Io ho aggredito la Grecia* (Milan: Rizzoli, 1946), pp. 51–2.

139 AUSSME, EMERGENZA G, 24 October 1940: M-3/1.

140 Visconti Prasca, *Io ho aggredito la Grecia*, pp. 93–4, 112, 125, 166–7.

141 Mussolini to Graziani, 26 October 1940: Montanari, *Le operazioni in Africa settentrionale* I, pp. 147–8.

142 Graziani to Mussolini, 29 October 1940: Canosa, *Graziani*, pp. 253–5.

143 Promemoria per il Duce, 27 October 1940: *DSCS* II/2, pp. 113–15.

144 Emanuele Grazzi, *Il principio della fine (L'impresa di Grecia)* (Rome: Faro, 1945), pp. 233–6.

145 Colloquio tra il Capo del governo, Mussolini, ed il Cancelliere del Reich, Hitler, 28 October 1940: *DDI* 9/V, no. 807, pp. 771–5.

146 Mussolini to Graziani, 29 October 1940: Montanari, *Le operazioni in Africa settentrionale* I, p. 149.

147 Seduta del 2 Iuglio 1940: *Verbali delle riunioni tenute dal Capo di SM Generale* I, pp. 70–1.

148 Esplorazione dell'Aviazione R. Marina e dell'Armata Aerea, 20 June 1940: Mattesini, *Corrispondenza di Supermarina* I/1, p. 408.

149 AUSSME, Supermarina: Relazione sulle operazioni navali dei giorni 6, 7, 8 & 9 luglio 1940, n.d., p. 17: I-4/10/4; Francesco Mattesini, *La battaglia*

di Punto Stilo (Rome: Ufficio Storico dell'Ufficio Storico della Marina, 2001), p. 17.

150 Mattesini, *La battaglia di Punta Stilo*, pp. 18–22, 26, 125; F. H. Hinsley et al., *British Intelligence in the Second World War* (London: HMSO, 1979), vol. I, p. 209.

151 Jack Greene and Alessandro Massignani, *The Naval War in the Mediterranean 1940–1943* (London: Chatham, 2002), p. 68; Mattesini, *La battaglia di Punta Stilo*, p. 31.

152 Relazioni sulle operazioni navali dei giorni 6, 7, 8 & 9 luglio 1940, p. 41.

153 Pricolo to Comando Supremo–Stato Maggiore Generale, 17 July 1940: Mattesini, *Corrispondenza di Supermarina* I/1, pp. 491–2.

154 Erminio Bagnasco, *La portaerei nella Marina italiana. Idee, progetti e realizzazioni dalle origini ad oggi* (Rome: Rivista Marittima, 1989), pp. 56–71.

155 Pricolo to Stamage [Badoglio]: Intervento di Armera a favore di unità operanti delle varie Forze Armate, 23 August 1940: Mattesini, *Corrispondenza di Supermarina* I/1, pp. 497–501.

156 Situazione delle forze nemiche e possibilità di azione, 2 September 1940: *ibid.*, pp. 643–4.

157 Badoglio to Cavagnari, 16 September 1940: *ibid.*, pp. 678–9.

158 Necessità di nuove costruzioni di torpediniere e navi scorta [Mussolini], 10 October 1940: *ibid.*, pp. 753–4.

CHAPTER 4

1 Mario Montanari, *L'esercito italiano nella campagna di Grecia* (Rome: Ufficio Storico dello Stato Maggiore dell'Esercito, 1999), p. 159.

2 Galeazzo Ciano, *Diario 1937–1943* (Milan: Rizzoli, 1980), p. 474 (31 October 1940); Quirino Armellini, *Diario di guerra. Nove mesi al Comando Supremo* (Milan: Garzanti, 1946), p. 134 (1 November 1941).

3 Seduta del 3 novembre: *Verbali delle riunioni tenute dal Capo di SM generale*, vol. I: *26 gennaio 1939–29 dicembre 1940* (Rome: Ufficio Storico delle stato Maggiore dell'Esercito, 1983), pp. 113–18.

4 Trasporto e sbarco a Prevesa di reparti del R. Esercito, 3 November 1940: Francesco Mattesini, *Corrispondenza e direttive tecnico-operative di Supermarina* (Rome: Ufficio Storico della Marina Militare, 2000), vol. I, tomo 2, pp. 834–6.

5 ACS, Roatta to Graziani, 24 November 1940 [referring to 4 November]: Carte Graziani 58/47/9.

6 Seduta del 1 novembre 1940: *Verbali delle riunioni tenute dal Capo di SM generale* I, pp. 107–12; Armellini, *Diario di guerra*, pp. 133, 136–7 (3 and 4 November 1940).

7 Badoglio to Graziani, 7 November 1940: *DSCS* II/2, pp. 127–8.

8 NARS, Roatta to Soddu, 8 November 1940: T-821/127/fr.000070–5.

9 NARS, Azioni aeree in Grecia, 3 November 1940: T-821/127/fr.000084.

10 Pricolo to Mussolini, 20 November 1940: *DDI* 9/VI, no. 141, pp. 149–50.

11 Graziani to Badoglio, 14 November 1940: Mario Montanari, *Le operazioni in Africa settentrionale*, vol. I: *Sidi el Barrani (Giugno 1940–Febbraio 1941)* (Rome: Ufficio Storico dello Stato Maggiore dell'Esercito, 2000), pp. 152–3.

12 AUSSME, Armellini to Stato Maggiore Regia Marina, 9 November 1940: I-4/7/11.

13 Verbale della riunione tenuta nella sala di lavoro del Duce a Palazzo Venezia il 10 novembre 1940–XIX: Emilio Faldella, *L'Italia e la seconda guerra mondiale. Revisione di giudizi* (Bologna: Cappelli, 1960), pp. 760–7.

14 Armellini, *Diario di guerra*, pp. 146–7 (11 November 1940).

15 Ciano, *Diario*, p. 478 (13 November 1940).

16 AUSSME, Resoconto dei colloqui tenuti ad Innsbruck nei giorni 14 e 15 novembre 1940 tra il Maresciallo Keitel ed il Maresciallo Badoglio [1st meeting 14 November 1940], pp. 1–7: L-13/44/8.

17 AUSSME, Riunione del giorno 15 novembre, pp. 1–3, 4, 7–9: L-13/44/8.

18 AUSSME, Terza riunione (pomeriggio del 15 novembre): L-13/44/8.

19 AUSSME, Notizie sulla situazione germanica, 17 November 1940: L-13/45/4.

20 BA-MA, Von Rintelen to von Tippelskirch, 17 November 1940: RH 2/2936.

21 'Alle gerarchie provinciali del PNF', 18 November 1940: OO XXX, p. 36.

22 Ciano to Mussolini, 18 November 1940: Malcolm Muggeridge, ed., *Ciano's Diplomatic Papers* (London: Odhams, 1948), pp. 408–9; Ciano, *Diario*, pp. 479–801 (8–19 November 1940).

23 Hitler to Mussolini, 20 November 1940: *DDI* 9/VI, no. 140, pp. 145–9.

24 David Irving, *The Rise and Fall of the Luftwaffe* (London: Weidenfeld and Nicolson, 1973), pp. 111–12.

25 Missione aerea tedesca a Roma per colloquio circa l'intervento aereo germanico nella guerra sul Mediterraneo, 6 December 1940: Francesco Mattesini and Mario Cermelli, *Le direttive tecnico-operative di Superaereo* (Rome: Stato Maggiore Aeronautica Ufficio Storico, n.d.), vol. I, tomo 1, pp. 436–43.

26 Soddu to Sorice, 17 November 1940: *DDI* 9/VI, no. 124, All., pp. 130–1.

27 Mario Cervi, *The Hollow Legions: Mussolini's Blunder in Greece 1940–1941* (London: Chatto & Windus, 1972), p. 164.

28 Geloso to Soddu, 28 November 1940; Soddu to Geloso, 28 November 1940: Montanari, *L'esercito italiano nella campagna di Grecia*, pp. 300, 301.

29 *Ibid.*, p. 229.

30 Giuseppe Santoro, *L'aeronautica italiana nella seconda guerra mondiale* (Rome: Esse, 1957), vol. I, pp. 149, 159, 166, 172–4, 178, 180, 199.

31 Montanari, *L'esercito italiano nella campagna di Grecia*, p. 210.

32 Promemoria N.1224, 13 November 1940; Promemoria N.292, Situazione dell'esercito metropolitano, 19 November 1940: *DSCS* II/2, pp. 161–6, 175–8.

33 Mussolini to Hitler, 22 November 1940: *DDI* 9/VI, no. 146, pp. 157–8.

34 Ciano, *Diario*, p. 483 (30 November 1940); Giuseppe Bottai, *Diario 1935–1944* (Milan: Rizzoli, 2001), p. 235 (30 November 1940).

35 Piero Pieri and Giorgio Rochat, *Badoglio* (Turin: UTET, 1974), pp. 763–7.

36 Montanari, *L'esercito italiano nella campagna di Grecia*, p. 323.

37 Ciano, *Diario*, pp. 484–5 (4 December 1940); Giordano Bruno Guerri, *Galeazzo Ciano. Una vita 1903/1944* (Milan: Bompiani, 1979), p. 499; Alfieri to Ciano, 7 and 8 December 1940: *DDI* 9/VI, nos. 256, 258, pp. 245–6, 247–8.

38 Carlo Cavallero, *Il dramma del Maresciallo Cavallero* (Milan: Mondadori, 1952), p. 89.

39 Angelo Iachino, *Tramonto di una grande marina* (Milan: Mondadori, 1966), pp. 228–9.

40 Promemoria del Comandante in Capo della II squadra navale Ammiraglio Iachino consegnato a Taranto il 10 ottobre 1940 al Sottosegretario di Stato e Capo di Stato Maggiore della Regia Marina Ammiraglio Cavagnari: Mattesini, *Corrispondenza di Supermarina* I/2, p. 761.

41 Cavagnari to Iachino, 12 October 1940: *ibid.*, pp. 762–3.

42 Promemoria per il sottocapo di Stato Maggiore, 27 October 1940; Direttive per la condotta della guerra con i sommergibili nel Mediterraneo (Cavagnari), 30 October 1940: *ibid.*, pp. 841–7, 848–50.

43 Notizie sulla situazione alle ore 06.00 del 12 novembre 1940; Relazione sull'attacco aereo alla base di Taranto della notte sul 12 novembre 1940: *ibid.*, pp. 884, 885–8.

44 Campioni to Maristat, 21 November 1940; Cavagnari to Campioni, 27 November 1940: *ibid.*, pp. 915–19, 920–1.

45 Appressamento della situazione in mediterranea [German naval general staff], 14 November 1940: Mattesini, *Corrispondenza di Supermarina* I/2, pp. 891–3; Gerhard Schreiber, *Revisionismus und Weltmachtstreben. Marineführung und deutsch-italienische Beziehungen 1919–1944* (Stuttgart: Deutsche Verlags-Anstalt, 1978), pp. 301–2.

46 Supermarina to *Vittorio Veneto* [Campioni], 26 November 1940: Mattesini, *Corrispondenza di Supermarina* I/2, p. 938.

47 Missione di guerra dei giorni 26–27–28 novembre 1940 [Campioni], 9 May 1941: *ibid.*, pp. 940–1.

48 Cavagnari to Commandants 1st and 2nd squadrons, 30 November 1940: *ibid.*, p. 947.

49 Promemoria (Cavagnari), 2 December 1940: *ibid.*, pp. 958–61.

50 Bottai, *Diario*, pp. 231, 235 (15 and 30 November 1940).

51 Fabio De Ninno, *Fascisti sul mare. La Marina e gli ammiragli di Mussolini* (Bari: Laterza, 2017), pp. 224–5.

52 Esame della situazione marittima sull'attuale fase di conflitto, 6 December 1940; Possibilità operative in cooperazione con la marina germanica, 12 December 1940: Mattesini, *Corrispondenza di Supermarina* I/2, pp. 962–7, 976–7.

53 Apprezzamento della situazione, 30 December 1940: *ibid.*, pp. 1,046–50.

54 Riccardi to Superaereo, 14 December 1940; Santoro to Supermarina, 20 December 1940; Guzzoni to Supermarina and Superaereo, 16 December 1940: *ibid.*, pp. 952, 953–4, 1,016.

55 Graziani to Badoglio, 14 November 1940: *DSCS* II/2, pp. 172–3.

56 IWM(D), Ausserungen General Perinos, generalstabschef der Luftflotte V am 14.10.40, 31 October 1940: EDS AL 1061.

57 Giuseppe Conti, *Una guerra segreta. Il Sim nel secondo conflitto mondiale* (Bologna: Il Mulino, 2009), pp. 154–6; Cesare Amé, *Guerra segreta in Italia 1940–1943* (Milan: Edizioni Bietti, 2011), pp. 57–9.

58 Fondazione Bondoni Pastorio, Tellera to 'Cetty' [Zete Tellera], 31 December 1940: Archivio Tellera.

59 AUSSME, ASI Situazione Forze terrestre, 7 December 1940: L-13/44/15.

60 Extraordinarily, in February 1942 the army general staff's figures for total losses in North Africa between June 1940 and January 1941 were 661 dead, 1,479 wounded and only 4,642 missing/prisoners of war; by May 1941 the latter figure had risen to 114,747: AUSSME, Perdite Africa, 6 February 1942: H-9/11.

61 AUSSME, Situazione politico-militare [Marras], 12 December 1940; Atteggiamenti tedeschi nei riguardi della nostra situazione militare, 13 December 1940: L-13/45/4; SIM to Comando Supremo SMG, 15 December 1940: I-4/7/11.

62 T. Graziani, 12 December 1940; T. Mussolini to Graziani, 12 December 1940: Montanari, *Le operazioni in Africa settentrionale* I, pp. 230, 232.

63 T. Graziani to Mussolini, 14 December 1940: Romano Canosa, *Graziani. Il maresciallo d'Italia, dalla guerra d'Etiopia alla Repubblica di Salò* (Milan: Mondadori, 2005), p. 262; Ciano, *Diario*, p. 488 (15 December 1940); Armellini, *Diario di guerra*, p. 215 (14 December 1940).

64 AUSSME, N.345, Roatta to Guzzoni, 13 December 1940: I-4/13/12.

65 Appunto per il Duce preparato il 16 dicembre 1940: Mattesini, *Corrispondenza di Supermarina* I/2, pp. 1,007–15.

66 Ugo Cavallero, *Diario 1940–1943* (Rome: Ciarrapico, 1984), p. 26 (18 and 19 December 1940).

67 AUSSME, Situazione carburante, 11, 21 and 27 December 1940: H-9/9/2; Situazione combustibile liquidi, 8 December 1940: L-13/44/9.

68 AUSSME, Produzione munizioni, 28 November 1940; Situazione carri M 13, 22 December 1940: L-13/44/9; Potenzialità produttiva armi e munizioni, 9 December 1940: H-9/9/2.

69 AUSSME, Efficienza delle divisioni dell'esercito al 15 dicembre 1940: L-13/44/9.

70 AUSSME, Concorsi germanici nella attuale situazione militare, 14 December 1940: I-4/7/11; Armellini, *Diario di guerra*, p. 219 (16 December 1940).

71 Diario Storico N-8/1341, 19 December 1940, cited in Pier Paolo Battistelli, 'La "guerra dell'Asse". Condotta bellica e collaborazione militare italo-tedesca 1939-1943', Tesi di dottorato Università degli Studi Padova, 2000, p. 202.

72 *DSCS* II/1, p. 584.

73 AUSSME, Colloquio dell'Ecc. il generale Guzzoni con il generale von Rintelen tenuto alla presenza dell'Ecc. Roatta il giorno 20.12 [1940]: L-13/45/4; Da richiedere al Reich, 23 December 1940: L-13/44/14; Enno von Rintelen, *Mussolini l'Alleato. Ricordi dell'addetto militare tedesco a Roma (1936-1943)* (Rome: Corso, 1952), p. 113.

74 Favagrossa to Mussolini, 15 December 1940; Ciano to Alfieri, 17 December 1940: *DDI* 9/VI, nos. 297, 308, pp. 282-4, 290-2.

75 AUSSME, TS.2578/A, 2579/A, 2580/A [Marras], 28 December 1940: I-4/7/11.

76 AUSSME, T. Guzzoni to Marras, 29 December 1940: I-4/7/11.

77 AUSSME, Punti di vista germanica [Roatta], 30 December 1940: I-4/7/11.

78 AUSSME, Colloquio italo-tedesco nei giorni 30-31 dic[embre] [19]40: L-13/45/4; Ts. 2585/A, 2586/A, 2587/A, 2584/A [Marras], 30 December 1940: I-4/7/11; T. Trattative per concorso Tedesco alle operazioni nel bacino mediterraneo, 31 December 1940: L-13/46/1.

79 AUSSME, Verbale dei colloqui con la parte germanica per la richiesta di materiali bellici per l'esercito, 30 December 1940: L-13/45/4.

80 AUSSME, Stato efficienza R R Navi al 26 dicembre 1940: L-13/44/15; Francesco Mattesini, *L'attività aerea italo-tedesca nel mediterraneo. Il contributo del 'X Fliegerkorps', gennaio-maggio 1941* (Rome: Ufficio Storico Stato Maggiore Aeronautica, 2003), pp. 57-8.

81 AUSSME, Situazione aeronautica, 25 December 1940: L-13/44/15.

82 Riepilogo situazione aerea nel Mediterraneo, c. 15 December 1940: Mattesini, *Corrispondenza di Supermarina* I/2, p. 1,004. This amounted to approximately two-thirds of the total force of 324 planes.

83 AUSSME, Nota del Duce, 31 December 1940: I-4/7/11.

84 Hitler to Mussolini, 31 December 1940: *DDI* 9/VI, no. 385, pp. 380-4.

85 Fondazione Bondoni Pastorio, Tellera to 'Cetty' [Zete Tellera], 31 December 1940: Archivio Tellera.

86 Montanari, *Le operazioni in Africa settentrionale* I, pp. 244-83.

87 Faldella, *L'Italia e la seconda guerra mondiale*, p. 319.

88 Guzzoni to Mussolini, 7 January 1941: Montanari, *Le operazioni in Africa settentrionale* I, All. 58, pp. 639-41.

89 AUSSME, T. Armellini to Marras, encl. Note by Guzzoni, 8 January 1941: L-13/46/10.

90 Graziani to Mussolini, 6 January 1941: Canosa, *Graziani*, pp. 267–9; *DSCS* III/2, pp. 19–23.

91 Armellini, *Diario di guerra*, p. 255 (6 January 1941).

92 *Fuehrer Conferences on Naval Affairs 1939–1945* (Annapolis, MD: Naval Institute Press, 1990), pp. 169–70 (8 and 9 January 1941); von Rintelen to Comando Supremo SMG, 10 January 1941: *DSCS* III/2, pp. 65–6.

93 AUSSME,Ts.18A,19A,MarrastoWarMinistry,12January1941:N-8/1448.

94 Jack Greene and Alessandro Massignani, *The Naval War in the Mediterranean 1940–1943* (London: Chatham, 2002), pp. 133–5.

95 Graziani to Guzzoni, 12 January 1941: Battistelli, 'La "guerra dell'Asse"', p. 213.

96 Fondazione Bondoni Pastorio, Tellera to 'Cetty' [Zete Tellera], 9 January 1941: Archivio Tellera.

97 AUSSME, Argomenti trattati nelle riunioni del 19 gennaio a Berchtesgaden tra il sottocapo di s.m. generale generale Guzzoni e il maresciallo Keitel e il generale Jodl del comando supremo Tedesco: L-13/44/11.

98 AUSSME, Esposizione del Fuehrer sulla situazione politico militare, 20 January 1941: N-8/1448; Gerhard Schreiber, Bernd Stegemann and Detlef Vogel, *Germany and the Second World War*, vol. III: *The Mediterranean, South-East Europe, and North Africa 1939–1941* (Oxford: Clarendon Press, 1995), p. 244.

99 BA-MA, Von Rintelen to von Tippelskirch, 17 December 1940: RH 2/2936.

100 BA-MA, Von Matzky to von Rintelen, 14 March 1941: RH 2/2936.

101 Fondazione Bondoni Pastorio, Tellera to 'Cetty' [Zete Tellera], 23 January 1941: Archivio Tellera.

102 AUSSME, Mussolini to Graziani, 6 February 1941: N-8/1448A.

103 Mussolini to Graziani, 30 January 1941: Montanari, *Le operazioni in Africa settentrionale* I, p. 345.

104 Battistelli, 'La "guerra dell'Asse"', p. 216.

105 Hitler to Mussolini, 5 February 1941: *DDI* 9/VI, no. 540, pp. 543–5.

106 AUSSME, Mussolini to Graziani, 6 February 1941: H-9/10/10.

107 Graziani to Mussolini, 9 February 1941: Montanari, *Le operazioni in Africa settentrionale* I, pp. 657–8.

108 AUSSME, Mussolini to Cavallero, 1 January 1941: H-9/10/10.

109 Cavallero, *Diario*, pp. 13–16, 25 (7, 8, 18 December 1940).

110 Operazioni in Albania, 12 December 1940: Mario Montanari, *La campagna di Grecia*, vol. II *Documenti* (Rome: Ufficio Storico dello Stato Maggiore dell'Esercito, 1980), pp. 627–8.

111 Sintesi della riunione tenuta il 27 dicembre 1940 – XIX al Ministero della Guerra: Mattesini, *Corrispondenza di Supermarina* I/2, p. 1,033.

112 Mario Roatta, *"Otto milioni di baionette"* (Milan: Mondadori, 1946), p. 133; Cervi, *The Hollow Legions*, p. 179.

113 AUSSME, Mussolini to Cavallero, 24 December 1940: H-9/10/10.

114 Cavallero Diary, 26 December 1940; Cavallero Diary, 27 December 1940; Direttive operative n.7 per le operazioni contro la Grecia, 27 December 1940: Montanari, *La campagna di Grecia* II, pp. 634–5, 637–8, 639.

115 Ubaldo Soddu, 'Memorie e riflessioni di un Generale (1933–1941)' (unpubl. mss), pp. 277, 288.

116 Mussolini to Cavallero, 1 January 1941: OO XXX, pp. 184–5; Cavallero, *Diario*, p. 48 (2 January 1941).

117 Mussolini to Graziani, 9 January 1941: OO XLII, p. 45.

118 Cavallero, *Diario*, pp. 27, 28, 30, 33–4, 48, 68, 81–2 (21, 23, 25, 27 December 1940, 2, 17 January 1941, 1 February 1941).

119 AUSSME, Sintesi della riunione tenuta al Ministero della Guerra il 1 gennaio 1941, pp. 2, 3: H-10/1/6.

120 Ottavo rapporto del gen. Pricolo a Mussolini, 17 January 1941: Montanari, *La campagna di Grecia* II, pp. 717–23.

121 AUSSME, Promemoria per il Duce, 6, 8, 12, 21, 22, 29 January 1941, 18, 23 February 1941; Albania, 8 February 1941; Libia, 24 February 1941: H-5/20/4.

122 Montanari, *L'esercito italiano nella campagna di Grecia*, p. 462 (18 January 1941).

123 Ciano, *Diario*, p. 499 (16 January 1941).

124 AUSSME, Ts. 2648/A, 26/A, 59/A, Marras to Rome, 4, 13 and 15 January 1941: L-13/46/1.

125 Cavallero Diary, 14 January 1941: Montanari, *L'esercito italiano nella campagna di Grecia*, p. 510.

126 Mussolini to Rossi, 21 January 1941: Montanari, *La campagna di Grecia* II, p. 731.

127 AUSSME, Riunione tenuta . . . il 25 gennaio [1941], pp. 4–9 (original emphasis): H-10/1/6.

128 Montanari, *L'esercito italiano nella campagna di Grecia*, pp. 528, 570–1.

129 Conflitto italo-greco, 13 December 1940: *La campagna di Grecia* Montanari, II, pp. 625–6.

130 Discorso al Teatro Adriano di Roma, 23 February 1941: OO XXX pp. 49–58.

131 Montanari, *L'esercito italiano nella campagna di Grecia*, pp. 536–7.

132 *Ibid.*, pp. 604–5, 606 fn.

133 Cervi, *The Hollow Legions*, p. 233.

134 TNA, SRIG 267, 12 September 1943: WO 208/4187.

135 Cavallero, *Diario*, pp. 114–15 (14 March 1941). Influential Greek officers were indeed attempting to persuade Germany to mediate in the conflict, but failed: Schreiber, Stegemann and Vogel, *Germany and the Second World War* III, pp. 471–2.

136 AUSSME, Sintesi degli argomenti trattati nella riunione tenuta dal DUCE il 20 marzo 1941, pp. 1–3, 6: H-10/12; Cavallero, *Diario*, pp. 122–4 (20 March 1941).

137 Cervi, *The Hollow Legions*, p. 240.

138 AUSSME, Von Rintelen memorandum, 8 April 1941: N-8/1449.

139 Amé, *Guerra segreta in Italia 1940–1943*, pp. 88–90.

140 AUSSME, Mussolini to Roatta, 9 April 1941: N-8/1449.

141 Montanari, *La campagna di Grecia* II, p. 943.

CHAPTER 5

1 IWM(D), Ghisa; Combustibili liquidi: Speer Collection FD 1940/44 Part 2, Fabriguerra Reports and drafts Italian war production and essential war materials production, 1939–40.

2 AUSSME, Consumo benzina, 13 March 1941: H-9/10.

3 Assegnazione materiali per acceleramento costruzioni naviglio mercantile, 3 March 1941: Francesco Mattesini, *Corrispondenza e direttive tecnico-operative di Supermarina* (Rome: Ufficio Storico della Marina Militare, 2001), vol. II, tomo 1, pp. 99–101.

4 Servizio dei cc.tt. della Squadra Navale, 14 May 1941; Costruzioni per la Marina da Guerra, 8 July 1941; Trasporti per l'A.S.I., 29 May 1941: Mattesini, *Supermarina* II/1, pp. 489–91, 599–601, 498; Situazione strategica e possibilità operative nel Mediterraneo, 15 July 1941: Mattesini, *Supermarina* II/2, p. 755.

5 IWM(D), Marina, pp. 17–18: Speer Collection FD 1940/44 Part 1, Fabriguerra Reports and Drafts Italian war production.

6 IWM(D), Aeronautica, pp. 1, 2: Speer Collection FD 1940/44 Part 1; Vera Zamagni, 'Italy: How to Lose the War and Win the Peace', in Mark Harrison, ed., *The Economics of World War II: Six Great Powers in International Comparison* (Cambridge: Cambridge University Press, 1998), table 5.11, p. 196.

7 IWM(D), Armi portatili, pp. 71–2: Speer Collection FD 1940/44 Part 1; Nicola Pignato and Filippo Cappellano, *Le armi della fanteria italiana (1919–1945)* (Parma: Albertelli Edizioni Speciali, 2008), pp. 71–2.

8 IWM(D), Fabbriguerra Notiziario #5, pp. 362–3: Speer Papers FD 1940/44 Part 2; Zamagni, 'Italy', table 5.3, p. 184.

9 Mussolini to Hitler, 23 June 1941: *DDI* 9/VII, no. 299, pp. 285–7. The last sentence, in Mussolini's original manuscript version, was removed from the typescript copy.

10 AUSSME, Appunto per il Duce, 24 June 1940: I-4/10/3.

11 Emanuele Beraudo di Pralormo, *Il mestiere delle armi. Diari 1939–1950* (Pralormo: Associazione Piemonte Ambiente da Scoprire, 2007), vol. I, pp. 201, 204; Mario Montanari, *Politica e strategia in cento anni di guerre italiane*, vol. III: *Il periodo fascista*, tomo II, *La seconda guerra mondiale* (Rome: Ufficio Storico dello Stato Maggiore dell'Esercito, 2007), p. 31.

12 Guglielmo Nasi, *Venticinque anni d'Africa* (unpubl. memoir), cited in Luigi Goglia, 'La guerra in Africa nel 1940', in R. H. Rainero and A. Biagini, eds., *L'Italia in guerra. Il I° anno – 1940* (Rome: Commissione italiana di storia militare, 1991), p. 187; MacGregor Knox, *Mussolini Unleashed 1939–1941: Politics and Strategy in Fascist Italy's Last War* (Cambridge: Cambridge University Press, 1982), pp. 152–3; Andrew Stewart, *The First Victory: The Second World War and the East Africa Campaign* (New Haven, CT: Yale University Press, 2016), p. 73, gives British numbers; for Italian estimates of British numbers (9,600 men), see Montanari, *La seconda guerra mondiale*, p. 309.

13 Trezzani to Badoglio, 25 August 1940: Montanari, *La seconda guerra mondiale*, p. 315.

14 Knox, *Mussolini Unleashed*, pp. 153–4.

15 Amedeo di Savoia (Duca d'Aosta) to Badoglio, 11 September 1940: Montanari, *La seconda guerra mondiale*, p. 316.

16 Stewart, *The First Victory*, pp. 111–12, 118, 152.

17 Goglia, 'La guerra in Africa nel 1940', pp. 180–1.

18 Beraudo di Pralormo, *Diari 1939–1950* I, pp. 191–2, 203.

19 Mussolini to Amedeo di Savoia, 11 January 1941: Montanari, *La seconda guerra mondiale*, p. 322.

20 AUSSME, A.O.I.-Intendimenti operative britannici contro il nostro impero, 15 January 1941: N-8/1488.

21 Stewart, *The First Victory*, p. 162.

22 *Ibid.*, pp. 132, 136.

23 Mussolini to Amedeo di Savoia, 20 February 1941; Amedeo di Savoia to Mussolini, 25 February 1941: Montanari, *La seconda guerra mondiale*, pp. 329–30.

24 Nasi to Comando Supremo and Ministero Africa Italiana, 17 August 1941: *DSCS* IV/2, pp. 201–2.

25 AUSSME, Perdite Africa (dal dicembre 1940), 9 January 1942: H-9/11.

26 Stewart, *The First Victory*, pp. 141, 146–7.

27 NARS, Reconquista dell'Impero (Guzzoni), 6 May 1941; Reconquista Impero, 22 June 1941: T-821/144/fr.163, 4.

28 Operazioni aeree iniziali interessanti la guerra marittima (Cavagnari), 16 May 1939; Operazioni aeree iniziali interessanti la guerra marittima (Pricolo), 6 June 1939: Francesco Mattesini, *Corrispondenza e direttive tecnico-operative di Supermarina*, vol. I tomo 1: *Maggio 1939–Luglio 1940* (Rome: Ufficio Storico dello Stato Maggiore della Marina Militare, 2000), pp. 49–50, 51–2.

29 Investimento di Malta, 18 June 1940: *ibid.*, pp. 393–6.

30 Emilio Faldella, *L'Italia e la seconda guerra mondiale. Revisione di giudizi* (Bologna: Cappelli, 1960), p. 313 fn. 17.

31 Richiamo [Pricolo], 19 February 1941: Mattesini, *Supermarina* II/1, p. 208.

32 Promemoria N.31 per il convegno di Merano, 10 February 1941: *ibid.*, pp. 211–19.

33 Gerhard Schreiber, *Revisionismus und Weltmachtstreben. Marineführung und deutsch-italienische Beziehungen, 1919–1944* (Stuttgart: Deutsche Verlags-Anstalt, 1978), pp. 305–9.

34 Promemoria. Azione di Capo Matapan (27–28/3/1941), 7 April 1941 [Fioravanzo]: Mattesini, *Supermarina* II/1, p. 302.

35 Alberto Santoni, 'La battaglia di Matapan', in R. H. Rainero and A. Biagini, eds., *L'Italia in guerra: Il 2° anno – 1941* (Rome: Commissione italiana di storia militare, 1992), pp. 422–4.

36 Santoni, 'La battaglia di Matapan', pp. 419–33; Jack Greene and Alessandro Massignani, *The Naval War in the Mediterranean 1940–1943* (London: Chatham, 2002), pp. 148–60. Relazione sull'azione di Capo Matapan 26, 27, 28 Marzo 1941: Mattesini, *Supermarina*, II/1, pp 304–13.

37 Possibilità di azione a massa aereo-navale contro la flotta inglese nel Mediterraneo, 28 May 1941; Azione aereo-navale a massa contro la flotta inglese nel Mediterraneo, 14 June 1941: Mattesini, *Supermarina* II/1, pp. 539–49, 551–2.

38 Iachino to Riccardi, 18 May 1941: Angelo Iachino, *Tramonto di una grande marina* (Milan: Mondadori, 1966), pp. 252–3.

39 Addestramento della Squadra Navale, 10 June 1941: Mattesini, *Supermarina* II/1, p. 592.

40 Greene and Massignani, *The Naval War in the Mediterranean*, pp. 236–8.

41 *DSCS* IV/1, pp. 177, 184, 342, 570, 587, 652–3 (24 May, 25 May, 14 June, 13 August, 15 August, 23 August 1941); Verbali della Riunione tenuta il pomeriggio del giorno 22 agosto 1941, *DSCS* IV/2, pp. 256–7.

42 Richard Hammond, 'An Enduring Influence on Imperial Defence and Grand Strategy: British Perceptions of the Italian Navy, 1935–1943', *International History Review*, vol. 39, no. 5, 2017, pp. 825, 826.

43 SIM 'counted' three enemy armoured divisions, a motorized division and a dozen infantry divisions in Cyrenaica and Egypt, whereas in reality the enemy's forces amounted to two armoured divisions and three infantry divisions: Montanari, *La seconda guerra mondiale*, p. 451.

44 AUSSME, Sintesi della riunione tenuta . . . il 3 marzo 1941, p. 2: H-10/1/6.

45 AUSSME, Verbale della riunione del 18 marzo 1941: H-10/1/6.

46 Guzzoni to Gariboldi, 28 March 1941: Mario Montanari, *Le operazioni in Africa settentrionale*, vol. II: *Tobruk (marzo 1941–gennaio 1942)* (Rome: Ufficio Storico dello Stato Maggiore dell'Esercito, 1993), p. 38.

47 Directive, 13 April 1941: *ibid.*, p. 114.

48 *Ibid.*, pp. 123 fn. 8, 146–7.

49 AUSSME, Relazione sullo spirito delle truppe, 2 April 1941: H-5/20/4.

50 AUSSME, Sintesi argomenti trattati dal Sottosegretario di Stato nella riunione del I° maggio 1941, p. 2 [original emphasis]: H-10/1/6.

51 Galeazzo Ciano, *Diario 1937–1943* (Milan: Rizzoli, 1980), p. 518 (30 May 1941).

52 Operazioni offensive in Egitto, 9 May 1941: Pier Paolo Battistelli, 'La "guerra dell'Asse". Condotta bellica e collaborazione militare italo-tedesca 1939–1943', Tesi di dottorato Università degli Studi Padova, 2000, p. 274.

53 AUSSME, Promemoria sulle principali questioni in corso, 18 May 1941, p. 3: H-9/10/10.

54 Gambara to Roatta, 23 May 1941: Lucio Ceva, *Le forze armate* (Turin: UTET, 1981), pp. 573–81.

55 Lucio Ceva, 'L'alto Comando delle Forze Armate in Italia durante il regime fascista (1925–1943)', in *idem.*, *Teatri di guerra. Comandi, soldati e scrittori nei conflitti europei* (Milan: Franco Angeli, 2005), pp. 76–7.

56 Ugo Cavallero, *Diario 1940–1943* (Rome: Ciarrapico, 1984), p. 198 (11 June 1941).

57 AUSSME, Monthly reports: I-3/123/1.

58 Colloquio Cavallero–Keitel, 2 June 1941: *DDI* 9/VII, no. 201, pp. 196–204; AUSSME, Sintesi del colloquio tra il maresciallo Keitel e il generale CAVALLERO del giorno 2 giugno 1941 al Brennero: L-13/44/12.

59 Appunto, 10 June 1941 (von Rintelen): Montanari, *Le operazioni in Africa settentrionale* II, pp. 798–9.

60 Promemoria N.308 Programma di trasporti per l'Africa Settentrionale, 4 May 1941: Mattesini, *Supermarina* II/1, pp. 426–8.

61 Trasporti per l'ASI, 29 May 1941: *ibid.*, p. 498.

62 AUSSME, Trasporti marittimi in ASI, 13 July 1941, pp. 3, 5–6: H-10/8/4.

63 In fact, Riccardi's figures were too low: in June he managed to ship 125,000 tons of materiel to Libya.

64 Protezione aerea ai convogli da e per la Libia, 29 May 1941: Mattesini, *Supermarina* II/1, pp. 499–500.

65 Ajmone Cat to Comandante Superiore Forze Armate in Africa Settentrionale, [?6] June 1941: *DSCS* IV/2, pp. 138–41.

66 Gariboldi to Comando Supremo, 1 June 1941: *DSCS* IV/2, pp. 60–3.

67 Roatta to Cavallero, 10 July 1941: Montanari, *Le operazioni in Africa settentrionale* II, pp. 273–80.

68 Bastico to Cavallero, 26 July 1941: *DSCS* IV/2, pp. 124–33.

69 Appunto per il Duce, 5 August 1941: Montanari, *Le operazioni in Africa settentrionale* II, pp. 301–2.

70 Cavallero to Bastico, 5 August 1941: *DSCS* IV/2, pp. 145–7.

71 Cavallero, *Diario*, p. 219 (6 August 1941).

72 Cavallero to Keitel, 6 August 1941: Battistelli, 'La "guerra dell'Asse"', p. 308.

73 Appunti relative alla riunione avvenuta dalle ore 9.45 all ore 10.45 per esame situazione, 8 August 1941: *DSCS* IV/2, pp. 163–6.

74 Appunti relative successivea riunione, 8 August 1941: *DSCS* IV/2, pp. 167–70.

75 Verbali del colloquio tra l'Eccellenza Cavallero e il Maresciallo Keitel, 25 August 1941 (morning): *DSCS* IV/2, pp. 280–4.

76 Promemoria, 10 September 1941; Esame critica della preparazione, della condotta e dei risultati della nostra guerra subacquea, 9 December 1941: Mattesini, *Supermarina* II/2, pp. 965–6, 1,301–3.

77 Hammond, 'British Perceptions of the Italian Navy', p. 823.

78 Raeder to Riccardi, 12 July 1941: Mattesini, *Supermarina* II/2, pp. 751–2.

79 Situazione strategica e possibilità operative nel Mediterraneo, 15 July 1941: *ibid.*, p. 754.

80 Promemoria relative ai cinque punti indicate nell'appunto concernente la lettera del Führer al Duce del 20 luglio 1941–XIX, 2 August 1941; Riccardi to Bastico, 6 September 1941: *ibid.*, pp. 770, 795.

81 Operazioni navali dei giorni 25–26–27–28 settembre 1941/XIX [Riccardi], 3 October 1941: *ibid.*, pp. 985–93; Greene and Massignani, *The Naval War in the Mediterranean*, pp. 181–91.

82 Giorgio Giorgerini, 'Il problema dei convogli e la guerra per mare', in Rainero and Biagini, eds., *L'Italia in guerra. Il 2° anno – 1941*, pp. 405–6, 416–17.

83 Lucio Ceva, *La condotta italiana della guerra. Cavallero e il Comando supremo 1941/1942* (Milan: Feltrinelli, 1975), p. 165 n. 20; Montanari, *Le operazioni in Africa settentrionale* II, p. 299.

84 Cavallero to Pricolo, 21 October 1941: *DSCS* V/2, p. 47.

85 Relazione sommaria sull'azione del 9 novembre, 14 November 1941: Mattesini, *Supermarina* II/2, p. 1,164.

86 Greene and Massignani, *The Naval War in the Mediterranean*, pp. 193–6.

87 Giuseppe Conti, *Una guerra segreta. il Sim nel secondo conflitto mondiale* (Bologna: Il Mulino, 2009), p. 167; AUSSME, EGITTO – Sintesi di prossima offensive Britannica, 11 November 1941; Z/131007 [SIE], 13 November 1941: N-3/520/A.

88 Montanari, *Le operazioni in Africa settentrionale* II, pp. 438–634; Martin Kitchen, *Rommel's Desert War* (Cambridge: Cambridge University Press, 2009), pp. 150 –73; Jack Greene and Alessandro Massignani, *Rommel's North Africa Campaign, September 1940–November 1942* (Conshohocken, PA: Combined Books, 1994), pp. 102–22.

89 Rommel for Cavallero, [3?] December 1941: *DSCS* V/2, pp. 103–4.

90 Cavallero to Bastico, 9 December 1941; Cavallero to Bastico, 12 December 1941: Cavallero, *Diario*, pp. 275–7.

91 Appunto per il DUCE, 13 November 1941; Azione aero-navale nella notte sul 22 novembre 1941; Verbale della riunione del giorno 4 dicembre 1941; Mattesini, *Supermarina* II/2, pp. 1,175–6, 1,189–91, 1,217–19.

92 Relazione sintetica sull'operazione del 16–19 dicembre 1941, 30 December 1941: *ibid.*, p. 1,246.

93 *DSCS* V/1, pp. 799–867 (16, 17, 18, 19 December 1941).

94 Ugo Cavallero, *Comando Supremo. Diario 1940–43 del Capo di S.M.G.* (Bologna: Cappelli, 1948), pp. 158, 175 (3 and 27 December 1941).

95 Mussolini to Hitler, 29 December 1941: *DDI* 9/VIII, no. 79, pp. 71–3.

96 Hitler to Mussolini, 29 December 1941: *DDI* 9'VIII, no. 80, pp. 73–81.

97 AUSSME, Perdite Africa, 6 February 1942: H-9/11.

98 AUSSME, FRONTE CIRENAICO: Rilievi sulle operazioni britanniche ed elementi informative tratti da un rapporto di un osservatore Americano, 23 December 1941: N-3/520/B.

99 *DSCS* V/1, p. 847 (22 December 1941).

100 Enrico Cernuschi, 'Breaking "ULTRA": The Cryptologic and Intelligence War between Britain and Italy, 1931–1943', in John Jordan, ed., *Warship 2018* (Oxford: Osprey, 2018), pp. 86, 96. Cernuschi attributes the intelligence breakthrough to an escapee, Lieutenant Luigi Tomasuolo.

101 J. Calvitt Clarke III, *Russia and Italy against Hitler: The Bolshevik-Fascist Rapprochement of the 1930s* (New York: Greenwood Press, 1991), pp. 77–91.

102 Rosaria Quartararo, *Italia-URSS 1917–1941. I rapporti politici* (Naples: Edizioni Scientifiche Italiane, 1997), p. 220.

103 Mussolini to Hitler, 5 January 1940: *DDI* 9/III, no. 33, pp. 21–2.

104 Manfredi Martelli, *Mussolini e la Russia. Le relazioni italo-sovietiche dal 1922 al 1941* (Milan: Mursia, 2007), pp. 311–14, 318, 345, 351; Quartararo, *Italia-URSS 1917–1941*, pp. 238–9.

105 AUSSME, N.115A, 13 July 1940: L-13/45/3; N. 2019/A, 25 October 1940: L-13/45/4; Esposizione del Fuehrer sulla situazione politico militare, 20 January 1941: L-13/44/3.

106 AUSSME, GERMANIA: Situazione militare e intendimenti operativi, 24 January 1941: N-8/1448.

107 SIM: Germania, opinioni di ambienti militari tedeschi circa gli attuali ed i futuri avvenimenti, 5 March 1941: *DSCS* III/2, pp. 252–3; AUSSME, URSS – Attività sovietica alla frontiera romena, 28 January 1941: N-8/1448.

108 Marras to War Ministry, 7 May 1941: *Le operazioni delle unità italiane al fronte russo (1941–1943)* (Rome: Ufficio Storico dello Stato Maggiore dell'Esercito, 2000), pp. 519–20.

109 AUSSME, GERMANIA – Misure precauzionali attuate nei confronti della Russia, 14 April 1941; URSS – propaganda Britannica e misure sovietiche a frontiere occidentale, 23 April 1941: N-8/1449.

110 Conti, *Una guerra segreta*, pp. 194–5.

111 Cavallero, *Diario*, p. 188 (30 May 1941).

112 Ciano, *Diario*, p. 520 (2 June 1941); Giuseppe Bottai, *Diario 1935–1944* (Milan: Rizzoli, 2001), pp. 270, 272 (5 and 7 June 1941).

113 *DSCS* IV/1, p. 304 (9 June 1941).

114 AUSSME, DSCS. Uff. Op., 14 June 1941: N-8/1438.

115 Marras to War Ministry, 17 June 1941: *Le operazioni delle unità italiane al fronte russo*, pp. 523–4.

116 Cavallero Diary, 21 June 1941: *Le operazioni delle unità italiane al fronte russo*, pp. 526–7.

117 Pietro Pastorelli, *L'esaurimento dell'iniziativa del'Asse* (Milan: ISPI, 1967), p. 33, quoted in Conti, *Una guerra segreta*, p. 472 fn. 351. According to one source the Italian Embassy in Berlin knew the date of the attack on Russia in advance, thanks to indiscretions on the part of the German Foreign Office: Cristiano Ridomi, *La fine dell'ambasciata a Berlino 1940–1943* (Milan: Longanesi, 1972), p. 78.

118 Mussolini to Petacci, 3 p.m., 22 June 1941; Ciano to [unknown], 13 September 1941: Ugo Guspini, *L'orecchio del regime. Le intercettazioni telefoniche al tempo del fascismo* (Milan: Mursia, 1973), pp. 189, 190–1.

119 Bottai, *Diario*, p. 276 (5 July 1941).

120 Jürgen Förster, 'Il ruolo dell'8a armata italiana dal punto di vista tedesco', in Enzo Collotti, ed., *Gli italiani sul fronte russo* (Bari: De Donato, 1982), p. 230.

121 Appunti del Col. Valfré di Bonzo, Addetto Militare a Bucarest sui procedimenti tattici sovietici, 22 July 1941: *Le operazioni delle unità italiane al fronte russo*, pp. 58–67.

122 Mussolini to Roatta, 14 July 1941: Battistelli, 'La "guerra dell'Asse"', p. 250; Relazione per lo stato maggiore generale sulla posizione politico-militare, 24 July 1941: OO XXX, pp. 112–13.

123 Programma di materiali di armamento e produzione mensile stilato dall'Esercito, [26 August 1941]: *DSCS* IV/2, pp. 273, 276–7.

124 Giovanni Messe, *La guerra al fronte russo. Il corpo di spedizione italiano in Russia (CSIR)* (Milan: Mursia, 2005), p. 42 (20 July 1941); *DSCS* IV/1, p. 551 (11 August 1941).

125 Cavallero Diary, 17 and 23 July, 12 August 1941: *Le operazioni delle unità italiane al fronte russo*, pp. 577–8, 581.

126 AUSSME, Promemoria per il Duce, giugno 1941, p. 2; Per il Duce – Notizie varie della capitale, 29 June 1941: H-5/20/4.

127 Bastian Matteo Scianna, 'Myths and Memories: The Italian Operations on the Eastern Front (1941–1943) and their Contested Legacies during the Cold War', Dr. Phil. Dissertation Universität Potsdam, 2017, p. 110.

128 *Le operazioni delle unità italiane al fronte russo*, pp. 537–41.

129 Thomas Schlemmer, *Invasori, non vittime. La campagna italiana di Russia 1941–1943* (Roma-Bari: Laterza, 2009), p.19.

130 Scianna, 'Myths and Memories', pp. 226–30.

131 AUSSME, Promemoria per il Duce, giugno 1941, p. 3: H-5/20/4.

132 Mario Isnenghi, 'La campagna di Russia nella stampa e nella pubblicistica fascista', in Collotti, ed., *Gli italiani sul fronte russo*, pp. 405, 409.

133 AUSSME, Il II Corpo italiano al fronte russo (1942–1943), 30 April 1943, p. 16: N1-11/1552/5.

134 Amedeo Osti Guerrazzi and Thomas Schlemmer, 'I soldati italiani nella campagna di Russia', *Annali dell'Istituto storico italo-germanico in Trento*, vol. XXXIII, 2007, p. 410.

135 Hitler to Mussolini, 20 July 1941; Mussolini to Hitler, 24 July 1941: *DDI* 9/VIII, nos. 288, 299, pp. 273–7, 285–7.

136 Ceva, *La condotta italiana della guerra*, pp. 63, 80–1, 210–13; Battistelli, 'La "guerra dell'Asse"', pp. 255–6, 266–73.

137 ASAM, Notizie sull'aviazione russa, 30 July 1941: INF 4/1.

138 ASAM, Interrogatorio di prigionieri russi, 28 June 1941, pp. 2, 3 (original emphasis): INF 7/1.

139 ASAM, Stralcio della promemoria in data 10 agosto 1941 inviato dal comandante d'aviazione del CSIR; Magli to Santoro, 27 August 194; Santoro to Magli, 28 August 1941: SIOS 11/124.

140 ASAM, Relazione compiuta dal ten. colonnello Porporati presso l'Aeronautica del CSIR dal 27/9 al 21/10/41, p. 2: SIOS 11/135.

141 Bianca Ceva, *Cinque anni di storia italiana 1940–1945* (Milan: Edizioni di Comunità, 1964), p. 53 (31 July and 13 August 1941).

142 *Ibid.*, pp. 53–4 (6 September 1941).

143 Cavallero, *Diario*, p. 222 (15 August 1941); *DSCS* IV/1, pp. 619, 627, 642 (19, 20, 22 August 1941).

144 Verbale del colloquio tra l'Eccellenza Cavallero e il Maresciallo Keitel, 25 August 1941 (mattino and sera): *DSCS* IV/2, pp. 280–1, 288. Drafts with handwritten corrections in AUSSME, L-13/44/13.

145 Verbali del colloquio tra l'Eccellenza Cavallero e il Maresciallo Keitel, 25 August 1941: *DSCS* IV/2, pp. 280–4.

146 Messe, *La guerra al fronte russo*, p. 71; Messe to Maria [Messe], 28 agosto [1941]: Giovanni Messe, *Lettere alla moglie. Dai fronti Greco-albanese, russo, tunisino e dalla prigionia 1940–1944* (Milan: Mursia, 2018), pp. 119–20.

147 Ridomi, *La fine dell'ambasciata a Berlino*, pp. 86–7.

148 Procedimenti d'impiego alla fronte russa, 21 September 1941: *Le operazioni delle unità italiane al fronte russo*, pp. 632–7.

149 AUSSME, Operazioni alla fronte russa, 11 September 1941; La situazione militare, 6 October 1941: I-4/3/7.

150 AUSSME, Per il Duce: Notizie varie dalla capitale, 14, 28 September 1941: H-5/20/4.

151 AUSSME, No. 1045/S, Visita alla fronte Sud, 1 October 1941 (Marras), p. 5: I-4/3/7.

152 TNA, SRIG #58, 4 June 1943: WO 208/4185.

153 ASAM, Indumenti invernali per il personale aeronautica destinato al 'CSIR', 1 August 1941, 2 August 1941, 10 September 1941: SIOS 11/128; *DSCS* IV/1, pp. 499, 561, 579 (4, 12, 14 August 1941); Filippo Cappellano, '"Scarpe di cartone e divise di tela ..." Gli stereotipi e la realtà sugli equipaggiamenti invernali delle truppe italiane in Russia nella seconda guerra mondiale', *Storia militare* anno X, n. 101, February 2002, pp. 20–2.

154 Messe to Maria [Messe], 16 and 19 January 1941, 8 and 11 October 1941: Messe, *Lettere alla moglie*, pp. 94, 85, 122, 123; Luigi Longo, *Giovanni Messe. L'ultimo maresciallo d'Italia* (Rome: Ufficio Storico dello Stato Maggiore dell'Esercito, 2006), pp. 143–4.

155 Messe, *La guerra al fronte russo*, pp. 124–5 (26 October 1941).

156 Ceva, *Cinque anni*, p. 59 (24 November 1941).

157 Cappellano, '"Scarpe di cartone e divise di tela ..."', p. 22.

158 Cesare Amé, *Guerra segreta in Italia 1940–1943* (Milan: Edizion Bietti, 2011), p. 92.

159 Conti, *Una guerra segreta*, p. 197 (5 September 1941).

160 Maria Gabriella Pasqualini, *Breve storia dell'Organizzazione dei Servizi d'Informazione della R. Marina e R. Aeronautica 1919–1945* (Rome: Ministero della Difesa, 2013), p. 239.

161 Ceva, *Cinque anni*, p. 67 (27 December 1941).

162 Hitler to Mussolini, 29 December 1941: *DDI* 9/VIII, no. 80, pp. 73–81.

163 NARS, Le operazioni militari germaniche nel 1941, [8] January 1942, pp. 4, 6, 12–14; La campagna invernale in Russia, n.d. [but after 12 February 1942]: IT 3033 T-821/252/ff.12–.

164 H. James Burgwyn, 'The Legacy of Italy's Participation in the German War against the Soviet Union: 1941–1943', *Mondo contemporaneo* no. 2, 2011, p. 180; Nicolas G. Virtue, '"We Istrians Do Very Well in Russia": Istrian Combatants, Fascist Propaganda, and Brutalization on the Eastern Front', in Emanuele Sica and Richard Carrier, eds., *Italy and the Second World War: Alternative Perspectives* (Leiden: Brill, 2018), pp. 292–3; Loris Rizzo, *Lo sguardo del potere: La censura militare in Italia nella seconda guerra mondiale 1940–1945* (Milan: Rizzoli, 1984), p. 111 (letter of 6 May 1942).

CHAPTER 6

1 'In viaggio', 19 June 1940 [Roatta]: Giacomo Carboni, *Memorie segrete 1935–1948. 'Più che il dovere'* (Florence: Parenti, 1955), p. 101.

2 Pavelić to Anfuso, 6 March 1941: *DDI* 9/VI, no. 688, pp. 669–70.

3 H. James Burgwyn, *Empire on the Adriatic: Mussolini's Conquest of Yugoslavia 1941–1943* (New York: Enigma Books, 2005), pp. 21–31.

4 Attività croata nel territorio di occupazione (Ambrosio), 23 April 1941: Alberto Becherelli and Paolo Formiconi, *La quinta sponda. Una storia dell'occupazione italiana della Croazia 1941–1943* (Rome: Ufficio Storico Stato Maggiore della Difesa, 2015), p. 46.

5 Situazione politica della Croazia (SIM), 10 May 1941: *DSCS* IV/2, pp. 18–19.

6 Croazia (SIM), 7 May 1941: *DSCS* IV/2, p. 12.

7 *DSCS* IV/1, p. 168 (23 May 1941).

8 Albania – Conflitti tra Albanesi e Montenegrini, 4 June 1941: *DSCS* IV/2, p. 64.

9 Slovenia, Dalmazia e Croazia. Sintesi della situazione, 8 June 1941: *DSCS* IV/2, pp. 80–1.

10 Croazia – propaganda comunista (SIM), 4 June 1941: *DSCS* IV/2, pp. 64–5; Eric Gobetti, *Alleati del nemico. L'occupazione italiana in Jugoslavia (1941–1943)* (Bari: Laterza, 2013), pp. 35–6.

11 I nuovi alleati del bolscevismo (SIM), 10 August 1941: *DSCS* IV/2, p. 195.

12 Gobetti, *Alleati del nemico*, pp. 43–4.

13 Pier Paolo Battistelli, 'La "guerra dell'Asse". Condotta bellica e collaborazione militare italo-tedesca, 1939–1943', Tesi di dottorato Università degli studi Padova, 2000, pp. 344–8.

14 Burgwyn, *Empire on the Adriatic*, p. 51.

15 Davide Rodogno, *Il nuovo ordine mediterraneo. Le politiche di occupazione dell'Italia fascista in Europa (1940–1943)* (Turin: Bollati Boringhieri, 2003), pp. 233–5.

16 Nicolas G. Virtue, 'Royal Army, Fascist Empire: The Regio Esercito on Occupation Duty, 1936–1943', PhD University of Western Ontario, 2016, p. 290.

17 Situazione politica in Croazia (Ambrosio to SME Ufficio Operazioni), 23 July 1941: *DSCS* IV/2, pp. 180–9.

18 Foreign Ministry Croatian Office to Comando Supremo,? [1–11] August 1941: *DSCS* IV/2, pp. 208–12.

19 Giacomo Scotti and Luciano Viazzi, *Occupazione e guerra italiana in Montenegro. Le Aquile delle Montagne Nere* (Milan: Mursia, 1987), p. 75.

20 NARS, Situazione Montenegro [Pirzio Biroli], 22 July 1941: T-821/356/fr. 677–81.

21 Scotti and Viazzi, *Le Aquile delle Montagne Nere*, p. 127.

22 AUSSME, Stralcio della relazione N.3 dalla Commissione di Stato jugoslava per l'accertamento dei misfatti commessi degli occupatori e dai loro coadiutori, p. 1: N1-11/2555(1)/8/1.

23 AUSSME, Relazione sull'attività svolta dal Governatore del Montenegro Generale d'Armata PIRZIO BIROLI Alessandro dal luglio 1941 al luglio 1943, 23 January 1945, pp. 2, 6, 9, 10: N1-11/2555(1)/8/1/2.

24 Scotti and Viazzi, *Le Aquile delle Montagne Nere*, pp. 184–5, 241.

25 *Ibid.*, pp. 242–3, 249. According to the partisans' figures the Italians lost 1,855 dead and wounded and another 2,970 men captured.

26 Federica Saini Fasanotti, *Etiopia 1936–1940. Le operazioni di polizia coloniale nelle fonti dell'esercito italiano* (Rome: Ufficio Storico dello Stato Maggiore dell'Esercito, 2010), pp. 260, 273–4, 284, 290.

27 NARS, Montenegro, 2 August 1941, p. 5: T-821/356/fr.648–58.

28 Ispezione delle truppe nel Montenegro e situazione politica, 27 August 1941: *DSCS* V/2, p. 20.

29 AUSSME, Relazione . . . del Generale d'Armata PIRZIO BIROLI, p. 14.

30 Addestramento invernale. Controguerriglia, 26 September 1941: *DSCS* V/2, pp. 41–3.

31 Situazione nel Montenegro, 25 October 1941: *DSCS* V/2, pp. 74–5.

32 Rodogno, *Il nuovo ordine mediterraneo*, pp. 172, 190, 407–10.

33 Burgwyn, *Empire on the Adriatic*, pp. 95–6.

34 Giacomo Scotti and Luciano Viazzi, *L'inutile vittoria. La tragica esperienza delle truppe italiane in Montenegro 1941–1942* (Milan: Mursia, 1989), pp. 49–50.

35 Montenegro (Pirzio Biroli), 12 August 1941: *DSCS* IV/2, pp. 239–46.

36 Memoria sulla situazione politico-militare, 24 July 1941: cited in Battistelli, 'La "guerra del'Asse"', p. 357.

37 Provvedimenti per fronteggiare attuale situazione in Croazia, 4 August 1941; Ambrosio to Ufficio Operazioni Stato Maggiore Regio Esercito, 12 August 1941: *DSCS* IV/2, pp. 148–9, 290–4.

38 AUSSME, Relazione contro l'accusa di criminalità di guerra [Robotti], 16 July 1945, p. 3: N1-11/2555(1)/7/1/1.

39 Situazione militare in Slovenia, 15 October 1941: *DSCS* V/2, pp. 70–3.

40 Azioni contro ribelli, 23 October 1941: Virtue, 'Royal Army, Fascist Empire', p. 453.

41 Amedeo Osti Guerrazzi, *The Italian Army in Slovenia: Strategies of Antipartisan Repression, 1941–1943* (New York: St Martin's Press, 2013), p. 34 (22 October 1941).

42 AUSSME, Relazione [Robotti], p. 6.

43 Burgwyn, *Empire on the Adriatic*, p. 103; Osti Guerazzi, *The Italian Army in Slovenia*, pp. 25–9, 37; Virtue, 'Royal Army, Fascist Empire', p. 455.

44 Appunto (von Rintelen), 17 December 1941; Appunto per il generale di divisione Enno von Rintelen, 18 December 1941: *DSCS* V/2, p. 97.

45 Galeazzo Ciano, *Diario 1937–1943* (Milan: Rizzoli, 1980), pp. 567–8 (15–16, 17 December 1941); Ambrosio to Cavallero, 18 December 1941: *DDI* 9/VIII, no. 40, pp. 33–5.

46 AUSSME, Dal DUCE – 18-XII-41: H-10/12.

47 *DSCS* V/1, pp. 832–3 (20 December 1941).

48 Battistelli, 'La "guerra dell'Asse"', pp. 368–74.

49 Burgwyn, *Empire on the Adriatic*, p. 103.

50 Amedeo Osti Guerrazzi, *Noi non sappiamo odiare. L'esercito italiano tra fascismo e democrazia* (Turin: UTET, 2010), p. 101 (19 January 1942).

51 Saini Fasanotti, *Etiopia 1936–1940*, p. 263.

52 Ugo Cavallero, *Diario 1940–1943* (Rome: Ciarrapico, 1984), pp. 276 (11 December 1941), 310, 315 (4 and 13 January 1942).

53 Promemoria, 10 January 1942: Battistelli, 'La "guerra dell'Asse"', pp. 376–7.

54 FLE, Pietromarchi Diary, 19, 22 January 1942.

55 Giacomo Zanussi, *Guerra e catastrofe d'Italia*, vol. I: *Giugno 1940 Giugno 1943* (Rome: Corso, 1946), pp. 180–1.

56 Matteo Dominioni, *Lo sfascio dell'Impero. Gli italiani in Etiopia 1936–1941* (Bari: Laterza, 2008), pp. 177, 205–15; Saini Fasanotti, *Etiopia 1936–1940*, pp. 353–6. According to the contemporary official account the gas did not work.

57 Ambrosio to Cavallero, 23 January 1942: *DDI* 9/VIII, no. 195, p. 207.

58 Pietromarchi to Ciano, 13 February 1942, enclosing Keitel to Cavallero, 4 February 1942; Pietromarchi to Ciano, 16 February 1942; Magli to Pietromarchi, 24 February 1942, enclosing Cavallero to Keitel, 18 February 1942: *DDI* 9/VIII, nos. 263, 274, 314, pp. 285–7, 307–9, 314.

59 Mario Cuzzi, 'I Balcani, problemi di un'occupazione difficile', *Italia in guerra. Il 3° anno 1942* (Rome: Commissione italiana di storia militare, 1993), p. 343; Osti Guerrazzi, *The Italian Army in Slovenia*, pp. 57, 59.

60 Osti Guerrazzi, *The Italian Army in Slovenia*, pp. 57–8, 168 fn. 21.

61 Battistelli, 'La "guerra dell'Asse"', pp. 417–18.

62 Giuseppe Santoro, *L'aeronautica italiana nella seconda guerra mondiale* (Rome: Esse, 1957), vol., p. 240.

63 Burgwyn, *Empire on the Adriatic*, pp. 74–5.

64 Zanussi, *Guerra e catastrofe d'Italia* I, pp. 222, 234–6; Virtue, 'Royal Army, Fascist Empire', p. 456.

65 Circolare N.3C, 1 March 1942: Gianni Oliva, *'Si ammazza troppo poco'. I crimini di guerra italiani 1940–1943* (Milan: Mondadori, 2007), pp. 174–99.

66 Burgwyn, *Empire on the Adriatic*, pp. 137–8; Osti Guerrazzi, *The Italian Army in Slovenia*, pp. 60–1, 63.

67 Cavallero to Keitel, 18 February 1942: *DSCS* VI/2, pp. 79–80.

68 Ambrosio to Cavallero, 5 March 1942: *DDI* 9/VIII, no. 339, p. 377.

69 Roatta to Ambrosio and Ciano, 6 March 1942; Verbale relative alla riunione tenuta ad Abbazia il 3 marzo 1942 [Point 10]: *DDI* 9/VIII, nos. 345, 339 All., pp. 384–7, 377–9.

70 Zanussi, *Guerra e catastrofe d'Italia* I, p. 216.

71 Battistelli, 'La "guerra dell'Asse"', pp. 390–9; Becherelli and Formiconi, *La quinta sponda*, pp. 67–70; Burgwyn, *Empire on the Adriatic*, pp. 146–53.

72 Operazioni italo-tedesche-croate in Bosnia orientale, [May 1942]: *DSCS* VII/2, p. 57.

73 Battistelli, 'La "guerra dell'Asse"', p. 403 fn. 506.

74 Scotti and Viazzi, *L'inutile vittoria*, p. 380.

75 Appunto relative alla situazione politica nei territori annessi della Dalmazia, 1 June 1942: *DSCS* VII/2, pp. 125–6.

76 AUSSME, VENEZIA GIULIA – Attività ribelli, 27 June 1942; VENEZIA GIULIA – Propaganda antitaliana, 28 June 1942; VENEZIA GIULIA – Attività ribelli, 8 July 1942: N-3/520/Q, N-3/520/R/1.

77 Cavallero, *Diario*, pp. 391, 393, (14 and 18 May 1942); FLE, Pietromarchi Diary, 21 May 1942; Rodogno, *Il nuovo ordine mediterraneo*, p. 404.

78 Osti Guerrazzi, *The Italian Army in Slovenia*, pp. 66, 67.

79 Oliva, 'Si ammazza troppo poco', pp. 126–7.

80 Loris Rizzi, *Lo sguardo del potere. La censura militare in Italia nella seconda guerra mondiale 1940–1945* (Milan: Rizzoli, 1984), pp. 115–16.

81 Becherelli and Formiconi, *La quinta sponda*, p. 98 fn. 55.

82 Osti Guerrazzi, *Noi non sappiamo odiare*, pp. 211–13.

83 Rodogno, *Il nuovo ordine mediterraneo*, p. 403.

84 Gobetti, *Alleati del nemico*, p. 70.

85 Osti Guerrazzi, *The Italian Army in Slovenia*, pp. 72–8.

86 Gobetti, *Alleati del nemico*, pp. 74–5; Ex-Jugoslavia: situazione della ribellione, 22 June 1942: *DSCS* VII/2, p. 143.

87 Pirzio Biroli to Ciano, 1 December 1941: *DDI* 9/VII, no. 796, pp. 810–11.

88 Cuzzi, 'I Balcani', p. 366.

89 FLE, Pietromarchi Diary, 1 June 1942.

90 AUSSME, CROAZIA – Situazione nella 3a zona, 28 June 1942: N-3/520/Q.

91 Sgombro della 3a zona e sgombero parziale della 2a zona della Croazia, 2 July 1942: *DSCS* VII/2, p. 257.

92 AUSSME, CROAZIA – Accordi italo-croati relative alla 2a e 3a zona, 7 July 1942: N-3/520R/1 [original emphasis].

93 Roatta to Gandin, 11 August 1942: *DSCS* VII/2, pp. 312–13.

94 AUSSME, CROAZIA – Creazione di speciali gruppi di combattimento, 3 July 1942: N-3/520R/1.

95 Situazione politica, economica e militare, 9 June 1942: *DSCS* VII/2, p. 151.

96 Virtue, 'Royal Army, Fascist Empire', p. 473.

97 Robotti to Roatta, 29 July 1942: Osti Guerrazzi, *The Italian Army in Slovenia*, pp. 101–2.

98 Cavallero, *Diario*, pp. 443–4 (31 July 1942).

99   Cuzzi, 'I Balcani', p. 362.

100 Virtue, 'Royal Army, Fascist Empire', p. 264.

101 Burgwyn, *Empire on the Adriatic*, pp. 243–9; Osti Guerrazzi, *The Italian Army in Slovenia*, pp. 115–19.

102 Burgwyn, *Empire on the Adriatic*, pp. 174–6.

103 FLE, Pietromarchi Diary, 20, 24, 28 August, 13 September 1942; Zanussi, *Guerra e catastrofe d'Italia* I, pp. 264–6.

104 Rodogno, *Il nuovo ordine mediterraneo*, pp. 434, 437, 447, 456–8, 467–71; Emanuele Sica, *Mussolini's Army in the French Riviera: Italy's Occupation of France* (Urbana, IL: University of Illinois Press, 2016), pp. 162–73.

105 Zanussi, *Guerra e catastrofe d'Italia* I, pp. 258, 271–3.

106 Santoro, *L'aeronautica italiana*, pp. 247–8 (21 October 1942).

107 Casertano to Ciano, 20 November 1942: *DDI* 9/IX, no. 329, pp. 324–5, 240.

108 Colloquio Ciano–Hitler, 18 December 1942; Secondo colloquio, 18 December 1942; Cavallero to Mussolini, 18–19 December 1942; DDI 9/IX, nos. 414, 415, 422, pp. 408–12, 416–17, 422–5; Ciano, *Diario*, pp. 678–9 (19–20 December 1942).

109 *DSCS* IX/1, p. 28 (3 January 1943).

110 Riunione tenuta dall'Eccellenza il Capo di stato maggiore generale il 3 gennaio 1943: Antonello Biagini and Fernando Frattolillo, eds., *Verbali delle riunioni tenute dal Capo di SM generale*, vol. IV: *10 gennaio 1943–7 Septtembre 1943* (Rome: Ufficio Storico dello Stato Maggiore dell'Esercito, 1985), p. 6; Cavallero, *Diario*, p. 646 (3 January 1943); Renzo De Felice, *Mussolini l'alleato*, vol. I *L'Italia in guerra 1940–1943*, tomo 2: *Crisi e agonia del regime* (Turin: Einandi, 1990), p. 438; Castellani to Ciano, 18 January 1943: *DDI* 9/IX, no. 510, p. 516.

111 AUSSME, Criminali di guerra italiani secondo gli jugoslavi (Berardi), 18 February 1946, p. 7: N1-11/2555(1)/6/4/1.

112 Becherelli and Formiconi, *La quinta sponda*, pp. 93, 95.

113 IWM(D), Colloquio con le LL. EE. Roatta e Robotti, 4 February 1943; Colloquio con l'Eccellenza Roatta, 9 February 1943: EDS AL 2761/2F; Colloquio col generale Warlimont avvenuto il giorno 27 Febbraio 1943: EDS AL 2761/4.

114 IWM(D), Riunione con il generale Warlimont ed i generali Rossi e Gandin, 6 February 1943: EDS AL 2761/4.

115 Hitler to Mussolini, 16 February 1943: *DDI* 9/X, no. 31, pp. 40–2.

116 IWM(D), Riunione a Palazzo Venezia del giorno 26.2.1943: EDS AL 2761/1.

117 IWM(D), Colloquio con generale Warlimont giorno 27 [February 1943] ore 9.20; Colloquio col generale Warlimont (alle ore 10), 27 February 1943: EDS AL 2761/4.

118 Forze e compiti di Supersloda, 11 February 1943: *DSCS* IX/2, p. 218.

119 Difesa Madrepatria, 12 January 1943; Appunto del Capo di SMG al Duce, 17 February 1943; Situazione e compiti della 2a Armata-Possibilità di riduzione di forze, 25 February 1943: *DSCS* IX/2, pp. 138–9, 170–1, 208–14.

120 Jacomoni to Ciano, 27 and 28 January 1943: *DDI* 9/IX, nos. 554, 558, pp. 555, 559–60.

121 IWM(D), Colloquio con l'Eccellenza Gambara, 5 March 1943: EDS AL 2761/2.

122 IWM(D), Colloquio colle Eccellenze Pirzio Biroli e Robotti, 3 March 1943; Continuazione colloqui giorno 3 marzo ore 16.30: EDS AL 2761/2; Mussolini to Hitler, 9 March 1943: *DDI* 9/X, no. 95, pp. 128–32; Burgwyn, *Empire on the Adriatic*, p. 221.

123 NARS, Promemoria sulla difesa della Grecia, nella sua funzione di porta della Balcania, 27 March 1943, pp. 9–14, 16, 18, 20: T-821/354/958 ff.

124 Bastianini to Mussolini, 28 February 1943; Ambrosio to Mussolini: Argomenti da trattare nel noto convegno, 6 April 1943: *DDI* 9/X, nos. 52, 97, pp. 76–7, 251–2.

125 Colloqui con Eccellenza Rosi ed Eccellenza Robotti, 12 April 1943: *DSCS* IX/2, pp. 331–2; Ambrosio to Mussolini, Colloquio di Klessheim (Salzburg), 12 April 1943: *DDI* 9/X, no. 220, p. 290.

126 Battistelli, 'La "guerra dell'Asse"', p. 474.

127 Becherelli and Formiconi, *La quinta sponda*, p. 162 fn. 17; Burgwyn, *Empire on the Adriatic*, pp. 218–19.

128 Battistelli, 'La "guerra dell'Asse"', pp. 471–2.

129 AUSSME, Situazione generale. Orientamenti, 3 May 1942, pp. 1–2, 4: L-13/105/1.

130 Gobetti, *Alleati del nemico*, p. 159 (19 June 1943).

131 *Ibid.*, p. 109 (6 July 1943).

132 NARS, Questione cetnica, 1 September 1943, p. 4: T-821/355/122 ff.

133 Gobetti, *Alleati del nemico*, pp. 160–1.

134 Battistelli, 'La "guerra dell'Asse"', p. 350.

135 Pirzio Biroli to Comando Supremo, 4 June 1941: *DSCS* IV/2, pp. 77–8.

136 Bulgaria – Situazione nei territori occupati, 4 September 1941: *DSCS* V/2, p. 29; Francesco Guida, 'L'evoluzione politico-militare del fronte balcanico nel 1941', in R. H. Rainero and A. Biagini, eds., *L'Italia in guerra. Il 2° anno – 1941* (Rome: Commissione italiana di storia militare, 1992), pp. 19–20.

137 Marco Clementi, *Camicie nere sull'Acropoli. L'occupazione italiana in Grecia (1941–1943)* (Rome: Derive Approdi, 2013), pp. 49–51.

138 AUSSME, Ordine di disciplina nei territori occupati, 14 May 1941; Direttive, 22 June 1941; T.0213434, 18 July 1941: L-13/105/5.

139 AUSSME, Radio cifre #0215226, 20 August 1941: L-13/105/5.

140 Rodogno, *Il nuovo ordine mediterraneo*, p. 188 (26 July 1941) [original emphasis].

141 Clementi, *Camicie nere sull'Acropoli*, p. 34; Rodogno, *Il nuovo ordine mediterraneo*, pp. 202, 209–10.

142 AUSSME, Situazione politica nei territori sottoposti alla nostra giurisdizione, 1 November 1941: L-13/105/5.

143 Mark Mazower, *Inside Hitler's Greece: The Experience of Occupation, 1941–1944* (New Haven, CT and London: Yale University Press, 2001), p. 31.

144 AUSSME, Situazione economica e organizzazione civile nei territori occupati, 14 November 1941, pp. 3–5: L-13/105/5.

145 Clementi, *Camicie nere sull'Acropoli*, pp. 109–32; Mazower, *Inside Hitler's Greece*, p. 41.

146 Mussolini to Hitler, 22 July 1942 [original emphasis]; Giannini to Ciano, 15 October 1942; *DDI* 9/IX, nos. 21, 224, pp. 22–7, 231–3.

147 Clementi, *Camicie nere sull'Acropoli*, p. 60.

148 FLE, Pietromarchi Diary, 24 June 1942; Mazower, *Inside Hitler's Greece*, p. 124.

149 AUSSME, Circolazione di militari fuori servizio, 7 June 1942; Operazioni contro il banditismo, 22 July 1942: L-13/105/5.

150 AUSSME, Direttive per la lotta contro le bande, 8 October 1942: L-13/105/5.

151 AUSSME, Sistema degli ostaggi, 19 August 1942: L-13/105/5.

152 AUSSME, Incendio di abitati, 20 November 1942: L-13/105/5 [original emphasis].

153 Rodogno, *Il nuovo ordine mediterraneo*, pp. 410–12; Clementi, *Camicie nere sull'Acropoli*, pp. 182–3.

154 Cuzzi, 'I Balcani', pp. 371–6; AUSSME, T. Supergrecia to III Corps, 1 December 1942: L-13/105/5.

155 NARS, Riflessi della situazione politico-militare sull'opinione pubblico ateniese, 9 December 1942, pp. 2, 5–6: T-821–356/ff.610–.

156 Notizie dalla Grecia, 19 January 1943; Promemoria per il Duce – Notizie dalla Grecia, 1 April 1943; Promemoria per il Duce – Notizie dalla Grecia, 16 April 1943: *DSCS* IX/2, pp. 155–9, 294–5, 347.

157 Clementi, *Camicie nere sull'Acropoli*, pp. 186–92. In 2009 the Italian ambassador to Greece formally admitted Italian responsibility for the massacre.

158 AUSSME, Illecita speculazione nei territori occupati, 16 May 1943: L-13/105/2.

159 Mazower, *Inside Hitler's Greece*, p. 146.

160 AUSSME, Rapporto in data 11 giugno 1943 del ten. colonello CC. RR. A. Faedda: L-13/105/2.

161 AUSSME, Elenco degli ufficiali risultati implicati negli accertamenti circa comportamento e tenore di vita: H-5/34/2.

162 AUSSME, Mussolini to Geloso, 10 July 1943: L-13/105/2; Geloso to Mussolini, 15 July 1943: L-13/105/8.

163 NARS, Notizie dalla Grecia, 2 July 1943: T-821/355/ff.235–.

164 Clementi, *Camicie nere sull'Acropoli*, pp. 167, 185–6.

165 *Ibid.*, pp. 209–11.

166 *Ibid.*, p. 221.

167 Mazower, *Inside Hitler's Greece*, p. 152.

CHAPTER 7

1 AUSSME, SUA – Conclusione ciclo addestrativo dell'esercito per il 1941, 7 December 1941: N-3/520B.

2 'Per la dichiarazione di guerra agli Stati Uniti', 11 December 1941: OO XXX, pp. 140–2; Galeazzo Ciano, *Diario 1937–1943* (Milan: Rizzoli, 1980), pp. 565–6 (11 December 1941).

3 Fabio De Ninno, 'The Italian Navy and Japan, the Indian Ocean, Failed Cooperation and Tripartite Relations (1935–1943)', *War in History*, September 2018, pp. 1–25.

4 AUSSME, SUA – Produzione bellica, 15 November 1941; Diario Storico Servizio Informazioni Esercito, 8 January 1942: N-3/520A, N-3/520.

5 AUSSME, SUA – Apprezzamenti del capo del servizio informazioni in merito alla situazione politico-militare, 5 February 1942: N-3/520/F.

6 ASAM, Produzione aeronautica bellica degli Stati Uniti Americani, 1 July 1942; Grafici produziche [*sic*] bellica degli Stati Uniti, 22 September 1942: INF 7/2.

7 ASAM, Promemoria di servizio per il Capo del SIA, 16 March 1943: INF 18/1.

8 Wesley F. Craven and James L. Cate, eds., *The Army Air Forces in World War II* (Washington DC: Office of Air Force History, 1983), vol. 6, pp. 352, 405.

9 AUSSME, Sviluppi della collaborazione nel campo militare fra l'URSS e le Potenze democratiche, 21 June 1942: N-3/520/Q.

10 Ugo Cavallero, *Diario 1940–1943* (Rome: Ciarrapico, 1984), pp. 472–3 (30 August 1942).

11 Antonello Biagini, Fernando Frattolillo and Silvio Saccarelli, eds., *Verbali delle riunioni tenute dal Capo di SM Generale*, vol. III *10 gennaio 1942 – 31 dicembre 1942* (Rome: Ufficio Storico dello Stato Maggiore dell'Esercito, 1985), p. 786 (30 August 1942).

12 Cavallero, *Diario*, p. 326 (27 January 1942).

13 NARS, Impiego del CSIR nella campagna invernale e nella prossima campagna primaverile, 15 January 1942: T-821/256/fr.27.

14 Giovanni Messe, *La guerra al fronte russo. Il corpo di spedizione italiano in Russia (CSIR)* (Milan: Mursia, 2005), pp. 179, 189, 190–4.

15 FLE, Pietromarchi Diary, 16 May 1942.

16 Giacomo Zanussi, *Guerra e catastrofe d'Italia* (Rome: Corso, 1945), vol. I, p. 124.

17 Ugo De Lorenzis, *Dal primo all' ultimo giorno. Ricordi di guerra 1939–1945* (Milan: Longanesi, 1971), pp. 164–5, 187.

18 Jürgen Förster, 'Il ruolo dell'8a armata italiana dal punto di vista tedesco', in Enzo Collotti, ed., *Gli italiani sul fronte russo* (Bari: De Donato, 1982), p. 246.

19 Messe, *La guerra al fronte russo*, pp. 211–17.

20 AUSSME, Colloquio dell'Eccellenza Cavallero con il Maresciallo Keitel nel castello di Klessheim, 29 April 1942, p. 2: L-13/44/13.

21 Cavallero, *Diario*, pp. 391–3 (16 May 1942).

22 TNA, SRIC 217, 10 August 1943: WO 208/4186.

23 AUSSME, URSS – Potenziale industriale bellico, 3 February 1942: N-3/520/F.

24 ASAM, Attuale efficienza dell'Arma Aerea dell'Unione Sovietica e previsioni sul suo sviluppo fino all'anno 1942, enc. with Informazioni sul nemico, 3 December 1941: INF 4/3.

25 David M. Glantz and Jonathan House, *When Titans Clashed: How the Red Army Stopped Hitler* (Lawrence, KS: University Press of Kansas, 1995), p. 306; V. Hardesty and I. Grinberg, *Red Phoenix Rising: The Soviet Air Force in World War II* (Lawrence, KS: University Press of Kansas, 2012), p. 368. I am grateful to Professor Evan Mawdsley for the latter reference.

26 *Le operazioni delle unità italiane al fronte russo (1941–1943)* (Rome: Ufficio Storico dello State Maggiore dell'Esercito, 2000), pp. 188–94; Giorgio Scotone, *Il nemico fidato. La guerra di sterminio in URSS e l'occupazione alpine sull'Alto Don* (Trento: Panorama, 2013), p. 147.

27 De Lorenzis, *Dal primo all' ultimo giorno*, pp. 169–70.

28 Cavallero Diary, 25 July 1942: *Le operazioni delle unità italiane al fronte russo*, p. 645.

29 Messe, *La guerra al fronte russo*, pp. 235–8; *Le operazioni delle unità italiane al fronte russo*, pp. 217–33.

30 Difesa del Don, 2 August 1942: *Le operazioni delle unità italiane al fronte russo*, pp. 649–51.

31 Zanghieri to divisional commanders, 1 August 1942: *ibid.*, pp. 648–9.

32 Loris Rizzi, *Lo sguardo del potere. La censura militare in Italia nella seconda guerra mondiale 1940–1945* (Milan: Rizzoli, 1984), p. 111 (letters of 6 May 1942 and 30 June 1942).

33 *Ibid.*, p. 99 (letter of 17 October 1942).

34 Nicolas G. Virtue, 'Fascist Italy and the Barbarization of the Eastern Front, 1941–1943', MA dissertation University of Calgary, 2007, pp. 79–80, 88–90, 91–2, 94–6; Bianca Ceva, *Cinque anni di storia italiana 1940–1945* (Milan: Edizioni di Comunità, 1964), p. 112 (20 February 1942).

35 Marina Rossi, 'Lo spirito militare del Corpo di Spedizione in Russia nei giudizi del Servizio Informazioni dell'Armata Rossa (1941–1946)', in Piero Del Negro, ed., *Lo spirito militare degli italiani* (Padua: Centro interuniversitario di studi e ricerche storico-militare/Commissione italiana di storia militare, 2002), pp. 107, 110.

36 Giorgio Vitali, *Savoia ha caricato signor Generale* (Florence: MEF, 2004), pp. 97–104.

37 Gariboldi to Messe, 25 August 1942: *Le operazioni delle unità italiane al fronte russo*, p. 664.

38 Messe to Gariboldi, 26 August 1942; Messe to Gariboldi, 27 August 1942: Messe, *La guerra al fronte russo*, pp. 260, 261–3.

39 Aldo Giambartolomei, 'La campagna in Russia del CSIR e dei suoi veterani nell'Armir', in R. H. Rainero and A. Biagini, eds., *L'Italia in guerra. Il 3° anno – 1942* (Rome: Commissione italiana di storia militare, 1993), p. 294.

40 Messe to Mussolini, 31 August 1942; Messe to Gariboldi, 23 September 1942: Luigi Longo, *Giovanni Messe. L'ultimo maresciallo d'Italia* (Rome: Ufficio Storico dello Stato Maggiore dell'Esercito, 2006), pp. 184–5.

41 *Le operazioni delle unità italiane al fronte russo*, pp. 305–8, 684–5.

42 Filippo Cappellano, '"Scarpe di cartone e divise di tela . . . ": Gli stereotipi e la realtà sugli equipaggiamenti invernali delle truppe italiane in Russia nella seconda guerra mondiale', *Storia militare* anno X, n. 101, February 2002, pp. 22–4, 27, 29; Giorgio Rochat, 'Le truppe italiane in Russia 1941–1943', *Storia militare* anno XI, no. 115, April 2003, pp. 39–42.

43 Scotone, *Il nemico fidato*, pp. 173–4, 176.

44 Stefano Basset and Filippo Cappellano, 'L'esercito italiano e la guerra anti-partigiana in Russia (1941–1943)', in Olga Dubrovina, ed., *Battaglie in Russia. Il Don e Stalingrado 75 anni dopo* (Milan: Unicopli, 2018), pp. 128–30; Emilio Tirone, 'La politica italiana verso la popolazione civile e i prigionieri di guerra sul fronte russo', in *ibid.*, pp. 192–7.

45 Vladimir V. Korovin, 'Azioni militari dei partigiani sovietici contro gli eserciti tedeschi, italiani e ungheresi negli anni 1942–1943', in Dubrovina, ed., *Battaglie in Russia*, pp. 39–71.

46 Carlo Gentile, 'Alle spalle dell'ARMIR. Documenti sulla repressione anti-partigiana al fronte russo', *Il Presente e la Storia* no. 53, June 1998, pp. 159–181; Thomas Schlemmer, *Invasore, non vittime. La campagna italiana di Russia 1941–1943* (Roma-Bari: Laterza, 2009), pp. 44–67; 'Il ricordo della campagna di Russia', in *La campagna di Russia. Nel 70° anniversario dell'inizio dell'intervento dello CSIR, Corpo di spedizione italiano in Russia* (Rome: Edizioni Nuova Cultura, 2013), pp. 43–4.

47 Scotoni, *Il nemico fidato*, pp. 185–90, 239–40; Nicolas G. Virtue, '"We Istrians Do Very Well in Russia": Istrian Combatants, Fascist Propaganda, and Brutalization on the Eastern Front', in Emanuele Sica and Richard Carrier, eds., *Italy and the Second World War: Alternative Perspectives* (Leiden: Brill, 2018), p. 297.

48 NARS, CSDIC (Main)/Y 15, First detailed interrogation of CARELLI, Adriano, 20 November 1944; CSDIC/CMF/Y 10, First detailed interrogation of EMER Guido, 17 October 1944: RG 457 Box 145.

49 Thomas Schlemmer, 'Italy', in David Stahel, ed., *Joining Hitler's Crusade: European Nations and the Invasion of the Soviet Union, 1941* (Cambridge: Cambridge University Press, 2018), pp. 149–50.

50 Cavallero, *Diario*, p. 471 (28 August 1942); TNA, Appunto per il Duce, 24 October XX [1942], pp. 12, 14: GFM 36/240/fr.046367, 04369.

51 Sergio Pelagalli, *Il generale Efisio Marras addetto militare a Berlino* (1936–1943) (Rome: Ufficio Storico dello Stato Maggiore dell'Esercito,1994), pp. 193–4.

52 Pier Paolo Battistelli, 'La "guerra dell'Asse". Condotta bellica e collaborazione militare italo-tedesca 1939–1943', Tesi di dottorato Università degli Studi Padova, 2000, p. 827.

53 AUSSME, Relazione del Generale di Brigata Cesare Rossi Comandante la Fanteria Divisionale – sugli avvenimenti bellici svoltesi al fronte russo nell'ottobre 1942–gennaio 1943, pp. 2–3 (25 October–22 November [1942]): N1-11/1555/10.

54 Bastian Matteo Scianna, 'Myths and Memories: The Italian Operations on the Eastern Front (1941–1943) and Their Contested Legacies during the Cold War', Dr. Phil. Dissertation Universität Potsdam, 2017, pp. 154–8.

55 *Le operazioni delle unità italiane al fronte russo*, pp. 327–8, 331–2, 334–5; Nicola Pignato and Filippo Cappellano, *Le armi della fanteria italiana (1919–1945)* (Parma: Albertelli Edizioni Speciali, 2008), p. 48.

56 Relazione del Gen. Fassi sulla visita all'8a Armata al Fronte Est, 7 January 1943: *DSCS* IX/2, p. 81.

57 Von Weichs, 15 December 1942: *Le operazioni delle unità italiane al fronte russo*, p. 696.

58 *Le operazioni delle unità italiane al fronte russo*, pp. 382–3; Scianna, 'Myths and Memories', p. 218.

59 AUSSME, Relazione del Generale di Brigata Cesare Rossi, p. 7 (19 December 1942).

60 AUSSME, Contegno alleati tedeschi [Generale Roberto Lerici], 14 May 1943, p. 2: N 1–11/1555/9.

61 Schlemmer, *Invasori, non vittime*, pp. 136–9; Scianna, 'Myths and Memories', p. 176 fn. 943.

62 Nuto Revelli, *Mai tardi* (Turin: Einaudi, 1989), pp. 118, 129, 138, 148, 182, 194, 195, 201.

63 Eugenio Corti, *Few Returned: Twenty-Eight Days on the Russian Front, Winter 1942–1943* (Columbia, MO: University of Missouri Press, 1997), pp. 49, 59, 138.

64 AUSSME, Relazione sul contegno degli alleati tedeschi all'inizio e durante il ripiegamento, March 1943, pp. 31, 36: N1-11/1555/2.

65 AUSSME, Relazione del Generale di Brigata Rossi, p. 13 (24 December 1942); Relazione del generale di brigata N. Capizzi (*Ravenna*), pp. 66–7: N1-11/1552/18.

66 AUSSME, Relazione del Tenente Colonnello Rizzo sulla Divisione fanteria 'Ravenna' in Russia, p. 91: N1-11/1552/13.

67 AUSSME, Relazione sul ciclo operativo 19 dicembre 1942–17 gennaio 1943 [Lerici], pp. 9–15: N1-11/1555/9.

68 Scotoni, *Il nemico fidato*, pp. 206–7, 228–9.

69 Gariboldi to commander of *Alpini*, 16 January 1943; von Weichs, 17 January 1943: *Le operazioni delle unità italiane al fronte russo*, p. 710.

70 Ordine di Operazione n.2 [Nasci], 18 January 1943: *Le operazioni delle unità italiane al fronte russo*, p. 712.

71 Scianna, 'Myths and Memories', p. 18.

72 TNA, Pagine di valore di eroismo di gloria (17 January–1 February 1943) [6th *Alpini* regt. *Tridentina* division]: GFM 36/317/fr.059276–059309.

73 Giorgio Rochat, *Le guerre italiane 1935–1943. Dall'impero d'Etiopia alla disfatta 1935–1943* (Turin: Einaudi, 2005), pp. 392–3. Generals Pascolini, Ricagno and Battisti were released by the Soviets on 5 May 1950.

74 Battistelli, 'La "guerra dell'Asse"', pp. 882–3, explores the varying figures produced at the time and afterwards.

75 By comparison, all twenty-one generals of the other two Italian corps (II and XXXV) got out safely, two of twenty regimental commanders fell in battle and four were taken prisoner: Scianna, 'Myths and Memories', p. 244 fn. 1,424.

76 Scotoni, *Il nemico fidato*, p. 293.

77 Valdo Zilli, 'Gli italiani prigionieri di guerra in URSS. Vicende, esperienze, testimonianze', in Enzo Collotti, ed., *Gli italiani sul fronte russo* (Bari: De Donato, 1982), pp. 295–321; Nuto Revelli, *Mussolini's Death March: Eyewitness Accounts of Italian Soldiers on the Eastern Front* (Lawrence, KS: University Press of Kansas, 2013); Hope Hamilton, *Sacrifice on the Steppe: The Italian Alpine Corps in the Stalingrad Campaign, 1942–1943* (Oxford: Casemate, 2016); Bastian Matteo Scianna, *The Italian War on the Eastern Front 1941–1943: Operations, Myths and Memories* (Cham, Switzerland: Springer Nature; London: Palgrave Macmillan, 2019).

78 Förster, 'Il ruolo dell'8a armata italiana dal punto di vista tedesco', pp. 254–5.

79 Battistelli, 'La "guerra dell'Asse"', pp. 884–6.

80 Evening Situation Report, 4 March 1943: Helmut Heiber and David M. Glantz, eds., *Hitler and his Generals: Military Conferences 1942–1945* (New York: Enigma Books, 2003), p. 77.

81 Mariano Gabriele, 'L'offensiva su Malta (1941)', in R. H. Rainero and A. Biagini, eds., *L'Italia in guerra: il 2° anno –1941* (Rome: Commissione italia-lia di storia militare, 1993), pp. 437–8, 440, 441–6.

82 Hitler to Mussolini, 29 October 1941: *DDI* 9/VIII, no. 693, p. 707.

83 Mariano Gabriele, 'L'offensiva su Malta (1941)', p. 447 (2 December 1941); Richard L. DiNardo, *Germany and the Axis Powers: From Coalition to Collapse* (Lawrence, KS: University Press of Kansas, 2005), pp. 67–70.

84 Jack Greene and Alessandro Massignani, *The Naval War in the Mediterranean 1940–1943* (London: Chatham, 1998), pp. 200–4; Gerhard Schreiber et al., *Germany and the Second World War*, vol. III: *The Mediterranean,*

South-East Europe, and North Africa 1939–1941 (Oxford: Clarendon Press, 1995), pp. 722–4.

85 Colloquio del Capo del Governo, Mussolini, con il Maresciallo del Reich, Goering, 28 January 1942: *DDI* 9/VIII, no. 211, p. 232.

86 Greene and Massignani, *The Naval War in the Mediterranean*, p. 207; James J. Sadkovich, *The Italian Navy in World War II* (Westport, CT: Greenwood, 1994), pp. 228, 236, 237.

87 Giorgio Giorgerini, 'Il problema dei convogli e la guerra per mare', in Rainero and Biagini, eds., *L'Italia in guerra: Il 2° anno – 1941*, p. 414.

88 Lucio Ceva, *La condotta italiana della guerra. Cavallero e il Comando Supremo 1941/1942* (Milan: Feltrinelli, 1975), pp. 102–6.

89 Angelo Iachino, *Tramonto di una grande marina* (Milan: Mondadori, 1966), p. 260.

90 Trasporti marittimi in ASI, 13 July 1941: Ceva, *La condotta italiana della guerra*, pp. 165–7.

91 Giorgerini, 'Il problema dei convogli', pp. 416–17.

92 Cavallero, *Diario*, p. 379 (21 April 1942).

93 Colloquio Cavallero–Keitel (Klessheim), 29 April 1942: *DDI* 9/VIII, no. 493, p. 546.

94 Mariano Gabriele, 'L'Operazione "C3" (1942)', in Rainero and Biagini, *L'Italia in guerra. Il 3° anno – 1942*, pp. 423–5, 425–7.

95 Mussolini to Hitler, 20 June 1942; Hitler to Mussolini, 23 June 1942: *DSCS* VII/2, nos. 80, 81, pp. 197–8, 199–200.

96 *DSCS* VI/1, 23 June 1942, pp. 425–6, 429.

97 Enno von Rintelen, *Mussolini l'Alleato* (Rome: Corso, 1952), p. 160.

98 AUSSME, Relazione mensile dell'Ufficio Propaganda ASI, 31 December 1941: I-4/23/3.

99 AUSMM, Perdite del naviglio mercantile in Mediterraneo, n.d.: LIII/3/BA. I am particularly grateful to Dr Fabio De Ninno for this source.

100 *La marina italiana nella seconda guerra mondiale*, vol. I: *Dati statistici* (Rome: Ufficio Storico della Marina Militare, 1972), pp. 32–7. No two sets of figures ever seem quite to agree, perhaps because of the different ways in which ships and shipping can be counted.

101 *Seconda controffensiva italo-tedesca in Africa settentrionale da El Agheila a El Alamein (gennaio–settembre 1942)* (Rome: Ufficio Storico dello Stato Maggiore dell'Esercito, 1971), p. 13; Mario Montanari, *Politica e strategia in cento anni di guerre italiane*, vol. III, *Il periodo fascista*, tomo 2: *La seconda guerra mondiale* (Rome: Ufficio Storico dello Stato Maggiore dell'Esercito, 2007), p. 557.

102 Martin Kitchen, *Rommel's Desert War* (Cambridge: Cambridge University Press, 2009), p. 188.

103 Cavallero, *Diario*, pp. 314, 322, 323 (11, 22, 23 January 1942).

104 Montanari, *La seconda guerra mondiale*, p. 567 (25 January 1942).

105 Cavallero, *Diario*, pp. 331, 335–6, 340 (1, 5, 9 February 1942).

106 AUSSME, Melchiorri to?, 31 December 1941; Efficienza morale e spirito delle truppe (Bastico), 9 February, 21 February, 9 March 1942: I-4/23/3.

107 Cavallero, *Diario*, pp. 344, 346–7 (21 February, 24 February 1942); Kitchen, *Rommel's Desert War*, p. 206.

108 Cavallero to Bastico, 12 February 1942: *Seconda controffensiva italo-tedesca*, All. 17, p. 328.

109 Cavallero, *Diario*, p. 345 (22 February 1942).

110 Promemoria, 13 March 1942 [Barbasetti di Prun]: Ceva, *La condotta italiana della guerra*, pp. 212–3.

111 Riunione, 4 and 5 March 1942: *ibid.*, pp. 203–4, 205.

112 Giuseppe Mancinelli, *Dal fronte dell'Africa settentrionale (1942–1943)* (Milan: Rizzoli, 1970), pp. 46–9.

113 *DSCS VI/1*, 5 May 1942, pp. 35–7.

114 *Seconda controffensiva italo-tedesca*, pp. 91–2.

115 Mancinelli, *Dal fronte dell'Africa settentrionale*, pp. 78–80.

116 John Ferris, 'The British Army, Signals and Security in the Desert Campaign, 1940–42', *Intelligence and National Security*, vol. 5, no. 2, April 1990, pp. 284–5.

117 Patrick John Rose, 'British Army Command Culture 1939–1945: A Comparative Study of British Eighth and Fourteenth Armies', PhD University of London, 2008, chapter 2.

118 Jack Greene and Alessandro Massagnani, *Rommel's North Africa Campaign, September 1940–November 1942* (Conshohocken, PA: Combined Books, 1994), p. 156.

119 Cavallero, *Diario*, pp. 399–400 (6 June 1942).

120 Appunto per il Duce, 9 June 1942: *DSCS VII/2*, pp. 131–3.

121 Verbale della riunione del 10 giugno 1942 fra Cavallero . . . e il Maresciallo Kesselring: *DSCS VII/2*, pp. 136–9.

122 Evan Mawdsley, *The War for the Seas: A Maritime History of World War II* (New Haven, CT, and London: Yale University Press, 2019), p. 294.

123 Mancinelli, *Dal fronte dell'Africa settentrionale*, p. 118.

124 *Ibid.*, p. 127; Montanari, *La seconda guerra mondiale*, p. 606.

125 Biagini, Frattalillo and Saccarelli, eds., *Verbali delle riunioni tenute dal Capo di SM Generale* III no. 178, p. 613, 19 June 1942.

126 *DSCS VII/2*, 23 June 1942, pp. 425–9.

127 Cavallero to Mussolini, 23 June 1942: *DSCS VII/1*, p. 201.

128 *DSCS VI/1*, 25 June 1942, pp. 445–7; Cavallero, *Diario*, 25 June 1942, pp. 414–15.

129 Operazioni in Egitto, 26 June 1942; Direttive del Duce . . . all'Eccellenza il Comandante superiore Forze Armate Africa Settentrionale, 27 June 1942; *DSCS VII/2*, pp. 280–1, 281–2.

130 Montanari, *La seconda guerra mondiale*, p. 611.

131 AUSSME, Z/115421, 23 June 1942: N-3/520/Q.

132 Mario Montanari, *The Three Battles of El Alamein (June–November 1942)* (Rome: Ufficio Storico dello Stato Maggiore dell'Esercito, 2007), pp. 63–81; Kitchen, *Rommel's Desert War*, pp. 252–5.

133 AUSSME, Predisposizioni ed orientamenti in relazione all'attuale situazione in Mediterraneo, 5 July 1942: H-9/11.

134 Mancinelli, *Dal fronte dell'Africa settentrionale*, pp. 142, 144.

135 Montanari, *The Three Battles of El Alamein*, pp. 111–15.

136 *Ibid.*, pp. 134–5.

137 Bastico to Rommel, 16 July 1942: Montanari, *The Three Battles of El Alamein*, p. 154.

138 *DSCS* VII/1, 17 July 1942, pp. 652–4.

139 Montanari, *The Three Battles of El Alamein*, pp. 157, 158 fn. 84.

140 Considerazione sulla situazione militare [Mussolini], 19 July 1942: *DSCS* VII/2, pp. 287–9.

141 Ciano, *Diario*, p. 638 (23 July 1942).

142 De Ninno, 'The Italian Navy and Japan', pp. 19–22.

143 AUSSME, Appunti circa riunione avvenuta presso Comando Supremo il giorno 18 luglio 1942, pp. 2–3; Sintesi riunione presso Ecc. Capo di SM ore 9 del 26/8/42, pp. 1–2: H-10/8/5.

144 Montanari, *The Three Battles of El Alamein*, p. 190; *Seconda controffensiva italo-tedesca*, pp. 209, 220–3; Cavallero, *Diario*, pp. 453–5, (11 August 1942).

145 Montanari, *The Three Battles of El Alamein*, pp. 220–6; Kitchen, *Rommel's Desert War*, p. 298.

146 AUSSME, Questioni di rilievo emergenti dalle relazioni sul servizio 'P' e sulla censura, 3 September 1942: I-4/13/10.

147 Montanari, *The Three Battles of El Alamein*, p. 289.

148 Mancinelli, *Dal fronte dell'Africa settentrionale*, pp. 169–70.

149 Battistelli, 'La "guerra dell'Asse"', p. 659.

150 Funzionamento organi di Comando Armata corazzata italo-tedesca, 30 September 1942: *DSCS* VIII/2, pp. 33–4; Mancinelli, *Dal fronte dell'Africa settentrionale*, pp. 172–7.

151 Cavallero, *Diario*, pp. 491, 493–4, 494–5 (24, 27, 30 September 1942).

152 Comunicazione dell'Armata corazzata Africa, 6 October 1942: *DSCS* VIII/2, pp. 36–7.

153 AUSSME, Riunione operative del giugno 7 [1942]: H-10/9/2.

154 Promemoria della riunione operativa del 7 ottobre 1942: *DSCS* VIII/2, p. 53.

155 Riunione 9 October 1942: *DSCS* VIII/1, pp. 364–7; Alberto Santoni, *Il vero traditore. Il ruolo documentato di ULTRA nella guerra del Mediterraneo* (Milan: Mursia, 2005).

156 Cavallero, *Diario*, pp. 513–14 (23 October 1942).

157 AUSSME, Stumme to corps and divisional commanders, 20 October 1942: I-4/23/3.

158 AUSSME, Relazione sullo spirito e morale delle truppe, 20 October 1942; Relazione sullo spirito e morale delle truppe, 23 October 1942: I-4/23/3.

159 Mancinelli, *Dal fronte dell'Africa settentrionale*, p. 191.

160 Paolo Morisi, *The Italian Folgore Parachute Division: Operations in North Africa, 1940–1943* (Solihull: Helion, 2016), pp. 100, 104, 112–23, 123–31.

161 Montanari, *The Three Battles of El Alamein*, p. 447.

162 Mancinelli, *Dal fronte dell'Africa settentrionale*, p. 198.

163 Kitchen, *Rommel's Desert War*, p. 338.

164 Montanari, *The Three Battles of El Alamein*, p. 478; Kitchen, *Rommel's Desert War*, pp. 340, 344.

165 Cavallero, *Diario*, p. 533 (2 November 1942).

166 Morisi, *The Italian Folgore Parachute Division*, pp. 159–60.

167 Montanari, *The Three Battles of El Alamein*, pp. 497–8 fn. 95.

CHAPTER 8

1 Mussolini to Hitler, 1 November 1942: *DDI* 9/IX, no. 270, pp. 281–2.

2 Alfieri to Ciano, 31 December 1942: *DDI* 9/IX, no. 454, p. 467.

3 AUSSME, Intendimenti operative germanici [Marras], 14 November 1942: L–13/46; also Grazioli to Mussolini, 15 December 1942: *DDI* 9/IX, no. 379, pp. 372–5.

4 Riunione, 2 September 1942: Antonello Biagini, Fernando Frattolillo and Silvio Saccarelli, eds. *Verbali delle riunioni tenute dal Capo di S M Generale, vol. III: 10 gennaio 1942–31 dicembre 1942* (Rome: Ufficio Storico dello Stato Maggiore dell' Esercito, 1985), no. 251, pp. 797–8.

5 Riunione, 3 September 1942: *ibid.*, no. 252, p. 804.

6 Riunione, 7 September 1942: *ibid.*, no. 255, p. 813.

7 AUSSME, Programma esercito 1943, 7 September 1942; Programma ridotto esercito 1943, 12 September 1942: I-4/42/13.

8 AUSSME, Programma R. Marina 1943, 3 September 1942; Marina mercantile, 9 September 1942: I-4/42/15.

9 AUSSME, Verbali della riunione tenute il giorno 10 ottobre 1942 – XX – a Palazzo Venezia presso il DUCE sull'argomento: Potenziamento delle FFAA, pp. 1–5: H-10/12.

10 *Ibid.*, p. 10.

11 *Ibid.*, p. 15.

12 *Ibid.*, pp. 21–3.

13 AUSSME, Sintesi degli argomenti trattati nella riunione indetta dall'Ecc. Il Capo di SM Intendente presso lo SMRE il 28 corrente alle ore 9, 29 December 1942: H-10/9/3.

14 AUSSME, Programma esercito 1943, 28 January 1943: H-10/12.

15 AUSSME, Promemoria N.3, Acceleramento della costruzione del naviglio sottile, 20 January 1943: H-10/12.

16 AUSSME, Relazione sulla produzione aeronautica, 28 January 1943: H-10/12.

17 AUSSME, Verbale della riunione tenuta il giorno 28 gennaio 1943 a Palazzo Venezia presso il Duce sull'argomento: Potenziamento delle FFAA, pp. 2–9: I-4/42/13.

18 Ibid., pp. 13, 14.

19 Ibid., p. 18.

20 Ibid., pp. 23, 24.

21 Ibid., p. 47.

22 IWM(D), Colloquio del 13 febbraio 1943 ore 12.25 a Palazzo Venezia, p. 1: EDS AL 2761/1.

23 IWM(D), Colloquio con l'Ecc. Riccardi, 4 February 1943: EDS AL 2761/2C.

24 NARS, Relazione sul ciclo operativo 16 novembre 1942–4 febbraio 1943 [Bastico], p. 4: T-821/9/fr.000117–.

25 Giuseppe Mancinelli, Dal fronte dell'Africa settentrionale (1942–1943) (Milan: Rizzoli, 1970), pp. 236–7.

26 Ugo Cavallero, Diario 1940–1943 (Rome: Ciarrapico, 1984), 21 November 1942, pp. 584–5.

27 DSCS VIII/1, p. 977 (6 December 1942).

28 Martin Kitchen, Rommel's Desert War (Cambridge: Cambridge University Press, 2009), p. 393.

29 Mancinelli, Dal fronte dell' Africa settentrionale, p. 240.

30 Bastico to Cavallero, 15 December 1942: Relazione sul ciclo operativo, All. 9.

31 Colloquio Mussolini – Goering, 6 December 1942: DDI 9/IX, no. 381, p. 377.

32 Mussolini to Ciano, 16 December 1942: DDI 9/IX, no. 410, p. 404.

33 Galeazzo Ciano, Diario 1937–1943 (Milan: Rizzoli, 1980), p. 678 (18 December 1942).

34 Ciano to Mussolini, 19 December 1942; Ciano to Mussolini, 22 December 1942: DDI 9/IX, nos. 418, 430, pp. 418–19, 433–40; Mario Montanari, Le operazioni in Africa settentrionale, vol. IV: Enfidaville (novembre 1942–maggio 1943) (Rome: Ufficio Storico dello Stato Maggiore dell'Esercito, 1993), p. 251 (quoting Lanza, 19 December 1942).

35 Sintesi del colloquio delle ore 12 con il Führer, partecipano Ciano, Ribbentropp [sic], Cavallero, Keitel, Schmidt, 18 December 1942: DSCS VIII/2, pp. 112–15.

36 Cavallero to Mussolini, 19 December 1942; Cavallero to Mussolini, 18–19 December 1942: DDI 9/IX, nos. 421, 422, pp. 422, 422–5.

37 Cavallero to Bastico, 1 January 1943: Relazione sul ciclo operativo, All. 17: DSCS IX/1, 1 January 1943, pp. 8–9.

38 *DSCS* IX/1, 6 January 1943, p. 51.

39 Bastico to Rommel, 19 January 1943; Bastico to Comando Supremo 'Per il Duce', 20 January 1943: Relazione sul ciclo operativo, All. 20, 21: *DSCS* IX/1, 20 January 1943, p. 163.

40 NARS, Relazione chiesta col foglio 102/S del 30.3.43 (brig. gen. Roberto Buoni), 11 April 1943, p. 3: T-821/355/fr.586–92; Difesa ad oltranza di Tripoli, 9 January 1943: *DSCS* IX/2, pp. 88–9.

41 NARS, Relazione sull'attività svolta in Libia nel periodo 5 marzo 1942 XX–20 febbraio 1943 XXI, May 1943 (gen. V. Palma), p. 6: T-821/355/ fr.571–84.

42 TNA, SRIG 236, 18 August 1943: WO 208/4186.

43 Luigi Longo, *Giovanni Messe. L'ultimo maresciallo d'Italia* (Rome: Ufficio Storico dello Stato Maggiore dell'Esercito, 2006), p. 227.

44 Giovanni Messe, *La mia armata in Tunisia. Come finì la guerra in Africa* (Milan: Mursia, 2004), pp. 140–1.

45 IWM(D), Ambrosio Project #46 Questionnaire Concerning Events in Italy, 1 February–8 September 1943, pp. 1, 2: EDS 163 AL 1880.

46 Appunto del Capo di SMG al Duce, 17 February 1943: *DSCS* IX/2, p. 171.

47 *DSCS* IX/1, 27 January 1943, p. 233.

48 Montanari, *Le operazioni in Africa settentrionale* IV, p. 351.

49 Messe to Ambrosio, 8 February 1943: *ibid.*, p. 639.

50 Operations in the Western Desert and Tripolitania. Italian XXI Corps. July '41–Jan '43 by It. Gen. Enea Navarini, n.d.: https://wp.me/phMWI-1HY, accessed 11/03/2018.

51 NARS, Condanna a morte del fante [name removed], 2 January 1943: T-821/486/fr.432.

52 NARS, Ordine e disciplina, 17 January 1943: T-821/486/fr.405.

53 IWM(D), Colloquio del 10 febbraio 1943 ore 19.45 a Palazzo Venezia, p. 3: EDS AL 2761/1.

54 NARS, Disciplina, 12 January 1943: T-821/486/fr.431.

55 NARS, Punizioni, 26 January 1943: T-821/486/fr.438.

56 AUSSME, Relazione sullo spirito delle truppe. Impressioni e commenti di carattere generali, March 1943, April 1943; Notizia dalla Corsica, 23 March 1943, p. 3: H-1/58/9.

57 Montanari, *Le operazioni in Africa settentrionale* IV, p. 324; Kitchen, *Rommel's Desert War*, pp. 431–7.

58 IWM(D), Colloquio del 1° marzo 1943 ore 19.45 a Palazzo Venezia: EDS AL 2761/1.

59 IWM(D), Riunione col Maresciallo Rommel presso il Duce al Palazzo Viminale 9.3.43 ore 12, p. 6: EDS AL 2761/1.

60 Mussolini to Hitler, 9 March 1943: *DDI* 9/X, no. 95, pp. 128–32.

61 Hitler to Mussolini, 14 March 1943: *DDI* 9/X, no. 116, pp. 149–52.

62 IWM(D), Riunione col grande ammiraglio Doenitz presso il Duce a Palazzo Venezia il giorno 15 marzo 1943: EDS AL 2761/1.

63 For a detailed comparison, see Longo, *Giovanni Messe*, pp. 278–82. 1st Army had 341 mortars, 8th Army 200.

64 Messe, *La mia armata*, p. 205.

65 Mussolini to Hitler, 26 March 1943: *DDI* 9/X, no. 159, p. 200.

66 AUSSME, La battaglia di Mareth e la manovra da Mareth all'Akarit 16–31 marzo 1943 [Messe], 5 April 1943: N-8/1492/123bis. Montanari, *Le operazioni in Africa settentrionale* IV, pp. 681–93, indicates the cuts.

67 Appunto per il Duce, 24 March 1943: Montanari, *Le operazioni in Africa settentrionale* IV, p. 429.

68 AUSSME, Ts. Mussolini to Hitler (via Marras), 25 March 1943, 1 May 1943: L-13/46/8; Mussolini to Hitler, 26 March 1943: *DDI* 9/X, no. 159, pp. 199–200.

69 Montanari, *Le operazioni in Africa settentrionale* IV, pp. 447–50.

70 Ambrosio to Messe, 5 April 1943; Ambrosio to von Arnim, 5 April 1943: Messe, *La mia armata*, pp. 227–8.

71 Longo, *Giovanni Messe*, pp. 308–12.

72 IWM(D), Colloquio Duce – Feldmaresciallo Kesselring giorno 12-4-43, p. 3: EDS AL 2761/1.

73 Messe, *La mia armata*, pp. 257–8.

74 *Ibid.*, pp. 269–70; Longo, *Giovanni Messe*, pp. 321–2.

75 TNA, GRIG 90, 20 September 1943: WO 208/4179.

76 Montanari, *Le operazioni in Africa settentrionale* IV, pp. 515, 569.

77 TNA, SRIG 105, 30 June 1943: WO 208/4185.

78 TNA, SRIG, 28 May 1943: WO 208/4185.

79 IWM(D), Verbale della riunione tenutasi presso il Duce a Palazzo Venezia il 4/5/43, pp. 1–4, 5: EDS AL 2761/1A.

80 IWM(D), Verbale della riunione tenutasi presso il Duce a Palazzo Venezia il 5 maggio 1943, pp. 2–4: EDS AL 2761/1A; AUSSME, Diario Storico del Comando Supremo, 5 May 1943, pp. 14–15: N-8/1444.

81 TNA, GRIG 4, 20 May 1943: WO 208/4179.

82 Longo, *Giovanni Messe*, p. 344.

83 TNA, GRIG 1, 17 May 1943: WO 208/4179.

84 Montanari, *Le operazioni in Africa settentrionale* IV, p. 550.

85 Franco Papili, 'Rapporto sui convogli', in *La battaglia dei convogli. Atti del convegno Napoli 22 maggio 1993* (Rome: Ufficio Storico della Marina Militare, 1993), pp. 40–1.

86 Giorgio Rochat, *Ufficiali e soldati. L'esercito italiano dalla prima alla seconda guerra mondiale* (Udine: Gaspari, 2000), p. 200.

87 Valerio Castronovo, *Giovanni Agnelli. Il fondatore* (Turin: UTET, 2003), pp. 450–2.

88 AUSSME, Rapporti a Sua Maestà il Re Imperatore, 12 January 1943, 23 March 1943, [-] April 1943, [-] May 1943: H-10/10/1.

89 *DSCS* VIII/1, 27 November 1942, p. 902.

90 AUSSME, Rapporto alla Maestà del Re Imperatore, 12 January 1943, pp. 8, 9, 10: H-10/10/1.

91 I owe this information to Mr Dan Zamansky.

92 IWM(D), Colloquio con l'Eccellenza Fougier, 27 February 1943: EDS AL 2761/2D.

93 TNA, SRIG 44, 28 May 1943: WO 208/4185.

94 Giacomo Zanussi, *Guerra e catastrofe d'Italia* (Rome: Corso, 1946), vol. I, p. 282; Luigi Marchesi, *Dall'impreparazione alla resa incondizionata 1939–1945: memorie di un ufficiale del Comando Supremo* (Milan: Mursia, 2001), p. 34.

95 Egidio Ortona, *Diplomazia di guerra. Diari 1937–1943* (Bologna: Il Mulino, 1993), p. 201 (22 February 1943).

96 Appunto del Capo di SMG al Duce, 17 February 1943: *DSCS* IX/2, p. 170.

97 NARS, Riccardi to Ambrosio, 23 February 1943; Situazione strategica del Mediterraneo nel caso che la occupazione della Tunisia venga mantenuta, 18 February 1943: T-821/140 fr.001019–20, 001021–29.

98 Studio operativo, 21 February 1943: Francesco Mattesini and Mario Cermelli, *Le direttive tecnico-operative di Superaereo* (Rome: Stato Maggiore Aeronautica Ufficio Storico, 1992), vol. II, tomo 2, pp. 569–85.

99 Ambrosio to Goering, [?] April 1943: *DSCS* IX/2, pp. 296–301.

100 Appunto del Capo di SMG al Duce, 24 March 1943: *DSCS* IX/2, pp. 238–41.

101 IWM(D). Colloquio del 29 marzo 1943 – ore 12.45 a Palazzo Venezia: EDS AL 2761/1.

102 Mario Caracciolo di Feroleto, '*E Poi?*' La tragedia dell'esercito italiano (Rome: Corso, 1946), pp. 57–9.

103 IWM(D), Colloquio con l'Ecc. Favagrossa, 7 February 1943; Colloquio con l'Eccellenza Favagrossa, 31 March 1943: EDS AL 2761/2H.

104 IWM(D), Colloquio con Eccellenza Ago, 7 March 1943: EDS AL 2761/6V; AUSSME, Costituzione GU corazzate, 28 March 1943: N-8/1492/103.

105 Produzione Bellica, 30 March 1943: *DSCS* IX/2, pp. 282–3.

106 IWM(D), Riunione tenuta dal Duce a Palazzo Venezia 30.3.43: EDS AL 2761/1A.

107 IWM(D), Rapporto del Generale Amé, 6 March 1943, p. 2: EDS AL 2761/4I.

108 Impiego dei sommergibili nazionali, 10 March 1943; Riccardi to Ambrosio, 27 March 1943: *DSCS* IX/2, pp. 242–3, 248–55.

109 IWM(D), Riunione del Duce sulla situazione Marina Mercantile Palazzo Venezia – ore 17 – 10 marzo 1943: EDS AL 2761/1A.

110 *DSCS* IX/1, 9 January 1943, p. 77.

III Host Venturi [Minister for Communications] to Comando Supremo, 16 January 1943: *DSCS* IX/2, pp. 134–7.

112 Situazione della difesa c.a. della Sicilia, n.d. [attached to Rossi to Ambrosio, 14 February 1943]: *DSCS* IX/2, p. 173.

113 IWM(D), Colloquio con Eccellenza Roatta, 14 marzo 1943; Colloquio con Eccellenza Roatta, 17 March 1943; Colloquio con Eccellenza Caracciolo, 21 March 1943: EDS AL 2761/2F.

114 IWM(D), Colloquio con Generale von Warlimont avvenuto il giorno 27 febbraio 1943, pp. 5–8: EDS AL 2761/4I.

115 Corsica, 25 February 1943: *DSCS* IX/2, p. 182.

116 AUSSME, Visita alla Corsica, 15 January 1943, p. 5: N-9/2081.

117 IWM(D), Colloquio del giorno 13 marzo [1943] a Palazzo Venezia: EDS AL 2761/1.

118 NARS, Possibili azioni nemiche, 5 April 1943: T-821/140/ff.001001–3.

119 Colloqui del Capo di SMG con Eccellenza Rosi, 13.4.43: *DSCS* IX/2, p. 338.

120 Amé to Ambrosio, 19 April 1943: *DDI* 9/X, no. 244, pp. 317–18.

121 IWM(D), Riunione a Palazzo Vidoni 29 April 1943: EDS AL 2761/6V.

122 Zanussi, *Guerra e catastrofe d'Italia*, I, pp. 292–4.

123 IWM(D), Riunione a Palazzo Venezia, 2 May 1943, pp. 1–24: EDS AL 2761/6V.

124 *Ibid.*, pp. 25, 27, 28, 29, 31.

125 AUSSME, Situazione generale. Orientamenti, 3 May 1943: L-13/105/1.

126 AUSSME, T. Mussolini to Hitler (via Marras), 13 May 1943: L-13/46/8.

127 IWM(D), Riunione svoltasi a Palazzo Venezia il 13 maggio 1943, pp. 2–3: EDS AL 2761/1A.

128 AUSSME, T. Hitler to Mussolini (via Marras), 14 May 1943: L-13/46/5.

129 Ortona, *Diplomazia di guerra*, p. 190 (16 December 1942); Renzo De Felice, *Mussolini l'alleato, vol. I: L'Italia in guerra 1940–1943*, tomo 2: *Crisi e agonia del regime* (Turin: Einaudi, 1990), pp. 1,271–4, 1,301.

130 Paolo Puntoni, *Parla Vittorio Emanuele III* (Bologna: Il Mulino, 1993), pp. 121–2 (27 February 1943).

131 Appunti per il Duce, 1 March 1943, 11 March 1943, 14 March 1943: Lucio Ceva, 'Momenti della crisi del Comando Supremo', in Romain H. Rainero, ed., *L'Italia in guerra. Il 4° anno – 1943* (Rome: Commissione italiana di storia militare, 1994), pp. 116–17.

132 Puntoni, *Parla Vittorio Emanuele III*, p. 125, (13 March 1943).

133 De Felice, *Crisi e agonia del regime*, pp. 1,053, 1,078–86.

134 Argomenti di trattare in noto convegno, 6 April 1943: *DSCS* IX/2, pp. 319–22.

135 Alfieri to Bastianini, 3 March 1943; Bastianini to Alfieri, 7 March 1943; Bastianini to Mussolini, [6 April 1943]; Bastianini to Ribbentrop, 21 April 1943: *DDI* 9/X, nos. 71, 89, 196, 198, 252, pp. 101–4, 122, 249–51, 253–4, 326–7.

136 Giovanni Tassini, 'Madrid 1943; tre colloqui col Caudillo', *Nuova Storia Contemporanea*, vol. VI, pt 1, January–February 2002, pp. 93–130.

137 Colloquio Bastianini – Ribbentrop, 7 April 1943: *DDI* 9/X, no. 203, pp. 258–9.

138 Tra il Duce e il Führer [Ambrosio], 12 April 1943: *DSCS* IX/2, pp. 323–30.

139 Franco Catalano, *L'economia italiana di guerra 1935–1943* (Milan: Istituto nazionale per la storia del Movimento di Liberazione, 1969), pp. 82–3.

140 Lucio Ceva, 'Ripensando all'8 settembre', in Claudio Dellavalle, ed., *8 settembre 1943. Storia e memoria* (Milan: Franco Angeli, 1989), pp. 8–10.

141 Ortona, *Diplomazia di guerra*, p. 211 (26 March 1943); Puntoni, *Parla Vittorio Emanuele III*, p. 127, (3 April 1943).

142 IWM(D), Riunione a Palazzo Chigi circa richieste di mezzi bellici alla parte germanica, 18 April 1943: EDS AL 2761/4I.

143 Bastianini to Mussolini, 19 April 1943: *DDI* 9/IX, no. 242, pp. 309–13; IWM(D), Colloquio con il Gen. von Rintelen, 19 April 1943, p. 2: EDS AL 2761/4I.

144 Alfieri to Mussolini, 12 April 1943: *DDI* 9/X, no. 221, pp. 292–4; Puntoni, *Parla Vittorio Emanuele III*, p. 128, (12 April 1943).

145 'Mussolini e il Re mio Padre: 25 luglio' (Umberto II): www.reumberto.it/maurano.htm, accessed 2 February 2018; Puntoni, *Parla Vittorio Emanuele III*, p. 121, (23 February 1943).

146 Appunto del Capo di SMG al Duce, 14 January 1943: *DSCS* IX/2, p. 109.

147 Marchesi, *Dall'impreparazione alla resa incondizionata*, p. 37.

148 AUSSME, Questioni di rilievo emergenti dalle relazioni sul servizio 'P' e sulla censura, 3 September 1942: I-4/13/10.

149 AUSSME, Manifestazioni sovversive, 22 March 1943: H-5/1/3.

150 NARS, Relazione sulla battaglia della Tunisia letta alla radio dall'Ecc. Il Capo di SM Generale il giorno 13-5-43 XXI: T-821/128/fr.462–.

CHAPTER 9

1 ASAM, N.407, SIA to Superaereo, 30 January 1943: INF 4/3.

2 ASAM, Ambrosio to Rosi, Riccardi and Fougier, 15 February 1943, enclosing Le intenzioni degli anglo-americani nella zona mediterranea, 27 January 1943: INF 4/3.

3 ASAM, Amé to Fougier, 30 April 1943, enclosing Possibili intenzioni operative del nemico nel Bacino del Mediterraneo, 28 April 1943: INF 23/5.

4 AUSSME, Colloquio a Palazzo Venezia, 6 May 1943: H-10/12.

5 ASAM, Incremento dei mezzi da sbarco in Medit. Occidentale [SIM], 7 May 1943; Mezzi da sbarco nemici in Mediterraneo centrale e occidentale [Super-

marina], 8 June 1943; Situazione dei mezzi da sbarco nel Mediterraneo al 5 giugno e fisionomia del loro raggruppamenti [SIM], 9 June 1943: INF 23/5.

6 ASAM, N.1045, SIA to Superaereo, 16 May 1943; N.2553, SIA to Super-aereo, 22 May 1943; N.0266, SIA to Superaereo, 27 May 1943; N.3069, SIA to Superaereo, 14 June 1943: INF 23/5.

7 ASAM, T. Aeritalia Berlin, 8 May 1943; Teucci to Superaereo, 24 May 1943: INF 23/5.

8 Potenze anglosassoni. Campagna allarmistica diretta a disorientare i servizi informativi dell'Asse, 19 February 1943, quo. Giuseppe Conti, *Una guerra segreta. Il Sim nel secondo conflitto mondiale* (Bologna: Il Mulino, 2009), p. 368.

9 Intendimenti nemici nel Mediterraneo centro-orientale, 16 May 1943, quoted in Conti, *Una guerra segreta*, p. 377.

10 ASAM, Appunto 5 June 1943, encl. with Previsioni di carattere militare, 14 June 1943: INF 4/5; Conti, *Una guerra segreta*, p. 373.

11 Amé circular, 28 June 1943: Maria Gabriella Pasqualini, *Carte segrete dell' intelligence italiana 1919–1949* (Rome: Edizione Fuori Commercio, 2007), p. 234.

12 AUSSME, Diario Storico del Comando Supremo, 30 June 1943: N-8/1444.

13 Cesare Amé, *Guerra segreta in Italia 1940–1943* (Milan: Bietti, 2011), p. 142; Alberto Santoni, *Le operazioni in Sicilia e Calabria (luglio–settembre 1943)* (Rome: Ufficio Storico dello Stato Maggiore dell'Esercito, 1989), pp. 51–6.

14 AUSSME, Appunti relativi al colloquio svoltosi a Palazzo Venezia il 17 maggio 1943, pp. 1–3: H-10/12.

15 Giacomo Zanussi, *Guerra e catastrofe d'Italia* (Rome: Corsi, 1946), vol. I, pp. 314–15.

16 Santoni, *Le operazioni in Sicilia e in Calabria*, pp. 66, 70.

17 AUSSME, Riunione a Palazzo Venezia del 5 giugno 1943: H-10/12.

18 Ambrosio to Riccardi, 16 June 1943; Riccardi to Ambrosio, 23 June 1943: Admiral Renato Sicurezza, 'Le operazioni in Tunisia e nell'Italia meridionale: l'aspetto navale', in Romain H. Rainero, ed., *L'Italia in guerra. Il 4° anno – 1943* (Rome: Commissione italiana di storia militare, 1994), pp. 46, 47–51.

19 ASAM, N.986, Comando Supremo to Superesercito, Supermarina, Super-aereo, 23 May 1943: INF 23/5.

20 Santoni, *Le operazioni in Sicilia e Calabria*, pp. 107–8, 110–11.

21 TNA, SRIG 104, 30 June 1943: WO 208/4185.

22 TNA, SRIG 179, 29 July 1943: WO 208/4186.

23 TNA, SRIG 106, 30 June 1943: WO 208/4185; SRIG 321, 8 October 1943: WO 208/4187. In fact, the decision to surrender was taken by the island's commander, Captain Bernardini, after consulting his immediate subordinates: Santoni, *Le operazioni in Sicilia e Calabria*, p. 122.

24 Mario Caracciolo di Feroleto, 'E Poi?' La tragedia dell'esercito italiano (Rome: Corso, 1946), p. 123.

25 AUSSME, Diario Storico del Comando Supremo, 18 June 1943: N-8/1444; Preparazioni morale dei combattenti, 18 June 1943: cited in Santoni, Le operazioni in Sicilia e Calabria, p. 125.

26 IWM(D), Colloquio con Eccellenza Roatta, 19.6.1943; Colloquio con Eccellenza Roatta, 30.6.1943: EDS AL 2761/2B; AUSSME. Forza delle unità in Corsica, 16 June 1943: N-8/1498/All.849; Zanussi, Guerra e catastrofe d'Italia vol. II, pp. 21–22.

27 Difesa della Sicilia, 27 June 1943: Santoni, Le operazioni in Sicilia e Calabria, pp. 490–1.

28 IWM(D), Giudizio sulla situazione, 23 June 1943: EDS AL 2761/1A.

29 IWM(D), Appunti sul colloquio svoltasi a Palazzo Venezia il 25 giugno 1943: EDS AL 2761/1A.

30 AUSSME, Ambrosio to OKW: Problema aereo del Mediterraneo (giugno 1943), 17 June 1943: N-8/1498.

31 AUSSME, Produzione bellica – Nuovi programmi 1944, 21 June 1943 [original emphasis]: N-8/1498/all. 1109.

32 ASAM, Problemi del dopoguerra, 15 March 1943; Verbale delle riunione fatte presso il IVo Reparto dello Stato Maggiore nei giorni 14 e 21 aprile 1943 circa i problemi del dopoguerra; fonogramma n.4/183742, 21 June 1943: SIOS 29/249.

33 'Gli imperiosi doveri dell'ora', 24 June 1943: OO XXXI, p. 196.

34 TNA, SRIG 130, 15 July 1942: WO 208/4185; Santoni, Le operazioni in Sicilia e Calabria, p. 72.

35 Mussolini to Hitler, 12 July 1943; Hitler to Mussolini, 13 July 1943: DDI 9/X nos. 499, 505, pp. 647–8, 652–4.

36 AUSSME, T. 1157/S, Marras to Comando Supremo, 20 July 1943: L-13/46/8.

37 Santoni, Le operazioni in Sicilia e Calabria, pp. 94–5, 150.

38 Angelo Iachino, Tramonto di una grande marina (Milan: Mondadori, 1966), pp. 285–6.

39 IWM(D), Appunti relativi al colloquio a Palazzo Venezia del giorno 13 luglio 1943: EDS AL 2761/1A.

40 Santoni, Le operazioni in Sicilia e Calabria, pp. 227–8; IWM(D), Appunti relativi alla riunione a Palazzo Venezia del 15.7.43, p. 7: EDS AL 2761/1A.

41 TNA, GRIG 116, 22 October 1943; GRIG 82, 26 August 1943: WO 208/4179; SRIG 227, 16 August 1943: WO 208/4186.

42 Santoni, Le operazioni in Sicilia e Calabria, pp. 279–80.

43 Giuseppe Santoro, L'Aeronautica italiana nella seconda guerra mondiale (Rome: Esse, 1957), vol. II, p. 556.

44 Situazione generale degli aeromobile al 31 luglio 1943: Gregory Alegi, 'Le operazioni in Tunisia e nell'Italia meridionale: l'aspetto aereo', in Rainero,

ed., *L'Italia in guerra. Il 4° anno* – *1943*, pp. 80–1. In all, the *Regia Aero-nautica* had 359 fighters fit for combat.

45 Santoro, *L'Aeronautica italiana nella seconda guerra mondiale*, II, p. 551; Santoni, *Le operazioni in Sicilia e Calabria*, p. 225.

46 [A]pprezamento di Superaereo sulla situazione alle ore 20.00 del giorno 24 luglio 1943: Santoni, *Le operazioni in Sicilia e Calabria*, pp. 335–6.

47 *Ibid.*, pp. 385–9, 398.

48 AUSSME, Relazione sullo spirito delle truppe, July 1943: H-1/58/9.

49 NARS, Mantenimento della disciplina e dell'ordine, 27 July 1943 [original emphasis]: T-821/140/fr.001073–5.

50 AUSSME, Promemoria per l'Eccellenza, 13 July 1943; Ambrosio to Keitel, 18 July 1943: L-33/44/16.

51 Egidio Ortona, *Diplomazia di guerra. Diari 1937–1943* (Bologna: Il Mulino, 1993), pp. 252–5 (19 July 1943).

52 AUSSME, Convegno di Feltre (19 luglio 1943) Sintesi esposizione del Fuehrer [*sic*], 20 July 1943: H-10/12.

53 Colloquio Ambrosio – Keitel, 19 July 1943: *DDI* 9/X, no. 530, pp. 685–6.

54 AUSSME, Diario Storico del Comando Supremo, 3 July 1943: N-8/1444.

55 Renzo De Felice, *Mussolini l'alleato*, vol. I *L'Italia in guerra 1940–1943*, tomo 2: *Crisi e agonia del regime* (Turin: Einaudi, 1990), pp. 1,327, 1,330–2, 1334–5; F. W. Deakin, *The Brutal Friendship: Mussolini, Hitler, and the Fall of Fascism* (Harmondsworth: Penguin, 1966), pp. 439–46; Mussolini, 'Pensieri pontini e sardi' (19 August 1943), *OO* XXXIV, pp. 296–8.

56 Colloquio del Capo di stato maggiore generale, Ambrosio, con il Capo di stato maggiore della Wehrmacht, Keitel, 19 July 1943: *DDI* 9/X, no. 533, pp. 693–6.

57 Paolo Puntoni, *Parla Vittorio Emanuele III* (Bologna: Il Mulino,1993), p. 126 (16 March 1943); Giacomo Carboni, *Memorie segrete 1935–1948. 'Più che il dovere'* (Florence: Parenti, 1955), pp. 183, 185–6, 196; De Felice, *Crisi e agonia del regime*, pp. 1,165–8; Piero Pieri and Giorgio Rochat, *Badoglio* (Turin: UTET, 1974), pp. 777–9.

58 Luigi Marchesi, *Dall'impreparazione alla resa incondizionata 1939–1945. Memorie di un ufficiale del Comando Supremo* (Milan: Mursia, 2001), p. 37; Giuseppe Castellano, *Come firmai l'armistizio di Cassibile* (Verona: Mondadori, 1945), pp. 37, 48.

59 Colloquio del Direttore generale degli Affari d'Europa e del Mediterraneo, Vitetti, con il Ministro del Real Casa, Acquarone, 9 June 1943: *DDI* 9/X, no. 406, p. 530.

60 Zanussi, *Guerra e catastrofe d'Italia*, II, pp. 17–18, 32; Carboni, *Memorie segrete*, p. 199.

61 Enrico Cernuschi, 'La rivolta dei generali. Il confronto sotterraneo tra la MVSN e il Regio Esercito, 1939–1943', *Storia Militare*, pts 1 and 2, August and September 2004 [electronic copy kindly supplied by the author].

62 Pietromarchi Diary, 22 July 1943: cited in De Felice, *Crisi e agonia del regime*, pp. 1,337–8.

63 Puntoni, *Parla Vittorio Emanuele III*, p. 142 (22 July 1943).

64 AUSSME, Maj.-Gen. Ernest Ferone to the Chief of the Army General Staff, n.d. [but after 2 March 1944]: H-5/1/1.

65 Carboni, *Memorie segrete*, pp. 208–9.

66 Evening Situation Report, 25 July 1943; Midday Situation Report, 26 July 1943; meeting of the Führer with Field Marshal von Kluge, 26 July 1943: Helmut Heiber and David M. Glantz, eds., *Hitler and his Generals: Military Conferences 1942–1945* (New York: Enigma Books, 2003), pp. 201–11, 218–34, 253.

67 Sorice to Comando Supremo, 29 July 1943; Senise to Questore di Roma [chief of police], 27 July 1943: Pietro Zullino, ed., *il 25 luglio* (Milan: Mondadori, 1973), pp. 120, 115.

68 Pieri and Rochat, *Badoglio*, pp. 784–5 fn. 1.

69 Zanussi, *Guerra e catastrofe*, II, pp. 40–2.

70 IWM (D), War Diary of Comando Supremo 1.2–3.9.43, 26, 27, 28, 29, 30 July 1943: EDS AL 2763/4.

71 AUSSME, Note by Marras, 8 November 1972; Lanza to Fecia di Cossato, 30 July 1943, p. 2: L-13/46/3.

72 TNA, Secret Report by General Major Lahousen on Canaris Secret Organization, Part II, pp. 16–17; Sidelights on the Developments of the '20th of July' in the *Amt/Ausland, Abwehr*, for the end of 1939–middle of 1943, p. 9: KV2/173. I am grateful to Dr Brian Sullivan for this reference. In his memoirs Amé, who dated the meeting to 2–3 August, said nothing about plots to kill the two men: Amé, *Guerra segreta in Italia*, pp. 184–6.

73 AUSSME, Promemoria, Roatta to Ambrosio, 4 August 1943: N-8/1504B

74 NARS, Promemoria [Ambrosio], 5 August 1943, p. 4: T-821/251/fr.908–10.

75 IWM(D), War Diary of Comando Supremo, 5 August 1943: EDS AL 2763/4.

76 NARS, Condotta politico-militare della guerra da parte dell'Asse, 31 July 1943, p. 9: T-821/251/fr.000921–31.

77 Colloquio Guariglia–Ribbentrop, 6 August 1943; Colloquio Ambrosio–Keitel, 6 August 1943: *DDI* 9/X, nos. 610, 611, pp. 771–81, 781–8.

78 AUSSME, Grandi Unità per la difesa del territorio metropolitano [Ambrosio], 8 August 1943: N-8/1504B.

79 AUSSME, Appunto, 12 August 1943: N-8/1504C.

80 NARS, Diary of Giuseppe Castellano, General, Italian Royal Army, 30 and 31 July 1943, pp. 16–17, 19: RG 226, Entry 210, Box 359 'Castellano, G. 15, 012'. This diary differs in several respects from Castellano's published memoir and contains much material not found in the account Castellano produced for Ambrosio at the end of 1943: Il Capo della missione militare italiana presso il Comando in capo delle forze alleate, Castellano, all'Ispettore

generale dell'esercito, Ambrosio, 15 December 1943: *DDI* 9/X, documenti allegati no. 3, pp. 945–57. It was obtained by the Italian section of the OSS without Castellano's knowledge and a translation forwarded to General William Donovan on 2 August 1944. Once again grateful thanks to Dr Brian Sullivan.

81 Plan of Action, 9 August 1943: Diary of Giuseppe Castellano, Part I, pp. 29–31.

82 Diary of Giuseppe Castellano, Part I, p. 25, 9 August 1943.

83 *Ibid.*, p. 28, 12 August 1943; Castellano, *Come firmai l'armistizio di Cassibile*, p. 82.

84 AUSSME, Movimento GU, 12 August 1943: N-8/1504C.

85 AUSSME, Riunione di Bologna (Villa Federzone), 15 August 1943, pp. 4–6: H-10/8/6.

86 *Ibid.*, pp. 9–10, 14, 15–16.

87 *Ibid.*, pp. 17, 19–20, 25–6, 29–30.

88 AUSSME, Ambrosio to Ministero degli Esteri, Riunione di Bologna del 15 corrente, 17 August 1943: N-8/1504C; Ambrosio to Foreign Minister [Guariglia], 17 August 1943: N-8/1504D.

89 AUSSME, Von Rintelen to Comando Supremo, 17 August 1943: N-8/1504C.

90 AUSSME, Colloqui preparatori tra Feldmaresciallo ROMMEL e i Comandanti della 4a e 8a Armata italiana [von Rintelen], 20 August 1943; Proposta per il regolamento dei rapporti tra i comandi [von Rintelen], 21 August 1943; Ambrosio to von Rintelen, 21 August 1943: N-8/1504D.

91 AUSSME, Osservazioni sulla carta [von Rintelen], 21 August 1943: N-8/1504D.

92 AUSSME, Rapporto alla Maestà del Re Imperatore, 19 August 1943: H-10/10/1. In all there were forty-three divisions in Italy, but seventeen of them were poorly equipped coastal defence divisions.

93 Claudia Baldoli and Marco Fincardi, 'Italian Society under Anglo-American Bombs: Propaganda, Experience, and Legend, 1940–1945', *Historical Journal*, vol. 52, no. 4 (December 2009), pp. 1,018, 1,028.

94 AUSSME, Difesa della madrepatria, 4 August 1943: N-8/1504B.

95 AUSSME, Rapporto alla Maestà del Re Imperatore, 15 August 1943: H-10/10/1.

96 Filippo Stefani, 'L'8 settembre e le forze armate italiane', in Rainero, ed., *L'Italia in guerra. Il 4° anno – 1943*, pp. 145, 173–4; Zanussi, *Guerra e catastrofe d'Italia*, II, p. 144; Marco Patricelli, *Settembre 1943. I giorni della vergogna* (Bari: Laterza, 2009), pp. 44–5.

97 Ruggero Zangrandi, *1943: 25 luglio 8 settembre* (Milan: Feltrinelli, 1964), p. 195.

98 AUSSME, Mezzi corazzati disponibili presso i depositi, unità complementi, centri di addestramento, 22 August 1943: N-8/1504/D.

99 Mario Caracciolo di Feroleto, 'E Poi?', p. 127.

100 AUSSME, Promemoria riservato personale del giorno 7 settembre 1943: H-5/1/3.

101 AUSSME, Rossi to von Rintelen, 27 August; Comando Supremo to von Rintelen, 26 August; von Rintelen to Comando Supremo, 27 August 1943: N-8/1504D.

102 AUSSME, Situazione carburanti e carboni, Ambrosio to Badoglio, 29 August 1943: N-8/1504D.

103 Account of a meeting held in the residence of the British ambassador in Lisbon, 18 August 1943, 2200 hours: Diary of Giuseppe Castellano, Part II, Attachment 3c.

104 Diary of Giuseppe Castellano, Part III, p. 1, 27 August 1943. The observation was not included in his published account: Castellano, *Come firmai l'armistizio di Cassibile*, pp. 125–6.

105 Raffaele Guariglia, *Ricordi 1922–1946* (Naples: Edizioni Scientifiche Italiane, 1950), pp. 670–3; Diary of Giuseppe Castellano, Part III, pp. 2–3, 28 August 1943 (not included in his published memoir).

106 Diary of Giuseppe Castellano, Part III, pp. 5–6, 29 August 1943.

107 Carboni, *Memorie segrete*, pp. 241–4.

108 Romain Rainero, 'Il 25 luglio: i quarantacinque giorni', in Rainero, ed., *L'Italia in guerra. Il 4° anno – 1943*, p. 86; Puntoni, *Parla Vittorio Emanuele III*, p. 175 (27 September 1943).

109 Zangrandi, *1943*, p. 455.

110 Diary of Giuseppe Castellano, Part I, p. 7.

111 Castellano, *Come firmai l'armistizio di Cassibile*, pp. 144, 222–3.

112 Diary of Giuseppe Castellano, Part II, Attachment 3, Summary of Conversations held on 31 August 1100 hrs to 1300 hrs between General Smith and General Castellano, pp. 1–2, 3–5; Castellano to Ambrosio, 15 December 1943: *DDI* 9/X, documenti allegati no. 3, pp. 945–57; Castellano, *Come firmai l'armistizio di Cassibile*, pp. 133–45, 219–23.

113 AUSSME, Rapporto a Sua Maestà il Re Imperatore, July 1943: H-5/1/13.

114 AUSSME, Morale delle truppe, 25 August 1943: H-5/1/6.

115 AUSSME, Ambrosio to Badoglio, 31 August 1943: N-8/1504D.

116 Elena Agarossi, *A Nation Collapses: The Italian Surrender of September 1943* (Cambridge: Cambridge University Press, 2006), pp. 82–3, 86, follows an account by the navy minister, Admiral de Courten, written shortly after 8 September, and also a letter from the *Comando Supremo* to Castellano on 6 September 1943, found by her, which refers to a six-division landing in the Naples-Salerno area. Roatta seems to have worked out from the location of enemy landing craft that the target was the Naples–Salerno region on 6 September.

117 Zanussi, *Guerra e catastrofe*, II, p. 137; Marchesi, *Dall'impreparazione alla resa incondizionata*, pp. 70–1; Agarossi, *A Nation Collapses*, pp. 88, 164 fn. 108

118 Comando Supremo to Castellano, 6 September 1943: Carboni, *Memorie segrete*, pp. 262–4; Mario Roatta, *Otto milioni di baionette* (Milan: Mondadori, 1946), pp. 306–7; Zanussi, *Guerra e catastrofe*, II, pp. 170–1; Mario Roatta, *Diario 6 settembre–31 dicembre 1943* (Milan: Mursia, 2017), p. 53 (6 September 1943). Afterwards both Ambrosio and Roatta denied that this letter ever existed.

119 AUSSME, Rapporto alla Maestà del Re Imperatore, 2 September 1943: H-10/10/1.

120 Patricelli, *Settembre 1943*, pp. 44–5, 51–2.

121 Caracciolo di Feroleto, '*E Poi?*', pp. 141–2, 151–2.

122 Promemoria N.1, 6 September 1943; Promemoria N.2, 6 September 1943: Stefani, 'L'8 settembre e le forze armate italiane', pp. 175–80, 181–3.

123 NDU, Mission to Rome [General Maxwell Taylor], 9 September 1943; Log of General Maxwell Taylor, 82nd Airborne Division, and Colonel W. T. Gardiner, 51 Wing, Troop Carrier Command [Gardiner]: 'Mission to Rome' file, Maxwell Taylor Papers; Carboni, *Memorie segrete*, p. 273.

124 Guariglia, *Ricordi*, p. 715.

125 Marchesi, *Dall'impreparazione alla resa incondizionata*, pp. 76–80; Carboni, *Memorie segrete*, pp. 282–5; Puntoni, *Parla Vittorio Emanuele III*, pp. 162–4 (8 September 1943); Agarossi, *A Nation Collapses*, p. 95. Ivone claims that Guariglia declared that the armistice conditions must be fulfilled but the evidence he cites does not support this: Diomede Ivone, *Raffaele Guariglia tra l'ambasceria a Parigi e gli ultimo 'passi' in diplomazia (1938–1943)* (Naples: Editoriale Scientifica, 2005), p. 126.

126 Zanussi, *Guerra e catastrofe*, II, p. 194.

127 Roatta, *Diario 6 settembre–31 dicembre 1943*, p. 63 (8 September 1943); Roatta, *Otto milioni di baionette*, p. 332.

128 Patricelli, *Settembre 1943*, pp. 61 [Ambrosio], 54, 111–12.

129 Roatta, *Diario 6 settembre–31 dicembre 1943*, p. 64 (9 September 1943); Puntoni, *Parla Vittorio Emanuele*, pp. 163–4 (9 September 1943).

130 Puntoni, *Parla Vittorio Emanuele III*, pp. 148, 151–2 (28 July, 3–4 August 1943).

131 IWM(D), Colloquio con Eccellenza de Courten, 4 agosto 1943 ore 18: EDS AL 2761/2C.

132 Direttive per azioni navali per contrastare sbarchi nemici nell'Italia meridionale, August 1943; Direttive per azioni navali per contrastare sbarchi in Albania, Grecia occidentale e Morea, September 1943: Francesco Mattesini and Mario Cermelli, *Le direttive tecnico-operative di Superaereo*, vol. II: *Gennaio 1942–Settembre 1943* (Rome: Ufficio Storico dello Stato Maggiore Aeronautica, 1992), tomo 2, pp. 1,030–40, 1,061–70.

133 Ezio Ferrante, 'L'8 settembre e il dramma della Marina italiana', *Politica militare* anno IV, no. 4, November–December 1982, pp. 69–75; Patricelli, *Settembre 1943*, pp. 116–21; William H. Garzke, Jr, and Robert O. Dulin,

Jr, *Battleships: Axis and Neutral Battleships in World War II* (Annapolis, MD: Naval Institute Press, 1985), pp. 405–10 (who list 596 survivors from a crew of 1,849).

134 Santoro, *L'Aeronautica italiana nella seconda guerra mondiale* II, p. 569; Alegi, 'Le operazioni in Tunisia e nell'Italia meridionale: l'aspetto aereo', pp. 81–2.

135 Supeaereo to Aerosquadra 3a, 8 September 1943; Aeronautica for Super-aereo, 8 September 1943; Supeaereo to Aerosquadra 1a etc., 8 September 1943: Mattesini and Cermelli, *Le direttive tecnico-operative di Super-aereo*, II/2, pp. 1,075–7.

136 Patricelli, *Settembre 1943*, pp. 121–4.

137 Claretta Petacci, *Verso il disastro. Mussolini in guerra. Diari 1939–1940* (Milan: Rizzoli, 2011), p. 240 (12 November 1939).

AFTERWORD

1 TNA, GRIG 117, 22 October 1943: WO 208/4179; SRIG 11, 22 May 1943: WO 208/4185.

2 Ubaldo Soddu, 'Memorie e riflessioni di un Generale (1933–1941)' (unpubl. mss), pp. 7–9.

3 Giuseppe Castellano, *Come firmai l'armistizio di Cassibile* (Verona: Mondadori, 1945), p. 11.

4 TNA, SRIG 158, 26 July 1943: WO 208/4186.

5 Antonio Sema, '1914–1934: Guerra e politica secondo Mussolini', in Virgilio Ilari and Antonio Sema, *Marte in Orbace. Guerra, esercito e milizia nella concezione fascista della nazione* (Ancona: Nuove Ricerche, 1988), pp. 18–51.

6 Virgilio Ilari, *Storia del servizio militare in Italia*, vol. III: *'Nazione militare' e 'Fronte del lavoro' (1919–1943)* (Rome: Rivista Militare, 1990), p. 350.

7 Mussolini to Oviglio, 5 September 1924: Renzo De Felice, *Mussolini l'alleato, vol. I: L'Italia in guerra 1940–1943*, tomo 1: *Dalla guerra 'breve' alla guerra lunga* (Turin, Einaudi, 1990), tomo 1, p. 77.

8 Colloquio del Capo del governo, Mussolini, con il maresciallo del Reich, Goering, 28 January 1942: *DDI* 9/VIII, no. 211, p. 236.

9 Ugo Cavallero, *Diario 1940–1943* (Rome: Ciarrapico, 1980), p. 481 (7 September 1942).

10 Cristiano Andrea Ristuccia, 'The Italian Economy under Fascism: 1934–1943. The Rearmament Paradox', DPhil University of Oxford, 2008, pp. 99–103.

11 Seduta del 5 giugno 1940: Carla Mazzaccara and Antonello Biagini, eds., *Verbali delle riunioni tenute dal Capo di SM Generale*, vol. I: *26 gennaio*

1939–29 December 1940 (Rome: Ufficio Storico dello Stato Maggiore dell' Esercito, 1983), p. 58; ACS, Roatta to Graziani, 27 September 1940: Carte Graziani 58/47/9.

12 Lucio Ceva, *La condotta italiana della guerra: Cavallero e il Comando supremo 1941/1942* (Milan: Feltrinelli, 1975), p. 37; Ugo Cavallero, *Diario 1940–1943* (Rome: Ciarrapico, 1984), p. xxxvi.

13 TNA, SRIG 1, 17 May 1943: WO 208/4185.

14 Lucio Ceva, 'Quelques aspects de l'activité du Haut Commandement italien dans la guerre en Méditerranée (mai 1941–août 1942)', in *La guerre en Méditerranée 1939–1945. Actes du Colloque International tenu à Paris du 8 au 11 avril 1969* (Paris: Editions du Centre National de la Recherche Scientifique, 1971), p. 88.

15 TNA, SRIG 243, 23 August 1943; SRIG 133, 13 July 1943: WO 208/4186; GRIG 67, 24 July 1943: WO 208/4179.

16 TNA, GRIG 2, 18 May 1943 (generals Orlando and Berardi): WO 208/4179.

17 On this concept see Eric Lohr and Joshua Sanborn, '1917: Revolution as Demobilization and State Collapse', *Slavic Review*, vol. 76, no. 3, Fall 2017, pp. 703–9.

18 Patrick Bernhard, 'Behind the Battle Lines: Italian Atrocities and the Persecution of Arabs, Berbers, and Jews in North Africa during World War II', *Holocaust and Genocide Studies*, vol. 26, no. 3, Winter 2012, pp. 425–46.

19 TNA, GRIG 7, 19 May 1943; GRIG 18, 29 May 1943: WO 208/4179.

20 'L'ultimo discorso alla Camera dei Fasci e delle Corporazioni', 2 December 1942: OO XXXI, pp. 119–33.

21 Aurelio Lepre, *L'occhio del Duce. Gli italiani e la censura di guerra 1940–1943* (Milan: Mondadori, 1992), pp. 73, 76.

22 AUSSME, Notizia fiduciaria, 31 December 1942: I-3/175/1. The B-29 could carry a bomb load of 20,000 lbs (ten US 'short' tons) and had a range of 4,100 miles.

23 USAMHI, Memorandum #6 Action in Yugoslavia, 21 April 1940: William Donovan Papers Box 74B.

Bibliography

ARCHIVES

Archivio Centrale di Stato
  Fondo Badoglio
  Fondo Graziani
Archivio dei Musei del Risorgimento e di Storia Contemporanea, Comune di Milano
  Quaderni Pariani
Archivio di Stato di Venezia
  Archivio Pariani
Archivio Storico dell'Aeronautica Militare
  INF
  SIOS
Archivio Storico del Ministero degli Affari Esteri
  Affari Politici: Grecia
  Ufficio di coordinamento del Gabinetto 1936–1943
Archivio dell'Ufficio Storico dello Stato Maggiore dell'Esercito
  F-3 Carteggio Sussidiario Prima Guerra Mondiale
  F-9 Commissione di Difesa – Consiglio dell'Esercito e varie corporazioni e comitati
  F-18 Oltre Mare Spagna – Gabinetto
  H-1 Ministero della Guerra – Gabinetto
  H-3 SIM – Notiziari stati esteri – Bollettini – 2a Guerra Mondiale
  H-5 Stato Maggiore del Regio Esercito
  H-9 Carteggio del Capo del Governo
  H-10 Verbali riunioni: SSS alla guerra – Comando Supremo – Capo SMG – Capo SMRE – Capo del Governo
  I-3 Carteggio versato dallo Stato Maggiore Difesa
  I-4 Carteggio Stato Maggiore Generale – Comando Supremo – Stato Maggiore Difesa
  L-3 Studi Particolari
  L-13 Documentazione acquista dal 1968

L-14 Carteggio Sussidiario Stato Maggiore Regio Esercito
M-3 Documenti Forze Armate Italiani restituiti dagli USA (già in mano tedesca)
N-1–11 Diari Storici
Bundesachiv-Militärarchiv
   RH 2/2936
Fondazione Bondoni Pastorio
   Archivio Tellera
Fondazione Luigi Einaudi
   Pietromarchi Diary
Fondazione Wilsoniana
   Fondo Riccardi
Imperial War Museum, Duxford
   Enemy Documents Section
   Speer Collection FD 1940/44
Istituto per la Storia dell'Età Contemporanea/www.archivionline.senato.it
   Fondo Gasparotto
National Archives and Records Service
   T-821
National Defense University
   Maxwell Taylor Papers
The National Archives
   GFM 36
   WO 208/4179
   WO 208/4185
   WO 208/4186
   WO 208/4187
United States Army Military History Institute
   William Donovan Collection

BOOKS

Seconda offensive Britannica in Africa settentrionale e ripiegamento italo-tedesco nella Sirtica orientale (18 novembre 1941–17 gennaio 1942), Rome: Ufficio Storico dello Stato Maggiore dell'Esercito, 1951.

L'esercito italiano tra la 1a e la 2a guerra mondiale, Rome: Ufficio Storico dello Stato Maggiore dell'Esercito, 1954.

In Africa settentrionale. La preparazione al conflitto. L'avanzata su Sidi el Barrani (ottobre 1935–settembre 1940), Rome: Ufficio Storico dello Stato Maggiore dell'Esercito, 1955.

Seconda controffensiva italo-tedesca in Africa settentrionale da El Agheila a El Alamein (gennaio–settembre 1942), Rome: Ufficio Storico dello Stato Maggiore dell'Esercito, 1971.

La marina italiana nella seconda guerra mondiale, vol. I: *Dati statistici*, Rome: Ufficio Storico della Marina Militare, 1972.

Le truppe italiane in Albania (Anni 1914–20 e 1939), Rome: Ufficio Storico dello Stato Maggiore dell'Esercito, 1978.

Fuehrer Conferences on Naval Affairs 1939–1945, Annapolis, MD: Naval Institute Press, 1990.

La campagna di Russia. Nel 70° anniversario dell'inizio dell'intervento dello CSIR, Corpo di spedizione italiano in Russia, Rome: Edizione Nuova Cultura, 2013.

Agarossi, Elena, *L'Italia nella sconfitta. Politica interna e situazione internazionale durante la seconda guerra mondiale*, Naples: Edizioni Scientifiche Italiane, 1985.

Agarossi, Elena, *A Nation Collapses: The Italian Surrender of September 1943*, Cambridge: Cambridge University Press, 2006.

Amé, Cesare, *Guerra segreta in Italia 1940–1943*, Milan: Edizioni Bietti, 2011.

Argentieri, Luigi, *Messe soggetto di un'altra storia*, Bergamo: Burgo Editore, 1997.

Arielli, Nir, *Fascist Italy and the Middle East, 1933–1940*, Basingstoke: Palgrave Macmillan, 2010.

Armellini, Quirino, *Diario di guerra. Nove mesi al Comando Supremo*, Milan: Garzanti, 1946.

Attanasio, Sandro, *Gli italiani e la guerra di Spagna*, Milan: Mursia, 1974.

Badoglio, Pietro, *La guerra d'Etiopia*, Milan: Mondadori, 1936.

Badoglio, Pietro, *Italy in the Second World War*, Oxford: Oxford University Press, 1948.

Bagnasco, Erminio, *La portaerei nella Marina italiana. Idee, progetti e realizzazioni dalle origini ad oggi*, Rome: Rivista Marittima, 1989.

Bargoni, Franco, *L'impegno navale italiano durante la guerra civile spagnola (1936–1939)*, Rome: Ufficio Storico della Marina Militare, 1992.

Bastianini, Giuseppe, *Uomini, cose, fatti. Memorie di un ambasciatore*, Milan: Vitagliano 1959.

Baudino, Carlo, *Una guerra assurda. La campagna di Grecia*, Milan: Istituto Editoriale Cisalpino, 1965.

Becherelli, Alberto and Paolo Formiconi, *La quinta sponda. Una storia dell'occupazione italiana della Croazia 1941–1943*, Rome: Ufficio Storico Stato Maggiore della Difesa, 2015.

Ben-Ghiat, Ruth, *Fascist Modernities: Italy, 1922–1945*, Berkeley, CA: University of California Press, 1996.

Beraudo di Pralormo, Emanuele, *Il mestiere delle armi. Diari 1939–1950*, Pralormo: Associazione Piemonte Ambiente da Scoprire, 2007.

Biagini, Antonello and Alessandro Gionfrida, eds., *Lo Stato Maggiore Generale tra le due guerre (Verbali delle riunioni presiedute da Badoglio dal 1925 al 1937)*, Rome: Ufficio Storico dello Stato Maggiore dell'Esercito, 1997.

Biagini, Antonello, Fernando Frattolillo, Carlo Mazzaccara and Silvio Sacca-relli, eds., *Verbali delle riunioni tenute dal Capo di S M Generale*, Rome: Ufficio Storico dello Stato Maggiore dell'Esercito, 1983–5.

Bottai, Giuseppe, *Diario 1935–1944*, Milan: Rizzoli, 2001.

Botti, Ferruccio and Virgilio Ilari, *Il pensiero militare italiano dal primo al secondo dopoguerra*, Rome: Ufficio Storico dello Stato Maggiore dell'Esercito, 1985.

Burdick, Charles B., *Germany's Military Strategy and Spain in World War II*, Syracuse, NY: Syracuse University Press, 1968.

Burgwyn, H. James, *Il revisionismo fascista. La sfida di Mussolini alle grandi potenze nei Balcani e sul Danubio 1925–1933*, Milan: Feltrinelli, 1979.

Burgwyn, H. James, *Empire on the Adriatic: Mussolini's Conquest of Yugoslavia, 1941–1943*, New York: Enigma Books, 2005.

Burgwyn, H. James, *Mussolini Warlord: Failed Dreams of Empire 1940–1943*, New York: Enigma Books, 2012.

Campbell, Ian, *The Addis Ababa Massacre: Italy's National Shame*, London: Hurst, 2017.

Canevari, Emilio, *Graziani mi ha detto*, Rome: Magi-Spinetti, 1947.

Canevari, Emilio, *La guerra italiana. Retroscena della disfatta*, Rome: Tosi, 1948.

Canevari, Emilio, *La fine del maresciallo Cavallero*, Rome: 'Latinità', n.d. [c. 1950].

Canosa, Romano, *Graziani. Il maresciallo d'Italia, dalla guerra d'Etiopia alla Repubblica di Salò*, Milan: Mondadori, 2005.

Carboni, Giacomo, *Memorie segrete 1935–1948. 'Più che il dovere'*, Florence: Parenti, 1955.

Carloni, Mario, *La campagna di Russia. Gli eroici combattimenti sostenuti dal 60 Bersaglieri durante la ritirata del dicembre 1942*, Genoa: EFFEPI, 2010.

Caracciolo di Feroleto, Mario, *'E Poi?' La tragedia dell'esercito italiano*, Rome: Corso, 1946.

Caracciolo di Feroleto, Mario, *Memorie di un Generale d'Armata. Mezzo secolo nel Regio Esercito*, Padua: Nova Charta, 2006.

Cassata, Francesco, *'La Difesa della Razza'. Politica, ideologia e immagine del razzismo fascista*, Turin: Einaudi, 2008.

Castellano, Giuseppe, *Come firmai l'armistizio di Cassibile*, Verona: Mondadori, 1945.

Castronovo, Valerio, *Giovanni Agnelli. Il fondatore*, Turin: UTET, 2003.

Catalano, Franco, *L'economia italiana di guerra. La politica economica-finanziaria del fascismo dalla guerra d'Etiopia alla caduta del regime 1935–1943*, Milan: Istituzione nazionale per la storia del movimento di liberazione, 1969.

Cavallero, Carlo, *Il dramma del Maresciallo Cavallero*, Milan: Mondadori, 1952.

Cavallero, Ugo, *Comando Supremo. Diario 1940–43 del Capo di S.M.G.*, Bologna: Cappelli, 1948.

Cavallero, Ugo, *Diario 1940–1943*, Rome: Ciarrapico, 1984.

Cernuschi, Enrico, *Domenico Cavagnari. Storia di un Ammiraglio*, Rome: Rivista Marittima, 2001.

Cervi, Mario, *The Hollow Legions: Mussolini's Blunder in Greece 1940–41*, London: Chatto & Windus, 1972.

Cervi, Mario, ed., *l'8 settembre*, Milan: Mondadori, 1973.

Ceva, Bianca, *Cinque anni di storia italiana 1940–1945*, Milan: Edizioni di Comunità, 1964.

Ceva, Lucio, *La condotta italiana della guerra. Cavallero e il Comando supremo 1941/1942*, Milan: Feltrinelli, 1975.

Ceva, Lucio, *Le forze armate*, Turin: UTET, 1981.

Ceva, Lucio, *Teatri di guerra. Comandi, soldati e scrittori nei conflitti europei*, Milan: Franco Angeli, 2005.

Ceva, Lucio, *Spagne 1936–1939. Politica e guerra civile*, Milan: Franco Angeli, 2010.

Ceva, Lucio and Andrea Curami, *La meccanizzazione dell'esercito fino al 1943*, Rome: Ufficio Storico dello Stato Maggiore dell'Esercito, 1989.

Chiaravelli, Emilia, *L'Opera della marina italiana nella guerra italo-etiopica*, Milan: Giuffrè, 1969.

Ciano, Galeazzo, *Diario 1937–1943*, Milan: Rizzoli, 1980.

Clarke, J. Calvitt, III, *Russia and Italy against Hitler: The Bolshevik-Fascist Rapprochement of the 1930s*, New York: Greenwood Press, 1991.

Clementi, Marco, *Camicie nere sull'Acropoli. L'occupazione italiana in Grecia (1941–1943)*, Rome: Derive Aprodi, 2013.

Collotti, Enzo, ed., *Gli italiani sul fronte russo*, Bari: De Donato, 1982.

Collotti, Enzo, *Fascismo e politica di Potenza. Politica estera 1922–1939*, Milan: RCS, 2000.

Conti, Giuseppe, *Una guerra segreta. Il Sim nel secondo conflitto mondiale*, Bologna: Il Mulino, 2009.

Cornwell, John, *Hitler's Pope: The Secret History of Pius XII*, New York: Penguin Books, 1999.

Corti, Eugenio , *Few Returned: Twenty-Eight Days on the Russian Front, Winter 1942–1943*, Columbia, MO: University of Missouri Press, 1997.

Cova, Alessandro, *Graziani. Un generale per il regime*, Rome: Newton Compton, 1987.

Coverdale, John F., *Italian Intervention in the Spanish Civil War*, Princeton, NJ: Princeton University Press, 1975.

D'Avanzo, Giuseppe, *Ali e poltrone*, Rome: Ciarrapico, 1976.

Deakin, F. W., *The Brutal Friendship: Mussolini, Hitler, and the Fall of Fascism*, Harmondsworth: Penguin, 1966.

De Biase, Carlo, *Aquila d'Oro. Storia dello Stato Maggiore Italiano (1861–1945)*, Milan: Edizioni Borghesi, 1970.

De Felice, Renzo, *Mussolini il Duce*, vol. I: *Gli anni del consenso 1929–1936*, Turin: Einaudi, 1974.

De Felice, Renzo, *Mussolini il Duce*, vol. II: *Lo stato totalitario 1936–1940*, Turin: Einaudi, 1981.

De Felice, Renzo, *Mussolini l'alleato*, vol. I: *L'Italia in guerra 1940–1943*, tomo 1: *Dalla guerra 'breve' alla guerra lunga*, Turin: Einaudi, 1990.

De Felice, Renzo, *Mussolini l'alleato*, vol. I: *L'Italia in guerra 1940–1943*, tomo 2: *Crisi e agonia del regime*, Turin: Einaudi, 1990

Del Boca, Angelo, ed., *Le guerre coloniali del fascismo*, Bari: Laterza, 1991.

Del Boca, Angelo, ed., *I gas di Mussolini*, Rome: Riuniti, 1996.

Dellavalle, Claudio, ed., *8 settembre 1943. Storia e memoria*, Milan: Franco Angeli, 1989.

De Lorenzis, Ugo, *Dal primo all' ultimo giorno. Ricordi di guerra 1939–1945*, Milan: Longanesi, 1971.

De Ninno, Fabio, *I sommergibili del fascismo. Politica navale, strategia e uomini tra le due guerre mondiali*, Milan: Unicopli, 2014.

De Ninno, Fabio, *Fascisti sul mare. La Marina e gli ammiragli di Mussolini*, Bari: Laterza, 2017.

DiNardo, Richard L., *Germany and the Axis Powers: From Coalition to Collapse*, Lawrence, KS: University Press of Kansas, 2005.

Di Rienzo, Eugenio, *Ciano*, Rome: Salerno, 2018.

Dominioni, Matteo, *Lo sfascio dell'Impero. Gli italiani in Etiopia 1936–1941*, Bari: Laterza, 2008.

Donosti, Mario [Mario Luciolli], *Mussolini e l'Europa. La politica estera fascista*, Florence: Edizioni Leonardo, 1945.

Dubrovna, Olga, ed., *Battaglie in Russia. Il Don e Stalingrado 75 anni dopo*, Milan: Unicopli, 2018.

Faldella, Emilio, *L'Italia e la seconda guerra mondiale. Revisione di giudizi*, Bologna: Cappelli, 1960.

Fantoni, Euclide, *Con il 20 Reggimento Bersaglieri nella vigilia e nella lotta*, Rome: n.p., 1963.

Favagrossa, Carlo, *Perché perdemmo la guerra*, Milan: Rizzoli, 1946.

Ferrante, Ezio, *Il pensiero strategico navale in Italia*, Rome: Rivista Marittima, 1988.

Focardi, Filippo, *La rimozione delle colpe della seconda guerra mondiale*, Bari: Laterza, 2013.

Fucci, Franco, *Emilio De Bono – Il maresciallo fucilato*, Milan: Mursia, 1989.

Gallinari, Vincenzo, *L'esercito italiano nel primo dopoguerra 1918–1920*, Rome: Ufficio Storico dello Stato Maggiore dell'Esercito, 1980.

[Gallinari, Vincenzo], *Le operazioni del giugno 1940 sulle Alpi occidentali*, Rome: Ufficio Storico dello Stato Maggiore dell'Esercito, 1994.

Garzke, William H., Jr, and Robert O. Dulin, Jr, *Battleships: Axis and Neutral Battleships in World War II*, Annapolis, MD: Naval Institute Press, 1985.

Gin, Emilio, *L'ora segnata dal destino. Gli Alleati e Mussolini da Monaco all'intervento settembre 1938–giugno 1940*, Rome: Nuova Cultura, 2012.

Giusti, Maria Teresa, *I prigionieri italiani in Russia*, Bologna: Il Mulino, 2003.

Giusti, Maria Teresa, *La campagna di Russia 1941–1943*, Bologna: Il Mulino, 2016.

Gobetti, Eric, *Alleati del nemico. L'occupazione italiana in Jugoslavia (1941–1943)*, Bari: Laterza, 2013.

Gooch, John, *Mussolini and his Generals: The Armed Forces and Fascist Foreign Policy, 1922–1940*, Cambridge: Cambridge University Press, 2007.

Gooch, John, *The Italian Army and the First World War*, Cambridge: Cambridge University Press, 2014.

Gorla, Giuseppe, *L'Italia nella seconda guerra mondiale. Diario di un Milanese ministro del Re nel governo di Mussolini*, Milan: Baldini and Castoldi, 1959.

Grandi, Dino, *La politica estera dell'Italia dal 1929 al 1932*, Rome: Bonacci, 1985.

Graziani, Rodolfo, *Fronte Sud*, Milan: Mondadori, 1938.

Graziani, Rodolfo, *Ho difeso la patria*, Rome: Garzanti, 1948.

Grazzi, Emanuele, *Il principio della fine (L'impresa di Grecia)*, Rome: Faro, 1945.

Greene, Jack and Alessandro Massignani, *Rommel's North Africa Campaign, September 1940–November 1942*, Conshohocken, PA: Combined Books, 1994.

Greene, Jack and Alessandro Massignani, *The Naval War in the Mediterranean 1940–1943*, London: Chatham, 2002.

Grimaldi, Ugo Alfassio and Gherardo Bozzetti, *Dieci giugno 1940 il giorno della follia*, Bari: Laterza, 1974.

Guariglia, Raffaele, *Ricordi 1922–1946*, Naples: Edizioni Scientifiche Italiane, 1950.

Guerri, Giordano Bruno, *Galeazzo Ciano. Una vita 1903/1944*, Milan: Bompiani, 1979.

Guspini, Ugo, *L'orecchio del regime. Le intercettazioni telefoniche al tempo del fascismo*, Milan: Mursia, 1973.

Hamilton, Hope, *Sacrifice on the Steppe: The Italian Alpine Corps in the Stalingrad Campaign, 1942–1943*, Oxford: Casemate, 2016.

Harrison, Mark, ed., *The Economics of World War II: Six Great Powers in International Comparison*, Cambridge: Cambridge University Press, 1998.

Heiber, Helmut and David M. Glantz, eds., *Hitler and his Generals: Military Conferences 1942–1945*, New York: Enigma Books, 2003.

Hinsley, F. H. et al., *British Intelligence in the Second World War*, London: HMSO, 1979.

Hippler, Thomas, *Bombing the People: Giulio Douhet and the Foundations of Air Power Strategy, 1884–1939*, Cambridge: Cambridge University Press, 2013.

Iachino, Angelo, *Tramonto di una grande marina*, Milan: Mondadori, 1966.

Ilari, Virgilio, *Storia del servizio militare in Italia*, vol. III: '*Nazione militare*' e '*Fronte del lavoro*' (*1919–1943*), Rome: Rivista Militare, 1990.

Ilari, Virgilio and Antonio Sema, eds., *Marte in Orbace. Guerra, esercito e milizia nella concezione fascista*, Ancona: Nuove Ricerche, 1988.

Irving, David, *The Rise and Fall of the Luftwaffe*, London: Weidenfeld and Nicolson, 1973.

Ivone, Diomede, *Raffaele Guariglia tra l'ambasceria a Parigi e gli ultimi 'passi' in diplomazia (1938–1943)*, Naples: Editoriale Scientifica, 2005.

Kertzer, David I., *The Pope and Mussolini: The Secret History of Pius XI and the Rise of Fascism in Europe*, Oxford: Oxford University Press, 2014.

Kirkpatrick, Ivone, *Mussolini: Study of a Demagogue*, London: Odhams, 1964.

Kitchen, Martin, *Rommel's Desert War*, Cambridge: Cambridge University Press, 2009.

Knox, MacGregor, *Mussolini Unleashed 1939–1941: Politics and Strategy in Fascist Italy's Last War*, Cambridge: Cambridge University Press, 1982.

Knox, MacGregor, *Common Destiny: Dictatorship, Foreign Policy, and War in Fascist Italy and Nazi Germany*, Cambridge: Cambridge University Press, 2000.

Knox, MacGregor, *Hitler's Italian Allies: Royal Armed Forces, Fascist Regime, and the War of 1940–1943*, Cambridge: Cambridge University Press, 2000.

Labanca, Nicola, *La Guerra d'Etiopia 1935–1941*, Bologna: Il Mulino, 2015.

Lehmann, Eric , *Le ali del potere. La propaganda aeronautica nell'Italia fascista*, Turin: UTET, 2010.

Lepre, Aurelio, *L'occhio del Duce. Gli italiani e la censura di guerra 1940–1943*, Milan: Mondadori, 1992.

Lessona, Alessandro, *Memorie*, Rome: Edizione Lessona, 1963.

Longo, Luigi Emilio, *L'attività degli addetti militari italiani all'estero fra le due guerre mondiali (1919–1939)*, Rome: Ufficio Storico dello Stato Maggiore dell'Esercito, 1999.

Longo, Luigi Emilio, *La campagna italo-etiopica (1935–1936)*, Rome: Ufficio Storico dello Stato Maggiore dell'Esercito, 2005.

Longo, Luigi Emilio, *Giovanni Messe. L'ultimo maresciallo d'Italia*, Rome: Ufficio Storico dello Stato Maggiore dell'Esercito, 2006.

Lorenzelli, Dante, *La divisione 'Superga' nella tormenta (1940–1943)*, Rome: Tipografia Regionale, 1954.

Luciolli, Mario, *Palazzo Chigi. Anni roventi*, Milan: Rusconi, 1976.

Mack Smith, Denis, *Mussolini's Roman Empire*, Harmondsworth: Penguin Books, 1979.

Mallett, Robert, *The Italian Navy and Fascist Expansionism 1935–1940*, London: Frank Cass, 1998.

Mallett, Robert, *Mussolini and the Origins of the Second World War*, Basingstoke: Palgrave Macmillan, 2003.

Mallett, Robert, *Mussolini in Ethiopia, 1919–1935: The Origins of Fascist Italy's African War*, Cambridge: Cambridge University Press, 2015.

Mancinelli, Giuseppe, *Dal fronte dell'Africa settentrionale (1942–1943)*, Milan: Rizzoli, 1970.

Marchesi, Luigi, *Dall'impreparazione alla resa incondizionata 1939–1945: memorie di un ufficiale del Comando Supremo*, Milan: Mursia, 2001.

Martelli, Manfredi, *Mussolini e la Russia. Le relazioni italo-sovietiche dal 1922 al 1941* Milan, Mursia, 2007.

Mattesini, Francesco, *Corrispondenza e direttive tecnico-operative di Supermarina*, vol. I, tomo 1: *Maggio 1939–Luglio 1940*, tomo 2: *Agosto 1940–Dicembre 1940*, Rome: Ufficio Storico della Marina Militare, 2000.

Mattesini, Francesco, *La battaglia di Capo Teulada (27–28 novembre 1940)*, Rome: Ufficio Storico della Marina Militare, 2000.

Mattesini, Francesco, *Corrispondenza e direttive tecnico-operative di Supermarina*, vol. II, tomo 1: *Gennaio 1941–Giugno 1941*, tomo 2: *Giugno 1941–Dicembre 1941*, Rome: Ufficio Storico della Marina Militare, 2001.

Mattesini, Francesco, *La battaglia di Punta Stilo*, Rome: Ufficio Storico della Marina Militare, 2001.

Mattesini, Francesco, *L'attività aerea italo-tedesca nel Mediterraneo. Il contributo del 'X Fliegerkorps' gennaio–maggio 1941*, Rome: Ufficio Storico Stato Maggiore dell'Aeronautica, 2003.

Mattesini, Francesco and Mario Cermelli, *Le direttive tecnico-operative di Superaereo*, vol. I, tomo 1, 2: *Aprile 1940–Dicembre 1941*, Rome: Stato Maggiore Aeronautica Stato Maggiore, n.d.

Mattesini, Francesco and Mario Cermelli, *Le direttive tecnico-operative di Superaereo*, vol. II, tomo 1, 2: *Gennaio 1942–Settembre 1943*, Rome: Stato Maggiore Aeronautica Ufficio Storico, 1992.

Matucci, Paolo, *Federico Baistrocchi Sottosegretario (1933–1936)*, Florence: Pagnini editore, 2006.

Maugeri, Franco, *From the Ashes of Disgrace*, New York: Reynal and Hitchcock, 1948.

Mawdsley, Evan, *The War for the Seas: A Maritime History of World War II*, New Haven, CT, and London: Yale University Press, 2019.

Mazower, Mark, *Inside Hitler's Greece: The Experience of Occupation, 1941–1944*, New Haven, CT and London: Yale University Press, 2001.

Messe, Giovanni, *La mia armata in Tunisia. Come finì la guerra in Africa*, Milan: Mursia, 2004.

Messe, Giovanni, *La guerra al fronte russo. Il corpo di spedizione italiano in Russia (CSIR)*, Milan: Mursia, 2005.

Messe, Giovanni, *Lettere alla moglie. Dai fronti Greco-albanese, russo, tunisino e dalla prigionia 1940–1944*, Milan: Mursia, 2018.

Minniti, Fortunato, *Fino alla guerra. Strategia e conflitto nella politica di potenza di Mussolini 1923–1940*, Naples: Edizioni Scientifiche Italiane, 2000.

Mockler, Anthony, *Haile Selassie's War*, Oxford: Oxford University Press, 1984.

Mondini, Marco, *La politica delle armi. Il ruolo dell'esercito nell'avvento del fascismo*, Rome-Bari: Laterza, 2006.

Montanari, Mario, *La campagna di Grecia*, vol. I: *Testo*, vol. II: *Documenti*, vol. III: *Schizzi e fotografie*, Rome: Ufficio Storico dello Stato Maggiore dell'Esercito, 1980.

[Montanari, Mario], *L'esercito italiano alla vigilia della 2a guerra mondiale*, Rome: Ufficio Storico dello Stato Maggiore dell'Esercito, 1982.

Montanari, Mario, *Le operazioni in Africa settentrionale*, vol. IV: *Enfidaville (novembre 1942–maggio 1943)*, Rome: Ufficio Storico dello Stato Maggiore dell'Esercito, 1993.

Montanari, Mario, *Le operazioni in Africa settentrionale*, vol. II: *Tobruk (marzo 1941–gennaio 1942)*, Rome: Ufficio Storico dello Stato Maggiore dell'Esercito, 1995.

Montanari, Mario, *L'esercito italiano nella campagna di Grecia*, Rome: Ufficio Storico dello Stato Maggiore dell'Esercito, 1999.

Montanari, Mario, *Le operazioni in Africa settentrionale*, vol. I: *Sidi el Barrani (giugno 1940–febbraio 1941)*, Rome: Ufficio Storico dello Stato Maggiore dell'Esercito, 2000.

Montanari, Mario, *Politica e strategia in cento anni di guerre italiane*, vol. III, tomo 1: *Le guerre degli anni trenta*, Rome: Ufficio Storico dello Stato Maggiore dell'Esercito, 2005.

Montanari, Mario, *Politica e strategia in cento anni di guerre italiane*, vol. III, tomo 2: *La seconda guerra mondiale*, Rome: Ufficio Storico dello Stato Maggiore dell'Esercito, 2007.

Montanari, Mario, *The Three Battles of El Alamein (June–November 1942)*, Rome: Ufficio Storico dello Stato Maggiore dell'Esercito, 2007.

Morisi, Paolo, *The Italian Folgore Parachute Division: Operations in North Africa 1940–1943*, Solihull: Helion, 2016.

Moseley, Ray, *Mussolini's Shadow: The Double Life of Count Galeazzo Ciano*, New Haven, CT, and London: Yale University Press, 1999.

Muggeridge, Malcolm, ed., *Ciano's Diplomatic Papers*, London: Odhams, 1948.

Oliva, Gianni, *"Si ammazza troppo poco". I crimini di guerra italiani 1940–1943*, Milan: Mondadori, 2007.

Orlando, Taddeo, *Vittoria di un popolo. Dalle battaglie di Tunisia alla guerra di liberazione*, Rome: Corso, 1946.

Ortona, Egidio, *Diplomazia di guerra. Diari 1937–1943*, Bologna: Il Mulino, 1993.

Osti Guerrazzi, Amedeo, *Noi non sappiamo odiare. L'esercito italiano tra fascismo e democrazia*, Turin: UTET, 2010.

Osti Guerrazzi, Amedeo, *The Italian Army in Slovenia: Strategies of Antipartisan Repression, 1941–1943*, Basingstoke: Palgrave Macmillan, 2013.

Overy, Richard, *The Bombing War: Europe 1939–1945*, London: Penguin Books, 2013.

Palma, Paolo, *Il telefonista che spiava il Quirinale 25 luglio 1943*, Soveria Mannelli [Catanzaro]: Rubbettino, 2006.

Paoletti, Ciro, *Dalla non belligeranza alla guerra parallela. L'ingresso dell'Italia nella Seconda Guerra Mondiale per paura dei Tedeschi, 1938–1940*, Rome: Commissione Italiana di Storia Militare, 2014.

Pasqualini, Maria Gabriella, *Carte segrete dell'intelligence italiana 1919–1949*, Rome: Ministero della Difesa-Edizione Fuori Commercio, 2007.

Pasqualini, Maria Gabriella, *Breve storia dell'Organizzazione dei Servizi d'Informazione della R. Marina e R. Aeronautica 1919–1945*, Rome: Ministero della Difesa, 2013.

Patricelli, Marco, *Settembre 1943. I giorni della vergogna*, Rome-Bari: Laterza, 2009.

Pedriali, Ferdinando, *Guerra di Spagna e aviazione italiana*, Pinerolo: Società storica pinerolese, 1989.

Pedriali, Ferdinando, *L'Aeronautica italiana nelle guerre coloniali. Guerra etiopica 1935–36*, Rome: Stato Maggiore Aeronautica Ufficio Storico, 1997.

Pedriali, Ferdinando, *L'Italia nella guerra aerea. Da el-Alamein alle spiagge della Sicilia (4 novembre 1942–9 luglio 1943)*, Rome: Ufficio Storico dello Stato Maggiore Aeronautica, 2010.

Pelagalli, Sergio, *Il generale Efisio Marras addetto militare a Berlino (1936–1943)*, Rome: Ufficio Storico dello Stato Maggiore dell'Esercito, 1994.

Petacci, Claretta, *Verso il disastro. Mussolini in guerra. Diari 1939–1940*, Milan: Rizzoli, 2011.

Pieri, Piero and Giorgio Rochat, *Badoglio*, Turin: UTET, 1974.

Pignato, Nicola and Filippo Cappellano, *Le armi della fanteria italiana (1919–1943)*, Parma: Albertelli Edizioni Speciali, 2008.

Puntoni, Paolo, *Parla Vittorio Emanuele III*, Bologna: Il Mulino, 1993.

Quartararo, Rosaria, *Italia-URSS 1917–1941. I rapporti politici*, Naples: Edizioni Scientifiche Italiane, 1997.

Rainero, R. H. and A. Biagini, eds., *L'Italia in guerra. Il 1° anno – 1940*, Rome: Commissione italiana di storia militare, 1991.

Rainero, R. H. and A. Biagini, eds., *L'Italia in guerra. Il 2° anno – 1941*, Rome: Commissione italiana di storia militare, 1992.

Rainero, R. H. and A. Biagini, eds., *L'Italia in guerra. Il 3° anno – 1942*, Rome: Commissione italiana di storia militare, 1993.

Rainero, Romain H., ed., *L'Italia in guerra. Il 4° anno – 1943*, Rome: Commissione italiana di storia militare, 1994.

Revelli, Nuto, *Mai tardi*, Turin: Einaudi, 1989.

Revelli, Nuto, *Mussolini's Death March: Eyewitness Accounts of Italian Soldiers on the Eastern Front*, Lawrence, KS: University Press of Kansas, 2013.

Ridomi, Cristiano, *La fine dell'ambasciata a Berlino 1940–1943*, Milan: Longanesi, 1972.

Rizzi, Loris, *Lo sguardo del potere: La censura militare in Italia nella seconda guerra mondiale 1940–1945*, Milan: Rizzoli, 1984.

Roatta, Mario, *"Otto milioni di baionette"*, Milan: Mondadori, 1946.

Roatta, Mario, *Diario 6 settembre–31 dicembre 1943*, Milan: Mursia, 2017.

Rocca, Gianni, *I disperati: La tragedia dell'Aeronautica italiana nella seconda guerra mondiale*, Milan: Mondadori, 1991.

Rochat, Giorgio, *Militari e politici nella preparazione della campagna d'Etiopia: Studio e documenti 1932–1936*, Milan: Franco Angeli, 1971.

Rochat, Giorgio, *Italo Balbo*, Turin: UTET, 1986.

Rochat, Giorgio, *L'esercito italiano in pace e in guerra*, Milan: RARA, 1991.

Rochat, Giorgio, *Guerre italiane in Libia e in Etiopia: Studi militari 1921–1939*, Treviso: PAGUS, 1991.

Rochat, Giorgio, *Ufficiali e soldati: L'esercito italiano dalla prima alla seconda guerra mondiale*, Udine: Gaspari, 2000.

Rochat, Giorgio, *Le guerre italiane 1935–1943: Dall'impero d'Etiopia alla disfatta*, Turin: Einaudi, 2005.

Rodogno, Davide, *Il nuovo ordine mediterraneo. Le politiche d'occupazione dell' Italia fascista in Europa 1940–1943*, Turin: Bollati Boringhieri, 2003.

Rossi, Francesco, *Mussolini e lo stato maggiore. Avvenimenti del 1940*, Rome: "Regionale" [1951].

Rovighi, Alberto and Filippo Stefani, *La partecipazione italiana alla guerra civile spagnola (1936–1939)*, Rome: Ufficio Storico dello Stato Maggiore dell'Esercito, 1992.

Sadkovich, James J., *The Italian Navy in World War II*, Westport, CT: Greenwood, 1994.

Saini Fasanotti, Federica, *Etiopia 1936–1940. Le operazioni di polizia coloniale nelle fonti dell'esercito italiano*, Rome: Ufficio Storico dello Stato Maggiore dell'Esercito, 2010.

Santoni, Alberto, *Le operazioni in Sicilia e in Calabria (luglio–settembre 1943)*, Rome: Ufficio Storico dello Stato Maggiore dell'Esercito, 1989.

Santoni, Alberto, *Il vero traditore. Il ruolo documentato di ULTRA nella guerra del Mediterraneo*, Milan: Mursia, 2005.

Santoro, Carlo Maria (ed.), *Italo Balbo: Aviazione e potere aereo: Atti del Convegno Internazionale del Centenario 1896–1996*, Rome: Aeronautica Militare, 1998.

Santoro, Giuseppe, *L'aeronautica italiana nella seconda guerra mondiale*, Rome: Esse, 1957.

Saz, Ismael and Javier Tusell, *Fascistas en España. La intervención italiana en la Guerra Civil a través de los telegramas del 'Missione Militare Italiana in Spagna' 15 Diciembre 1936–31 Marzo 1937*, Rome: Escuela Española de Historia y Arqueología, 1981.

Scalise, Guglielmo, *C'era una volta. Il . . . settimo*, Milan: Cavallotti, 1974.

Scaroni, Silvio, *Con Vittorio Emanuele III*, Milan: Mondadori, 1954.

Schlemmer, Thomas, *Invasori, non vittime: La campagna italiana di Russia 1941–1943*, Roma-Bari: Laterza, 2009.

Schreiber, Gerhard, *Revisionismus und Weltmachtstreben: Marineführung und deutsch-italienische Beziehungen 1919–1944*, Stuttgart: Deutsche Verlags-Anstalt, 1978.

Schreiber, Gerhard, Bernd Stegemann and Detlef Vogel, *Germany and the Second World War*, vol. III: *The Mediterranean, South-East Europe, and North Africa 1939–1941*, Oxford: Clarendon Press, 1995.

Scianna, Bastian Matteo, *The Italian War on the Eastern Front, 1941–1943: Operations, Myths and Memories*, Cham, Switzerland: Springer Nature; London: Palgrave Macmillan, 2019.

Scotoni, Giorgio, *Il nemico fidato. La guerra di sterminio in URSS e l'occupazione alpine sull'Alto Don*, Trento: Panorama, 2013.

Scotti, Giacomo and Luciano Viazzi, *Occupazione e guerra italiana in Montenegro. Le Aquile delle Montagne Nere*, Milan: Mursia, 1987.

Scotti, Giacomo and Luciano Viazzi, *L'inutile vittoria. La tragica esperienza delle truppe italiane in Montenegro 1941–1942*, Milan: Mursia, 1989.

Sica, Emanuele, *Mussolini's Army in the French Riviera: Italy's Occupation of France*, Urbana, IL: University of Illinois Press, 2016.

Sica, Emanuele and Richard Carrier, eds., *Italy and the Second World War: Alternative Perspectives*, Leiden: Brill, 2018.

SIFAR, *Il servizio informazioni militare italiano dalla sua costituzione alla fine della seconda guerra mondiale*, Rome: Stato Maggiore della Difesa, 1957.

Stahel, David, ed., *Joining Hitler's Crusade: European Nations and the Invasion of the Soviet Union, 1941*, Cambridge: Cambridge University Press, 2018.

Stefani, Filippo, *La storia della dottrina e degli ordinamenti dell'esercito italiano. Da Vittorio Veneto alla 2a Guerra Mondiale*, Rome: Ufficio Storico dello Stato Maggiore dell'Esercito, 1985.

Stewart, Andrew, *The First Victory: The Second World War and the East Africa Campaign*, New Haven, CT: Yale University Press, 2016.

Stockings, Craig and Eleanor Hancock, *Swastika over the Acropolis: Reinterpreting the Nazi Invasion of Greece in World War II*, Leiden: Brill, 2013.

Strang, G. Bruce, *On the Fiery March: Mussolini Prepares for War*, Westport, CT: Praeger, 2003.

Strang, G. Bruce, ed., *Collision of Empires: Italy's Invasion of Ethiopia and its International Impact*, Farnham: Ashgate, 2013.

Sweet, J. J. T., *Iron Arm: The Mechanization of Mussolini's Army, 1920–1940*, Westport, CT: Greenwood Press, 1980.

Tranfaglia, Nicola, *La prima guerra mondiale e il fascismo*, Turin: UTET, 1995.

Trevor Roper, H. R., ed., *Hitler's War Directives*, London: Pan, 1966.

Trizzino, Antonino, *Navi e poltrone*, Milan: Longanesi, 1966.

van Creveld, Martin, *Hitler's Strategy 1940–1941: The Balkan Clue*, Cambridge: Cambridge University Press, 1973.

Visconti Prasca, Sebastiano, *Io ho aggredito la Grecia*, Milan: Rizzoli, 1946.

Vitali, Giorgio, *Savoia ha caricato signor Generale*, Florence: MEF, 2004.

Volterra, Alessandro, *Sudditi coloniali. Ascari eritrei 1935–1941*, Milan: Franco Angeli, 2005.

von Rintelen, Enno, *Mussolini als Bundesgenosse. Erinnerungen des deutschen militärattaches in Rome 1936–1943*, Tübingen and Stuttgart: Rainer Wunderlich Verlag Hermann Leins, 1951. Italian edition: *Mussolini l'Alleato. Ricordi dell'addetto militare tedesco a Roma (1936–1943)*, Rome: Corso, 1952.

Warlimont, Walter, *Inside Hitler's Headquarters 1939–1945*, London: Weidenfeld and Nicolson, 1964.

Zangrandi, Ruggero, *1943: 25 luglio–8 settembre*, Milan: Feltrinelli, 1964.

Zanussi, Giacomo, *Guerra e catastrofe d'Italia*, Rome: Corso, 1945.

Zullino, Pietro, ed., *Il 25 luglio*, Milan: Mondadori, 1973.

Articles and chapters

Alegi, Gregory, 'Le operazioni in Tunisia e nell'Italia meridionale: l'aspetto aereo', in R*omain H.* Rainero, ed., *L'Italia in guerra. Il 40 anno–1943*, Rome: *Commissione* italiana di storia militare, 1994, pp. 55–82.

Ambrosini, Luigi, 'Recherches sur les thèmes impérialistes dans les programmes et les livres de textes de culture fasciste (1925–1941)', *Guerres mondiales et conflits contemporains* no. 161, January 1991, pp. 51–66.

Baldoli, Claudia, 'L'Italia meridionale sotto le bombe, 1940–44', *Meridiano* no. 82, 2015, pp. 37–57.

Baldoli, Claudia and Marco Fincardi, 'Italian Society under Anglo-American Bombs: Propaganda, Experience, and Legend, 1940–1945', *Historical Journal*, vol. 52, no. 4, December 2009, pp. 1,017–38.

Bernhard, Patrick, 'Behind the Battle Lines: Italian Atrocities and the Persecution of Arabs, Berbers, and Jews in North Africa during World War II', *Holocaust and Genocide Studies*, vol. 26, no. 3, Winter 2012, pp. 425–46.

Burgwyn, H. James, 'The Legacy of Italy's Participation in the German War against the Soviet Union: 1941–1943', *Mondo contemporaneo* no. 2, 2011, pp. 161–81.

Cappellano, Filippo, '"Scarpe di cartone e divise di tela . . ." Gli stereotipi e la realtà sugli equipaggiamenti invernali delle truppe italiane in Russia nella seconda guerra mondiale', *Storia militare* anno X, no. 101, February 2002, pp. 20–30.

Cappellano, Filippo, 'Il Sim e la prima controffensiva britannica in Africa settentrionale', *Mondo contemporaneo* no. 1, 2008, pp. 123–48.

Carrier, Richard, 'Some Reflections on the Fighting Power of the Italian Army in North Africa, 1940–1943', *War in History*, vol. 22, no. 4, November 2015, pp. 503–28.

Cecchini, Ezio, 'Organizzazione, preparazione e supporto logistico della campagna 1935–1936 in Africa Orientale', *Memorie Storiche Militari*, 1979, pp. 9–38.

Cernuschi, Enrico, 'La rivolta dei generali. Il confronto sotterraneo tra la MVSN e il Regio Esercito, 1939–1943' [electronic copy provided by the author].

Cernuschi, Enrico, 'Breaking "ULTRA": The Cryptologic and Intelligence War between Britain and Italy, 1931–1943', in John Jordan, ed., *Warship 2018*, Oxford: Osprey, 2018, pp. 85–97.

Ceva, Lucio, 'Quelques aspects de l'activité du Haut Commandement italien dans la guerre en Méditerranée (mai 1941–août 1942)', in *La guerre en Méditerranée 1939–1945. Actes du Colloque International tenu à Paris du 8 au 11 avril 1969* (Paris: Editions du Centre National de la Recherche Scientifique, 1971), pp. 86–93.

Ceva, Lucio, 'Altre notizie sulle conversazioni militari italo-tedesche alla vigilia della seconda guerra mondiale (aprile–giugno 1939)', *Il Risorgimento* anno XXX, no. 3, October 1978, pp. 151–82.

Ceva, Lucio, 'La campagna di Russia nel quadro strategico della guerra fascista', in Enzo Collotti, ed., *Gli italiani sul fronte russo*, Bari: De Donato, 1982, pp. 163–93.

Ceva, Lucio, 'Aspetti politici e giuridici dell'Alto Comando militare in Italia (1848–1941)', *Il Politico* anno XLIX, no. 1, 1984, pp. 81–120.

Ceva, Lucio, 'Influence de la guerre d'Espagne sur l'armement et les conceptions d'emploi de l'aviation de l'Italie fasciste', in *Adaptation de l'arme aérienne aux conflits contemporains et processus d'indépendance des armées de l'Air des origines à la fin de la Seconde Guerre mondiale. Colloque international 4 au 7 settembre 1984*, Paris: Fondation pour les Études de Défense Nationale, 1985, pp. 191–9.

Ceva, Lucio, 'Il diario del Maresciallo Cavallero', *Rivista Storica Italiana* anno XCVII, fasc. 1, 1985, pp. 296–319.

Ceva, Lucio, 'Ripensando all'8 settembre', in Claudio Dellavalle, ed., *8 settembre 1943. Storia e memoria*, Milan: Franco Angeli, 1989, pp. 7–20.

Ceva, Lucio, 'Ripensare Guadalajara', *Italia Contemporanea* no. 192, September 1993, pp. 473–86.

Ceva, Lucio, 'L'ultima vittoria del fascismo Spagna 1938–1939', *Italia Contemporanea* no. 196, September 1994, pp. 519–35.

Ceva, Lucio, 'Momenti della crisi del Comando Supremo', in Romain H. Rainero, ed., *L'Italia in guerra. Il 4° anno – 1943*, Rome: Commissione italiana di storia militare, 1994, pp. 101–33.

Ceva, Lucio, 'Voci dai vari "fronti"', in Anna Lisa Carlotti, ed., *Italia 1939–1945. Storia e memoria*, Milan: Vita e Pensiero, 1996, pp. 173–204.

Ceva, Lucio, 'L'opinione pubblica in Italia sulla guerra civile di Spagna (1936–1939)', in *Le forze armate e la nazione italiana (1915–1943). Atti del convegno di studi tenuto a Roma nei giorni 22–24 ottobre 2003*, Rome: commissione italiana di storia militare, 2004, pp. 227–50.

Cuzzi, Marco, 'I Balcani, problemi di un'occupazione difficile', in R. H. Rainero and A. Biagini, eds., *Italia in guerra–il 3° anno 1942*, Rome: Commissione Italiana di storia militare, 1993, pp. 343–76.

Cuzzi, Marco, 'L'opinione pubblica italiana e lo scoppio della guerra', in *Le forze armate e la nazione italiana (1915–1943). Atti del convegno di studi tenuto a Roma nei giorni 22–24 ottobre 2003*, Rome: Commissione italiana di storia militare, 2004, pp. 323–51.

De Grand, Alexander, 'Mussolini's Follies: Fascism in its Imperial and Racist Phase, 1935–1940', *Contemporary European History*, vol. 13, no. 2, May 2004, pp. 127–47.

De Ninno, Fabio, 'The Italian Navy and Japan, the Indian Ocean, Failed Cooperation and Tripartite Relations (1935–1943)', *War in History*, 2018: https://doi.org/10.1177/0968344518777270.

Di Rienzo, Eugenio and Emilio Gin, 'Quella mattina del 25 luglio 1943. Mussolini, Shinrokuro Hidaka e il progetto di pace separata con l'URSS', *Nuova rivista storica*, vol. 95, pt 1, January–April 2011, pp. 1–88.

Di Rienzo, Eugenio and Emilio Gin, 'L'ambigua intesa. L'URSS e le potenze dell'asse 1939–1941', *Nuova rivista storica*, vol. 96, pt 2, January–April 2012, pp. 1–112.

Faggione, Gabriele, 'I piani operativi italiani e tedeschi per l'occupazione della Svizzera (1939–1941)', *Bollettino dell'Ufficio Storico Stato Maggiore dell'Esercito*, 2018, pp. 139–212.

Ferrante, Ezio, 'L'8 settembre e il dramma della Marina italiana', *Politica militare* anno IV, no. 4, November–December 1982, pp. 69–75.

Ferrari, Dorello, 'La mobilitazione dell'esercito nella seconda guerra mondiale', *Storia Contemporanea* anno XIII, no. 6, December 1992, pp. 1,001–46.

Ferris, John, 'The British Army, Signals and Security in the Desert Campaign, 1940–42', *Intelligence and National Security*, vol. 5, no. 2, April 1990, pp. 254–91.

Förster, Jürgen , 'Il ruolo dell'8a armata italiana dal punto di vista tedesco', in Enzo Collotti, ed., *Gli italiani sul fronte russo*, Bari: De Donato, 1982, pp. 229–59.

Gabriele, Mariano, 'L'offensiva su Malta (1941)', in R. H. Rainero and A. Biagini, eds., *L'Italia in guerra. Il 2° anno – 1941*, Rome: Commissione italiana per la storia militare, 1992, pp. 435–50.

Gabriele, Mariano, 'L'Operazione "C 3" (1942)', in R. H. Rainero and A. Biagini, eds., *L'Italia in guerra. Il 3° anno – 1942*, Rome: Commissione italiana per la storia militare, 1993, pp. 409–34.

Gabriele, Mariano, 'Le premesse', in *La battaglia dei convogli. Atti del convegno Napoli 22 maggio 1993*, Rome: Ufficio Storico della Marina Militare, 1993, pp. 14–25.

Gentile, Carlo, 'Alle spalle dell'ARMIR: documenti sulla repressione antipartigiana al fronte russo', *Il Presente e la Storia* no. 53, June 1998, pp. 159–81.

Giambartolomei, Aldo, 'La campagna in Russia del CSIR e dei suoi veterani dell'Armir', in R. H. Rainero and A. Biagini, eds., *L'Italia in guerra. Il 3° anno – 1942*, Rome: Commissione italiana di storia militare, 1993, pp. 273–96.

Giannini, Amedeo, 'Pietro Badoglio', *Rivista di Studi Politici Internazionali*, vol. 23, no. 4, Ottobre–Decembre 1956, pp. 639–44.

Giorgerini, Giorgio, 'Il problema dei convogli e la guerra per mare', in R. H. Rainero and A. Biagini, eds., *L'Italia in guerra. Il 2° anno – 1941*, Rome: Commissione italiana per la storia militare, 1992, pp. 399–418.

Goglia, Luigi, 'La guerra in Africa nel 1940', in R. H. Rainero and A. Biagini, eds., *L'Italia in guerra. Il 1° anno – 1940*, Rome: Commissione italiana di storia militare, 1991, pp. 177–91.

Guida, Francesco, 'L'evoluzione politico-militare del fronte balcanico nel 1941', in R. H. Rainero and A. Biagini, eds., *L'Italia in guerra. Il 2° anno – 1941*, Rome: Commissione italiana di storia militare, 1992, pp. 13–25.

Hammond, Richard, 'An Enduring Influence on Imperial Defence and Grand Strategy: British Perceptions of the Italian Navy, 1935–1943', *International History Review*, vol. 39, no. 5, 2017, pp. 810–35.

Knox, MacGregor, 'The Sources of Italy's Defeat in 1940: Bluff or Institutional Incompetence?', in Carole Fink, Isabel V. Hull and M. Knox, eds., *German Nationalism and the European Response, 1890–1945*, Norman and London: University of Nebraska Press, 1985, pp. 247–66.

Knox, MacGregor, 'The Italian Armed Forces, 1940–1943', in Allan R. Millett and Williamson Murray, eds., *Military Effectiveness*, vol. III: *The Second World War*, Boston, MA: Allen and Unwin, 1988, pp. 136–79.

Labanca, Nicola, 'Chi ha studiato il "consenso" alla guerra d'Etiopia?', in *Le forze armate e la nazione italiana (1915–1943). Atti del convegno di studi tenuto a Roma nei giorni 22–24 ottobre 2003*, Rome: Commissione italiana di storia militare, 2004, pp. 201–26.

Mack Smith, Denis, 'Mussolini as a Military Leader', University of Reading: The Stenton Lecture, 1974.

Magistrati, Massimo, 'La Germania e l'impresa italiana di Etiopia', *Rivista di Studi Politici Internazionali*, vol. 17, no. 4, 1950, pp. 563–606.

Meier-Welcker, Hans, 'Zur deutsch-italienischen Militärpolitik und Beurteilung der italienischen Wehrmacht vor dem Zweiten Weltkrieg', *Militärgeschichtlicher Mitteilungen*, vol. 7, no.1, 1970, pp. 59–93.

Melchioni, Maria Grazia, 'Pietro Badoglio', *Rivista di Studi Politici Internazionali*, vol. 23, no. 4, Ottobre–Dicembre 1956, pp. 639–44.

Minniti, Fortunato, 'Il problema degli armamenti nella preparazione militare italiana dal 1935 al 1943', *Storia Contemporanea* anno X, no. 1, 1978, pp. 5–61.

Minniti, Fortunato, 'Profilo dell'iniziativa strategica italiana dalla "non belligeranza" alla "guerra parallela"', *Storia Contemporanea* anno XVIII, no. 6, December 1987, pp. 1,113–95.

Minniti, Fortunato, 'Piano e ordinamento nella preparazione italiana alla guerra negli anni trenta', *Dimensioni e problemi della ricerca storica* no. 1, 1990, pp. 1–42.

Minniti, Fortunato, 'Oltre Adua. Lo sviluppo e la scelta della strategia operative per la guerra contro l'Etiopia', *Società di storia militare*, Quaderno, 1993, pp. 85–142.

Minniti, Fortunato, '"Il nemico vero". Gli obiettivi dei piani di operazione contro la Gran Bretagna nel contesto etiopico (maggio 1935–maggio 1936)', *Storia Contemporanea* anno XXVI, no. 4, August 1995, pp. 575–602.

Minniti, Fortunato, 'Gli ufficiali di carriera dell'esercito nella crisi del regime', in Angelo Ventura, ed., *Sulla crisi del regime fascista 1938–1943*, Marsilio: Istituto Veneto per la storia del Resistenza, 1996, pp. 75–123.

Navarini, Lt. Gen. Enea, 'Operations in the Western Desert and Tripolitania, Italian XXI Corps. July '41–Jan 143', https://wp.me/phMWI-1HY.

Nuti, Leopoldo, 'Italo Balbo e la politica estera fascista', in Carlo Maria Santoro, ed., *Italo Balbo. Aviazione e potere aereo. Atti del Convegno Internazionale del Centenario 1896–1996*, Rome: Aeronautica Militare, 1998, pp. 49–75.

O'Hara, Vincent P. and Enrico Cernuschi, 'The Other ULTRA: Signal Intelligence and the Battle to Supply Rommel's Attack toward Suez', *Naval War College Review*, vol. 66, no. 3, Summer 2013, pp. 117–38.

Osti Guerrazzi, Amedeo, '"Schonungsloses Handeln gegen den bösartigen Feind". Italienische Kriegführung und Besatzungspraxis in Slowenien 1941/42', *Vierteljahrshefte für Zeitgeschichte*, vol. 62, no. 4, 2014, pp. 537–67.

Osti Guerrazzi, Amedeo and Thomas Schlemmer, 'I soldati italiani nella campagna di Russia', *Annali dell'Istituto storico italo-germanico in Trento*, vol. XXXIII, 2007, pp. 385–417.

Palayret, Jean-Marie, 'La tentative d'alliance militaire franco-italienne et son échec 1935–1940', in Anne-Claire de Gayffier-Bonneville, ed., *Sécurité et coopération militaire en Europe, 1919–1955*, Paris: L'Harmattan, 2005, pp. 212–35.

Papili, Franco, 'Rapporto sui convogli', in *La battaglia dei convogli: Atti del convegno Napoli 22 maggio 1993*, Rome: Ufficio Storico della Marina Militare, 1993, pp. 26–44.

Pardini, Giuseppe, 'La "non scelta" del Maresciallo De Bono', *Nuova Storia Contemporanea*, vol. V, pt 3, May–June 2001, pp. 109–31.

Pelagalli, Sergio, 'Il generale Pietro Gazzera al ministero della Guerra (1928–1933)', *Storia Contemporanea* anno XX, no. 6, December 1989, pp. 1,007–58.

Perfetti, Francesco, 'Vittorio Emanuele, Umberto e il "25 luglio" mancato', *Nuova Storia Contemporanea*, vol. VI, pt. 5, September–October 2002, pp. 31–40.

Preston, Paul, 'Mussolini's Spanish Adventure: From Limited Risk to War', in Paul Preston and Ann L. Mackenzie, eds., *The Republic Besieged: Civil War in Spain 1936–1939*, Edinburgh: Edinburgh University Press, 1996, pp. 21–51.

Rainero, Romain H., 'Il 25 luglio: i quarantacinque giorni', in Romain H. Rainero, ed., *L'Italia in guerra. Il 4° anno – 1943*, Rome: Commissione italiana per la storia militare, 1994, pp. 83–100.

Rochat, Giorgio, 'Mussolini, chef de guerre (1940–1943)', *Revue d'histoire de la Deuxième Guerre mondiale* no. 100, October 1975, pp. 43–66.

Rochat, Giorgio, 'Memorialistica e storiografia sulla campagna italiana di Russia 1941–1943', in Enzo Collotti, ed., *Gli italiani sul fronte russo*, Bari: De Donato, 1982, pp. 465–82.

Rochat, Giorgio, 'Lo sforzo bellico 1940–43. Analisi di una sconfitta', *Italia Contemporanea* no. 160, September 1985, pp. 7–24.

Rochat, Giorgio, 'L'impiego dei gas nella guerra d'Etiopia, 1935–1936', *Rivista di Storia Contemporanea* no. 1, 1988, pp. 74–109.

Rochat, Giorgio, 'I servizi di informazione e l'alto comando italiano nella guerra parallela del 1940', *Studi Piacentini* no. 4, 1988, pp. 69–83.

Rochat, Giorgio, 'L'aeronautica italiana nella guerra d'Etiopia (1935–36)', *Studi Piacentini* no. 7, September 1990, pp. 97–123.

Rochat, Giorgio, 'Il fascismo e la preparazione militare al conflitto mondiale', in Angelo Del Boca, Massimo Legnani and Mario G. Rossi, eds., *Il regime fascista. Storia e storiografia*, Bari: Laterza, 1995, pp. 151–65.

Rochat, Giorgio, 'Una ricerca impossibile. le perdite italiane nella seconda guerra mondiale', *Italia Contemporanea* no. 201, December 1995, pp. 687–700.

Rochat, Giorgio, 'La guerra di Grecia', in Mario Isnenghi, ed., *I luoghi della memoria. Strutture ed eventi dell'Italia Unita*, Bari: Laterza, 1997, vol. II, pp. 347–63.

Rochat, Giorgio, 'L'esercito di Mussolini visto dalla Francia', *Storia e Memoria* no. 2, 2003, pp. 29–43.

Rochat, Giorgio, 'Le truppe italiane in Russia 1941–1943', *Storia militare* anno XI, no. 115, April 2003, pp. 39–47.

Rossi, Marina, 'Lo spirito militare del Corpo di Spedizione in Russia nei giudizi del Servizio Informazioni dell'Armata Russa (1941–1946)', in Piero Del Negro, ed., *Lo spirito militare degli italiani. Atti del Seminario Padova, 16–18 novembre 2000*, Padua: Centro inter-universitario di studi e ricerche storico-militare/Commissione italiana di storia militare, 2002, pp. 107–16.

Sadkovich, James J., 'Understanding Defeat: Reappraising Italy's Role in World War II', *Journal of Contemporary History*, vol. 24, 1989, pp. 29–61.

Sadkovich, James J., 'The Italo-Greek War in Context: Italian Priorities and Axis Diplomacy', *Journal of Contemporary History*, vol. 28, 1993, pp. 439–64.

Sadkovich, James J., 'Italian Morale during the Italo-Greek War of 1940–1941', *War & Society*, vol. 12, no. 1, May 1994, pp. 97–123.

Sadkovich, James J., 'Anglo-American Bias and the Italo-Greek War of 1940–1941', *Journal of Military History*, vol. 58, no. 4, October 1994, pp. 617–42.

Sadkovich, James J., 'The Indispensable Navy: Italy as a Great Power, 1911–43', in N. A. M. Rodger, ed., *Naval Power in the Twentieth Century*, Annapolis, MD: Naval Institute Press, 1996, pp. 66–76.

Sadkovich, James J., 'Some Considerations Regarding Italian Armored Doctrine Prior to June 1940', *Global War Studies*, vol. 9, no. 1, 2012, pp. 40–74.

Santarelli, Lisa, 'Muted Violence: Italian War Crimes in Occupied Greece', *Journal of Modern Italian Studies*, vol. 9, no. 3, 2004, pp. 280–99.

Santoni, Alberto, 'Il vero traditore', in *La battaglia dei convogli. Atti del convegno Napoli 22 maggio 1993*, Rome: Ufficio Storico della Marina Militare, 1993, pp. 45–54.

Schlemmer, Thomas, 'Italy', in David Stahel, ed., *Joining Hitler's Crusade: European Nations and the Invasion of the Soviet Union, 1941*, Cambridge: Cambridge University Press, 2018, pp. 134–57.

Schröder, Josef, 'La Germania e i suoi Alleati nella Seconda Guerra Mondiale. Un contributo sulla politica degli obiettivi bellici di Hitler', *Storia Contemporanea* anno VII, no. 4, December 1976, pp. 751–81.

Sema, Antonio, '1914–1934: Guerra e politica secondo Mussolini', in Virgilio Ilari and Antonio Sema, *Marte in Orbace. Guerra, esercito e milizia nella concezione fascista della nazione*, Ancona: Casa Editrice Nuove Ricerche, 1988, pp. 15–118.

Setta, Sandro, 'Cesare Maria de Vecchi di Val Cismon. Diario 1943', *Storia contemporanea* anno XXIV no. 6, dicembre 1993, pp. 1,057–1,113.

Sicurezza, Admiral Renato, 'Le operazioni in Tunisia e nell'Italia meridionale: l'aspetto navale', in Romain H. Rainero, ed., *L'Italia in guerra. Il 4° anno – 1943*, Rome: Commissione italiana di storia militare, 1994, pp. 33–51.

Smyth, Howard McGaw, 'The Command of the Italian Armed Forces in World War II', *Military Affairs*, vol. 15, no. 1, Spring 1951, pp. 38–52.

Stefani, Filippo, 'L'8 settembre e le forze armate italiane', in R. Rainero, ed., *L'Italia in guerra il 4° anno – 1943*, Rome: Commissione italiana di storia militare, 1994, pp. 137–94.

Sullivan, Brian R., 'A Fleet in Being: The Rise and Fall of Italian Sea Power, 1861–1943', *The International History Review*, vol. X, no. 1, February 1988, pp. 106–24.

Sullivan, Brian R., 'The Italian-Ethiopian War, October 1935–November 1941: Causes, Conduct and Consequences' in A. Hamish Ion and E. J. Errington, eds., *Great Powers and Little Wars: The Limits of Power*, Westport, CT: Prager, 1993, pp. 167–201.

Sullivan, Brian R., 'Fascist Italy's Military Involvement in the Spanish Civil War', *Journal of Modern History*, vol. 59, no. 4, October 1995, pp. 697–727.

Sullivan, Brian R., 'The Primacy of Politics: Civil-Military Relations and Italian Junior Officers, 1918–1940', in Elliott V. Converse III, ed., *Forging the Sword: Selecting, Educating, and Training Cadets and Junior Officers in the Modern World*, Chicago, IL: Imprint Publications, 1998, pp. 65–81.

Sullivan, Brian R., 'More than Meets the Eye: The Ethiopian War and the Origins of the Second World War', in Gordon Martel, ed., *The Origins of the Second World War Reconsidered: A. J. P. Taylor and the Historians*, New York: Routledge, 1999, pp. 178–203.

Sullivan, Brian R., 'Downfall of the Regia Aeronautica, 1933–1943', in Robin Higham and Stephen J. Harris, *Why Air Forces Fail: The Anatomy of Defeat*, Lexington, KY: The University Press of Kentucky, 2006, pp. 135–76.

Tassini, Giovanni, 'Madrid 1943. Tre colloqui col Caudillo', *Nuova Storia Contemporanea*, vol. VI, pt 1, January–February 2002, pp. 93–130.

Tirone, Emilio , 'La specificità del comportamento umanitario italiano durante le operazioni sul fronte russo (1941–1943)', *Bollettino dell'Ufficio Storico Stato Maggiore dell'Esercito* 2017, pp. 113–45.

Toscano, Mario, 'Le conversazioni militari italo-tedesche alla vigilia della seconda guerra mondiale', *Rivista Storica Italiana* anno LXIV, fascicolo 3, December 1952, pp. 336–82.

Trifković, Srdjan, 'Rivalry between Germany and Italy in Croatia 1942–1943', *The Historical Journal*, vol. 36, no. 4, December 1993, pp. 879–904.

Tsirpanlis, Zacharias N., 'The Italian View of the 1940–41 War: Comparisons and Problems', *Balkan Studies*, vol. 23, no. 1, 1982, pp. 27–79.

Vinci, Stefano , 'La reforma fascista dell'esercito italiano', in L. Martínez Peñas and M. Fernández Rodríguez, eds., *Amenazas y orden público: efectos y respuestas, de los Reyes Católicos al Afghanistán contemporaneo*, Madrid: Asociación Veritas para el Estudio de la Historia, el Derecho y las Instituciones, 2013, pp. 129–74.

Virtue, Nicolas G., '"We Istrians Do Very Well in Russia": Istrian Combatants, Fascist Propaganda, and Brutalizatiòn on the Eastern Front', in Emanuele Sica and Richard Carrier, *Italy and the Second World War: Alternative Perspectives*, Leiden: Brill, 2018, pp. 275–98.

Virtue, Nicolas G., 'Religion, Race, and the Nation in *La tradotta del Fronte Giulio*, 1942–1943', *Modern Italy*, vol. 23, no. 4, 2018, pp. 373–93.

Visani, Alessandro, 'Il gesuita di Mussolini. Piero Tacchi Venturi e le leggi razziali del 1938', *Roma moderna e contemporanea*, vol. XIX, no. 1, 2011, pp. 103–20.

Zamagni, Vera , 'Italy: How to Lose the War and Win the Peace', in Mark Harrison, ed., *The Economics of World War II: Six Great Powers in International Comparison*, Cambridge: Cambridge University Press, 1998, pp. 177–223.

Zilli, Valdo, 'Gli italiani prigionieri di guerra in URSS: vicende, esperienze, testimonianze', in Enzo Collotti, ed., *Gli italiani sul fronte russo*, Bari: De Donato, 1982, pp. 295–321.

Dissertations, theses, and unpublished manuscripts

Arielli, Nir, 'Fascist Italy and the Middle East, 1935–1940', PhD University of Leeds, 2008.

Battistelli, Pier Paolo, 'La "guerra dell'Asse". Condotta bellica e collaborazione militare italo-tedesca 1939–1943', Tesi di dottorato Università degli Studi Padova, 2000.

Budden, M. J., 'British Policy towards Fascist Italy in the Early Stages of World War II', PhD University of London, 1999.

Donohue, Alan, 'Hitler as Military Commander: From *Blau* to *Edelweiss*', PhD Trinity College Dublin, 2015.

Fiore, Massimiliano, 'The Clash of Empires: Anglo-Italian Relations in the Middle East and the Origins of the Second World War, 1935–1940', PhD University of London, 2008.

Gabriele, Mariano, 'The Influence of Malta on the Mediterranean War, 1940–1943' (unpublished mss in the author's possession).

Miller, Dawn M., 'Italy Through the Looking Glass: Aspects of British Policy and Intelligence concerning Italy, 1939–1941', PhD University of Toronto, 1997.

Panebianco, Ivan, 'Gli Arditi. Dalla guerra di trincea alla guerra fratricida (1917–1921)', Tesi di laurea Università degli Studi Pisa, 2007–8.

Pecher, André, 'Friedrich Oskar Ruge (1894–1985). Lebenswelt, Rolle und Selbstverständnis eines Marineoffiziers von 1915 bis 1945', Dr. Phil. Dissertation Helmut-Schmidt-Universität Hamburg, 2017.

Ristuccia, Cristiano Andrea, 'The Italian Economy under Fascism: 1934–1943. The Rearmament Paradox', DPhil University of Oxford, 2008.

Rose, Patrick John, 'British Army Command Culture 1939–1945: A Comparative Study of British Eighth and Fourteen Armies', PhD University of London, 2008.

Scianna, Bastian Matteo, 'Myths and Memories: The Italian Operations on the Eastern Front (1941–1943) and their Contested Legacies during the Cold War', Dr. Phil. Dissertation Universität Potsdam, 2017.

Sica, Emanuele, 'Italiani Brava Gente? The Italian Occupation of Southeastern France in the Second World War, 1940–1943', PhD University of Waterloo, 2011.

Soddu, Ubaldo, 'Memorie e riflessioni di un Generale (1933–1941', unpubl. mss.

Sullivan, Brian R., 'A Thirst for Glory: Mussolini, the Italian Military and the Fascist Regime, 1922–1936', PhD Columbia University, 1984.

Virtue, Nicolas G., 'Fascist Italy and the Barbarization of the Eastern Front, 1941–1943', MA dissertation, University of Calgary, 2007.

Virtue, Nicolas G., 'Royal Army, Fascist Empire: The Regio Esercito on Occupation Duty, 1936–1943', PhD University of Western Ontario, 2016.

Index